MW00628526

The Neurobehavioral and Social-Emotional Development of Infants and Children

The Norton Series on Interpersonal Neurobiology
Allan N. Schore, Ph.D., Series Editor
Daniel J. Siegel, M.D., Founding Editor

The field of mental health is in a tremendously exciting period of growth and conceptual reorganization. Independent findings from a variety of scientific endeavors are converging in an interdisciplinary view of the mind and mental well-being. An interpersonal neurobiology of human development enables us to understand that the structure and function of the mind and brain are shaped by experiences, especially those involving emotional relationships.

The Norton Series on Interpersonal Neurobiology will provide cutting-edge, multidisciplinary views that further our understanding of the complex neurobiology of the human mind. By drawing on a wide range of traditionally independent fields of research—such as neurobiology, genetics, memory, attachment, complex systems, anthropology, and evolutionary psychology—these texts will offer mental health professionals a review and synthesis of scientific findings often inaccessible to clinicians. These books aim to advance our understanding of human experience by finding the unity of knowledge, or consilience, that emerges with the translation of findings from numerous domains of study into a common language and conceptual framework. The series will integrate the best of modern science with the healing art of psychotherapy.

A NORTON PROFESSIONAL BOOK

The Neurobehavioral and Social-Emotional Development of Infants and Children

ED TRONICK

W. W. Norton & Company
New York • London

Copyright © 2007 by Ed Tronick

For information about permission to reproduce
selections from this book, write to
Permissions, W. W. Norton & Company, Inc.,
500 Fifth Avenue, New York, NY 10110

Manufacturing by TechBooks
Production Manger: Leeann Graham

Library of Congress Cataloging-in-Publication Data

Tronick Edward.
The neurobehavioral and social-emotional development of infants and children / Ed Tronick.
     p. cm. — (A Norton professional book)
   Includes bibliographical references and index.
   ISBN-13: 978-0-393-70517-1
   ISBN-10: 0-393-70517-X
    1. Pediatric neuropsychology.   2. Biological child psychiatry.   3. Child psychology.
I. Title.

RJ486.5.T76 2007
618.92'8 — dc22

                                  2006047203'

ISBN 13: 978-0-393-70517-1
ISBN 10: 0-393-70517-X

W. W. Norton & Company, Inc., 500 Fifth Avenue, New York, N.Y. 10110
www.wwnorton.com

W. W. Norton & Company Ltd., Castle House, 75/76 Wells St., London W1T 3QT
0 9 8 7 6 5 4 3 2 1

For Pearl

Contents

PART V. DYADIC EXPANSION OF CONSCIOUSNESS AND MEANING MAKING

Acknowledgments

This book has been an integrating process of the past and the present. Jerome Bruner and Berry Brazelton are always sitting on my shoulder whispering ideas and encouragement. So is Uri Bronfenbrenner, who once said to me that I should observe mothers interacting with their babies to understand the formation of relationships. James Gibson taught me that the stimulation was always meaningful and afforded action.

Alexandra Harrison has been a most wonderful collaborator. We have co-created the dyadic expansion of consciousness hypothesis. She also brought me a deep understanding of psychodynamic thinking and an authentic moment-to-moment vision of how therapy actually works. Much of my thinking, indeed much of this book, is really hers, and I am sure new things will emerge in the future.

George Downing and Stephen Ruffins have regulated me and co-created with me. No one was ever more thoughtful and supportive than Barry Lester, who, in his challenges to the notion of regulation, helped to instantiate it for me. I could not have completed this book without them.

My research work over the past 15 years with my colleagues at the Child Development Unit—Katherine Weinberg, Marjorie Beeghly, Karen Olson, and Jacob Ham—prove how meaning can be better made in collaborative relationships. Important early collaborators were Andrew Gianino, Gilda Morelli, and Jeff Cohn. Much of the work in this book is theirs.

John Gottman, Lauren Adamson, and Beatrice Beebe have all expanded my thinking. My work with the Boston Process of Change Group, particularly with Lou Sander and also with Dan Stern, was very rewarding and changed my thinking about many ideas, people, and relationships. Arnold Modell made it clear that not everything is dyadic, though our engagements always are.

Dawn Skorczewski helped me think and write clearly. I also want to thank Deborah Malmud for her persistence and her colleagues Andrea Costella and Vani Kannan for their fine editorial work.

Three others have been critical to my work. Betty Woo took care of everything that needed to stay in the background and made my work on this book possible by helping me make sense of the world. From watching my daughter,

Anna Yarbrough, regulate a class of middle school students, I learned new dimensions of regulation. A rather amazing process that makes dyadic regulation seem simple.

And from the moment I met her, my wife Marilyn Davillier changed my sense of my self in the world, but I did not know then that she would expand my consciousness beyond the information given and its own boundaries. She taught me to see new ways of making meaning and the meaning of relationships.

The Neurobehavioral and Social-Emotional Development of Infants and Children

Introduction

Why are some infants, children, and adults happy and robust and others sad and withered? How are mothers and infants similar to and different from therapists and patients? What are the developing infant's capacities for neurobehavioral self-organization? How are early infant–adult interactions organized? How are self- and mutual regulation related to developmental processes? Is there a process that can explain normal as well as abnormal development? Is the process of "meaning making," in which humans make sense of themselves in relation to the world, only in their heads, or is it in their bodies as well? This broad set of questions is addressed and looped back to in this book, which compiles my writing and thinking over the past 30 years.

A central goal of this book is to present my Mutual Regulation Model (MRM) of infant–adult interaction. The MRM sees infants as part of a dyadic communicative system in which the infant and adult mutually regulate and scaffold their engagement with each other and the world by communicating their intentions and responding to them. This book presents my thinking and research that led to the MRM and its elaboration into ideas about meaning making, biopsychological states of consciousness, and how they are expanded in engagement with others and the world.

From my first studies of infants ducking to avoid virtual objects on a collision course with them (Ball & Tronick, 1971; see Chapter 28), to my studies of infants making sense of their interactions with depressed mothers (Tronick & Weinberg, 1997; see Chapter 20), the focus of my research has been on the nature of how people live in the world and how they change both themselves and their relation to the world over moments, hours, days, and years. My aspiration is to develop a theory that has the qualities of being experientially-near and clinically authentic, broad and integrated, and developmental and culturated at its core. This goal is hardly in hand—it is a work in progress—but I offer this version of the theory as one step in an ongoing effort towards its development.

PSYCHOBIOLOGICAL STATES OF CONSCIOUSNESS

My organizing idea is, as Bruner (1990) stated, that humans are makers of meaning about their relation to the world. They are purposeful. This idea of private meaning is explored in theories as divergent as psychoanalysis to Socratic exploration in cognitive-behavioral theory. My MRM theory weds Bruner's view of humans as meaning-makers with dynamic systems theory. It sees humans as complex systems, as hierarchical multileveled psychobiological systems that constantly work to gain energy and meaningful information to make sense of their place in the world. This sense-of-oneself in the world equals the totality of meanings, purposes, intentions, and biological goals operating in every moment on every component and process at every level of the system from molecules to awareness.

The Sense-of-Oneself in the World

This totality of meanings can be conceptualized as a psychobiological state of consciousness. A state of consciousness (the whole of an individual's self-organization) guides an individual's engagement with others, with the world of things, and with their engagement with themselves. To use Walter J. Freeman's phrase, consciousness is how individuals thrust themselves into the world (Freeman, 2000). Of course, as psychobiological states, states of consciousness are not unique to humans, but in humans they contain unique species-specific qualities of human meaning making processes and experience. And parenthetically, the lack of consideration of species-specific qualities is what renders fallible arguments about chimpanzees or any other animal having awareness and consciousness equivalent to humans. Certainly they may have consciousness, but it is a chimpanzee form of consciousness, not a human form.

The private meaning of one's place in the world can be thought of as a psychobiological state of consciousness, an assemblage of the totality of meanings, purposes, intentions, and the like, from every component of the multiple levels of organization and functioning of the individual. Using the term *consciousness* can be misleading, for in my usage it does not imply that the individual is aware of the private meaning. Rather, the private meaning is inherent in the organization of the flow of an individual's psychobiological state as he or she acts in the world.

To capture what I mean by a *state of consciousness*, consider the multilevel cascade of meaning, both in and out of awareness—including emotions and thoughts, perceptions and actions, as well as feelings in your arms, feet, gut, and hands—as the wash of adrenalin flows through you when your plane is thwacked and shaken in flight by mother nature punishing humans hubris, because we all know it is impossible for something *so big* to fly. The multilayered totality of this state of consciousness is not and could not be completely *in* awareness. Indeed, much of being in the world is *out* of awareness, including most of the processes that produce experience. And we must not forget that states of consciousness and awareness for that matter are not singular concepts but rather broad terms referring to many forms of consciousness and awareness: reflective alertness, preconscious, unconscious, dynamic unconscious, reverie, daydreaming, the multiple states of sleep, meditation, and mindfulness, and even the biologically-oriented physiologic, neurologic, endocrine, and other somatic states. The *knowing* in a state of consciousness is like Bollas's "unknown known" (Bollas, 1987). However, there is even more that is unknown, because what is unknown is not only in the un- or preconscious. The unknown is also *in* and *of* our biopsychological organization and the processes that generate meaning, much of which are not available to consciousness. But no little internal observer is needed to catch the meaning; it is inherent in our biopsychological state of consciousness.

On the other hand, in some ways a biological state of consciousness is also about being *in* the world and the processes creating that "being in." Put yourself in the shoes of a 1 year old and try to experience and actually express the flow of her meanings as she watches her mother go toward the door leaving her with an unknown stranger, only to see her mother stop, turn around, come back, feel her mother pick her up, and hear her say "You are coming with me!" The child's sense of this event (and perhaps yours, too) is not only an unconscious awareness, but it is *in* all of her being.

Expanding States of Consciousness

I believe that successful growth or expansion of states of consciousness is governed by principles from dynamic systems theory that require all living systems—humans included—to garner energy and information from the world in order to maintain and increase the complexity and coherence of the organization and structure of their states of consciousness (i.e., their sense of self and their place in the world). The three ways of expanding complexity and coherence are: (1) interacting and communicating with people, (2) acting on things, and, as Modell (1993) would argue, (3) engaging our private selves. When humans are successful in appropriating meaning into themselves, our biopsychological state moves away from entropy, becomes information-rich, exists at the edge of chaos, and new properties (meanings) emerge. When humans are unsuccessful in appropriating meaning, the biopsychological state dissipates, loses complexity, and properties of the system are either lost or become fixed.

A particularly effective way of growing and expanding complexity occurs when two or more individuals convey and apprehend (i.e., take hold of) meanings from each other to create a dyadic state of consciousness. This dyadic state contains more information than either individual's state of consciousness alone, and when individuals co-create a dyadic state they can appropriate meanings from it into their own states of consciousness and increase its complexity. This is referred to as the Dyadic Expansion of States of Consciousness Model, which is elaborated on in Part V of this book. The mutually expressed and apprehended co-created meaning of "WE are together" is more complex than the individually expressed message "I want to be with you," conveyed and understood, for example, by the simultaneous gaping smiles of an infant and her father.

IMPORTANT QUALITIES FOR A THEORY ON HUMAN DEVELOPMENT

It is important for the reader to understand each of the qualities I want my theorizing to have: being experientially near and clinically authentic, broad and integrated, and developmental and culturated at its core.

Clinically Authentic

My emphasis on an experientially-near and clinically authentic theory of human development derives from my recognition that good clinicians know things about how individuals experience and "do" life that researchers often don't know and can't "do." Though we must recognize that clinicians' intriguing descriptions can at times actually be little more than hermeneutic theoretical musings, more often than not they present us with experiential data about how people make sense of the world — important data that demand explication. Unfortunately, some clinicians themselves often have little appreciation for the way scientists think. This lack of appreciation may lead clinicians to undervalue what the researcher knows, or paradoxically, and far too often, to undervalue their own clinical knowledge. A case in point for some psychodynamically-oriented clinicians is when they embrace neuroscience's cold cognitive concept of unconscious processes without realizing that they are ignoring valuable aspects of the original concept of the "dynamic unconscious."

Reciprocally, some researchers fail to appreciate the phenomenon of a dynamic unconscious that demands explanation. So, the worlds of the clinician and the researcher have become somewhat polarized. But to give up grappling with the mysteriousness of the dynamic unconscious, projective identification, body memory, or the "spooky kookiness" (at least for me, when I first bumped into them) of the concepts of the "unknown known," the "analytic third," or the idea that thinking is fuzzy and illogical, is to give up the struggle to understand the all too real "lived" lives of clinicians' patients (and everyone, for that matter) and their mysteriousness.

Broad and Integrated

In order to begin the study of the meaning people make of themselves and their relation to the world, the theory must be broad and integrated. Much theorizing is based on deep, powerful but bounded insights (attachment, adaptation, ego, re-entry, or intersubjectivity), which in the hands of their adherents promise more than they can deliver. As a consequence, the concepts lose their focus and their explanatory power is diluted as they are stretched to account for more than they can encompass. Furthermore, when these concepts are investigated, the research is often weak because alternative hypotheses are not investigated. Take, for example, the vast body of correlated and predictive research on attachment theory. Much of the research "mothers" the theory because alternative conceptualizations are rarely evaluated against attachment theory, and causality is too often implied from the correlations. Moreover, in the hands of some attachment theory is extended to account for phenomenon as diverse as intersubjectivity or borderline personality. Similar critiques can be made of concepts such as projective identification, adaptation, and sensory integration. Far too often the result—especially in a clinical setting—is sectarian positions and incestuous blood feuds.

The alternative to eclecticism, however, is problematic because a theory can all too easily become an assemblage of unrelated pieces lacking a theoretical anchor. Clinicians are often eclectics, but their eclecticism lies in the fact that they have to decide what to *do* in the moment and cannot wait. On the other hand, eclecticism for a theorist or researcher is not imperative because they have the privilege of not having to act, of not knowing, and therefore being able to say they don't know without facing criticism. Unfortunately, sectarian, eclectic, and broad theories alike often fail the tests of being experience-near or clinically authentic. Consider artificial intelligence models, mathematical models of the mind, and a host of neuroscience models of the brain in which the experiencing individual is not even present.

Developmentally-oriented

Of particular concern for me is that much theorizing is a-developmental and fails to conceptualize each individual as actively engaged in a change process with him- or herself, others, and things. Many neuroscience and psychological models conceptualize the individual or the brain as if they, like Athena Goddess of Wisdom, emerged from Zeus's forehead fully formed. Another version of an a-developmental perspective is when theorists create virtual backward developmental histories from the adult state that inevitably lead to the kind of adult (often weirdly like the theorist himself, such as Freud and Piaget) that the theory purports to explain (known as "adult-endstate" models). Examples of adult-endstate models include seeking out infant precursors to borderline adults, or attributing adult cognitive capacities to infants. These endstate models fail to critically appreciate the uniqueness that emerges from the messiness, unpredictability, unique vicissitudes of development. They also fail to appreciate the complex multidirectional interaction of lived experience, genes, and brain structures, and the complexity of the emergent qualitative changes that occur during development. Therefore, such virtual developmental histories and adult-endstate models of lifespan development are hazardous for understanding human functioning, experience, and ontogenetic change, and for guiding clinical practice.

Though it is often difficult to keep in mind and to think through in its full complexity, it is necessary to recognize that experience, genes, and brain, as well as the structures and processes of all three, are not only fundamentally different at different ages, but their constant interplay is also different and makes for qualitative differences in the totality of the biopsychological organization of the individual in each moment over the lifespan. Attempting to understand how things continue to change must be a constant consideration because change affects what is happening now, and what is happening now affects the future. An infant experiencing the toxic stress of abuse for the first time is affected differently than a toddler, and the toddler who chronically experienced stress as an infant experiences it differently than the toddler who did not experience undue stress. These differences are not only differences in the content of the past, they are also constitutive, embodied, and embedded in the actual operation of the processes that generate the toddler's sense of place in the world.

The operation of systems, such as the hypothalamic pituitary access or the vagal systems, are experience-dependent. A history of toxic stress changes how processes operate and, in turn, how the individual functions in the world. The stressed toddler operates—sees the world—with greater vigilance and fearfulness, and the differences in this toddler's process of meaning making will continue to influence what she experiences as she gets older by constituting her very meaning making processes themselves. Though it is an overstatement, change in development argues for the idea of a continuous and ongoing process of *all* affecting *all*.

Culturated

Possibly the process least considered, least understood, least thought about, least incorporated into our biopsychological theorizing, developmental theorizing, and clinical work, is culture. Culture is often referred to, even deferred to, but only superficially and rarely well: "Of course culture is important. (Lets move on)." A large array of theories are "universalist"—we all evolved, we are all biological, every one of us carries around our hunter-gatherer genes and our opportunistic brains, such that the differences among different cultural communities is a matter of differences in the content filed in our brains. Along with being romanticized, the universalist view satisfies our Western fantasies for equality and equi-potentiality. What could be wrong with that? Unfortunately much of it, if not wrong, is wrongheaded, and certainly incomplete.

To start, memory, genes, the brain, and even culture hardly constitute file cabinets. Each is a complex of continuous dynamic processes. Equally important, each of these processes and others unnamed or not yet known are part of a multidirectional set of processes in which experience regulates and shapes, and, in turn, is regulated and shaped by, the same set of processes. Consider how language experience over the first few years of life modifies the very sounds an individual can discriminate—what the individual can actually *hear*, as well as what the individual can actually *speak*. This process is one that involves the interaction of experience, genes, and the brain, and how they work together to modify what an individual *can experience* and *can do* in the world. Infants in all cultures appear to start with the same capacities, but soon become French or Javanese or English listeners and speakers. They do have different content in their minds but more important, their brain processes have been tuned, structurally modified to *do* the language they have been exposed to, and nothing is more cultural than language.

This simultaneous narrowing and refining process may occur in other experiential domains as well. Research seems to suggest that early experience with the faces of one's ethnicity—the faces seen leaning over the crib—increases visual discriminative skills within a particular range of faces and diminishes visual skills outside of that range; that is, what is *seen* as well as the capacity for *seeing* is modified by the exposure. Thus, we can only imagine (and we have spent too little time in such imagining) how such differences in the way a *cultured* seeing, hearing, touching, smelling, playing, and interacting constitute what we *do* and *feel* in the world long before we understand the symbols of our culture.

Indeed, I previously thought it was foolish to argue that peoples who lived in the forest as foragers as opposed to pastoralists who lived on the plains *saw* the world differently. After all, perception created universal Kantian categories. I no longer think this. Much more likely these different peoples *experience* the world differently and they are *not* always able to experience the same thing in the same way. Efe (pygmy) infants interact with every individual in their group every day and will go to any one of them when distressed. As a consequence, their experience of the attachment landscape is one of secure bases wherever they look, as opposed to the singular (sometimes double) vision of Western infants, who usually only turn to their immediate caregiver. Thus it takes no great stretch of imagination to hypothesize that to the extent that the local fullness of all the domains of experience are cultured, so too will the biopsychological processes generating experience be cultured. And what domains of experience are not cultured?

In my view, culture is not an external factor with an arrow aimed at the individual. Rather, it is *inside* the individual as much as anything else is inside the individual. Oddly, seeing culture as inside the individual is a challenge for psychologists and neuroscientists even though so much of their work is getting inside peoples' heads in an effort to see how the inside affects the outside—for example, looking at how one's attachment to one's mother affects other relationships. Yet neither one's mother nor one's attachment to her is a-cultural. The way she moves and talks and interacts with her child as well as with others are not simply expressions of her uniqueness; they are a manifestation of a *cultured* uniqueness. Her "cultured way" is transferred to her child, affecting what the child experiences and how the child experiences him- or herself in the world.

Thus, the criteria for my theoretical perspective are as follows: experience-near and clinically informed, broad and integrative, developmental and culturated. And actually, there is another: The theory has to be testable and generative of hypotheses, not simply descriptive. It is especially important to keep this criterion in mind when so much of my thinking is influenced by dynamic systems theory, which is so general, experience-*far*, and powerfully descriptive. Dynamic systems theory is more easily used as a kind of meta-theory rather than a deeply instantiated psychological theory of how people live and make sense of their place in the world. Yet so much of my effort is aimed at instantiating it.

THE MUTUAL REGULATION MODEL

I will start with my Mutual Regulation Model (MRM) because it is foundational and intimately related to my thinking about the Dyadic Expansion of States of Consciousness Model, and the complexity and coherence of individuals' ways of being in the world (Beeghly & Tronick, 1994; Tronick, 1989). The MRM views the infant and the caretaker as parts of a larger regulatory system. Let's start with the MRM's view of the infant.

Infant Self-organizing Neurobehavioral Capacities

The MRM postulates that infants have self-organizing neurobehavioral capacities that operate to organize behavioral states (from sleep to alertness) and biopsychological processes—such as self-regulation of arousal, selective attention, learning and memory, social engagement and communication, neuroception, and acting purposefully in the world—that they use for making sense of themselves and their place in the world. In the first several chapters of this book I present research on this postulate.

My early work on neurobehavioral capacities was carried out with Berry Brazelton as we constructed the Neonatal Behavioral Assessment Scale (NBAS; Tronick 1987; see Chapter 1). The NBAS is a neurobehavioral scale used for evaluating infant capacities for self-soothing, habituation to disturbing events, regulation of states, differential attention to people and things, and interaction with adults. Infants' self-organized neurobehavioral capacities have been much elaborated upon since then, but when we first created the scale in 1970 the infant was viewed as undifferentiated and disorganized, reflexive with only all-or-none, either/or states of distress or sleep, harking back to Freud's original notions. At the time when Berry and I, along with Jerome Bruner, examined infants at the Mount Auburn Hospital in Cambridge, we felt like we were discovering a new species.

My later research utilized much more sophisticated techniques to investigate infant neurobehavior. In 1993, Linda Fetters and I used computerized kinematic analysis of movement and ultrasound brain imaging techniques to explore how brain lesions might compromise infant self-organization (Fetters, Chen, Jonsdottir, & Tronick, 2004; see Chapter 3). We found that infants with almost identical lesions would have radically different outcomes (e.g., cerebral palsy versus normal movements), suggesting that self-organization and (still) unknown features of experience (e.g., carrying patterns) play key roles in determining the quality of movement. In 1996, Barry Lester and I developed a new neurobehavioral scale, the NICU Network Neurobehavioral Scale (NNNS; Lester & Tronick, 2004; see Chapter 2). The NNNS makes a detailed assessment of the interplay between stressors and infant self-regulatory abilities. It is highly reliable because it is administered in a standard fashion and specifies what behavioral states (e.g., state 1 or 2 sleep, alertness) an item can be administered in (or not), because the biopsychological state of the infant affects his or her response characteristics to an item (e.g., looking at faces is different in quiet alertness compared to active alertness).

The differential reactivity in different self-organized states is a clear demonstration of how the sense of the world even newborns make is related to the biopsychological state of consciousness. We have used the NNNS to examine how stressors, such as in utero drug exposure or maternal depression, affect infant neurobehavioral organization as well as to predict long-term outcome. Using the NNNS we developed standardized data on newborn neurobehavioral organization (e.g., percentiles for different neurobehavioral performances on the items) for the first time (Fetters, Chen, Jonsdottir, & Tronick, 2004). And in longitudinal studies we saw relations of different NNNS profiles and outcomes at 7 and 8 years (Lester & Tronick, in preparation). These data will aid clinicians' evaluation of newborn neurobehavior and development and suggest forms of clinical interventions to foster development.

Mutual Regulation

Despite their impressive self-organizing neurobehavioral capacities, infants' capacities clearly have limits. Even were they sufficient in the moment to deal with an internal or external regulatory disruption, they would not be sufficient over time. An infant can utilize a number of mechanisms (e.g., crying, moving, and "fetaling up") to self-regulate homeothermy, but eventually these resources fail. A resolution to the limitation of self-organizing capacities occurred when I recognized that an infant could not be viewed as a self-contained system. Rather, we have to think of an infant as a sub-system within a larger dyadic regulatory system. The other sub-system is the caregiver. I saw this larger system as a dyadic system that functioned to scaffold an infant's limited regulatory capacities. Interestingly, coming from studies on infant neurobehavior, I concluded what Winnicott—coming from his clinical observations—had postulated some 50 years before: "No baby is without a mother" (Winnicott, 1964). However, for me the immediate question not dealt with by Winnicott was how was this regulation was guided and directed? After all, misapplied regulation could further dysregulate an infant. A caretaker calming a crying infant but leaving her exposed to too low a temperature actually disrupts the self-regulatory effect of crying, which warms the infant. Calming, in this case, exacerbates the demands on the infant.

My idea was that regulation was accomplished by the operation of a communication system in which the infant communicated its regulatory status to the caregiver, who responded to the *meaning* of the communication. An infant cry means something ("I am in trouble"), as does a bright alert look ("I am fine"). A parent does not see a baby's clenched hand as a fist, but without awareness knows the baby is stressed. If this postulate of the MRM was true, infants had to have organized communicative displays related to their internal state and to their external intentions and goals, and caregivers had to have capacities to apprehend and respond to the meaning of these messages. Also, as I will address later, keep in mind that the MRM is easily extended to the self-organizing capacities and limitations of adults and *their* need for external scaffolding, albeit around issues different than those of infants. Furthermore, the MRM can be extended to understand therapeutic change processes.)

In a sense, the end of the theory of the self-contained infant was also the end of one-person psychology. This formulation also overlays a deeper question pondered in multiple places in the book: Given their self-organizing capacities, what do infants (and adults) "know" about themselves and the world? We will come back to this question.

"Messy" Interactions, Intersubjectivity, and Reparation

My thinking about regulation and communication led to my studies of the organization of infant–adult (mothers and fathers and strangers) face-to-face interaction as presented in Part III of the book. I devised a technique using reel-to-reel videotape recorders and hand-cranked slow-motion to micro-analytically code the communicative expressions of infants and adults and their interactions. This technique now seems crude, but it functioned as a temporal microscope expanding time. In these groundbreaking studies we discovered the temporal organization of the dyadic communication system, contingencies of signaling (of meaning), synchrony and attunements (Tronick, 1989).

I developed statistical approaches to analyzing the time series streams of infant and adult communication, though as gently pointed out by my friend John Gottman, our initial application of these techniques was problematic. Later, using better techniques with guidance from John, we discovered the bidirectional (mutual) influence of the infant and the adult successfully challenging the idea that the infant was passive. Our results (Cohn & Tronick, 1988; see Chapter 16) demonstrated infants initiating contact and responding to turn-taking signals and to specific emotional displays in specific ways as well as signaling to their adult partner their evaluation of what the adult was doing. Our findings on infant self-organized capacities raised questions about one directional analogy of the therapeutic process (Tronick & Cohn, 1989; see Chapter 12).

It was at this time and in considering the mutuality of infant–adult interaction that I borrowed Habermas's concept of intersubjectivity and brought it into the developmental literature. *Intersubjectivity* is a concept about the exchange of meaning. I suggested that in the infant–adult interaction there is a mutual apprehension in which each understands what the other intends. Others (Trevarthen & Hubley, 1978) seized this concept more fully than I, but I felt that although intersubjectivity required an exchange process it glossed over and did not explain the nature of it. Critically, intersubjectivity does not explain how acquiring meaning and creating shared meaning states grows the complexity and coherence of the individual. Nonetheless, intersubjectivity is a pre-cognition to meaning- making, states of consciousness, and their dyadic expansion.

Initially, the organization of the infant-mother interaction seemed clear: It was bi-directional, synchronous, and coordinated. Indeed, these dyadic phenomena were impressive. Here were small infants actively engaged in a very fast (micro-second) exchange of information. But as my research progressed, findings began to emerge that demanded a different take on what was going on in the interaction. Among others, the most telling finding seemed to be that much of the time there was a lack of coordination between the infant and the adult. I felt compelled to characterize and understand what I saw as the "messiness" of the interactions. I described this messiness as a mismatch of the affective states and relational intentions that occurred when the infant and adult were conveying non-matching meanings: Infant: "I want you to look at me." Adult: "I want to look away." Most importantly, I recognized that re-achieving a matching state from a mismatching state was a mutually regulated reparatory process.

This view of the reparatory organization of the interaction was an alternative to the dominant view of the interaction as highly synchronized or attuned. The synchrony model of the interaction (to which many of us ascribed at the time, and to which some theorists still do) not only does not reflect the findings on interactions, it also romanticizes the mother–infant relationship. Further, it leads to pathological clinical judgments of the normal, typical, and ubiquitous messiness of infant–adult relationships. For that matter, messiness characterizes most if not all social relationships, such as Gottman's characterization of marital relationships (Gottman & Levenson, 1988). My idea of a messy reparatory organization of the interaction was also the foundation for the Boston Process of Change Group's view of psychoanalysis as a sloppy process (Boston Change Process Study Group, 2002).

The Still-Face Perturbation

To evaluate these hypotheses, I created the face-to-face/still-face (FFSF) paradigm. The paradigm is based on a simple a priori deduction: If infants are regulating the state of the interaction and themselves by responding to adult regulatory input, meanings, and intentions, then if the adult's communications are perturbated, the infant should detect this disruption, attempt to correct it, and react to it in meaningful ways. In the experiment, we instructed the adult to hold a still-face and not move or talk after a period of normal interaction with the infant. The now well-known results were dramatic. Infants attempted to solicit the mother's attention and when their efforts failed they looked away, withdrew, and expressed sad and angry affect. The infant was actively regulating the interaction and was apprehending and responding to the adult's perturbated communication. The critical implication is that in normal exchanges infants also apprehend and respond to the adult's expressed meaning.

With the creation of the FFSF paradigm, a number of studies followed including the creation of a simulated depression paradigm. Mothers were instructed to "Act the way you do on the days you feel blue;" none had trouble doing just that. In response, the infants became sad and withdrawn. Shortly thereafter, we began the first observational studies of the face-to-face interactions of depressed mothers and their infants. These studies opened up a field of developmental observations of infants with parents with a variety of behavioral disorders (e.g., mothers with borderline personality disorder; Apter-Danon, Devouche, Valente, & Le Nestour, 2004) as well as studies of the effects of interventions (e.g., George Downing's video micro therapy; Downing, 2003). We also studied other naturally occurring perturbations that we thought would have effects on infant self-regulation, maternal behavior, and their interaction. These included some of the first microanalytic studies of infants' or parents' blindness or deafness, infant facial anomalies, and medical status (e.g., drug exposure, prematurity). All of these disturbances of the communicative regulatory system had effects—but not always ill effects—as dyads, such as a sighted mother and a blind infant, somehow found ways to mutually regulate their interaction and each other.

Cultured and Other Perturbations

In a critical reversal of the experimental perturbation approach, I expanded my research to include naturally occurring perturbations such as the relation of culturated forms of self- and interactive regulation and experience. I found these studies profoundly interesting and several of them are presented in Part II of the book. They all made the same point: Western models of childrearing and development are severely limited and narrow.

The study of Quechua childrearing practices in high-altitude Peru demonstrated a form of "normal" caretaking that Western theorists would have considered to be a form of stimulus deprivation inevitably leading to pathological development (Tronick, Thomas, & Daltabuit, 1994; see Chapter 9). In Peru it did not, though I am sure the Quechua infants and adults experienced the world differently. Likewise, the study of the multiple caretaking system of Efe foragers living in the Ituri forest did not conform to universalist or evolutionary hypotheses or to attachment theory, with its concept of monotropy in the niche of human evolution (Tronick, Winn, & Morelli, 1985; see Chapter 8). Yet the system was "normal," and Efe infants became acculturated adults who "naturally" made sense of the world in an Efe-created culturated way.

In Kenya, Gusii mothers do not often engage in face-to-face play, a form of play thought to be required for normal development. When *asked* to engage in face-to-face play Gussii mothers turned away from their infants just as the infants were most focused on them and most excited. This is a behavior that would be labeled as pathological in the West, but functions to shape normal Gusii infants' experience of the world as a Gusii, not as a Western infant. The full implications of this work insist that not only do these different culturated individuals-in-groups have different experiences, but the very processes that generate experience are culturated (Tronick & Morelli, 1991; see Chapter 7).

MEANING MAKING

From thinking about reparation and therapeutic interactions and my research on culturated communication systems, depression, children with anomalies (cleft lip), and the range and variety of normal interactions, I came increasingly to realize that the communication system could not be seen as an "empty" process with referents only to measures of information (bytes) or only in terms of the qualities of the interaction (e.g., synchrony). Bruner (1990) has made the point forcefully that measures of information are uninformative as to what the information is about. In particular for the human communication system it is not *how much* information is being conveyed but what the information is *about*. Process terms can make vastly different phenomena equivalent. For example, privileging the qualities of the process of dancing (synchrony, complexity) masks the differences in the dance being performed (the tango, hip hop, etc.). Such terms are not uninteresting (who would want to be awkward?), but they ignore the kind of dance the dancers are doing together. People do need some yet-to-be-determined level of mutual regulation when they are doing something together, but they cannot be in synchrony without actually doing something together.

So, too, for the communication system. It is not always well-coordinated and smooth, but it must be filled with something, and the "somethings" are meaning, intentions, purposes, and the like. These meanings can be conveyed with different communication qualities (smoothly, disjointedly) and via different channels (language, facial expressions, moods, gestures), but some*thing* must be communicated. For me, the critical "somethings" are the individual's biopsychological state of consciousness, their experiential state, their intentions to act in the world, their cultural and somatic meanings, and their relational intentions to be with and to create new meanings with others. Furthermore, no alternative exists to seeing the known and unknown meaning of being in the world for every individual as distinct and unique.

USING THE THEORY TO THINK ABOUT PRACTICE

There is a relation (but very far from a strict relation) between the mutual regulation model of infant–adult interactions and the patient–therapist interaction, which was at the core of the work I did with the Boston Process of Change Group (Tronick, 1998). I saw that therapy, like infant–adult interactions, is a messy process of match-mismatch and reparation, with two active meaning making individuals in the room. I argued that reparation of messiness rather than synchrony might be a key change-inducing process in therapy and development. In development, reparation has the effect of the infant and adult coming to experience and implicitly know that the negative experience of a mismatch can be transformed into a positive, affective match, that the partner can be trusted, and that one can be effective in acting on the world. Also, in repairing interactive messiness new implicit ways of being together for the infant and adult are co-created and come to be implicitly known.

In the Boston Process of Change Group, we saw therapeutic analysis as a sloppy process with change occurring during moments of meeting when the sloppiness was repaired. Thus, in the reparation of mismatches in therapy, the patient who may be stuck in negative affect experiences its transformation into positive affect. Further, by working on the messiness of the therapeutic relationship the patient (and the therapist) comes to know new ways of being with the therapist and, in turn, with others. The reparation model and its findings clearly imply that relationships are dyadically regulated and that the infant and, in this case, the patient are active, intentional, and capable of making reparations in the relationship. But unlike the Boston Process of Change Group's findings, the implicit knowing that comes from being together is not sufficient to produce change. I felt that something else more classic in its origins was needed: a change in meaning, made by the infant or the patient, about their place in the world.

As I touched upon earlier, successful creation of a dyadic state of consciousness and selective appropriation of meaning from it, by the individuals creating it, expands the complexity of their individual states of consciousness and fulfills the principle of dynamic systems. But how is all of this systems theory experience-near and clinically relevant?

The Dyadic Expansion of States of Consciousness Model is experience-near because there are experiential consequences to the success or failure of the process of expanding the complexity and coherence of states of consciousness. When new information is selectively incorporated the individual experiences a sense of expansion, joy, and movement into the world. A successful increase in complexity leads to a sense of connection to the other person in the dyadic state, and a relationship to him or her emerges. Importantly, a sense of connection to one's self develops, accompanied by a feeling of solidity, stability, and continuity of the self. Additionally, the inherent momentum that comes from forming states leads to a sense of impelling certitude about one's place in the world—a sense, in or out of awareness, that "I know this (whatever it is) to be true." By contrast, when meaning is not incorporated, or incorporated unsuccessfully, the complexity of the state dissipates. The individual experiences a sense of shrinkage, sadness and/or anger, and a withdrawal and disconnection from the world, from others, and from his- or herself. The feeling of continuity in time is compromised. Thus, a variety of powerful experiential consequences travel with success or failure of expansion, not the least of which is that successful meaning making is the constitutive process of relationship formation.

Many implications of the expansion model in clinical work are presented in the following chapters. According to the principles of dynamic systems theory, letting go of old meanings requires giving up organization and certitude, and threatens the unpredictable but implicitly hoped for outcome of expansion. Change for a patient means risking dissipation and experiencing fear or even the terror of annihilation and the dissolution of the self. But change also means hope.

Another implication for therapeutic technique is that the therapist has to scaffold the patient's movement towards greater complexity and coherence rather than work on the resistance that arises for psychodynamic reasons. There are two sides to this scaffolding process. One side is to help regulate the affect that threatens the patient's willingness to risk change such that successful scaffolding then allows the patient's self-organized processes to make new meaning and fulfill his or her hopes. The second side of the scaffolding process comes from co-creating a dyadic state of consciousness, in which the patient and therapist can make new, more complex and coherent meanings together. As new meanings form, the patient's feelings of trust in his- or herself and the therapist increase, amplifying the possibility of change.

Because meanings come from multiple levels in the individual, some meanings may only be available to the therapist and/or the patient in certain states of receptivity. Alert interpretative states may detect the meaning in cognitions and language and produce insight, but Ogden's (1997) reverie states may be needed to apprehend meanings from preconscious or unconscious levels, and Downing's (2003) body work may be needed to reach meanings at other biopsychological levels. And because I believe that we have not identified all the ways that a therapist or a patient comes to reach certain levels of meaning, there will be meanings that may be available to one or the other that are not apprehended and cannot be formulated yet produce change.

There also is the somewhat vicious clinical implication of complexity-governed selection: The selective force of complexity operates moment-to-moment to maximize coherence and complexity of the individual's state of consciousness and, like natural selection, it is blind to the state the system is moving toward. As a consequence, complexity is not necessarily adaptive in either the short or the long run (adaptation being an appropriate adjustment to external or internal circumstances) because increasing complexity hardly equals successful adaptation).

For example, an individual may stay in a destructive relationship or have a self-debilitating sense of place in the world because these may be the only ways in which to maintain or perhaps increase complexity in the moment. These are solutions in the moment, but in the long run they may lead to the preclusion of engagement with the social world or other ways of being in the world that could be expansive. In these patients, dissipation and terror are a constant threat and the need for the therapist and the patient to co-create mutual strategies to modulate these affective states is essential. More generally, complexity-governed selection as a moment-by-moment process adds to our understanding of how patients persist in living in an experiential world filled with sadness and fear that cuts them off from the world and themselves, and may ultimately lead to generating non-linear techniques for inducing change. For example, with her patients Alexandra Harrison uses repetition of the same interactive sequence for prolonged periods to demonstrate that sudden state changes can emerge from "repetition of the same" (Harrison, 2003; see Chapter 36).

CONCLUSION

I believe the theoretical perspective presented in this book addresses a host of other questions: What are the different types of meaning-making processes? Is meaning and its making and the remembrance of the past actually a multi-leveled, biopsychological process as I argue, or is meaning only in the mind? What induces us to change? What is the nature of psychological change and what principles govern it? What is the relation between meaning making and mutual regulation? Why and how are relationships so important to human development? What makes relationships unique, and is there such a thing as a prototypical (attachment) relationship? What makes us stay in a painful relationship? What principles govern our moment-to-moment actions versus our developmental pathway over a lifespan?

How many of these questions and others the MRM and the Dyadic Expansion of States of Consciousness Model can help us answer will be yours to judge. Certainly, these two models will not answer all of these questions but I think they will provide purchase on many of them. Importantly, rather than being purely descriptive in nature, the biopsychological instantiation of these ideas in dynamic systems theory will, I think, allow us to make deductions about how people experience and live in the world and how they change both themselves and their relation to world.

If I experience too much certitude about this, it likely emerges because I feel I have found a secure base in the Norton Series on Interpersonal Neurobiology. This series is at the dynamically forming critical edge of developmental psychology, relational neurosciences, therapeutic processes, and dynamic systems theory. The editors have "scaffolded" me to talk about, explore, and co-create emergent understandings out of the creative messiness embedded in my ideas of self- and mutual regulation, reparation, meaning making, states of consciousness, and their expansion. Of course, that is the simple goal of the book: to present these ideas, explore them, and encourage us together—virtually, and hopefully at times together, in real time and space—to co-create a more coherent and complex understanding of these ideas, and of ourselves in the world.

REFERENCES

Apter-Danon G. G. R., Devouche, E.,Valente, M., Le Nestour, A. (2004). *Role of maternal mood and personality disorder in mother-infant interactive and regulatory capacities: Implications for interventions.* Paper presented at the International Conference of Infant Studies, Chicago, 2006.

Ball, W., & Tronick, E. Z. (1971). Infant responses to impending collision: Optical and real. *Science, 171,* 818–920.

Beeghly, M. & Tronick, E. Z. (1994). Effects of prenatal exposure to cocaine in early infancy: Toxic effects on the process of mutual regulation. *Infant Mental Health Journal, 15*(2), 158–175.

Bollas, C. (1987). *The shadow of the object: Psychoanalysis of the unthought known.* New York: Columbia University Press.

Boston Change Process Study Group (Harrison, A. M., L.-R. K., Morgan, A. C., Bruschweiler-Stern, N., Naham, J. P., Stern, D. N., Sander, L. W., Tronick, E. Z.) (2002). Explicating the implicit: The local level of microprocess of change in the analytic situation. *International Journal of Psychoanalysis, 83,* 105–162.

Bruner, J. (1990). *Acts of meaning.* Cambridge, MA: Harvard University Press.

Cohn, J. F., & Tronick, E. (1988). Mother-infant face-to-face interaction: Influence is bidirectional and unrelated to periodic cycles in either partner's behavior. *Development Psychology, 24,* 386–392.

Downing, G. (2003). Video Microanalyse Therapie: Einige Gundlagen und Prinzipien. In H. Scheuerer-English, G. J. Suess, & W. Pfeifer (Eds.), *Wege Zur Sicherheit: Bindungswissen In Diagnostik Und Intervention* (pp. 51–68.). Gottengin: Geissen: Psychosocial Verlag.

Fetters, L., Chen, Y. P., Jonsdottir, J., & Tronick, E. Z. (2004). Kicking coordination captures differences between full term and premature infants with white matter disorder. *Human Movement Science, 22*(6), 729–748.

Freeman, W. J. (2000). *How brains make up their mind.* New York: Columbia University Press.

Gottman, J. M., & Levenson, R. (1988). The social psychophysiology of marriage. In P. Noller & M. A. Fitzpatrick (Eds.), *Perspectives on marital interaction* (pp. 182–200). San Diego, CA: College-Hill.

Harrison, A. M. (2003). Change in psychoanalysis: Getting from A to B. *Journal of the American Psychoanalytic Association, 51,* 221–257.

Lester, B. M., & Tronick, E. Z. (2004). The Neonatal Intensive Care Unit Network Neurobehavioral Scale (NNNS). *Pediatrics, 113*(3), 631–699.

Lester, B. M., & Tronick, E. Z. (in preparation). Predictions of outcome at 6 to 8 years from the Neonatal Intensive Care Unit Network Neurobehavioral Scale (NNNS) administered in the newborn period in a sample of infants born preterm.

Modell, A. (1993). *The private self.* Cambridge, MA: Harvard University Press.

Ogden, T. (1997). *Reverie and interpretation: Sensing something human.* Lanham, MD: Rowman & Littlefield.

Trevarthen, C., & Hubley, P. (1978). Secondary intersubjectivity: Confidence, confiding, and acts of meaning in the first year. In A. Lock (Ed.), *Action, gesture, and symbol: The emergence of language* (pp. 183–229). New York: Academic Press.

Tronick, E. Z. (1987). The Neonatal Behavioral Assessment Scale as a biomarker of the effects of environmental agents on the newborn. *Environmental Health Perspectives, 74*, 185–189.

Tronick, E. Z. (1989). Emotions and emotional communication in infants. *American Psychologist, 44*(2), 112–119.

Tronick, E. Z. (1998). Interactions that effect change in psychotherapy: A model based on infant research. *Infant Mental Health Journal, 19*, 1–290.

Tronick, E. Z., & Cohn, J. F. (1989). Infant-mother face-to-face interaction: Age and gender differences in coordination and the occurrence of miscoordination. *Child Development, 60*, 85–92.

Tronick, E. Z., & Morelli, G. A. (1991). Foreword: The role of culture in brain organization, child development, and parenting. In J. K. Nugent, B. M. Lester, & T. B. Brazelton (Eds.), *The cultural context of infancy: Multicultural and interdisciplinary approaches to parent-infant relations* (2nd ed., pp. ix–xiii). Norwood, NJ: Ablex Publishing.

Tronick, E. Z., Thomas, R. B., & Daltabuit, M. (1994). The Quechua manta pouch: A caretaking practice for buffering the Peruvian infant against the multiple stressors of high altitude. *Ch Dev, 65*, 1005–1013.

Tronick, E. Z., & Weinberg, M. K. (1997). Depressed mothers and infants: Failure to form dyadic states of consciousness. In L. Murray & P. J. Cooper (Eds.), *Postpartum depression and child development* (pp. 54–81). New York: Guilford Press.

Tronick, E. Z., Winn, S., & Morelli, G. (1985). Multiple caretaking in the context of human evolution: Why don't the Efe know the Western prescription for child care? In M. Reite & T. Field (Eds.), *The Psychobiology of attachment and separation* (pp. 293–322). Denver, CO and Miami, FL: Harcourt Brace Jovanovich.

Winnicott, D. W. (1964). *The child, the family, and the outside world*. Baltimore, MD: Penguin Books.

PART I

NEUROBEHAVIOR

The Neonatal Behavioral Assessment Scale as a Biomarker of the Effects of Environmental Agents on the Newborn

The transient and somewhat undifferentiated organization of the newborn's brain and the typically nonspecific and overlapping effects of different environmental agents on the newborn conspire to produce complex and difficult problems for marking the effects of environmental agents on the newborn. These problems can, in part, be overcome by using newly developed instruments for assessing the newborn's behavior. In this essay, I will briefly present characteristics of the newborn brain as well as characteristics of the effects of environmental agents that create assessment problems. Second, I will describe the behaviors of the newborn and the use of the Neonatal Behavioral Assessment Scale (Brazelton, 1984) to resolve some of the problems of assessment. Third, I will suggest a general strategy for correcting some of the problems remaining after application of this assessment scale. I focus on assessment techniques. This essay is not a comprehensive review of the effects of environmental agents, but to some extent an attempt to broaden the definition of what is considered a teratogenic effect.

THE PROBLEM OF ASSESSMENT

The newborn brain, compared to the older brain, is less differentiated and integrated (Peiper, 1963). It is thought to have considerable redundant structure or capacity—a capacity that decreases with maturation (Prechtl, 1981b). The newborn brain is as unique to the newborn period as it is to any developmental period (Prechtl, 1981b). Indeed, many of its structures, forms of organization, and functions are thought to be transient and characteristic of this and no other period of development (Anokhin, 1984). One reason for the uniqueness is that brain maturation is not simultaneous in all areas. Rather, maturation proceeds at different rates for different areas depending on which areas are necessary for performing the functions characteristic of a specific developmental period. This means that as it develops, the brain undergoes qualitative changes such as the presence but later disappearance of radial glial cells that function as a guiding framework for migrating neurons, or the presence of supernumerary synaptic contacts and axons and their later reductions (Rakic, 1978; Redfern,1970; Scheibel, Davies, & Scheibel, 1973; Silver, 1978). Additionally, the uniqueness of the newborn brain is the result of the fact that inputs must take place during limited periods of time to have their normal effects. Finally, a critical reason for this uniqueness is that the brain's normal functioning and development are under the control of internal processes as they interact with environmental input (Spinelli, Jensen, & Viana di Prisco, 1980). Obviously, the environmental input of special importance is that provided by the caregiver. Caregiving must be precisely adapted to the properties of the newborn so that it too has a form in the newborn period that is different from the form it will have in other periods (Redfern, 1970; Tronick, Als, & Brazelton, 1979).

These features of the infant's brain appear to create a number of problems of assessment. The newborn is likely to present fewer specific biomarkers to assess than its older counterpart. Some of the available biomarkers are transient and may hold little importance for later functioning. Others certainly are the precursors of later functions, but their transformation during development is unknown. The biomarkers available are likely to be more difficult to quantify than are those of the older child. This makes it difficult to assess subtle and sometimes even large distortions in their form, their time of appearance, and their coordination with other functions. Last, because their form and timing are modified by the environment, the quality of the environment may need to be assessed if one wants to predict their developmental outcome.

Unfortunately, what we know of the nature of the effects of environmental agents on the newborn does not help us to resolve these issues. If we knew the unique specific effect or even the general effects of different environmental agents on the newborn's functioning, then we could look for that effect with some disregard for other problems (Weiss & Spyker, 1974). However, our knowledge suggests that the effects of different agents are likely to be overlapping, subtle, and invasive of many areas of integrated functioning of the newborn (Fein, Schwartz, Jacobson, & Jacobson, 1983; Hutchings, 1978; Jacobson, Jacobson, Schwartz, Fein, & Dowler, 1984; Seposki, 1985). For example, the most studied environmental agents are the pain-killing agents used in obstetric procedures (Seposki, 1985). The hospital-based use of these agents gives us access to a large number of subjects, some control over their experience, and more detailed information on the history of the subject's exposure and other confounding variables (Tronick et al., 1976). Analgesic agents such as the various barbiturates have been found to modify electrophysiological characteristics of the brain, disrupt infants' sleep-wake cycles, disorganize their sucking patterns, decrease their responsiveness to environmental events, and produce overactivity, excessive crying, and hypertonicity (Brakbill, 1976; Brazelton, 1971; Hughes, Eheman, & Brown, 1948; Kron, Stein, & Goddard, 1966; Lester, Als, & Brazelton, 1982). Many similar effects are seen when the obstetric medication is one of the anesthetic agents such as lidocaine (Lester et al., 1982; Scanlon & Hollenback, 1983; Seposki, 1985; Tronick et al., 1976). Some differentiation is possible between the effects of these drugs; for example, barbiturates tend to produce hypertonia with decrements in alertness, whereas lidocaine tends to produce hypotonia without associated effects on alertness. But, for the most part, their effects are similar and generalized. Moreover, modifications of each of these behaviors has been found to affect the caretaking the infant receives (Brazelton, 1971; Brazelton, Koslowski, & Main, 1974; Richards & Bernall, 1972; Seposki, 1985; Tronick et al., 1979).

The first point, then, is that assessment of the teratogenic effects of environmental agents on the newborn's development is a complicated and difficult task because of the nature of development and the nature of the toxic effects. Furthermore, the importance of caretaking to normal development suggests that the definition of teratology may need to be expanded once again (Sameroff & Chandler, 1975; Tronick et al., 1976). According to the history of this field, the definition of teratology was easily expanded from the mortal effects of different agents to morphological effects. Later, with some difficulty, it was expanded to encompass functional effects. I think now we may need to add distortions of the infant's behavior that alter the caregiver's behavior (Bell, 1971; Sameroff & Chandler, 1975).

NEWBORN BEHAVIORAL CAPACITIES

What type of test can we use to assess the newborn? Before we can answer this question, we need to know what capacities of the newborn we can assess. Recent research has demonstrated that newborns possess a rich and complex set of behaviors for regulating their internal states and their exchanges with the environment (Tronick et al., 1976). These behaviors provide a good basis for assessment.

A fundamental self-regulatory capacity of the newborn is the ability to organize five different behavioral states: two kinds of sleep states, two kinds of awake or alert states, and one kind of distress state (Anders & Weinstein, 1972; Prechtl, 1981b; Prechtl & Beintema, 1964; Wolff, 1959). Each of these states is made up of a qualitatively different and coherent organization of physiological systems, such as respiration and heart rate; electrophysiological systems, such as electroencephalogram; and behavioral systems, such as motor tone and motility (Prechtl, 1974). These states are conceptualized as reflecting changes in the mode of activity of the nervous system. They function to change the nature of the input-output relations between the newborn and the environment by modifying the responsiveness of the newborn to different stimuli. For example, the infant's auditory responsiveness is greater in State 2 sleep than in State 1 sleep, whereas most of its proprioceptive reflexes are greater in State 1 sleep than in State 2 sleep (Prechtl, 1972). Visual responses are available only in the two awake states (Prechtl, 1972). An infant who was unable to organize his states or was unable to control their sequencing would be unable to set up reliable relations between himself and the environment.

The infant has two abilities for selectively modifying his responsiveness within behavioral states. The first is habituation, the ability not to respond to an environmental stimulus that is either disrupting the newborn's state organization or has no functional significance to the newborn (Tronick et al., 1976). Habituation is sometimes thought to be a primitive form of learning. For example, infants are able to inhibit their motor responses and startle responses to repeated disturbing sounds. An infant whose capacity for habituation was disturbed would be at the mercy of disruptive environmental stimuli.

The second selective capacity is the infant's ability to orient to and process information from the environment. Infants can look, listen, smell, touch, and taste with amazing facility (Eimas, Siqueland, Juzczyk, & Vigorito, 1971; Engen, Lipsitt, & Kaye, 1963; Fantz, 1961; Kearsley, 1973; Tronick et al., 1976). Infants can make coordinated head and eye movements and visually locate and discriminate among different targets (Fantz, 1961). They can turn their heads toward and localize a sound (Tronick et al., 1976). They can discriminate among different tastes and differentiate the odor of their mother's milk from the odor of another mother's milk (MacFarlane, 1975). They are capable of coordinating information between different perceptual systems and between perceptual and motor systems. For example, newborns are able visually to identify an object that they have previously sucked on but not seen, or imitate another person's facial expression (Meltzoff & Moore, 1977).

Clearly, the infant's behavior is not simply a compilation of reflexes. For example, the exploratory behavior of the infant's head and mouth as it searches for the nipple and its latching onto it when it is found, followed by the coordination of breathing with sucking and swallowing is indicative of complex motor control systems (Prechtl, 1958). So is the change in the infant's neutral facial expression to an expression of interest when he turns toward and sees the source of a sound he has been searching for when he finally locates it (Brazelton, 1984). Importantly, many of the infant's behaviors, including facial expressions, cries, tremors, startles, and even behavioral states function to change and guide the behavior of the newborn's caretaker (Osofsky & Danzger, 1974; Tronick et al., 1976). An infant who is fussy and moving in a discoordinated fashion receives different caretaking than a newborn who is awake and alert with relaxed, fluid movements. This suggests the possibility that the infant in part controls his own development by modifying the caretaking he receives.

The infant thus displays an impressive array of behavioral capacities that lend themselves to functioning as biomarkers in the form of an apical assessment.

Apical assessments are procedures that assess the overall ability of the organism to adapt to its situation (Hutchings, 1978). An apical assessment is a comprehensive test that examines a variety of functions. Successful performance requires the integration of intact subsystems. To be effective, an apical assessment must be quantifiable, able to detect subtle differences in performance, and reliable. This means assessing the newborn's integrated actions that function to regulate its internal state and its exchanges with the environment, primarily the animate environment of caregivers.

There are several assessments that have attempted to meet these criteria (Amiel-Tisson, Barrier, & Schnider, 1982; Graham, Matarazzo, & Caldwell, 1956; Prechtl & Beintema, 1964; Rosenblith, 1961; Saint-Anne Dargassies, 1977; Touwen, 1976). The Neonatal Behavioral Assessment Scale developed by the pediatrician Brazelton is the most successful effort to date (Als, Tronick, Lester, & Brazelton, 1977; Brazelton, 1984; Lasaer, 1979; Parmalee, Kopp, & Sigman, 1976; Prechtl, 1981b; Sameroff, 1978). Brazelton's scale is an integration and systematization of clinical knowledge of the newborn, the nature of the effects of the newborn's behavior on its caregivers, and our increased understanding of the newborn's functioning derived from developmental research. The scale is a valid and reliable instrument (Als et al., 1977; Brazelton, 1984; Lester, 1979; Sameroff, 1978) that can detect subtle differences in performance. It uses reflexes and 26 behavioral performance items to assess seven domains of infant functioning (Table 1.1; Lester, 1979): habituation, orientation, motor performance, range of state, regulation of state, autonomic regulation, and reflexes. To put this in other words, the Brazelton examination looks inward at an infant's capacities to maintain physiological homeostasis, to organize his states of consciousness, and defend himself against disruptions of these states by external stimulation. The scale also looks outward at the infant's capacities to engage the environment and the effect that the infant's form of engagement might have on the environment. The examination of an infant by a trained examiner takes about 30 to 40 minutes.

Research with the Brazelton scale has demonstrated its usefulness in detecting deviations in performance as biomarkers produced by environmental agents, most often obstetric medications, but also for PCBs; recreational drugs, including marijuana, tobacco, and caffeine; and other factors such as subclinical and clinical malnutrition (Als et al., 1977; Fein et al., 1983; Jacobson, et al., 1984; Lester & Dreher, 1987; Lester et al., 1982; Parke et al., 1972; Tronick et al., 1979). For example, Jacobson et al. (1984) and Fein et al. (1983) found abnormal behavioral development in a group of infants whose mothers had chronic exposure to PCBs. The strongest relationships were found between the consumption level of contaminated fish and the infant's organization of behavioral state, motor performance, and physiological regulation. Specifically, the exposed infants had more jerky, unbalanced, cogwheel motor movements, a greater number of abnormal reflexes, and fewer state changes. No deviations were noted in their orientation performance. These effects remained after likely

TABLE 1.1   Brazelton Scale Items That Are Included in the Seven A Priori Clusters

Cluster	Brazelton scale item
Habituation	Response decrement to: light, rattle, bell, pin prick
Orientation	Inanimate visual (red ball)
	Inanimate visual (rattle)
	Animate visual (face)
	Animate auditory (voice)
	Visual and auditory (face and voice)
	Alertness
Motor performance	Tonus
	Motor maturity
	Pull-to-sit
	Defensive movements
	Activity
Range of state	Peak of excitement
	Rapidity of buildup
	Irritability
	Lability of state
Regulation of state	Cuddliness
	Consolability
	Self-quieting
	Hand-to-mouth
Autonomic regulation	Tremors
	Startles
	Lability of skin color
Reflexes	Number of abnormal reflexes

Source: From Lester (1979).

confounders were removed from the data. The results are consistent with the reports in the animal literature (Jacobson et al., 1984). These results, along with the results from the effects of obstetric medication, indicate that environmental agents do have disruptive effects on several areas of behavioral functioning and that these effects can be detected by the Brazelton assessment.

I have argued that we consider not only functional disturbances, but also their effects on the caretaking environment as part of evaluation of the teratogenic effects of environmental agents. For example, I found, using the Brazelton examination, that Guatemalan infants who had experienced malnutrition in utero had poor motor tone and poorly organized states of alertness, were unresponsive to stimuli, had weak cries, and had a behavioral state characterized by sleep and a lack of distress or even fussiness (Tronick et al., 1979).

Because their mothers nursed them in response to their signals of distress, these infants were fed less often and became even weaker and less responsive. In the United States, I have seen similar behavioral effects in a group of clinically normal but slightly underweight infants and similar effects on the caretaking provided by their parents (Als et al., 1977).

Like all apical tests, the Brazelton scale has a number of limitations. It is not specific as to the underlying mechanism causing the developmental distortion because it examines performances based on the integration of many processes. Second, it is susceptible to the intrusion of other factors affecting the performance rather than the one of concern. This may be partially resolvable through the use of statistics and clinical experience. Third, as sensitive and comprehensive as the Brazelton scale is, it is not sufficient. This brings me to my final point in regard to a strategy for assessment.

An assessment strategy should begin with two or three repetitions of the examination during the newborn period. Repeated assessments have been found by Lester to document more subtle effects than a single examination (Brazelton, 1984). Critically, repeated assessments help us to distinguish transient acute physiological effects from longer term effects on the central nervous system, and they provide some information on the infant's capacity to recover from an insult (Parmalee et al., 1976). Then, following these repeated assessments and guided by the results, more sensitive and specific assessments should be attempted. These assessments would be: a full neurological assessment (Amiel-Tison et al., 1982; Lasaer, 1979; Sainte-Anne Dargassies, 1977); 24-hr observation of sleep and awake states (Amiel-Tisson et al., 1982; Parmalee et al., 1976); visual attention or auditory attention studies (Fantz, 1961); cry analysis when the quality of distress states and the infant's ability to achieve them appear disrupted (Lester, 1979; Lester & Dreher, 1987); and studies of caretaker–infant interaction to assess the impact of these behavioral distortions on the caretaking environment (Brazelton et al., 1984).

CONCLUSION

The nature of infant development and the nature of the effects of environmental agents conspire to produce great difficulties for the assessment of teratogenic effects. Given what we now know about the behavioral capacities of the infant, an apical test such as the Brazelton scale resolves some, but not all, of the difficulties. Such a test must be embedded in a larger strategy of assessment. I have argued that the definition of teratogenic effects must be expanded to include the distortion of the caretaking provided to the infant that may be produced by the distortion in his behavior.

I have focused on assessment and not on a presentation of the teratogenic effects of environmental agents on newborn behavior and caretaking. However, animal models and models of the adult, the young child, and even the fetus are not easily applied to the infant. There are few well-worked-out models of such effects on human newborns. Our methods of assessment only begin to evaluate the behavior of the infant; knowledge and research are limited. Yet it is extremely sobering that whenever we have looked for such effects, we have found them, and we have only begun to look.

CHAPTER 2

Behavioral Assessment Scales: The NICU Network Neurobehavioral Scale, the Neonatal Behavioral Assessment Scale, and the Assessment of the Preterm Infant's Behavior

The NICU Network Neurobehavioral Scale (NNNS) was designed for the neurobehavioral assessment of drug-exposed and other high-risk infants. It is based on the Neonatal Behavioral Assessment Scale (Brazelton, 1973). This chapter focuses on the NNNS but also reviews other assessment scales as relevant.

Infant assessment, historically, has been strongly influenced by the current dominant theoretical view of the infant and of the mind or brain. Prior to the turn of the century, the infant was viewed as diffusely organized, unstructured, and lacking in sensory capacities and motor abilities. No examinations existed because there was "nothing" to evaluate.

At the turn of the century, infant functioning was associated with the model of reflexes developed by Sherrington (1906). Much of this work was based on studies of the spinal frog and the view that the single neuron was the fundamental unit of the nervous system. This model was elaborated by learning theorists who viewed reflex, like the neuron, as the building block of behavior. During this period, Peiper (1928) began his exploration of the newborn's reflexes, eventually publishing a standard neurological text on newborn neurobehavior. Critical demonstrations of reflexes in anencephalic infants supported the idea that the infant operates only at the spinal level.

Reflex models began to be supplemented by models of more generalized motor functioning. Andre-Thomas (1960) and Saint-Anne Dargassies (1977) developed an examination that focused on the motor tone of the infant in which tone involved passive and active components. They were influenced by models of the brain that were beginning to focus on mass action as enunciated by Lashley (1951) in the United States and those that included inhibitory and excitatory centers, concepts that would not be fully incorporated into thinking about infants for another 25 years. Critically, this idea led to the view that the infant could modulate behavior, not just act in an all-or-none fashion. Concepts of active and passive tone became part of the dominant view of infant assessment and the model started to evolve into one of control or feedback systems, with the thermostat as the mechanical metaphor.

A major advance by Prechtl (Prechtl & Beintema, 1964) was his introduction of the concept of state. Descriptively, states were differentiated, structured organizations of the brain and associated physiology that affected how the infant responded to the same stimulus. The same stimulus resulted in different responses in different states, introducing a substantive change in the view of the infant's neurobehavioral functioning. The brain, not just the spinal cord, was involved in the infant's responses and, more important, the infant's brain was active. When state was considered, the neurobehavioral organization of the infant became more apparent. State, the organization of its components and their sequential organization over time, became assessable features of the infant's neurological status. An intact brain was capable of organizing states whereas a damaged brain could not. This advance was derived from early work on sleep and electroencephalograph activity in which it was demonstrated that the brain is not simply quiescent when the organism is asleep but shows differentiated states with different electrical, physiological, and behavioral concomitants. Thus, even when asleep the brain was active. Prechtl's formulation of "state" decimated the reflex model of the infant.

Examination of the infant's neurological status became a feature of standard care. These examinations viewed the infant as active, as in part responsible for generating the responses, and as able to modulate performance. New research demonstrated that even asphyxiated infants and anencephalic infants generated variable reflexes, that healthy infants modulated their responses, and that modulation and state-dependent responsiveness were characteristics of the infant. Simple stimulus–response reflex models were no longer tenable—there was a brain in the baby.

In the 1950s and exploding into the 1960s through 1990s, developmental researchers demonstrated highly complex functioning in the infant. Fantz, Fagan, and Miranda (1975) demonstrated preferential gaze, and much research followed showing that neonates were capable of complex highly differentiated hand movements (Twitchell, 1965), discrimination of sounds (Eimas, 1975; Eimas & Miller, 1980; Eimas, Siqueland, Jusczyk, & Vigorito, 1971), instrumental conditioning (Papousek, 1967), affective behaviors in response to stimuli (Wolff, 1966), detection of odors (Engen, Lipsitt, & Kaye, 1963), coordination of movement and speech (Condon & Sander, 1974a), and different cry patterns (Wolff, 1966; Wasz-Hockert, Lind, Vuorenkoski, Partanen, & Valanne, 1968). The infant also engaged in socially focused activities (Brazelton, Koslowski, & Main, 1974).

As this competent infant arrived on the scene, it was also recognized that the infant had abilities to control (regulate) its own level of arousal and to habituate, a rudimentary form of learning. The recognition of infant functional competence contributed to the development of assessments of more complex forms of behavior. Rosenblith (1961) developed a scale that incorporated qualities of infant orientation, habituation, tone, and reflexes. Brazelton and colleagues (Brazelton, 1973) developed the Neonatal Behavioral Assessment Scale (NBAS), which included items focused on the infant's capacity to self-regulate and to interact with animate and inanimate stimuli. Thus, for the first time the infant's social competence was assessed, or at least the infant's competencies in a social context. With these advances and influences from the formulation of the concept of temperament, the field of assessment moved beyond the evaluation of neurological integrity toward assessment of individual differences. The NBAS focused on assessing the infant in a social context and emphasized how the infant's individual differences affected caretaking and development.

NEONATAL BEHAVIORAL ASSESSMENT SCALE

General Description

The NBAS consists of 28 behavioral items scored on a 9-point scale and 18 reflex items scored on a 4-point scale. The reflex items were included to provide some information about neurological status and to manipulate the baby to produce changes in state. The second edition of the NBAS included seven supplementary 9-point rating scales called qualifiers, designed to summarize the quality of the infant's responsiveness and the amount of input the infant needed from the examiner to elicit the desired responses. The supplementary items were based on scales developed by Horowitz and Linn (1984) in the Kansas version of the NBAS and by Als, Lester, Tronick, and Brazelton (1982) in the Assessment of the Preterm Infant's Behavior (APIB), discussed later. The Kansas version is also notable for scoring the infant's "modal" rather than "best" performance, a trademark of the NBAS. The NBAS takes 30–45 minutes to administer in a quiet, dimly lighted room. An additional 20–30 minutes are needed to score the exam.

A number of data reduction schemes have been proposed for the NBAS, including factor analytic solutions. Most studies use the seven clusters of habituation, orientation, motor, range of state, regulation of state, autonomic stability, and reflexes (Lester, Als, & Brazelton, 1982). The clusters are derived by rescoring items so that higher scores represent clinically better performance. However, the direction of some of the items cannot be determined from the cluster score as the original items have to be reexamined. For example, a low score on the motor cluster indicates poor motor performance, but one cannot determine whether the infant is hypertonic or hypotonic without inspecting the individual item scores that comprise the cluster.

Training

The NBAS requires training in handling the infant and scoring the exam. The interactive nature of the exam and the emphasis on eliciting best performance place serious training demands on examiners. Brazelton has established training centers to meet these needs. Certification to perform the exam requires both reliability in administration, based on clinical judgment of the trainer, and reliability in scoring, based on agreement within 1 point on the 9-point rating scales. Training is a several-step process in which trainees are taught the exam, observe several exams, and then practice on their own until ready for a certification test, with periodic consultation of feedback from a certified trainer. Most trainees practice with 20–25 babies before they are ready for certification, although this number is affected by prior experience with handling newborn infants.

Reliability and Validity

Test–retest reliability of the NBAS shows low to moderate correlations, most slightly above or below .30, a finding that has been used as a criticism of the test. However, it has also been suggested that test–retest correlations are appropriate only when the construct measured is expected to be stable (Lester, 1984). A 5-year-old's IQ should be relatively stable from day to day, but the first month of life is a period of rapid change; therefore, behavior may not be stable during this time. Brazelton (1984) has argued that clinically one might worry about infants who show minimal change during the neonatal period. Brazelton suggested that the infant's pattern of change over repeated exams, called recovery curves, might be the best predictor of infant adaptation to the postnatal environment. Most studies have not found evidence for the long-term predictive validity of the NBAS, although some pilot data on the recovery curve idea looked promising (Lester, 1984). Most investigators view the NBAS as a valid description of the contemporary behavior of the infant but not a predictor of long-term development. As a description of current behavior, it is useful to help parents understand the strengths and vulnerabilities of their newborn.

Studies of normal infants raised questions about what might affect the expression of behavior of newborn infants. Brazelton and his colleagues pioneered studies of factors (e.g., obstetric medication) and medical conditions (e.g., low birth weight) that affected the infant's neurobehavioral organization. Thus, with its focus on individual differences and the factors that affect those differences, as well as its conceptualization that these differences affect the caregiver's behavior and infant long-term development, the NBAS became the dominant neonatal behavioral assessment in the field. This use of the NBAS confirmed the emerging view that infant development was determined by a complex interactionist perspective. It has been used in several developmental studies of at-risk infants, cross-cultural factors, and intervention. As such, the

NBAS is the benchmark neurobehavioral examination, the "parent" of the NNNS and several other examinations.

ASSESSMENT OF THE PRETERM INFANT'S BEHAVIOR

The APIB was developed by Als et al. (1982) to develop an "ethogram" of the preterm infant's behavioral repertoire. The APIB is based on the NBAS but focuses on the unique characteristics of the preterm infant.

The APIB yields 285 raw scores, most of which are scored on 9-point scales. These are reduced to 32 summary scores organized into five behavioral systems: physiological (e.g., respiratory patterns and skin color), motor (e.g., tonus, posture, and movements), state (level of consciousness, with states also described as diffuse or well defined), attentional-interactive (alertness and ability to attend to social stimuli and inanimate objects), and regulatory (regulatory activity of the infant to maintain itself in a balanced, well-modulated state). The APIB includes ratings of the amount of facilitation by the examiner needed to bring out the infant's best performance. The APIB is administered by organizing the test items of the NBAS into six packages of maneuvers that reflect increasingly challenging and complex interactions: (1) sleep-distal, (2) uncover-supine, (3) low tactile, (4) high tactile, (5) vestibular, (6) attentional-interaction. Time to administer the exam is comparable to the NBAS (30–45 minutes), but because of the number of items, scoring is labor intensive.

The predictive and construct validity for the APIB was reported by Als (1997) on a sample of 160 term and preterm children studied through 9 months of age. The APIB has also been used as an outcome measure to study the effect of intervention in the neonatal intensive care unit (NICU; Als, 1994) with a companion NICU intervention based on the same model as the APIB. The APIB requires extensive training. According to Als (1994, 1997), the conceptual basis of the APIB necessitates training in neurodevelopment and human evolution in addition to training in the assessment itself.

NICU NETWORK NEUROBEHAVIORAL SCALE

General Description

The NNNS was developed as an assessment for the at-risk infant, especially substance exposed, and was meant to have broad applicability. It is a comprehensive assessment of both neurological integrity and behavioral functioning, including withdrawal and general signs of stress.

The NNNS was developed for the National Institutes of Health for the multisite Maternal Lifestyles longitudinal study (Lester, 1998) of prenatal drug exposure and child outcome in preterm and term infants. The demands of this project required an examination that evaluated risk status and toxic exposures in a wide range of infants of varying birthweights, which could be reliably used at multiple sites. The exam needed to broadly assess the infant at risk, not just a single group such as preterm infants or only drug-exposed infants, for two major reasons. First, most drug-exposed infants are term, not preterm, infants. Second, prenatal drug exposure often occurs in the context of multiple risk factors. These factors may be biological, such as prematurity or intrauterine growth retardation, or social, such as poverty, poor nutrition, and lack of prenatal care, which also have biological consequences for the infant. Therefore, the exam needed to be sensitive to the many risk factors that affect infant neurobehavior and to assess a variety of domains of functional status. Moreover, there was a broader need for an examination that was standardized. The idea was to provide a comprehensive evaluation of the neurobehavioral performance of the high-risk and substance-exposed infant during the perinatal period; neurobehavioral organization, neurological reflexes, motor development, active and passive tone, and signs of stress and withdrawal.

The NNNS draws on prior examinations in addition to the NBAS, including "The Neurological Examination of the Full-Term Newborn Infant" (Prechtl, 1977), "Neurological Examination of the Maturity of Newborn Infants" (Amiel-Tison, 1968), *Neurobehavioral Assessment of the Preterm Infant* (Korner & Thom, 1990), and the APIB (Als et al., 1982). Signs of stress and withdrawal observed during a neurobehavioral examination were scored to the Neonatal Abstinence Score (Finnegan, 1986). Use of the examination was not restricted to a particular type of infant (e.g., drug exposed) or to a limited age (e.g., full-term or preterm); it could be used for a variety of infants and for infants of varying gestational ages.

The NNNS assesses and scores the full range of infant neurobehavioral performance; assesses infant stress, abstinence and withdrawal, neurological functioning, and some features of gestational age assessment; and specifically and procedurally evaluates behavioral states and frames the assessment of other behaviors within states. It can be used with low- and extremely high-risk infants once they are stable and well out into the postnatal period; has a standardized administrative format that "removes" the examiner from the behavior assessed; evaluates the quality of the examination; was designed to have internal validity and appropriate statistical properties; was designed to generate summary scores for the major domains of neurobehavioral performance, as well as stress and withdrawal; and was designed to be sensitive to the effects of drugs and other risk conditions based on empirical literature.

Description of the NNNS Examination

The exam should be performed on medically stable infants in an open crib or isolette. It is probably not appropriate for infants less than 28 weeks gestational age; the upper age limit may also vary, with a reasonable upper limit of 46 weeks (corrected or conceptional age).

Neurological Status

Neurological items were selected to provide a valid assessment of the neurological integrity and maturity of the infant, based on their demonstrated clinical utility and empirical validation, as well as being chosen to represent the various schools such as the French angles method (Amiel-Tison, 1968) and the primitive reflexes method (Prechtl, 1977). Many items were omitted because they were redundant with other items or because they have shown little utility in research studies. The number of neurological items was limited to balance with the behavioral part of the exam so that it could be completed in less than 30 minutes and would not unduly fatigue or stress the infant. Infant state is specified for each reflex. The NNNS identifies normal or best responses, if applicable, but a wide range of normal is recognized and the best response is meant only as a point of reference. A normal, abnormal, or suspect neurological scoring system is also included.

A crucial part of the neurological assessment is the assessment of muscle tone, which is assessed under both active and passive conditions. Active tone is assessed while observing spontaneous motor activity, including efforts at self-righting. Passive tone can be assessed during posture, scarf sign, popliteal angle, forearm and leg recoil, and forearm and leg resistance. Both may be influenced by infant state, position (i.e., prone, supine, or supported upright), or the effects of postural reflex activity. When assessing muscle tone, both the distribution (proximal vs. distal) and the type of tone (extensor vs. flexor) should be described, as in the developing infant, proximal tone in the neck and trunk may differ from distal tone in the extremities. For example, in the preterm infant, flexor tone develops first in the lower extremities, in contrast to the more mature full-term infant, who demonstrates uniform flexion.

Stress/Abstinence Scale

Most work documenting signs of stress in drug-exposed infants involves signs of abstinence or withdrawal, usually in infants of heroin-addicted or methadone-dependent mothers. Less potent opiates have been identified as precipitating a neonatal opiate abstinence syndrome and some nonopiate central nervous system depressants have also been implicated.

In work to date with cocaine-exposed infants, neonatal abstinence symptomatology does not appear to be increased. However, abstinence may occur from the depressants and narcotics used concomitantly with cocaine. Cocaine-exposed infants may show additional signs of stress such as lethargy in which the infant is unable to maintain a quiet awake state or crying during social interaction.

In addition, other signs of stress have been added that have been described in cocaine-exposed, or other high-risk infants, including preterms (Als et al., 1982).

NNNS Procedure

In the NNNS, items are administered in packages with each package beginning with a change in focus or position. The order of administration is relatively invariant. Table 2.1 presents a list of the maneuvers or packages and their respective items in the preferred order of administration.

During the preexamination observation the infant is asleep, prone, undressed, and covered. Initial state is scored using the traditional 1–6 criteria described by Prechtl (1974). All other items include criteria for why an item is not administered in addition to criteria for scoring the behavioral response. The response decrement items are administered with infant in State 1 or 2 and coded on scales that include criteria for when the infant stops responding ("shutdown") and criteria for when the item is discontinued. During unwrap and supine, the infant's posture, skin color, and movement are observed and scored on scales that include, when appropriate, criteria for normal responsiv-

TABLE 2.1   Packages of Neurobehavioral Items in Preferred Order of Administration

Package	Items
Preexamination observation	Initial state observation
Response decrement	Response decrement to light; response decrement to rattle; response decrement to bell
Unwrap and supine	Posture; skin color; skin texture; movement; response decrement to tactile stimulation of foot
Lower extremity reflexes	Plantar grasp; babinski; ankle clomus; leg resistance; leg recoil; power of active leg movements; popliteal angle
Upper extremity and facial reflexes	Scarf sign; forearm resistance; forearm recoil; power of active arm movements; rooting, sucking; hand grasp; truncal bone; pull-to-sit
Upright responses	Placing; stepping; ventral suspension; incurvation
Infant prone	Crawling; stimulation needed; head raise in prone
Pick up infant	Cuddle in arm; cuddle on shoulder
Infant supine on examiner's lap	Orientation (order not determined); animate visual and auditory—animate visual, animate auditory; inanimate visual and auditory—inanimate visual, inanimate auditory
Infant spin	Toric deviation of head and eyes; nystagmus
Infant supine in crib	Defensive response; asymmetrical tonic neck reflex; foot withdrawal reflex; Moro reflex
Postexamination observation	Postexamination state observation

ity, hyporesponsivity, and hyperresponsivity. Skin texture is also scored for the presence of specific conditions. The seven lower extremity reflexes, nine upper extremity and facial reflexes, four upright and three infant prone responses are administered with the infant in State 3, 4, or 5 and include classic reflexes, measures of tone and angles, scored on scales that also include, where appropriate, criteria for normal responsivity, hyporesponsivity, and hyperresponsivity. The infant, in State 4 or 5, is picked up and cuddled and scored separately for cuddle in arm and shoulder. The six orientation items are then administered with the infant still in State 4 or 5, on the examiner's lap. The types of handling procedures used to keep the infant in State 4 or 5 during the orientation package are scored along with the orientation responses. The infant is picked up for the spin items, returned to the crib for the final set of reflexes, and observed for the postexamination period.

Alternatives to this order may be required with some infants. For example, it may be necessary to administer the orientation items after pull-to-sit. This decision is based on whether or not best performance during the orientation would be elicited immediately after pull-to-sit or after the cuddle items. However, the order is not changed simply because the infant is in an alert state after pull-to-sit. Rather, the examiner continues with the standard order and administers the orientation in its proper sequence. For some infants, the examiner may need to rearrange the packages but can maintain the preferred sequence within the packages, whereas for others, the items must be administered without regard for the preferred order of either packages or items within packages. The extent of deviation from the standard order may provide critical information about the infant's functional status. Finally, although every effort should be made to start with a sleeping infant, this is not always possible and the response decrement items cannot be administered first.

Table 2.2 shows the items on the Stress/Abstinence Scale divided into organ systems. Each item is scored as present/absent with definitions provided in the manual if the examiner observed the event during the exam.

Inability to Achieve Quiet Awake State (State 4): Data Reduction and Scoring

Missing Data

Specific codes are used to identify reasons an item cannot be scored. Each item contains only codes that are logical outcomes of the specific manipulation or observation. Codes may indicate that the item was started but discontinued because the infant's response lasted too long (e.g., habituation items), that the item was not administered because the infant did not respond after gentle prodding (e.g., habituation items), that the item was started but discontinued because the infant changed to an inappropriate state, that the item was not administered because the infant was in an inappropriate state, or that the item was inadvertently skipped by the examiner.

TABLE 2.2   Stress/Abstinence Scale

Organ System	Items
Physiological	Apnea; tachypnea; labored breathing; nasal flaring; bradycardia; tachycardia; desaturation
Autonomic nervous system	Sweating; spit up; hiccoughing; sneezing; nasal stuffiness; yawning
Central nervous system	Abnormal sucking; choreiform movements; athetoid postures and movements; tremors; cogwheel movements; startles; hypertonia; back arching; fasting; cortical thumb; myoclonic jerks; generalized seizures; abnormal posture
Skin	Pallor; mottling; lividity; overall cyanosis; circumoral cyanosis; periocular cyanosis
Visual	Gaze aversion during orientation; pull down during orientation; fuss/cry during orientation; obligatory following during orientation; end-point nystagmus during orientation; sustained spontaneous nystagmus; visual locking; hyperalertness; setting sun sign; roving eye movements; strabismus; tight blinking; other abnormal eye signs
Gastrointestinal	Gagging/choking; loose stools, watery stools; excessive gas, bowel sounds
State	High pitch cry; monotone pitch cry; weak cry; no cry; extreme irritability, abrupt state changes

Asymmetrical Reflex Scores

For many reflexes, the left and right sides are evaluated separately. The scoring system is designed to reveal systematic asymmetries across items.

Summary Scores

Summary scores were developed a priori and tested in the Maternal Lifestyles study sample of 1,388 infants. Half the sample was randomly selected and used to test the internal consistency of the summary scores without any information about the characteristics of the infants (i.e., exposure status and birth weight). Alpha coefficients were computed on the summary scores and found to be acceptable. The summary scores were then computed for the entire sample and found to be stable. The summary scores include Habituation, Orientation, Amount of Handling, State, Self-Regulation, Hypotonia, Hypertonia, Quality of Movement, Number of Stress/Abstinence Signs (which can be also computed by organ system), and Number of Nonoptimal Reflexes. Alpha coefficients ranged from .59 to .81 with a median of .71.

Biobehavioral Basis

The term *neurobehavioral* is critical to understanding the NNNS. The term *neurobehavior* was developed to characterize older children and refers to an expanded neurological examination which involves sophisticated observation of higher cortical function and motor output that is often combined with an assessment of the maturation of the central nervous system or a search for minor neurological indicators. Here the term is used broadly to reflect the idea that all human experiences have psychosocial as well as biological or organic contexts. *Neurobehavioral* recognizes bidirectionality—that biological and behavioral systems dynamically influence each other and that the quality of behavioral and physiological processes is dependent on neural feedback. *Neurobehavior* becomes the interface of behavior and physiology and includes neurophysiological mechanisms that mediate specific behaviors or psychological processes.

These processes are affected by multiple risk factors. Thus, the NNNS was designed to measure processes of biobehavioral organization determined by multiple risk factors. Because much of the biobehavioral organization of the infant is determined by the combination of multiple biological and social risk factors, the exam must be sensitive to the broad range of behaviors that high-risk infants present.

Drug exposure is one such major biological factor and provides a good model for understanding multiple risk factors. Much is known about the mechanism of action of specific drugs and there is concern that illegal (cocaine, opiates, marijuana) and legal (alcohol and tobacco) drugs may act as behavioral teratogens, altering fetal brain development and subsequent function. Typically, the mechanisms of action are constructed as individual agents, such as cocaine, on dopaminergic systems or alcohol on inhibitory amino acid systems. However, recent evidence suggests that in addition to these specific effects, there is a mechanism of action common to all drugs of abuse that centers on activation of specific neural pathways that project from the pons and midbrain to more rostral forebrain regions, including the amygdala, medial prefrontal cortex, anterior cingulate cortex, ventral palladium, and nucleus accumbens (Malanga & Kosofsky, 1999). Regardless of the site of initial binding of a drug in the brain, there may be a final common pathway for drug action that affects neurotransmitter systems. The behavioral expressions of these effects are not known. This approach also supports the multiple-risk model because it could imply that polydrug exposure acts in a cumulative or synergistic fashion on the same neurotransmitter systems. There is a cumulative effect of risk factors that places increased stress on the nervous system, which in turn affects behavior, and these effects may be different from the effects of the individual risk factor.

Therefore, the NNNS was designed to be generically sensitive to the range of behaviors that at-risk infants display and also to attend to the specific dimensions affected by multiple risk factors. Neurological integrity, tone and posture, behavior and signs of stress, and withdrawal were included to assess a variety of functional domains and to be useful for the range of high-risk infants.

Reliability and Validity

Training to reliability criteria, including separate criteria for the administration of scoring, was established for the Maternal Lifestyles study. A training video and manual were developed. Twelve examiners at four sites were initially trained to reliability and periodically rechecked during the 2-year period of data collection. Approximately 1,400 1-month-old infants were given the NNNS, providing a database with a cross-section of infants that vary in birthweight, substance exposure, race/ethnicity, social class, and geographical location.

Test–retest reliability was established in two ongoing studies of preterm infants: one in the United States, the other in India, tested at 34, 40, and 44 weeks gestational age. In both studies, the INNS summary scores showed statistically significant correlations ranging from .30 to .44 across the three tests.

Validity of the NNNS was first documented in a study of full-term newborns (Napiorkowski et al., 1996). Infants with cocaine and alcohol exposure were compared with infants with alcohol exposure alone and those without prenatal drug exposure. Differences were found between the cocaine/alcohol and alcohol groups as well as between these groups and the unexposed group, showing the sensitivity of the NNNS to the effects of cocaine and alcohol. Preliminary analysis from the Maternal Lifestyles study used a multivariate analysis in which the effects of each drug (cocaine, opiates, marijuana, alcohol, and tobacco) and birth weight were tested (covaried) with the effects of all other covariates controlled. Specific independent effects of cocaine, opiates, alcohol, tobacco, and birth weight on the various NNNS summary scores were found (Lester, 1998), demonstrating the NNNS is sensitive to several classes of legal and illegal drugs in term infants and to the effects of prematurity with and without prenatal drug exposure. The sample size of 1,400, approximately half exposed and half comparison infants, is not a standardization sample in the traditional sense but is a large sample relative to those used to standardize most infant tests. The NNNS has also been used in a study of temperament in 150 preterm infants in India and is currently being used in a National Institutes of Health study of very-low-birth weight infants with and without neonatal white matter lesions in the brain.

DEVELOPMENTAL MODEL

Our developmental model of the neonate has certainly come a long way since Sherrington's initial "spinal frog" model and the early reflex models. However, although the NNNS embraces many of the constructs of the competent infant, we are equally impressed with the immaturity, poorly differentiated, and limited nature of the infant. The newborn can only do so much, and much of what it can do is affected by the very conditions under study, level of prematurity, effects of pre- and perinatal conditions, and so on.

With the NNNS, we try to portray a comprehensive and integrated picture of the infant without weighting any specific functional domains. This holistic view assumes that an accurate assessment of the infant includes evaluation of classical reflexes, tone, posture, social and self-regulatory competencies, and signs of stress.

The high-risk infant is viewed as struggling to maintain a balance between competing demands. The preterm infant is trying to maintain physiological homeostasis in the face of external stimulation. Internal demands such as maintaining respiratory and metabolic control are competing with external demands—stimulation that increases respiratory and metabolic demands. The drug-exposed infant may be experiencing withdrawal or disturbances in monoaminergic systems that can result in hyper- or hyporesponsivity. The assessment of these infants is complex—a simple assessment of reflexes alone will miss higher order functioning, regulatory capacities, and coping strategies. Likewise, a focus on social interactive capacities will miss basic neurological functions that may determine current and future behavior. In addition, how information is gathered is critical. With the NNNS, some behaviors are observed (e.g., state, posture, and signs of stress), and others are elicited (reflexes, motor responses, social interaction) and interpreted in the context of the infant being challenged. Some responses require scaffolding; that is, the examiner provides a certain amount of stage setting for the behavior to appear. How much scaffolding or stage setting is necessary to produce a behavior is as important as the actual behavior elicited. For example, an infant who is able to track a visual stimulus, who does not need to be swaddled, and who shows minimum respiratory instability and few signs of stress is clearly different than an infant with the same visual tracking ability who requires substantial facilitation by the examiner and shows physiological and behavioral signs of stress.

The concept of state-dependent performance is an important principle of the NNNS. The NNNS requires that items be administered in specific states and that when they are elicited they are only administered a set number of times. This state dependency and the inherent variability of behavior in early infancy require flexibility of administration. However, when an examination is unstructured, a number of problems arise. The primary problem is that different examiners may do the examination differently and elicit different behavioral qualities in the infant. Thus, the scoring may reflect the examiner–infant interaction rather than the infant's performance when faced with a standard challenge.

The NNNS attempts to balance flexibility and structure in several ways. First, state-dependent administration (SDA) is inherently structured and sensitive. Second, the NNNS has a relatively invariant sequence of item administration in that the specified sequence is one strongly preferred by experienced examiners because most infants can achieve it. Thus individual differences in examiner style are minimized. The exam allows for modification, but the order of administration and deviations from the standard sequence are recorded.

SDA is facilitated by the use of packages of items that allow the examiner to maximize the number of items administered when the infant is an appropriate state.

Finally, the NNNS contains codes for the reason an item was not administered. These reasons include examiner error but, more important, the failure of the infant to be in an appropriate state. This information is useful for explaining why the preferred order may have been varied. It also provides critical information on the performance of the infant.

SDA helps achieve several critical standardization goals. First, SDA ensures the comparability of how state affects performance. SDA emphasizes the state-dependent features of infant responsiveness. At the same time, it does not fall into the trap of having to do items in a rigid order at all costs. SDA increases the likelihood that the infant's performance is due to the characteristics of the infant per se, rather than the examiner's skills in trying to elicit optimal behavior. SDA facilitates the administration of the examination in the standard order. Finally, SDA also minimizes the time needed to administer the examination because handling procedures aimed at bringing out optimal performance are eliminated, especially the need for time-outs and soothing of the infant.

TRAINING REQUIREMENTS

Use of the NNNS requires certification, and certification procedures have been established that require meeting specified critieria in areas of administration and scoring. Training programs are available in the United States, Europe, South America, and Southeast Asia. There is also a Spanish version of the manual. In general, the recommended training process is for the trainee to practice the exam with intermittent feedback from either a trainer or an already trained examiner until such time as the trainee feels that he or she is ready for the certification test. Through telemedicine, videoconferencing is also being used from remote locations to provide introductory background and didactic material, to observe a live exam that includes interaction between the examiner and observers in the remote sites, and to give feedback to trainees as they examine infants in remote sites. The certification test can be arranged by contacting a trainer. Our experience is that the amount of practice that trainees need depends on prior experience, comfort in handling young infants, and clinical acumen. A training kit is available that includes the necessary equipment (standard 8″ flashlight, red ball, red rattle, bell, foot probe, head supports, manual, and scoring form). Introductory and debriefing scripts as well as scripts appropriate to specific items are provided in the manual.

IMPLICATIONS

Information from the NNNS can be used for research and clinical practice. Clinical applications include developing a profile of the infant to write a management plan for the infant while in the hospital, evaluation of the infant close to discharge as part of the discharge plan, and transition to home that includes involving the caretakers in the exam. Postdischarge, the exam can be used to determine which infants qualify for early intervention services. The long-term goal is to provide standardized norms for the NNNS at selected gestational ages to be used for the evaluation of at-risk infants prior to and in the few months following hospital discharge. At Women and Infant's Hospital (Providence, Rhode Island) the NNNS is used for the evaluation and behavioral management of infants in the intensive care nursery and for drug-exposed infants.

It is a luxury to be able to choose from a variety of neonatal assessments, reflecting how far the field of neonatal assessment has progressed. The NNNS is appropriate for some uses and not appropriate for others. There are measures for specific purposes, such as the Neurobehavioral Assessment of the Preterm Infant (Korner & Thom, 1990) for assessment of maturity and other procedures that measure aspects of neurological function. Although the NNNS includes these domains, if this were the only interest, there would be no reason to do a full NNNS exam. Similarly, for work with full-term healthy infants, the NBAS should be used, because many of the behaviors measured by the NNNS that would have to be scored will not occur; it would be overkill. The NNNS is also not appropriate for highly detailed assessments of specific functions. Although the exam includes some classical reflexes, measures of tone and posture, preterm behavior, and stress abstinence, it does not provide the level of detail needed if the focus were only on one of these domains. For example, the exam includes items from the Finnegan scale (Finnegan, 1986) that are used to measure drug withdrawal but does not include all the items or specific cutoffs. Therefore, it would be inappropriate to use the NNNS the way the Finnegan is used to determine drug treatment for addicted infants. Similarly, the NNNS does not provide the detail about preterm behavior that the APIB (Als et al., 1982) provides. The NNNS is best suited for use with infants at risk, term or preterm, when the interest is in providing estimates of a broad range of neurobehavioral function.

CHAPTER 3

Kicking Coordination Captures Differences Between Full-Term and Premature Infants With White Matter Disorder

Leg coordination patterns, specifically intralimb coordination of prematurely born infants with documented brain damage, have been used in attempts to predict later movement problems (Droit, Boldrini, & Cioni, 1996; Vaal, van Soest, Hopkins, Sie, & van der Knaap, 2000; van der Heide, Paolicelli, Boldrini, & Cioni, 1999). Some controversy exists in the literature regarding the best predictive method (Cioni, Ferrari, & Prechtl, 1992; Droit et al., 1996; van der Heide et al., 1999), but regardless of method, early atypical leg coordination appears to be related to later movement problems, including cerebral palsy (CP). The major neuropathology in premature infants that has been associated with motor deficits such as atypical leg coordination is thought to be neonatal white matter disorder (WMD). In the literature, the term WMD includes not only infants with periventricular leukomalacia (PVL) but also infants with perinatal telencephalic leukoencephalopathy and periventricular hemorrhagic infarction (e.g., Grade IV interventricular hemorrhage or IVH, ventriculomegaly, and/or hydrocephalus ex vacuo; Kuban, Leviton, Pagano, & Dammann, 1997; Leviton & Paneth, 1990). The literature suggests that approximately 60–90% of infants with WMD are later given a diagnosis of CP in varying grades of severity (Fawer & Calame, 1991; Leviton & Paneth, 1990; Monset-Couchard et al., 1988; Paneth, Rudelli, & Monte, 1990). The etiology of these motor handicaps is thought to be neonatal injury to the periventricular white matter (e.g., necrosis of axons; impairment of myelination), predominantly in areas containing the corticospinal tracts, which pass near the lateral ventricles and involve motor pathways (Truwit, Barkovich, Koch, & Ferriero, 1992; Volpe, 1992). Approximately 75% of infants with WMD have lesions in areas of the brain

containing the corticospinal tracts. The corticospinal tracts to the legs pass clos-
est to the lateral ventricles, which could explain the high incidence of early atypical leg movements and later spastic diplegia associated with WMD (Fedrizzi et
al., 1996; Kuban & Levitan, 1994; Truwit et al., 1992; Volpe, 1992b).

Our study explores the relation of WMD to intralimb coordination patterns
of the legs in premature infants with very low birth weight (VLBW). This is a
report from the first month of life from infants whom we will follow longitudinally to determine long-term motor outcome. Our primary interest is in the
early identification of atypical or abnormal movement in order to identify early
on those infants who eventually will be diagnosed with CP. Although the relation of VLBW, WMD, and movement disorder (including CP) has been identified in previous studies, there have been no studies that have identified and
quantified these relations as early as the first few weeks of life. This early identification serves two purposes: (1) early treatment for the movement problems,
and (2) specific description of the nature of the movement problem in order
to design effective treatment.

Leg coordination patterns of healthy, normally developing infants are characterized first by a predominant coupling among leg joints (hip, knee, ankle)
such that all joints tend to flex or extend in temporal synchrony (Piek, 1996;
Thelen, 1985). These, usually tight, couplings give way to the dissociation
(decoupling) of joints as the ability to assemble joint combinations of flexion
and extension emerges (Piek, 1996; Thelen, 1985). The newborn begins to
decouple leg joint motion during the very first months of life, first distally in
the hip-ankle pair. Further dissociation among all joint combinations in the
legs occurs in subsequent months as evidence of more complex coordination.

Studies of healthy premature infants without documented brain damage
have identified delayed but not necessarily atypical coordination patterns
(Geerdink, Hopkins, Beek, & Heriza, 1996; Piek & Gasson, 1999). Prematurely
born infants evidence a somewhat different trajectory of both interlimb and
intralimb leg coordination during the first months of life, although there is a
lack of agreement across studies as to the exact description of their trajectories
(Geerdink et al., 1996; Piek & Gasson, 1999). Jeng, Chen, and Yau (2002) summarized the current research on premature infants and identified causes for
this apparent lack of agreement including sample characteristics, study design,
and precise measures for study.

The few studies of premature infants with documented brain damage have
identified atypical coordination patterns, but the description of these patterns
varies (Droit et al., 1996; Vaal et al., 2000; van der Heide et al., 1999). The
inability of infants with brain lesions to decouple intralimb joints has been
reported by Vaal et al. (2000), but a consistent relation of the coupling strength
and brain damage was not demonstrated until infants were 26 weeks (approximately 4 months) postterm. In a study by Droit et al. (1996), infants at 37–39
weeks postmenstrual age (not quite at term age) with brain damage had longer
pauses between the flexion and extension phases of intralimb kicks (intrakick

pauses) and fewer pauses between kicks (interkick pauses) in comparison to infants without brain damage. These differences were not apparent at the earlier ages (younger than 26 weeks postterm) that were tested. A recent study by van der Heide et al. (1999) found no differences in intralimb couplings at 1 or 3 months of age between preterm infants with brain lesions and preterm (PT) infants. The cross-sectional design of their study and the use of nonparametric statistics increased the likelihood of a Type II error, as stated by the authors.

Our study quantifies kicking of VLBW infants with WMD and compares their kicking to a group of VLBW infants without WMD and a group of infants born full term (FT). We chose to study infants at 1 month of age in order to test the assumption that PTWMD infants would not show the typical decoupling of leg joints (out-of-phase movements) characteristic of both FT and PT infants in the first months of life. A more complete quantitative description of the characteristics of this failure to decouple the limb joints will give us the ability to plan an intervention strategy that might promote typical kicking behavior. We have previously demonstrated that healthy infants can learn to increase the amount of out-of-phase compared to more typical in-phase (all joints flex or extend together) kicking when they are reinforced by a mobile (Chen, Fetters, Holt, & Saltzman, 2002). Our goal is to identify characteristics of atypical kicking very early and design a similar intervention aimed at promoting typical kicking behavior and thus potentially reducing the long-term consequences of WMD on movement.

METHOD

Participants

Infants participated in a larger, ongoing prospective cohort study. We compared three groups of infants: 10 premature infants born VLBW and WMD (PTWMD), 10 premature infants born VLBW without WMD (PT), and 10 FT infants. Premature infants were born between 24 and 31 weeks, 6 days gestational age (GA). GA was based on date of in vitro fertilization that was superordinate to GA based on ultrasound (US) that was superordinate to GA based on the mother's last menstrual period, which was superordinate to GA based on obstetrical exam, which was superordinate to physician estimate of GA. Groups were matched on mother's education and race, infant's gender, and additionally the two PT groups were matched on GA. Subject characteristics are listed in Table 3.1. We recruited all infants from the nurseries at Brigham and Women's and Beth-Israel Hospitals in Boston, Massachusetts.

Identification of WMD

Infants were classified into the WMD group if they had periventricular white matter lesions and/or severe (Grade IV) hemorrhage and/or ventriculomegaly,

TABLE 3.1 Demographic Information

	FT (*n* = 10)	PT (*n* = 10)	PTWMD (*n* = 10)
Gender			
Male	4	5	6
Female	6	5	4
Race			
Caucasian	8	9	6
African American	2	0	2
Hispanic	0	1	2
Gestational age at birth (weeks)	39.7 (1.2)	27.3 (1.9)	28.3 (2.4)
Birth weight (g)	3608.5 (411.7)[a]	1009.5 (304.9)	1132.5 (270.2)
Days on ventilation	0	54.9 (58.2)	37.1 (31.4)
Age (days GA)	33.7 (7.4)	32.0 (6.1)	40.4 (3.7)[b]
Weight at testing (kg)	4.51 (0.55)	3.85 (0.45)[c]	4.35 (0.53)

[a]*Significantly different from PT and PTWMD infants.*
[b]*Significantly different from PT infants.*
[c]*Significantly different from PTWMD and FT.*

as documented by high-resolution serial US or magnetic resonance imaging (MRI) in the newborn period (Table 3.2). For an infant to be classified as having WMD, the "worst scan" had to fulfill the following criteria/rules:

1. At 40 weeks GA, an MRI that evidenced WMD (IVH Grade IV, ventriculomegaly, hyperintensity in the white matter, hypointensity in the white matter).
   Or if not available:
2. A last scan, either a US or MRI, at greater than 1 month of life which identified WMD.
   Or if not available:
3. US between day of life 21–30 which identified WMD, with an accompanying US from any time point with corresponding WMD identification.
   Or if not available:
4. The infant was not recruited.

For a PT infant to be classified as free of WMD, all MRI and/or US scans had to be free of findings and one of the scans (either US or MRI) had to be made after 1 month GA. A pediatric radiologist with a specialization in MRI performed all classifications. All FT infants had a normal pediatric physical assessment done by a pediatrician at discharge from the hospital.

TABLE 3.2   MRI and US Findings for PTWMD Infants

PTWMD1
  MRI   Mild to moderate white matter damage in the frontal and parietal lobes (bilateral), moderate VM, PVL
  US   Germinal matrix hemorrhage

PTWMD2
  MRI
  US   Germinal matrix hemorrhage, mild ventriculomegaly

PTWMD3
  MRI   Moderate white matter damage in the frontal, parietal, occipital, temporal lobes (bilateral), severe VM, PVL
  US   Germinal matrix hemorrhage, PVL

PTWMD4
  MRI   Mild to moderate atrophy in the internal capsule and basal ganglia (bilateral), moderate VM, no PVL
  US   PVL

PTWMD5
  MRI   Mild to moderate white matter damage in the frontal, parietal, temporal lobes (bilateral), severe VM, PVL
  US

PTWMD6
  MRI   Severe white matter damage in the frontal, parietal, occipital, temporal lobes (bilateral), severe VM, PVL
  US   Intraventricular hemorrhage, severe ventriculomegaly, uncertain periventricular echo densities

PTWMD7
  MRI   Moderate whole brain atrophy, moderate VM, PVL
  US   Intraventricular hemorrhage, ventriculomegaly, shunt placement

PTWMD8
  MRI   Mild right frontal lobe atrophy/hemorrhage, PVL
  US   PVL

PTWMD9
  MRI   Moderate whole brain atrophy, mild VM, PVL
  US   Germinal matrix hemorrhage, PVL, ventriculomegaly

PTWMD10
  MRI   Moderate whole brain atrophy, severe VM, no PVL

FIGURE 3.1. Infant testing setup.

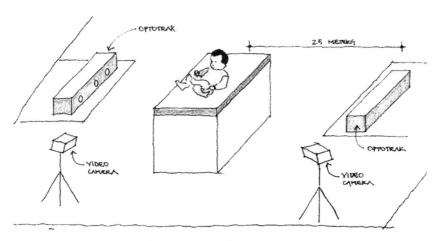

Apparatus and Procedure

Testing took place in the Developmental Motor Control laboratory at Sargent College of Health and Rehabilitation Sciences, Boston University, when the infants were 44 weeks GA (43–45.6 weeks GA). Parents signed a consent form prior to participation in the study, in accordance with the policies of Boston University Institutional Review Board and the respective hospital. The research assistant responsible for recruitment knew group status; all other researchers were masked to infant group.

Instrumentation and Experimental Setup

Three-dimensional time-position (kinematic) data were collected at 100 Hz using an OPTOTRAK 3020 System with two banks of position sensors.*Each position sensor consisted of three sensors (cameras) connected in series to a Compaq Prolinea 5133 computer through the OPTOTRAK System's PT Unit.

The two OPTOTRAK position sensors were placed horizontally across from each other on both sides of the central testing area (a table in the middle of the room), each at a distance of approximately 1.9 m from the border of the central testing area (Figure 3.1). Prior to data collection the testing area was calibrated by moving a rigid body frame consisting of 20 infrared light-emitting diodes (IREDs) throughout the viewing volume. The root-mean-squared error in the calibration was always less than 0.7 mm for each data collection session.

In addition to the kinematic data, movements were recorded with three video cameras (Panasonic Wv BL600) with a right lateral, overhead, and frontal view of the infant. The OPTOTRAK data and video image were synchronized in time during data collection (Figure 3.1).

*Northern Digital Inc., 403 Albert Street, Waterloo, Ontario, Canada, N2L 3V2.

Infant Testing Procedure

On arrival at the lab, infants were undressed and weighed on an electronic scale (Health o meter), and subsequently placed supine on a table in the central testing area. All infants were naked during testing. The midline position of the head was maintained for all infants during testing by the use of a horseshoe-shaped support pillow surrounding infants' heads. IREDs were taped to the skin using double-sided sticky EKG collars. A total of 12 IREDs were placed bilaterally in the following places: midline of trunk (below the 10th rib), the anterior superior iliac spine (ASIS), the hip (greater trochanter), knee (lateral aspect of knee joint line), ankle (lateral malleoli), and the distal end of the fifth metatarsal. During the testing session, the experimenter was in visual and verbal contact with the infant as needed to keep the infant in State 4 (i.e., alert and not crying). Spontaneous leg movement trials were recorded bilaterally from the infants with each trial lasting 30 seconds. The number of trials recorded was dependent on the number of leg movements produced during each trial with a range from four to seven trials.

Data Reduction

Position data were converted into three-dimensional coordinates using a direct linear transformation algorithm in OPTOTRAK system software. All data were viewed from videotape and OPTOTRAK display program in Data Analysis Package (DAP; Northern Digital, Inc.) to determine the beginning and end frames of a kick. A kick start was the onset of a continuous leg movement of foot, ankle, knee, and hip markers moving toward the body for which: (a) the infant's foot moved at least five consecutive frames (one frame = 10 ms), and (b) the hip joint angle change exceeded 11.5°. The end of the kick was the frame of peak extension amplitude following a flexion movement (Chen et al., 2002; Jensen, Ulrich, Thelen, Schneider, & Zernicke, 1994).

Data were not extracted for analysis if more than 20 consecutive frames (>200 ms) were missing or if the missing data occurred at peak flexion or peak extension, as these specific data points were used for analysis. Single leg movements that passed these exclusion criteria, those that were an isolated movement, and those that came from bouts of leg movements were extracted using the DAP software and subsequently used for the kinematic analysis. Then 122 leg movements were defined for analysis from the 30 infants (FT = 40, PT = 40, PTWMD = 42). Each infant contributed 2–5 kicks for analysis. For all three groups, the majority of the leg movements analyzed came from bouts of leg movements.

Where necessary, the extracted data were interpolated using a second-order polynomial interpolation (DAP program). All data were filtered using a fifth-order Butterworth with a cutoff frequency of 6 Hz. The cutoff frequency was determined from power spectrum analysis results of the position data from all infants, and on all three axes (x, y, z) of all IREDs. Joint angle data were calculated from the filtered position data. Angle velocities of hip, knee, and ankle joints were calculated from the angle data using a fourth-order central difference algorithm. All dependent measures were computed using Matlab (Mathworks, Inc., Natick, MA).

Dependent Measures

Kick Phases. A *flexion phase* was defined as a decrease in hip angle of at least 11.5° until peak flexion was reached. *Duration of flexion phase* was calculated as the time it took for 95% of the change in hip angle to occur from beginning of flexion to peak flexion.

Intrakick pause was the time interval between flexion phase and extension phase, and was defined as the time around peak flexion between less than 5% of the overall change in angle of flexion phase and less than 5% of the overall change in joint angle in extension phase.

Extension phase was defined as a continuous increase of hip angle from peak flexion until movement stopped or a change in direction of movement occurred. *Duration of extension phase* was calculated as the time it took for 95% of the change in hip angle to occur from peak flexion to end of extension. These criteria are consistent with previous kicking literature (Chen et al., 2002; Jeng et al., 2002; Jensen et al., 1994).

Joint Angles. We obtained the joint angle positions of hip, knee, and ankle at: (a) beginning of flexion phase, (b) end of flexion phase, (c) peak flexion, (d) beginning of extension phase, and (e) end of extension phase; 180° represents full extension of the hip and knee joints and full plantar flexion of the ankle joint. The larger the number, the more extended the joint. Angles at these four positions were used either as the dependent measure or to compute measures.

Amplitude of flexion and extension phases in hip, knee, and ankle joints were obtained and peak velocities of flexion and extension phases of hip, knee, and ankle joints were computed. Again, these definitions are consistent with the literature (Chen et al., 2002; Jeng et al., 2002; Jensen et al., 1994).

Intralimb Coordination Intralimb coordination was assessed with the analysis of joint correlations, discrete relative phase (DRP), and the relation of joint angle amplitude to peak velocity. Joint correlations were computed using Pearson correlation coefficients (r) at zero lag between hip, knee, and ankle joint angle trajectories for all leg movements extracted for each infant. Correlation between joint angle trajectory pairs was assessed continuously. All joint angle correlations were converted to Fisher Z scores for each infant to allow comparison of correlations (r) between infants and between groups (FT, PT, and PTWMD; Chen et al., 2002; Jeng et al., 2002; Jensen et al., 1994).

Relative phase of joint angle data indicate the relation (difference) of joint angles over time. Continuous relative phase describes this continuous relation over the time of leg movement, while DRP indicates the joint relations at specific

FIGURE 3.2. Leg joint angles: hip, solid line; knee, large dashed line; ankle, small dashed line; arrows at points of discrete relative phase: (1) peak flexion velocity, (2) flexion phase offset, (3) peak flexion, (4) extension phase onset, (5) peak extension velocity.

Relative Phase of Leg Joint Angles

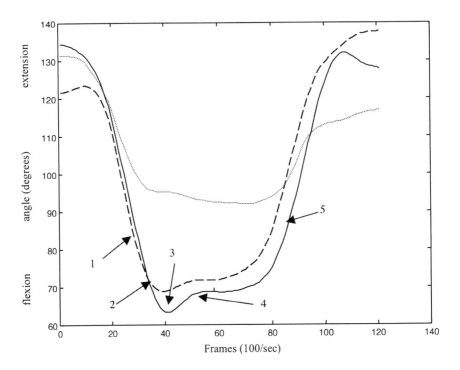

points in the leg movement. After data were normalized, the phase angles for hip, knee, and ankle were computed from the angular position/velocity data after the method of van Emmerik and Wagenaar (1996). Then we computed DRP at four discrete points in the kicking movement: end of flexion phase and beginning of extension phase (point of joint reversal) and flexion and extension peak velocities (see Figure 3.2). These were chosen, as they are points of potential need for control. Values approaching 0 indicate more in-phase patterns, whereas values approaching π (3.1415) indicate more out-of-phase patterns.

In order to test the relation between amplitude of the movement phases and their peak velocities, we computed Pearson r correlations and transformed to Fisher Z for significance testing.

A custom-written MatLab (The Mathworks, Inc., Natick, MA) program was used to compute all dependent measures.

Statistical Analysis

It was not possible to match pairwise on all criteria in this study sample; however, maternal education and race, and infant gender did not differ among groups. In addition, gestational age and birth weight at birth did not differ significantly between the preterm groups. The average age at testing was significantly different, $F(2, 27) = 5.63$, $p < 0.01$, between preterm groups with the PTWMD group on average 8 days older than the PT group, PT = 32.0 days (SD = 6.1), PTWMD = 40.4 days (3.7), FT = 33.7 days (7.4; see Table 3.1). ANOVA with group (FT, PT, and PTWMD) as the between-subject factor was used for all variables. Post hoc analyses of significance of difference between groups consisted of Bonferroni t tests for multiple comparisons. The α level of significance was set at 0.05 for overall F values and 0.0167 for post hoc comparisons. StatView (SAS Institute, Inc.) and SAS (version 7.0, SAS Institute, Inc.) were used for all statistical analysis. Values of p between .02 and .08 are reported as approaching significance.

RESULTS

Kick Phase Durations

The FT group had the longest duration of the extension phase of the hip, overall—$F(2,117) = 3.90$, $p = .02$; with a significant difference ($p = .01$) between FT and PT groups, and between FT and PTWMD ($p = .02$), but there was no difference ($p = .88$) between PT and PTWMD groups (see Table 3.3). The

TABLE 3.3   Duration of Movement Phases (s); Mean (SD)

	FT ($n = 10$)	PT ($n = 10$)	PTWMD ($n = 10$)
Number of leg movements	40	40	42
Hip			
Flexion	0.34 (0.22)	0.38 (0.24)	0.36 (0.27)
Intrakick pause	0.18 (0.22)	0.16 (0.11)	0.17 (0.15)
Extension	0.60 (0.34)[a]	0.44 (0.28)	0.46 (0.21)
Knee			
Flexion	0.28 (0.20)	0.32 (0.22)	0.31 (0.18)
Intrakick pause	0.14 (0.11)	0.16 (0.11)	0.23 (0.24)
Extension	0.64 (0.40)[a]	0.47 (0.34)	0.42 (0.21)
Ankle			
Flexion	0.38 (0.21)	0.37 (0.26)	0.34 (0.26)
Intrakick pause	0.17 (0.10)	0.17 (0.13)	0.22 (0.16)
Extension	0.48 (0.38)	0.37 (0.23)	0.39 (0.26)

[a]*Significantly different from PT and PTWMD.*

FT group again had the longest duration of the extension phase of the knee, overall $F(2,117) = 4.80$, $p = .01$; with the greatest difference ($p = .004$) between the FT and PTWMD groups. The difference approached significance ($p = .03$) between FT and PT, but there was no difference ($p = .47$) between PT and PTWMD groups. The extension phase of the ankle joint was not significant among groups, $F(2, 117) = 1.21$, $p = .30$.

There were no significant differences among groups in duration of flexion phases in hip, knee, and ankle, $F(2,117) = 0.30$, $p = .74$ for hip joint; $F(2,117) = 0.42$, $p = .66$ for knee joint; $F(2,117) = 0.28$, $p = .76$ for ankle joint). Nor were there significant differences in duration of intrakick pause in hip and ankle joint, $F(2,117) = 0.06$, $p = .94$ for hip joint; $F(2,117) = 1.85$, $p = .16$ for ankle joint. The difference among groups for duration of intrakick pause in the knee approached significance, $F(2,117) = 3.16$, $p = .05$; however, only the difference between the FT and the PTWMD groups was significant ($p = .02$); FT and PT ($p = .57$); PT and PTWMD ($p = .07$).

In general, the extension phase durations were longer for the FT infants in comparison to the two premature groups, while the flexion and intrakick phase durations were similar among groups.

Joint Angles

The PTWMD group was significantly more extended at the hip and knee joint at the beginning of the flexion phase, overall $F(2, 117) = 4.91$, $p = .01$ for hip: $p = .003$ between FT and PTWMD, approached significance ($p = .03$) between PT and PTWMD, with no difference ($p = .45$) between FT and PT; overall $F(2,118) = 10.78$, $p < .0001$ for knee: $p < .0001$ between FT and PTWMD, $p = .002$ between PT and PTWMD, and $p = .17$ between FT and PT; see Table 3.4). Ankle angle at beginning of the flexion phase was significantly different among all groups, but the PT group had the most extended angle and the FT group again the most flexed, overall $F(2,318) = 7.92$, $p = .0006$; $p = .0001$ between FT and PT, and approached significance ($p = .04$) between FT and PTWMD, and between PT and PTWMD ($p = .06$). Thus, the PT and FT infants began their movements from similar hip and knee postures, both groups being more flexed than the PTWMD infants.

The FT infants had significantly smaller hip and knee flexion angles (more flexed at peak flexion than the PT group, overall $F(2,117) = 4.31$, $p = .02$ for hip; $p = .01$ between FT and PT. This difference approached significance ($p = .03$) between FT and PTWMD, and was not significant ($p = .58$) between PT and PTWMD; overall $F(2,117) = 12.23$, $p < .0001$ for knee; $p = .002$ between FT and PT, $p < .0001$ between FT and PTWMD, and not significant between PT and PTWMD ($p = .09$). Peak flexion at the ankle was also significantly different among all groups, overall $F(2,117) = 8.13$, $p = .0005$; however, the findings were different at the ankle in comparison to the hip and knee. The PT group had the largest flexion peak angle (most extended) and

TABLE 3.4 Joint Angles and Angle Excursions; Mean (SD) in Degrees

	FT (n = 10)	PT (n = 10)	PTWMD (n = 10)
Number of leg movements	40	40	42
Hip joint excursion			
Flexion	55.97 (14.92)[a]	49.95 (14.35)	57.73 (13.57)[a]
Extension	53.31 (17.52)	49.45 (15.5)	51.59 (17.0)
Hip angle			
Initiation of flexion	131.54 (17.67)	133.98 (11.8)	141.04 (12.47)[b]
Peak flexion	72.34 (16.85)[c]	81.13 (14.40)	79.64 (12.30)
End of extension	134.94 (17.96)	136.76 (12.23)	143.75 (12.77)[b]
Knee joint excursion			
Flexion	55.4 (17.20)	51.18 (14.25)	57.9 (16.38)
Extension	53.13 (23.08)	53.22 (16.72)	52.65 (17.33)
Knee angle			
Initiation of flexion	125.44 (19.45)	130.98 (15.8)	142.58 (15.93)[b]
Peak flexion	65.87 (16.23)[c]	76.87 (17.98)	82.53 (10.95)
End of extension	127.36 (20.96)	133.84 (16.07)	145.1 (16.49)[b]
Ankle joint excursion			
Flexion	22.09 (12.17)	26.11 (11.16)	32.37 (14.58)[b]
Extension	20.49 (12.09)	22.59 (8.43)	29.69 (13.66)[b]
Ankle joint position			
Initiation of flexion	119.94 (13.20)[a]	131.71 (12.69)	126.08 (13.34)[a]
Peak flexion	97.52 (15.64)[a]	104.15 (11.30)	91.62 (13.57)[a]
End of extension	121.80 (12.65)[c]	133.15 (13.06)	128.85 (14.08)

[a]*Significantly different from PTs.*
[b]*Significantly different from FTs and PTs.*
[c]*Significantly different from PTs and PTWMDs.*

the PTWMD group the smallest angle (most flexed). The difference was significant ($p = .0001$) between PT and PTWMD, and approached significance ($p = .04$) between FT and PT, and between FT and PTWMD ($p = .05$).

As shown in Figure 3.3, these joint angle variables together suggest that infants in the three groups move their legs in different spaces in relation to their bodies. As we would expect, the FT infants tend to be more flexed and move within a tighter flexion space. While the PT group does not extend as much as the PTWMD group, they do not flex as tightly as the FT group. The PTWMD move from and within a more extended space in relation to their bodies and relative to the other groups.

There were significant differences among groups in the magnitude of the hip joint excursion in the flexion phase, overall $F(2,117) = 3.29$, $p = .03$; with a significant difference ($p = .01$) between PT and PTWMD, a difference approaching significance ($p = .05$) between PT and FT, and no significant

FIGURE 3.3. Characteristic postures and joint angle changes of the three groups of infants during leg movements. The FT and PT infants start their leg movements from a more flexed position (solid lines) than the PTWMD infants. At peak flexion (dashed line), PT have a smaller flexion angle in hip and knee than do either the PT or PTWMD infants.

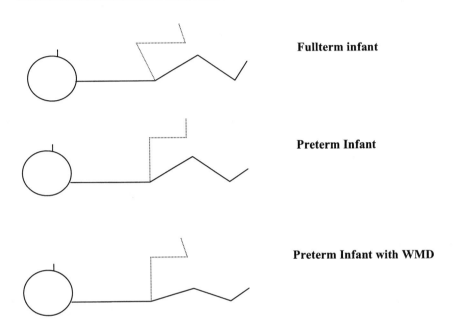

Fullterm infant

Preterm Infant

Preterm Infant with WMD

difference ($p = .58$) between FT and PTWMD. The PT group had significantly smaller hip joint excursions during the flexion phase of the leg movement in comparison to the PTWMD or FT group. There were no significant differences among groups in knee joint excursions in the flexion phase, $F(2,117) = 1.93$, $p = .15$. There was a significant difference among groups in magnitude of the ankle joint excursion in the flexion phase. The PTWMD group had larger excursions than did the PT and FT groups, overall $F(2,117) = 6.71$, $p = .002$); a difference that was significant ($p = .0004$) between FT and PTWMD, approached significance ($p = .03$) between PT and PTWMD, and was not significant ($p = .18$) between FT and PT.

There were no significant differences among groups in the hip or knee excursions in the extension phases, $F(2,117) = 0.71$, $p = .50$ for hip joint; $F(2,117) = 0.007$, $p = .99$ for knee joint, but there was a significant difference among groups, overall $F(2,117) = 6.91$, $p = .002$, in magnitude of ankle joint excursion for extension phase: $p = .001$ between FT and PTWMD, $p = .008$ between PT and PTWMD, and no significant difference ($p = .42$) between FT and PT.

TABLE 3.5 Joint Angle Peak Velocities (deg/s); Mean (*SD*)

Joint	FT	PT	PTWMD
Number of leg movements	40	40	42
Hip			
Flexion	322.41 (113.09)	283.51 (116.25)	332.39 (136.42)
Extension	214.68[a] (77.53)	269.75 (134.75)	252.89 (100.12)
Knee			
Flexion	351.06 (140.81)	308.16 (137.05)	358.54 (136.12)
Extension	201.04[b](92.43)	296.44 (147.30)	317.34 (134.10)
Ankle			
Flexion	138.15[a] (122.66)	156.72 (84.18)	200.17 (122.57)
Extension	102.18[c] (63.79)	132.28 (60.22)	189.03[d] (122.37)

[a]*Significantly different from PTs.*
[b]*Significantly different from PTs and PTWMDs.*
[c]*Significantly different from PTWMDs.*
[d]*Significantly different from FTs and PTs.*

There were no significant differences in flexion phase peak velocities among groups for either the hip or knee joints, $F(2,121) = 1.80$, $p = .17$ for hip joint, and $F(2,121) = 1.42$, $p = .25$ for knee joint (see Table 3.5). The differences among groups in flexion phase peak velocity of the ankle joint approached significance, overall $F(2,121) = 3.43$, $p = .04$, with a significant difference ($p = .01$) only between FT and PTWMD, but no significant difference ($p = .09$) between PT and PTWMD, or between FT and PT ($p = .45$). The PTWMD group had significantly higher peak velocities than the FT infants.

The FT group had lower peak velocities in the extension phase of the hip than did the PT group. Although the overall group differences approached significance, overall $F(2,120) = 2.60$, $p = .08$, the difference between FT and PT was the only comparison that approached significance ($p = .03$; $p = .10$ between FT and PTWMD, and $p = .58$ between PT and PTWMD). The FT group also had significantly lower peak velocities in the extension phase at the knee than both of the preterm groups, overall $F(2,120) = 9.99$, $p < .0001$ for the knee, $p = .002$ between FT and PT, $p < .0001$ between FT and PTWMD, and $p = .40$ between PT and PTWMD. The pattern was similar for the ankle, with the FT group having lower peak velocities, overall $F(2,120) = 7.90$, $p = .001$ for the ankle, with significant differences ($p = .0002$) between FT and PTWMD and $p = 0.01$ between PT and PTWMD; but no significant difference ($p = .22$) between FT and PT.

These results generally support the findings of longer duration and slower velocities of extension phases at the hip, knee, and ankle for FT infants.

TABLE 3.6   Interjoint Correlations (Pearson's *r*); Mean (*SD*)

	FT (*n* = 10)	PT (*n* = 10)	PTWMD (*n* = 10)
Number of leg movements	40	40	42
Hip-knee	0.92 (0.15)	0.93 (0.07)	0.89 (0.14)
Hip-ankle	0.72 (0.38)	0.77 (0.20)	0.88 (0.12)[a]
Knee-ankle	0.64 (0.46)	0.72 (0.19)	0.86 (0.12)[a]

[a]*Significantly different from FT and PT.*

Intralimb Coordination

All groups had significant correlations of the knee-ankle and hip-ankle pairs (0.64–0.88); however, the PTWMD group had significantly higher correlation coefficients of these joint pairs in comparison to the FT and PT groups, overall $F(2,119) = 5.28$, $p = .01$ for knee-ankle pair; $p = .01$ between FT and PTWMD, $p = .004$ between PT and PTWMD, and $p = .73$ between FT and PT; for hip-ankle pair, overall $F(2,119) = 4.18$, $p = .02$; $p = .01$ between FT and PTWMD, $p = .01$ between PT and PTWMD, and $p = .97$ between FT and PT (Table 3.6). There were larger standard deviations of the ankle-hip and ankle-knee correlations in the FT group in comparison to either of the preterm groups. There were no significant differences between groups in the knee-hip correlation coefficients, $F(2,118) = 2.26$, $p = .11$. All groups had high positive knee-hip correlations with values ranging from 0.89 to 0.93.

The FT group tended to have larger DRP values, particularly for the hip-ankle and knee-ankle pairs (zero values are in-phase). DRP for hip-ankle pairs approached a significant difference among groups at peak flexion, overall $F(2,127) = 3.57$, $p = .03$; but only the comparison between FT and PTWMD approached significance ($p = .04$); $p = .31$ between PT and PTWMD, and $p = .31$ between FT and PT. The DRP for the knee-ankle pair was significantly different among groups, overall $F(2,127) = 7.09$, $p = .001$, with a significant difference ($p = .0005$) between FT and PTWMD, and between FT and PT ($p = .005$), but no significant difference ($p = .49$) between PT and PTWMD.

There were no significant differences at peak velocity of flexion phase for hip-ankle pairs, overall $F(2,127) = 2.37$, $p = .09$. The differences approached significance for knee-ankle pairs, overall $F(2,127) = 2.95$, $p = .05$, with a significant difference ($p = .02$) between FT and PTWMD, a difference approaching significance ($p = .06$) between PT and PTWMD, and no significant difference ($p = .65$) between FT and PT. DRP for knee-ankle pairs also approached significance among groups at flexion end, overall $F(2,127) = 5.72$,

TABLE 3.7 Discrete Relative Phase

	Flexion End		Peak Flexion		Extension Onset		Peak Flexion Velocity		Peak Extension Velocity	
	Mean	SD	Mean	SD	Mean	SD	Mean	SD	Mean	SD
Hip-knee										
PTWMD	0.33	0.44	0.28	0.41	0.45	0.44	0.56	0.46	0.55	0.58
PT	0.31	0.27	0.22	0.19	0.29	0.27	0.28	0.24	0.34	0.44
FT	0.43	0.47	0.33	0.44	0.31	0.48	0.45	0.46	0.39	0.35
Hip-ankle										
PTWMD	0.50	0.59	0.51	0.58	0.59	0.55	0.55	0.48	0.55	0.53
PT	0.65	0.60	0.49	0.48	0.51	0.45	0.81	0.55	0.88	0.66
FT	0.79[a]	0.76	0.82[a]	0.81	0.78	0.83	0.81	0.85	0.71	0.78
Knee-ankle										
PTWMD	0.50	0.50	0.45	0.52	0.50	0.49	0.64	0.58	0.64	0.63
PT	0.75[a]	0.56	0.54[b]	0.49	0.52[b]	0.37	0.92[a]	0.61	0.95[a]	0.68
FT	0.98[a]	0.86	0.92[a]	0.79[a]	0.79	0.78	0.99[a]	0.90	0.79	0.86

[a]*Significantly different from PTWMD.*
[b]*Significantly different from FT.*

$p = .004$; $p = .001$ between FT and PTWMD, approaching significance ($p = .08$) between PT and PTWMD, and no significant difference ($p = .11$) between FT and PT, and at *extension onset*, overall $F(2,127) = 3.26$, $p = .04$; $p = .02$ between FT and PTWMD, $p = .04$ between FT and PT, and $p = .88$ between PT and PTWMD. DRP for hip-ankle pairs approached significance among groups at peak velocity of extension phase, overall $F(2,127) = 2.67$, $p = .07$; but only the difference between PT and PTWMD was significant ($p = .02$); $p = .26$ between FT and PTWMD, and $p = .23$ between FT and PT (see Table 3.7). PTWMD most often had smaller discrete relative phase values (values approaching 0 indicating in-phase movements) in comparison to both PT and FT infants for the hip-ankle and knee-ankle comparisons. This supports the joint angle correlation data, which demonstrated a tighter coupling of joints for the PTWMD group between knee-ankle and hip-ankle joints.

Intralimb coordination, specifically organization within joints, is depicted in phase plane portraits in Figure 3.4a–c. Joint angle data have been normalized to between –1 and 1. One example of a typical FT infant's phase plane portrait shows the variability that is typical of this group. The PT infant's portrait depicts increasing constraints (regularity), while the PTWMD has a highly constrained (regular) portrait which is also consistent within this group.

One hallmark of skilled movements is a linear relation between movement amplitude and peak velocity (i.e., larger movements have higher peak velocities; Cooke, 1987; Heriza, 1988). We used correlation coefficients (Pearson r) to test the relation between these variables in the three groups (see Table 3.8). We found significant correlations in the flexion and extension phases between movement amplitudes and peak velocities in hip, knee, and ankle joints for both the FT and the PT groups ($p < .0001$ for FT and $p < .01$ for PT). However, we found no significant relation between movement amplitude and its peak velocity in any joint for the PTWMD group ($p = .96$ for PTWMD).

FIGURE 3.4. (a) Phase portrait of ankle angle of an FT infant portrays the variability in kicking pattern that is characteristic of this group. (b) Phase portrait of ankle angle of a PT infant portrays the reduced variability in comparison to FT infants in the kicking pattern that is characteristic of this group. (c) Phase portrait of the ankle joint of PTWMD infant portrays the reduced variability in kicking pattern in comparison to both FT and PT that is characteristic of this group.

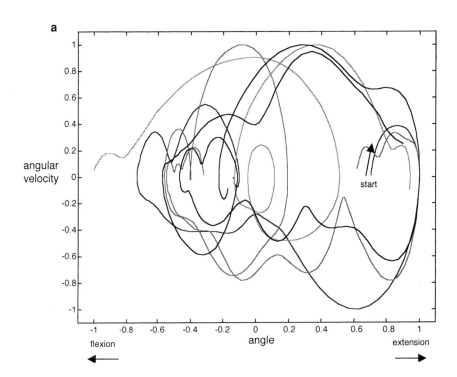

FIGURE 3.4. *Continued*

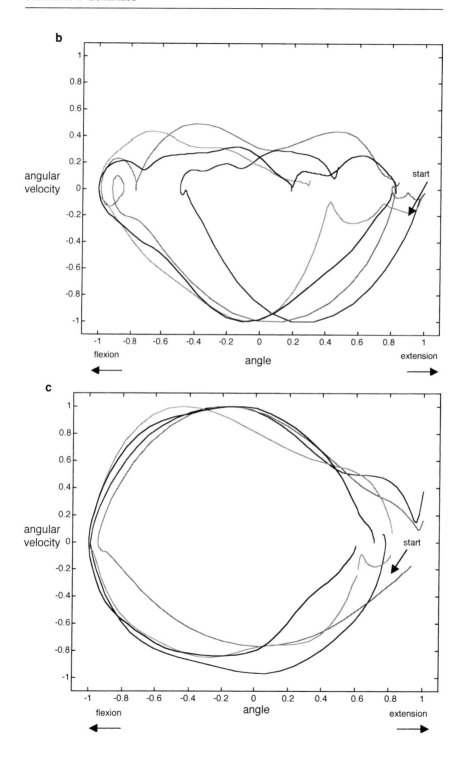

TABLE 3.8   Correlations (Pearson r) Between Joint Amplitude and Joint Peak Velocity

	FT	PT	PTWMD
Hip			
Flexion	0.69[a]	0.65[a]	0.07
Extension	0.57[a]	0.28[a]	0.24
Knee			
Flexion	0.66[a]	0.64[a]	0.11
Extension	0.53[b]	0.33	0.02
Ankle			
Flexion	0.49[a]	0.60[a]	0.30
Extension	0.61[b]	0.25	0.29

[a]*Significantly different from PTWMD.*
[b]*Significantly different from PT and PTWMD.*

DISCUSSION

Our data consistently describe atypical coordination patterns for premature infants with white matter disorder even as young as 1 month of age. The intralimb coordination of leg movement in our healthy 1-month-old infants born at term and born prematurely with VLBW is characterized by in-phase combinations in the proximal joint pairs (i.e., hip-knee) but begins to decouple at distal joints (i.e., knee-ankle; hip-ankle). The coordination of 1-month-old infants with WMD, however, is characterized by a persistent in-phase pattern at all joints and shows little evidence of the expected decoupling. The coordination patterns are found in the correlation measures, the measures of DRP, and depicted in the phase plane portraits. Our findings are consistent with findings of others for FT and PT, but have not been reported for PTWMD at this young age (Droit et al., 1996; Jeng, Yau, & Teng, 1998; Piek & Gasson, 1999; Vaal et al., 2000; van der Heide et al., 1999).

Developmental dissociation of intralimb joints begins in the ankle at 1-2 months of age and occurs later in the knee and hip joint in healthy FT infants (Thelen, 1985) and PT infants without WMD (Jeng et al., 1998; Piek & Gasson, 1999). The PT group, while more constrained (lower SD) than the FT group also shows a beginning disassociation of the ankle joint from the other joints, as depicted by lower correlation values in the PT group than the PTWMD group and a larger SD. This constrained coordination pattern evident in the PTWMD infants may be the first evidence of impending movement dysfunction as development progresses. Since VLBW infants with WMD have a high incidence of spastic diplegic CP, persistence of the in-phase pattern may be the first diagnostic sign of CP.

The characteristics of the extension phase of movement are different among groups. The extension phase of leg movement in kicking is mostly passive, influenced by the elastic properties of the leg and the effects of gravity (Thelen, 1985; Thelen & Fisher, 1983). The longer duration of the extension phase of hip and knee joint in the FT infants is consistent with findings of higher flexor muscle tone in FT infants, which could slow the extension movement, and increased extensor tone in PT infants, which could speed up the extension movement (Heriza, 1988). FT infants tended to be more flexed in kicking and WMD infants kicked with higher velocities.

Although brain lesions clearly have an impact on intralimb coordination, there are other constraints (e.g., the ratio of leg mass and muscle strength) on this coordination that need further investigation. One constraint to the emergence of out-of-phase movements may be the limited contexts for leg movements in the first months of life. Patterns of movement emerge within context and if context is limited, then so are the emergent patterns. The characteristics of kicking that we have described here and that others have reported are measured during bouts of spontaneous kicking. Exploratory play in the first months of life is typically exclusive to eyes and hands. Legs are left free to kick and become most useful for weight-bearing tasks such as sitting, crawling, and walking. Recently, we have demonstrated that an out-of-phase pattern can be learned (significantly increases in frequency) by 4-month-old FT, infants through contingent mobile reinforcement (Chen et al., 2002). A contingent learning paradigm using the legs could be the basis of an early intervention program to facilitate more typical intralimb coordination patterns in PTWMD infants when the in-phase patterns persist.

What is particularly striking in our data is not only the persistence of the in-phase pattern, but also the very limited variability in leg patterns in PTWMD infants. The small SDs of the correlations of the joint pairs in the PTWMD infants support the restricted variability of movement that has been reported in other samples with neurological impairments (Wagenaar & Van Emmerik, 1994). Typical movement includes variability, which supports adaptability. When movement variability is limited, the adaptability of the movement to the constraints of the context is also limited.

A remarkable characteristic of the infants with WMD is the lack of coordination between the amplitude and velocity of movement. The typical amplitude-velocity positive correlation that is reported in skilled movement and was apparent in both the FT and PT groups was absent in the infants with WMD. This could provide an additional early signal of atypical coordination in these infants.

WMD typically damages the corticospinal axons, but the cortical neurons are often less damaged or spared (Eyre, Miller, Clowry, Conway, & Watts, 2000; Eyre, Taylor, Villagra, & Miller, 2001). These neurons may then create intracortical connections that do not support the expected developmental course for movement (Marin-Padilla, 1997). Eyre et al. (2000) suggested that early intervention may induce the regrowth of corticospinal axons through the cystic areas typically seen in WMD. According to Eyre, this regrowth then will support the cortical input to spinal motor centers and facilitate normal development. What remains unclear in this cited work is the meaning of early intervention. We believe that the reinforcement of typical movement patterns through learning paradigms may be one critical form of early intervention. We have successfully demonstrated that premature infants as young as 1 month of age with WMD have atypical movement patterns. Our research efforts now will be focused on the relation of these atypical patterns to long-term movement problems, including CP, and to the potential for changing these aberrant patterns.

CHAPTER 4

Late Dose-Response Effects of Prenatal Cocaine Exposure on Newborn Neurobehavioral Performance

Early observations suggesting significant neonatal neurobehavioral dysfunction associated with prenatal exposure to cocaine raised clinical and public health concerns. (Chasnoff, Burns, Schnoll, & Burns, 1985; Frank, Bresnahan, & Zuckerman, 1993; Frank et al., 1988). Subsequent findings were neither as striking nor as consistent as the initial observations (Beeghly & Tronick, 1994; Coles et al., 1992; Dow-Edwards, 1991; Hutchings, 1993a; Lester & Tronick, 1994; Frank et al., 1988; Zuckerman et al., 1989). The most consistent behavioral finding is a decrement in the newborn's ability to habituate in the immediate postpartum period. (Eisen et al., 1991; Mayer, Granger, Frank, Schottenfeld, & Bornstein, 1993). However, other studies have not found this effect or have found different effects. (Chasnoff et al., 1985; Coles, 1993; Coles et al., 1992; Fetters & Tronick, 1994; Napiorowski et al., 1996; Schneider & Chasnoff, 1992). Several studies have not found any neurobehavioral effects after in utero cocaine exposure (Frank et at., 1988; Lloyd & Abiden, 1985; MacGregor et al., 1987; Neuspiel, Hamel, Hochberg, Greene, & Campbell, 1991; Ryan, Ehrlich, & Finnegan, 1987). Complicating this issue further, a number of studies (Chasnoff et al., 1988; Coles et al., 1992; Fulroth, Phillips, & Durant, 1989) have found interactive effects of cocaine with other substances, principally alcohol and marijuana, or with other risk conditions, such as lack of prenatal care (Coles et al., 1992; Eisen et al., 1991; Napiorkowski et al., 1996). Last, several investigators have found effects later in the newborn period rather than immediately after birth (Coles et al., 1992; Neuspiel et al., 1991).

These inconsistent findings may be attributable to small sample sizes, which preclude control for confounding variables, to the variability of doses and timing of exposure, and to the timing of assessments (Beeghly & Tronick, 1994; Coles, 1993; Coles et al., 1992; Frank et al., 1988, 1993; Hutchings, 1993; Mayes et al., 1993). Few studies have effectively controlled for confounding variables (Beeghly & Tronick, 1994), and in one study in which confounding variables were covaried, the critical variable of birth weight was not controlled for (Coles et al., 1992). Several investigators have suggested that weak or inconsistent results would be expected, because neurobehavioral effects will be seen only with high levels of exposure (Corwin et al., 1992; Mirochnick, Meyes, Cole, Herren, & Zuckerman, 1991). Studies showing little or no effect may be obscuring effects caused by heavy exposure by evaluating lighter and heavier users (e.g., samples identified solely by self-report or by self-report and urine assays) as a single group. It also has been argued that women who are the heaviest users are less likely to participate in studies, leading to ascertainment bias (Dow-Edwards, 1991).

The current study was designed to determine whether a dose effect of pre-natal cocaine exposure on neonatal neurobehavioral performance could be demonstrated in a representative sample of urban full-term infants of English-speaking mothers. The study also aimed to see whether effects were found early or late in the newborn period. The effects of selected confounding factors were controlled for using statistical techniques.

METHODS

Sample Construction

Sample Selection Criteria

The sample was recruited on the postpartum floor of Boston City Hospital from October 1990 to March 1993. Cocaine-exposed mother-infant dyads were matched when possible by ethnicity (African American and African Caribbean versus other) to unexposed dyads. All mother-infant dyads met the following criteria at delivery: (1) infant gestational age of 36 weeks or older; (2) no requirement for Level III (neonatal intensive) care; (3) no obvious major con-genital malformations; (4) no diagnosis of fetal alcohol syndrome in the neona-tal record; (5) no history of human immunodeficiency virus seropositivity noted in the mother's or infant's medical record; (6) the mother's ability to commu-nicate fluently in English; (7) no indication by toxic screen or history in the medical record of the mother's use during pregnancy of illegal opiates, methadone, amphetamines, phencyclidine, barbiturates, or hallucinogens; and (8) mother 18 years of age or older. These criteria were established to exclude infants with known major risk factors for developmental impairment that might confound or obscure the effects, if any, of in utero cocaine exposure. In par-ticular, these criteria excluded any preterm infants and infants with significant intrauterine growth retardation (IUGR) whose neurobehavior, compared with the neurobehavior of clinically healthy, full-term infants, might be compro-mised by these risk factors as well as more vulnerable to the effects of cocaine exposure.

Method of Exposure Classification

Previous research has demonstrated that a combination of self-report and biological markers—urine or meconium assays—maximizes identification of cocaine use in pregnancy (Zuckerman et al., 1989). All dyads were classified as exposed or unexposed based on a biological marker of the infant or the mother. After the identification of exposure status, classification of mothers as lighter or heavier users was done with a combination of information from interviews and biological markers obtained by clinicians and study personnel (see below).

Interview

The mothers were interviewed about their drug use history at intake on the postpartum floor using an adaptation of the Addiction Severity Index (Zuckerman et al., 1989). This interview provides information on the chronicity of the mothers' drug use and the frequency of use of drugs, including cigarettes and alcohol, before and during pregnancy.

Biological Markers—Methods of Meconium and Urine Analysis

As previously described (Mirochnick et al., 1991), meconium samples were analyzed for the presence of benzoylecgonine (a cocaine metabolite), opiates, amphetamines, benzodiazapines, and cannabinoids by a modification of the methods of Mirochnick et al. (1991) and Ostrea, Brady, and Parks (1989). Maternal urine samples were analyzed at recruitment for benzoylecognine, opiates, amphetamines, benzodiazepines, and cannabinoids by radioimmunoassay (RIA) using commercial kits (Abuscreen RIA; Roche Diagnostics Systems, Inc., Montclair, NJ).

Subject Exposure Classification

All mother-infant dyads had at least one biological marker, urine or meconium, which confirmed their exposure or lack of exposure to cocaine during pregnancy. In this sample, the mean days of self-reported cocaine use during pregnancy was 20.6 (range, 0 to 264) days. The mean meconium concentration was 1,143 (range, 0 to 17,950) ng of benzoylecognine/g of meconium. Heavy use was considered a priori to be the top quartile of meconium concentration for cocaine metabolites (>3,314 ng of benzoylecognine/g of meconium) or the top quartile days of self-reported use (>61 days) during pregnancy. All other use was classified as lighter (Mirochnick et al., 1991).

Procedures

Recruitment

Trained interviewer-recruiters screened maternity and nursery records 7 days a week and then sought informed consent from eligible women who, with their infants, met the selection criteria. Women with clinically documented prenatal cocaine use were recruited as exposed mothers, and those without such use were recruited as provisionally unexposed comparison mothers.

Of the 192 known cocaine-using mothers invited to participate, 123 (64%) agreed to join the study. Of the 646 mothers who were not clinically known cocaine users, 134 (21%) agreed to join the study. Of these 257 participants, 5 were excluded from further analysis, because their unexposed status could not be confirmed by biological assay. One additional woman was dropped because of a meconium test that was deemed unreliable. Of this sample of 251 dyads, 128 were provisionally considered unexposed, and 123 were considered provisionally exposed. Based on the results of the study of biological assays, 15 unexposed dyads were reclassified as exposed, yielding a study sample of 138 exposed and 113 unexposed dyads.

Within the cocaine-exposed group, no statistically significant differences in maternal age, parity, ethnicity, or mode of payment for medical care were observed among the mothers who were recruited, refused, or were not approached. It was not possible to assess levels of use of the exposed mothers who refused to participate. Within the nonexposed group, mothers who were recruited were significantly more likely ($p = .03$ by chi squared test) to be primiparous than those not approached or those who refused to participate (33% vs. 20% vs. 24%, respectively). These groups did not differ on the other parameters. Thus, aside from the difference in parity, our sample was representative of the general obstetric population from which they were drawn. When infants who had the week 3 Neonatal Behavioral Assessment Scale (NBAS) examination were compared with those who were examined only in the early newborn period, no significant differences in maternal characteristics (including substance use) were found.

Sample

A total sample of 251 infants received the NBAS examination in the newborn period or at the week 3 visit. In the immediate postpartum period, complete data were available on 224 dyads: 101 of the 224 dyads were nonusers; 79 were light users; and 44 were heavy users. At the week 3 visit, complete data were available on 205 dyads: 94 nonusers, 73 light users, and 38 heavy users. Thus, 7 heavy users, 6 light users, and 6 nonusers were lost to follow-up.

Physical Examination and Record Review

Within 8 to 72 (mean, 48) hours, a study pediatrician masked to exposure status assessed the infant's gestational age using the method of Dubowitz, Dubowitz, & Goldburg (1970). In addition, each infant was given a physical examination for minor and major congenital anomalies. The pediatrician carried out anthropometric measures of recumbent length on a Holtain Infantometer and head circumference using a plastic-coated tape (Zuckerman et al., 1989). Reliability was regularly assessed on the anthropometric measures and was maintained at .95 for head and length measurements using an intra-class correlation coefficient. After performing the physical examination, the pediatrician reviewed the infant's neonatal record and completed the Hobel index (Finnegan, 1981) for neonatal complications. A trained research assistant abstracted the mother's medical record to complete the prepartum, intra-partum, and postpartum Hobel risk indices for the mothers (Hobel, Youkeles, & Forsythe, 1979).

Neurobehavioral Assessment

As the most valid and standardized extant measure of neonatal behavior, the NBAS (Finnegan, 1981; MacGregor et al., 1987; Oro & Dixon, 1987) has been the instrument of choice in the majority of studies evaluating the effects of in utero cocaine exposure on newborn behavior. The NBAS consists of 28 behavioral items scored on a 9-point scale that describe the range of an infant's behavioral responses to social and nonsocial stimuli as the neonate moves from sleeping to awake and crying states as well as the infant's central neuro-organizational capacity to process and react to stimuli. Additionally, the NBAS contains nine supplementary quali-fier items. In contrast to the NBAS behavioral item scores, which focus on spe-cific aspects of the infant's performance, the supplementary items rate the quality of the infant's performance during the course of the examination (e.g., "robust-ness" varies from the infant appearing very fragile to energetic with no signs of exhaustion during the course of the examination), as well as difficulties the exam-iner had in examining the infant (e.g., "examiner persistence" varies from maxi-mal effort to elicit responses to no special examiner maneuvers needed to elicit responses during the course of the examination). Thus, the qualifier scores are similar to clinical judgments of the infant's quality of performance.

In this study, the NBAS was administered to the infants during the early neona-tal period (mean age, 51 hours) and during the third week of life (mean age, 17 days). Serial NBAS examinations are more accurate and better predictors of behav-ior (Lester, 1984; Lester et al., 1991) and permit the evaluation of drug effects when the infants are no longer possibly acutely intoxicated by maternal cocaine. The newborn examination was administered in a quiet room off the nurseries. The week 3 examination was administered in a quiet room in the primary care pedi-atric clinic before the infant received a physical examination. All examiners were masked to infant drug exposure status and trained by a certified NBAS trainer to standard levels of reliability, that is, 90% reliability within one scale point on all items. Reliability was maintained at this level during the course of the study.

Data Reduction of the NBAS

The NBAS supplementary qualifier items were analyzed item by item. The NBAS behavioral item raw scores were reduced to cluster scores in two ways. Seven neurobehavioral clusters were calculated using the method of Lester (1984): habituation, orientation, state regulation, range of state, autonomic stability, motor organization, and reflexes. Two additional clusters (developed by Lester & Tronick, in press), excitability and depression, were also calculated. The excitability and depression clusters are hypothesized to be related to the direct effects of cocaine on the central nervous system and to indirect effects mediated through IUGR (Lester et al., 1991). Thirteen NBAS items are used to construct the excitability and depression scales (see appendix and Lester & Tronick, in press, for details).

Data Analysis

Least-squares regression models were carried out on the NBAS data to evaluate the differences among the groups uncontrolled for covariates. These multivariate group analyses are conservative, because they make no assumption about the relations among the three groups. Two-tailed tests (p values) were used. After these analyses, multiple regression analyses were performed on the NBAS measures, controlling for covariates. Some covariates were examined but dropped from the final model because they had no significant relation to outcome. Variables dropped from analysis included infant gender, maternal education, ethnicity, parity, and number of prenatal visits. Covariates entered in the model included age at examination, birth weight, maternal anesthesia (general, local, or none—used only in the newborn analysis), prepartum Hobel risk score (any positive risk item vs. none), maternal age, marijuana use, log average daily volume of alcohol, and log average daily number of cigarettes. Birth weight was entered as a z score to adjust for gender and gestational age. Head circumference and length were dropped from the analyses, because birth weight was found to be a better predictor of the dependent measures than these variables.

The birth weight z scores were obtained by taking gender-specific least-squares regressions of birth weight on the Dubowitz gestational age, with squared and cubic terms included. Data for these models were obtained in a previous study (Zuckerman et al., 1989) of more than 1,200 infants whose mothers had received prenatal care and who were delivered at the hospital. Predicted birth weight values for the current sample were generated using the parameter estimates from the above models. The difference of each infant's birth weight and the predicted values, referred to as residuals, were computed. Z scores for these residuals were computed using the mean and SD of the residuals from the previous study sample as population values.

Multivariate trend analyses were carried out to evaluate dose-response relations. The three groups (unexposed, lightly exposed, and heavily exposed) were assigned values of 0, 1, and 2, respectively. The values 0, 1, and 2 are not interval values but only ordinal values, representing an increase in exposure. Multivariate trend analyses were then applied to the slopes of the data for the cluster and qualifier scores over these groups. Dose-response relations would be represented by a significant trend across the means.

RESULTS

Maternal Characteristics

Table 4.1 presents data on maternal characteristics for each exposure group. As would be expected from the matching procedures, there were no significant ethnic differences among the groups. The non-cocaine-using mothers were younger than the light or heavy users (24.8 vs. 27.7 vs. 26.7 years, respectively; $p = .0001$). The exposed and unexposed groups did not differ in parity, education, percentage of private insurance, or percentage of cesarean section.

Table 4.2 presents data on maternal cigarette, alcohol, and marijuana use during pregnancy. Cigarette and alcohol use were determined by self-report on the Addiction Severity Index. Marijuana use was determined by a positive self-report or any positive urine or meconium assay. Women who used cocaine prenatally, and heavy users more than lighter users, were significantly more likely

TABLE 4.1 Characteristics of Mothers of Infants With Neonatal Behavioral Assessment Scale Examinations

	Exposure to Cocaine			
Characteristic	Nonuse (n = 101)	Light (n = 79)	Heavy (n = 44)	*p*
Ethnicity, %				
White, Hispanic, and other	9	18	15	.001
African-American and Caribbean	91	82	85	
Age, y*	24.8a	27.7b	26.7b	.0001
Payment status, %				
Public	80	72	70	.03
Private	10	4	3	
Self	10	24	27	
Education, %				
Not high school	33	40	44	.40
High school	48	48	47	
Any college	19	11	8	
Marital status, %				
Married	16	2	5	.005
Separated or divorced	9	7	11	
Never married	75	91	84	
Parity, primiparous, %	43	29	33	.10
Cesarean section, %	20	14	9	.22
Any Hobel prenatal risk, %	39	24	31	.10

Different letters indicate significant differences between groups, and shared letters indicate no significant difference ($p < .05$ by Tukey test).

TABLE 4.2 Maternal Use of Cigarettes, Alcohol, and Marijuana

| | Exposure to Cocaine | | | |
Maternal Use	Nonuse (n = 101)	Light (n = 79)	Heavy (n = 44)	*p*
Cigarettes, %				
None	86	37	14	.001
≤ ½ pack/d	4	26	39	
> ½ and <1 pack/d	6	22	27	
≥1 pack/d	4	15	20	
Average no. of drinks, %				
None	96	60	36	.001
<1/d	4	37	50	
≥1/d	0	3	14	
Marijuana use, %	9	33	40	.001

to have used cigarettes, alcohol, and marijuana, as reported in other studies (Bateman, Ng, Hansen, & Heagerty, 1993; Feldman, Minkoff, McCalla, & Salwen, 1992; Frank et al., 1988; Handler, Kistin, Davis, & Ferre, 1991; Petit & Coleman, 1990; Zuckerman et al., 1989).

Infant Characteristics

Data on infant characteristics in each exposure group are presented in Table 4.3. The three exposure groups did not differ on Apgar scores at 1 and 5 minutes. No significant differences among the groups on the Hobel neonatal risk index were found. Birth weight and length differed among the three groups ($p < .0001$).

TABLE 4.3 Clinical Characteristics of Infants With Neonatal Behavioral Assessment Scale Data

| | Exposure to Cocaine | | | |
Characteristic	Unexposed (n = 101)	Light (n = 79)	Heavy (n = 44)	*p*
Apgar <7 at 1 min, %	10	6	8	.63
Apgar <7 at 5 min, %	1	0	3	.43
Weight, g*	3356a	3058b	2931b	.0001
Length, cm*	49.13a	47.98b	47.06b	.0001
Head circumference, cm*	34.93a	34.20ac	33.60c	.001
Ponderal Index	2.87	2.79	2.81	.64

*Different letters indicate significant differences between groups, and shared letters indicate no significant difference ($p < .05$, by Tukey test).

Unexposed infants weighed more and were longer than lightly and heavily exposed infants. Unexposed and lightly exposed infants had significantly larger occipital head circumferences than heavily exposed infants ($p < .001$) but did not differ from each other. Ponderal indices did not differ significantly among groups. Relatedly, meconium benzoylecgonine concentration was negatively related to birth weight ($r = -.27$; $p = .01$) and length ($r = -.32$; $p = .01$; Mirochnick et al., 1991).

Neurobehavioral Performance

In Table 4.4 and Table 4.5, analyses of the data on neurobehavioral performance of study infants controlled and uncontrolled for confounders during the newborn period and the third week of life are presented. Confounders included age at examination, birth weight, maternal anesthesia (general, local, or none— used only in the newborn analysis), prepartum Hobel risk score (any positive risk item vs. none), maternal age, marijuana use, log average daily volume of alcohol, and log average daily number of cigarettes.

At the newborn examination, uncontrolled for confounders, prenatal cocaine exposure was significantly associated in a dose-related fashion with habituation ($p < .03$) and with all but three supplementary qualifier items ($p = .04$; Table 4.5). Significant effects for habituation ($p = .02$) and motor maturity ($p = .04$) were found using multivariate trend analysis. At the week 3 examination, prenatal cocaine exposure had significant univariate associations with NBAS cluster scores for reflexes ($p = .04$), state regulation ($p = .01$), autonomic stability ($p = .03$), excitability ($p = .0004$), and three of the qualifier scores ($p = .02$; Table 4.5). At week 3, trend analyses revealed significant univariate dose-response effects for reflexes ($p = .001$), state regulation ($p = .005$), autonomic stability ($p = .009$), and excitability ($p = .001$).

After controlling for confounding variables, cocaine exposure was no longer significantly associated with habituation or the NBAS qualifiers at the newborn examination. In contrast, at the week 3 examination, when confounding variables were controlled for, the level of prenatal cocaine exposure continued to be independently associated with state regulation ($p = .02$) and excitability ($p = .007$) but not with reflexes ($p = .48$), autonomic stability ($p = .28$), or any of the NBAS qualifier scores. Trend analyses continued to be significant for state regulation ($p = .01$) and excitability ($p = .05$) after controlling for confounders.

Various covariates were also significantly related to different neurobehavioral scores at the two examinations, but no significant interactions between these covariates and the level of exposure were observed. These covariate effects at the early examination were: (1) habituation cluster—the older the infant at the time of examination, the poorer the performance ($p = .004$); (2) orientation cluster—infants of mothers who received anesthesia during delivery performed better ($p = .04$); and (3) reflex cluster—infants with higher birth weight z scores performed better ($p = .04$).

TABLE 4.4   Neonatal Behavioral Assessment Scale Clusters in the Newborn Period and at 2 to 3 Weeks: Unadjusted Means and SEs*

| | Exposure to Cocaine | | | | | | p | |
| | Unexposed | | Light | | Heavy | | | |
Scale Item	Mean	SE	Mean	SE	Mean	SE	Un-adjusted	Adjusted
Newborn								
Examination	n = 101†		n = 79†		n = 44†			
Habituation	6.54	0.19	5.90	0.22	5.75	0.28	.03	.18
Orientation	5.32	0.16	4.99	0.19	5.11	0.20	.37	.88
Motor	5.22	0.07	5.10	0.08	4.94	0.12	.13	.50
Reflex	3.35	0.27	3.68	0.34	4.05	0.43	.38	.95
State								
regulation	5.04	0.12	5.11	0.16	4.96	0.20	.83	.74
State range	3.48	0.07	3.40	0.08	3.56	0.08	.44	.34
Autonomic								
stability	5.84	0.11	5.61	0.12	5.64	0.18	.33	.79
Excitability	0.19	0.01	0.21	0.02	0.18	0.03	.52	.35
Depression	0.21	0.02	0.22	0.02	0.24	0.03	.85	.96
2- to 3-week								
Examination	n = 94†		n = 73†		n = 38†			
Habituation	6.39	0.37	6.15	0.36	5.67	0.71	.59	.59
Orientation	5.93	0.15	5.85	0.16	5.60	0.19	.46	.74
Motor	5.49	0.08	5.54	0.07	5.49	0.09	.88	.31
Reflex	2.95	0.31	3.47	0.31	4.37	0.49	.04	.48
State								
regulation	4.69	0.14	4.50	0.13	3.98	0.19	.01	.02
State range	3.57	0.08	3.41	0.09	3.62	0.13	.28	.30
Autonomic								
stability	6.45	0.10	6.27	0.11	5.98	0.14	.03	.28
Excitability	0.14	0.01	0.14	0.01	0.24	0.03	.0004	.007
Depression	0.15	0.02	0.14	0.02	0.12	0.03	.44	.30

*Analyses compare categories of in utero cocaine exposure for infants with complete data on marijuana use, natural log of prenatal average daily volume of alcohol, natural log of prenatal average daily cigarettes, the presence of any Hobel prenatal risk factors, any general anaesthesia, any opiate labor medications, infant age at examination, and birth weight z score adjusted for gender and gestational age. Numbers of infants at newborn examination: unexposed = 101; light = 79; and heavy = 44. Numbers of infants at 2- to 3-week examination: nonuse = 94; light = 73; and heavy = 38.

†The actual n varies for particular items, because infants may have been in the wrong state to administer an item, or items were not administered or missed.

TABLE 4.5 Neonatal Behavioral Assessment Scale Supplementary Qualifier Item Ratings in the Newborn Period and at 2 to 3 Weeks: Unadjusted Means and SEs*

| | Exposure to Cocaine | | | | | | p | |
| | Unexposed | | Light | | Heavy | | | |
	Mean	SE	Mean	SE	Mean	SE	Un-adjusted	Adjusted
Newborn Examination	n = 101†		n = 79†		n = 44†			
Quality of responsiveness	5.68	0.19	5.27	0.71	4.91	0.30	.08	.45
Cost of attention	6.07	0.13	5.41	0.13	5.34	0.14	.0001	.09
Persistence	5.51	0.13	5.08	0.13	4.93	0.15	.01	.27
Irritability	5.60	0.21	5.45	0.24	5.44	0.27	.86	.79
Robustness	6.13	0.13	5.51	0.15	5.37	0.16	.0004	.15
Regulatory capacity	6.18	0.15	5.68	0.18	5.43	0.19	.02	.24
State regulation	6.64	0.12	6.29	0.13	6.14	0.17	.04	.69
Balance motor tone	6.62	0.18	5.86	0.19	5.68	0.29	.003	.51
Reinforce value of infant	5.90	0.20	5.29	0.24	5.25	0.28	.07	.47
2- to 3-Week Examination	n = 94†		n = 73†		n = 38†			
Quality of responsiveness	6.63	0.18	6.38	0.20	5.89	0.28	.09	.62
Cost of attention	6.46	0.15	6.18	0.15	5.74	0.17	.02	.39
Persistence	6.21	0.16	5.78	0.15	5.79	0.19	.10	.75
Irritability	6.27	0.23	6.27	0.25	5.43	0.41	.12	.26
Robustness	6.85	0.18	6.55	0.16	6.21	0.19	.08	.74
Regulatory capacity	6.82	0.16	6.74	0.15	6.29	0.21	.14	.42
State regulation	7.12	0.11	6.95	0.13	6.63	0.14	.06	.55
Balance motor tone	7.01	0.19	6.29	0.23	6.11	0.30	.01	.89
Reinforce value of infant	6.60	0.21	6.37	0.25	5.47	0.35	.02	.31

*Analyses compare categories of in utero cocaine exposure for infants with complete data on marijuana use, natural log of prenatal average daily volume of alcohol, natural log of prenatal average daily cigarettes, the presence of any Hobel prenatal risk factors, any general anaesthesia, any opiate labor medications, infant age at examination, and birth weight z score adjusted for gender and gestational age. Numbers of infants at newborn examination: unexposed = 101; light = 79; and heavy = 44. Numbers of infants at 2- to 3-week examination: unexposed = 94; light = 73; and heavy = 38.
†Actual n may vary.

At the week 3 examination, covariate associations included: (1) reflex clus-ter—a higher birth weight z score was associated with better performance (p = .05); (2) regulation of state cluster—older infants performed better (p = .006), as did infants with no prenatal risk by Hobel criteria (p = .03); and (3) auto-nomic stability cluster—infants of mothers who used alcohol performed more poorly (p = .03).

DISCUSSION

This study is the first to document human dose-response effects of in utero cocaine exposure on the neurobehavioral performance of the infant (Dow-Edwards, 1991; Hutchings, 1993; Richardson & Day, 1991). In this sample, after controlling for covariates, heavier maternal use of cocaine was associated with poorer regulation of arousal (i.e., state regulation and excitability) late in the newborn period but not in the immediate postpartum period. Significant dose effects were found in this sample of infants for habituation and motor per-formance in the immediate postpartum period and later in the newborn period for reflexes and autonomic stability, as well as on the supplementary qualifier items, but these effects disappeared when potentially confounding variables were controlled for analytically.

The study's prospective, longitudinal design overcomes, at least in part, many of the methodological problems of earlier research. Examiners were masked to exposure status. Importantly, the sample represents the spectrum of the cocaine-using population of medically indigent, English-speaking women in Boston. The sample was drawn from a general obstetric population of mothers, and the newborns were clinically healthy, full-term, and free of heroin, methadone, barbiturates, phencyclidine, and amphetamines. The sample is not biased against heavier cocaine users, who may not enroll in prenatal care (Dow-Edwards, 1988, 1991, 1993), or who do not give birth in hospitals. In Boston, virtually all women receive prenatal care and give birth in hospitals. Of course, some of the heaviest-using mothers may still have been missed. Missing the heaviest users might have occurred if one were to assume that they are more likely to refuse to participate, even though refusers and compilers did not dif-fer with respect to demographic or clinical characteristics. However, were such a bias to occur, it would work against finding dose-related effects.

Thus, heterogeneity of the amount of use, as indicated by the newly devel-oped composite index based on self-reports and meconium assays (Mirochnick et al., 1991), was large enough to detect dose-related neurobehavioral effects, even though meconium measurement has been generally thought to be only an all-or-none measurement. Although unmeasured confounders may have affected neurobehavioral performance, the finding of significant dose-response effects after controlling for many covariates suggests a specific effect of cocaine on new-born neurobehavioral performance. Indeed, the dose-response relationships found are likely to underestimate the effects of prenatal exposure because of the exclusion of preterm, IUGR, and other at-risk infants from the sample and the possibility that some of the heaviest-using mothers were still missed.

The emergent independent effects of cocaine at 3 weeks postpartum on state regulation and excitability reflect an impairment in the infant's ability to modulate arousal. These effects are not likely to be attributable to the direct acute exposure of the infant after delivery. First, cocaine-using women are routinely discouraged from breast-feeding at Boston City Hospital, so that direct mother-to-infant transfer of cocaine is likely to end at delivery, with the exception of passive postnatal exposure. Second, after in utero exposure, cocaine metabolites clear the newborn's body in 7 days, as assessed by RIA methods (Frank et al., 1993). Third, if the effect seen were attributable to acute infant intoxication, one would expect to see other neurobehavioral effects. These effects were not observed. Fourth, similar to other studies (Coles et al., 1992; Neuspiel et al., 1991), effects are seen late rather than early in the newborn period.

These late-emerging neurobehavioral effects might be expected if in utero cocaine exposure is associated with evolving neuroanatomical damage (Dixon, 1994) or disruption of the neurotransmitter systems (e.g., the monoaminergic system, which is thought to control the modulation of arousal and attention; Dow-Edwards, 1988; Kaltenbach & Finnegan, 1988). Dysfunction of this or other systems might result in the observed effects and even an infant withdrawal syndrome. Little in these findings supports the hypothesis that the exposed newborn's neurobehavior is compromised because of IUGR, for two reasons: (1) the effects of cocaine persist after controlling for birth weight adjusted for gender and gestational age (Lester & Tronick, 1994; Zuckerman et al., 1989); and (2) IUGR was not associated with the depression cluster among the cocaine-exposed infants, as Lester and Tronick (1994) have hypothesized and found in previous research (Beeghly & Tronick, 1994; Lester et al., 1991).

The habituation effect found in this study replicates and extends previous findings (Eisen et al., 1991; Mayes et al., 1991). This effect was no longer significant after controlling for confounders, as was the case in other studies (Dow-Edwards, 1991; Eisen et al., 1991; Mayes et al., 1991). Similarly, as in other studies (Dow-Edwards, 1991; Eisen et al., 1991; Mayes et al., 1991) the significant associations of in utero cocaine exposure with week 3 motor, reflex, and autonomic stability clusters were no longer significant after controlling for covariates. Thus, these effects could not be specifically attributed to cocaine but, rather, are related to other risk factors, such as maternal anesthesia, alcohol, birth weight, and prenatal risk (Coles et al., 1992; Lester & Tronick, 1994; Neuspiel et al., 1991).

The effects of a combination of factors are evident in the findings for the NBAS supplementary qualifier items. These clinical judgments demonstrate that exposed newborns at both the early and late examinations were judged to have less regulatory capacity, poorer state regulation, poorer motor tone, and less responsivity than the nonexposed infants. Moreover, the exposed infants were more difficult to examine and less rewarding to the examiner. However, unlike the findings for the specific neurobehavioral items, the clinically recognizable differences for the supplementary qualifier items were not statistically significant after adjusting for covariates. Clinicians correctly judge cocaine-exposed infants to have poorer functional status than unexposed infants, but it is incorrect simply to attribute their dysfunction to maternal cocaine use. Rather, these findings indicate that cocaine exposure is a marker for a number of other adverse lifestyle factors that contribute to the infant's poorer functioning. Thus, the clinician needs to consider not only cocaine but these other factors when managing the care of the exposed mother and her infant.

Caution must be exercised in generalizing these results to other populations in which the mix of risk factors and other exposures may be different from those reported here. Moreover, it is important to note that although neurobehavioral effects were found that were consistent with previous reports, several domains of newborn functioning (e.g., orientation) were unaffected. With the exception of the dose-response relationships for excitability and state regulation at 2 to 3 weeks, which indicate specific neonatal neurobehavioral effects of maternal cocaine use, other domains of neurobehavioral functioning of even the heavily exposed infants were indistinguishable from the those of the unexposed infants (Coles, 1993).

For the pediatric provider, prenatal cocaine exposure should serve as a flag that the infant is likely to show clinically detectable compromised neurobehavioral status throughout the newborn period. These characteristics make the infants both more sensitive to disruptive caregiving and more difficult to care for, leading to a self-reinforcing process that may exacerbate initial neurobehavioral impairments. Thus, in utero cocaine exposure needs to be prevented. However, when prevention fails, intervention with the caregiver-child dyad can be beneficial in limiting further neurobehavioral dysfunction caused by the disruption of mutual regulatory processes that determine extrauterine development (Beeghly & Tronick, 1994).

In summary, this research documents a dose-related association between the level of in utero cocaine exposure and neurobehavioral performance during the late newborn period. In addition, our findings indicate that a combination of other factors, including cocaine, compromises newborn neurobehavioral performance. In utero cocaine exposure thus has a measurable effect on the exposed newborn's emerging neurobehavioral capacity to regulate arousal. It is not known whether this problem progresses developmentally, but it would be critical to know its course, because regulation of arousal and attention is critical to learning. Longitudinal studies focusing on the development of infants' capacity to regulate arousal and attention are warranted, especially in the context of social interaction (Beeghly & Tronick, 1994).

APPENDIX

The 13 NBAS items and their criterion scores that make up the excitability scale are: tone, more than 6; motor maturity, less than 4; cuddliness, less than

3; consolability, less than 4; peak of excitement, less than 7; rapidity of buildup, more than 6; irritability, more than 5; activity, more than 6; tremulousness, more than 5; startles, more than 4; lability of skin color, more than 7; lability of state, more than 3; and self-quieting, less than 3. For the depression scale, the items are: orientation to a ball, less than 4; to a rattle, less than 4; to a face, less than 4; to a voice, less than 4; to a face and voice, less than 4; to alertness, less than 4; tone, less than 4; pull-to-sit, less than 4; defensive reaction, less than 4; rapidity of buildup, less than 4; irritability, less than 3; and activity, less than 4. Infants are assigned one point for each NBAS item on which the infant meets or exceeds the criteria for excitability or depressed behavior. However, rules must also be applied that take account of performances that are dependent on one another, which in turn affect the cluster scores (e.g., the failure of an infant to achieve a state of 4 is associated with the infant's scores on the orientation items, which in turn affects the depression cluster score). Additionally, the score is averaged to allow for missing values. A complete manual with rules of combination is available from Lester and Tronick (in press).

CHAPTER 5

Similar and Functionally Typical Kinematic Reaching Parameters in 7- and 15-Month-Old In Utero Cocaine-Exposed and Unexposed Infants

The effects of intrauterine cocaine exposure on infant neuromotor functioning and development remain unclear. The emergent interpretation from what Lester (Beeghly & Tronick, 1994; Lester, 1994, 1999) termed second-wave studies is that although there are definite effects of intrauterine exposure, the effects are small. Moreover, many of these effects appear to resolve during the second year of life and may only indicate an initial slowing of development or an alternative trajectory of development (Chiriboga, Bateman, Brust, & Hauser, 1993; Fetters & Tronick, 1996, 2000; Volpe, 1992a). Importantly, it is still unclear whether any of the effects identified to date have clinical or functional implications.

Based on the pathophysiology of cocaine's effect on the central nervous system (CNS; Eyler & Behnke, 1999; Fetters & Tronick, 1996; Kosofsky & Wilkins, 1998; Mayes, 1994; Mayes, Granger, Frank, Schottenfeld, & Bornstein, 1993; Mirochnick, Meyer, Cole, Herren, & Zuckerman, 1991; Needlman, Zuckerman, Anderson, Mirochnick, & Cohen, 1993; Volpe, 1992), one might expect intrauterine cocaine exposure to have specific, permanent effects on infant motor functioning as well as on affect, attention, and arousal. Additionally, in utero exposure to cocaine also may indirectly affect infant outcome via the maternal fetal cardiovascular system with its resultant fetal hypoxic effects (Lester, LaGasse, & Bigsby, 1998; Lester & Tronick, 1994; Livesay, Ehrlich, & Finnegan, 1987; Villar, Smeriglio, Martorell, Brown, & Klein, 1984; Zuckerman, 1996). These indirect effects are expected to be global. The pathophysiological pathways are not mutually exclusive. As a consequence, it would be expected that there would be developmental deficits in motor performance (e.g., effects on reaching and later effects on fine motor performance) to be produced by their action.

This pathophysiological interpretation faces the problem that in human studies the effects of intrauterine exposure are, at most, erratically observed and weakly demonstrated (Durand, Espinoza, & Nickerson, 1990; Lester, 1999). This inconsistent detection of effects is often attributed to lack of sufficiently sensitive measurement techniques (e.g., omnibus developmental tests such as the Peabody Developmental Motor Scales; Dow-Edwards, 1991; Folio & Fewell, 1983; Hutchings, 1993a, 1993b; Jacobson & Jacobson, 1996; Kosofsky, 1998; Kosofsky & Wilkins, 1998; Zuckerman, 1991). Our goal in this study was to attempt to overcome some of these measurement limitations by utilizing a precise, quantifiable method of analysis, kinematic analysis, to evaluate the effect of in utero cocaine exposure on infant motor functioning. Kinematic recording of movement patterns (e.g., reaching) generates a set of quantitative parameters of movement rather than coarser measures such as judgments of success or failure of movement, or qualitative judgments of movement dimensions (e.g., smooth). The utility and precision of kinematic analysis has been demonstrated in developmental studies of infants and children. Kinematic measures have been demonstrated to be sensitive to age-related changes in reaching. With development, the number of movement units (MU; i.e., number of zero crossings in acceleration during a movement making up a reach; Brooks, 1974; von Hofsten, 1979; see Table 5.1 for definitions) decreases from 2 to 3 MU at 3 to 5 months to slightly more than 1 MU at 9 to 12 months (Fetters & Todd, 1987; von Hofsten, 1979). In descriptive terms, with development the reach becomes less jerky. Reach durations range from 500 to 2,000 ms for the youngest infants and decrease to 800 to 1,000 ms in the older infants (Fetters & Todd, 1987; Kluzik, Fetters, & Coryell, 1990). Rose-Jacobs and Fetters (1989) and von Hofsten (1979) reported that as the infant develops, the first MU covers an increasing proportion of the total reach distance. Finally, reaches tend to become straighter with development. Further attesting to the validity of the method, kinematic studies of healthy preterm infants, infants and children with CNS pathophysiology, and children with other medical conditions have detected compromises in the kinematic parameters of movement that were undetected with clinical assessments (Claman & Zeffiro, 1986; Fisk & Goodale, 1988; Heriza, 1991; Lough, Wing, Fraser, & Jenner, 1984; Rose-Jacobs & Fetters, 1989; Thelen, 1986; Thelen et al., 1991; Wagenaar & Beek, 1992; Wagenaar & Van Emmerick, 1994). However, it is important to note that like other forms of precise measurement (e.g., MRI or assays of human neurotransmitters), utilization of kinematic analysis limits studies to small sample sizes (e.g., often $n = 10$ or less). As a consequence, there is a trade-off between the precision of measurement, sample characteristics and biases, and the control and the evaluation of covariates.

In this study, we longitudinally evaluated the reaching of 34 infants (19 exposed, 15 unexposed) at two ages, 7 months and 15 months, using kinematic

TABLE 5.1 Demographics (Means and *SD*s in Parentheses)

	Number Exposed/Unexposed	Exposed	Unexposed	*p*
Gender	19/15			
Male		12	5	.0842
Female		7	10	
Race	19/15			
African American		15	8	.2596
Hispanic		3	6	
Caucasian		1	1	
Weight (g)				
Birth	18/14	3018 (508)	3321 (425)	.0832
1 month	14/12	4302 (514)	4500 (406)	.2937
4 months	14/13	6896 (847)	7103 (854)	.5320
7 months	16/13	8330 (778)	8715 (958)	.2419
15 months	15/13	11181 (1452)	10906 (1557)	.6327
Alcohol (yes)	18/15	17	1	.0001
Tobacco (yes)	17/15	13	4	.0048
Hobel 2 (no prenatal)	18/15	6.2 (6.5)	5.8 (8.5)	.8727
Hobel	18/15	10.8 (8.4)	9.7 (8.8)	.7006
Maternal education	19/15			.1312
No high school (HS)		8	4	
HS		9	5	
HS plus		2	6	
Maternal age (years)	19/15	27.9 (3.4)	23.1 (5.0)	.0021
Parity	19/15	3.6 (2.3)	2.3 (1.2)	.0628

techniques. We hypothesized that the exposed infants in comparison to the unexposed infants would have compromised kinematic parameters of reaching at each age. More specifically, we expected that the exposed infants' reaches compared to the unexposed infants' reaches would have (a) a larger number of MUs (i.e., jerkier) making up the reach, (b) smaller MUs making up the reach, (c) less proportional distance covered in the first MU of the reach, (d) less direct reach paths, and (e) longer reach durations. Nonetheless, we expected that these parameters would improve with age for infants in both groups. Additionally, given the high-risk profiles of infants in both groups (e.g., low socioeconomic status, maternal alcohol and tobacco use, birth weight below group mean), we expected that both of these groups of high-risk infants would perform more poorly than lower risk infants studied in similar paradigms in other studies (Hurt et al., 1995; Ostrea, Brady, Gause, Raymundo, & Stevens, 1992).

METHOD

Subjects

Sample Selection Criteria

Subjects were recruited from the regular (well-baby) newborn nurseries of the Joint Program in Neonatology at the Brigham and Women's and Beth Israel Deaconess Hospitals, Boston. The study was approved by each institution's institutional review boards, and mothers signed informed consent. All mother-infant dyads met the following selection criteria: (a) mother at least 18 years of age; (b) infant birth weight equal to or greater than 2,000 g (in these hospitals, infants with birth weights of ≤2,000 g are considered "well" and stay in the well-child nurseries unless they develop a complication); (c) no obvious major congenital malformations; (d) NICU stay for none other than drug-related reasons, minor routine observation, or septic workup (which had to be negative); (e) no requirement for mechanical ventilation: (f) no stigmata of fetal alcohol syndrome on neonatal examination; (g) no evidence of seropositivity for HIV; (h) mothers free of seizure disorders or requiring medication for any psychiatric illness; (i) infant discharged to mother's or foster mother's care from the hospital; and (j) mother's willingness to give informed consent. These criteria were chosen to exclude infants with known major risk factors for developmental impairment (other than cocaine use and other high-risk social risks that travel with cocaine exposure) that might confound the effects of cocaine exposure.

Method of Exposure Classification

Mothers were identified as cocaine users on the basis of their medical record history of cocaine use during pregnancy, or on the basis of urine positive toxic screens for cocaine metabolites in the infant following delivery, in the mother at delivery, or within 1 week before delivery (for details, see Fetters & Tronick, 1996). Unexposed mother-infant pairs had no record of substance abuse, and each had a negative urine at the time of delivery. The lack of exposure for the control infants was further confirmed with radioimmunoassay of meconium for cocaine, opiates, phencyclidine, amphetamine, and marijuana (Ostrea et al., 1992).

Recruitment

To control for changes in hospital care, unexposed infants were accepted as matches for exposed infants if delivered no more than 2 months apart. Matches were found for each exposed infant within this time window. Cocaine-exposed and unexposed mother-infant dyads were matched by self-reported race (African American, Hispanic, Caucasian) and mother's education and income (indexed by method of health insurance payment). Unexposed dyads that were similar in self-reported race, education, and income to the exposed dyads were preferentially approached for recruitment. This was done to ensure that the exposed and unexposed groups were similar in sociodemographic characteristics. A research assistant contacted 119 of the 178 mothers who met the inclusion criteria. The remaining 59 mothers were not contacted because of technical problems (e.g., they had been discharged). Of the 119 mothers, 59 (49%) agreed to participate (35 exposed dyads and 24 unexposed). Nine mother-infant dyads were excluded from the study. In the exposed group, two infants were excluded from the study because the mothers were found to be established users of heroin. One infant died from sudden infant death syndrome. Four exposed infants were excluded for missing appointments. In the control group, two mothers were excluded for not keeping appointments.

The final sample consisted of 28 exposed and 22 unexposed mother-infant dyads. The numbers of accepters and refusers are typical of many studies of intrauterine exposure, and the dropout rate is somewhat lower than often reported. For analytic purposes, the sample was comprised of 34 infants (19 exposed and 15 unexposed) who had usable kinematic data at both ages, which is required for repeated measures statistical analyses. To our knowledge, this is the largest sample size to date for kinematic analysis of infants exposed to cocaine.

Sample Demographics and Medical Data

Table 5.1 presents the basic medical and sociodemographic information on the exposed and unexposed infants and mothers. As expected, mothers of exposed infants used significantly more alcohol and tobacco, were older, and had higher parity.

Procedure

Testing was carried out at 7 and 15 months of infant age in the child observation laboratory of the Child Development Unit of Children's Hospital, Boston. Infants sat in an infant chair placed in a semicircular cutout section of a wooden table with the mother/caretaker at one side and the examiner facing the child. The examiner sequentially presented two toys to the infant within reaching distance at the infant's midline: a rattle (i.e., a clear plastic box, 2.5 × 2.5 × 6.0 cm, filled with unpopped popcorn) and a two-part Lego doll and chair. Each toy was presented for five trials each or until infants were no longer interested in the toy. Infants were videotaped using two wall-mounted video cameras (Model WV-D5100, Panasonic Co., Seacaucus, NJ) placed in front and above on each side of the infant, 90 degrees orthogonal to each other. Videotaping continued throughout the entire testing session. The video recordings were digitized at 60 Hz using the Peak Performance motion analysis system (Peak Performance Technologies, Englewood, CO). Reflective spheres (1 cm diameter) were placed (a) on the infant's head at the middle of the forehead attached with double-sided tape and (b) secured on foam bracelets that were attached with Velcro strips to the infant's wrists. Incandescent light was beamed toward the reflective markers, creating high-intensity luminescence from the markers. The two video cameras, time synchronized with SMPTE time code, were mounted to allow full views of all markers. The luminescence of the markers was detected on the videotape via custom software in the Peak Performance system. The centers of the different spheres were computer digitized to represent the head, limbs, or toys. The two tapes from the two cameras were digitized to create a three-dimensional representation (x, y, z coordinates) of the markers. After calibration, using a three-dimensional rigid cube with a 24-marker array, there was a 2-mm positional calibration error. Digitized raw data were filtered at 5 Hz. Marker velocities and accelerations in x, y, and z coordinates were calculated from the filtered position data using a fourth-order central difference algorithm, and marker tangential velocity and acceleration were calculated. Data were further managed with custom software.

Data Reduction

Reaches were selected from the continuous videorecording if they met the following criteria: (a) Although the starting position was unrestricted, subjects' hands had to be at rest when the object was placed in front of them on the table, and (b) all markers were in view of the cameras.

Calculation of the Dependent Variables

Five variables describing absolute values of infants' reaches were computed from the kinematic data, and four variables were derived from these variables to characterize the features of the reach (see Table 5.1). The absolute variables were (a) MT: total movement time, measured in frames at 60 frames per second, from the start of the reach to first contact with the object; (b) MU: the number of movement units calculated as the number of zero crossings of acceleration; (c) PATH: the actual path traveled by each hand (from start point to first touch of the object); (d) PEAK VELOCITY: the peak velocity achieved during a reach; and (e) DIST: the straight-line path (shortest path) between the starting point of the hand and the object.

   Unlike experiments with older children or adults, the experimenter has little control over where infants place their hands at the start of a trial; thus the variables DIST and PATH are dependent on the starting point of the infants' hands. To adjust for the effect of different starting points, we derived four additional variables (Table 5.2): (f) straightness ratio (SR) distance to the object (DIST) divided by the length of the reach (PATH). Higher SR values represent shorter reaches (note that because the marker was not placed at the tips of the fingers but further back on the wrists, PATH could be shorter than the DIST between the starting point and the object). (g) PATH/MU: the length of the reach (PATH) divided by the number of MU. (h) %MU1: the length of the first MU divided by the total length of the reach (PATH). Values of %MU1

TABLE 5.2   Dependent Variables

Movement time (MT)	Total movement time measured in total number of frames from start to object touch
Movement units (MU)	Number of movement units
Distance of reach (PATH)	Actual distance of the path of the infant's reach (from start point to touch object) measured in mm
Peak velocity (PV)	Peak velocity measured in mm
Distance (DIST)	Distance (displacement) of the direct path between start point and object measured in mm
Straightness ratio (SR)	PATH/DIST (distance of reach/distance of direct path between start point and object)
PATH	Path divided by number of movement units
%MU1	Percentage of PATH covered by the first movement unit
PPV	Percentage of the PATH at which peak velocity was achieved

represent the proportional distance of the first MU. (i) PPV: percentage of the PATH at which peak velocity was reached.

Determination of a Movement as a Reach

Two coders, blind to group membership, reviewed videotapes of the testing sessions to extract reaching movements. Reaches were selected from the continuous video recording if they met the following criteria: (a) Although the starting position was unrestricted, subjects' hands had to be at rest when the object was placed in front of them on the table, and (b) all markers were in view of the cameras. Forty reaches were excluded (7%) from analysis because they did not meet criteria. A reach began at the frame of first visible movement of the hand and ended at first hand contact (any part of hand or fingers) of the object. The agreement for determining a reach was 98% between the coders.

DATA ANALYSIS

Dependent Measures

For each dependent variable (e.g., MU, PATH) and because a different number of reaches was used from different subjects, an average, minimum, and maximum value for each subject (all variables) were calculated. Averages were used to characterize the central tendency, and minimum and maximum values were used to examine extreme performance in either direction. The three measures for each dependent variable were highly and significantly correlated (i.e., all values of the average of each of the dependent variables and its minimum and maximum value were significantly correlated, $p < .01$, between .707 and .844), indicating that the difference in the expression of each variable had no effect on the results. Only the analysis of the average values was used in the statistical analysis of this report.

Analysis of Exposure and Age Effects

To examine the hypothesis that the exposed infants would have reaches with different kinematic properties at each age than the unexposed infants, a 2×2 (Drug Status $\times$ Infant Age) repeated measures analysis was performed with each of the dependent measures. Infants were included only if they had data at both 7 and 15 months of age, resulting in a sample of 34 subjects at both 7 and 15 months (19 exposed) with a total of 317 reaches (mean number of reaches $= 4.25$, range $= 1-9$). No significant differences were found for the number of reaches by exposure group at either age (all t tests, $ps > .10$).

Exposure Status

Table 5.3 presents the results for the kinematic variables of the infant reaches by exposure group and age. Although there were no differences for PATH or MU, which requires caution regarding the finding, exposed infants compared to unexposed infants covered a greater distance on average per MU (PATH/MU, $p = .01$). The data suggested that exposed infants had straighter reaches (SR, $p = .08$) and covered more of the total distance of the reach with their first MU (%MU1, $p = .07$), although the conventional level of significance was not reached for either variable. There were no significant interactions between exposure status and age.

Age

Compared to the reaches of infants at 7 months of age, infants' reaches at 15 months of age were faster (MT, $p = .001$), had significantly fewer MU (MU, $p = .0001$), had a longer path to the target (PATH, $p = .001$), had a higher peak velocity (PV, $p = .004$), covered more distance per MU (PATH/MU, $p = .0001$), and covered a larger proportion of the total path with the first MU (%MU1, $p = .0001$).

Cumulative Risk

To test the hypothesis that neurobehavioral outcome is primarily determined by an accumulation of risk factors, a measure of risk previously developed (Fetters & Tronick, 1996) was evaluated as a potential covariate. The measure of risk included one point for each of the following variables: Hollingshead (1979) socioeconomic status level of 4 or 5, use of alcohol, use of tobacco, birth weight less than total group median (exposed or control), minority group membership,

TABLE 5.3 Group and Age Means for the Kinematic Dependent Variables

| | Group | | | | | | Age | | | | | |
| | Exposed | | Unexposed | | | | 7 Months | | 15 Months | | | |
Variable	Mean	SD	Mean	SD	F	P	Mean	SD	Mean	SD	F	P
MT (frames, 60/s)	46.84	21.47	51.65	16.78	0.85	.363	56.09	24.14	41.62	9.66	12.31	.0015
MU (#)	1.82	1.24	2.074	0.98	0.90	.351	2.50	1.35	1.35	0.34	24.31	.0001
SR (ratio)	0.849	0.21	0.755	0.18	3.258	.810	.782	0.22	0.837	0.18	1.355	.2539
PATH (mm)	167.3	52.7	155.6	51.3	0.82	.373	147.9	53.9	176.8	46.6	4.98	.336
DIST (mm)	187.5	22.4	201.6	26.7	1.50	.125	184.9	34.0	202.2	37.3	3.16	.86
PV (mm/s)	445.6	147.8	401.7	162.4	1.42	.244	374.9	155.5	479.5	136.3	9.70	.0041
PATH/MU (mm)	126.8	55.6	100.7	47.0	6.99	.013	82.6	44.6	199.1	39.0	36.77	.0001
%MU1	0.615	0.261	0.510	0.227	3.42	.075	0.440	0.237	0.702	0.192	24.10	.0001
PPV (%)	0.546	0.175	0.541	0.167	0.015	.9038	0.534	0.200	0.554	0.138	0.008	.6337

Note: See definitions of acronyms in Table 5.2.

maternal education below high school, a score on the Hobel (Hobel, Youkeles, Forsythe, 1979), subject hospitalization, poor infant health as described by the mother, and intervention by a physical or occupational therapist.

In both groups, risk had very limited variability; all but four infants had four or more risk factors (range = 2–10), a score that placed almost all infants in a high-risk category. Infants in the exposed group had more risk factors (mean = 6.5, SD = 1.9) than infants in the unexposed group (mean = 4.8, SD = 1.4, t = 4.89, p < .001). Correlations between risk and each of the dependent measures at 7 and 15 months were calculated, but in no case did risk significantly correlate with a measure (ps >. 10). Thus, aside from limited power given the sample size, cumulative risk did not function as a meaningful covariate in this sample.

DISCUSSION

Our hypothesis that the kinematic parameters of reaching would be compromised in infants exposed to cocaine in utero was not confirmed. Nonetheless, the kinematics of the reaches of the exposed infants were subtly different than the reach kinematics of unexposed infants. The exposed infants' reaches covered more distance on measures of average distance per MU, and there was a weak indication that distance covered in the first MU was greater and that their reaches were straighter. These findings might suggest that exposed infants were more effective in scaling and assembling the components of reaching and better managed the internal and external forces of movement during a reach compared to the unexposed infants. However, only the finding for average distance per MU was reliable, whereas the other measures were only trends. Furthermore, unlike the age differences, the actual differences were small and scattered.

Nonetheless, the findings indicate that reaches of exposed infants were not compromised compared to unexposed infants. We found little evidence for a specific compromising effect of cocaine or for an indirect compromising effect of cocaine associated with cocaine's effect on intrauterine growth, which is associated with a general compromise of motor performance (for a review, see Tronick & Beeghly, 1999). The findings also do not support Billman, Nemeth, Heimler, and Sasidharan's (1996) hypothesis that there is improved performance in exposed infants based on a genetically determined differential sensitivity to cocaine among different racial groups. Further, though the most widely accepted hypothesis is that in utero cocaine exposure has a disruptive effect on the nigrostriatal and mesolimbic extrapyramidal dopaminergic pathways (Chiriboga et al., 1993) or on the trophic function of aminergic neurotransmitters during early fetal development (e.g., Kosofsky & Wilkins, 1998; Volpe, 1992a), there was nothing in our findings to support this interpretation. Clearly, more work is needed to understand the mechanisms underlying the developmental effects of intrauterine cocaine exposure, but our findings did not find a compromise associated with exposure.

We had expected that both the exposed and unexposed infants in our study would perform more poorly than the lower risk infants (Fetters & Todd, 1987; Rose-Jacobs & Fetters, 1989; von Hofsten, 1979). This hypothesis also was not confirmed. The performance of these high-risk infants regardless of exposure was similar to the performance reported in the literature for healthy, low-risk infants. For example, comparable movement times (between .5 and 1 second) have been previously reported for infants in the age range of our subjects (Fetters & Todd, 1987; von Hofsten, 1979). Movement units between 1 and 2, such as those we found in this study, also have been reported for healthy infants in several studies (Fetters & Todd, 1987; Rose-Jacobs & Fetters, 1989; von Hofsten, 1979). Peak velocities occurring halfway into the reach are typical for adults performing a simple point-to-point reaching task, a finding that is similar to the peak velocity time in this study (Abend, Bizzi, & Morasso, 1982; Fetters & Todd, 1987). Importantly, there were no Group × Age interactions, indicating that the exposed and unexposed infants had similar developmental changes in their reaching characteristics and that the developmental changes observed in these groups were similar to findings in other studies on low-risk infants.

The lack of functional compromise is supported by an analysis of the grasping behavior in this cohort of infants (Chen & Fetters, 2004). Chen and Fetters (2004) found that the features of object grasping of the exposed infants were not different from unexposed comparison infants or from those reported in the published literature for low-risk infants. Thus, regardless of exposure status, the kinematic reaching performance of the infants in this study as well as their grasping fits within the range of the performance of healthy, low-risk infants.

There are several reasons to view the findings in this study with caution. Several methodological limitations of this study, primarily associated with the small sample size, must be considered. Matching is a weak technique, especially in small samples in which undetectable biases can be present. For example, there are disproportionate numbers of different ethnic groups in the two groups and a high proportion of males. Though undetected, there may still be differences between the accepters and refusers in the two groups associated with self-selection biases. Though less likely, the large number of women who were excluded for technical reasons (e.g., early discharge) may have had unknown effects on sample characteristics. The small numbers precluded effective evaluation of other possible mediating and moderating factors that are known to affect motor performance. For example, Dempsey and colleagues (Dempsey et al., 2000; Jacobson & Jacobson, 1996) documented the role of tobacco as a factor that affects performance as does alcohol, but both could not be evaluated and were left as background variables. Relatedly, the cumulative risk analysis lacked power. Importantly, there was not a strong, coherent pattern of altered reaching associated with exposure.

On the other hand, exposure status was determined by bioassay and self-report. Examiners were blind to exposure status, as were the analyzers of the kinematic data. Though limited as a measure, cumulative risk was not related to the difference in performance between the groups, and it favored the unexposed group. The findings for age demonstrate the sensitivity of the kinematic technique and certainly support the precision and validity of kinematics as a measurement technique. The kinematic technique is both a more objective measure and a more sensitive measure of performance than many other procedures that have found compromised effects associated with exposure.

In sum, although there may be some subtle differences in the reaches of exposed infants as measured by precise kinematic methods compared to unexposed infants, there is no marked difference in their performance. However, one kinematic feature of reaching appears to favor the performance of the exposed infants, and although it is only one among many nonsignificant findings, it may be worthy of further investigation (Billman et al., 1996; Chasnoff, Griffith, Freier, & Murray, 1992; Koren, Graham, Shear, & Einarson, 1989). Importantly, the reaching performance of both of these groups of high-risk infants compares favorably to the performance of healthy, low-risk infants. It seems unlikely that reaching of either the exposed or unexposed group is functionally compromised. The apparent lack of functional compromise in these infants is encouraging, but it should not lead us to disregard the differences observed. With development, even small effects may derail the development of later-emerging capacities. Clearly, more longitudinal studies in different contexts using kinematic analysis are needed to unravel any subtle effects of cocaine exposure on the different components of reaching and other aspects of motor functioning.

PART II

CULTURE

CHAPTER 6

Introduction: Cross-Cultural Studies of Development

The articles in this special section on cross-cultural studies of development are powerful examples of how cross-cultural work can inform developmental theory. Each documents an "experiment in nature," and they are good experiments indeed. They cover topics from sleeping arrangements to language development and represent a process of growing sophistication in cross-cultural work. Rather than relying on unsystematic and unreliable but compelling narratives, these studies use systematic and sophisticated methodologies and theories.

All of them make use of a set of standard instruments ranging from Q-sorts to facial coding schemes to interviews and questionnaires. Such methods, developed for studying subjects in technologically advanced societies, have produced a substantial body of literature. However, in earlier cross-cultural studies, such instruments were used without much consideration of the fit between instrument and subject in context. One need only recall the critiques of the use of the strange situation in other cultures to get a sense of this problem. However, in these reports, the researchers have been careful to evaluate the usefulness of their methods with their subjects in the context of their studies. Nakagawa, Teti, and Lamb (1992), for example, carefully evaluated the responses of their Japanese subjects to the questionnaires they were using. This allowed for the questionnaires to be adjusted to get at the constructs of stress and harmony that Nakagawa et al. were interested in studying. Bornstein and colleagues (1992) in Argentina, Paris, and Japan evaluated the effectiveness of their language coding schemes for each of the language communities they were observing. They found that the method worked across cultures, an interesting finding in itself. This attention to the fit between methods and the subject in context is an important methodological advance.

Each of the studies also strikes a good balance between descriptiveness and theory testing. Certainly a great value of cross-cultural studies is that they enhance our sense of human variation. At the same time, when that description is guided by theory, our understanding is greatly enriched. Nakagawa et al.'s (1992) evaluation of an ecological model derived primarily from studies of American populations is called into question by the observations of Japanese sojourners. The observation of the multiple caretaking pattern of the Efe by Tronick, Morelli, and Ivey (1992) not only expands our vision of what form human caretaking may take but confronts head-on theoretical assumptions about the developmental patterning and sequencing of relationships during the first years of life.

Nor do these studies simplistically attribute effects to culture, as if culture were a single and solitary force. Camras, Oster, Campos, Miyake, and Bradshaw (1992) invoke a strong hereditary and ontogenetic argument to explain their findings, but they critically incorporate cultural factors as modifying these more universal factors. Richman, Miller, and LeVine (1992) invoke cultural and educational factors to understand the differences observed in parental responsiveness. Morelli, Rogoff, Oppenheim, and Goldsmith (1992) are able to interpret sleeping arrangements in terms of developmental and cultural factors. Thus there is no dichotomy here between nature and nurture but an attempt to integrate these factors in more complex interpretations.

There is also an interesting subtlety to these studies; each one emphasizes that the basic process shaping the phenomenon under study has to do with the mutual exchange between or among the child and his or her caretaker or caretakers (Tronick, 1989). This process is essentially social, communicative, and regulatory. Even where universal biological factors appear prominent, there is a recognition that the child's development is a cultural construction by individuals interacting with individuals. To me this idea unites these studies and makes it evident that cross-cultural studies are no longer exotic distractions but fundamental to our understanding of human development. We can only hope for more of them.

CHAPTER 7

The Role of Culture in Brain Organization, Child Development, and Parenting

The chapters in this volume present the reader with a varied set of studies on the relations between newborn behavioral organization, parenting, and culture. It is striking to us that, despite the diversity of these studies' settings and of the researchers' backgrounds, there is an underlying perspective that unifies the different works and helps create a more integrated picture of the factors shaping development.

This perspective promotes the view that development can only be understood by studying the interplay of infant characteristics, including biological and temperamental factors, and parenting practices that are shaped by sociocultural and ecological factors. It is a complex, transactional perspective; scholars who adopt it are faced with the difficult task of taking into account the multiplicity of factors affecting development while not losing sight of the issues under study. For example, examining the relation of infant behavior and culture while considering ecological factors is extremely difficult because these factors come from radically different domains. One solution to the challenges posed is provided by recent theorizing about brain development that allows us to integrate these factors into a more unified model.

The transactional position, which is a radical shift from the perspective that sees sociocultural experiences as modifying only what the brain learns or stores, argues that structural as well as functional characteristics of the brain are modified by culturally shaped pre- and postnatal experiences. In the following passage, pediatric neurologist Heinz Prechtl clearly expresses this view:

> The effects of the selective pressure on the pre-programmed maturation of the nervous system [and related changes in behavior] should not be considered without taking into account the influence of the caregiver. There is an inevitable

process of matching between the offspring and care-giver through mutual influences. Put differently, the young will only survive and grow and develop properly if the mothering and nursing repertory of the care-giver is precisely adapted to the properties of the young and vice versa. . . . [Thus] our interest shifts from the seemingly limited [behavioral] abilities of the young organism to their astonishing competence to cope with a large variety of specific demands of internal regulation as well as adaptation and responsiveness to environmental features. (Connelly & Prechtl, 1981, p. 199)

Prechtl's position is broad; nonetheless, he is very specific that nonneurological factors such as "mothering and nursing repertory" and caregiver's and infant's behavioral characteristics are among the primary forces shaping the organization of the infant's brain. The interdependence of biology and culture is clear; to the extent that culture modifies caregiving (e.g., mothering) and the coregulation of caregiver and infant behavior, then to that extent does culture affect the developing brain. Culture and infant behavior now take their rightful place in a transactional perspective alongside biological factors (e.g., nutrition, deprivation, toxic insults, drug exposure, ecological stresses) that are known to affect features of the brain. Indeed, each of these factors can be seen to be involved in a dynamic developmental process of transactions between the organization of the infant's brain and behavior, and the parenting the infant receives.

The studies in this volume attend to the organization of infant behavior and parenting as they are modified by culture. While the description of culture is approached in many different ways (e.g., interviews with informants, historical records, literature reviews), the Brazelton Neonatal Behavioral Assessment Scale (BNBAS) is used in each of the studies for assessing the organization of the infant's behavior.

The BNBAS presents us with two simultaneous views of the infant. One view looks "inward" and evaluates the status of the infant's central nervous system by assessing the functional organization of the infant's behavior. The second view looks "outward" at the impact of the infant's behavior on the behavior of its caregivers. The quantified characterization of the infant's neural and behavioral repertoire is the type of information required by Prechtl to understand the relation among behavior, brain development, and culture. Moreover, the use of the BNBAS by all of the researchers provides a unifying methodological theme. This is effective strategy for the volume because it helps bridge the research described in the different chapters.

We have developed a model, the caregiver-child strategy model, that is useful in framing our understanding of the chapters in this volume. While this model is sharply focused on child-caregiver interactions and the strategies child and caregiver develop to manage their interactions, it also maintains a background focus on parenting practices as embedded within the sociocultural and ecological system. The caregiver-child strategy model views the child and the caretaker as having proximal and distal goals. The child's proximal goals are to regulate internal physiological, behavioral, and affective states and, at the same time, engage the social and physical world. The child's distal goals are survival, growth, and development, and eventual reproductive success, economic self-sufficiency, and the acquisition of culturally appropriate behaviors.

To accomplish these goals, children use what we have termed resource acquisition strategies. These strategies are the set of regulatory physiological and behavioral processes for maintaining internal regulation, instrumental behaviors for acquiring resources from the inanimate environment and, most centrally, communicative behaviors for modifying caregiver activities in order to procure psychological and physical resources. The organization of the infant's basic resource acquisition strategy is what is assessed by the BNBAS. The behaviors making up these elemental strategies include self-comforting, orientation, alertness, facial expressions, vocalizations, and gestures. With development, the infant's resource acquisition strategies will be elaborated, most uniquely, into a universal culture-specific form—speech—which, as argued by Vygotsky, will serve as a form of self-regulation and communication.

Caretakers have proximal and distal goals that are similar but not identical to their offspring's goals. They also have strategies, called caretaker investment strategies, for achieving these goals (see LeVine, 1977, for a discussion of these strategies). While caregiver investment strategies necessarily include Prechtl's maternal and nursing behaviors, their most fundamental characteristic is the capacity of the caregiver to understand and act on the child's communicative displays in culturally appropriate ways. These child and caregiver strategies are reciprocal adaptive processes that ensure the accomplishment of the caretaker and offspring's success. Essentially, their mutual adaptation is a communicative process because without communication there can be no effective regulation between the child's resource acquisition strategy and the parental investment strategy.

Strategies vary among people from different communities because caregivers draw on culturally based knowledge to guide their decision making (LeVine, 1977). Culture tailors the phylogenetically based aspects of caregiver investment strategies to the locally specific, relatively stable, social and physical features of the environment. Most important, culture helps define those features of the child's behavior and communication that require attention and response, as well as the culturally appropriate form of the response. Needless to say, culture is not the exclusive factor influencing investment strategies, but one of several factors (e.g., ecological, phylogenetic, demographic).

To put the strategic model in more mechanistic terms, the infant can be seen as a device for garnering resources from the environment to help accomplish its goals. Caregivers often provide the necessary resources because their goals overlap with the goals of their infant. Yet, while there is no question that children actively influence the care they receive, a child's ultimate dependence on caregivers effectively limits the extent to which he or she modifies their strategies; that is, the child has no choice but to make his or her acquisition strategies conform to the caregiver's strategies, including the cultural components making them up. Thus, the child's strategies take on a cultural form as does his or her central nervous system from the moment it begins to act. To quote Prechtl again, "Within limits, a new intact but biologically different brain may be formed, with a rather different functional repertoire" (Connelly & Prechtl, 1981, p. 212).

To illustrate this caregiver-child strategy model, consider some of our work on the Efe and their system of care. The Efe are a people of short stature who live in the Ituri rainforest of northeastern Congo. Efe women give birth to infants whose average weight is 2.4 kg and average length 43.4 cm (Winn, Morelli, & Tronick, 1989). U.S.-born infants born at this weight and length would be considered at risk for medical complications. While this also may be the case with Efe neonates, we believe that the caregiving strategy adopted by the Efe mitigates against threats to infant survival and, at the same time, communicates cultural messages to the infant and community members alike.

Efe child-rearing practices must deal with immediate hazards to survival such as dehydration and long-term hazards to social functioning such as antisocial behaviors. How is this accomplished? Nursing the infant by individuals in addition to the mother may increase the infant's fluid balance, reducing the small infant's vulnerability to dehydration. Multiple nursing may also foster the development of social capacities for relating to many different individuals, and the development of multiple secure bases for attachment. The competencies emerging from these social experiences serve infants well throughout their lifetime. Infants and toddlers are often left in the camp in the care of others while their mothers forage for forest foods (Morelli, 1987), a practice unlike that observed among foraging communities such as the !Kung (Draper, 1976). Further, mortality is high among the Efe, leaving many infants motherless or parentless. Thus, the ability to form trusting relationships with a variety of individuals is likely to be important for the Efe infant. In addition, the Efe—adults and children alike—are almost always in social and often physical contact with one another and are largely dependent on each other for their survival. The ability to get along with community members appears to be an essential part of Efe living, and the parental investment strategy of the Efe fosters this ability. Clearly, the form that Efe infant and caregiver strategies take will be different from that observed in other communities. And one can only speculate that the Prechtilian brain of these infants and their adult caregivers will differ as well.

The chapters in this volume provide many exemplars of the interplay of caregiver and infant strategies. Each chapter documents infants' behavioral organization at birth using the BNBAS, and most authors relate this organization to the infant's and mother's medical status during the perinatal period. Many of the chapters examine the relation between caregiving strategies and infant behavioral organization, and how this relation changes in the first year of life. Finally, some authors consider the role cultural institutions such as hospitals play in the type of care the infant receives. Most important, however, each study examines the relation between sociocultural features like caregiving practices and infant development.

These studies have helped set the direction for future research, and we should continue to conduct research that expands our knowledge of the diversity of practices. However, we must also begin to select for study communities that allow us to examine more systematically our assumptions about culture and development. For example, we selected the Efe of the Congo for study because their system of care will help us understand the process by which infants develop relationships with their caregivers.

The task we have identified is somewhat daunting, in that it requires detailed specification of cultural belief systems, ecological factors, caregiver and infant strategies, and the interplay among them. Nonetheless, the effort will be worthwhile. With carefully chosen research questions, and communities that best allow these questions to be addressed, we will broaden our understanding of the relations among culture, infant behavior and neurological organization, and caregiving.

CHAPTER 8

Multiple Caretaking in the Context of Human Evolution: Why Don't the Efe Know the Western Prescription for Child Care?

The most widely accepted model of the caretaking environment of the human infant at birth and into the second year of life is that it should provide relatively continuous care and almost constant contact between the infant and mother, with frequent nursing bouts of short duration (Blurton Jones, 1972; Bowlby, 1969; Fishbein, 1976, Hinde, 1979). An often-drawn implication from this view is that the requirements of continuous care and contact are satisfied by only one caretaker—the mother—and that the infant forms his or her first and primary relationship with this caretaker (e.g., monotropy) and progresses with development toward a multiplicity of relationships (Bowlby, 1969; Mahler, Pine, & Bergman, 1975; Rutter, 1981; Spitz, 1965). The initial newborn period is often referred to as the period of bonding, and the outcome of this period as attachment. Although the views of monotropy and bonding are actually independent, they are compatible and complementary and often related to one another in arguing that a lack of maternal care or extensive multiple caretaking has detrimental effects on the infant's social, emotional, and cognitive development (Bowlby, 1958; Klaus & Kennell, 1976).

The continuous care and constant contact model rests on an integration of several perspectives: (1) evolutionary views of our species; (2) comparative data from other species, especially within the class Mammalia; (3) psychological views of the immaturity and dependency of the human infant; and (4) psychological views of infant development and maternal caretaking.

The continuous care and constant contact model is an impressive integration of these diverse formulations, and it has generated a set of hypotheses about early child care and its effect on a child's development. However, this model seems to have become rather prescriptive as to the nature of our caretaking as well as current medical practices. In this chapter, we want to evaluate the model with some preliminary observations from our study of the Efe. The Efe (Pygmies) are seminomadic and live in the Ituri Forest of the Congo. These people are traditionally classified as hunters and gatherers. These observations suggest that some of the interpretations from the model are overgeneralizations of specific observations and that these interpretations have become rather rigid formulations of both our biology and our psychology, especially regarding the primary role of the mother in providing care and the concept of monotropy. Although we want neither to argue against the use of biological and evolutionary data for helping us formulate our thinking and our practices nor to argue against the bonding view of delivery practices, we do want to make the point that, although not all forms of child care practices are possible, the range available to us from our biology is wide indeed and that it is for us to decide where we will fall within that range. The data on the Efe help us to see the range of human possibilities and to make it clear that our decisions about child care practices are really decisions about cultural values: about what we want our children to become.

CONTINUOUS CARE AND CONTACT MODEL

A major part of the supportive evidence for the continuous care and constant contact model comes from an integration of evolutionary theory with psychological, comparative, and physiological data. This view asserts that the genetic determinants of our behavior and physiology evolved during a time when hunting and gathering was the major form of human subsistence, until some 12,000 years ago (Lee & DeVore, 1968). Because of the nature of the adaptations occurring during our evolutionary history, many of our current adaptations to contemporary ecological-environmental pressures result from nongenetic changes brought about through the process of learning. Although learning allows us flexibility in dealing with these demands, the range of this flexibility is constrained by our genetic heritage.

Hunting and gathering as a way of life was characterized by sociality and cooperation among our hominid ancestors. Small groups of 10 to 50 or more people composed of several families engaged in cooperative hunting, gathering, and tool manufacture. There were male-female pair bonds with sex-role specialization and cooperative child care, symbolic communication and language, and social rules and culture. The cognitive capacities of these large-brained protohumans were powerful and flexible. They included long-term memory and cognitive maps of the environment, along with temporal schedules of future events, capacities for generating language and social rules, and, following Mead's suggestions, the abilities of empathy and self-awareness (Fishbein, 1976; Mead, 1934). These last capacities shade over into the emotional realm where we would suggest the following emotional qualities to have evolved in the hunting and gathering social context: affectionate bonds to other group members, strong group identification, inhibition of intragroup aggressiveness, and general gregariousness. These prosocial behaviors were adaptive in that they predisposed individuals to group living, which affords certain advantages to group members (Kellerman, 1981). Prosocial behaviors also fostered caretaking of extremely dependent neonates and children who were marked by a prolonged period of immaturity (Hamburg, 1968).

Psychologists and psychiatrists argue from a psychological perspective that these prosocial behaviors—especially nurturant behaviors—are critical for the infant's normal motor, cognitive, social, and emotional development, and as such are available only in a context where the infant has continuous and constant access to a primary caretaker (Bowlby, 1958; Lozoff, Brittenham, Trause, Kennell, & Klause, 1977; Spitz, 1965). This argument was buttressed by the findings on the effects of maternal deprivation in human (Bowlby, 1951; Rutter, 1981) and nonhuman primates (Harlow & Harlow, 1965, 1969), institutionalized care in children (Provence & Lipton, 1962; Spitz & Wolf, 1946), and isolation rearing in monkeys (Mitchell, 1968; Sackett, 1968). Bowlby (1969) more than other theorists explicitly relies on bioevolutionary theory and data to support the position of maternal care and monotropy. But others as well, notably Mahler, Spitz, Kohut, and Kernberg, strongly imply a biological, better read as maturational, basis to their theorizing on the mother-infant relationship. Mahler et al. (1975) titled their book *The Psychological Birth of the Human Infant,* and almost everyone who has written on the topic writes of the transition of the infant over the first year from a physiological to a psychological being. Bowlby (1969) argued that, in "the environment of evolutionary adaptedness," a set of behavioral systems evolved that ensured contact, or at least proximity, between the newborn or young child and his or her caregiver because of the selective pressure of predation on humans. Alexander (1977) argued that primate sociality in general arose from predation pressures, some of it from other primates. These selective pressures favored the evolution of proximal psychological mechanisms—elaborate emotional and behavioral systems—that motivated these proximity-maintenance behaviors and fostered a reciprocal attachment between infant and mother (i.e., the formation of an affectionate tie). This attachment developed over the first year, and although the infant was dependent on care, the infant also made an active contribution to the care it received. This last aspect was a major revision of previous arguments.

Psychologists prior to the arguments made by Bowlby (1969) had argued that the infant was undifferentiated motorically and perceptually and made no contribution to the caregiving it received. Bowlby and others (Bell, 1971) were strongly influenced by ethological theorizing. This theorizing emphasized the lock and key relationship between the environment, including the social environment, and the behavior of the organism. Transporting this view to the human mother-child relationship, Bowlby saw the infant as being predisposed, often referred to as preadapted, to form an attachment to one person. Similarly, the British (Balint, 1966; Guntrip, 1971; Winnicott, 1975) and later the

American schools of object relations theorists (Kohut, 1971; Loevinger, 1976; Mahler et al., 1975) incorporated evolutionary ideas on human adaptations and concepts developed by ego psychologists, especially those concerning coping rather than just defense (Freud, 1937). They argued that the infant was innately object (person-relationship) seeking and that this was an evolutionary accomplishment, as opposed to an ontogenetic accomplishment, as was thought by earlier analytically oriented theorists. Thus, in earlier views the infant was dependent on care solely because of his or her physiological and psychological immaturity, whereas in later views the infant required care not only because of this immaturity but because of the predisposition for social engagement.

Predisposition, like notions of panadaptiveness, is a weak argument because, although it does place the mother-child relationship in the framework of evolutionary theory, it is a pre-explanation (i.e., a priori) with little force. But these ideas were rescued by powerful empirical data on infant competencies. This research, initially focused on infant visual competencies, soon encompassed findings demonstrating auditory, gustatory, tactile, and olfactory competencies (for reviews of the literature, see Atkinson & Braddwick, 1982; Lipsitt, 1977; Tronick, Als, & Brazelton, 1979). And quickly on the heels of these discoveries came the demonstrations by Brazelton, Koslowski, and Main (1974) and others (Als, 1977; Beebe & Stern, 1977; Hodapp & Mueller, 1982; Stern, 1977; Trevarthen, 1977; Tronick, 1980) of the infant's social capacities and the still ongoing findings on infant abilities to imitate and form expectancies about different individuals in social interactions (Cohn & Tronick, 1983; Field, 1982; Field, Woodson, Greenberg, & Cohen, 1982; Meltzoff & Moore, 1977). The infant with such an armamentarium of capacities could easily be seen, then, as adapted to social exchange and, by easy implication, as being capable of the early formation of a social relationship.

Bonding, although actually a phenomenon hypothesized to characterize parents, becomes another argument supporting the view of monotropy and of mother as provider of infant care (Klaus & Kennell, 1976). The concept of bonding, like the concept of imprinting, hypothesized a sensitive period during which exposure of the mother to the newborn infant produced an emotional response in the mother that not only bonded her to her infant but aided her in becoming a more effective parent. The exposure worked because the infant presented stimuli to the parent that elicited this preadapted response, which was primed by the birthing process. Although this research has been criticized (Lamb & Hwang, 1982; Svejda, Pannabecker, & Emde, 1982), there is little doubt that a human newborn powerfully affects the adults exposed to it. Although not originally formulated as part of the maternal care and monotropy configuration, bonding (inadvertently) fits in because it presents the reciprocal side of the mother becoming "monofantic" as the infant becomes monotropic. Furthermore, it implies the necessity of the bonding process for optimal parenting, including somewhat prescriptive practices of early (and prolonged) visual and physical contact of a mother and her newborn.

A particularly timely and supportive cross-cultural study of these views was conducted by Konner (1976) on the !Kung. The !Kung are savannah-dwelling hunters and gatherers whose way of life and child-rearing practices closely approximated those hypothesized for ancestral hunters and gatherers. Konner observed that a !Kung infant was in physical contact with its mother 70–80% of the time during the first year of life and in contact with someone else almost all of the rest of the time. These infants were nursed often, four or more times an hour, and for short bouts (Konner & Worthman, 1980). Caretaking was affectionate, and the infant progressed smoothly from a primary relationship with the mother to broader social relationships. Although Konner noted it, the observation that the !Kung mother did not give her infant colostrum was an often forgotten abberation in an otherwise striking confirmation of the continuous care and contact model.

Psychological theorizing, then, has unified related but nonetheless separable concepts—maternal care, monotropy, and bonding—into one configuration. Although there is variability among authors in the strength with which they argue this position, maternal care, monotropy, and bonding are viewed as the standard against which to evaluate caretaking practices. This configuration is a forceful account of the emotional and behavioral adaptations observed in the mother and infant. It gains even more force when it is seen as only one of another set of adaptations critical for the child's development. This second set of adaptations, involving the physiological needs of the infant and the means by which these needs are met, lends further support to the continuous care and contact model of child rearing and the implications that it is the mother who has to provide the care and that the infant is monotropic. To examine this, we start with the content of human milk.

It is now well established that human milk supplies the infant with a full complement of nutritional requirements (Lawrence, 1980). One of the important features of this feeding system is that the nutritional content of milk remains fairly constant over relatively large variations in maternal intake (Lawrence, 1980). This characteristic makes it a highly efficient system and one that reduces the risk of energy supply variation to the vulnerable infant. Fat content, an important component of breast milk, is indirectly related to mammalian feeding schedules (frequency of nursing bouts) and directly related to mammalian sucking frequency (frequency of sucking within a nursing bout; Blurton Jones, 1972; Lawrence, 1980). For example, lagomorphs (rabbits and hares) have very high fat content in their milk and feed every 12 to 24 hours. In contrast, most primates that carry their infants have low fat content in their milk and feed on demand. Humans, following this primate pattern, have low fat content in their milk. Sucking frequency is highest in mammals with high fat content in their milk (e.g., lagomorphs) and lowest in mammals with low fat content in their milk (e.g., primates). Sucking frequency is relatively independent of the deprivation state of the infant, indicating an inherited relationship between frequency of sucking within a nursing bout and frequency of nursing bouts (Wolff, 1968). These data support the constant contact model by arguing that the human infant is a rather continuous feeder requiring rather continuous caretaking.

Aside from nutrition, other qualities of the maternal caregiver seem to compensate for the immaturity of the neonate and young infant. Small infants are especially vulnerable to fluid imbalance, given the relationship of their surface area and volume, and the immaturity of their renal functioning (Almroth, 1978; Schaffer & Avery, 1971). Clinically, as little as 10% loss of fluids produces signs of physiological stress and 15% loss results in a moribund infant. The effects of this immaturity are exacerbated by fevers, hot or cold environments, and humidity, and the smaller the infant, the more vulnerable it is to such stresses. However, it is established that human milk provides the infant with sufficient fluids, and this is even true in hot and humid climates where the specific gravity (1.005–1.015) and osmolarity of urine samples remain in the normal range for exclusively breast-fed infants (Almroth, 1978).

Another aspect of fluid balance regulation is used as evidence supporting the hypothesis of constant care. Infants that are cached—hidden and left alone or with other siblings—do not spontaneously urinate or defecate (Ben Shaul, 1962). Human infants are not cached and spontaneously urinate and defecate. Further support for this hypothesis draws from the findings that cached infants tend not to cry spontaneously. In contrast, human infants cry spontaneously, and picking up the infant is the most effective method of quieting him or her (Korner & Thoman, 1970).

Continuous care and contact further compensate for the infant's immature temperature regulatory system (Schwartz & Rosenblum, 1983). Als (1977) has suggested that human infants are ventral-ventral creatures. Dark lipid fat is thinnest on their ventral surface and thickest on their dorsal surface. When in ventral contact with another person, infants readily accept heat and lose it more slowly, making them easily and efficiently incorporated into the maternal thermoregulatory system. In an intriguing paper, Schwartz and Rosenblum (1983) argued that the initial pattern of care is largely determined by problems of temperature regulation. Using allometric curves, they came to the conclusion that the infants of the smaller primates, who are usually large relative to their mothers, actually demand the greatest amount of parental investment (i.e., continuous care and contact). This finding in part reflects the tremendous energy demands of small mammals, as is the situation for fluid balance regulation.

Continuous care and contact strikingly compensate for the inadequacies of the infant's immune system in almost unbelievably elegant ways (Lawrence, 1980; Schaffer & Avery, 1971). The infant at birth transits from a sterile to a contaminated environment with few self-generated protective immune system mechanisms in place and little of the transplacentally provided protection that characterizes several mammalian species. Colostrum and, following it, mature milk, however, provide cellular and humoral antipathogenic agents along with other specific protective factors to the infant. The cellular components found in colostrum and milk include macrophages, lymphocytes, neutrophils, and other cells, with concentrations similar to those found in peripheral blood, except that macrophages replace neutrophils as the predominant cell in milk. Macrophages are large complex phagocytes and serve several functions, one of which is to phagocytose (encapsulate and usually destroy) microorganisms, such as fungi and bacteria.

Lymphocytes are found in the form of T- and B-lymphocytes, which synthesize humoral antibodies (immunoglobulins IgG, IgA, and IgM). Head and Beer (1978) postulated that lymphocytes are incorporated into the suckling's tissues, providing short-term adoptive immunization for the newborn. The T and B cells found in colostrum and milk have been shown to have reactivities not found in peripheral blood. They exhibit responses to viral antigens of rubella, cytomegalovirus, mumps, and poliovirus. These cells are also reactive against organisms invading the intestinal tract. In addition to the IgA, IgG, and IgM synthesized by the T- and B-lymphocytes, the infant receives other classes of humoral factors directly from the breast milk. Secretory IgA (sIgA) is probably the most important of these, constituting 90% of all the immunoglobulins in colostrum and milk. This sIgA provides protection of the gastrointestinal tract's mucous membranes against viruses such as poliovirus and bacteria such as *Escherichia coli*. Neonatal diarrhea, which is due to various bacterial infections, but especially to *E. coli*, is best managed by breast milk and its higher concentration (relative to serum) of IgA. The levels of these immunoglobulins are much higher in colostrum than in mature milk, but they drop off rapidly over the first 4 to 6 days. However, because the overall volume of mammary secretion is higher in mature milk, the absolute levels of immunoglobulins are more constant than would first appear (Lawrence, 1980).

Another humoral factor in breast milk, in addition to these immunoglobulins, is bifidus factor (Gyorgy, 1953). Bifidus factor supports the growth of *Lactobacillus bifidus*, the normal flora of the intestine, which is inhibitory to the growth of certain pathogenic bacteria, such as *Staphylococcus aureus*, *Shigella*, and Protozoa. Additional antipathogenic agents are supplied as well.

Colostrum and breast milk, then, can be seen as important in immunizing and helping the infant to fight infection. Further, this mechanism is not solely unidirectional, but rather a dynamic process. This is to say that an infant in contact with his or her mother is likely to share her immunological exposure. However, if through some external contact the infant is exposed to something the mother has not been exposed to, the infant through contact with her is likely to expose her to the pathogen and then benefit by her response to that pathogen. Important, and distinct in function, is the suggestion that maternal T and B cells induce immunological tolerance and host-graft reactions in the neonate (Lawrence, 1980).

In summary, the data show that an intricate system of psychological and physiological adaptations evolved to meet the needs of the neonate and young child. The proponents of the continuous caretaking model argue more or less forcefully that these systems develop in the context of an intense and initially exclusive relationship between the infant and the mother. However, the infant's requirement of relatively continuous care can be satisfied in a number of different ways: mother as exclusive caretaker; mother as the primary caretaker, assisted by one or a few others; or caretaking shared by a few stable individuals (Rutter, 1981). Furthermore, an infant's attachment—its quality, intensity, singularity, or multiplicity—should vary according to his or her caretaking environment. We maintain, therefore, that the conditions stated by the proponents of the continuous caretaking model are culturally bound and that there exist alternative strategies to meet the needs of the neonate and young child that do not produce a maladjusted adult. The child-rearing practices of the Efe illustrate one such alternative strategy.

SELECTED OBSERVATIONS OF EFE CHILD-REARING PRACTICES

The Efe, because of their way of life and their ecological setting, are a highly relevant people for evaluating the continuous care and contact model. The Efe are thought by some (DeVore, personal communication, 1979; Turnbull, 1962) to be the earliest known inhabitants of the Ituri Forest. But for how long and whether they have always had an association with other people, as they do now, remains controversial (Bailey, personal communication, 1983). The Efe live in virilocal bands, with 6 to 50 residents, and although some bands have relatively stable membership with a consistent set of families, there is a great deal of flexibility in membership.

The Efe in this study area are traditionally classified as hunters and gatherers. In this view, subsistence is gained totally from forest foods. The Efe men hunt duiker, elephant, monkeys, and birds, using bows and arrows, nets, traps, snares, and spears, and the women gather forest fruits and roots. Whether or not the Efe ever subsisted in this manner remains unknown, but it is clear that they do not now. Bailey and Peacock (1988) and our own observations indicate that, although the Efe do hunt and gather forest foods for their own consumption, some of those resources are traded to local villagers, the Walese, for cultivated foods, cloth, and iron. More important, the Efe exchange labor for Walese resources. There is a clear division of labor, with men devoting their time to hunting and women devoting their time to gathering in the forest and to laboring in Walese fields. Cultivated foods provide the largest proportion of their caloric intake (Bailey & Peacock, 1982).

The Efe are seminomadic. The pattern of movement over a year partly reflects seasonal variation in the availability of forest and cultivated foods and affects Efe work patterns and social organization. For approximately 7 months of the year, they live in encampments near a Walese village, often on the perimeter of the village's fields. During this period the Efe women, in particular, engage in seasonally appropriate horticultural activities and receive cultivated foods in exchange. Most Efe do not plant gardens of their own. For the remaining 5 months of the year, the Efe move deeper into the forest to camps 1 to 3 days' walk from the villages, where they hunt and gather honey, fish, forest fruits, and roots (Bailey & Peacock, 1982).

The Efe practice polygamy, although monogamy is more common. Polygamy typically occurs when a women seems unable to have any children or has had children but is now postmenopausal. The Efe practice sister exchange. When a man from one clan wishes to marry a woman from another clan (there are strong cultural taboos against intraclan marriage), he must provide a girl for one of the men in that band to marry. Upon birth, each girl is given to a boy or a man in her group, often a brother, but possibly a cousin or uncle, who can exchange her for a bride from another band. Some bands will have exchanged several times over the years, and a woman may find herself married into a group where there are women from her clan: sisters, cousins, or aunts. But perhaps just as commonly, an Efe woman comes into a group of unknown and unrelated individuals. Intermarriage occurs between Walese women and Efe men.

The Walese are slash-and-burn agriculturalists living in permanent villages of 15 to 100 or more people. Their work activity cycle is entrained to the seasonally appropriate tasks of clearing fields and planting, weeding, and harvesting their crops of manioc, bananas, peanuts, rice, small amounts of coffee, and such other casual foods as sweet potatoes, corn, squash, and beans. They hunt and fish but subsist mainly on cultivated foods.

The Walese are thought to have lived in the forest for 300 to 400 years. Originally, they inhabited villages deep in the forest, but during the Belgian colonization, they were ordered out of the forest onto the roads, where the Belgians were better able to control and exploit them. The Walese are organized into virilocal groups and, like the Efe, some Walese practice polygamy. Unlike the Efe, however, Walese men generally buy their brides with a commercial resource (local currency, chickens, metal).

Slash-and-burn cultivation has modified the forest close to the villages. The primary forest of this northeastern portion of Zaire is dominated by two climax species of leguminous hardwoods: *Cynometra alexandri* and *Brachystegia laurentii*. These produce an uneven overstory of 120 to 140 feet, shading a diverse midstory of 40 to 60 feet and a sparse undercover. The agriculturalist's practice of clearing fields that are planted for only 2 years and then abandoned has resulted in a patchwork of climax forest and varying stages of successional growth (Wilkie, personal communication, 1982). The current concentration of villagers along the road has produced a band 1–4 km wide on both sides of the road that is intensely exploited, never reaching a climax state prior to recultivation. It is along this 25 km of the road built by the Belgians, now deteriorated to a barely passable track, that our project site is located. There are approximately 500 to 600 Walese and 400 to 500 Efe in this area (Bailey & Peacock, 1988).

The project is collaborative, including biological anthropologists, ecologists, public health practitioners, physiologists, biologists, and ourselves. Work to date and in progress has provided complete demographic and anthropometric data on the study population, information on their health status and their sanitary practices, data on forest productivity, and descriptions of adult activity patterns and social exchanges. The study of child care practices utilizes naturalistic observations distributed throughout the day to describe the daily activities and social exchanges of Efe and Walese children, starting at birth and continuing through the first 3 years of life. Some of the observations of the earliest caretaking practices, particularly those of the Efe, are relevant to the discussion at hand. But we want to emphasize that these observations are preliminary and more on the order of single examples rather than complete data analyses. They should not be taken as general characterizations of child-rearing practices of these people because we have already observed exceptions to each of them. In choosing these observations, there is no attempt to make a complete description of these practices but rather to emphasize examples that are relevant to our questions of bioevolutionary theorizing.

At birth, an Efe mother is not the first person to hold the infant. The Efe have a strong belief that the infant should not be born onto the floor, nor should the mother be the first to hold him or her. This belief precludes Efe women from going off and having their infants on their own. Rather, the common practice seen in all our observations of Efe births is that another woman serves as midwife, though she does not have specialized training. This woman receives the infant, bathes him or her with cold water, and cuts the umbilical cord following the delivery of the placenta. The infant is then wrapped in a light cloth and passed among most of the women in the group. The father and other men are not present in the delivery hut, but the newborn is shown to them at the door of the hut or may be brought outside for viewing and then returned to the hut.

Several hours may pass before the infant is given to the mother. If a lactating woman is in the band, she will nurse the infant over the first days of life. If none is present, a lactating woman from a nearby Efe camp or Walese village will be called to feed the infant. In the latter case, this woman may suckle the infant only two or three times a day for the first days of life because she has to interrupt her work and come to the camp to nurse the infant. The mother will also suckle the infant during this time, but her colostrum is not viewed as nutritional.

Over the next few days, the infant will be kept in or around the hut, held in mother's lap or laid next to her when she sleeps, or held by another woman or girl while the mother is engaged in other tasks. When the mother's task requires a longer out-of-camp trip (1–2 weeks postpartum), she may take a caretaker with her who, if competent, will carry the infant and give him or her to the mother only when the infant needs feeding or is inconsolable. Alternatively, women often go out in groups together and child care is shared at the work site. Mothers do leave their infants in camp for short periods, up to an hour. When their infants get upset, other caretakers try to comfort the infant, putting him or her to the breast whether or not they are lactating. In fact, these other-than-mother attempts at comforting occur even when the mother is present. However, if their attempts are unsuccessful, the caretakers will fetch the mother or have the infant carried to her. This pattern of assistance, caring for the infant while the mother engages in other tasks, continues as the infant gets older. These observations indicate that, over the first half year of life and particularly over the first few weeks, whether in camp or out, the infant is almost always held in close bodily contact and seldom if ever put down or left alone. Access to a breast is virtually constant and upon demand. However, the mother, although present, may not be—indeed (with respect to holding and carrying) tends not to be—the sole caregiver of the infant. Rather, infants have multiple caretakers whose interactions with them are typically playful and sensitive. For example, in one 1-hour session, a 4-month-old was transferred nine times among six different people.

To summarize, Efe infants during the first 6 months of life and to a lesser extent throughout the following year and a half experience multiple caretaking, including nursing by women other than the mother. Aside from the caretaking aspects, their interactions with these other-than-mother caregivers can be characterized as playful and responsive. And although infants are left with other-than-mother caregivers for periods of time, the mother is available with some delay to comfort the infant if the caregivers are unsuccessful. Infants also sleep with their mothers, which provides a long and reiterated period of exclusive caretaking. Through the second half year of life and for some unspecified time into the second year, the infant has a more focalized relationship with the mother, but it is in the context of relationships with other familiar and willingly available persons.

It is also useful to examine some of the child care practices of the other population in our study site—the Walese agriculturalists. Since the Walese and Efe have lived as neighbors for at least several generations, and possibly for hundreds of years (Schebesta, 1933; Schweinfurth, 1874), it is not surprising that many of their practices are very similar.

To begin with, there appear to be very few differences in birthing practices between Efe and Walese. A Walese midwife will have much the same responsibilities as her Efe counterpart. The Walese newborn is received, bathed, and examined by another woman, passed around for other village members to hold, and generally not returned to his or her mother for several hours. Like the Efe, the Walese see the mother's colostrum as harmless, but useless, and summon another lactating woman to nurse the newborn until the mother's "milk" arrives. A preliminary examination of transfer rates of the newborn over the first few weeks indicates that Walese infants are handled by many people: siblings and other children, co-wives, and other women in the village. Over the first few months, Walese infants may in fact be left in the village under the care of others more often than Efe infants, as most of the Walese woman's out-of-village trips are to her field or garden, which is typically only a few hundred meters from the village. On those occasions when mother is going to her garden for an extended work period, she will, like the Efe, take a sibling or other child with her to watch her infant or coordinate her trip with other mothers such that child care can be shared while they work. This pattern is quite similar to that of other African agriculturalists, such as the Gusii (LeVine, 1979).

Although differences exist between Efe and Walese child care, which become more pronounced as the children get older, the similarities are striking. Of course, this is only a preliminary description, but it illustrates that these two groups—one a seminomadic transitional hunting and gathering people, the other a relatively sedentary group of slash-and-burn agriculturalists—are meeting the early biological and psychological needs of their newborns in much the same way.

Efe and Walese child care raises questions about the use of physiological and psychological data to support maternal caretaking and monotropy as the only strategy satisfying the requirements of the continuous care model. Alternative strategies exist. Consideration of Efe and Walese practices, within the context of the social-ecological environment, provides insight into the immediate beneficial consequences of these contemporary practices. These considerations indicate that maternal caretaking and monotropy are conceptually too limiting and that we need to focus on the transactions that take place between an individual and his or her physical-social environment.

The life of the Efe is that of continuous social contact. There are few solitary tasks or settings. It requires that an individual be socially skilled in avoiding disruptive conflict, minimally aggressive within the group, cooperative, and in general committed to the overall successful functioning of the group, which includes strong group identification and group attachment. At the same time because of the fissioning of bands, possibly because the demands for cooperative existence are too great, with its resulting frequent change in the group's social composition, the individual's functioning must not be too disrupted by these changes and losses. Efe child rearing beginning at birth must fulfill these as well as biological demands. How do the Efe practices meet these demands?

EFE PRACTICES: SOCIAL AND BIOLOGICAL DEMANDS

Let us start with the observations of infant transfer and shared nursing. From the continuous contact model perspective, these practices should entail physiological and psychological costs for the neonate. However, several factors mitigate these effects because there is greater flexibility to these biopsychological constraints than is typically discussed. Moreover, we show that mother and infant can actually benefit from these practices.

One potential cost of infant transfer and shared nursing is exposure to foreign pathogens. Yet, among populations of low density, not only is there less risk of epidemic infections, but there is some indication that the group is more homogeneous with respect to pathogens than are more dense populations (Armelagos & McArdle, 1975; Dunn, 1968). Such homogeneity is probably facilitated by food and utensil sharing and the amount of physical contact that goes on in the group. Being fed and held by someone other than mother in a small group is not likely to expose the infant to foreign pathogens. In fact, this analysis suggests that bonding as part of an antipathogen system may not have been very significant to our hunter-gatherer ancestors. Rather, its importance may have developed as a cultural characteristic with the advent of forms of human subsistence that increased population density such that there were strangers, human and otherwise, in the environment.

Additionally, although it is true that colostrum contains a high concentration of antipathogenic factors, its volume is low when compared to mature milk, and so the absolute number of antipathogenic factors is more constant than would first appear (Lawrence, 1980). Infants being nursed by a woman with a mature milk supply incur no risk in regard to disease protection. In fact, the nursing by other than mother may have other advantages for the infant.

Efe infants average 2.4 kg at birth. This low birth weight exacerbates the normal vulnerability of the human newborn to fluid loss. Fluid replacement simply with water may not be sufficient because it may not restabilize the physiological osmolarity of the body, and of course sterile water is not available to the Efe. Being nursed by a woman with a mature milk supply, a supply 1.5 to 7 times larger than the volume of colostrum, would significantly attenuate this risk (Lawrence, 1980). Furthermore, being nursed by several women during the neonatal period may permit the Efe infant to grow at an increased velocity. This increased velocity of growth would shorten the duration of time that the infant remains at greatest mortality risk. Bertram (1976) has made this point for the suckling of other mothers' infants by lions, but surprisingly it is not made for those primate species that nurse other mothers' infants (Hrdy, 1976).

The Efe infants' small size places them at greater risk for temperature instability and its consequent effects. Transfer and the attendant handling and movement may increase the activity level of the infant, resulting in greater heat production. This is supported by our observation that when we examined the infants, which required a breaking of ventral-ventral contact, they often became irritable. Note that because of the nursing pattern, infants have a larger volume of milk available to them for heat production. Multiple functions, physiological and psychosocial, are served by those transfer practices, and as we will see, other benefits accrue as well. However, an additional point needs to be made regarding bioevolutionary thinking in this context.

From the perspective of evolutionary theory, particular adaptations function in the context of the entire life cycle of the individual. Thus, an adaptation at one point in time may incur some costs at that time that are offset at some later point in time (Konner, 1977a). This perspective needs to be applied to the Efe data as well. The greater vulnerability of Efe infants to dehydration and temperature stress arises because of their small size. Nursing and handling may overcome some of these risks, but possibly not completely. However, there is a hypothesized advantage later in life to the small size of the Efe.

The proximal physiological mechanism for the height of the Efe is attributed now to a low level of Growth Factor I (Merimee, Zapf, & Froesch, 1981). But it is not only that the Efe are short that is of importance. They have long limbs relative to their trunk size and a different distribution of fat than their more temperate climate relatives (Bailey, personal communication, 1983). Billig (personal communication, 1982) has hypothesized that the evolutionary and physiological significance of their morphology is that it maximizes nonevaporative modes of heat loss, especially convection and radiation. He views these as adaptations to an environment where the mean radiant temperature is low because of the high moisture content in the air, cloud cover, and vegetation that blocks direct sunlight. These characteristics make evaporative heat loss inefficient. This adaptation confers an advantage to Efe adults in the form of more effective thermoregulation. Additionally, it allows for a conservation of other minerals, especially salt, which is scarce. It appears that the Efe growth pattern is one of being born small, with growth proceeding at similar velocities to larger individuals. This initial small size may impose some additional risk on the infant, although it is expected to have a larger benefit over the entire life cycle.

This pattern of multiple caretaking at birth raises obvious questions concerning the issue of bonding. However, to the extent that neonates elicit bonding responses in adults who are exposed to them, although the bonding may be less well formed or intense than in the mother, it increases the likelihood that an exposed adult will invest resources in the infant. Other benefits accrue to the infant from the multiple bonding situation: (1) increased likelihood of adoption were the mother to die; (2) increased overall quality of care received; that is, a somewhat awkward girl may provide better care than a busy harried mother; reciprocally, (3) the mother may be a better and healthier caretaker because she is relieved of some caretaking chores; (4) increased infant sense of security resulting in increased exploration of its environment; or at least, (5) wider and more varied social exposure. These benefits to the infant are much like the benefits that accrue to nonhuman primates in groups that engage in alloparenting (Hrdy, 1976). Other people benefit as well.

Mothers probably receive two direct immediate benefits. The first is freedom to engage in work. Whiting (1980) has argued persuasively that the pattern of caretaking an infant receives is most strongly influenced by the form of work the mother must engage in. Only preliminary data are available, but it appears that Efe infants are often left in the care of someone else when the mother is either working on camp tasks or foraging in the field or forest. For the latter tasks, the mother gains by not having to be continually responsible for the care and transport of her infant. This reprieve allows the Efe mother to carry back more food and resources, as well as to go faster or cover more distance. The distance traveled and to some extent the weight of foods carried for a successful trip, rather than the availability of alternative caretakers, probably accounts for the difference from the !Kung pattern in which mothers take their infants with them. It is our impression that the !Kung women go much further to forage than do Efe women, which would require leaving their infants behind for much longer periods of time than is required for the Efe (Konner, 1976, 1977). A second benefit is that mothers also receive some respite from the demands of caring for a young infant, a hard to evaluate, but nonetheless obvious and important benefit. Field (1983), for example, has argued that child abuse is more likely to occur in societies where mothers are seldom relieved of their child care responsibilities.

The other-than-mother caregivers gain, too. First, they probably incur some reciprocal obligations to be redeemed from the mother in the future. This is especially true when a mother shares her food with the caretakers or caretakers' children. Lancaster (1971) and Hrdy (1976) argued that young girls gain by learning how to mother. Under the supervision of the infant's mother and other adults, young girls soon get over their clumsiness and awkwardness and become better prepared to mother their own children.

There may be an additional benefit to this system as well. Young girls marry out of their band into their husband's band, a band of strangers, but maybe not all strangers. We are examining kinship records to see if the band a bride is married into has, as one of its members, an older woman who was a caretaker to the bride when the bride was an infant. Such a woman would be likely to have a good deal of affection for the bride and so help ease this very difficult transition.

The greater primary caretaking involvement of the mother that develops in the latter part of the first year is not an exclusive involvement. There is still much caretaking by others, and similar benefits as accrued earlier accrue to each of the individuals involved. The infant has more caretakers readily available with a concomitantly greater sense of security and opportunity for exploration of the social and inanimate environment. Mother can readily free herself of the burdens of child care when required, and others may benefit because of the resources shared with them and obligations engendered. Young girls gain in mothering experience.

This accounting makes it clear that there are few physiological or social costs and likely some benefits attributable to the Efe child care pattern. But what of the psychological costs? Or more generally, what type of personality might be formed by the Efe practices, and how does it relate to multiple caregiving? Essentially, we think there are few psychological costs and tentatively suggest that the Efe personality formed by these practices would be clearly bounded with sharp distinctions between self and other. Individuals would have multiple attachments, with greater intensity for the mother than for others, but all oriented toward and based on current interchanges rather than past emotional involvements. They would also have a strong group identification and be oriented toward contemporaneous events. This characterization does not arise out of the continuous care and contact model, which is not really a model of personality formation. But it also does not fit with its associated hypotheses of maternal care and the psychological requirement of monotropy, which are hypotheses of personality formation. Rather, we would suggest that what seems to be required is a process-oriented theory of personality formation that explains the transduction of Efe child-rearing practices into personality structures and, more generally, how cultural practices affect personality formation. We think that Sander's theory of personality development, with its focus on regulation of exchanges between organism and environment, begins to do just that.

A MODEL OF REGULATION OF EXCHANGES BETWEEN ORGANISM AND ENVIRONMENT

Sander (1975, 1977) has theorized that personality formation arises out of a process of mutual regulation of exchanges between the organism and the environment, animate and inanimate. The young organism is a configuration of subsystems—physiological (temperature, nutritional, fluid, eliminatory, hormonal, and so on) and behavioral (sleep-wake state organization and cycling, reflexes, perceptual, ideational, affective, and so on)—each requiring stabilization of functioning and temporal coordination among themselves and with the exogenous environment. The organism as a system and each of the subsystems as well possess regulators to fulfill these tasks, but their initial capacity is limited and incompletely developed. Successful functioning requires input from the external environment, and this input, referred to by Sander as entraining stimuli, must be specifically fitted in form and temporal organization to the requirements of the regulator. When the fit is incorrect, regulation is either more slowly achieved or not achieved depending on the extent of the lack of fit. For example, as already discussed, the human infant's immune system is only partially in place and must be provisioned by specific inputs from the outside if it is to operate effectively. Another example at a more behavioral level, emphasizing the temporal relationship of the regulators and entraining stimuli, is the demonstration by Sander and his colleagues that, although there is some endogenous temporal organization to the sleep-wake cycling of the human infant, it is strikingly influenced by the timing of the caretaking provisioned to it. Caretaking that is phase synchronized to the infant's endogenous cycle leads to faster establishment of diurnal cycling in the infant than does caretaking provisioned at a regular but arbitrary tempo. Importantly, over time the infant's cycling becomes increasingly independent of the caretaking routine, and later in development, infants with different sleep-wake cycle organization have different patterns of visual attention.

These examples highlight significant aspects of this theory. First, with appropriate provisioning of entraining stimuli, the internal regulators become increasingly capable of accomplishing their tasks without input, although initially their success in functioning is tightly coupled to the entraining input. The organism can be characterized as increasingly self-regulatory—for example, the infant's increased capacity to have longer bouts of sleep. Second, as the independent capacity of regulators to stabilize and control particular tasks increases, the organism can go on to engage in new developmental tasks. For example, the infant can devote more regulatory capacity to the organization of visual attention only after organizing the sleep-wake cycle. More generally, Sander speaks of a developmental hierarchy of tasks during the first 3 years of life, starting with the regulation of preemptive physiological and state variables moving onto and through the regulation of social exchanges, the focalization of a relationship, and later still, the formation of the self. Concomitantly, as tasks at one level are accomplished, as the regulators become self-regulatory and less tightly coupled to input, the organism becomes responsive to different entraining stimuli that vary along a dimension of physiological to psychological. For example, as the infant achieves coordination and stabilization of its preemptive states of hunger with its demand for food provisioned at appropriate times, the infant can begin to engage in social exchanges in which emotional regulators require social-emotional displays to achieve stabilization and coordination. This development is evidenced in the infant's increasing engagement with and discrimination of social input, as well as in a growing sensitivity to distortions of that input (Tronick, 1980).

A third aspect is that the decoupling of the regulator from entraining stimuli corresponds to an increase in the endogenous organization or structure of the regulator. This structure, the characteristic organization of its functioning, is then in some sense a representation of the history of the input the organism has received from the environment, although the representation is hardly a one-to-one transformation. To return to the sleep example, the history of the infant's caretaking is represented in the structure of the infant's sleep regulator as manifest in its endogenously generated sleep-wake cycle. But as Sander points out, not all aspects of the caretaking history affect the structure of the regulator, but only those that specifically fit its requirements at a particular time. The rest of the input goes by unprocessed and without effect; it might be thought of as noise. Moreover, Sander emphasizes that, even for those entraining stimuli that do fit, it is only in their reiteration that they have a powerful effect on the structure of the regulator. By contrast, and to emphasize how specific inputs specifically affect a regulator's structure, take Piaget's theory. There, although input is necessary for the development of cognitive structures, those structures become increasingly abstract and divorced from any particular features of the input. Last, following from the postulate of hierarchy of tasks and the physiological-psychological continuum of entraining stimuli, the "representation" of the past moves from being reflected in how regulators are operating to increasingly emotional and cognitive forms of representation (quotation marks no longer required).

Caretaking from this perspective can be seen as provisioning the child with entraining stimuli appropriate in content and timing to the task the child is attempting to regulate. Initially, the content and temporal organization of the entraining stimuli complete the regulators and allow them to function. There is a tight coupling of regulator and input. With development, the regulators become increasingly self-controlled and the form of that control reflects the cumulated and reiterated characteristics of the entraining stimuli that they have been exposed to.

Sander's theory is a theory of biological regulation in much the same way that evolutionary theory is reliant on the concept of adaptation. And it is similar to notions of predispositions in that, although there are constraints initially present and emerging in the organism as it attempts to regulate its interchange with the external environment, the constraints are not limited or rigid. Rather the final form achieved is a product of their initial structure, the input encountered, and its reiterated resolutions over time. This perspective opens the way to monotropy and other types of caregiving without prescribing any particular form and opens the way to our understanding the diversity and individuality of caretaking and individuals.

In terms of Efe personality formation, the early multiple caretaking is expected to limit the development of a sharply focused single-figure orientation by the infant and enhance feelings of attachment to many members of the group. Lancaster has put it this way:

> Any behavior pattern which reduces or limits the frequency of interaction between mother and offspring, such as passing around of infants in langurs, works against the development of a strong geneology by diffusing social contacts. In other words, certain behavior patterns can alter the sharpness of focus of the mother-infant bond so that the developing infant seeks social patterns among members of the social group who do not belong to its geneology. (1976, p. 15)

In Sander's terms, *sharply focused* is equivalent to a very tight coupling of bioemotional entraining stimuli and the infants' social-emotional regulator, whereas, *diffusely focused* is equivalent to a decoupling of input and regulator.

The Efe child care pattern can be seen as exposing the infant to a diversity of entraining social stimuli requiring regulation and eventual internalization. Caretaking tasks, such as nursing, or social interchanges, such as face-to-face play, can be conceptualized as exchanges of social-emotional signals (entraining stimuli) in which the infant and partner attempt to mutually regulate the task at hand—feeding for the former and social coordination for the latter. This multiplicity of social entraining stimuli eventuates in an internal regulator for social interactions that is less narrowly focused in two ways. First, and most obviously, because each of the individuals that interacts with the infant is stylistically different, the infant needs to develop the regulatory capacity to adjust to these differences. Second, it has been hypothesized that the mismatching of social signals during an interchange, a lack of coordination of entraining stimuli and endogenous regulator, is a fundamental part of an inducing process producing development of the capacity of the infant's social regulator (Tronick, Als, & Adamson, 1979). It would be expected that the Efe infant would experience more of the mismatching and that his or her capacity for social regulation would be more broadly based. By contrast, a monofed or monoplayed with infant has only one stylistic set of entraining stimuli and concomitant mismatches to regulate such that the form of its initial regulations will be tightly coupled to that input and the eventual endogenous structure of its regulator will be more strongly influenced by that set. Thus the "mono" infant's attachment would be quite sharply focused.

Of course, it is possible that too many stylistically different caregivers and too many mismatches would have detrimental effects on an infant. One would expect such effects to be manifest in the affective tone of the infant and the interaction. As noted already, the typical affect of Efe adult-infant interchanges is positive and playful. Similar in their way are the results of studies of quality day care centers in the United States (Kagan, Kearsley, & Zelazo, 1975) as well as those in Russia (Bronfenbrenner, 1970) and China (Kessen, 1975) on the enhancement of children's social skills and the formation of multiple attachments along with a primary attachment.

This pattern of Efe child care can be readily seen as leading to multiple attachments and group identification, and it is difficult not to be reminded of Bettelheim's (1969) controversial accounting of the personality structure of adults reared in the Israeli kibbutz system of child care. Bettelheim argued that the goal of kibbutz child rearing was to rid the individual of the inward-oriented, self-conscious personality of the ghettos of Europe; to change the nature of the mother-family relationship, especially the role of women; and to raise an adult who was literally happier and more vigorous and oriented toward work and society. To do that, the kibbutzniks engaged in group rearing of their children, with a strong de-emphasis of the mother's role and a raising to preeminence of the peer group's role. Bettelheim saw this as a successful process. He saw adults as strongly identified with the group, as having multiple attachments characterized as less intimate.

Bettelheim's interpretation from the perspective of analytic theory was that these characteristics arose because the young child did not have a continuous relationship with one caregiver and so the fear of loss and its opposite, capacity for intimacy, were not engendered. This lack of intimacy, we would suggest, can be more usefully conceptualized as a less tight initial coupling and later structuring of the infant's social-emotional regulators to the social-emotional entraining of stimuli of one person. The Efe form of intimacy, although different from that described for kibbutz-raised children, is nonetheless expected to be influenced by the multiple caretaking pattern.

The adult side to this interaction must also be put in place. Efe mothers are probably less sharply focused (not to be read as less caring) on their infants. At birth and continuing through the first months of life, they share their caregiving and they maintain their focus on work. Both would be expected to lead to a less intense involvement with the infant. A similar argument can be made for the caregivers. They too have other involvements, and importantly, they are not always related to the infant.

This less tight coupling or nonsingular coupling of internal regulators and exogenous entraining social stimuli should further produce well-formed personality boundaries or self-other distinctions as well as an orientation toward contemporaneous here-and-now events. From Sander's perspective, regulators that are confronted by a diversity of input that they successfully regulate will become more differentiated and more quickly self-regulatory. This should be the case for the Efe child. The Efe child, to successfully regulate a diversity of exchanges, needs to devote a lot of effort to the immediate input it is receiving. This is different from the child who interacts with only one person, where it is possible to more easily base current regulation on past history in the interaction. Moreover, the diversity of input allows for increasingly fine discriminations of exogenous social input. And the hypothesized greater number of mismatches of entraining stimuli and endogenous processes leads to more rapid and complete self-other differentiation.

Chodorow (1978), from the different but not unrelated theoretical perspective of object relations, developed a similar argument to account for self-other differentiation as it relates to mothering. The question of how maternal sensitivity, identification, and emotionality is developed in daughters in their interactions with their mothers and how it is not developed in sons was the focus of her inquiry. She saw mothers as having a strong projective identification with their daughters as well as a strong empathic understanding of them; a tight coupling of social-emotional regulators. This identification is unique to mothers and daughters. This process allows for a greater intimacy to develop between mother and daughter, and because of their interactions within this intimacy, the daughter develops the same capacities as the mother. Obviously, according to Chodorow, there is a greater enmeshing of mother and daughter such that the daughter has more diffuse personality boundaries and difficulty in establishing her sense of self.

The intimacy and enmeshing do not characterize the mother-son relationship, although they may in other cultures, nor do they characterize the father-daughter relationship. The father, because he has not participated in the early symbiotic mother-child relationship and the physiopsychological relationship of pregnancy before it, and because of the boundedness of the paternal personality with its characteristics of objectivity, lack of emotion, and lesser capacity for intimacy, interacts with his daughters with an orientation toward reality. This interaction from Chodorow's perspective, and one that is supported by descriptive research on the quality of father-daughter relationships (Johnson, 1975), is crucial to the daughter's formation of a reality orientation and clear personality boundaries. Fathers, for Chodorow, bring reality to their children and crucially to their daughters. As the Zinacanteco say, "Mothers hold their children in close, fathers hold them up toward the sky and show them the world." For the Efe, one might say that many people hold the infant up to the sky and show him the world.

Efe children will be different from Western children at all levels of development, including the regulation of infectious processes, hunger, sleep-wake cycles, face-to-face interactions, attachments, self, and intimacy, to the extent that the provisioning of entraining stimuli around each of these issues is different. A more radical prediction comes out of this regulatory process: Each individual will be structured differently to the extent that his or her regulatory entraining experiences differ. Such a view of individual regulatory strategies could ultimately be readily related to individual strategies of maximizing reproductive success.

The Efe data and the previous examples, along with a multiplicity of uncited examples on child rearing, make it clear that the biological and psychological constraints have a broad range, that there is flexibility in selecting within that range, and that a culturally biased child-rearing process is often the arbiter of that selection. There may be a predisposition in the infant toward monotropy, as evidenced by the Efe infant in the second half year of life. But its form is uniquely structured by the Efe infant's experience of a multiplicity of caretakers in the first half year of life and the continuation of that care into the second half year and beyond.

In some portions of American society, infants and mothers and possibly fathers are in almost intimate and continuous contact with one another from birth. This situation is not a biological given, nor is it even strongly supported by empirical Western data. We have somehow forgotten Robson's (1967) observations that some mothers do not report loving their infants until the infants are 6 to 10 weeks old, Rutter's (1981) statement that separations during the first 6 months of life do not have any detrimental effects, and Harlow's observations that early separations have few if any effects. Mothers of many readers of this essay delivered under general anesthesia; did they not bond and attach? Adoptive parent-child relationships seem secure and loving, and so on. One might even argue, as did Hinde (1983), that not until the infant is capable of mobility does a fear of strangers and a focalized attachment begin to make sense.

These arguments, however, still miss the point. As Kurland has stated about models of genetic influences: "A 'norm of reaction model' for gene effects portrays the individual's genotype as a mechanism that developmentally maps specific environments onto specific behavior, physiology and morphology. The proximate cause of any behavior is therefore necessarily environmental" (1979, p. 146).

For humans, what we must come to see is that the environment, particularly the social-cultural environment, is the selective force within the range. We live in a time when our technology makes us even more flexible regarding biological constraints. But flexibility is what characterizes human biological adaptations. Biology is no more the destiny of the Efe than it is for us. Our current views of the early mother-child and father-child relationships have been couched in a limited viewpoint rather than in a broadly based biological perspective that includes culture as the most important human adaptation. When we want fathers at the birth of their infants, it has nothing to do with physiological constraints or primate evolution; male presence at birthing is an unprecedented occurrence. Rather, their presence is a question of cultural choices about the kind of people we want fathers to become by having them experience the unique form of intimacy of so singular an event as birth. But human societies have always made such choices, except that now, perhaps with a growing knowledge of our biology in its broadest sense and with a greater self-awareness, we can come to see that our practices are determined by our choices rather than by hidden irrevocable forces.

CHAPTER 9

The Manta Pouch: A Regulatory System for Peruvian Infants at High Altitude

People who live at high altitudes must adapt to a variety of environmental stressors. There is not only hypoxic stress, but also extremes of temperature, high radiant solar energy, and high aridity. Infants, with their limited regulatory capacities, are especially vulnerable to these stressors. Although there may be some fetal acclimatization processes, high-altitude infants appear to have no specific adaptations to their environment. On the contrary, there is evidence that intrauterine adaptations place the high-altitude infant at greater risk than is true for a low-altitude baby. The placenta of the high-altitude native woman weighs more than that of her low-altitude counterpart, presumably in order to increase its capacity to deliver oxygen to the fetus. This increase in size reduces the possibility of fetal hypoxia, but is also associated with a significant reduction in birth weight.

How, then, does the human newborn survive a harsh, multiple-stress environment at birth, and how does it become acclimatized to the conditions it must live in? These questions were investigated in a study of the practices of Quechua residents in the Nunoa district of the altiplano in southern Peru. The project is described in detail in the August 1994 issue of *Child Development*.

The Nunoa Quechua live in permanent settlements about 4,000 meters, where they practice a mixed economy of pasturalism and agriculture (Figure 9.1a–c). The partial pressure of oxygen is 62% of that at sea level, relative humidity ranges from 10% to 60% depending on the season, and cosmic radiation is about five times its sea-level value. It can freeze any night of the year and does on an average of 340 days a year. The diurnal variation in temperature is greater than seasonal variation, with a mean range of 20°C per day, and in addition, temperature in the sun and in the shade can vary by more than 25°C.

FIGURE 9.1. The Nunoa Quechua live in permanent settlements in the altiplano of southern Peru, where they practice a mixed economy of pasturalism and agriculture.

a

b

FIGURE 9.1. *Continued*

c

In order to protect their infants from the multiple stresses of this harsh environment, the Quechua have devised a remarkable and elegant solution—the manta pouch, a wrapping system that provides a hospitable and portable microenvironment for the young child (Figure 9.2a–d). The practice of arranging the child in the pouch requires experience and skill. The infant is first dressed in diaper cloths, hats, sweaters, and leggings, and then wrapped in a poncho. Next it is wrapped tightly with arms at its sides in one or more blankets, and a cloth belt is used to swaddle it further. This belting around the already blanket-wrapped infant immobilizes it except for its head. Indeed, when the child is picked up at its midsection and held in the air, it does not bend.

The infant is covered with several more blankets, the last of which is put on so that a flap covers its face. When wrapping is complete, the infant is placed in a carrying blanket or manta. This, too, is folded so that it covers the infant's face. The infant is then picked up in the manta by the mother, swung behind her, and placed on her back. The loose ends of the blanket are tied securely across her chest, and the infant is thus carried within a tightly sealed pouch (see Figures 9.3c–e and 9.4).

The environment within this pouch is significantly different from the outside environment. Mothers allowed us to insert thermal and oxygen probes into the pouches with the understanding that there would be minimal disturbance to the "seal" of the pouch. While the ambient relative humidity was 25.8%,

FIGURE 9.2. A mother wraps and ties her child in several layers.

a

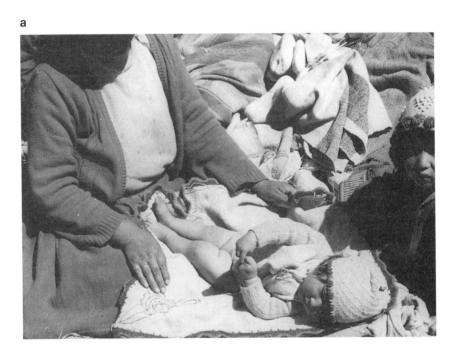

b

FIGURE 9.2. *Continued*

c

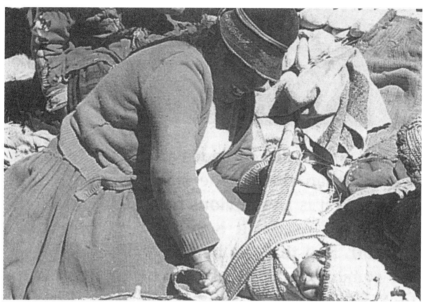

d

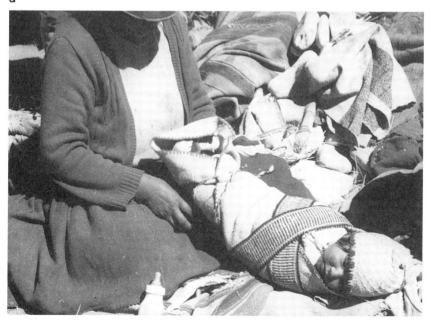

within the manta it was found to be 38%. The ambient temperature averaged 13.2°C, whereas the temperature inside the first layer of the pouch averaged 20.5°C. The temperature close to the infant's body surface averaged 26.1°C. The temperature within the manta, furthermore, was relatively stable even when exposed to the extremes of sun and shade that characterize this environment. The manta pouch, then, creates a warmer, more humid, and more stable environment for the infant.

But the pouch also provides an oxygen level that is lower than that in the surrounding environment, and it is less obvious how this might serve the infant's needs. It is conceivable that it is a trade-off, and that the benefits related to raising and stabilizing temperature and humidity make up for the costs to the infant in lowering the oxygen level. There is another possible explanation though. It may be that the reduction in the level of oxygen serves to reduce the infant's metabolic rate, and thereby results in significant energetic savings. How might this work?

A primary result of reducing the oxygen level in the pouch is to increase the relative level of carbon dioxide, and with it the likelihood that the infant will sleep. Energetic demands are reduced at least two times in sleep compared to more active states, and these additional calories can be readily utilized for the infant's growth and maintenance. There is a radical analogy here to bats: In some species of bat, when the pregnant female is stressed she goes into a state of torpor, and fetal development is inhibited until the mother resumes her normal state. One can wonder if the Quechua infant in the pouch does not go into a torporlike state that is even lower in its energetic demands than normal sleep states. Such a state has never been described in humans. But could be investigated. It might be especially important for our thinking about the care of acutely ill infants.

Other characteristics of the manta pouch also contribute to the likelihood of increased amounts of sleep. Swaddling, stable temperatures, and the rhythmic movement of the mother are all conducive to sleep. The lack of visual stimulation and the muffling of sound make sleep still more likely.

The microenvironment of the pouch serves not only to buffer the infant from the extreme stress of the high-altitude environment and to reduce caloric expenditure; there are other protective effects as well. The increase in humidity in the pouch reduces the likelihood of respiratory infection associated with dryness, and also limits the infant's exposure to the dense smoke from cooking fires inside the huts. Finally, the manta pouch may limit the infant's exposure to pathogens produced by, for instance, the coughing of others and wind-blown fecal material.

We observed that the youngest infants were typically found not only in a horizontal position but also with their feet toward the side of the manta that went over the mother's shoulder, so that their feet tended to be slightly elevated, a position that would tend to increase blood flow to their heads. As they got older, we found that their positions were changed to the upright, the manta was opened, and the swaddling was loosened. These modulations would serve to acclimatize infants gradually to the environmental stressors of the altiplano (Figure 9.3a–e).

One cost of the manta pouch may be that the Quechua infant is deprived of stimulation relative to infants in other situations. Such deprivation has been

FIGURE 9.3. Older babies, who spend longer periods of time unwrapped, are still in the pouch for parts of the day.

a

FIGURE 9.3. *Continued*

b

c

d

FIGURE 9.3. *Continued*

e

hypothesized to result in slowed and even damaged mental development. The only study assessing behavioral and mental development in high-altitude Quechua infants did find that their developmental quotients were lower than sea-level children at 2 years. However, in a study of Guatemalan infants who also experienced some deprivation, little or no effects were found later in development. The swaddling and carrying of the infant might also be expected to delay motor development. However, extensive studies of the Navaho show that while there may be some initial delay due to the use of the cradleboard, such delays are not permanent.

Other cultural factors must also be considered. Among Quechua herders, parents expect that by the age of 6 or 7 years their children will be able to care for and guard their herds, the family's most valuable resource. This is a demanding task that requires high degrees of vigilance and diligence, as well as an ability to tolerate a lack of social interchange. One can speculate that being raised in the manta pouch with its restrictions on movement and its general lack of social and object stimulation may dampen the children's activity levels and demands for social interaction and stimulation. The characteristic behavior of Quechua children may be seen from the Western perspective on childbearing as a result of deprivation. On the other hand, the

FIGURE 9.4. The baby in the Manta Pouch is swung onto the mother's back and tied securely across her chest.

actively exploring 6-year-old of the West would be seen by the Quechua as dysfunctional.

While the manta pouch is not the only answer to raising infants at high altitude, it works well for the Quechua in the context of their lives. It is a remarkable piece of cultural technology, lightweight and portable, made from local materials, and reusable later for other purposes (Figure 9.4).

CHAPTER 10

Mother-Infant Interaction Among the Gusii of Kenya

The daily interaction between an infant and his caregivers has been hypothesized as the process through which the infant develops a sense of himself as a separate person of family and of culture (Kohut, 1971; Whiting & Whiting, 1975). Caudill and Weinstein (1969) demonstrated how cultural values infused and shaped the interactions of Japanese and American mothers and their infants. Japanese mothers saw their infants as independent biological beings that had to be incorporated into the culture and made interdependent. American mothers saw their infants as dependent beings who had to be helped to become independent. Specific infant-mother interactions during the course of daily caretaking reflected these cultural expectations. For example, Japanese mothers slept with their infants, fed them, and performed caretaking activities on a sleeping infant while American infants most often slept alone. Sleep, as a sign of independence, was seldom interrupted. In both cultures, the infants were the unknowing focus of the universal process of gaining a culture-specific sense of self.

One segment of caretaking patterns that has become the focus of recent research is infant-caretaker face-to-face playful interaction (Brazelton, Koslowski, & Main, 1974; Stern, 1974b). Face-to-face interaction makes up only a small proportion of an infant's experience, but it is thought to be a particularly significant and intimate form of interaction. There are several reasons for this: First, because of its intimacy, it becomes the earliest and most basic form of communication and one in which the infant can develop the capacity to regulate the behavior of others. He learns the rules of joint regulation of interchanges with people in general, providing him with an expectancy for social responsiveness to his own behavior (Tronick, Als, & Brazelton, 1977). Second, speech and conversation are thought to be based on face-to-face interaction and becomes a developmental product of it (Tronick, Als, & Adamson, 1979).

Sophisticated capacities essential to affective and cognitive development are built upon the structure that can be seen in the face-to-face situation. Finally, the infant in the en face position learns the language of emotional expression, his own and others'. Most important (Tronick et al., 1977), the infant grows to understand the mutual effects of these emotional expressions, and upon these mutual exchanges his or her sense of attachment is first formed.

The structure of infant-adult exchanges has been described in some detail (Als, Tronick, & Brazelton, 1979; Tronick, Als, & Brazelton, 1980b). Positive states of dyadic interaction characterized by smiles and vocalizations cycle and alternate among neutral and negative states; the latter are exemplified by fusses, pouts, frowns, and cry faces for the infant, and neutral or sober expressions for the adult (Brazelton et al., 1974). The rhythmic nature of these interactions is seen in the behavior of both infant and caregiver. Furthermore, the movement within the interaction is characterized by both partners changing state together in order to achieve greater synchrony of affective states rather than by one partner leading or following the other (Brazelton, Tronick, Adamson, Als, & Wise, 1975). This mutual regulation of the interaction can be seen when the structure of the interaction is examined microscopically. The structure has been characterized as dialogic, conversational, or synchronous. Infants as young as 1 month can participate in this mutuality in interaction with familiar adults. Even within the caretaking unit, the infant can participate in the specific joint regulation of the interaction with different partners in accordance with the goals and expectations for these differing interactions (Dixon, Yogman, Tronick, & Brazelton, 1981; Yogman, 1977). Interactions with unfamiliar people lack this essential conversational quality.

Prior to this volume, almost all of the studies of face-to-face interaction had been of American, English, and other Western European mother-infant pairs. Exceptions might be the ethological descriptions of caretaker-infant interaction, for example, the observational studies of Konner (1977b) on the !Kung and Goldberg (1972) on the Zambians. But these descriptive studies were not subjected to detailed microbehavioral analyses of the structure of the interactions.

The study reported here on mother-infant face-to-face interaction among the Gusii is aimed at beginning to decipher the structure within these cross-cultural observations. This attempt to bring these basic observations under more careful scrutiny was designed to answer specific questions on both universal and culture-specific aspects of early mother-infant interaction: Would such interactions show a cyclic structure? Would they have both dialogic and synchronous structural elements, and which would predominate? Would the systems of analysis designed in this culture allow complete analysis of the interactions in another (how ethnocentric is the system itself)? What was the nature of the mutuality achieved in the interaction and how was it achieved? Who led and who followed? Could one see from the elements of the interaction the goals of the partners? In what way might these goals reflect culture-specific expectations for infants and the socialization of children in general? Our thoughts were that the structural elements—the nature of the behavioral displays, the cycling of affective states, the dialogic and synchronous structure—would all be found in these interactions and would represent their universality, whereas their quantity and the signal value of the elements of negotiation—who leads, who follows, the signal behaviors represented, the evidence of goal direction—would reflect culture-specific elements.

THE GUSII

The Gusii are a Bantu-speaking agricultural minority tribe living in the densely populated highlands of southwestern Kenya. Ethnographic material has been collected over the past 50 years and provides some detail on all aspects of life (R.A. Le Vine & Le Vine, 1966; Mayer, 1951). Clan affiliation is the basis of patrilineal, patrilocal patterns of living and allows for the cultivation of small plots of land in cooperation with members of an extended family. Tribal survival and the smooth functioning of clan units is monitored by elders working under traditional systems of rules for the settlement of disputes, the inheritance of land, the enforcement of moral behavior, and the adherence to ritual (R.A. Le Vine & Le Vine, 1966). The goal for each person is to fit into the modal role of a hard worker in tilling the soil, to meet the expectations of the kinship system of obligations and to raise children with these same expectations (R.A. Le Vine, 1980a).

The patterns of social interchange are governed by implicit rules for every situation. These serve to make clear age and sex divisions among tribe members and to avoid the display of any intense affect, as it is seen as a possible disruptive force. The face-to-face situation may call up strong feelings; hence it is particularly regulated. Conversation can be uncoupled from gaze in the enface position and often is. A typical adult-adult interaction often occurs with completely averted gaze. Conversations occur with the participants at a 90° or greater angle to each other. Interactions of adjacent generations and cross-sex partners (e.g., mother-son, father-in-law/daughter-in-law) call up the most strict restrictions on face-to-face interaction. The buildup of either positive or negative feeling is avoided in this manner.

The power of gaze in interpersonal relationships is seen in the elaborate Gusii belief system built upon concepts of the "evil eye" and the danger of being seen at vulnerable periods of life (S. LeVine, 1979). Some individuals, usually women, are said to be afflicted with the capacity to bring illness or misfortune to children by simply looking upon these young ones, and thereby affecting incorporation of small particles normally present on the skin. Children can be protected from this evil eye by certain practices such as wearing small charms, and so on (LeVine, 1963). Although only a few people are unfortunate enough to inflict this specific injury on children, the danger in being looked at directly by anyone seems to be a constant theme behind many beliefs and practices (S. LeVine, 1979; R. A. LeVine, 1980b).

Rituals among the Gusii reflect the dangerous aspect of gaze. For example, practices proscribed at the birth of premature infants, ceremonies of circumcision for young boys and girls, reconciliations and rituals of funerals, all include seclusion of a vulnerable person, protecting that individual from being seen during an important life transition. Interestingly, the danger for the weakened person is thought to be most severe from close relatives and neighbors. These individuals may harbor jealousness and resentments, leading them to invoke sorcery or witchcraft directed at their kin. One requires the most protection from persons most closely related by kinship and physical proximity.

Greeting behavior among the Gusii is also strictly governed, with proscribed forms and sequences demanded in any encounter, no matter how familiar the person or how frequent the meeting. Slips or mistakes in the regularity of these exchanges would lead to interpersonal tension, embarrassment, and apprehension. There is some suggestion that this greeting behavior as well as other ritualistic practices are increasing in importance among the Gusii rather than decreasing (R. A. LeVine, 1980a).

These practices and beliefs among the Gusii are in marked contrast to our own culture's emphasis on face-to-face encounters. We believe that eye-to-eye contact is universally and absolutely necessary for affective communication. In fact, in our culture, gaze avoidance is seen as a violation of mutual trust and arouses suspicion of malintent or insincerity.

Early parent-child relationships among the Gusii are characterized by avoidance of eye-to-eye contact and restraint in playful interactions. The almost continuous physical contact between the mother and her infant does not encourage other kinds of social intimacy, because the infant is rarely held in a face-to-face posture and, therefore, does not often achieve eye-to-eye contact (R. A. LeVine, 1979). Affectionate and social behaviors are rarely directed toward the baby, nor is the infant regarded as capable of communicative intent other than to signal hunger or distress (LeVine & LeVine, 1966; New, 1979). The mother sees her job as to respond to these signals appropriately and to safeguard the cleanliness and health of her infant. Enhancing social development or cognitive growth are not part of her culture-specific parental goals. The long-term adaptiveness of these norms in late childhood and adulthood can be seen in maintenance of incest taboos and strict discipline. Extended to infancy and early childhood, these practices may be protective for both partners in a culture where infant mortality has been high. Mothers may have needed a ritualized method to dampen the intensity of their feelings for infants they may lose. These deeply engrained beliefs are absorbed by young children early in life and are manifest in their own behaviors. In their extensive comparative analysis of the behavior of children from six cultures, the Whitings (Whiting & Whiting, 1975) found the Gusii children to be the least attention seeking of all children studied. The regulation and diffusion of direct face-to-face contact becomes part of their behavioral repertoire very early.

In a series of naturalistic observations (coded in the home by trained native observers with a technique adapted from Clarke-Stewart, 1973), insights into the social environment of the infant have been summarized. Gusii infants with a median age of 12 months or less are held on an average of 58% of the time (Hitchcock, 1979). The mean level of holding drops to 18% when the median age is 12 to 20 months. Before 5 months, mothers held their babies over half of the time, but after that less than half of this holding was attributed to mothers; the rest to child caretakers of 5 to 8 years of age (*omereri*). Young children are assigned to care for infants in order to allow mothers to return to crop cultivation or housework. Only in families where the father's income was low and there was little land for the mother to till was the mother the sole caretaker; in these cases she held her baby 70-80% of the time (Hitchcock, 1979).

Looking directly at their infants was represented in a range of 2–21% of the mothers' behaviors at 3 months, but by 6 months it represented less than 10% of all interactional behaviors (New, 1979). Talking to infants at 3 months was even less and varied from 0–10% seen in all responses. A mother is likely to respond to cries or demands of an infant but not to initiate or to respond to contented vocalizations. Using as a comparative base the mean proportion of all caretaker behaviors in response to contented infant behaviors, mothers at both 3 and 6 months appeared to initiate less than did other caretakers. However, they did respond more to their infants' cries and demands than did other caretakers. Maternal responsiveness to less than 10% of 3-month-old infant vocalizations as opposed to 50% responses to frets or cries, conforms to the Gusii belief that infants are not regarded as capable of social interactions (R.A. LeVine, 1963; New, 1979). As infants are held on the hip or back most of the time, this allows for little enface interaction. Communication appears to be mediated through touch rather than gaze. The infant's social experience is bounded by the demands of external circumstances (e.g., mother's work) and is based on the child's vegetative needs rather than his need for social stimulation. Mutual regulation of social interaction is seen as neither possible nor desirable.

In short, Gusii babies were not being exposed to the same type of social experience, nor did the mothers have the same goals as are present in our culture. Gusii babies were rarely played with in a face-to-face situation. This caretaking pattern, then, seems to be a way of visualizing cultural norms for interpersonal communication, as well as of defining the particular expectations for mothers and their infants.

METHOD OF STUDY

Videotapes of face-to-face interactions of Gusii infants and their mothers from a single market area were analyzed. These mothers and infants were part of a larger multifaceted, longitudinal study of parenting and early child development.

Because of the semitropical climate and living arrangements of the Gusii, most of the taping was done outdoors at the homes of the subjects. In a typical outdoor filming arrangement, the infant was seated in an American infant seat with the mother seated or kneeling on the ground in front of him (Figure 10.1). An assistant held a tarpaulin curtain to contain the interaction and to decrease

FIGURE 10.1. In-field situation for taping of mother-infant social interaction.

FIGURE 10.2. Image recorded by videotape of Gusii mother-infant interaction. Digital timer superimposed prior to analysis.

distracting stimuli. Another assistant held up a mirror with which to reflect the mother's image on the camera. This allowed one video camera to record a face-to-face image of both mother and infant. The video camera and microphone were placed about 15 feet from the interacting pair. Figure 10.2 demonstrates the resultant video image.

The mothers were instructed in this situation, as in the American laboratory situation, to "talk to your baby," "play with your baby," "get your baby's attention." Two and a half minutes of this playful interaction were recorded. Infants were taped biweekly from 2 to 12 weeks and at monthly intervals till 6 months of age. The final data set includes sequential sessions of nine mother-infant pairs with a mean duration of 2 minutes 22 seconds (Range: 1 minute 22 seconds to 3 minutes 10 seconds).

The taping was done when the infant was in a quiet, alert state and all distracting elements (e.g., chickens, older children) had been cleared from the area. Mothers were allowed to see the tapes after each session. Mothers (and infants) became accustomed to the situation and participated eagerly. However, they continued to preserve their own judgment as to the value of such observations, considering them a pleasant waste of time. They specifically said it was silly to talk to a baby.

TABLE 10.1   Examples of Criteria for Monadic Phase Coding

Infant	Mother

A.
Neutral to negative affect, but not crying or fussing
Gaze away from mother
Posture neutral to slumped
Head position variable
  a) fully to part-side away with or without focused attention elsewhere
  b) any position, totally involved in object or hand play
	Aversion (2)
	Neutral to negative affect
	Gaze away from infant
	Distance medium to far back
	Head position variable, toward to part-side away
	Vocalizations variable
	  a) none to infant
	  b) may or may not vocalize to another adult
	Contact with infant variable, none to simple touch

B. Affect slightly negative Head and/or gaze predominantly toward the mother Posture slumped to neutral	*Monitor (3)* Affect neutral to slightly negative Gaze intermittent or lidded Body in neutral position No contact of infant Head may be partially turned away
C. Affect neutral to positive Bright look to simple smile Head and gaze toward mother Eyes open and alert Body upright Vocalizations positive or none	*Set (5)* Affect neutral to positive Face bright or with simple smile Vocalizations of all types except abrupt and/or negative Body and head orientation toward infant in medium to close position Touches may include containment or none
D. Affect greater than neutral Head and gaze totally oriented to mother Posture upright Face variables, from simple smile to coo face Vocalizations variable, from none to positive vocalization to laugh Movement variable, from none to large limb movements	*Play (6)* Affect greater than neutral Body, head and gaze fully oriented to infant Vocalizations variable, from none to low burst-pause narrative, playful-stern or non verbal sounds and laugh Contact with infant variable, from none to simple touch or tapping

In order to understand the meaning of the face-to-face data, we had also gathered medical, social, and psychological information on the mothers while pregnant, and pediatric and Brazelton Neonatal Behavioral Assessments (Brazelton, 1973) in the newborn period, as well as naturalistic observations in the homes and cognitive testing over the next 15 months. The face-to-face data then can be understood within this context in order to allow us to make meaningful interpretation of its goals within this culture. The mother-infant pairs as well as the whole market population were well known to the authors.

The videotapes are analyzed by scoring behavioral phases for mother and infant. American studies have led to the development of a system of analysis by which the interaction could be divided into segments of identifiable behavioral clusters or phases displayed by each interactant (Tronick et al., 1977). Individual behavioral clusters can be characterized by seven monadic phases: (1) avoid/protest, (2) avert, (3) monitor, (4) elicit (mother only), (5) set, (6) play, and (7) talk. Each monadic phase has specific mutually exclusive behavioral descriptors built upon the microscopic observations of component behaviors. The composite cluster can be reliably (>.85) scored directly from the videotapes. Examples of the descriptors for several of these phases for mother and infant are shown in Table 10.1. The phases constitute the continua in the degree of attention to the other in the dyad (7 to 1). It is scored as positive to negative in affect (7 to 1), and in this way provides an ordinal scaling system. This system was used to analyze the Gusii tapes by identifying the monadic phase for mother and infant for each one = quarter second of interaction. Technical problems including lighting difficulties and marginal resolution account for the exclusion of 6% of the time of the taped material. Scrutiny of these missing data verifying that there is no systematic bias in these exclusions; these reflect random events in the field conditions of the study.

RESULTS

Global Description of the Interactions

Gusii mothers entered the interaction with their infants by sitting at a medium close distance from the child's seat. They appeared relaxed and comfortable within the interaction. They gave the prescribed stylized greeting with a simple smile followed by a short pause. The infant would attend brightly and might or might not smile. Mothers often would initiate a repetitious verbal pattern using single words or phrases, ones we often heard them use in the course of daily caretaking (e.g., "kira, kira, kira" [be quiet, don't complain, be content]; or "issi, issi, issi" [you see, attend here]; or "seca, seca, seca" [smile]). Their repetitive phrases might or might not accompanied by tapping of the infant's arm, leg, or occasionally chin, or very prominently, the face. These taps would typically occur in short clusters of four rapid beats followed by a pause. Although reminiscent of the mother-infant "game" as defined by Stern (1974b), these sequences did not vary upon each repetition, nor were they elaborated upon during the course of the interaction. These sequences were repeated unchanged for several repetitions. They seemed to be used to maintain steady attention from the infant rather than as elicitations.

"Baby talk" in its most exaggerated form was not heard. However, mothers did use dialogue broken by long pauses to interact with the infants. Some mothers did raise the pitch of their usually low voices, but dramatic changes in inflection were not used. The action for the mothers' part, then, was carried along steadily using voice and through touch. Facial expression had little variation. The mothers smiled pleasantly or had an alert, open expression throughout most of the interactions. Gaze was generally toward the infant but appeared to have a grossly distracted quality. Slow motion and stop-frame review of the tapes indicated that the mothers' gaze was broken by brief glances away from the infant and was frequently directed at some part of the infant's body other than the face. Movement of the mother was very limited and was generally restricted to small head movements rather than large shifts of body position. The overall intensity of the interaction seemed less than those seen in the American sample; one had the feeling that there was less of a sense of hovering by the African mothers.

Infants responded to their mothers' attentions with pleasure. Dramatic aversions of gaze or posture were very rare. Cooing vocalizations were accompanied by big kicks of the legs and large smiles. Uniformly positive affect was present. Infants were usually content and interested in the interaction. Occasionally an infant would wiggle in the chair with arms extending out or up. This behavior appeared to signal that the infant wanted or expected to be picked up by the mother. When mothers left at the end of the designated time, few infants showed the dramatic change in affect common in similar American sequences. They seemed quite competent to redirect their attention toward objects in the surrounding environment. Their affect remained neutral to positive as they casually scanned the environment.

Some of the infants laughed out loud, with lots of movement and vocalization. These peaks in affective display produced a mixed response in mothers: Some giggled nervously; others' faces became devoid of expression and turned away. The infant would then display less dramatic, though still positive behaviors. Even these abrupt shifts in mother's attention produced little change in the infant's affective level; positive affect, only slightly dampened prevailed. The cyclic nature of the interactions was not immediately apparent. In the field, the sessions seemed very flat and in certain ways monotonous. It is only upon review that the rhythmic quality was seen. The cyclic modulation is smooth and regular but much more subtle than in American interactions. At first inspection, the mother's momentary gaze aversions appeared random and seemed to give the whole interaction a distracted quality. Only after closer scrutiny does one see that these are closely linked to the infant's peaks of affective display and as such are important junctures in the interactions.

Individual differences in pacing and style were apparent among the African mother-infant pairs. Temperamental characteristics of the infants themselves seemed to be the basis of some of that variation. For example, one very large, placid infant vocalized frequently and smiled often; body movements were very rare. His affective peaks or periods of withdrawal were signaled by cessation of vocalization. His mother, a relaxed older woman with many children, responded by participating in the dialogues. She extended the rhythm of that interchange to touch by moving slightly forward and tapping the infant with each vocalization in a very pleasant, moderately excited way. In this case, the infant seemed to determine the pacing of the interaction, and the mother its complexity. In another case, the infant seemed vigilant, quiet, and relatively stoic throughout the interactions. His mother gave repeated, stylized greetings as if she too sensed his reticence to engage in the interaction. When initiated, the dialogue was carried by gentle tapping games and quiet reciprocal vocalizations. His mother had an unwavering, broad smile and a low-pitched voice that she used to gently draw him out. In addition to the gaze aversion, this mother used her hands to hold down the child's arms if his movements became large or tremulous. The whole interaction was dampened by these maneuvers.

Another mother was more dramatic in her response to the slightly withdrawn infant; she readjusted the infant's head when she attempted to turn away. Although she would not accept disengagement, within an attentive state she was very nonintrusive. Long dialogues with the infant were present but were modulated by a flurry of eye blinks by this mother. She did not turn away herself but did avert gaze by blinking when the intensity of the interaction began to build.

One of the interactions with a temperamentally negative and irritable infant was quite uncomfortable to watch. The child's mother used taps and an unusual hissing sound to get the attention of a solemn, slumped-over infant. This sound coupled with the child's name appeared to be a greeting, recognized as such by both participants. Several short-lived engagements followed these greetings but were terminated by the infant turning away. The mother then repeated this greeting behavior to begin the cycle again. Finally, the infant put up her hand in a real avoidance posture and made some swipes toward the mother's face. The mother's forthright and relatively aggressive personality was clear in her persistence and insistence with this very difficult infant. The interaction appeared uncomfortable to the onlooker as these two negotiated their patterns of early communication.

Although almost all the Gusii mothers appeared relaxed and calm, two of the mothers seemed very calm and slightly distanced from the interaction. Their style outside the face-to-face situation was consistent with this mode. The shifts and modulations in these interactions were slow and smooth and the whole sessions were more obviously rhythmic on even casual inspection.

The observations of these individual differences only serve to highlight how the more generalized influence of culture is modified but not suppressed by the specific temperamental and situational characteristics of the mother and infant pairs. There was no Gusii stereotype but rather a range of behavioral displays and patterns that were clearly different from the American mother-infant pairs interacting within the same structure.

Microanalysis of the Interaction

Proportion of Time and Duration of Each Phase for the Gusii Infants

The monadic phase system is used to describe the infants' performance during the interaction. Table 10.2 presents the percentage of time each phase occurs in an interaction and the duration of each phase. The relatively large standard deviations and ranges indicate large individual differences. Except for infant protest, each phase made up a significant proportion of the interaction with monitor and set being the modal state. Monitor also had the largest mean and median duration. Talk and play had the shortest durations, and next to protest, the smallest proportion of total time. Avert and protest had relatively long mean durations (6.4 and 7.0 seconds, respectively).

Combining phases shows that the infants spend 25% disengaged (Phases 1 and 2), 40% neutrally engaged (Phases 3 and 5), and 32% positively engaged (Phases 6 and 7). Periods of high attention and positive affect are brief and few in number. Infants spend longer periods in phases at the midportion of the range of possible behaviors.

Infant Transitions

The ordering of transitions from one state to another was examined to determine how the infants change among the phases over the course of the interaction.

TABLE 10.2 Behavioral Phases of Gusii Infants

Percentage of Time	Mean	SD	Range	States
Phase:1 Protest	5.1	11.1	0–33 }	Disengaged
2 Avert	20.8	19.7	0–50 }	25 ± 17
3 Monitor	19.0	28.4	0–90 }	Neutrally engaged
5 Set	21.1	17.9	0–53 }	40 ± 23
6 Play	19.5	16.3	0–47 }	Positively engaged
7 Talk	13.3	14.1	0–41 }	32 ± 16

Duration in Seconds	Mean	SD	Range
Phase:1 Protest	7.0	2.3	4.5–9.1
2 Avert	6.4	5.7	0.7–17.0
3 Monitor	8.2	11.2	0.2–37.0
5 Set	5.2	5.5	1.8–18.0
6 Play	3.0	1.9	0.5–6.5
7 Talk	1.7	0.6	1.1–2.7

FIGURE 10.3. Examples of mother-infant interaction laid out sequentially using sequential monadic phases.

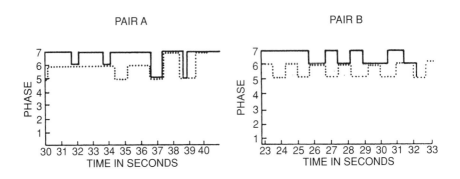

Figure 10.3 gives examples of a graphing of these interactions. In each, the phase is plotted on the ordinate and time intervals of one-quarter second along the abscissa. A horizontal line indicates the phase and its duration and a vertical line indicates a phase transition. The phases are ranked from positive to negative along an affective dimension to allow for sequential relationships in the data but not to imply any judgment of the behaviors scored.

Figure 10.3 shows the cycling among the negative, neutral, and positive phases that have been described for infants in interactions in our own country. This cyclic quality was seen in all the Gusii mother-infant interactions. The infants cycle from neutral or positive engagement and back to negative an average of 3.3 times per minute. Two other significant features of the infants' transitions among phases were noted. Only 2% of the transitions were from phases 1/2 to 6/7 or vice versa, the extremes of the scale; 76% were from within the neutral to positive range. The usual transitions were in a narrow range along the attentional continuum, one-step transitions. Second, infants typically changed from one phase to the next adjacent phase. For example, Gusii infants moved from play to talk, and play to set, but seldom from talk to monitor or avert. One-step transitions (i.e., modulations from one phase to adjacent one) constituted 51% of infant changes; two-step transitions, 32%; and three- and four-step transitions, a total of only 8%. Thus, regardless of an infant's predominant phase, transitions took place within a narrow range.

Proportion of Time and Duration of Each Phase for the Gusii Mothers

Table 10.3 presents the data on proportion of time spent in each phase and the duration of each phase. The relatively large standard deviations and ranges indicate that there were large individual differences. However, Gusii mothers spent the greatest proportion of time in set (.34) and next in play (.20). They spent a total of only 7% of the time disengaged (Phases 1 and 2). The mean duration

TABLE 10.3   Behavioral Phases of Gusii Mothers

Percentage of Time	Mean	SD	Range	State
Phase: 1 Avoid	4.1	3.3	1–11 ⎫	Disengaged
2 Avert	3.8	3.3	2–12 ⎭	7 ± 3
3 Monitor	13.6	9.3	14–27 ⎫	Neutrally
4 Elicit	11.1	11.3	1–35 ⎬	engaged
5 Set	34.0	14.9	11–58 ⎭	47 ± 13
6 Play	20.5	11.7	0–41 ⎫	Positively engaged
7 Talk	11.7	12.1	0–37 ⎭	31 ± 11

Duration, Seconds	Mean	SD	Range	
Phase: 1 Avoid	1.1	0.5	0.5–2.0	
2 Avert	3.0	1.9	1.3–7.6	
3 Monitor	2.5	1.3	1.2–5.0	
4 Elicit	1.7	0.8	0.9–3.7	
5 Set	2.1	1.0	0.7–3.6	
6 Play	1.4	.4	0.8–2.0	
7 Talk	1.2	.2	0.8–1.6	

of avert was 3.0 seconds, representing the longest phase duration. This was a very long behavioral unit in our experience with American tapes. Monitor had the next longest mean duration, 2.5 seconds. Play and talk were relatively shortlived (1.4, and 1.2 seconds, respectively). Combining the phases into "disengaged" (Phases 1 and 2), .07; "neutrally engaged" (Phases 3 and 5), .47; "positively engaged" (Phases 6 and 7), .31; and "elicit" (Phase 4), .11 completed the analysis.

Maternal Transitions

Maternal transitions among the phases were analyzed in the same manner as the infant fluctuations. Examples are plotted in Figure 10.3. These again show the cyclic pattern of transitions along the affective and attentional continuum. This is, again, the modal pattern of the Gusii mothers. On the average, Gusii mothers cycled from being neutrally or positively engaged to negatively engaged 4.4 times a minute. Mothers tended not to go directly from the extreme negative phases (1 and 2) to positive phases (6 and 7). The largest proportion of their transitions were one-step transitions. These accounted for 71% of transitions, even a greater proportion than the one-step infant fluctuation. Two-step transitions constituted 17% of the total. Three- and four-step changes accounted for only 9% of changes. Again, the fluctuations were, by and large, within a narrow range; 64% percent were within the neutral to positive category. When in the disengaged phases (1 and 2), the transition was to the positive states 1% of the time, and to neutral 4%; 2% of the time, the mother went to the other of the disengaged states.

TABLE 10.4   Percentage of Time in Joint Phases for Gusii Mother-Infant Pairs (Matched Pairs Highlighted on the Diagonal)

| | Maternal Phase | | | | | | | |
| | 1 | 2 | 3 | 4 | 5 | 6 | 7 | |
Infant Phase	*Avoid*	*Avert*	*Monitor*	*Elicit*	*Set*	*Play*	*Talk*	*Total*
1 Protest	0	0	0.8	1.5	1.1	.9	.2	4.5
2 Avert	1.6	**0.5**	3.6	4.2	5.6	2.2	2.1	19.8
3 Monitor	0.8	0	**1.0**	2.0	7.2	1.4	1.6	14.0
5 Set	0.6	1.6	4.9	1.1	**7.5**	3.8	2.7	22.2
6 Play	0	0.6	1.1	0.5	5.9	**7.7**	4.3	20.1
7 Talk	0	0.4	1.7	0.2	6.5	5.2	**1.4**	15.2
Total	3.0	3.1	13.1	9.5	33.8	21.2	12.3	

Note. *Truncation of the matrix during calculations accounts for the discrepancy of values of infant and maternal percentages of time in phases on this table in comparison with Tables 10.1 and 10.2.*

Relational Aspects of the Interaction

Examination of the behavior of both partners in the interaction simultaneously provides some understanding of the amount of synchrony in the interactions. Table 10.4 represents the proportion of time that infant and mother are in joint phases. Both partners were simultaneously in positive monadic phases 18.6% of the time (Phases 6 and 7) and were in mutually negative states only 2.1% (Phases 1 and 2). Patterns were in the neutral categories synchronously (Phases 3 and 5) 20.6% of the time. When the specific patterns of the "conjoint" state are examined in detail, it can be seen that the infant more frequently displayed behavior characteristics of a more affectively positive state than did his mother at that time. For example, the percentage of time when the mother was in a neutral state while the infant was in a positively engaged state was 15.2%. The portion of time when the reverse occurred (i.e., mother positively engaged and infant neutral) was .5% of the time. Overall, the proportion of time the infant had a more positive affective state than the mother was 40%; the mother was more positive 31% of the time.

Dyadic Transitions

Two additional analyses were made to determine the nature of the changes that define the cyclic quality in the interaction. The first is an assessment of events when mother and infant are both in the same state (about 40.3% of interaction time). Using the occurrence of this matched state as a marker, this analysis looked at the transition to the conjoint or disjoint states. Sixty percent of the time the mother initiated the move out of the matched joint state and only

40% of the time was the infant responsible for this change. Mothers initiated the alterations more frequently, and further adjustments were then necessary to return the interaction to the matched state. If the infant made the initial transition, the mother followed this change in level of attention or affect and returned to a joint state of match 34% of the time; the infant, however, followed her change only 5.8% of the time. Mothers appeared to be responsible for the readjustment toward the synchronous state six times more frequently than were the infants. The second analysis examines how the mother responded to the infant as he changed into a positive phase (6 or 7). Fifty-six percent of the time she followed the infant by altering her behavior into positive engagement (Phases 6 or 7). However, 39% of the time, she changed to the less positive states of 5 or 3. Five percent of the time she turned away from the interaction, behavior characterized in the avoid phase, Phase 1.

DISCUSSION

Gusii mother-infant face-to-face interaction was seen to be organized in a cyclic flow of affective behaviors similar to interactions described in our own culture (Brazelton et al., 1975). This organization suggests an underlying universal form. The monadic phase scoring system, a descriptive system developed within our culture, described the behaviors seen in the Gusii mother-infant interactions as well. The range and quality of affective behaviors were similar across the different cultures, but were used differentially. The emergence of play and talk episodes, with the modulation of voice effective for sustaining infant attention, were seen in this cultural setting as well as our own. Adult behavior, including speech in all cultures described to date, had an infantilized form when interacting with young infants. This seems to reflect the universal awareness of the capacities of young infants. The infants displayed a full range of behaviors within our system in spite of a very different social experience.

Brazelton et al. (1974) hypothesized that the cyclic acceleration and deceleration of affective behavior during interactions becomes basic to the organization of the interaction. Such cycles of affect and attention were clearly evident in the Gusii interaction. Additionally, as has been described in American interactions, there is a high degree of predictability as to both the change of affective direction and the size of that change for infant and mother. Infants and mothers moved among the states in a regular fashion, that is, rarely from avert to play or vice versa, and changing between states in one step apart predominating. The orderliness of each participant's behavior permitted or resulted in the successful negotiation of frequent joint interactive states. These were evident in a large proportion of matched states and in synchronous ("chorusing together") interchanges and transitions.

Yet some of these features showed culturally specific features. Comparisons to American infant-mother interactions highlight differences in the behavior of the Gusii mother (Tronick, Als, & Brazeltons, 1980b).* We think these differences reflect Gusii cultural regulations of face-to-face interaction and the expression of intense emotions. Gusii mothers play and talk to their infants a similar proportion of time as do American mothers, 31% versus 32%, but the duration of these two phases among the Gusii (1.4 and 1.2 seconds, respectively) is shorter than for the American mothers (3.6 and 3.4 seconds). Gusii mothers look away from the infant a greater proportion of time than do American mothers (7% of the time versus 4.8% for Phases 1 and 2). Both of these comparisons suggest a different investment in sustaining affectively charged episodes, because avert behaviors serve to dampen and diffuse any buildup of affective display and to limit its duration. Play sequences of short duration do not allow time for this buildup of affect to occur either. A smooth, even interaction appears to be the goal for the Gusii mothers. This contention is supported by the fact that Gusii mother-infant interactions achieve a match state 40% of the time, whereas American interactions achieve it only 19.8%. The interactions are in steady balance between partners most commonly, and as a result there is a certain monotony or evenness to them. They do not show the peaks of affective excitement seen in interaction in this country. Only 8.1% of the time are the Gusii interactions in joint positive states (talk or play) as compared to 17% in joint positive states in American interactions. Synchrony is achieved most frequently in the neutrally engaged states (12% American vs. 20.6% Gusii).

Differences do not appear to be related to the availability of the Gusii infants. The infants' behavior on the tapes and as analyzed by the microscoring system looks like that of American infants. Fully 32% of the time they are in play or talk as compared to 19% of the time for American infants. Talk, the more excited of the two phases, accounts for most of this difference, 13% versus 3%. Of critical importance is that 39% of the time when the infant goes to play or talk, the Gusii mother goes to set or monitor (Phases 3 and 5), and 5% of the time she goes to avert/avoid (Phases 1 and 2). The mother's response to these displays of positive affect seem to be to dampen, diffuse, or diminish the affective level of the interaction. In the United States the goal for mothers seems to be to build upon, amplify, or extend these infant behaviors. Every attempt is made to sustain play and talk episodes up to the limits of the infant's capacities.

Expansion and elaboration of the infant's displays is the usual response for U.S. mothers. Gusii mothers do not appear to want this high intensity in the interactions with their infants; their behavior reflects this difference. They have a repertoire of repetitive vocalizations, taps, head nods, and fixed facial expressions. These stylized behaviors give an evenness, a flatness to the interactions. The analysis of the size of state transitions supports and specifies those clinical impressions of the steadiness and regularity of the Gusii interactions. American

*American mother-infant interactions have been described using the monadic phase system and this study is presented descriptively here as a contrast to the Gusii data only. The data are published in detail elsewhere (Tronick, Als, & Brazelton, 1980b).

mothers change among phases in one-step units 38% of the time and in two-step units 51% of the time. The two-step changes serve to heighten and exaggerate the interaction, to turn up the "gain." Gusii mothers change 71% of the time in one-step units and only 17% of the time in two-step units. This would seem to lessen the exaggerated quality of their behavior and the affective intensity of the interaction. The interaction remains contained within a narrow range of affect and attention. This containment reflects the mothers' underlying concern about the experience as well as the expression of intense emotion in any interpersonal exchange. Such intensity may be dangerous, and the anxiety that is produced by this buildup demands to be quickly diffused. The narrow range of the state transitions represents a very automatic fine tuning of the interaction in response to culturally determined rules for interpersonal exchange. These observations do not imply that the Gusii mothers are unresponsive to their own individual infants. They respond sensitively to their infants' behaviors, as shown by the frequency with which they match their own behavior to that of their infant and the frequency with which they alter their behavior after the infant makes a transition in the interaction (34% of the time). Even the occurrence of negative phases (1 and 2) seems to be linked to the infant's behavior episodes of positive display rather than either randomly or as markers of disinterest. The mother's modulation of the interaction speaks to a sensitivity to the infant within a matrix of culture-specific expectancies and goals.

These comparisons add clarification to the goals of American mothers' face-to-face interactions. American mothers behave in a fashion that intensifies the level of affect expressed; they share the infant's most excited behaviors. Intensity of interaction may represent a prototype of expectations for our children's interactions with other people and events in their environment. We value an individualistic, dynamic, and aggressive approach to life in general and to interpersonal experience in particular. The interactions we have with our children appear to reflect these goals and to prepare our children to be ready for this intensity. A strong sense of self as a separate, autonomous individual is built within these early interactions with sensitive caretakers (Kohut, 1971). This may be appropriate for a culture dependent on individual initiative and assertiveness. The interactions of mother and infant can be seen as uniquely suited to the cultural goals and expectations.

The long-term adaptiveness of the Gusii behavior in social encounters can be seen by looking at it in context. Tribal solidarity is essential for the survival of a small tribe surrounded by unrelated neighbors. Close living situations for an extended family, with sons, their several cowives and their children, all living off the same land, put many stresses on the interpersonal sphere. Extremes of negative affective display could cause family disruptions and even tribal divisions; extremes of positive affect set up jealousies or reveal dangerously sensitive areas of the self. Both extremes are to be avoided. One's self must be defined not by unique characteristics, but rather by participation in the kin system and by being a good worker in one's expected role (LeVine, 1980b). The elaborate set of implicit and explicit rules that govern social interaction are designed to protect the Gusii from those dangerous extremes and to reinforce compliance with role expectation. They serve to preserve a constancy and evenness in all the affairs of life that is clearly economical and advantageous to all members. Greater self-assertiveness or even conspicuous self-esteem do not meet these societal needs.

The Gusii infant is learning these lessons in his own culture at a very young age. In the earliest interactions with his mother, he is shown how to ration the periods of intense affective display carefully, to keep them under control and to avoid the dangerous extremes. Individual initiative is contained within firm boundaries. The definition of self is made within an implicit set of rules that give clear messages as to the expectations of those around him. Repetitiveness and formality safeguard interactions within safe limits.

Face-to-face interaction appears to have an underlying universal structure that is modified by specific cultural goals and expectancies. As in Caudill and Weinstein's (1969) studies, it is striking how early these cultural aspects begin to permeate the infant-caregiver interaction. It is our feeling that the interaction does not simply reflect the developmental process but rather forms the base of that process. That is, the infant's cumulative and iterative daily experiences of engagement in a culturally specific universal form shapes the infant's development of self.

PART III

INFANT SOCIAL-EMOTIONAL
INTERACTION

Interactive Mismatch and Repair: Challenges to the Coping Infant

Researchers on infancy—we among them—have typically talked about mother-infant interaction in terms of synchrony, reciprocity, matching, coherence, and attunement. These descriptions attempt to capture those periods of engagement that say that all is well in the young infant-mother partnership. For the individual, they are times of pleasure and delight.

We expected to see many such periods as we studied face-to-face interaction of 18 normal mother-infant pairs when the babies were 3, 6, and 9 months old. Our study population was in many ways optimal: Mothers had averaged two years' post–high school education; infants had been born after uneventful pregnancies; all were from intact families and lived in the bucolic surroundings of Amherst, Massachusetts.

But our videotapes of mother-infant interactions had some surprises in store. First, infants were in social play only 15% of the observation time at 3 months, 13% at 6 months, and 25% at 9 months. Second, the variability of play among these infants was quite large. Third, the proportions of observation time that infants and mothers were in matching behavioral states—for example, mother in play and infant in play; mother and infant looking at one another; or mother and infant sharing attention to objects—were 28% at 3 months, 30% at 6 months, and 34% at 9 months. We define such matches as acting the same way at the same time. When we examined matched periods of play alone, the proportions were even smaller—13%, 10%, and 21% at 3, 6, and 9 months. The variability, again, was large (Figure 11.1).

We wondered about this large portion of the time when mother and infant were not displaying positive emotions and especially about the 70% of the time when mother and infant were not in matching stage, were not in synchrony.

FIGURE 11.1. Proportion of mother-infant matches in any state (any match), matches in social play (soc. match) (with standard deviation).

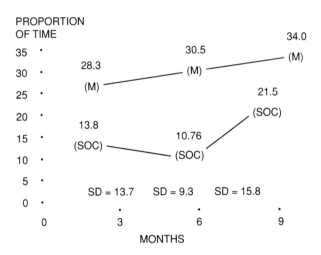

"STRESS BUILDS CHARACTER"

Our view begins with the injunction New England has been preaching to the rest of the country for years: Stress builds character. Specifically, there is often a mismatch between the infant's expectations and the state of the interaction, or between the behaviors of the partner and the behaviors of the infant. These mismatches stress the infant by generating negative emotions, but the infant has coping behaviors for repairing them to turn a mismatch into a match and the negative emotions into positive emotions. Developmentally, the experience of repairing these mismatches has several positive benefits for the infant. First, the infant's sense of effectance or mastery is increased. Second, his coping capacities are elaborated. And third, following Spitz's formulation, with the reiteration and accumulation of the experience of successfully repairing mismatches in his daily interactions with his mother, the infant internalizes a pattern of interactive coping that he brings to interactions with other partners. Indeed, to the extent that the infant successfully copes, to that extent will the infant experience positive emotions and establish a positive affective core.

But there is a darker side to the New England injunction: The infant who employs his coping strategies unsuccessfully and repeatedly fails to repair mismatches begins to feel helpless. This infant eventually gives up attempting to repair the mismatches and increasingly focuses his coping behavior on self-regulation in order to control the negative emotion generated. He internalizes a pattern of coping that limits engagement with the social environment and establishes a negative affective core. Ironically, when this infant utilizes these coping behaviors in potentially normal interactions, they distort those interactions as well, engendering a cycle that reinforces his inwardly focused style of coping, a style that may eventually become pathological.

COPING BEHAVIORS OF THE INFANT

What coping behaviors does the infant have? Gianino, following Brazelton and Beebe, has described six coping behaviors utilized by infants (Table 11.1). First, the infant can signal his partner with his emotional displays and other behaviors to correct the mismatch. For example, frowns communicate the infant's dissatisfaction with the interaction and convey the message "change what you are doing." If signaling does not work, the infant can focus on himself, that is, self-comfort, and buffer himself from the interactive stress. The infant can also focus on objects. If these do not work, the infant can attempt to disengage from the interactive stress by withdrawing, averting, or even trying to escape.

These strategies are crucially different from one another. When the infant utilizes his emotional signaling skills, he preserves his goal of maintaining social engagement. When he switches to objects, he gives up that goal. And when the infant utilizes any of the other coping strategies, he sacrifices social engagement and even engagement with objects in order to maintain internal

---

TABLE 11.1   Infant Coping Behaviors

1. SIGNAL: Infant acts in a way that function to modify mother's behavior.
   Positive—Signalling with positive affective tone, e.g., coo face
   Neutral—Signalling with neutral affective tone e.g., pick-me-up gesture
   Negative—Signalling with negative affective tone, e.g., fuss

2. ALTERNATE FOCUS: Infant focuses attention on something other than mother.
   Object—Infant focuses on object with or without manipulation of it, e.g., strap of chair
   Self—Infant focuses on part of own body, e.g., toes

3. SELF-COMFORT: The infant uses own body or object to provide self-comforting stimulation
   Oral—Sucks on part of body or object, e.g., fingers
   Self-Clasp—Clasps hands together
   Rock—Infant rocks from side to side or to and fro

4. WITHDRAWAL: Infant utilizes motor, attentional and perceptive processes to minimize social engagement.
   Motor—Infant gives-up postual control
   Perceptual—Infant looks "dull'" or "glassy-eyed'"

5. ESCAPE: Infant attempts to increase his physical distance from mother by turning, twisting or arching away.

6. AVERT/SCAN: Infant looks away from the mother but does not successfully maintain attention to something else.

emotional regulation. Thus self-regulation and interactive regulation are two sides of one regulatory process.

To demonstrate the infant's repertoire of coping behaviors, we presented infants in our study with an unresolvable mismatch: the challenge of the still-faced mother. In the still-face manipulation, the mother is in the normal face-to-face position with her infant, but she remains expressionless and unresponsive. It is as if the mother is saying hello and good-bye at the same time, leaving the infant trapped between the two messages. In early work with T. Berry Brazelton, we had described a pattern of eliciting, but we had seen other coping patterns as well. In this study, we wanted to document these other coping patterns and to evaluate if these infants evidenced stable individual differences if coping.

In fact, our videotapes of infants and their still-faced mothers amply illustrated the variety of coping behaviors these babies used to attempt repair of the mismatch of the still face. Some infants would repeatedly engage in positive elicits with smiles and vocalization. Other infants utilized negative elicits. Some mixed the two together. Other infants looked over at the mother and turned toward objects and did not look at the mother again. And some displayed stress and ragged breathing and fingering but were unable to elicit or turn toward objects, but could only self-comfort and stare into space.

INDIVIDUAL DIFFERENCES AND STABILITY IN COPING BEHAVIOR

To examine whether or not there were individual differences, or stability in coping behaviors, Gianino, Plimpton, and Tronick had 52 6-month-olds confront their mothers engaging in the still face on two occasions 10 days apart. They found strong and consistent evidence for stability in infant coping styles. Infants demonstrated stability in utilizing signaling, self-comforting, and focusing on objects (Table 11.2). In fact, they even demonstrated stability for the type of signals and type of self-comforting they employed.

These results are intriguing because they suggest that preferential orientations toward others, the self, and the world of things may already be in place by 6 months of age. As hypothesized by generations of psychodynamic therapists, these orientations may potentially be predictive of certain patterns of personality development and defensive patterns. But our observations occurred during experimentally produced stress. Could we see the same type of coping behavior in the normal interaction?

INFANT COPING WITH NORMAL INTERACTIVE STRESS

Normal interactive stress arises from many causes—mistiming of emotional signals, unclear signals, misreading of signals, differences in goals, and overloading or underloading of stimulation. More simply put, these stresses occur

TABLE 11.2　Correlation of Proportion of Time Spent in Different Coping Behaviors from Time 1 to Time 2

	RT1-T2
Signalling	43**
Positive	50**
Neutral	29**
Negative	35**
Self-Comforting	35**
Oral Self	31**
Oral Other	36**
Alternate Focus Objects	28**

*P < .05
**P < .01

because it is impossible for mother or infant to maintain mutual regulation over the course of an entire interaction. These stresses are normal, typical, and inherent to an interaction.

In one sequence we observed, for example, an infant was looking at her chair and comforting herself by sucking her finger. The mother attempted to elicit her attention, but the infant avoided her by looking first to one side, then the other. The mother then removed the baby's hand from her mouth. The mother moved back slightly, they established eye contact, and both smiled.

In another segment, we saw a mother establish eye contact with the infant, who averted, however, as the mother moved in closer. When the mother decreased some of her activity, the infant smiled, but when the mother moved in closer, the infant averted again.

Data analysis of these tapes of infants attempting to repair normally occurring mismatches demonstrated that when infants were confronted by a mismatch, 34% of these mismatches were repaired to a matching state by the next step in the interaction and 36% of the remaining mismatches were repaired by the second step. In other words, normal infants and their mothers are constantly moving into mismatch states and are then successfully repairing them. Furthermore, we found evidence that the infant's experience in repairing normal interactive mismatches was strongly related to the coping behaviors that baby employed when confronted by the more extreme interactive stress of the mother in still face. Using a scale developed in our laboratory by Ricks, we found that infants whose mothers were more responsive to their signals during the normal interaction were more likely to signal their mothers during the still face, less likely to evidence distress, and less likely to engage in scanning, a sign of disorganization. Similarly, in a preliminary analysis of a small number of subjects, we found that infants who experienced more repairs of mismatched states during the normal interaction were more likely to positively signal their mother and significantly less likely to utilize negative signals during the still face.

COPING STYLES REFLECTING FAILURE: INFANTS
OF DEPRESSED MOTHERS

If the kinds of coping behaviors we observed are beginning to stabilize by 6 months of age and if infants' experiences in the normal interaction are related to how they cope with stress, we would expect that infants who experience unrepaired mismatches on a constant basis would begin to stabilize coping styles that reflect that failure. In particular, they would become increasingly withdrawn and sad in their affect; they would resort to coping strategies that focused on self-regulation, and they would give up attempts to repair the interaction.

The work of Greenspan, Field, Clark, Zahn-Waxler, and others suggested that maternal depression would present the infant with such a stress. But before we studied real depression, we developed an experimental manipulation with Jeff Cohn in which mothers simulated depression. We asked mothers to flatten their facial expression, talk in a monotone, move slowly, and sit away from the infant—to act the way they do on the days they feel blue. (Normal mothers had no trouble following these instructions.) We saw this manipulation as more stressful than the still face, because though many of the mother's actions in the simulation are contingent on the infant's actions, they are inappropriate and produce repeated mismatches.

In one sequence, for example, an infant slumped in his chair and turned away from his mother. He did glance at her several times, but even when she straightened him up, he slumped away from her on the other side and eventually fussed and cried.

Our next step was to carry out a naturalistic study of 7-month-old infants whose mothers evidenced depressive symptoms and other signs of disturbance. This was done with Jeff Cohn, Karlon Lyons-Ruth, and Dave Connell. Findings from our preliminary analyses were similar to what we saw in the simulated depression study except that these infants looked much more distressed and disengaged than did the infants in the simulated situation. We found that:

- During face-to-face play, the depressed mothers engaged in positive social play less than 10% of the observation time and they looked away from their infants 20% of the time. Normal mothers engaged in play about 40% of the time and, as Stern has shown, almost never looked away.
- Infants of depressed mothers were only in social play about 5% of the time, whereas infants of normal mothers were in play about 13% of the time. We also observed a marked decrease in the percentage of time the infants of depressed mothers were able to focus on objects. In normal interactions, the 6-month-old infant spent about 41% of the time looking at objects, but infants of depressed mothers looked at objects only 20%

of the time. Not only, then, has prolonged exposure to this distortion of maternal behavior disturbed these infants' capacity to play, but it has even disrupted their engagement with the inanimate environment.

- Most important, just as we found in the normal interactions, there was a strong relation between what the mother did and what the infant did: Mothers who were more emotionally positive, even minimally so, had infants who were more positive—the correlation of maternal play and infant play was .51. Mothers who engaged in more intrusive behaviors, such as expressions of anger, had infants who looked away more—the correlation of maternal intrusiveness and infant avert was .54. Mothers who averted from their infants had infants who were more likely to protest—the correlation was .87.

SUMMARY AND DISCUSSION

Normal infants, in normal interactions with adults, experience a large number of mismatches in the interaction. Infants have coping behaviors for repairing the interactive mismatches and maintaining self-regulation, coping behaviors which are in large part successful and which begin to stabilize at around 6 months of age. Most important, the normal infant's use of coping behaviors is related to his experience in repairing mismatches in the normal interaction. When infants experience atypical interaction or unresolvable mismatches, as in the case of maternal depression, they decrease their deployment of coping skills aimed at repairing the interaction or even at maintaining engagement with the inanimate environment. More and more babies deploy coping behaviors aimed at maintaining self-regulation.

From this perspective, the pathways to normalcy or psychopathology appear as part of the same developmental process. The central event of the process is the mismatch. The critical developmental experience has to do with whether or not the infant's coping behaviors successfully repair the mismatch and maintain or fail to maintain self-regulation. We see no single traumatic juncture separating these pathways—only the slowly accumulated and eventually internalized experiences of the infant over time. When the coping functions well, the infant is able simultaneously to maintain self- and interactive regulation; when these twin achievements are not possible, self-regulation becomes the predominant goal.

Psychopathology may be an outcome of repeated unsuccessful efforts to repair mismatches. We have hypothesized that defensive behaviors can evolve out of the infant's attempts to cope with a history of chronic mismatches in his primary social relationships. The infant's interactive experience, constrained by possible temperamental qualities such as the orientations toward object engagement, people, or self-comforting that we uncovered, teaches the infant which coping behaviors are most effective in regulating his distress. But the transition from coping to defense occurs when the infant begins to employ his coping behaviors automatically, inflexibly, and indiscriminantly. Behaviors become defensive because they are adopted to preclude the experience of interactive stress—that is, to preclude the anxiety generated by the infant's interactive history. Such behaviors are unrelated to the infant's actual and current interactive situation. They are deployed even when they restrict his immediate and longer term options; even if they curtail his autonomy. The infant seems to need to self-regulate his affective state whatever the cost.

This view does not require that the infant be able to make a distinction between self and other in order to repair mismatches. In fact, it may be advantageous to an infant with a sensitive partner not to make the distinction, and instead to believe that all changes emanate from himself, since the resulting well-regulated interaction will further his sense of effectance. On the other hand, the inability to distinguish between self and other can be disadvantageous—indeed, deleterious—when the interactive partner is insensitive. In these circumstances, the infant's inability to discriminate the actual source of his distress will teach him that he is incapable of exerting any control over the social realm.

If we are to use these concepts and observations for assessment, attempting to predict future problems in a mother-infant relationship, we need to see synchrony or reciprocity or matching as the outcome of an active process of infant and mother coping. While its achievement marks the success of that process, it is the process of interactive mutual regulation, the process of coping and repairing mismatches, that is critical to the infant's development. We should expect to see dissynchrony in the normal interaction. We should also expect to see infant and mother persistently deploying coping behaviors to repair their mismatches and sometimes achieving success.

Following an examination of normal interaction, an assessment might also include a look at the infant coping with the still-faced mother. Like Ainsworth's strange situation, this experience is an age-appropriate stress. It is our belief that the infant's reaction to the still face reveals his expectations, based on the interaction's history and his affective core, and may predict the future. For us, seeing fusses, protests, and averts during the still face is a sign that the infant has an expectancy of a normally regulated interaction which is being violated. Indeed, we initially give a similar interpretation to much of the negative behaviors we see in normal interactions. We then look at the infant's reaction to the still face to see if he is telling us by his reaction to this stress that his usual interactive experience is appropriate.

We have so far focused on the mother as the disorganizing agent in the interaction. But she is not the only agent and may not even be the primary agent of disorganization. An infant is immature, has limited regulatory capacities, is slow to process and slow to respond. He is a difficult interactive partner. Much disorganization comes from the infant, but once disorganization starts to stabilize it no longer matters who was the initial cause. Both partners become complicit in maintaining the disorganization.

How can one intervene to undo this disorganization? It may be useful to provide infant and mother each with opportunities for satisfying interactive experiences with other partners. It is expected that these experiences will allow them to develop new interactive patterns that can then be brought into their own interaction. However, disorganization of an interaction, while a sign of a possible problem, may not require immediate intervention. "Holding back but still holding" the dyad may allow adult and infant the opportunity to experience the positive benefits of reparation. Such a strategy should also convey confidence in their capacities to cope; we believe that the dyad itself generates a more stable organization than the organization that occurs when we cut the reparation process short.

One more finding may help to focus us on this process and suggest new areas of exploration. In our study of Amherst mothers and their infants, we found that at 6 and 9 months of age, mother-daughter pairs were much more likely to be in match states than were mother-son pairs. This finding raises questions about the differential development of a sense of effectance, empathy, and coping skills in girls and boys. However, it serves to emphasize the potential centrality of the mismatch and its resolution as part of a normal developmental process.

CHAPTER 12

Emotions and Emotional Communication in Infants

How is it that some children become sad, withdrawn, and lacking in self-esteem, whereas others become angry, unfocused, and brittlely self-assertive, whereas still others become happy, curious, affectionate, and self-confident? As clinicians, researchers, and policymakers, our goal must be to understand the processes that lead to these outcomes, not just to generate indexes of them, so that problematic and compromised developmental outcomes can be prevented and remediated. Although the nature of these processes is not yet known, an answer is taking shape on the basis of recent work on the nature of infant-caretaker emotional communication.

The emerging answer is that the infant and adult are participants in an affective communication system. A central hypothesis is that the operation of this system has a major influence on how well the infant accomplishes his or her goals, the emotions the infant experiences, and the infant's developmental outcome. If this hypothesis is correct, then the key issue is to understand how this system works. We need to explore the inextricable links among infant emotions and behavior, caretaker emotions and behavior, and the success, failure, and reparation of interactive errors that the infant experiences when striving to accomplish his or her goals. Two contrasting examples of infant-mother interaction drawn from the work of Brazelton (Brazelton, Koslowski, & Main, 1974) will serve as a base for the initial exploration of the functioning of this affective communication system.

Imagine two infant-mother pairs playing the game of peekaboo. In the first, the infant abruptly turns away from his mother as the game reaches its "peek" of intensity and begins to suck on his thumb and stare into space with a dull facial expression. The mother stops playing and sits back, watching her infant. After a few seconds, the infant turns back to her with an interested and inviting expression. The mother moves closer, smiles, and says in a high-pitched, exaggerated voice, "Oh, now you're back!" He smiles in response and vocalizes. As they finish crowing together, the infant reinserts his thumb and looks away. The mother again waits. After a few seconds the infant turns back to her, and they greet each other with big smiles.

Imagine a second similar situation, except that after this infant turns away, she does not look back at her mother. The mother waits but then leans over into the infant's line of vision while clicking her tongue to attract her attention. The infant, however, ignores the mother and continues to look away. Undaunted, the mother persists and moves her head closer to the infant. The infant grimaces and fusses while she pushes at the mother's face. Within seconds, she turns even further away from her mother and continues to suck on her thumb.

I will not yet focus on the issue of who is responsible for the interactional errors in the second example. Instead, I will focus on the critical feature in each interaction: that the affective communications of each infant and mother actually change the emotional experience and behavior of the other. In both illustrations, the infants' looking away and thumb sucking convey the message that the infants need to calm down and regulate their emotional state. Each mother respects this message by waiting. Within seconds, the first infant looks back at his mother, communicating that he is ready to interact, and the mother responds by moving in closer with a smile, which her infant returns. Their smiles communicate their positive evaluations of what they are doing. In the second illustration, the mother waits but then disregards the infant's message and makes a vigorous attempt to solicit the infant's attention. The mother comes in closer and actively signals her infant to change what she is doing and attend to her. The infant responds by sharply turning away with strong negative affect, communicating to her mother that she should change what she is doing. The mother, however, ignores this message, and the infant becomes even more affectively negative as she tries to cope with her mother's continuing intrusiveness.

Now imagine that these episodes are prototypical for each dyad. That is, the first dyad routinely experiences reciprocal positive exchanges in which interactive errors are readily repaired, whereas the second dyad experiences repeated conflictual negative exchanges. There is no need to overcharacterize these interactions. Certainly, the first dyad experiences some conflictual interactions, and the second some reciprocal positive interactions. Given the difference in the balance of positive and negative exchanges in the two, however, it is hypothesized that the first infant will develop a tendency to look at his mother more, exhibit more positive affect, and experience less distress when he experiences stress than the second infant. The second infant, by contrast, will be more withdrawn and will exhibit more sadness. There is evidence to support this prediction (as I will show later), but first I will examine some of the theoretical assumptions underlying this hypothesis.

EMOTIONS, GOALS, AND OTHER- AND
SELF-DIRECTED REGULATORY BEHAVIORS

To begin with, infants, like all other creatures, have a multiplicity of goals (Bowlby, 1982; Trevarthen, 1974). These include goals for engaging the social and inanimate environments (e.g., interacting with others, maintaining proximity to the caretaker, engaging in interactions characterized by mutual delight and reciprocity, and acting on objects) and internal goals (e.g., maintaining homeostasis, establishing a feeling of security, experiencing positive emotions, and controlling negative emotions). To accomplish these goals, infants process information about their current state in relation to their goal. They evaluate whether they are succeeding or failing and then use that evaluation to guide actions aimed at accomplishing their goal or redirecting their efforts to other goals (Tronick, 1980). For instance, the first infant in the earlier example fulfills his interactive goal by affectively signaling his mother when he is ready to interact by looking at her and smiling. He also fulfills his goal to control his emotional state by turning away and sucking on his thumb. Thus, the infant is active, not passive.

Emotions play a critical part in this evaluative process. An evaluation by the infant that the goal is being accomplished results in a positive emotional state—joy or interest—motivating further engagement (e.g., the first infant smiles and continues to look at his mother). When the infant's evaluation is that the goal is not being accomplished, the infant experiences negative emotions. More specifically, if the infant's evaluation is that the obstacle blocking the achievement of the goal can be overcome, an emotional state of anger results, and the infant is motivated to try to remove the obstacle (e.g., the second infant has an angry facial expression and pushes her mother away). However, an evaluation that the obstacle cannot be overcome results in sadness and disengagement (e.g., the second infant eventually withdraws). Thus emotions motivate and organize the infant's behavior rather than disrupting it (Campos, Barrett, Lamb, Goldsmith, & Sternberg, 1983; Izard, 1978a).

Obviously, infants are not born fully equipped to accomplish these goals on their own. Infants' capacities are immature, limited, and poorly coordinated. Moreover, disruptions of infants' ongoing activities come from both inside and outside (e.g., from internal physiological states, such as hunger and uncontrolled affect, as well as from external obstacles). Given these limitations and disruptions, why don't infants typically fail to achieve their goals and continuously experience negative emotions?

To oversimplify, the answer is that the infant is part of an affective communication system in which the infant's goal-directed strivings are aided and supplemented by the capacities of the caretaker. An infant's affective displays function as messages that specify the infant's evaluation of whether he or she is succeeding in achieving a goal. The caretaker "reads" this message and uses it to guide his or her actions for facilitating the infant's strivings. Gianino and Tronick (1988) have labeled these affective displays *other-directed regulatory behaviors* to capture their function of regulating the behavior of the infant's partner.

Consider the following example, in which the infant's goal is to get a just-out-of-reach object. The 6-month-old infant stretches his hands out toward the object. Because he cannot get hold of it, he becomes angry and distressed. He looks away for a moment and sucks on his thumb. Calmer, he looks back at the object and reaches for it once more. But this attempt fails too, and he gets angry again. The caretaker watches for a moment, then soothingly talks to him. The infant calms down and, with a facial expression of interest, gazes at the object and makes another attempt to reach for it. The caretaker brings the object just within the infant's reach. The infant successfully grasps the object, explores it, and smiles. In this illustration, the caretaker reads the infant's affective displays, uses this information to facilitate the infant's goal-directed activities, and helps to change the infant's emotional state. More specifically, the caretaker is responsible for the reparation of the infant's failure into success and the simultaneous transformation of his negative emotion into a positive emotion (Gianino & Tronick, 1988).

There is a second important feature to this illustration. The infant is not solely dependent on the caretaker to control the negative affect he experiences. He has several coping behaviors available: looking away, self-comforting, and even self-stimulation. These behaviors control the infant's negative affect by shifting his or her attention away from a disturbing event or substituting positive for negative stimulation (Rothbart & Derryberry, 1984). For example, looking away reduces infants' heart rates during stress, and thumb sucking can calm distressed infants.

Gianino and Tronick (1988) have labeled these coping behaviors *self-directed regulatory behaviors*, suggesting that they function to control and change the infant's own affective state (Beebe & Stern, 1977). When successful, these behaviors, like the infant's other-directed regulatory behaviors, shift the infant's negative emotional state to a more positive emotional state so he or she can pursue goal-directed engagements with people and objects. In the aforementioned example, the infant attempted to reach the object again only after calming himself down by looking away and sucking on his thumb.

Clearly, the distinction between self-directed and other-directed behavior is not hard and fast. Self-directed behavior can function as communication, conveying the infant's evaluation of success or failure and his or her emotional state to a caregiver. The caregiver may then act on this communication to aid the infant's accomplishment of internal and external goals. This also occurred in the illustration.

Other-directed and self-directed regulatory behaviors are part of the infant's normal repertoire for coping with sadness, uncontrolled anger, and the extremes of positive affect, which can turn into distress. They enable the infant to control the potential disruptive effects of these emotions and their extremes on his or her goal-directed activities. These coping behaviors make it possible for the infant to accomplish the dual simultaneous tasks of controlling his or her emotional state while interacting with people or acting on the inanimate world.

Some of the most dramatic effects of regulatory behaviors on infant emotions are seen when the mother's behavior is manipulated so that the infant is prevented from successfully achieving the goal for reciprocal interaction. Such manipulations may involve distorting the mother's affective behavior by instructing her to act in an unresponsive manner (i.e., remaining still faced while looking at her infant) or to behave in a disruptive manner (i.e., interacting in an emotionally flat and withdrawn fashion, which simulates the disengagement of some depressed mothers; Cohn & Tronick, 1983; Tronick, 1980).

Confronted by these manipulations, most 3-month-old infants initially signal to their mothers with facial expressions, vocalizations, and gestures in an attempt to get their mothers to resume their normal behavior. The infants' message is that their mothers should change what they are doing. When these other-directed behaviors fail to achieve that goal, the infants express negative emotions and use self-directed regulatory behaviors in an attempt to control their emotional responses. They look away and self-comfort. These reactions occur even when the mothers are still faced for only a few seconds. Moreover, the infants' negative affect and utilization of self-directed regulatory behaviors do not end simply upon the resumption of normal behavior by their mothers, Rather, there is a continuation of the infants' negative mood and reduction in visual regard of their mothers for the next few minutes. This finding suggests that even 3-month-old infants are not simply under the control of the immediate stimulus situation but that events have lasting effects, that is, they are internally represented. These effects will be related to defensive behavior and psychopathology later in this chapter. For now, I will focus on the implication from these studies that infant emotions are specific and meaningful reactions to the infant's active processing and appreciation of the mother's and others' affective behavior.

THE ORGANIZED NATURE OF INFANT EMOTIONS

Two-month-old infants make a fundamental distinction between people and objects (Brazelton et al., 1974; Trevarthen, 1974). Prereaching infants presented with an object look intently at it, sit up straight, remain relatively still, and punctuate their fixed gaze with swiping movements and brief glances away. Presented with people, infants' posture is more relaxed, and their movements are smoother. They become active at a slower pace and then look away for longer periods of time than they do with objects. Furthermore, infants give full greeting responses to people but not to objects. Simply stated, infants communicate with people and act instrumentally on objects.

Young infants can also discriminate the facial expressions of others (Malatesta & Izard, 1984). For example, infants look more at facial expressions of joy than anger. More significantly, it appears that the emotional content of different maternal emotional expressions are appreciated by infants (i.e., they lead to different infant emotions). When newborns are in a quiet, alert state, looking at them and gently talking to them can produce a smile. Wolff (1963) described how the infant's smile is first regularly elicited by a vocalization and then by the face. More recent research suggests that 10-week-old infants react to maternal facial and vocal displays of anger with anger but have fewer angry responses when their mothers pose sadness (Lelwica & Haviland, 1983). Moreover, infant reactions are even influenced by their appreciation of the context surrounding the event (e.g., a mother wearing a mask elicits laughter, whereas a stranger wearing the same mask elicits distress and fear; see Sroufe, 1979a).

Campos and his colleagues (Campos et al., 1983) made a classic observation of how 10-month-old infants appreciate (i.e., appraise; Bowlby, 1982) the affective expressions of others and modify their own actions on the basis of that appreciation. They found that when 10-month-old infants are exploring the surface of the visual cliff (i.e., an apparatus that presents an apparent but not real drop-off), they will look to their mothers when they come to the "drop-off" if the apparent depth is ambiguous as to its "danger." When their mothers pose a fearful or angry face, most infants will not cross. But when their mothers pose a joyful face, most infants will cross. Infants react similarly to maternal vocalizations conveying fear or joy. Interestingly, the expressions and vocalizations of other adults have a similar effect. It is remarkable that infants actively seek out affective information from another person not only to supplement their information about the event but even to override their own appreciation and perception of the event. Clearly, the emotional state of others is of fundamental importance to the infant's emotional state. And carefully note that this importance is not the result of passive processes such as mirroring. Rather, it results from the infant's active use of another's emotional expression in forming his or her appreciation of an event and using it to guide action.

Infants are well equipped to convey their appreciations and their emotional states. Young infants make nearly all the muscle movements that are used by adults to express the primary emotions (Ekman & Oster, 1979). Izard (1978a) has identified facial expressions of interest, joy, disgust, surprise, and distress in young infants. Weinberg (1989) and Hamilton (1989) have identified facial expressions of sadness and anger in 3- to 6-month-olds, Furthermore, a quite dramatic phenomenon is that newborns can imitate the components of the facial expressions of surprise, fear, and sadness (Field, Woodson, Cohen, Garcia, & Greenberg, 1983). Although these findings on imitation are controversial, they provide evidence of infants' ability to discriminate facial expressions and their ability to express that discrimination in differentiated ways. Hand postures and variations in motor tone are also indicative of infant affective behavioral states, as are variations of infant vocalizations (Fogel & Hannan, 1985; Papousek & Papousek, 1987).

Far less work is available on the relations among different expressive systems. However, Weinberg (1989) has found that in normal interactions, specific facial expressions are related to specific behaviors. In 6-month-olds, for example, facial expressions of joy are more likely to occur when the infant is looking at the mother, positively vocalizing, and using gestural signals, whereas facial expressions of sadness occur when the infant is looking away and fussing, but not crying. These data demonstrate well the organized quality of the infant's affective system.

Varied and differentiated as the infant's affective repertoire is, it may still be underestimated. The variety and subtlety of facial expressions still elude our categorical schemes. Mow many types of smiles are there? How many forms are there of what we broadly label distress?

Moreover, past research has focused too much on facial expressions and not enough on gestures, postures, and vocalizations and their relations. Most critically, researchers need to put the infant in situations that evoke infant goals, evaluations, and strivings in order to elicit the infant's full affective repertoire. If this is not done, then the repertoire will not be available for observation. In these situations, researchers also must carefully consider moods rather than just the brief affective expressions they have concentrated on in the past. Recurrent moods, or what Emde (1983) has referred to as the infant's affective core, are critical to infant functioning because they systematically modify the infant's experience of events and bias the infant's response to them.

Regardless of what the infant's affective repertoire is eventually discovered to be, it is well established that parents are acutely sensitive to their infant's emotional expressions and behavior. Parents attend to their infant's direction of gaze and modify their behavior on the basis of it. They maintain a somewhat distant (40 cm) observational distance when their infant is looking at something other than themselves, but they move to a dialogic distance of about 22.5 cm when their infant looks at them (Papousek & Papousek, 1987). Parents also "frame" their infant's gaze by looking at their infant until the infant looks away from them (Kaye & Fogel, 1980). Cohn and Tronick (1987) have found that when the infant looks away, parents use facial expressions, vocalizations, and gestures to solicit their infant's attention back to themselves, but that when eye-to-eye contact is established, parents change their affective behavior. For instance, parents often give an initial greeting in which they tilt their head slightly back, raise their eyebrows, and open their eyes and mouth wide (Papousek & Papousek, 1987).

Emde (1983) has found that parents categorize infant facial expressions along three dimensions: (a) hedonic tone, from positive to negative affect; (b) activation, from sleep to excitement; and (c) orientation, from internal to external (i.e., sleepy or bored to interested or curious). Most mothers also discriminate the discrete emotions of anger, fear, surprise, joy, interest, and sadness in their 1-month-old infants. The mothers use facial, vocal, and behavioral expressions to make their judgments. Malatesta (Malatesta & Izard, 1984) found further specificity in parental responses to infants' facial expressions of emotion. Mothers respond with contingent imitation to their infants' more fully formed categorical emotional expressions (e.g., anger and joy) than to the more "random" facial movements (e.g., twitches or half smiles). Moreover, infant expressions of sadness and anger produce affective responses of sadness or anger in their mothers.

In sum, parents and other adults appear to operate on the assumption that a child has better information about what he or she wants than they do. Consequently, they attend to and act on a wide range of affective behaviors to aid the child's accomplishment of his or her goals.

NORMAL AND ABNORMAL INFANT-ADULT AFFECTIVE COMMUNICATION

Infant and adult affective communicative capacities make possible mutually coordinated infant-adult interactions. After a decade of controversy, it is now well established that the face-to-face interactions of infants and adults starting as young as 3 months are bidirectional (i.e., mutually regulated) rather than just being the product of adult social skills. That is, infants modify their affective displays and behaviors on the basis of their appreciation of their mothers' affective displays and behavior (Cohn & Tronick, 1987; Lester, Hoffman, & Brazelton, 1985). For instance, infant smiles and vocalizations are contingent on specific maternal affective turn-taking signals (Cohn & Tronick, 1987). Of course, adults make similar modifications.

This coordination has led to characterizations of the mother-infant interaction as typically being reciprocal, synchronous, or coherent These terms and others like them are attempts to capture the quality of the interaction when it is going well. Methods of assessment have been developed on the basis of this type of characterization; that is, a "good interaction" is a coordinated interaction. However, such terms overcharacterize just how well the interaction typically goes. Coordination, regardless of infant age during the first year, is found only about 30% or less of the time in face-to-face interactions, and the transitions from coordinated to miscoordinated states and back to coordinated states occur about once every 3 to 5 seconds (Tronick & Cohn, 1989). Thus, a more accurate characterization of the normal interaction, and a better basis for assessment, is that it moves frequently from affectively positive, mutually coordinated states to affectively negative, miscoordinated states and back again. But if this is the characterization of normal interaction, what is the characterization of abnormal interaction?

I (Tronick, 1980) have summarized several descriptions of infants who chronically experienced miscoordinated interactions. These infants repeatedly engaged in self-directed regulatory behaviors (e.g., they turned away, had dull-looking eyes, lost postural control, orally self-comforted, rocked, and self-clasped). These cases were extreme, but in examining a more typical population of mothers with high levels of depressive symptomatology for depression, Cohn and I (Cohn & Tronick, 1989) have found that not only are the interactions of these mothers and their infants disturbed in ways similar to those seen in the extreme cases but that the affective and regulatory reactions of the infants are related to the affect and behavior of their depressed mothers.

In general, during these interactions there are few periods when infant and mother are mutually positive, and only a few of the interactions evidence any contingency between the infant's and mother's affective behavior. As a group, the depressed mothers look away from their infants more, are angrier and more intrusive, and display less positive affect than normal mothers. Cohn and Tronick (1989) found that 7-month-old infants of the most disengaged mothers show the greatest amounts of protest, that the infants of the most intrusive mothers look away the most, and that the infants of the most positive mothers, little as that is, express more positive affect. Similarly, Hamilton (1989) found that 3-month-old infants' affective expressions are strongly related to maternal reports of their own affect. Three-month-old infants whose mothers reported more anger expressed more anger, whereas infants of mothers who reported more sadness expressed more distress.

My interpretation is that depressed mothers, in different ways for different mothers, fail to appropriately facilitate their infant's goal-directed activities. Their interactive behaviors and affect are poorly timed or often intrusive. Their affective displays are negative (e.g., anger, sadness, irritability), conveying the message that the infant should change what he or she is doing. This message and way of interacting is an obstacle to successful interaction, precludes the infant's achievement of his or her interactive goal, and leads to a predominance of negative affect and self-directed regulatory behavior by the infant. Thus, a general characterization of abnormal interactions is that the participants are stuck in affectively negative miscoordinated interactive states, and their messages calling for change are disregarded.

Now let me return to my opening question: How is it that some children become happy and curious, whereas others become sad and withdrawn, and still others become angry and unfocused? My answer is that these different outcomes are related to the working of the affective communication system in which the infant participates, especially to the balance of the child's experience of success or failure during his or her social-emotional interactions. Gianino and I (Gianino & Tronick, 1988) think of the normal, often-occurring, miscoordinated interactive state as an *interactive error*, and the transition from this miscoordinated state to a coordinated state as an *interactive repair*. The achievement of a coordinated state successfully fulfills the infant's interactive goal and engenders positive affect, whereas an interactive error fails to fulfill that goal and engenders negative affect.

In normal interactions, the infant experiences periods of interactive success and interactive error and frequent reparations of those errors. Emotionally, the infant experiences periods of positive affect and negative affect and frequent transformations of negative to positive affect; hence, experiences of negative emotion are brief. In abnormal interactions, the infant experiences prolonged periods of interactive failure and negative affect, few interactive repairs, and few transformations of negative to positive affect.

Gianino and I (Gianino & Tronick, 1988) have argued that the experience of success and reparation of interactive errors and negative affect that typifies normal interactions has several developmentally enhancing effects that lead to positive outcomes. The experience of interactive reparation and the transformation of negative affect into positive affect allow the infant to elaborate his or her other-directed affective communicative and self-directed regulatory capacities and to use them more effectively, that is, to be able to maintain engagement with the external environment in the face of stress. With the accumulation and reiteration of success and reparation, the infant establishes a positive affective core, with clearer boundaries between self and other (Emde, 1983). From this experience, the infant develops a representation of himself or herself as effective, of his or her interactions as positive and reparable, and of the caretaker as reliable and trustworthy.

In some initial work on normal interactions, Gianino and I (Gianino & Tronick, 1988) found that infants who experience more repairs during normal interactions are more likely to attempt to solicit their mothers' normal behavior when their mothers are acting in a disturbing, stressful manner (i.e., still faced). These infants, on the basis of their experience of normal interactions, have a representation of the interaction as reparable and of themselves as effective in making that repair. Infants who experience fewer repairs are less likely to solicit their mothers and more likely to turn away and become distressed. In addition, infants who exhibit specific affective tendencies, such as smiling or distress, to this stressful behavior by their mothers at a first laboratory visit exhibit similar affective tendencies on a second visit 2 weeks later. Stability across visits was also found for such self-directed regulatory behaviors as self-comforting. Six-month-olds are already establishing an affective coping style and a representation of self and other.

By contrast, in abnormal interactions the chronic experience of failure, nonreparation, and negative affect has several detrimental effects on developmental outcome. The infant establishes a self-directed style of regulatory behavior (i.e., turning away, escaping, becoming perceptually unavailable) to control negative affect and its disruptive effects on goal-directed behavior. Indeed, regulation of negative affect becomes the infant's primary goal and preempts other possible goals. This self-directed style of regulatory behavior precludes the infant's involvement with objects, potentially compromising cognitive development, and distorts the infant's interactions with other people. With the reiteration and accumulation of failure and nonreparation, the infant develops a representation of himself or herself as ineffective and of the caretaker as unreliable.

I (Tronick, 1980) have found that those infants who chronically experienced miscoordinated interactions disengaged from their mothers and the inanimate environment and distorted their interactions with other people. Similar effects are seen in the infants of depressed mothers: They have more negative interactions with unfamiliar adults, and those infants who are more negative during face-to-face interactions are also more negative in other situations (Tronick & Field, 1986). Of course, an infant could completely give up the goal of engaging his or her mother. However, the young infant may not be able to give up this goal, and even if he or she could, the consequences might be even more severe (Bowlby, 1982).

From this perspective, the pathways leading to the varieties of normalcy and psychopathology derive from the divergent experiences infants have with success, reparation of failure, and the transformation of negative emotions to positive emotions. Typically, there is no single traumatic juncture or special moment separating these pathways, only the slowly accumulated interactive and affective experiences with different people and events in different contexts that shape the regulatory processes and representations of the infant over time.

A major pathway leading to the variety of normal individual outcomes, one that is often disregarded, is the difference in emotional experience of individuals due to exposure to different cultural practices of socializing affect and behavior. For example, among the Gusii of Kenya, a people with strict rules about who may look at whom during face-to-face interactions, a mother is likely to look away from her infant at just that moment when the infant gets most affectively positive. In response, the infant's affect becomes more neutral, and he or she may look away. American mothers, at least the ones we study in our laboratories, almost never look away from their infants but, rather, get quite excited themselves. In response, American infants get even more excited and positive. Thus, Gusii infants internalize one set of interactive experiences and American infants another.

Framed by cultural bounds, the most important cause of the varieties of normal outcome are the strikingly different experiences individuals have with affective communication, interactive success, and emotional reparation during their reiterated daily exchanges with others. For instance, Cohn and I (Tronick & Cohn, 1989) have found large individual differences in the ability of mother-infant pairs to maintain coordinated interactive states. In addition, Cohn and I reported that mother-son pairs are in well-coordinated states about 50% more of the time than mother-daughter pairs at 6 and 9 months. These differences have important consequences for the emotional responsiveness and the formation of the self in individual males and females.

There are many pathways to psychopathology. From the perspective of mutual regulation, psychopathology is likely to arise in situations where there is persistent and chronic interactive failure. In these situations, the infant is forced to disengage from people and things because the infant has to devote too much regulatory capacity to controlling the negative affect he or she is experiencing (Main, 1981). Eventually and paradoxically, to the extent that these self-directed regulatory behaviors are successful in controlling the negative affect and containing its disruptive effects, the infant begins to deploy them automatically, inflexibly, and indiscriminately. Thus, what were normal self-regulatory behaviors become pathological or "defensive" because they are used to preclude the anticipated experience of negative affect, even in situations where negative affect might not occur. The infant gives up attempting to appreciate the nature of the immediate situation and instead approaches new situations already withdrawn and biased to act inappropriately. This severely constricts the infant's engagement with the world, future options, and even autonomy and may lead to failure to thrive, depression, and other forms of infant psychopathology.

But of course one must be cautious. Pathology is not necessarily the outcome of abnormal interactive experiences; indeed, some effects may be positive. For example, the infant of a depressed mother might become exceedingly sensitive to her emotional state in order to read her better and to better regulate the interaction. Such sensitivity may be useful when the infant interacts with others. Moreover, experience with poorly coordinated interactions is likely to have different effects at different developmental points. For example, experience with a depressed mother will have one effect during the infant's first months of life, when the mother's behavior may disrupt her infant's early emotional experience, and a different effect at the end of the first year, when depressed behavior will be more likely to disrupt the infant's newly emerging forms of autonomy.

This account has focused on the caretaker as the critical factor affecting, especially disrupting, the affective communication system. But the infant is an agent as well. Although the infant's capacities are impressive, they are still limited, so that the infant is not always able to play his or her role in the interaction effectively. Furthermore, individual differences in temperament make different infants quite different interactive partners. In the opening examples, the first infant might be temperamentally more active and better able to control affect, whereas the second infant might be more sensitive to stimulation and more inhibited. These sorts of differences place different demands on interactive partners, make infants differentially reactive, and lead to different outcomes.

More generally and critically, many factors affect the child's developmental outcome. Even a partial list would include prematurity, malnutrition, illness, the infant's other interactive experiences, and factors such as social support, stress, and self-esteem that affect the mother's behavior with her infant. Indeed, the list is a long one, but the principle is that any factor, no matter how distant, that consistently modifies the infant's affective experience modifies the infant's outcome to some degree.

CONCLUSION

This perspective on affective communication can be extended to the older child. The older child experiences new emotions—shame and guilt to name two—and has a more structured self to be affected by success and failure (Lewis, 1987). The older child also moves on to more complex and demanding tasks with people, objects, and ideas. These tasks place new demands on the child's ability to control his or her affect and on the caretaker to supplement the child's capacities. Problems children have with tantrums, impulse control, and conduct disorders, and even the risk taking of adolescents, may be viewed as arising out of children's experiences with mutual regulation and their ability to self-regulate.

The regulation of emotions, self and other, interactive success, and affective reparation are in fact lifetime issues (Stern, 1985). How adults manage these functions is determined in their current circumstances by their regulatory style and their conscious and unconscious representation of their past. Given the transformational nature of development, it would be foolish to assert that the infant's regulatory style and representations determine those of the adult, but it would be equally foolish to assert that they are without long-term influence. Certainly the way in which the adult-as-child regulated and represented the circumstances and the emotions he or she experienced accrue to the adult.

Thus, the infant, the child, and the adult act on the world, regulate emotional states, and communicate affectively. And for all of them, the working of the communicative process—its degree of interactive coordination and affective reparation—is what is critical to their outcome. Of course we need to know more. To do that we need to look in great detail at the daily reiterated workings of this emotional communication system. This will take a major effort and commitment. Indeed the time may have arrived for researchers to reinvent the systematic study of the development of individuals looked at one at a time. However, intervention need not wait for that full understanding. We already know that many interventions—from close-up ones such as interactive coaching, parental therapy, respite care for the child and parent, and daycare to more distant ones such as prenatal care, health care, and jobs—will modify the child's experience and lead to positive developmental outcomes. We should put them in place.

CHAPTER 13

The Mutual Regulation Model: The Infant's Self and Interactive Regulation and Coping and Defensive Capacities

COPING WITH INTERACTIVE STRESS IN INFANCY

Psychopathology in infancy is often attributed to abnormal interactive experiences. For example, social withdrawal (Bakeman & Brown, 1977; Brazelton, Kowslowski, & Main, 1974; Field, 1977; Massie, 1978; Stern, 1971, 1977), failure to thrive (Greenspan, 1982), and depression (Cohn & Tronick, 1983; Zahn-Waxler, McKnew, Cummings, Davenport, & Radke-Yarrow, 1984) have been linked to aberrant interpersonal relations. The underlying view is that the infant who experiences abnormally stressful interactions learns to cope with them in a particular fashion, but that his learned pattern of social interaction and coping is also abnormal. Consequently, when the infant utilizes his pattern in other, potentially normal, interactions, it distorts them, making them abnormal, too. This engenders an insidious, self-reinforcing, interactive cycle in which the infant's repeated distortion of otherwise normal interactions stresses him, compelling him again and again to adopt his coping response, which further reinforces the learned, or internalized, aberrant pattern.

Unfortunately, the interactive details of such abnormal social exchanges typically remain unexamined, as do the specific ways in which infants cope with interactive stress (but see Brazelton et al., 1974; Massie, 1978; Stern, 1971). In addition, none of the available data indicate when an infant's pattern of coping with an interactive stress becomes a stable individual characteristic. Thus the connection between the infant's manner of coping with interaction stress and other developmental changes remains unclear (Campos, Barrett, Lamb, Goldsmith, & Sternberg, 1983; Gianino, 1982, 1985; Hodapp & Mueller, 1982; Parke & Asher, 1983).

In this chapter, we present a system for describing the infant's capacities for coping with stressful interactions, and we summarize data on the developmental changes and stability of these capacities. Our work has been guided by what has become known as the mutual regulation model of social engagement. In particular, we have elaborated on the model's hypothesis that the infant's coping capacities develop from his behavioral repertoire for regulating social and object engagement.

THE MUTUAL REGULATION MODEL

The mutual regulation model (MRM) of mother-infant interaction (Brazelton, 1982; Brazelton et al., 1974; Tronick, 1980, 1982) proposes that mother and infant have an interactive goal and a set of capacities to help attain the goal. It suggests that their goal is to achieve a state of mutual regulation, or reciprocity, and that to attain it they jointly regulate the interaction with interactive behaviors. The MRM further proposes that the interactive behaviors are primarily affective displays.

Research supporting the MRM's assumption of the infant's active role in the regulation of his interactions includes studies such as those on the infant's differential reactions to mothers, fathers, and strangers (Dixon et al., 1981; Parke, 1979; Parke, O'Leary, & West, 1972); significant differences between the observed distribution of mother-infant joint behaviors and their expected distribution predicted from the distributions of their independent behaviors (Bullowa, 1975; Tronick, Krafchuk, Ricks, Cohn, & Winn, 1985); specificity and modification in the infant's response to distortions in his partner's behaviors (Beebe, Jaffe, Feldstein, Mays, & Alson, 1985; Cohn & Tronick, 1983; Fogel, Diamond, Langhorst, & Demos, 1983; Trevarthen, 1977; Tronick, Ricks, & Cohn, 1982); contingencies between infant smiles and vocalizations and specific maternal turn-yielding signals (Anderson, Vietze, & Dokechi, 1977; Mayer & Tronick, 1985); and contingencies between infant averting and maternal behaviors (Bloom, 1977; Brazelton et al., 1974; Field, 1977; Massie, 1978; Stern, 1977).

Studies by Stern (1974a), Brazelton et al. (1974), Tronick, Als, and Adamson (1979), and Beebe and Stern (1977) support the MRM's assumption that the interactants have a goal of achieving a state of reciprocity. Note that *reciprocity* is used to cover a range of somewhat unspecified terms, such as *matching, attunement, synchrony, mutual delight, mutual regulation,* and so on. These terms are nonequivalent, but in the current context the differences are not central, with one exception. These terms differ in the relative weight they give to the interactive process as opposed to the interactive outcome, or goal. The process is a feedback-regulated control system, which primarily operates as an affective process.

The goal is some interpersonal state, such as intimacy, connectedness, sociality, oneness, love, attachment. Reciprocity, for example, focuses on the process, while mutual delight focuses on the hedonic outcome.

In support of its claim that the infant's affective system plays a crucial role in regulating social interaction, the MRM contends that the infant's affective system is differentiated at birth. Following models suggested by Izard (1978b) and Campos et al. (1983), the MRM proposes that by the middle of the infant's first year he has the capacity to experience and express at least seven primary emotions, that is, joy, interest, sadness, anger, fear, surprise, and distress. According to this view, each of the infant's affective responses entails a qualitatively different evaluation of the events impinging on him. The infant's affective responses are said to be evaluative in the sense that they invest these events with personal significance and meaning; there is no implication that the process involves higher order cognitions or conscious reflection. To accomplish this evaluation—referred to as an appraisal by Bowlby (1969) and as an appreciation by Campos et al. (1983)—the infant's affective system appraises the impinging events in terms of their bearing on his current goals. The appraisal process is differentiated in that each of the infant's emotions expresses a different categorization of how the impinging events affect the infant's goal attainment. For instance, the difference between an infant's joyful, angry, and sad response, according to Campos et al., is due to the following difference in the infant's appraisal: A joyful response occurs when the infant's appraisal is that he is obtaining his goal; an angry response occurs when the infant's appraisal is that his goal is being obstructed but that it is obtainable under the circumstances, that is, given the stimulus conditions; and a sad response occurs when the infant's appraisal is that his goal is being obstructed such that it is unobtainable under the circumstances.

These recent advances in our understanding of the development and complexity of the infant's affective system have supported the MRM's claim that the infant's affective responses have an important interpersonal function. The function, to communicate the infant's ongoing appraisal of the interaction, is accomplished because the infant's appraisal is automatically expressed through his affective displays. This affords the infant significant communicative power, particularly with a sensitive and responsive partner, enabling him to initiate, modify, and maintain the exchange.

Although the MRM contends that the interactants have a goal of achieving a state of reciprocity, it emphasizes that such a state is not always achieved. Imperfections occur for a number of reasons: mistimed behavior; a misreading by one partner of the other partner's signals, producing behavior that does not match the expectation of the other; differences in each partner's immediate goal; or the older partner's attempt to encourage the infant to expand his capabilities (Tronick, Als, Adamson, Wise, & Brazelton, 1978). Moreover, instances of imperfection are remarkably common. In a study of 3-, 6-, and 9-month-old infants (Cohn, Krafchuk, Ricks, Winn, & Tronick, 1985), it was found that mother and infant were in mismatched states 70% of the time. This is hardly the romantic synchrony of mutual delight.

The MRM takes account of the imperfections inherent in the interactive process by proposing that a "normal disruption"—referred to here as a mismatch (Stern, 1977; Tronick, Als, & Brazelton, 1980b; Tronick, Krafchuk, et al., 1985;

Fafouti-Milenkovic & Uzgiris, 1979)—motivates the infant to adjust to it or modify it by employing his interactive skills. To do this, the infant employs the same affective displays and interactive behaviors that allow him to initiate, modify, and maintain the well-regulated interaction, since these also enable him to repair, avoid, or terminate a mismatched exchange.

During a normal interaction, positive affect is generated by well-regulated exchanges, and negative affect is generated by mismatched exchanges. Both positive and negative affect manifest themselves in affective expressions and, motivationally, in interactive behavior. Specifically, the infant's expressions of joy and interest indicate his positive emotional evaluation of the ongoing interaction and communicate to the partner that she should interact or continue to engage in what she is doing (Tronick, Als, & Adamson, 1979). The infant's negative appraisal of a mismatched interaction (Campos et al., 1983)—manifested in distress, anger, and sadness—signals to the partner to change her behavior. Together, positive and negative affect enable the infant to regulate the interaction to achieve mutual regulation. As noted earlier, however, this is true with one qualification. The infant's affective displays regulate the interaction when he is with a sensitive partner who is willing to modify her own behavior to match her reading of his communications.

An important implication of the MRM's position that the infant uses his affective system to regulate his interactions is that the infant has a capacity for regulating his affective responses (Brazelton, 1974; Field, 1977; McCall & McGhee, 1977; Spitz, 1965; Stern, 1974a, 1977). This follows because the infant must regulate two aspects of affect while interacting. The first aspect is the qualitative dimension, that is, the particular affective state the infant is feeling and expressing. The second aspect is the quantitative dimension, that is, the temporal and intensive parameters of affect, typically measured in terms of the threshold, latency, rise time, intensity, and recovery time of an affective occurrence. When a mismatch occurs, both types of affective self-regulation are usually facilitated through the communicative effects of the infant's affective expressions. With a sensitive partner, the infant's affective displays alter a mismatch, a situation which would continue to generate increasingly strong negative affect if allowed to continue. The interactive reparation accomplished by the infant's affective displays (with the partner's cooperation) fosters at least a reduction in negative affect, if not a change toward positive affect. In this sense, the infant's interactive repertoire facilitates his self-regulation of emotional states while he is interactively engaged.

This perspective casts a different light on what are commonly thought to be the important aspects of social interaction for the infant's development. Although it is generally agreed that mismatches are normal and occur with some frequency, many researchers, including ourselves, have typically proposed that the degree of reciprocity or mutual delight evidenced in an interaction is most important to the development of the infant. From the point of view of the MRM, reciprocity is still important, but the successful resolution of mismatches is more central, serving a multiplicity of developmental functions.

Psychodynamic theorists from Freud to Mahler, as well as developmentalists (Stechler & Halton, 1982; Trevarthen, 1977), have propounded that otherwise apparently frustrating experiences allow for self-other differentiation. Stern (1977) and Tronick, Als, and Adamson (1979) have argued that mismatches provide the infant with opportunities to further broaden and develop his interactive skills. Tronick (1980) has expanded on that claim by suggesting that insofar as the infant is able to repair mismatches, the infant is more likely to develop a sense of effectance in the interactive sphere. We propose two further functions of mismatches. First, mismatches compel the infant to develop his self-regulatory skills. Second, the infant's experience in managing mismatches develops his self-regulatory skills into skills which are useful for coping with prolonged, exaggerated, or aberrant forms of interactive stress. As we will argue in the Discussion, however, we also propose that the second function can be derailed if the interaction is chronically aberrant.

The facilitative effects of ordinary mismatches on normal development need to be contrasted to the potentially deleterious consequences of prolonged, exaggerated, or aberrant forms of interactive stress, what we call PRESAS (pronounced "presses") for short. PRESAS stress not only the infant's resources for regulating social exchanges, but also his capacity for regulating the accompanying negative affect. The MRM hypothesizes that when the infant experiences a significant and prolonged distortion of reciprocity, one he is unable to repair by altering the interaction to achieve his goal, the amount of stress and negative affect increases significantly (Gianino, 1982; Tronick et al., 1982).

Such effects have been consistently demonstrated in studies of relatively prolonged perturbations of the normal interaction. The studies include both experimental designs and clinical investigations. For example, there are studies of infants interacting with strangers (Dixon et al., 1981) or interacting with their mother while she remains still faced or simulates depression (Cohn & Tronick, 1983; Fogel et al., 1983; Gianino, 1982; Tronick, Als, Adamson, et al., 1978); and there are studies in which the infant's mother is clinically depressed (Tronick, Cohn, & Shea, 1986; Zahn-Waxler et al., 1984) or for other reasons behaves inappropriately (Massie, 1978, 1982; Stern, 1977). In all the studies, two things occur. On the one hand, the infant's attempts to repair the distortion through affective displays fail as long as the distortion persists, and on the other hand, negative affect is generated as long as the infant remains motivated to interact while continuing to fail in his reparative attempts. Consequently, the studies repeatedly show that the PRESAS tax the infant's capacity for sustaining interactive engagement while maintaining self-regulation (Brazelton et al., 1974; Gianino, 1982; Massie, 1978; Stern, 1974a; Tronick et al., 1982). Following Brazelton (1974), Gianino (1982) has observed that in order to manage the negative affect generated by PRESAS, even those experimentally induced, the infant is sometimes compelled to utilize other coping behaviors in addition to, or instead of, his interactive skills.

But one note of clarification is needed. There is no exact boundary between self-regulation and coping, just as there is no clear boundary between normal and abnormal input. In general, we try to use the term *self-regulation* when the infant is confronted by the mismatches and other imperfections characteristic of normal interactions and the term *coping* when the infant is attempting to regulate distortions that fall outside the normal range, that is, PRESAS. Thus, in this chapter we typically refer to "coping" behaviors because we are focusing on interactions we have experimentally manipulated to simulate PRESAS, even though they are short-lived simulations. But, more generally, we believe that from a developmental point of view there is a great deal of overlap between the sets of behaviors that serve self-regulatory and coping functions, with self-comforting being a notable exception. The primary difference is in the way the two sets of behaviors are deployed, for example, with regard to flexibility and persistence. Furthermore, as will be discussed at the end of this chapter, there are the additional complicated relations among self-regulatory, coping, and defensive behaviors.

According to Brazelton et al. (1974), even 1-month-old infants have several behavioral strategies for coping with stress, whether the stress is induced by the infant's interaction with people or objects. In addition to being able to signal both positively and negatively with affective displays, infants are able to reject or push away the stressful object; they are able to withdraw from the stressor by sharply turning or arching away and even by losing postural control, and they are able to decrease their perceptual receptivity to the stressful stimuli by what is in effect looking without seeing.

All four coping strategies produce a reduction in the amount of negative affect experienced by the infant. A significant difference between signaling and the other strategies is that by signaling the infant preserves his goal of maintaining engagement with the partner. Beebe (1975) has made a similar point. When the infant adopts any of the other coping strategies, he forgoes social engagement in order to maintain internal regulation.

Gianino (1982) has noted that when an infant turns away from his partner in an effort to terminate or avoid a stressful exchange, he can exert control over his attention process in one of two ways (Derryberry & Rothbart, 1984). In the first way, the infant can scan the environment without fixing his focus, causing his attention to remain free floating. In the second way, the infant can redirect his attention to a surrounding object, including his own body. Both allow the infant to reorient away from the stressful stimuli, enabling him to control the timing and duration of his focus on the stressor and, according to Brazelton et al. (1974), providing him with a recovery period. However, the two ways of controlling his attentional processes are not equivalent. Although scanning the surroundings without pausing to attend to the mother or a particular object allows the infant to reduce the stressful input, it precludes his engagement with the object world as well as his reengagement with the mother; this strategy is "autistic" in the nonpathological sense. By redirecting his attention to a particular object, however, the infant is able to avoid the stressful stimuli while at the same time retaining his capacity for engaging in an affectively positive activity.

Functionally, the attention directed to an object entails a switch in the infant's operative goals, since in withdrawing interest from his partner and attending to an object the infant becomes motivated more by object exploration than by social interaction. A potential advantage of coping with PRESAS by switching goal orientations from social engagement to object exploration is that the infant can make more adaptive use of his time and energy while maintaining his self-regulation.

INFANT COPING IN RESPONSE TO THE STILL-FACE, SIMULATED DEPRESSION, CLINICAL DEPRESSION, AND THE STRANGE SITUATION

To examine the infant's coping capacities, we have engaged in a number of studies in which we looked at the infant's reaction to a particular interactive stress, such as the mother behaving still faced. In this manipulation, the mother is in the normal face-to-face position, but she does not react at all to her infant; she remains expressionless and unresponsive. Tronick, Als, Adamson, et al. (1978) have argued that the still face is stressful because gaze contact functions as a crucial context marker that affects the regulative meaning of the accompanying emotional displays (Bloom, 1977; Fogel et al., 1983). In the still face, the mother's en face position and eye contact with her infant present him with a signal that invites social interaction, while her expressionless and unresponsive face denies it. It is as if the mother is saying hello and good-bye at the same time, leaving the infant trapped between the two messages. Insofar as the infant is primed for interaction by the mother's en face position and eye contact, as well as by his own interactive goals, the mother's still face often results in infant bids to initiate social interaction. Because the mother remains unresponsive, however, there is no possibility for the infant to repair the interaction; the infant's attempts are repeatedly frustrated. For this reason, the still face is a stress outside the normal range. Unless the infant is able to adopt some other measure to cope with his predicament, he will likely become increasingly distressed as the experiment continues.

To assess the infant's coping response to the interactive stress, Gianino (1982) developed the infant coping behavior system (ICBS). The system combines (a) observations by Brazelton et al. (1974) on how the infants respond to stress, (b) Gianino's hypothesis about the infant's use of object exploration as a coping strategy, and (c) elements of the modified monadic phase scoring system (Tronick, Als, & Brazelton, 1980b). The major categories of the system are presented in Table 13.1. Social Attend, Self-Comfort, and Escape were added after the first study, as will be discussed below. Coding with Gianino's system was done from videotapes on a slow-motion video deck.

In our first still-face study, we compared the behavior of 54 mother-infant dyads, 18 each at 3, 6, and 9 months (Gianino, 1982). Each dyad played normally for 2 minutes, experienced the still face for 2 minutes, and played again for 2 minutes. We found that the infant's tendency to use Object Attend

TABLE 13.1   Infant Coping Behavior System

1. Social-Attend: Looks at mother without signaling.
2. Signal: Acts in a way that functions to modify mother's behavior.
   Positive—Signals with a positive affective tone, e.g., smile or coo face.
   Neutral—Signals with neutral affective tone, e.g., pick-me-up gesture.
   Negative—Signals with negative affective tone, e.g., fuss or cry.
3. Object Attend: Focuses attention on something other than mother.
   Other—Focuses object with or without manipulation of it, e.g., strap of chair.
   Self—Focuses on part of own body with or without manipulation of it, e.g., toes.
4. Self-Comfort: Uses own body or object to provide self-comforting stimulation.
   Oral-Self—Sucks on part of body, e.g., fingers.
   Oral-Other—Sucks on object, e.g., strap of chair.
   Self-Clasp—Clasps hands together.
   Rock—Rocks from side to side or to and fro.
5. Escape: Attempts to increase the physical distance from mother by turning, twisting, or arching away.
6. Avert/Scan: Looks away from the mother, but does not successfully maintain attention to something else.
7. Withdrawal: Utilizes motor, attention, and perceptual processes to minimize social engagement.
   Motor—Gives up postural control.
   Perceptual—Looks dull or glassy-eyed.

increased with development. We also found that compared to 9-month-old infants, 3- and 6-month-olds were more likely to use Object Attend for either very brief or very long bouts. That is, 3- and 6-month-olds were less able than 9-month-olds to sustain their attention to an object or to withdraw it from an object once it was fixed. We believe this indicates the greater ability of 9-month-olds to modulate their attentional involvement with objects while interactively stressed and thus to use object exploration as an effective coping strategy without forsaking their goal of reengaging the mother. Piaget's (1968) observation that from 4 to 10 months the infant's horizon extends outward from his body to objects in the surround, manifesting itself in a change from primary to secondary circular reactions, was supported by our finding that the use of Self-Object Attend peaked at 3 months while that of Other-Object Attend peaked at 6 months. We were suprised to find that the frequency of Positive Signal did not increase with development, while the frequency of Negative Signal did. However, the mean bout length of Negative Signal dropped eightfold from 3 to 9 months, which suggests that 3-month-olds were least capable of soothing themselves once they became distressed enough to cry, and 9-month-olds were most capable. Furthermore, there is a qualitative change between 3 and 9 months in the use of Negative Signal that is not captured by the coding system in that the 3-month-olds appeared more distressed and the 9-month-olds more angry.

We also found that Motor and Perceptual Withdrawal were seldom used by these normal infants, particularly after they reached 3 months of age. This is not surprising since Motor and Perceptual Withdrawal are relatively primitive forms of coping, involving the type of pervasive disengagement from the surround more typical of very young infants. We also observed that the amount of body tension, evidenced in hand clenching and heavy breathing, decreased with development. For 3- and 6-month-olds, body tension is a somewhat primitive phenomenon. The younger infant is a more biosocial creature than the older infant and as such is more prone to relatively nonspecific physiological reactions to many forms of stress, including interactive stress (Sander, 1977).* The last finding we would like to mention was a significant decrease in the variability of the frequency of all coping behaviors, suggesting that as infants become older they become more alike in their coping tendencies.

In order to assess the organization and structure of the infant's response, a within-group analysis of the transition matrices at each age was performed with the infant's behavior scored using Tronick, Als, and Brazelton's (1980b) modified monadic phase scoring system. The monadic system was used because the ICBS was not exhaustive when first designed, which precluded a sequential analysis of the infant's behavior. In terms of the data presented here, the relevant differences between the ICBS and the Monadic Scoring System are twofold. First, Self-Comfort, Escape, and Withdrawal are scored in the ICBS but not in the monadic system. Second, Wary, a subcategory of "Social Attend," in which the infant looks at the mother warily, is scored in the monadic system, but not in the ICBS.

An integral feature of the organization of infant behavior at all three ages was the infant's tendency to cycle from Social Attend to Avert and from Avert to Object Attend (see Figure 13.1a–c). Regardless of age, infants first attempted to terminate and avoid the stressful interaction by averting their gaze from the mother. After averting, they were more likely to switch their attention from the interaction to the surround, as evidenced in the low probability that they would go from Avert to Social Attend and the increased probability that they would go from Avert to Object Attend. Among the significant main effects for age was a difference in how infants tended to respond after Object Attend. Whereas 9-month-olds were more likely than expected to Avert again after Object Attend, 6-month-olds were more likely than expected to Social Attend and 8-month-olds to Protest. This finding indicates the 3-month-old's greater difficulty with switching goals as a way of self-regulating. Furthermore, after Protesting, 9-month-olds were the only group who were more likely than expected to Object Attend, suggesting better coping capacity than 3- or 6-month-olds.

---

*While we are focusing on affective regulation for purposes of discussing coping, we agree with Sander (1962) that there are different tasks at different developmental periods which require other forms of regulation. As Sander notes, the task preceding the period we are discussing has to do with physiological regulation.

FIGURE 13.1a–c. The size of the circle represents the proportion of time infants were in each phase. The solid arrows are excitatory transitions, those conditional probabilities that significantly ($p < .05$) exceeded the independent probability of one transition, and broken arrows are inhibitory transitions, those conditional probabilities that significantly ($p < .05$) reduced the independent probability of the transition. The wider the arrow, the greater the likelihood of occurrence.

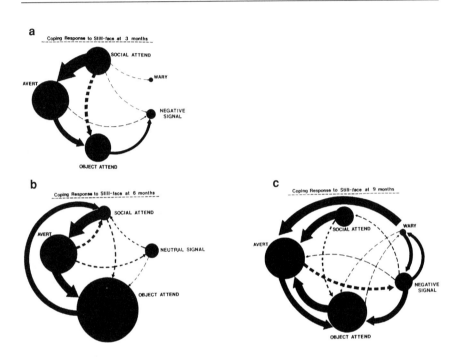

More generally, the developmental differences in the infant's coping response were marked by a significant increase to behavioral complexity and organization. There were increases in the number of coping behaviors from 3 to 9 months (225, 320, 348, respectively) and in the frequency of transitions from one behavior to another. Furthermore, there was an increase in predictability, in that the number of transitions that had a conditional probability significantly different from expected went from 6 at 3 months, to 8 at 6 months, to 13 at 9 months. In general, it was found that the older the infant, the more behavioral options he had available and the greater his capacity to employ these options to sustain self-regulation while interpersonally stressed.

In another study in our laboratory (Cohn & Tronick, 1983), we asked each mother to simulate depression with her 3½-month-old infant. Specifically, we asked the mother to flatten her affect, restrain the expressiveness of her voice, and to limit the use of her hands. Because simulated depression is a dynamic display, the mother mistimed and mismatched many of her infant's signals, making this a more stressful PRESAS than the still face. What we found was that there was less social engagement by the infant than in the still-face situation. In terms of the sequential organization of behavior, there was a very tight cycle of Avert, Wary, and Negative Signal, which the infant found difficult to escape from.

In order to better understand infant coping, Cohn and Tronick carried out a naturalistic study of 7-month-old infants whose mothers evidence depressive symptoms and other signs of disturbance (Cohn, Matias, Tronick, Connell, & Lyons-Ruth, 1986). The mothers were rated in the clinical range on the CES-D depression scale. The families were also participating in one of two clinical interventions. To better study the interactions of these dyads, the mothers were asked to play with their infants at their homes. In preliminary analyses, the findings appeared very much like what we found in our experimental studies except that these infants looked much more distressed and disengaged than did infants in the simulated situation. For example, the depressed mothers engaged in play less than 10% of the time, whereas normal mothers engaged in play more than 42% of the time (Tronick, Krafchuk, et al., 1985). A second finding is that there was a profound distortion in infants' behavior when they were interacting with their depressed mother. These infants played only about 5% of the time, whereas infants of normal mothers played about 13% of the time. Moreover, the extent of play by the mother was strongly related to the amount of play by the infant, with a correlation of .51. We believe this indicates the extent to which the mother's behavior was influencing the infant's behavior.

Looking at the same group of depressed mothers and infants, we also found a disruption in other aspects of the infant's behavior in addition to the amount of play. In particular, there was a marked decrease in the percentage of time the infants were able to focus on an object during the interaction. In a normal interaction, the 6-month-old infant spends about 41% of the time in Object Attend. When a normal interaction is disturbed, as in the still face, there is nonetheless a similar proportion of object engagement. In these situations, the infant directs his attention to objects as away of coping; that is, he switches his goal to object exploration as a away of maintaining self-regulation. However, when we look at the interactions of infants and their depressed mothers, there is a marked decrease in the proportion of time the infants engage objects. So not only has prolonged exposure limited the infants' available coping strategies by inhibiting his capacity to use Positive Signal to repair the distortion, it has also begun to disrupt the infant's emerging engagement with the inanimate environment.

The question we are now asking is when infants develop stable individual differences in dealing with stress. Some results have suggested that styles of coping are stabilizing around 6 months of age (Brazelton, 1974; Cohn & Tronick, 1983; Massie, 1977, 1978, 1982; Stern, 1971, 1977). However, the stability found in these studies was either short-term within-session effects, based on a few subjects, or drawn from clinical evidence. To address this situation, we completed a study in which we looked at the stability of infant reactions to the still face at 6 months of age (Gianino, 1985). We had 52 infants interact with their mothers on two occasions, separated by 7 days. We then compared infant coping behaviors on Visit 1 which their coping behaviors on Visit 2. Gianino's ICBS was used, modified to include three new codes based on the work reported earlier:

1. Self-Comfort—to capture the infant's attempts to use his own body or nearby objects to provide self-comforting stimulations includes the categories Oral-Self, Oral-Other, Rock, and Self-Clasp
2. Escape—to capture the infant's attempts to increase his physical distance from the mother by turning, twisting, or arching away and to distinguish this behavior from the more serious forms of Motor Withdrawal in which the infant gives up postural control and collapses in his seat
3. Social Attend—to capture the times the infant monitors the mother without attempting to Signal her and to make the scoring system exhaustive

The addition of Self-Comfort was particularly important, since our studies of simulated PRESAS indicated that infants often resorted to this coping behavior, sometimes to the exclusion of their other self-regulatory behaviors and sometimes in conjunction with them. Overall, we found that of the 33 correlations of behavior from Visit 1 to Visit 2 which we analyzed, 18 were significant, ranging between .29 and .50. Only Scan and Social Attend failed to exhibit stability for all three dependent measures (frequency, total duration, and bout length) from Visit 1 to Visit 2. Since the literature on the stability of discrete behaviors in infancy has seldom demonstrated significant relationships (Sroufe & Waters, 1977), correlations of this size suggest an emergent pattern of stability in coping strategies. We offer two examples (see Table 13.2). First, we found that the total duration of all three categories of Signal (Positive, Neutral, and Negative) were positively correlated, indicating that infants displayed some stable tendencies in their use of Signal when presented with a particular interactive stress.

TABLE 13.2   Correlations of Self-Regulatory Behaviors Visit 1 With Visit 2

Behavior	Total Frequency[a]	Total Duration[a]	Bout Length
Signal	.43[b]	.41[b]	.32[b]
Positive Signal	.36[b]	.50[b]	.20
Neutral Signal	−.03	.29[b]	.31[b]
Negative Signal	.22[b]	.35[b]	.20
Self-Comfort	.46[b]	.35[b]	.33[b]
Oral-Self	.47[b]	.31[b]	.45
Oral-Other	.30[b]	.34[b]	.32
Rock	.71[b]	.99[b]	.71

[a]*Total duration and bout length measured in seconds.*
[b]$p < .05$.

When these three categories were collapsed, the evidence for stability in the use of Signal was even stronger. Significant correlations were found in how often the infants signaled, how long they sustained each attempt, and the total time they employed it. If signaling the partner when distressed is an especially adaptive coping strategy, as we claim, then it is significant that 6-month-old infants are already exhibiting some stable individual differences in this regard. Second, we found that three out of the four categories of Self-Comfort (the exception being Self-Clasp) were significantly correlated for the same three measures, that is, frequency, total duration, and bout length. If tendencies to Self-Comfort in response to stress are predictive of certain patterns of personality developing and defensive parents, as hypothesized by generations of psychodynamic theorists, then evidence indicating the presence of stable individual differences in these tendencies at 6 months, at least in response to an interactive stress, suggests that certain aspects of character may be present as early as 6 months.

In a longitudinal study (Tronick et al., 1982), we related whether 6-month-old infants signaled or failed to signal (e.g., scanned) in response to the still face with their classification of attachment at 1 year, using Ainsworth's strange situation. From our perspective, the strange situation assesses the quality of the infant's ability to cope with an age-appropriate stress, that is, the mother leaving the infant in a strange situation. We found that those infants who signaled at 6 months were classified as securely attached at 1 year, while those infants who failed to signal were classified as insecurely attached. Thus there is evidence of stability between coping with an interpersonal stress at 6 months and interpersonal competence at 12 months.

The results of our two studies on the stability of individual differences in coping with interpersonal stress provide support for the view that two of the infant's more important coping strategies (Signal and Self-Comfort) are beginning to stabilize by 6 months. Remarkably, this is at least a month or two before most infants evidence a strong, discriminating attachment to their mother (Bowlby, 1969).

THE INTERCONNECTIONS AMONG SELF AND MUTUAL REGULATION, OBJECT EXPLORATION, COPING, AND DEFENSE

Our study of the ontogeny of infant coping behaviors from 3 to 9 months has shown that coping patterns are modified by the developmental level of the infant. Maturation and experience combine to expand the infant's initial self-regulatory repertoire. With development, the infant acquires greater skill and capacity in a number of areas. As Stern (1977) has pointed out, the infant's communicative repertoire, such as the range and use of facial expressions and vocalizations, broadens with development. At the same time, the infant's capacity to interpret the mother's expressions also increases as the infant begins to master subtleties of affective displays and social cues as well as nuances in the communicative meanings of changes in tempo and rhythm. The stabilization of the mother-infant relationship between 3 and 9 months facilitates this learning, enhancing the infant's ability to predict the mother's interactive patterns (Tronick et al., 1982). The enhancements in the infant's ability to signal and decode interactive behaviors enable the infant to more effectively communicate his appraisal of a distorted interaction.

A most dramatic change comes between 4 and 7 months with the incorporation of objects into the interaction, affording the infant greater flexibility in switching his immediate goal away from social interaction when such interaction proves overly stressful. Considering these factors together, an infant of 9 months of age will have notably more skills available than a 3-month-old for coping with such sources of interactive stress as occasional maternal unresponsivity to the infant's signals (Stern, 1977; Tronick et al., 1982). Additionally, the older the infant, the greater the complexity and flexibility of responses to interactive stress. Thus coping strategies are part of and arise out of the infant's behavioral repertoire for regulating social and object engagement. They are supplemented by the infant's ability to control his attentional, perceptive, and motor capacities, all of which afford him a further measure of behavioral and psychological control over the source of his distress.

It appears for at least some infants that coping patterns are beginning to stabilize by the time the infants reach 6 months of age and that the social competency exhibited in these emergent patterns might be related to the social competency evidenced in the infant's quality of attachment at 12 months (Tronick et al., 1982). Thus there is now evidence that infants have specific coping patterns and that they exhibit individual differences in the deployment of these coping patterns when confronted with an interactive stress. Furthermore, there is now reason to believe that a prolonged distortion of the interactive process, such as having a depressed mother, distorts and modifies both the infant's social and object skills.

We think these studies indicate that infant coping skills arise partly out of the infant's normal interactive behaviors. The skills required to regulate a normal interaction are employed whenever the flow of the interaction is disrupted by a mismatch. The negative affect which is briefly produced by a mismatch is typically modulated when the infant successfully regulates the interaction with his social skills. According to the MRM's account of the process, the infant signals the partner to change her mismatched behavior by expressing his appraisal that the interaction is distressing. The resulting change in the (sensitive and responsive) partner's behavior typically helps alleviate the infant's distress, since it alters the state of the interaction, which enables the infant to self-regulate his affective state. In short, interactive regulation and self-regulation complement each other: The infant's affective displays alter the partner's behavior and the interaction, which facilitates the infant's attempts to regulate his affective state. During those periods when the interactive stress is markedly prolonged, exaggerated, or distorted, however, the infant is unable to readjust the interaction. This engenders greater negative affect, which often compels the use of other regulatory—or what we call coping—strategies, such as self-comforting.

The intimate connection between self-regulation and interactive regulation within the MRM has led us to conclude that it is important to consider them together when discussing the infant's social behavior. Since even normal interactions typically involve a number of mismatches, we believe this point applies to normal as well distorted interactions. In a sense we are saying that the infant must be viewed from two perspectives, but that like the Necker cube the perspectives are on one object, the infant.

The first perspective views the infant as regulating his social interactions to achieve a goal-determined interactive state. Although this regulatory task has been given more attention than the task of self-regulation by researchers studying social interaction, there is still no consensus on how to classify the interactive goal. As mentioned earlier, in addition to Brazelton's (1974) suggested term *reciprocity*, which we use in this chapter to designate both a goal and a dynamic process, there are the concepts of mutual delight (Stern, 1977), affective attunement (Beebe & Stern, 1977), intersubjectivity (Trevarthen, 1977), coherence (Lester, Hoffman, & Brazelton, 1985), matching (Tronick, Als, & Adamson, 1979), and shared directional tendencies (Tronick et al., 1982). In spite of those differences, there is agreement that the infant's behavior is directed toward social interaction once the corresponding behavioral system has been activated by social stimuli or internal processes. There is also agreement that the infant's behavior is modified by the feedback he receives from his interactive partner. Bowlby (1969) employed the term *goal-corrects* to describe this type of complexly motivated behavior.

In the second perspective, once the infant has set a goal for social interaction, he must regulate a variety of emotions appropriate to the goal and the conditions confronted. Each of these emotions is qualitatively different from the others (or they include blends; cf. Ekman, 1980), and each has an intensity dimension. The infant must regulate both the quality, that is, which affective state predominates, and quantity, that is, the intensity or fullness within an affective state. Others (Brazelton, 1974; Field, 1977; Sroufe, 1979b; Stern, 1977) have argued that the infant is regulating a level or dimension of arousal. We believe this to be incorrect. Consider whether the infant is more aroused when smiling or when showing intense interest. Indeed, it is not at all clear how the arousal model accounts for the affective behavior specifically evidenced by the infant. Very similar critiques have been made of the "discrepancy hypothesis," which—although primarily a cognitive hypothesis—invokes a quantitative model of degree of discrepancy to account for the infant's differential reactions. In our view, the arousal which the infant must regulate is the intensity dimension of his affective states. But these differences notwithstanding, whatever we choose to call the "what" that is being regulated, these models agree it is something internal.

What may mine these two perspectives on the infant's regulatory tasks—one unobservable, endogenous, and subjective experiential, the other observable, exogenous, and interactive—is that both see the process of regulation as involving the affective system with its simultaneous dualities of internal states and internal experiences manifested in external emotional expressions and interactive communication. It is because the infant's internal affective regulators use the exogenous input he is receiving to help modify both his internal affective state and his interactive communication to his partner that self-regulation and interactive regulation can occur at the same time. Again, since the exogenous input emanating from a social partner can be modified through the infant's communicative behaviors when the partner is willing to be sensitively responsive to the infant's signals, the infant can regulate the interaction at the same time that he regulates his affective state. For example, when the infant smiles in response to maternal play, it is an act of self-regulation which has resulted in pleasure, indicating that the infant has achieved some goal, and it is a socially regulatory act, communicating that the partner should continue to engage in her activity. Thus regulation takes place inside and outside the organism.

This view does not require that the infant make a distinction between self and other. In fact, it may be advantageous to an infant with a sensitive partner not to make the distinction and instead believe that all changes emanate from himself, since the resulting well-regulated interaction will further his sense of effectance (Tronick et al., 1982). On the other hand, the inability to distinguish between self and other can be disadvantageous—indeed, deleterious—when the interactive partner is insensitive. With such a partner, the infant's inability to discriminate the actual source of his distress will teach him that he is incapable of a sense of effectance.

In this chapter, we have noted that the disruption of object engagement observed in infants interacting with their depressed mothers entails a disruption of their capacity to use such engagement as a self-regulatory, or coping, strategy. We recognize that the disruption in object engagement is directly due to a disruption in the behavioral system that controls object engagement rather than to a disruption in the system that controls social engagement (Brazelton et al., 1974; Trevarthen & Hadley, 1978; Tronick, Krafchuk, et al., 1985). However, we also believe that the two systems are organized hierarchically, with the social engagement system primary and the object engagement system partly dependent on it (Tronick, 1980). The disruption seen in object engagement occurs because the depressed mother's interaction profoundly disrupts the infant's ability to control his social engagement, and without that control the infant cannot go on to engage objects. This interpretation is similar to Ainsworth's interpretation of a balance between attachment and exploration. In her view, when the attachment is disrupted, causing the infant to feel insecure, the infant is unable to move on to explore the environment. We are making the further claim that when the infant has a history of abnormally stressful interactions, he becomes unable to recruit his object engagement system for self-regulatory purposes. The infant's ability to deploy his object engagement system to regulate his affective state as well as his involvement with objects parallels his ability to use his social skills for both self- and interactive regulation. From this point of view, he is able to use both systems for internal and external regulatory functions (the Necker cube, again).

As a last point, we might begin to think about the development of defensive behaviors. We introduce defensive behaviors into this discussion because we believe they have a functional relationship to coping behaviors in that both serve self-regulatory objectives. Since we are looking at the normal development of coping skills and arguing that they evolve out of the normal interaction, particularly aspects of the interaction that involve mismatching, we think it is important to consider the connection these functions have to the emergence of infant defensive skills. Drawing upon case studies by Brazelton, Young, and Bullowa (1971), Stern (1971, 1977), Massie (1977, 1978, 1982), and Adamson, Als, Tronick, and Brazelton (1977), Gianino (1982) has hypothesized that defensive behaviors can evolve out of the infant's attempts to cope with a history of chronic PRESAS to his primary social relationships. Experience, constrained by temperament (Derryberry & Rothbart, 1984) teaches the infant which coping behaviors are most effective in regulating the distress (Sullivan, 1953). The transition from coping behaviors to defensive behaviors occurs once the infant begins to employ them automatically, inflexibly, and indiscriminately, and thus even with a partner who does nothing to warrant them. They are defensive because they are adopted to preclude the experience of interactive stress, that is, to preclude the experience of anxiety generated by the infant's interactive experience. Once the infant begins to automatically deploy defensive behaviors, he will adopt them even if they are so extreme as to constrict his overall ability to maintain engagement with the surround and, more generally, even if they restrict his immediate and longer term options; in short, even if they curtail his autonomy. Such is the primacy of the infant's need to self-regulate his affective state.

To illustrate the difference we see between coping and defense, consider the following example. We have found that among normal infants a prolonged avert is a common response to an interactive stress. In a normal population an avert is adaptive since it allows the infant to self-regulate and does not preclude him from returning to the mother when she makes herself more available. As long as the mother is not habitually unavailable, the infant experiences many occasions in which he successfully engages her and many occasions in which he first averts from her to cope with a mismatch but then returns to find her ready to reengage him. With this interactive history, the infant develops a sense of confidence in his mother's availability (Ainsworth, Bell, & Stayton, 1974) and a sense of competence in his own ability to regulate mismatches (Tronick et al., 1982; White, 1959). But consider an infant who repeatedly resorts to an avert in order to cope with a mother who routinely rebuffs his social elicitations. We speculate that after many such experiences the infant will tend to automatically disengage from the mother in order to immediately minimize his distress. His tendency will be to disengage, perhaps involving himself in the surround, even before he has begun to interact with her. And with the cumulative impact of these experiences, he will develop a sense of ineffectance or helplessness and be biased toward withdrawal (Seligman, 1975). Furthermore, we expect that his sense of ineffectance and tendency toward withdrawal will be carried into his other relationships, even with partners who are more sensitive (Massie, 1978; Stern, 1977). We believe that in situations such as described in the hypothetical example above, the infant's deployment of his normal social skills fails to regulate the distorted interaction. As this begins to compel the infant to make self-regulation a preeminent goal, he begins to turn inward. Once the infant's experience with this kind of failure of interactive regulation is reiterated enough, he begins to withdraw and to come into new situations already withdrawn, already biased not to react to the situation appropriately. We think that the reiteration of experiences that prevent normal interactive regulation is the basis of the defensive patterns of behavior and, indeed, the pathology we see in failure to thrive, depressed, and withdrawn infants.

We believe that coping with an interpersonal stress is an important adaptive task for normal infants during the first year and that such coping may have a predictive relationship to later measures of social competency. Certainly more research is needed on the origin of individual differences in the patterning of coping strategies, or what we call coping styles. Research of this type is needed on both normal and at-risk populations and should consider variables such as infant temperament and maternal sensitivity. We believe the resulting data will broaden our understanding of both normal and abnormal developmental processes.

CHAPTER 14

Infant-Mother Face-to-Face Interaction: Age and Gender Differences in Coordination and the Occurrence of Miscoordination

To evaluate the extent to which infants and mothers are able to coordinate their behavior, the interactions of 54 mother-infant pairs—18 each at 3, 6, and 9 months of age—were videotaped. Coordination was evaluated with two measures: (1) matching—the extent to which mother and infant engage in the same behavior at the same time; and (2) synchrony—the extent to which mother and infant change their behavior with respect to one another. Mother-infant pairs increase their degree of coordination with infant age, but the proportion of time they are coordinated is small. Mother-son pairs spend more time in coordinated states than mother-daughter pairs. The results suggest that interactions be characterized in terms of their movement from coordinated to miscoordinated states rather than only in terms of their degree of coordination. The gender differences are discussed in terms of their importance for the developmental differences in females and males.

A feature of infant-caretaker face-to-face exchanges is the degree to which the pair is able to coordinate their behavior. Such coordination is thought to be critical for the establishment of a successful relationship and mutual understanding between the infant and the caregiver as well as the infant's learning and elaboration of social skills and conventional forms of communication and culture (Brazelton, Koslowski, & Main, 1974; Schaffer, Collis, & Parson, 1977; Stern, 1985; Trevarthen, 1977; Tronick, 1980; Tronick, Brazelton, & Als, 1978). Many terms—interactive synchrony, co-occurrence, attunement, matching, reciprocity, and coherence—have been used to describe this coordination. Each term is an attempt to describe the characteristic structure of the interaction and in particular a quality of the interaction that indicates that it is going well. Each term varies in the precision of its definition, what it sees as being coordinated (e.g., behaviors, clusters of behaviors, the temporal or directional characteristics of behaviors), and the extent to which it is a theoretical construct (e.g., reciprocity) or a more quantitative variable (e.g., co-occurrence). Because of these differences in definition, we defined two terms, matching and synchrony, as indices of coordination (see below).

There have been several studies of the degree to which infant and caretaker are able to achieve this coordination. These studies have looked at the coordination of different interactive characteristics: the coordination of movements, and movements with speech (Condon & Sander, 1974b; Dowd & Tronick, 1986), gaze patterns (Peery & Stern, 1976; Stern, 1971), clusters of behaviors (Bakeman & Brown, 1977; Cohn & Tronick, 1987; Fafouti-Milenkovic & Uzgiris, 1979; Fogel, 1977; Kaye & Fogel, 1980; Uzgiris, Benson, & Vasek, 1983), levels of engagement (Beebe & Gerstman, 1980; Lester, Hoffman, & Brazelton, 1985; Tronick, Als, & Brazelton, 1980), and the additive qualities of behaviors to produce the coordinated state of reciprocity (Brazelton et al., 1974). Depending on the definition employed, which often is related to the time unit analyzed and the method of analysis, coordination is found to occur 30%–40% of the time (Fogel, 1977, 1982; Pawlby, 1977; Tronick, Als, & Brazelton, 1980b; Uzgiris et al., 1983), as little as 12% (Lester et al., 1985), and sometimes not at all (Dowd & Tronick, 1986; Gottman & Ringland, 1981).

The differences in results are in part related to whether the researcher analyzed unselected or selected portions of an interaction. Selecting interactions according to some criteria (e.g., absence of negative affect) typically results in a greater proportion of the interaction being characterized as coordinated. Selected or not, the variability among pairs is generally considerable (Cohn & Tronick, 1987; Lester et al., 1985; Tronick, Als, et al., 1980b; Uzgiris et al., 1983). Developmental evidence exists that coordination increases with age (Pawlby, 1977; Uzgiris et al., 1983). Little evidence exists for sex differences, although some theoretical perspectives predict differences between mother-son and mother-daughter pairs (Chodorow, 1978).

The present study is an analysis of the normative course of coordination during the first year of life. For purposes of this study, coordination was defined and analyzed in two ways: (1) as behavioral matching, that is, the degree to which infant and mother are in the same behavioral state at the same time (Tronick, Als, et al., 1980b; Uzgiris et al., 1983); and (2) as synchrony, that is, how consistently the pair are able to move together over time regardless of the content of their behavior (Beebe, Jaffe, Feldstein, Mays, & Alson, 1985; Lester et al., 1985). These measures differ in that matching focuses on the content of the behaviors of mother and infant at one point in time (i.e., the achievement of a joint state) and can be assessed using standard statistical techniques such as analysis of variance for evaluating the proportion of time match states are achieved. The second focuses on how mother and infant change with respect to one another and can be analyzed using time series techniques (Beebe, 1982; Beebe et al., 1985; Cohn & Tronick, 1988; Gottman, 1977; Lester et al., 1985; Tronick, Als, & Brazelton, 1977).

From other work, we know that at 3, 6, and 9 months both mother and infant are responsible for the coordination observed (Cohn & Tronick, 1988). Neither the behavioral matching nor the synchrony measures used here evaluates who is responsible for the degree of coordination observed. But that issue is different from the issues of concern here, which are the extent to which mother and infant are able to coordinate their behaviors and if there are differences in relation to age and sex. It was expected that the degree of coordination as assessed with each of these measures would increase with age and that there would be no significant sex differences.

To evaluate these issues, the face-to-face interactions of mothers and infants at 3, 6, and 9 months of age were videotaped and coded with the monadic phase scoring system (Tronick, Als, et al., 1980b). This coding scheme segments the interaction into units of combinations of expressive behaviors for mother and infant (i.e., monadic phases). The phases allow for the determination of the degree to which mother and infant are matching the content of their interactive behaviors and the extent to which they are able to synchronize their behaviors when the phases are arranged along a univariate scale of affective/attentional involvement (Lester et al., 1985).

METHOD

Subjects

The sample consisted of three different groups of infant-mother pairs, 18 each at 3 (M = 98.4 days, SD = 3.8), 6 (M = 186.3 days, SD = 3.2), and 9 months (M = 280.6 days, SD = 3.9). Age groups were balanced for gender of the infant. Infants were all full-term Caucasians and from intact homes.

Study participants were recruited through birth announcements published in local newspapers in the Amherst/Northampton, Massachusetts, area. Potential participants were telephoned and told of our Infant Studies Program at the University of Massachusetts. Mothers who expressed interest in participating in the current study were scheduled to bring their infants to a taping session at a time when they judged that their infant would be alert.

Eighty-one mother-infant dyads were tested to produce the final sample of 54 mother-infant pairs. Eight infants who had sustained substantial medical complications were excluded, as their experiences might have biased the data in unknown ways. Three additional mother-infant pairs (one 3-month- and two 9-month-olds) were not included because of technical problems. An additional 9-month-old infant was excluded because the mother used an object during the taped episodes. Fifteen infants (four 3-, six 6-, and five 9-month-olds) were excluded because of fussing, operationally defined as crying for more than a minute prior to or during the taping session.

Setting and Equipment

The laboratory consisted of a video studio with an adjoining room. The studio was equipped with an infant seat mounted on a table, an adjustable stool for the mother to face the infant, two video cameras, and a microphone. One camera was focused on the mother and the other on the infant. Both pictures were transmitted through a digital timer and split-screen generator into a video recorder. Digital timer, split-screen generator, and video recorder were located in the adjoining room (see Als, Tronick, & Brazelton, 1979; Tronick, Als, et al., 1980b, for details).

Procedure

Mothers were greeted by an experimenter and escorted to the laboratory. Mothers were encouraged to make themselves and their infants comfortable in the adjoining room. Informed, written consent for her own and her infant's participation was obtained from the mother. Mothers were then interviewed and asked about the infant's perinatal status, general health, and other demographic information about the family.

Mother and infant were then escorted to the video studio and the infant was situated in the infant chair. The experimental procedure was explained to the mother. It consisted of three episodes: 2 minutes of normal interaction, followed by 2 minutes during which mothers either interacted normally or maintained a still face, followed by a final 2 minutes of normal interaction. Mothers were simply instructed to "play with your baby." At the end of the session, mothers were allowed to view the videotape of their interaction. Only the data for the first period of normal interaction are included in this report.

Coding

Videotapes were coded by teams of two coders using the monadic phases manual (Als et al., 1979; Tronick, Als, et al., 1980b). Monadic phases for mother and infant are: Protest (infant only), Avert, Pick-me-up gesture, Positive Away, Object Attend and Object Play, Social Attend, Social Play, and Talk (see Als et al., 1979; Tronick, Als, et al., 1980b, for details).

Monadic phases were coded with the tape running at normal speed. Whenever a change in phase was observed, the tape was reversed and replayed at normal or slow speed to determine the change point. Times, read from a digital display on the videotape, were rounded to the nearest .25 second (i.e., phases were coded to the nearest .25 second). To assess interobserver agreement, videotapes of 12 mothers and five babies were recoded by a second team of coders. Agreement, defined as both sets of coders observing the same phase within .5 second of the other, ranged from .81 to .97 for mothers' monadic phases and .90 to 1.0 for babies' phases (kappas = .60 and .72, respectively).

Data Reduction

We differentiated two types of matches: (1) Social Match—the proportion of time of the total interaction that the infant and mother were in Social Attend or Social Play at the same time; and (2) Object Match—the proportion of total time of the interaction that the infant and mother were in Object Attend or Object Play at the same time. We made this distinction because mutual engagement with objects as well as one's social partner both appear to be coordinated states, especially given the infant's interest in objects at this age (Kaye, 1982; Malatesta & Izard, 1984; Trevarthen, 1977). The definitions of these matching states are relatively global when compared to definitions used by others (e.g., Beebe et al., 1985; Brazelton et al., 1974). This feature increases the likelihood of finding matches. Matches involving Avert were not analyzed because the mothers were in Avert less than 1% of the time.

Synchrony, a term with many meanings, was defined as the proportion of shared variance at lag 0 as indexed by the square of the cross-correlation between each mother's and infant's time series. To generate this index of synchrony, the monadic phases were scaled along an affective/attentional dimension. A score of 1 assigned to Protest represented maximum negative involvement; a score of 9, assigned to Talk within the Social Play phase, maximum positive involvement (see Als et al., 1979; Tronick, Als, et al., 1980b, for details). For comparability with previous work, which used a similar scaling of attentional/affective involvement but a 1-second scoring interval (Als et al., 1979; Lester et al., 1985; Tronick, Als, et al., 1977), we averaged scaled scores within 1-second blocks. The cross-correlations were then computed using these scaled scores and used as the test statistic for synchrony. The relation of infant and mother behaviors at lags other than 0 were not computed because our focus was on the ability of infant and mother to coordinate their behavior at the same time and not at some temporal delay.

These definitions and our analyses utilize data from the entire interaction and not just portions that met some selection criteria. We thought that this was appropriate so as not to generate a supposed characterization of the interaction that in fact only represented a selected portion of the interaction.

RESULTS

Coordination in Individual Dyads

Mothers and babies could match each others' behavior or change together over time (synchrony) purely by chance. If this were the case, analyses of matching or synchrony would be of little interest. To rule out this possibility, we conducted two sets of analyses. The first was a chi-square test of independence to evaluate the null hypothesis that the distributions of mothers' and babies' monadic phases were independent. The second was to compute cross-correlation functions from the time series of each mother-infant pair. A finding of no statistically significant cross-correlations is sufficient to rule out synchrony between infant and mother (i.e., that the covariance between each mother's and baby's series was due to chance; see Cohn & Tronick, 1988, for details). Both sets of tests were performed separately for each mother-infant pair.

The joint distributions of mothers' and infants' monadic phases were not independent. For 52 of the 54 dyads, the chi-square tests ($df = 6$) were highly significant ($p < .01$). Similarly, all pairs had significant cross-correlations ($p < .05$). The results of these two analyses indicate that coordination is found in almost all of the individual dyads examined, that it is a dyad-by-dyad phenomenon and not simply the product of group analyses of the data.

Percentage of Time in Monadic Phases

The percentage of time that mothers and infants spent in each monadic phase was analyzed with univariate analyses of variance with age and sex of infant as the between-groups factors. Because percentages typically have skewed distributions, we used an arcsine transformation prior to these and all other analyses of percentage data. We were unable to use multivariate analyses of variance because of the absolute degree of association among the mothers' and infants' monadic phases. The results, therefore, are interpretable in terms of patterns of relations among measures rather than as independent tests.

Table 14.1 shows the means for the percentage of time that mothers and infants spent in each monadic phase. The percentages are pooled across sex of

TABLE 14.1   Mean Percentage of Mothers' and Infants' Time in Each Monadic Phase

	Avert	Obj Att	Obj Play***	Soc Att***	Soc Play*
Mother					
3 months	.7	19.9	1.4_a	35.4_a	42.6_a
6 months	.2	23.1	7.9_b	26.6_{ab}	42.2_a
9 months	.3	15.1	8.2_b	19.2_b	57.2_b

	Avert*	Obj Att***	Obj Play	Soc Att	Soc Play***
Infant					
3 months	36.4_a	21.0_a	1.9	25.3	15.5_a
6 months	21.5_b	40.8_b	1.5	23.0	13.2_a
9 months	26.3_b	24.6_a	3.5	20.4	25.1_b

Note. Obj = object; Att = attend; Soc = social. *Column means with dissimilar subscripts differ significantly, $p < .05$, Newman-Keuls, following the finding of a significant age effect for that behavior using a univariate analysis of variance as indicated by the asterisks.*
*p ($df = 2,51$) $< .10$.
**p ($df = 2,51$) $< .05$.
***p ($df = 2,51$) $< .01$.

infant since there were no differences due to this factor. Mothers showed an increase in Object Play, a decrease in Social Attend, and a trend ($p < .10$) toward an increase in Social Play from 3 to 9 months. These findings suggest that the mothers become more affectively positive and more willing to focus on objects as their infants develop. The infants show a decrease in averting. They have a peak interest in objects at 6 months, but at 9 months, this returns to the 3-month level. There is a growth in social play. These findings suggest that infants maintain their interest in social play over this time period and that a focus on objects does not come to dominate the interaction, as some have suggested (Kaye, 1982; Trevarthen, 1977).

Percentage of Matches

To analyze the percentage of object compared to social matches for age and gender effects, it was necessary to adjust for differences in the base rates of object and social phases. The adjusted, or relative, percentage of object matches was computed as the percentage of time in object match divided by the total time that mother or baby were in an object phase, and the adjusted percentage of social match as the total time in social match divided by the total time that mother or baby were in a social phase. These adjusted percentages were analyzed with an analysis of variance for correlated measures, with age and sex of infant as the between-groups factors.

The mean percentage of time in match states varied with infants' sex and age (Table 14.2). Matching was less at 3 months than at 6 and 9 months. Mother-son dyads were more likely than mother-daughter dyads to be in matching states. Social matches were more frequent than object matches.

TABLE 14.2 **Means and Standard Deviations for Adjusted Percentages of Object and Social Matches by Infants' Age and Sex**

	Object Match	Social Match
Mother-daughter dyads		
3 months	6 (9)	24 (18)
6 months	11 (11)	14 (9)
9 months	14 (13)	27 (13)
Mother-son dyads		
3 months	7 (7)	24 (19)
6 months	19 (14)	28 (13)
9 months	20 (20)	36 (19)

Note. F ratios, age: 3.64 (df = 2,48), $p < .05$, 3 < 6 = 9; sex: 5.98 (df = 1,48), $p < .025$, mother-daughter < mother-son; type of match: 20.17 (df = 1,48), $p < .001$; interactions: ns.

TABLE 14.3   Mean Synchrony Scores for Mother-Daughter and Mother-Son Dyads at 3, 6, and 9 Months

| | Synchrony Score | | | |
| | Mother-Daughter | | Mother-Son | |
Infant's Age	Mean	SD	Mean	SD
3 months	.20	.19	.11	.17
6 months	.09	.09	.23	.10
9 months	.11	.09	.22	.10

Note. F ratio for age × sex interaction is 3.24 (df = 1,48), p < .05.

Synchrony

Synchrony scores were analyzed with a univariate analysis of variance with age and sex of infant as the between-groups factors. The scores were transformed with Fisher's z transformation prior to analysis.

There was no age-related change in synchrony. The percentages of shared variance were similar at 3, 6, and 9 months (Table 14.3). However, we found a significant age × sex interaction. Mother-son dyads had higher synchrony scores than mother-daughter dyads at 6 and 9 months, $F(1,48) = 3.24$, $p < .05$.

Rates of Change Between Matching and Nonmatching States

To describe the movement of the interactions between coordinated and miscoordinated states, we evaluated the rate of change between the two states. Table 14.4 presents the rate of change between matching and mismatching states. The rate of change between matching and mismatching ranged from .20 to .32 per second. There were no age and no gender-of-dyad differences. The rate measure indicates that the interaction moves from matching to nonmatching states on a frequent basis.

TABLE 14.4   Rate of Change per 1 Second Between Matched and Mismatched States

| | Mother-Daughter | | | Mother-Son | | |
	3	6	9	3	6	9
Rate of change per 1 second	.24	.24	.24	.20	.32	.24

DISCUSSION

The matching of particular social-affective behaviors and of the temporal flow of these behaviors are features of infant-mother face-to-face interaction. These features can serve to establish mutuality or intersubjectivity between mother and infant (Beebe & Gerstman, 1980; Brazelton et al., 1974; Lester et al., 1985; Tronick, Als, et al., 1980b; Uzgiris et al., 1983). As expected, the ability of a mother-infant pair to coordinate their behavior increases with age. This probably reflects the increase in the infant's interactive skill and the interactive experience infant and mother have had together (Pawlby, 1977; Uzgiris et al., 1983). But, as opposed to typical earlier interpretations of similar results, we also must recognize that even in low-risk pairs matching/synchrony is less common than periods of mismatching and dissynchrony. More than 70% of the time of these interactions was spent in mismatched/dissynchronous states.

The rate-of-change data between matched and mismatched states demonstrate that the interaction frequently moves from coordinated states to less coordinated states. This movement has been noted before, but little attention has been paid to it. Brazelton et al. (1974) and Tronick, Als, and Adamson (1979) described periods of disengagement. Stern and Gibbon (1978) noted that periods of engagement came in bursts, implying that they were surrounded by periods of disengagement. Tronick, Als, et al. (1980b) described periods of mismatching, and Cohn and Tronick (1988) and Kaye and Fogel (1980) have noted that periods of coordination are stochastic in their distribution. Yet in each of these studies the focus and emphasis were on the ability of the infant and mother to be in coordinated states. We would now suggest that a characterization of the interaction that emphasizes the movement of the interaction from coordinated to miscoordinated states and back again is more accurate than one emphasizing matching/synchrony as the typical and critical feature of the interaction. This is a process-oriented characterization in which miscoordinated states and the transitions between them and coordinated states would be as critical to the quality of the interaction as is the coordinated state and its maintenance.

We (Gianino & Tronick, 1988; Tronick, 1980; Tronick, Cohn, & Shea, 1986; Tronick & Gianino, 1986b) have referred to the miscoordinated state as an interactive error and the transition from a miscoordinated state to a coordinated state as a process of repair. The reparatory process has been demonstrated in a number of studies. Infants attempt to repair experimentally induced interactive errors (Cohn & Tronick, 1983; Fogel, Diamond, Langhorst, & Demos, 1983; Tronick, Als, Adamson, Wise, & Brazelton, 1978). Tronick and Gianino (1986a) reported that during normal face-to-face interactions at 6 months of age, about one third of the interactive errors are repaired in the next step of the interaction. Cohn and Tronick (1983) found specific repair sequences at 3, 6, and 9 months and that infants, as well as their mothers, were responsible for the structure of the interaction (Cohn & Tronick, 1988). In this study, the repair rate ranged from about once every 3 seconds to once every 5 seconds. Reparations are typical features of the interaction.

What might be the developmental function of miscoordination and repair? Given the developmental changes in the infant and the interaction, it is likely that reparations serve different functions at different ages. We have suggested that for younger infants the reparation of interactive errors may induce the development of interactive skills (Spitz, 1965; Stern, 1977; Tronick, 1982) and the learning of the rules of interaction (Cohn & Tronick, 1983). Later in development, Tronick, Ricks, and Cohn (1982) have argued that the extent to which the infant is able to successfully repair interactive errors produces a sense of effectance, whereas an inability to successfully resolve them induces a feeling of helplessness. Tronick and Gianino (1986a) demonstrated that infants who experienced more repairs during normal interaction were more likely to elicit their mothers during experimentally manipulated per-turbated interactions. In the older infant, Stechler and Kaplan (1980), fol-lowing Winnicott (1975), argued that reparation may function to help in the formation of an early sense of self as the infant experiences discrepancies between his behavior and goals and his partner's behavior and goals (see also Tronick, 1980). These formulations and the data presented here suggest that more research focused on interactive errors and their repair would be extremely useful.

A significant gender difference was found in the degree of matching/ synchrony. Mothers and their sons were more likely to be in matching states than were mothers and their daughters. Haviland (1977) found that mothers tended to ignore their sons' expressions of pain but responded with a knitted brow to their daughters' expressions of pain. Moreover, when sons expressed anger it was reciprocated by a knitted-brow expression by the mother, whereas daughters' angry expression was responded to with an angry expression. These findings are suggestive of a different form of emotional attunement between mothers and their daughters compared to mothers and their sons (Stern, 1985). Such a difference would be expected to have important consequences for the emotional responsiveness and the formation of the self in females and males. For example, sons may develop a greater sense of their own effectance. These results tend to contradict the hypothesis by Chodorow (1978) of greater mater-nal empathy with daughters than with sons.

Last, these data and suggested conceptualization serve as a cautionary note to those concerned with the assessment of early interactive disorders and pos-sible pathologies. Normal interaction is not always well coordinated, and it is differentially coordinated between mothers and sons and mothers and daugh-ters. A lack of coordination is common and expected. It is normal, indeed. Assessments that focus on coordination or similar optimality characteristics are likely to see interactive failure or pathology when neither is present. An alter-native formulation is that assessment should focus on the interactants' capaci-ties to repair interactive errors and to move smoothly from miscoordinated states into coordinated states (Tronick & Gianino, 1986b). In such an interaction, both partners have the opportunity to experience reparation and to further elaborate their interactive and coping skills as well as gain a sense of effectance. To observe coordination in a dyad is phenomenally impressive, and to discover it was critical to our initial theorizing, but now we also need to look at and examine miscoordination and its reparation as a significant factor affecting the infant's development.

CHAPTER 15

The Transfer of Affect Between Mothers and Infants

The mutual regulation model (MRM) of early infant-caregiver social interchange proposed by Tronick (Gianino & Tronick, 1988) has characterized that interchange as a dyadic system in which emotional messages are exchanged between the partners functioning such that one partner achieves his or her own goals in coordination with those of the other partner (Tronick, 1980; Tronick, Als, & Brazelton, 1980b). The infant's behavior in this context meets the criteria usually advanced for goal directedness: persistence, use of multiple means to the same-end state, observance of a "stop rule" upon achievement of the goal, and appropriateness of actions (Bruner, 1970). The interactional goal in our culture is the achievement of a shared positive emotional state, mutual delight (Stern, 1974a). The infant's emotional displays coordinate social exchanges. They convey an evaluation of the partner's action, the state of the interaction, and also signal the infant's direction of action. For example, smiles typically indicate a positive evaluation and signal that the infant will continue his direction of action, whereas grimaces and frowns express a negative emotional state and signal a change in the infant's direction of action. To do this, the infant must have a repertoire of emotional displays; he must be able to appreciate the emotions displayed by his partner; and he must be able to organize his own displays in a coordinated fashion with the partner (Campos, Barrett, Lamb, Goldsmith, & Sternberg, 1983; Tronick, 1980, 1982).

From the perspective of the MRM, the ability of the partner and infant to mutually regulate the quality of the interaction has a fundamental effect on how the infant feels about himself—that is, on the child's feeling of effectance: the sense of what he can and cannot accomplish (White, 1959). When the child's social interactions result in a shared positive emotional state, the infant develops a sense of effectance. When such interactions do not accomplish this goal, the infant develops a sense of ineffectance or helplessness. Effectance can be thought of as modifying the infant's social style: the amount of persistence in following a direction of action and the extent to which a varied repertoire of means are mustered by the child. And although it is during social interaction, during the actual interchanges that the child's sense of effectance is structured, any factor such as maternal personality or stress that modifies how the mother interacts and responds to her infant will in turn affect the infant's sense of effectance.

The MRM's formulation is straightforward: the infant, through active deployment of his emotional signals, attempts to control the social environment. When the infant succeeds, positive emotions are generated and the infant gains a sense of effectance. When the infant fails, negative emotions are generated and a sense of ineffectance or helplessness results. The infant's success to some extent depends on the sensitivity—cooperation—of the mother in responding reciprocally to him. Emotions are not magically transferred from mother to infant, but rather the infant generates his own emotions as he processes the emotional input provided by the mother in relation to his own interactive goal.

The MRM applies to the mother as well. When the interaction goes well, the mother gains a sense of effectance; when it does not, she feels a sense of failure. But there is a difference as well. Because of the differences in their development, the infant's reactions are largely affected by the immediate external and internal stimuli; while the mother, obviously more developed, is not only capable of true empathy, she is affected by other factors—historical and social—that modify her self-esteem and in turn her interactions with her infant. When these historical factors are positive, the mother's sensitivity to her infant is increased; if they are negative, her behavior is disrupted and less sensitive. The disruption follows directly from the formulation that increases in anxiety are likely to disrupt complicated behavioral tasks, and interacting with an infant, though "natural," is complicated indeed. Thus the success or failure of mutual exchange generates emotional states in the infant which reflect not only the immediate situation but the effect of historical factors that impact on the mother's behavior.

This chapter presents a set of studies of normal mothers and infants. It illustrates how infant and maternal emotionality and effectance arise out of the quality of their social interactions as well as some of the factors that affect the quality of that interaction. To examine the effect of nonreciprocal signaling between mother and infant, mothers were asked to depress their affect during face-to-face interactions with their infants (Cohn & Tronick, 1983). This was accomplished through verbal instructions and by a videotape of a woman simulating a depressed interaction. This was a useful demonstration along with the particular instruction "act as you do on those days that you feel tired and blue." Few women had trouble following these instructions. The effect was to slow them down, eliminate all smiles or bright faces, limit their to-and-fro movements, and restrict their touching of their infants.

It was predicted that if the mother's behavior was distorted so that she conveyed primarily sad affect and did not facilitate the normal interactive goal, the infant would detect this distortion and engage in activities aimed at eliciting her normal response. It was also hypothesized that if the infant continued to try and continued to fail to elicit his mother's normal behavior, then he would also become emotionally depressed. This depressed affect, while a mirror of the maternal affect, is a product of the infant's own active emotional processing. These effects would be indicated by an increase in the proportion of time the infant was affectively negative and in the pattern of infant behavior during the interaction.

Twenty-four 3-month-old infants and their mothers were observed while the mother acted normally and in a depressed fashion, by turns. From the videotapes of the interaction, six infant affective states were coded: Look Away, Protest, Wary, Social Monitor, Brief Positive, and Play.

Figure 15.1 provides a schematic representation of the organization of infant behavior in each condition. Depressed-condition infants cycled among Protest,

FIGURE 15.1. Diagram of the state transitions for the depressed and normal conditions. The size of the circle represents the relative proportion of time spent in each state. The relative size of the conditional probabilities of event transitions is represented by the thickness of the arrows. Numbers are the exact conditional probabilities. Striped arrows indicate transitions where the conditional probability did not differ from the unconditional probability. Only the highest conditional probabilities are shown. (From Cohn & Tronick, 1983)

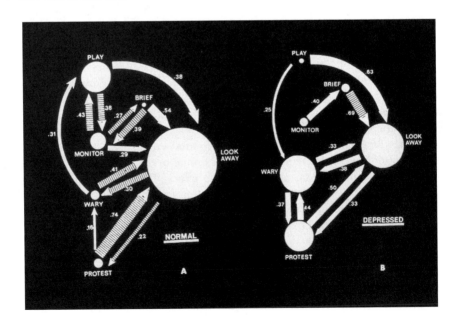

Wary, and Look Away. They also positively elicited (Brief Positive) more often than infants in the normal condition. Normal-condition infants evidenced a more positive emotional cycle—Brief Positive, Monitor, and Play. Second, there was an order effect. Infants were more upset in the normal interaction if they had experienced the depressed interaction first than infants who experienced the normal interaction first.

These data demonstrated a clear relationship between the quality of maternal affective displays and the infant's behavior. In this specific case, when maternal affect is experimentally depressed, infants organized their emotions very differently and they too begin to look depressed. Infants adapt to depressed affect on the part of the mother, and this adaptation persists into the next period of time in which the mother acts normally.

There are other examples of this process. Brazelton, Koslowski, and Main (1974), Stern (1971), and Massie (1978) have observed similar phenomena and have seen more longlasting consequences. Brazelton, Koslowski, and Main (1974)—in their study of face-to-face play of mothers and infants using frame-by-frame analysis—found that a mother, by not pausing during an interaction and allowing the infant to respond, produced turning away by the infant. They interpreted this pattern as a violation by the mother of the basic cyclic pattern of reciprocity. Most significantly, mothers who habitually engaged in this pattern had infants who, as they developed, deployed less and less visual attention to their mother.

Stern (1971), in an observational study of the interaction of a mother and her twins, found a rule violating pattern. With one twin, the pattern was one that repeatedly resulted in his turning away and, one might suggest, being turned off. He observed that as the mother approached the infant, he would begin to turn away and then, as the infant would start to turn toward the mother, she would begin to turn away. Thus, there was a vicious cycle. The cycle was time-consuming so that the mother and this twin interacted for longer periods of time than the mother and the other twin did, but it was an unsatisfying interaction.

This pattern was important because it constituted an important adaptive experience for the infant. It became a pattern with which the infant began to approach other situations. At 15 months this twin was more fearful and dependent than his brother. He refused prolonged eye contact and regularly performed gaze aversion in social situations. This pattern was clearly consistent with the earlier pattern.

Massie (1978), did frame-by-frame analysis of home movies parents had taken of their infants prior to the diagnosis of autistic-like psychosis. In some sense, the films were a prospective account of the early natural history of psychosis. For example in one case, Massie found a pattern of interaction in which positive approach by the infant produced turning away by her mother, followed by turning away of the infant and then turning toward the infant by the mother. At three years, when this infant was brought into a therapeutic setting, she no longer engaged in eye-to-eye contact with anyone and clearly behaved in an autistic-like fashion. This child showed normal developmental milestones during the first year and Massie attributed her aberrant outcome to this pattern of interaction.

In another study from our laboratory, Ricks (Ricks, 1981; Tronick, Ricks, & Cohn, 1982) has shown that the quality of the infant's interactive experience relates to the patterns of infant coping. Mothers were asked to distort the normal interaction by maintaining a still-face (Tronick, Als, Adamson, Wise, & Brazelton, 1978). Infants who elicited their mothers during the still-face were the infants of mothers who sensitively interacted with them during normal interactions. By contrast, infants of mothers who were, either over- or under-controlling had infants who failed to elicit. Under- and overcontrol do not allow the infant to have control over the interaction. Additionally there was the finding that infants who elicited at 6 months were more likely to be securely attached at one year than infants who had failed to elicit. Thus at six months and at one year infants of more sensitive mothers came into a stressful situation with a sense of their own effectance, expecting that what they do will make a difference. Infants at six months and one year whose mothers have been nor-reciprocal in their interactions came into new stressful situations with feelings of helplessness.

To follow up on these findings we are currently carrying out a study of the social interactions of depressed mothers and their young infants (Cohn, Connell, & Lyons-Ruth, 1984). Comprehensive developmental data are being collected on a group of 31 high-risk infants and their families. Project families are low SES (family income less than the poverty level) which have been referred by health providers or social workers because of disturbed maternal functioning. In particular, median maternal CES-Depression Scale scores are within the clinical range, mean scale score was 26 ($SD = 7$). The data presented are preliminary data on face-to-face interactions between eight 6-month-old Caucasian infant-mother pairs from the larger sample.

Mothers were asked to play with their infants for 2 minutes. A mirror placed at an angle to the mother permitted a single camera to record frontal views of both mother and infant. The filming of these interactions occurred in the families' homes, was preceded by 45 minutes of naturalistic observation and video-taping, and was conducted by two project staff, at least one of whom was well known to the families. Having at least one observer who was well-known to the mother was an attempt to reduce the stressfulness of the observation. The interactions were subsequently coded with a set of behavioral descriptors on a quarter-second time base.

Modal maternal behavior was neutral to negative (see Figure 15.2). Five of eight mothers were in Play less than 10% of the time. Only one mother was predominantly neutral to positive in affect expression. Mothers tended to sit back and away from their infants and either passively observe or else talk to them with relatively flat expression. One mother's paralinguistic expression, however, was frequently hostile and threatening.

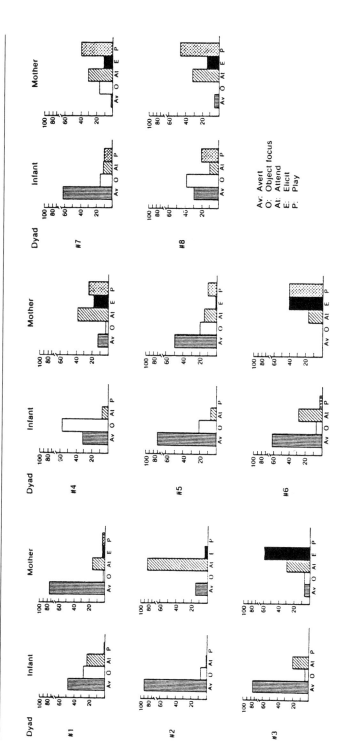

FIGURE 15.2. Percentage of interaction time in each monadic phase for each infant and mother.

Infant behavior was withdrawn and poorly regulated. Over 80% of infant time was spent in either Avert (62%) or Object Focus (20%). Attend accounted for only 13% of infant time and Play only 5%. On the few occasions when infants did direct gaze toward their mothers or become positive, these displays were attenuated. The mean durations of Attend and Play were each less than 2 seconds. Mean durations of Object Focus and Avert, conversely, were 4 and 7 seconds and both distributions were highly skewed. There was no significant variability across infants in any of these dependent measures.

A lag analysis of infant state transitions detected no sensitivity on the infant's part to his own prior behavior and at best only slight sensitivity to that of the mother. Infant state transitions were modeled adequately by a zero-order model. Inspection of dyadic state transitions yielded equivocal evidence of infant sensitivity to mother's previous state. On the few occasions when infants did become positive in affect expression, it was contiguous with maternal Play.

These interactions, therefore, were characterized by little joint visual regard and few bouts of positive engagement. Mothers tended to behave in a relatively detached manner, and even when they did attempt to engage their infants they were generally unsuccessful. Infant behavior was withdrawn, and those infant state transitions that did occur could not be reliably anticipated from the infant's prior behavior. At 6 months of age, these infants are responding in a manner that mirrors their mothers' lack of engagement and restricted range of affect expression. These data are strikingly unlike those which have been found in low-risk mother-infant pairs and suggest that the clinical antecedents of later distortions in infant development may be found in the fabric of social interactions as early as 6 months of age.

These studies support the MRM's hypothesis that the quality of the interaction between the mother and infant affects the infant's immediate emotional state and the infant's later interactions. Also the quality of the interaction affects the extent to which the infant feels either effective or helpless. One could argue that the mother's emotions are transferred to the infant. But that is too passive a view of the infant. The infant is not a mere recipient of maternal affect. The infant actively attempts to shape the interaction by processing the maternal emotional input and acting in terms of it and his own goal. When the infant is successful, when the mother's behavior conforms to his goal, the infant feels effective. During a distorted interaction when the infant's actions fail to modify her behavior, the infant begins to look distressed and helpless, and while that helplessness resembles the mother's state, it is not a mirroring of that state. It arises out of an active process that has failed. The infant's goal was one of reciprocity. He appreciates the mother's affective displays and attempts to change them. When he fails, he experiences distress and failure. This same process is hypothesized to account for depression in adults as well (Seligman, 1975).

These studies further emphasize that during the first year of life, infants evidence patterns of emotional reactivity that reflect their cumulated social and emotional history (Spitz, 1965). Historical factors, however, are more likely to influence the mother's behavior. To investigate this, we examined mothers' evaluations of their past relationships and in particular their self-esteem as it related to their infants' behavior. In an earlier study (Tronick, Ricks, & Cohn, 1982), it was demonstrated that mothers who evaluated their past relationships as more positive or had higher self-esteem were much more likely to have infants who at 1 year were securely attached. To investigate this prospectively, mothers' self-esteem was evaluated during the newborn period and its relationship to the quality of their interaction with their infants and their infants' behavior at 1 month were evaluated. The expectation was that mothers who had higher self-esteem would interact more sensitively with their infants and that their infants would be better organized behaviorally.

Thirty mother-infant pairs were randomly selected from the normal nursery of the Baystate Medical Center in Springfield, Massachusetts. The only criterion for inclusion in the study was that mother and infant had to be discharged home from the hospital together. This made for a generally healthy sample of infants and mothers. The infants ranged from 38 to 44 weeks gestational age and the group included infants with no health complications as well as infants with such health complications as transient tachypnea, feeding problems, minor anomalies such as a dislocated hip, and medical interventions such as phototherapy for elevated bilirubin levels.

Mothers were administered the Maternal Self-Report Inventory (MSRI; Shea, 1982; Shea & Tronick, 1982). This questionnaire is based on in-depth accounts of the feelings and attitudes of mothers toward pregnancy and motherhood that have been provided by Leifer (1977), Shereshefsky and Yarrow (1973), Greenberg and Hurley (1971), Blau et al. (1963), Schaefer and Bell (1958), Cohler, Wiess, and Grunebaum (1970), Bibring (1959), Benedek (1949), and Seashore, Leifer, Barnett, and Leiderman (1973). Their descriptions of maternal feelings and attitudes were derived from years of observations, clinical interviews with mothers, and data from questionnaires designed to identify and assess the critical factors comprising maternal adjustment to motherhood. From these reports, seven dimensions of maternal attitudes and feelings that comprise maternal self-esteem were identified. These dimensions have been found to be related to successful adaptation to motherhood and to infant development. These seven dimensions are: (1) maternal caretaking ability, (2) general ability as a mother, (3) acceptance of the baby, (4) expected relationship with the baby, (5) complications during labor and delivery, (6) parental influence, and (7) body image and maternal health. About 15 questions for each dimension, a total of 100 self-report items, were written to measure how a mother rates her own feelings on each. These questions were compiled in a self-report questionnaire on maternal self-esteem, the MSRI.

All items were written in the first person. Mothers were requested to indicate on a 5-point scale how accurately each statement described how they felt. Items from the seven dimensions were randomly intermixed throughout the scale and an equal number of positive and negative items were written for each dimension and randomly interspersed throughout the questionnaire in order to avoid response sets. This questionnaire was completed by the mothers 2 days after delivery. Reliability and validity analyses of the scale demonstrated that the MSRI is a highly reliable and valid measure of maternal self-esteem (Shea, 1982; Shea & Tronick, 1982).

All infants were examined using the Brazelton Neonatal Behavioral Assessment Scale (Brazelton, 1973). The Brazelton examination assesses the newborn's neurological intactness on 20 reflexes and the newborn's interactive behavior on 26 items. The interactive behaviors assessed include the infant's need for and use of stimulation, alertness, consolability, irritability, cuddliness, motor maturity, and ability to organize states. These interactive behaviors are summarized by four a priori scoring dimensions labeled interactive processes, motoric processes, state control, and physiological response to stress (Als, Tronick, Adamson, & Brazelton, 1976). Each dimension is scored such that high scores reflect poor performance and low scores reflect optimal performance. In the present study, the scores from the four dimensions were totaled to produce a summary score.

The quality of maternal and infant interaction at 1 month was assessed using a teaching task, designed by Spietz and Eyres (1977). In this assessment, the mother is asked to teach her infant two tasks, an easy and a hard task. The easy task for the 1-month-old infants was adapted from the Bayley Scales of Infant Development and involved teaching the infant to turn to look at a small shielded flashlight, and to follow the light as it was moved through several excursions from left to right. The hard task, also adapted from the Bayley Scales of Infant Development, involved teaching the infant to follow a red ring for at least 30 degrees to each side. Mothers were not given any instructions as to how to engage their infant in the tasks and if they asked, they were told to do what they felt would work best for their baby. The two tasks were presented in succession but the length of time spent on each task was determined by the mother and recorded by the investigator. The following standard instructions were given to each mother by the investigator: "I have two tasks I would like you to help your baby to learn. You may position your baby in any way that you like and take as much time as you wish. Just let me know when you are finished with the first task and then I will take a few notes and give you the second task." Following the first task, mothers were reassured that the second task was a difficult one and asked to do it with their infants.

At the end of each task, maternal and infant behaviors were rated using the manual and scoring sheet designed by Spietz and Eyres (1977). Two observers were present on more than 80% of the visits in order to check on interrater reliability. Interrater reliability across both teaching tasks ranged from .65 to .90, with a mean of .81.

Scores on these tasks consisted of a total maternal score, referred to as the Maternal Interactive score, with higher scores reflecting more positive and optimal maternal behaviors, and an Infant Interactive score, with lower scores reflecting more attentive and responsive infant behaviors. In addition, specific dimensions of the Maternal Interactive score were analyzed including Maternal Sensitivity and Techniques. Maternal Sensitivity scores reflect the degree to which the mother appears tuned into her infant's communication and task performance, and the frequency with which she responds to the infant's various cues, whether potent or subtle, during the task (Spietz & Eyres, 1977). The Techniques score reflects the success of various techniques such as infant positioning, task handling, and timing used by the mother to teach her infant the task. For both of these variables, a high score reflects more positive and optimal maternal behaviors.

Observations of the teaching task demonstrated that mothers who had higher self-esteem during the newborn period had a higher quality of interaction at 1 month with their infants (see Table 15.1). Maternal Interactive scores for the easy and hard tasks were significantly related to MSRI at 1 month with correlations of .34 ($p < .05$) and .24 ($p > .10$), respectively. Maternal Sensitivity score on the easy task was significantly related to MSRI score ($r = .40$, $p < .001$) but not on the hard task ($r = .20$, ns). Maternal Techniques score was significantly related to MSRI on the easy task ($r = .34$, $p < .05$) and on the hard task ($r = .36$, $p < .05$). There was no significant relationship between Infant Interactive scores and MSRI, although the correlations were in the appropriate direction. There was no relationship to infant behavior as measured by the Brazelton and the MSRI, though the relationship was in the predicted direction.

TABLE 15.1   Correlation of Maternal and Infant Behavior at 1 Month to Maternal Self-Report Inventory (MSRI) During Newborn Period

	Correlation to MSRI
Maternal Interactive score	
Easy task	.34**
Hard task	.24*
Maternal Sensitivity score	
Easy task	.40***
Hard task	.20
Maternal Techniques score	
Easy task	.34**
Hard task	.36**
Infant Interactive score	
Easy task	−.19
Hard task	−.17
Brazleton total score	−.18

*$p < .10$.
**$p < .05$.
***$p < .001$.

FIGURE 15.3. A diagram of the mutual regulation model representing the relationship of infant effectance and maternal self-esteem to the quality of the interaction and other factors.

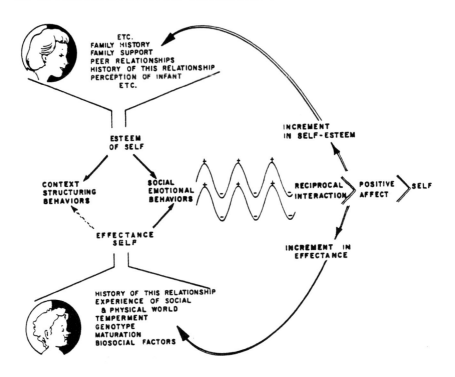

Figure 15.3 summarizes these studies and the MRM. It shows how a multiplicity of factors find their expression in the quality of the social exchanges that infants engage in. The entry point into the figure is the interaction—the actual behavioral exchange between a mother and her infant.

Mother and infant engage in social exchanges. When these engagements go smoothly with well-fitted-together positive and negative cycles of behavior, positive emotions are generated. This produces an increment in self-esteem for the mother and in effectance for the infant. In the study where mothers acted depressed, the reciprocal interaction was disrupted and negative affect was experienced by the infant.

To further substantiate that argument, we showed that mothers who were more sensitive to their infants during normal interactions had infants who at 6 months and at 1 year made strong and persistent efforts to overcome an interactive stress. On the other hand, infants whose mothers were either over- or undercontrolling during normal interactions had infants who failed to effectively cope with the stress. Such over- or undercontrolling patterns prevent the infant from having an effect on the interaction and produces a sense of ineffectance.

Other factors—not explored here—such as temperament, biosocial factors, experience in the inanimate world, and such modify the infant's sense of effectance and emerging self. Such factors affect the mother as well, but some that are especially relevant at her developmental level have to do with her familial history and sense of self-esteem. Each of these, as was found, affects her behavior with her infant.

Emotions then are transferred during the interaction through the form and quality of the social interaction of the mother and child. It is not a passive process for either but an active social engagement on both their parts.

It is our view that from the emotions generated during social exchanges, an emotional mood and interactive patterns become internalized in the child. They become part of the infant's affective core or prerepresentational self (Emde, 1983). Any specific interchange makes a trivial contribution to that stabilization. Spitz (1965) has emphasized it is the cumulation and reiteration of the positive and negative emotions generated in the daily social exchanges that is significant. But this should not be taken to mean that the interaction must always go smoothly. Far too often, we romanticize the mother-infant relationship and expect it to always be reciprocal. Rather, from the model of effectance one can see that some amount of dissynchrony varying with the child's developmental level can have positive effects. It provides the child with the opportunity to renegotiate the interaction. When that renegotiation is successful, the child will experience an increase in his sense of effectance. This formulation of the MRM is much more specific than the idea that some frustration or stress is necessary for development (Spitz, 1965). Of course, if the dissynchrony is too great, occurs too often, or is intractable to the infant's efforts, then a sense of helplessness is generated in the child.

The affective core biases the infant's evaluation of a new situation and his interactive patterns even before the information arising from the situation has been processed. The infant whose affective core is one of depression or possibly anxiety is biased to evaluate a new situation fearfully and to disengage from it even before confronting it. For the infant who regularly interacts with a depressed mother there will be a particular poignancy to the affective core that is internalized. The infant with a depressed mother will find that positive emotional displays are repeatedly greeted by negative displays, sadness, and anger by the mother. Even if the infant repeatedly attempts to elicit a positive maternal response, he will be met by failure and the infant will become sad himself. What is poignant here is that the infant comes to internalize an interactive pattern as part of the affective core in which his positive displays become related to sad feelings. Thus when the infant feels positive within himself, those positive feelings lead to sad feelings and withdrawal. When interacting with others, his withdrawal leads to their withdrawal. Thus he becomes trapped by his own depression from both inside and outside. This affective core acts as the infant's initial adaptive system. It structures the "meaning" of a situation for the infant and so regulates his interactive behavior.

CHAPTER 16

Mother-Infant Face-to-Face Interaction: Influence Is Bidirectional and Unrelated to Periodic Cycles in Either Partner's Behavior

D uring mother-infant face-to-face interactions, bidirectional influence could be achieved through either the entraining of periodic cycles in the behavior of each partner or through the stochastic organization of behaviors. To determine whether and how bidirectional influence occurs, we used both time- and frequency-domain techniques to study the interactions of 54 mother-infant pairs, 18 each at 3, 6, and 9 months of age. Behavioral descriptors for each mother and infant were scaled to reflect levels of affective involvement during each second of the interaction. Periodic cycles were found in infants' expressive behavior only at 3 months and not in mothers' behavior. Nonperiodic cycles, which were found in some mothers' and infants' behavior at each age, were more common. At no age was the occurrence of cycles in mothers' or infants' behavior related to the achievement of bidirectional influence. Similar proportions of mothers and infants were responsive to moment-to-moment changes in the other's behavior, except at 6 months when the proportion of mothers was higher. Bidirectional influence was brought about by the stochastic organization of behaviors rather than through the mutual entraining of periodic cycles.

Early mother-infant face-to-face interactions have a conversation-like pattern in which each partner appears to be responsive to the other. The assumption that this pattern is actually achieved by bidirectional influence has been seriously questioned in a series of papers (Gottman & Ringland, 1981; Thomas & Malone, 1979; Thomas & Martin, 1976). Few studies have rigorously tested the null hypothesis that during face-to-face interactions, moment-to-moment changes in the infant's behavior are independent of changes in the mother's behavior. Three studies that did test the null hypothesis (Gottman & Ringland, 1981; Hayes, 1984; Thomas & Malone, 1979) failed to reject it.

Two types of organization of the infant's behavior, periodic or stochastic, would permit the mother to create the semblance of bidirectional influence. *Periodic* events cycle on and off at regular, precise intervals, permitting highly accurate prediction of the timing of future events. A periodic cycle is deterministic in that the frequency, phase, and amplitude do not vary over time (Gottman, 1981). Alternatively, *stochastic* events are autocorrelated over short intervals; that is, sequences occur nonrandomly (e.g., smiles following the onset of visual regard; Kaye & Fogel, 1980). Depending on the type of autocorrelation, sequences may also be cyclic, but not periodic. Cohn and Tronick (1983), for instance, reported that during normal interactions infants displayed cycles of neutral and positive expressions. Because these cycles were stochastic (i.e., nonperiodic and, hence, variable in frequency, phase, and amplitude), they would not accurately predict infants' expressions over the long term.

These two types of behavioral organization have different implications for how bidirectional influence could occur. One hypothesis is that periodic cycles occur in both the infant's and the mother's behavior and that these cycles become synchronized through a process of mutual entrainment (Lester, Hoffman, & Brazelton, 1985; Schaffer, 1977b). A second hypothesis is that expressive behaviors are autocorrelated over short intervals but also cross-correlated with (i.e., contingent on) the preceding behavior of the partner (Cohn & Tronick, 1987; Kaye & Fogel, 1980). These hypotheses are not mutually exclusive; a third hypothesis, therefore, is that bidirectional influence occurs in both of these ways.

These hypotheses all posit active processing of social signals by the young infant and are consistent with the view that infants respond in specific and appropriate ways to their mother's communicative displays (Campos, Barrett, Lamb, Goldsmith, & Stenberg, 1983; Cohn & Tronick, 1983; Tronick, 1981). They differ in regard to how this responsiveness comes about.

Mutual entrainment hypotheses make greater demands on the infant's cognitive abilities because they assume that the infant can abstract relatively long periodicities from the mother's behavior. Lester et al. (1985) reported periodicities of 10 to 45 seconds. The accomplishment of this task would be all the more impressive in light of the fact that the mother's periodicity varies as she attempts to adjust to her infant's. Because face-to-face interactions seldom last more than several minutes, infants might have to accumulate experience over the course of many interactions before mutual entrainment could occur and bidirectional influence could be detected.

Data relevant to these hypotheses have been inconsistent. Brazelton, Koslowski, and Main (1974) described infants' attention to the mother as cycling on and off at four regular intervals per minute and hypothesized that these cycles were sinusoid, which implies periodicity. Nevertheless, they also claimed that the duration of cycles varied depending on the quality of the mother's behavior. Lester et al. (1985), on the other hand, appear to have assumed that any nonrandom temporal organization is periodic. Visual analysis of their graphs of mothers' and infants' spectral density functions suggests otherwise. Such graphs are characteristic of stochastic organization (see Appendix A for an example).

The present report uses both time- and frequency-domain techniques (Gottman, 1981; McCleary & Hay, 1980) with mother-infant pairs at 3, 6, and 9 months to define the organization of infants' behavior. Age 3 months was chosen because previous theory and some data about periodicity and bidirectional effects have focused on infants at this age (Brazelton et al., 1974; Gottman & Ringland, 1981; Kaye & Fogel, 1980; Stern, 1974a). Age 9 months was chosen because more recent data (Jasnow & Feldstein, 1986; Martin, 1981) suggest that by 9 or 10 months infants' behavior during face-to-face interactions is stochastic and influence is bidirectional. The organization of behavior may change with development, and the range of ages studied allowed us to investigate that possibility.

METHOD

Subjects and Procedures

The subjects were 18 infants, 9 boys and 9 girls, each at 3, 6, and 9 months of age. All were from middle-class families and had experienced no significant perinatal medical complications. Face-to-face interactions were videotaped in our laboratory using a split-screen procedure. Only the first of three 2-minute interactions are included in this report (additional details are reported in Cohn & Tronick, 1987).

Coding

Videotapes were coded using the *Monadic Phases Manual* (Tronick & Cohn, 1987), which is a revised version of a system described by Tronick, Als, and Brazelton (1980b; Als, Tronick, & Brazelton, 1979). Following Tronick (Tronick, Als, & Brazelton, 1977) and Lester et al. (1985), the monadic phases were scaled along an attentional/affective dimension. For our coding of monadic phases, this resulted in a 9-point scale; Lester et al. (1985) used a more differentiated coding of monadic phases that resulted in a 13-point scale.

Mother and infant monadic phases were scored separately by teams of two coders using a stop-frame procedure: Whenever a change in phase was observed, the videotape would be reversed and replayed at full and at slow speed to determine whether a change and what type of change in phase had occurred and the time of its occurrence. Times, read from the digital time display, were rounded to the nearest 0.25 second. For comparison, videotapes of 12 mothers and 5 infants were recoded by a second team of coders. Agreement, defined as the second team of coders' observing the same phase within 0.5 second of the first, ranged from 81% to 97% for mothers' monadic phases and from 90% to 100% for infants' monadic phases (κs = 60% and 72%, respectively).

Data Reduction

To achieve comparability with previous research that used a 1-second modified frequency scoring interval (Gottman & Ringland, 1981; Lester et al., 1985; Tronick, Als, et al., 1977) scaled scores were averaged within 1-second blocks. This produced a time series for each mother and infant of approximately 120 observations, which is sufficiently long for time series analysis. All analyses were of individual subjects.

Data Analysis

To determine whether a stochastic or a periodic process characterized the time series for each mother and infant, and as a preliminary step in the analysis of bidirectional influence, each univariate time series was modeled using time-domain autoregressive integrated moving average (ARIMA) analysis (Appendix B). Unlike the frequency-domain spectral analysis used by Lester et al. (1985), ARIMA analysis provides (orthogonal) parameter estimates of stochastic and periodic components in a time series. The two approaches are theoretically equivalent, but in practice the time domain approach may miss periodic processes that are rare and show little variance to a time series.

To guard against such errors, we computed spectral density functions (Appendix C) for each series and compared them with those expected on the basis of the fitted time domain model. When a spectral analysis indicated a periodicity not present in the model, we refit the series with a periodic parameter at a lag consistent with the spectral analysis.

As an initial step in the analysis of bidirectional influence, we first computed cross-correlation functions (CCFs) from the raw (or first-differenced, as appropriate) data for each mother-infant pair. These results were used to screen out dyads for whom no further analyses were warranted. A finding of no statistically significant cross-correlations (i.e., all cross-correlations within two standard deviations of zero) is sufficient evidence to rule out bidirectional influence. Where significant cross-correlations were found, we used Gottman's (Williams & Gottman, 1982) program Bivar (Appendix D) to test the null hypothesis that mother's and infant's behaviors are independent.

RESULTS

The time series for all but one of the mothers and one of the babies were stationary and did not require differencing. In the two cases that required differencing, first-order differencing was sufficient to bring about stationarity.

Is the Mother's Behavior Periodic?

The time-domain analyses showed no evidence of periodicity in any mother's time series, with the exception of one mother each at 3 and at 6 months. The absence of periodicity was confirmed by spectral analysis.

Is the Infant's Behavior Periodic?

At 3 months, the time series for 5 of 18 (28%) babies had a significant periodic component. Of these, 3 were identified during the initial time domain modeling; 2 others suggested periodicity after spectral analysis. The mean period was 10 seconds. The variance due to periodicity, however, was small relative to that accounted for by autoregression (see Is the Infant's Behavior Stochastic?, below). For these 5 babies, periodicity accounted for less than 3% of the variance in the univariate time series.

Only 1 of 18 infants at 6 months and none at 9 months showed any evidence of periodicity. Both of these proportions were below the 95% confidence interval for 3 months.

Is the Mother's Behavior Stochastic?

The mothers' series all had significant autoregressive parameters and, as noted before, no significant periodic parameters. Autoregression accounted for an average of 37% of the variance in the mothers' univariate time series; this proportion did not vary with age of the infant.

Four mothers at 3 months, 8 mothers at 6 months, and 6 mothers at 9 months had series that were fit by nonperiodic, cyclic AR(2) models. Estimated mean cycle durations were 16, 23, and 27 seconds at 3, 6, and 9 months, respectively. Neither the number of mothers with nonperiodic cyclic series nor the duration of the cycles varied with infant age.

Is the Infant's Behavior Stochastic?

The time series for all but one of the infants had significant autoregressive parameters. Autoregression accounted for an average of 36% of the variance in infants' univariate time series; this percentage did not vary with age of infant, nor did it differ from that for the mothers.

Nonperiodic, cyclic AR(2) models fit the series of 4 infants at 3 months, 8 infants at 6 months, and 4 infants at 9 months (an example from the 6-month data appears in Figure 16.1). Estimated mean cycle durations were 23, 18, and 17 seconds at 3, 6, and 9 months, respectively. Neither the number of babies with nonperiodic cycles nor the cycle durations varied with infant age. Table 16.1 summarizes these findings.

TABLE 16.1 Proportion of Mothers and Infants at Each Age Whose Univariate Time Series Included a Periodic or a Stochastic Nonperiodic Cycle

	Type of Cycle	
Dyad Member	Periodic	Stochastic, Nonperiodic
Mothers		
3 months	.06	.22
6 months	.06	.44
9 months	.00	.33
Infants		
3 months	.28	.17
6 months	.06	.44
9 months	.00	.22

Note. N = 18 mothers and 18 infants at each age. For all but 1 baby and no mother, the periodic cycle is in addition to a large stochastic component. The maximum number of cycles is, therefore, two: one stochastic and one periodic.

Are Changes in the Infant's Behavior Related to Changes in the Mother's Behavior?

The proportion of infants who responded to changes in their mother's behavior was similar to the proportion of mothers who responded to changes in their infant's behavior, except at 6 months (see Table 16.2). The size of bidirectional effects was also similar for both partners. When the bivariate models were significant, they increased the proportions of explained variance by 16% for mothers and 17% for infants.

Babies were more likely to respond to changes in their mother's behavior if the mother were responsive to changes in their behavior. Only one baby at each age showed a bidirectional effect when the mother did not.

To see whether the occurrence of cycles—either periodic or nonperiodic—in the infant's behavior was related to the achievement of bidirectional influence, we first compared the proportion of dyads in which both the mother's

TABLE 16.2 Proportion of Mothers and Infants at Each Age Who Were Responsive to Changes in the Other's Behavior

Infant's Age	Mothers	Infants	z
3 months	.55	.39	*ns*
6 months	.67	.33	2.03
9 months	.50	.39	*ns*

Note. N = 18 mothers and 18 infants at each age; z is the test statistic for the significance of the difference between two proportions.

and the infant's behavior was cyclic with the proportion predicted by chance (i.e., we tested to see whether the occurrence of cycles in the mother's behavior was independent of the occurrence of cycles in the baby's behavior). Second, we compared the proportion of infants whose behavior was both cyclic and bidirectional with the proportion predicted by chance (i.e., we tested to see whether the occurrence of cycles in the baby's behavior and the achievement of bidirectional influence were independent). Both proportions were nonsignificant ($z = -.01$, and $z = -.43$, respectively).

DISCUSSION

Mothers' and babies' time series, with few exceptions, were stationary. This finding is relevant to the generalizability of our other findings. Had we looked at longer interactions, of the length studied by Lester et al. (1985) or Gottman and Ringland (1981), would we have found otherwise? The available evidence suggests not. Gottman and Ringland analyzed three 3-minute interactions and found nonstationarity, but only at the longest cycles. They reported that the effect was not large. Letter et al. analyzed 80 3-minute interactions and found no evidence of nonstationarity, although they had first removed any linear trend. Cohn and Elmore (1987) analyzed 20 3-minute interactions and found few exceptions to stationarity. Thus, only one study has found nonstationarity and then only at the slowest frequencies. Moreover, the convergence between our findings and those of Lester et al., despite differences in length of interaction and method of analysis, argues for the robustness of our findings with respect to stationarity.

We found strong support for the belief that face-to-face interactions are a product of bidirectional influence. At 3 and 9 months, similar proportions of infants and mothers had significant bivariate models. At these ages, we also found that infants and mothers were equally influential in influencing the direction of the interaction. At 6 months, on the other hand, mothers were more likely to follow their infant's lead. The relative difference between mothers and babies at 6 months may be related to infants' increased interest in objects at this age (Cohn & Tronick, 1987).

Some previous studies that found bidirectional influence in mother-infant interactions have been seriously criticized on statistical grounds. Rigorous reanalyses of data from Jaffe, Stern, and Peery (1973) and from Tronick, Als, et al. (1977) failed to replicate the original findings (Gottman & Ringland, 1981; Thomas & Malone, 1979). A study by Hayes and Elliot (reported in Hayes, 1984) found that mothers' and infants' vocalizations were independent.

Two more recent studies, in addition to ours, have used appropriate analyses and found evidence of bidirectional influence (Beebe, Jaffe, Feldstein, Mays, & Alson, 1985; Lester et al., 1985). An important difference between these studies and previous ones is that they regarded expressive behavior as multimodal. Jaffe et al. (1973) and Hayes and Elliot (reported in Hayes, 1984) examined only individual response modalities (e.g., gaze or vocalization) or small numbers of interactions. Under these conditions, evidence of bidirectional influence may be less likely.

Several factors demonstrate that bidirectional influence was achieved through the stochastic organization of behaviors rather than through the mutual entrainment of periodicities. First, if periodicity were, as Lester et al. (1985) and others argue, a biologically based "fundamental property of early face-to-face mother-infant interactions" (pp. 22–25), we would have found a higher proportion of truly periodic cycles. We observed 54 mother-infant interactions and found periodic cycles in the time series of only 6 babies and 2 mothers, and even then periodicity accounted for little variance. It is possible, of course, that had we observed longer episodes of interaction we would have found a higher proportion of periodic cycles. However, the cycle durations that we observed were within the range reported by others (Brazelton et al., 1974; Lester et al., 1985).

Second, even if we were not to reject the mutual entrainment hypothesis on the grounds that too few infants or mothers showed truly periodic cycles, the total proportion of cycles, both periodic and nonperiodic, was still less than one would expect on the basis of Lester et al.'s characterization. No more than half of the babies showed any evidence of cycles, periodic or nonperiodic, at any age. The same was true of the mothers. Proponents of periodicity in infants' expressive behavior claim that it is always present. Our results clearly do not support that claim.

Third, even if the type and proportion of cycles that we found were consistent with the mutual entrainment hypothesis, the occurrence of cycles in the infant's behavior was independent of the occurrence of cycles in the mother's behavior. Furthermore, mothers or infants with cyclic behavior were no more likely to show responsiveness to their partner. Cyclic behavior and bidirectional influence were unrelated.

Our conclusions differ from those of Lester et al. but are consistent with their spectral data. Visual analysis of their spectral plots, as noted earlier, suggests stochasticity rather than periodicity, and our data confirm that impression.

A minor difference between our findings and theirs is that we found no more than two cycles (periodic plus stochastic) in any one time series. They identified three. This difference may be due to their practice of arbitrarily defining slow, medium, and fast cycles and averaging spectral densities within these ranges. This procedure may have overestimated the number of cycles, because one band of elevated frequencies, as occurs in AR(1) and AR(2) processes, could be counted as more than one cycle. Moreover, they used a 13-point scale, which may have resulted in the identification of additional cycles. In this connection, Lester et al. reported that the use of fewer scale points eliminated slower frequency cycles but did not otherwise influence the spectra.

Our findings seriously call into question the belief that infants' behavior during face-to-face interactions is periodic. In light of the results, spectral data previously cited in support of the periodicity hypothesis are better inter-preted as indicative of stochastic organization. Of course, it is possible that were infants' behavior described with a system other than the monadic phases (as we use or as used by Lester et al. and Gottman & Ringland) or were some discrete behavior, such as vocalization or gaze, studied, accept-able evidence of periodicity might be found. Further research is needed to explore this possibility.

The results provide an important basis for the use of sequential analysis to study mother-infant interactions. Sequential analysis is valid only if behavior is generated by a stationary, stochastic process. Were infants' behavior during interactions either nonstationary or periodic, its characterization by sequential analysis—and, consequently, findings from a large number of studies (e.g., Cohn & Tronick, 1983, 1987; Kaye & Fogel, 1980; Malatesta & Haviland, 1982; Stern, 1974a)—would be potentially invalid.

In summary, using rigorous data analytic techniques, we have confirmed that the conversation-like pattern of mother-infant face-to-face interactions at 3, 6, and 9 months is produced by bidirectional influence. Bidirectional influence is achieved through the stochastic organization of behaviors and not through mutual entrainment of periodic cycles. Periodic cycles accounted for some variance in infants' behavior at 3 months. Nonperiodic cycles were found in some mothers' and infants' behavior at each age. However, at no age was the occurrence of cycles in mothers' or infants' behavior related to the achieve-ment of bidirectional influence.

APPENDIX A

Different temporal organizations have characteristic spectral profiles. A sto-chastic second-order autoregressive organization—AR(2)—has one nonperiodic cycle when the two autoregressive parameter estimates meet the following con-dition: $a_1^2 + 4a_2 < 0$. The spectral density function will peak over a broad range of frequencies, which reflects the variability of the cycle. Figure 16.1 is an example from our data of an autoregressive organization of this type. In this example, $a_1 = .75$ and $a_2 = -.75$; therefore, $a_1^2 + 4a_2 = -0.40$.

When $a_1^2 + 4a_2 > 0$, an AR(2) organization is not cyclic, and the spectral density function will have no peak and will be similar to that of an AR(1) organ-ization, as exemplified in our data by Figure 16.2.

By contrast, the expected spectrum for a periodic cycle would peak over a narrow band of frequencies. (Were it not for measurement error, the spectrum for a periodic cycle would peak at a single frequency.)

Note that in both Figures 16.1 and 16.2, more than one frequency departs from the expectation for a random organization (i.e., white noise), as depicted by the dashed line in each figure. Significant spectral results cannot be inter-preted as facto evidence of periodicity (see Gottman, 1981, or Chatfield, 1980, for further reference).

FIGURE 16.1. Spectral density function for a stochastic organization with one nonperiodic cycle.

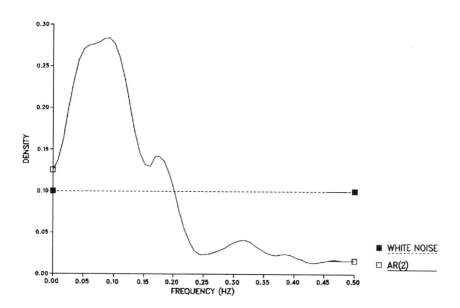

APPENDIX B

An integrated process is one that is nonstationary in mean, variance, or covariance and must be differenced prior to making estimates of AR or MA parameters. A time series generated by both stochastic and periodic processes would have orthogonal AR or MA parameters for each component.

ARIMA models are written in the form (p, d, q) (p, d, q), where p refers to the order of the autoregressive parameter(s); d to the order of differencing (typically $d = 0$ or 1); and q to the moving average parameter(s). The repetition of terms is for periodic processes; when they are all zero, they are usually omitted from notation. A stochastic autoregressive process would be written in the form $(p, 0, 0)$ $(0, 0, 0)$, or more briefly as $(p, 0, 0)$ or AR(p). A process with one autoregressive, stochastic component and one periodic component would be of the form $(p, 0, 0)$ $(p, 0, 0)$.

Univariate ARIMA modeling was performed using the time series program in Minitab (Ryan, Joiner, & Ryan, 1982) as implemented on the University of Pittsburgh's DEC-10 computer. The program subtracts the mean from each observation prior to analysis.

Following McCleary and Hay (1980), we used the following univariate mode-fitting procedure. First, each mother's and infant's series was examined for stationarity. A stationary series will have an autocorrelation function (ACF) that approaches zero as the distance between correlated observations (i.e., lag)

FIGURE 16.2. Spectral density function for a stochastic organization with no cycles.

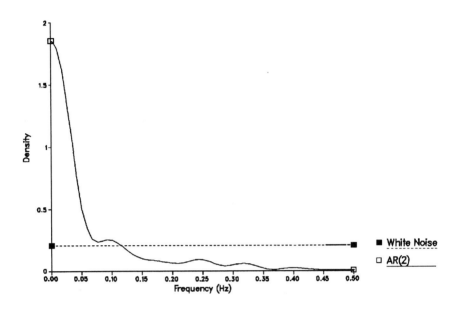

increases (Gottman, 1981). Any series for which the ACF did not behave in this way was differenced before making parameter estimates.

Second, both the ACF and the partial autocorrelation function (PACF) for each series were examined. Different types of time series have characteristic estimated ACFs and PACFs. For instance, the estimated ACF for a random process is zero; the estimated ACF for a nonperiodic AR(1) process decays exponentially. The estimated ACF for a periodic process will decay exponentially at periodic lags. For each series, after inspection of the ACF and PACF, a model was selected and fitted to the series. Model parameters had to be statistically sigificant, and the ACF of the residual series had to be acceptable by the following criteria: By visual inspection, no more than alpha (i.e., $\alpha = .05$) of the cross-correlations for the residual series could be significantly different from zero; cross-correlations for Lags 1–3 could not approach significance; and the Box-Pierce statistic, which is distributed as chi-square, had to be nonsignificant.

APPENDIX C

We used Gottman's (Williams & Gottman, 1982) spectral analysis program, which uses a Tukey-Hanning window. In general, we were not concerned with significance testing, because in each case the form of the spectral density function was known from the preceding time domain analysis. When an unanticipated peak in the spectrum did occur, we calculated the period of the cycle in seconds and then refit the time-domain model with a periodic term at that lag.

The parameter estimate for that lag was then tested for statistical significance ($p < .05$). An alternative test of significance would be to compute confidence intervals around the white-noise spectrum value.

APPENDIX D

Bivar is a bivariate time domain procedure that regresses each partner's behavior on both its own past (autoregression) and the past behavior of the other (cross-regression). It is an extension of the univariate modeling described in Appendix B with the following limitations: Differencing, if necessary to achieve stationarity, is assumed rather than included as a formal parameter; stochastic AR but not MA parameters are included; and no periodic parameters are included. The absence of MA parameters is of little consequence. The absence of periodic parameters would be, however, were a series strongly periodic.

Bivar uses a step-down procedure in which auto- and cross-regressive terms are systematically tested for significance and dropped as indicated. The bivariate models are:

$$M_t = \Sigma a_1 \times M_{t-1} + \Sigma b_1 \times B_{t-1} + e_t$$

and

$$B_1 = \Sigma c_1 \times B_{t-1} + \Sigma d_1 \times M_{t-1} + n_t,$$

where B_{t-1} baby's behavior at Time $t=1$, M_{t-1} = mother's behavior at Time $t=1$, and e_t and n_t = random noise or error at Time t. The baby's (or mother's) behavior is a function of both her own previous behavior and that of her partner. For both the mother and the infant, a likelihood-ratio procedure tests the significance ($p < .05$) of the difference between the larger bivariate and the smaller univariate model. The bivariate models reduce to univariate models when the cross-regressive coefficient is not significantly different from zero.

To reduce the likelihood of spurious findings, the univariate modeling and inspection of the CCF guided our choice of the number of parameters at which to begin the step-down procedure. The initial number of AR terms was set at one more than that found in the largest univariate AR model, which was a third-order autoregressive model—AR(3). The number of cross-regressive terms was individually set according to the CCF for a given dyad. For instance, if the CCF suggested that the baby was following the mother at a lag of 1–6 seconds, we set the initial number of cross-regressive terms at 6.

Bivar does not test for simultaneous cross-lag dependence. Most other bivariate time series programs do (e.g., BMDP IT). However, to correct this omission, we modified Bivar accordingly. We also subtracted the mean from each observation prior to analysis to aid interpretation and for consistency with the univariate analyses.

Beyond the Face: An Empirical Study of Infant Affective Configurations of Facial, Vocal, Gestural, and Regulatory Behaviors

The extent to which young infants' expressive modalities of face, voice, gesture, posture, and gaze form coherent affective configurations and whether these configurations relate to interactive events is of critical theoretical importance for our understanding of infant emotions and experience. Despite extensive work on individual modalities taken one at a time (e.g., Izard, Huebner, Risser, McGinnes, & Dougherty, 1980; Scherer, 1982; Stern, 1974b), and the creation of a priori configurations by us (Tronick, Als, & Brazelton, 1980b) and others (Beebe & Gerstman, 1980; Gaensbauer, Mrazek, & Emde, 1979), little empirical examination of these questions is available. In this chapter, we evaluate the coherence of infant expressive modalities and their relation to interactive events.

Empirical evidence on the coherence of expressive modalities and their relation to events would help clarify a number of issues. Findings of coherence and specificity to events would weaken the arguments that infants lack affective states, that infant affective states are diffusely organized, and that expressive modalities are unrelated to emotional states (Lewis & Michalson, 1982; Sroufe, 1963; Sroufe, 1979b). Coherence among expressive modalities would support the hypothesis that infants have discrete emotions (Izard, 1977; Izard & Malatesta, 1987) but not the argument that facial expressions constitute the primary index of affective states. Rather, coherence is consistent with the hypothesis that emotions are "tripartite complexes" composed of facial expressions, vocalizations, and body postures (Izard, 1977; Malatesta, 1981). Coherence as well as specificity may also lead to consideration of Kagan's (1984) and Fogel's (Fogel et al., 1992) suggestion that we attend more carefully to context and that context be included in our identification of affective states.

Findings on the co-occurrence of expressive modalities may have clinical and functional implications as well. Clinically, organized patterns of expressive modalities may serve as the basis for evaluating and describing atypical emotional and social behaviors in young infants. For example, Tronick, Beeghly, Fetters, and Weinberg (1991) proposed that infants exposed to cocaine in utero may have abnormal patterns of co-occurring facial expressions and regulatory behaviors. Abnormal configurations may characterize infants and children with cognitive, affective, and neurological disorders. We would also hypothesize that functionally the co-occurrence of affective behaviors would enhance the communicative value of the infant's affective displays by increasing the redundancy of the message conveyed by face, voice, and body. Evidence on the coupling and decoupling of affective behavior may shed light on Brazelton's (Brazelton, Koslowski, & Main, 1974) hypothesis that different behaviors can be substituted for one another to convey the same message. Substitutability contrasts with a position arguing for the primacy of facial expression as the major or even sufficient mode of affective communication.

The issue of the relation among different expressive modalities has been typically sidestepped by a priori solutions that have assumed coherence among modalities rather than empirically examining it. Several researchers have developed coding systems that cluster behaviors and facial expressions into affective states (Beebe & Gerstman, 1980; Gaensbauer, Mrazek, & Emde, 1979) or monadic phases (Tronick, Als, et al., 1980b) on an a priori basis. These systems purport to measure infant affect by combining information about facial and vocal expressions, posture, gaze, and type of activity. Some empirical evidence speaks to the validity of these a priori systems. Matias, Cohn, and Ross (1989), for example, reported strong correlations between MAX codes of facial expressions and monadic phases. Nonetheless, a priori clustering can incorrectly group unrelated behaviors and mask findings that a more empirical approach might uncover. For example, Weinberg and Tronick (1992) found gender differences in 6-month-old infants' facial expressions and behavior using a microanalytic scoring system that were undetected by the monadic phases clustering system.

There are some data that more directly evaluate the issues of coherence among expressive modalities and their relation to specific contexts. This research is both descriptive and empirical. Casaer (1979) described the co-occurrence of posture, motor tone, eye opening and closure, and hand positions for different states of sleep and wakefulness. Brazelton et al. (1974) suggested that the newborn's alert face is accompanied by smooth movements, eyes oriented toward mother, fleeting smiles, grimaces, and vocalizations. By contrast, they described periods of withdrawal as characterized by glazed or dull expressions, few vocalizations and smiles, little movement, and face and eyes oriented away from the mother. Empirically, some researchers have reported that discrete hand movements are associated with particular arousal and affective states (Fogel & Hannan, 1985; Legerstee, Corter, & Kienapple, 1990). Fogel and Hannan found that pointing tended to occur before or after mouthing and vocalizations, curling of fingers during vocalizations, and spreading of fingers when the infant was looking away from the mother. Legerstee further found that hand and arm movements are differentially organized when the infant is presented with different interactive and nonsocial events.

Michel, Camras, and Sullivan (1992) found coherence among 5- and 7-month-old infants' head, brow, and eye movements. Specifically, they found that raised-brow movements co-occur with head-up/eyes-up whereas knit brows co-occur with eyes down at 5 months and with head down at 7 months. They argued that these "coordinative structures" are not indicative of underlying emotional states. Rather, they suggested that a multiplicity of factors constrain the formation of motor components into larger structures and that one of these constraints is the recruitment of one set of muscles by another set of muscles (e.g., specific facial actions such as a brow movement recruiting other movements such as a head movement). This argument may be difficult to refute even with evidence of coherence of modalities, given that it breaks the linkage between the co-occurrence of behaviors and internal state. However, empirical evidence on the co-occurrence of affective modalities might clarify this issue. For example, since it is not obvious why certain muscles should recruit other muscles, especially those at a "distance" from one another (e.g., certain facial expressions and certain postures), findings of coherence among distant behaviors would tend to support arguments for an underlying motivational organization rather than recruitment.

The present research examined the relations among the modalities of face, voice, gesture, gaze, and self-regulatory and withdrawal behaviors during Tronick's face-to-face still-face paradigm (Tronick, Als, Adamson, Wise, & Brazelton, 1978). This paradigm was chosen because it has been demonstrated to elicit a wide range of affective behaviors from infants. The paradigm confronts the infant with an age-typical developmental task (face-to-face social interaction with the mother), an age-appropriate stress (the mother holding a still face and remaining unresponsive), and a reunion episode during which the infant and mother renegotiate the interaction after it has been disrupted by the still face (reunion face-to-face interaction with the mother). The infants' behavior was coded with the Infant Regulatory Scoring System (IRSS; Tronick & Weinberg, 1990), which is designed to separately characterize infant gaze, gestures, vocalizations, and self-regulatory and withdrawal behaviors. The infants' facial expressions were coded with Izard's AFFEX system (Izard & Dougherty, 1980). The extent to which individual expressive modalities formed organized affective configurations and whether these affective configurations were related to the different interactive contexts of the face-to-face still-face paradigm was evaluated.

METHOD

Subjects

Twenty-five male and 25 female 6-month-old infants and their mothers participated in this study. The infants ranged in age from 5 months 3 weeks to 6 months

1 week. All infants were healthy full-term Caucasians from intact homes. Subjects were recruited through birth announcements published in local newspapers. Potential participants were sent a letter describing the study and were then telephoned. Mothers who expressed interest in participating in the study were scheduled to bring their infant to the laboratory at a time when they thought their infant would be alert.

Laboratory Setting and Procedures

The laboratory instrumentation was based on the system originated by Tronick for recording face-to-face interactions (Tronick, Als., et al., 1978). The laboratory consisted of a video studio and an adjoining equipment room. The studio was equipped with an infant seat mounted on a table, an adjustable swivel stool for the mother, two cameras, a microphone, and an intercom. One camera was focused on the infant and one on the mother. Both picture signals were transmitted through a digital timer and split-screen generator into a single video recorder in order to produce simultaneous frontal views of the mother and the infant. The digital timer, split-screen generator, and video recorder were located in the equipment room, in which the experimenter timed the episodes and gave the mother instructions via the intercom.

When the mother and infant arrived at the laboratory, they were greeted by a female experimenter. After some initial conversation to make the mother and infant as comfortable as possible, informed written consent was obtained from the mother for her own and her infant's participation. The mother was then asked questions about the perinatal status and general health of the infant, and various demographic data about the family were collected. At the completion of the interview, the mother and infant were escorted to the video room, and the infant was placed in the infant seat. The mother and infant were then videotaped during the face-to-face still-face paradigm: a 2-minute face-to-face normal interaction for which the mother was instructed to play with the infant as she would at home, followed by a 2-minute still-face interaction for which the mother was instructed to keep a poker face, to look at the infant but not to smile, talk, or touch the infant, and a second 2-minute normal reunion interaction. At the end of the session, the mothers viewed the videotape of the interactions.

Coding of Data

Infant Behavior

The infants' behavior was coded using the IRSS (Tronick & Weinberg, 1990). The IRSS was derived from Tronick's Modified Monadic Phase Scoring System (Tronick, Als, et al., 1980b), observations by Brazelton and his colleagues (Brazelton et al., 1974) of the young infant's coping repertoire, and Gianino's (1985) research on self-comforting and exploratory behavior. The system codes

TABLE 17.1   Summary Description of the Major Codes of the Infant Regulatory Scoring System (IRSS)

IRSS Category	Description
Social Engagement	The infant looks or glances at the mother's face.
Object Engagement	The infant looks at or manipulates an object for 2 seconds or more.
Scans	The infant glances at objects or around the laboratory without focusing on an object for more than 2 seconds.
Vocalizations	The infant vocalizes with (1) neutral/positive, (2) fussy, or (3) crying vocalizations.
Gestures	The infant (1) gestures to be picked up or (2) moves his or her arms or legs in an organized manner in the direction of the mother (e.g., reaching).
Self-Comforting	The infant self-comforts by (1) sucking on his or her body (e.g., thumb sucking) or (2) sucking on an object (e.g., the chair strap).
Distancing, Escape/Get Away	The infant attempts to distance himself or herself from the mother by turning, twisting, or arching his or her body in the infant seat.
Autonomic Stress Indicators	The infant exhibits behaviors that indicate autonomic arousal such as spitting up, hiccuping, or tongueing.
Inhibition/Freezing	The infant inhibits his or her perceptual, motor, and/or attentional processes to minimize engagement with the mother and the surround (e.g., the infant is glassy-eyed).

eight dimensions of infant behavior: Social Engagement, Object Engagement, Scans, Signaling (i.e., vocalizations and gestures), Self-Comforting, Distancing, Inhibition, and Autonomic Stress Indicators (see Table 17.1 for a summary description of these codes). The Social Engagement, Object Engagement, and Scan codes are mutually exclusive, whereas the other codes can co-occur. It should be noted that all mothers are instructed not to use any toys during the face-to-face still-face paradigm. Therefore, Object Engagement refers to the infant looking at the chair, infant strap, clothing, and so on.

The coding was done by three coders from videotapes using 1-second time intervals. One coder scored Object Engagement, Social Engagement, and Scans, another Signaling, and a third Self-Comforting, Distancing, Inhibition, and the Autonomic Stress Indicators. A digital time display was used to track the intervals. This produced an absolute frequency count of the behaviors and maintained their temporal sequence to within a 1-second interval. The tape was run at normal speed although it was frequently stopped or run in slow motion to accurately determine the beginning and ending of shifts in infant behavior.

Infant Facial Expressions

The infants' facial expressions were scored using Izard's AFFEX system (Izard & Dougherty, 1980). AFFEX identifies 10 discrete emotions as well as blends of emotions. The 10 discrete emotions are interest, joy, surprise, sadness, anger, contempt, fear, shame/shyness/guilt, distress, and disgust. The tapes were scored using 1-second time intervals by coders who had been trained with Izard's training tapes and manuals and who were unfamiliar with the IRSS used to code the infants' behavior.

Reliability

To assess interobserver reliability, 20% of the first-play, still-face, and reunion-play episodes were recoded. Reliability was determined in two ways. First, following the procedure established by Cohn and Tronick (1987), agreement was defined as both coders scoring the same IRSS or AFFEX code in the same 1-second interval. This is an extremely stringent criterion requiring agreement by category and time. For example, lack of agreement can occur because the two coders code different behaviors or facial expressions in the same second or because they chose the same code but disagreed as to the exact second in which it occurred. Reliability (number of agreements divided by agreements plus disagreements) was calculated for each IRSS code and the AFFEX codes of joy, interest, sadness, and anger. The AFFEX-coded facial expressions of surprise, fear, disgust, distress, contempt, shame, and positive and negative blends occurred 1% of the time or less and were excluded from analysis. The mean percentage agreement for the IRSS and AFFEX codes was .91. Second, when there was sufficient variability in the codes, reliability was determined using Cohen's kappa. The mean kappa was .69.

Since both the IRSS and AFFEX codes were on the same time scale, it was possible to evaluate the extent to which the different IRSS-coded behaviors and AFFEX-coded facial expressions co-occurred.

RESULTS

Relation Between Facial Expressions and Behavior:
Affective Configurations

To test the hypothesis that infant facial expressions and behaviors form organized and coherent affective configurations, the relations between AFFEX-coded facial expressions and IRSS-coded behaviors were examined using a set of chi-square tests for mutually exclusive categories of IRSS behaviors. These analyses specified which behaviors were more as well as less likely than chance to co-occur with the facial expressions of joy, interest, sadness, and anger. Examination of behaviors that were more likely as well as less likely to co-occur with each facial expression is important for evaluating the meaning or function of a configuration. Table 17.2 presents descriptive data on the AFFEX facial expressions and IRSS behaviors. Tables 17.3–17.6 present the observed frequencies of co-occurrence of the AFFEX-coded facial expressions of joy, interest, sadness, and anger and each IRSS behavior displayed by the infants.

Four different affective configurations were found (see Table 17.7). One was a coherent affective configuration of Social Engagement (see Table 17.3). This configuration was characterized by person-oriented positive behaviors: facial expressions of joy, looks at the mother, neutral/positive vocalizations, and mouthing body parts. Specifically, the observed frequencies of the combinations

TABLE 17.2 Mean Proportion of Time (*M*), Standard Deviation (*SD*), and Number (*N*) of Infants Who Displayed Each AFFEX Facial Expression and IRSS Behavior Across the Episodes of the Face-to-Face Still-Face Paradigm

Facial Expressions and Behaviors	M	SD	N
Joy	.21	.23	49
Interest	.61	.25	50
Sadness	.03	.08	30
Anger	.05	.14	35
Look at mother	.39	.25	50
Look at objects	.41	.24	50
Scans	.19	.12	50
Signals	.40	.41	50
Neutral/positive vocalization	.10	.15	48
Fussy vocalization	.07	.12	35
Crying	.02	.12	7
Pick-me-up gesture	.03	.07	28
Gestural signals	.17	.20	50
Self-comforting	.08	.12	44
Mouthing body part	.04	.10	31
Mouthing object	.04	.08	34
Escape/get away	.02	.07	25
Autonomic indicators	.03	.07	27
Inhibition/freezing	.00	.00	0

Note. AFFEX codes are mutually exclusive. Look at mother, look at objects, and scans are also mutually exclusive, as are neutral/positive vocalization, fussy vocalization, and crying.

TABLE 17.3   Social Engagement: Observed Frequencies for the Co-occurrence
of the AFFEX Facial Expression of Joy and IRSS Behaviors

Joy Co-occurring With:		
Look at mother ↑ 2,948**	Look at objects ↓ 479**	Scans ↓ 347**
Neutral/positive ↑ 1,130**	Fussy ↓ 138**	Crying ↓ 19**
Pick me up ↓ 92**	Gestural signals 1,074	
Mouth body part ↑ 155**	Mouth object ↓ 53**	
Escape/get away ↓ 32**		
Autonomic stress ↓ 33**		

Note. ↑ and ↓ indicate that the observed value is greater than or less than expected.
*p < .05.
**p < .01.

TABLE 17.4   Object Engagement: Observed Frequencies for the Co-occurrence
of the AFFEX Facial Expression of Interest and IRSS Behaviors

Interest Co-occurring With:		
Look at mother ↓ 3,066**	Look at objects ↑ 5,541**	Scans ↑ 2,383**
Neutral/positive 662	Fussy 355	Crying 87
Pick me up 173	Gestural signals 1,417	
Mouth body part ↓ 371*	Mouth object ↑ 635*	
Escape/get away ↓ 132*		
Autonomic stress ↓ 150**		

Note. ↑ and ↓ indicate that the observed value is greater than or less than expected.
*p < .05.
**p < .01.

TABLE 17.5　Passive Withdrawal: Observed Frequencies for the Co-occurrence of the AFFEX Facial Expression of Sadness and IRSS Behaviors

Sadness Co-occurring With:		
Look at mother 195	Look at objects 143	Scans 113
Neutral/positive ↓ 14**	Fussy ↑ 200**	Crying 11
Pick me up 27	Gestural signals 135	
Mouth body part 5	Mouth object 3	
Escape/get away 35[a]		
Autonomic stress ↑ 35**		

Note. ↑ and ↓ indicate that the observed value is greater than or less than expected.
[a]Although the χ² was significant, one infant was responsible for more than half of the sadness/escape instances. When excluded from the analysis, the result was no longer significant.
*$p < .05$.
**$p < .01$.

TABLE 17.6　Active Protest: Observed Frequencies for the Co-occurrence of the AFFEX Facial Expression of Anger and IRSS Behaviors

Anger Co-occurring With:		
Look at mother 361	Look at objects ↓ 148**	Scans ↑ 246**
Neutral/positive ↓ 25**	Fussy ↑ 398**	Crying ↑ 222**
Pick me up ↑ 102**	Gestural signals ↓ 272*	
Mouth body part 8	Mouth object 3	
Escape/get away ↑ 129**		
Autonomic stress ↑ 137**		

Note. ↑ and ↓ indicate that the observed value is greater than or less than expected.
*$p < .05$.
**$p < .01$.

TABLE 17.7   Summary of Likely and Unlikely Co-occurrences of AFFEX
Facial Expressions and IRSS Behaviors

Likely Co-occurrences	Unlikely Co-occurrences
Social Engagement	
Facial expression of joy	Facial expression of joy
Look at mother	Look at objects
Neutral/positive vocalizations	Scans
Mouthing body part	Fussy vocalizations
	Crying
	Mouthing objects
	Pick-me-up gestures
	Escape/get away
	Autonomic stress indicators
Object Engagement	
Facial expression of interest	Facial expression of interest
Look at objects	Look at mother
Scans	Mouth body part
Mouthing objects	Escape/get away
	Autonomic stress indicators
Passive Withdrawal	
Facial expression of sadness	Facial expression of sadness
Fussy vocalizations	Neutral/positive vocalizations
Autonomic stress indicators	
Active Protest	
Facial expression of anger	Facial expression of anger
Scans	Look at objects
Fussy vocalizations	Neutral/positive vocalizations
Crying	Gestural signals
Pick-me-up gestures	
Escape/get away	
Autonomic stress indicators	

of AFFEX joy and IRSS look at mother, AFFEX joy and IRSS neutral/positive vocalizations, and AFFEX joy and IRSS mouthing body parts were significantly greater than the expected values for these combinations.

Importantly, facial expressions of joy were significantly less likely to co-occur with looking at objects or scans. Thus, facial expressions of joy were preferentially directed toward the mother rather than objects and occurred infrequently with scans, a gaze pattern hypothesized to be indicative of brief exploration of the environment (Tronick & Gianino, 1986a). The characterization of the Social Engagement configuration as positive person-oriented was further supported by the finding that AFFEX joy was significantly less likely than expected to co-occur with behaviors that preclude positive social engagement such as fussy vocalizations, crying, and escape/get away.

An inanimate environment Object Engagement configuration was found (see Table 17.4). This configuration was characterized by facial expressions of interest, sustained looking at objects, scans, and mouthing objects. Thus, the combinations of AFFEX interest and IRSS look at objects and AFFEX interest and IRSS scans were observed significantly more than expected by chance. AFFEX interest was also more likely than expected to co-occur with IRSS mouthing of objects, a behavior often thought to reflect self-comforting but which can also be seen as exploratory. Facial expressions of interest therefore appear to occur in conjunction with brief or sustained exploration of the environment. This characterization was further supported by the finding that AFFEX interest and IRSS look at mother and AFFEX interest and IRSS attempts to escape/get away were observed significantly less than expected.

A configuration of Passive Withdrawal was found (see Table 17.5). This configuration was characterized by facial expressions of sadness, fussy vocalizations, and autonomic stress indicators. AFFEX sadness was unlikely to co-occur with neutral/positive vocalizations and was not significantly less or more likely to co-occur with any particular gaze pattern or active protesting behavior (e.g., crying or escape/get away).

Last, a configuration of Active Protest was found (see Table 17.6). This configuration consisted of facial expressions of anger, scans, fussy vocalizations, crying, pick-me-up gestures, attempts to escape/get away, and autonomic stress indicators. Thus, the observed frequencies of AFFEX anger and each of these IRSS behaviors were significantly greater than was expected by chance. Together these behaviors form an affective configuration that reflects a protest state characterized by actions that function to indicate the infant's active displeasure. This characterization was further supported by the finding that AFFEX anger was unlikely to co-occur with looking at objects, indicative of engagement with the inanimate environment, or with neutral/positive vocalizations and gestural signals, which indicate a positive state and social engagement.

Higher-order combinations of AFFEX expressions and IRSS behaviors were evaluated using logistic regression. This analysis confirmed the previous analyses of the two-way combinations. For example, the combination of look at mother and neutral/positive vocalizations was 41 times more likely to co-occur with facial expressions of joy than with facial expressions of interest, sadness, or anger. The combination of looks at objects and mouthing objects was 15 times more likely to co-occur with facial expressions of interest than with facial expressions of joy, sadness, or anger. And the combination of scans and crying was 14 times more likely to co-occur with facial expressions of anger than with facial expressions of joy, interest, or sadness.

Specificity of Affective Configurations by Conditions

A repeated-measures one-way ANOVA using MANOVA test criteria with episodes as repeated measures was used to determine whether the affective configurations

TABLE 17.8   Mean Proportion (*M*), Standard Deviation (*SD*), and Number (*N*)
of Infants Who Displayed Each Affective Configuration During
Each Episode

Affective Configuration	Play 1	Still Face	Reunion	*F*
Social engagement				
M	.09a	.02b	.13c	32.51**
SD	.15	.04	.19	
N	43	32	46	
Object engagement				
M	.16a	.20b	.11c	21.90**
SD	.18	.21	.15	
N	50	50	50	
Passive withdrawal				
M	.00a	.01b	.01b	3.84*
SD	.01	.04	.05	
N	11	16	15	
Active protest				
M	.00a	.01b	.02b	8.54**
SD	.02	.04	.06	
N	13	24	22	

Note. Means with different letters differ significantly at p < .05.
*p < .05.
**p < .01.

were differentially distributed across the first-play, still-face, and reunion-play episodes. The ANOVA used the combined proportions of the two-way AFFEX-IRSS combinations that were part of each affective configuration. As can be seen in Table 17.8, the results support the hypothesis that each of the four configurations is specifically related to the interactive event the infant was experiencing. The affective configuration of Social Engagement (i.e., facial expressions of joy, looking at mother, neutral/positive vocalizations, and mouthing body parts) was most likely to occur during the reunion play episode and least likely to occur during the still-face episode. This is consistent with an interpretation that social engagement decreases when the mother is unavailable but increases to higher levels when the mother resumes normal behavior and the partners attempt to reestablish the interaction. The affective configuration of Object Engagement (i.e., facial expressions of interest, looking at objects, scans, and mouthing objects) was significantly more likely to occur during the still face than during the two play conditions, suggesting that the still face as compared to the other episodes may require the infant to disengage from the mother and preferentially focus on objects. Finally, the affective configurations of Passive Withdrawal (i.e., facial expressions of sadness, fussy vocalizations, and autonomic stress indicators) and

Active Protest (i.e., facial expressions of anger, fussy vocalizations, crying, pick-me-up gestures, escape/get away, and autonomic stress indicators) occurred rarely during the first-play but increased significantly during the still-face and the reunion-play episodes, indicating that both the still-face and the reunion-play episodes are stressful. Thus, the data indicate that affective configurations are context specific.

DISCUSSION

In this study, we found that expressive modalities are differently associated with one another to form affective configurations which are differentially distributed in meaningful ways among the episodes of the face-to-face still-face paradigm. These findings lend considerable empirical support to the assumptions that infants' emotional expressions are well organized and that they are systematically related to environmental events. This degree of multimodal coherence and specificity for different types of affective modalities has not been previously demonstrated.

The degree of affective organization and specificity weaken the positions that infant emotions are diffusely organized (Sroufe, 1979b) or that infants do not have emotions because their expressive displays are neither well organized nor related to specific events (Spitz, 1963). Organization and specificity in infant affective displays also weaken the argument that adults treat infants "as if" they are capable of affective communication and that out of this as-if process true communication emerges (Kaye, 1982; Schaffer, 1984). The organization and specificity of the infant's expressive configurations certainly provide the caregiver with a wealth of information about the infant's as-if emotions and intentions. However, it must be noted that during the still-face episode the infant is organizing his or her behavior without the caregiver's as-if responses. Thus, it would seem that the infant's affective organization is not as dependent on the caregiver's behavior as the as-if hypothesis suggests.

The hypothesis that facial expressions constitute the primary means for indexing emotions also seems weakened. The data suggest that we cannot view one expressive system as the primary index of emotions. Rather, we must begin to evaluate the extent to which different expressive behaviors convey affective information on their own and, more important, in relation to one another. Moreover, we may need to reevaluate our terminology and conceptualization of affective expressions. Typically we label affective configurations simply by the facial expression presumed to index a particular emotion. The results from this study suggest that this practice may be inadequate. This labeling system makes the infant's facial expression the criterion modality but disregards the infant's other behaviors which are also organized in a particular manner in association with a particular facial expression and a specific event. Terms may need to incorporate affective, behavioral, and contextual features. This more inclusive form of labeling emphasizes that the infant who is displaying a particular

facial expression (e.g., anger) is at the same time acting on the world in a particular fashion (e.g., signaling to be picked up while crying) in response to a
specific event (e.g., the still-faced mother).

The message value of each configuration may also need to be included or
implied in the label. This is what we have attempted to do in labeling the four
configurations. The first two affective configurations, Social Engagement and
Object Engagement, communicate the infant's intention to socialize with people and to act on objects. For the Social Engagement configuration, the message might be "I want to continue this interaction," whereas for the Object
Engagement configuration, the message might be "I want to continue exploring this object." Both configurations convey the infant's goal to continue an
engagement through a sustained pattern of looking and an inhibition of negative vocalizations, escape behaviors, autonomic stress indicators, and facial
expressions of sadness and anger. These characterizations are consistent with
the functionalist perspective on emotions, which hypothesizes that infants persist in engaging in behaviors that facilitate the attainment of their goals,
whether social or object oriented (Campos & Barrett, 1984; Campos, Barrett,
Lamb, Goldsmith, & Stenberg, 1983; Tronick, 1980).

The Social Engagement and Object Engagement configurations are differentially displayed to people and to objects. When the infants are looking at
their mothers, facial expressions of joy, positive vocalizations, and mouthing
body parts are most likely to occur. By contrast, when the infants are looking
at objects, they are most likely to display facial expressions of interest and to
mouth objects. These findings are consistent with previous research indicating
that infants rarely display positive affective expressions such as smiles or play
faces when focusing on an object (Cohn & Tronick, 1987) and that there are
marked differences in attention span, state behavior, and buildup of excitement
when infants are interacting with objects as contrasted to people (Brazelton et
al., 1974).

The third and fourth affective configurations convey dissimilar messages primarily differentiated on an active-passive dimension. The Passive Withdrawal
configuration conveys a passive state characterized by facial expressions of sadness, fussy vocalizations, autonomic stress indicators, and low levels of activity.
Importantly, crying and escape behaviors, both thought of as active forms of
protest, are unlikely features of this configuration. The message of this configuration might be "I give up, I am overwhelmed." This characterization is clearly
consistent with Campos's assumption that sadness motivates disengagement and
withdrawal (Barrett & Campos, 1987; Campos et al., 1983). By contrast, the
configuration of Active Protest communicates the infant's negative evaluation
of an event through vocal protests and active attempts to get away and be picked
up. The message might well be "Change this!" As suggested by Campos
(Campos & Barrett, 1984; Campos et al., 1983), this configuration appears to
be associated with attempts to remove obstacles and with determined efforts to
change frustrating circumstances.

Organizing facial expressions and behaviors into multimodal configurations means that the infant's messages are elaborated and clarified. The dynamic and flexible nature of the configurations (i.e., similar behaviors are substitutable) also permits the configurations to vary in form while still conveying a similar message (Brazelton et al., 1974). We would hypothesize that expressive flexibility serves important functions. An infant capable of expressing the same message in multiple ways may maximize the chance that the caregiver will eventually interpret the message and respond to it in an appropriate manner. The infant makes an initial communicative attempt using a particular affective configuration or sequence of configurations and then, based on the caregiver's response, makes another and somewhat different type of communicative effort.

Expressive flexibility also allows infants to adapt their behavior and affect to different contexts. For example, anger expressions and crying may be the most appropriate means of communication in one context, whereas anger expressions and pick-me-up gestures may be more effective in another context. Finally, one can hypothesize that the greater the infant's need to communicate something to the caregiver, the greater the number of expressive units the infant will utilize to form an affective configuration. Thus, the infant presents information to the caregiver that is increasingly explicit in regard to his or her own state and direction of action.

The argument made by Michel et al. (1992) that coordinative structures do not reflect underlying motivational or affective states is not easily evaluated. However, it is not clear that their hypothesis of muscle groups recruiting other muscle groups can account for the observed configurations. Why, for example, are facial expressions of anger associated with physical attempts to escape/get away? An alternative hypothesis is to view the organization of the infant's affective communicative system, as described here, as similar to Bruner's (1970) account of the organization of skilled performances. According to Bruner, skillful motor performances consist of motor modules that are sequentially ordered into larger units of skilled action guided by intention. Intentionality or goal directedness allows for the flexible deployment of different means to the same end (Bowlby, 1969). We would argue that, in the case of the infant's affective communicative system, facial expressions and behaviors can be seen as fundamental expressive units. These expressive units are concurrently and sequentially combined into larger affective configurations by an underlying motivational state or emotion. Their function is to convey messages about the infant's internal state and direction of action in a specific context. Thus, facial expressions of joy and positive vocalizations go together because the infant is motivated to make social contact with the mother, not simply because smiles somehow recruit vocalizations.

In conclusion, our view is similar to that advanced by Campos (Campos et al., 1983) and Izard (1977) that the organization and specificity of the infant's affective configurations can be most parsimoniously understood by postulating that infants have emotions. Stern (1985) elaborates on the underlying process when he argues that the basis for the infant's emotional experience is the multimodal input from different sensory modalities in association with feedback from the infant's actions and feedforward of the infant's control signals (also see Edelman, 1987). The multimodal affective configurations displayed by infants and their specificity to environmental events strongly demonstrate that infants are processing temporally coordinated sensory and behavioral input as well as regulatory and control signals from their actions. Certainly it is reasonable to suggest that so rich a configuration of information could form the basis for coherent emotional experiences. Indeed, we would hypothesize that the basic units of the infant's experience are these bounded configurations of affect and behavior. The change from one configuration to the next, with all its internal features, is the boundary between chunks of experience for the infant in relation to equally well-structured events.

Whatever the eventual resolution of these issues, the findings here suggest that infants' affective displays are organized into coherent affective configurations, that there is a variety of configurations which serve different communicative functions, that expressive modalities are substitutable within configurations, and that the configurations are related to environmental events. These characteristics of the normal infant's affective displays might serve as a basis for evaluating atypical expressive emotional displays and configurations in young infants.

PART IV

PERTURBATIONS: NATURAL
AND EXPERIMENTAL

CHAPTER 18

The Primacy of Social
Skills in Infancy

An understanding of the organization of behavior in any species must focus on its members' most central adaptations. Adaptations can be viewed as the solutions a species develops for the problems posed by the external environment. These problems are posed in two domains—the domain of exchanges with the inanimate environment and the domain of exchanges with the animate environment that is composed of members of the same and other species. For any given species, the relative importance of each domain varies in a species-specific fashion. Each species survives and develops by evolving a unique set of adaptations to a unique mixture of problems in each domain. For example, if one wanted to understand the organization of vegetatively reproducing species such as protozoa, the focus would be on their evolved tropisms to temperature, light, acidity and other physical features of the environment. This is because their unique pattern of adaptations is aimed primarily at regulating exchanges in the domain of the inanimate environment. In the human species, the solutions to problems of survival and development have been shaped around regulating exchanges in the animate domain. This is evidenced by the species-specific configuration of human adaptive features—food sharing, tool manufacture, division of labor and coordinated tasks, male-female reciprocity, the mother-infant dyad, and culture with its elements of symbolic communication, and rule giving and following. All of these involve regulating exchanges with conspecifics. An understanding, then, of the organization of human behavior must thus first and foremost focus on the adaptations that our species has evolved for regulating joint activities.

This perspective has several implications. It suggests that each member of our species functions primarily as a communicator and that our most central adaptation is our communicative competence. This competence makes for the skillful regulation of all our cooperative endeavors. Moreover, this communicative competence not only allows us to function in our cooperative contexts but is fundamental and underlies our competence in manipulating the inanimate environment as well. This allows for the viewing of communication with conspecifics and manipulation of objects as a process of skill development, with the communicative skill preceding and generating the object-related skills.

Furthermore, from a developmental perspective, it appears to me that, following the establishment of physiological regulation, the infant's next task is to develop a set of skills for regulating joint exchanges. This is a necessary developmental step, because without the ability to regulate interaction the infant would be unable to regulate object-oriented interactions. Such skills are developed during interactions with adults that have no functional goal. Their goal is the successful establishment of regulation per se. The developmental task is to fulfill a set of constraints that ensure incorporation into the species.

This chapter will explore three aspects of joint activity. First, the process by which mother and infant are able to coordinate their behaviors during face-to-face interaction is described. Second, forms of disturbance in the interaction that disrupt appropriate coordinations are discussed. And third, the consequences of disruptions on infant development are presented.

JOINT REGULATION OF MOTHER-INFANT INTERACTION

I wish to present a model of the process underlying the joint regulation of activity in which the mother and infant, or any two human communicants, are viewed as two interacting cybernetic systems. The two systems utilize a shared set of generative communicative rules. These communicative rules generate the communicative behavior of each participant and predictions about the other's communicative behavior.

When two people come together in an interaction, they must share a goal as to what they want to do together. Let us say it is to have a dialogue. Given this goal, they must have a lexicon of communicative acts whose meanings they share. For example, frowns mean stop and smiles mean continue. They must also share a generative interactive syntax that has a format which specifies one's own communicative performance and a prediction of the partner's communicative performance (e.g., when I am talking, you will be listening).

When an interaction is appropriately coordinated, the sequence of communicative acts emitted by each partner conforms to the prediction each of them has made about the other's behavior. One communicant talks while the other communicant listens, just as each of them had predicted. It is this mutual matching of communicative acts and predictions that is the basis of joint regulation. When prediction and behavior do not match, the interaction is disordered.

However, one other condition is required for well-coordinated joint activities: temporal coordination. Two communicators may share the same goal, lexicon of communicative acts, and interactive syntax, but if they cannot act in a temporally coordinated fashion, the interaction will fail to be coordinated. Just recall the last time you and a partner started talking at the same time (and realize how seldom it actually happens). Or, if you want to try an experiment, try mouthing words each time someone starts to talk to you and note the disruption.

In summary, this description indicates what goes into the coordinated regulation of joint activity. The critical feature is a sharing of functions in time. The regulation of joint activity depends on shared interactive rules, a shared lexicon of communicative acts, shared interactive rules, and shared time. Partners generate their own behavior and predictions of their partner's behavior. This conformation or disconformation is the basis of regulation.

The investigation of mother-infant synchrony is a somewhat special case of joint regulation of communicative acts. First, language is not yet part of the interaction. Second, the participants probably do not share the same temporal domain. They are at very different developmental levels.

Condon and Sander (1974a) have approached the problem of temporal coordination by extending work on adults back to infancy. Condon (Condon & Ogston, 1967) has described two types of synchrony: self-synchrony and interactive synchrony. In self-synchrony, changes in direction of an adult's movement are coordinated with the phoneme boundaries of his speech. In interactive synchrony, two adults interact and the changes in direction of their body movements are synchronous with the phoneme boundaries of their partner's speech. Thus, their movement changes are coordinated.

Further, this synchrony extends to the system of mutuality between the organism and the environment. Condon (1979) has shown that some autistic children are out of sync with environmental events. Their reaction to an environment event is delayed. They react to what has happened several hundredths of a second in the past, rather than to what happens in the immediate present.

Condon and Sander (1974a) have demonstrated that infants are capable of interactive synchrony in that they can coordinate their movements with adult speech. Such synchrony is remarkable since phoneme boundaries are psychological rather than physical entities and may be as short as one tenth of a second in duration. Several studies (Eimas, 1975) suggest that infants may structure speech into phonemes, but it seems well beyond simple explanation that infants are able to process events and respond to them as quickly as interactive synchrony requires.

It may be that infants integrate the rhythm of speech much in the way that adults synchronize themselves with the melody of music, but at the moment there is no clear explanation of the phenomenon of infant interactive synchrony. Certainly, more developmental work is required to follow up on a hypothesis that the ability of the newborn to self-synchronize and to interactively synchronize—its coherence, so to speak—may be a crucial measure of the intactness of its central nervous system.

Our research, on the other hand, has focused on communicative synchrony between infants and adults (Tronick, Als, & Brazelton, 1977). We sought to answer the question of whether infants and adults are able to synchronize the changes in their communicative acts. To do this, we videotaped face-to-face interactions between mothers and their 80- to 90-day-old infants and then described their communicative acts. Thus, eye direction, facial expression, head direction, and so on were described on a second-by-second basis. Every act for every second was then given a ranked score reflecting the positive or negative affective tone of that act. For example, smiles had a higher positive rank than frowns, and looking toward was more positive than looking away. The ranked scores were then summed separately for mother and infant and the relationships between these summed scores were established. It must be emphasized that the scaling was not done to scale the interaction or to scale each participant. Such scaling is fraught with problems. Rather, the scaling was performed to allow for examination of the relational aspect of the interaction.

This relational aspect was analyzed by correlating the summed scaled scores for each mother and infant pair. High positive correlations would indicate mother and infant changing in the same direction at the same time in terms of their affective tone. High negative correlations would indicate that they were changing in opposite directions at the same time, and low correlations would indicate that there was little or no relationship between their changes in affective tone.

As shown in Figure 18.1, there was a striking result. Correlations were often high and positive, but they were also often high and negative. Mother and infant were able to synchronize their displays but, paradoxically, they could be

FIGURE 18.1. Ten-second "running" correlations of infant and mother scaled sum scores. (From Tronick, Als, & Brazelton, 1977)

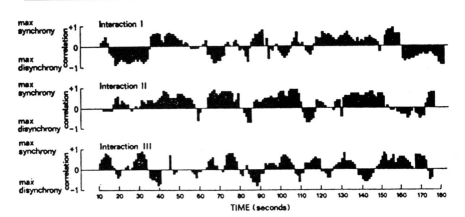

changing in exactly opposite affective directions. It may be as complicated a task to be out of phase with your partner as to be in phase, but it certainly does not possess the quality of being appropriately coordinated.

To analyze the question of appropriateness, the data were reanalyzed in the following manner. Three behavioral states were defined for mother and infant: (1) engaged—the communicator is looking toward his or her partner with a bright or smiling face and may be vocalizing or gesturing; (2) monitor—the communicator is looking toward his or her partner with a neutral or sober facial expression with no vocalization or gesturing; and (3) disengaged—the communicator is looking away from his or her partner with a cry, frown, or sober facial expression and may be crying or gesturing. Then three joint interactive states were defined: (1) match—the communicators are both in the same communicative behavioral state, engage-engage, disengage-disengage, monitor-monitor; (2) conjoint—the partners are in engage and monitor, or monitor and disengage; and (3) disjoint—the partners are in engage and disengage. When the three interactions were analyzed in this fashion, it became clear that, although the interactions might be synchronous, their coordinations were significantly different (see Figure 18.2). Interaction I is primarily disjoint and conjoint and Interaction II is primarily matched and conjoint. Interaction III is somewhat less matched than interaction II but much less disjoint than Interaction I (Tronick, Als, & Brazelton, 1980b).

These analyses demonstrate the extent to which mother and infant were able to appropriately coordinate their communicative behavioral states. Such coordination goes beyond synchrony in that it focuses on the relational appropriateness of the infant and mother behaviors.

What process underlies mother-infant communicative coordination? The answer, I think, lies in the joining of two cybernetic systems and the critical feature has to do with the mutual following of shared interactive rules. Such a model is suggested by studies which demonstrate the consequences of an inability to jointly follow these interactive rules.

FORMS OF DISTURBANCE IN FACE-TO-FACE INTERACTIONS

Some time ago we did an experiment in which the mother was asked to distort the normal interaction with her infant by establishing an en face position with the infant but to remain otherwise still in face and body (Tronick, Als, Adamson, Wise, & Brazelton, 1978). It was hypothesized that if the infant only has schemas for interesting displays, this change might be boring or interesting. However, if the infant has a set of interactive goals and a set of interactive rules that are used to make predictions about the mother's behavior, then the infant should attempt to reinstate a rule confirming interaction. That is exactly what happened.

FIGURE 18.2. Proportion of time in different joint interactive states and the types of state transitions. (From Tronick, Als, & Brazelton, 1977)

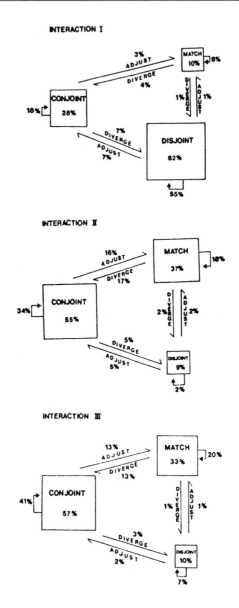

As the mother seated herself in front of her infant, the infant would establish eye-to-face contact and smile at the mother (Figure 18.3). When she failed to respond, the infant sobered but then might smile again. Following these greetings, the infant would begin a sequence of behaviors that involved looking toward the mother with a bright face, looking away, although probably

FIGURE 18.3. Sequential photo of infant's reaction to the mother in stil
Tronick, Als, Adamson, Wise, & Brazelton, 1978)

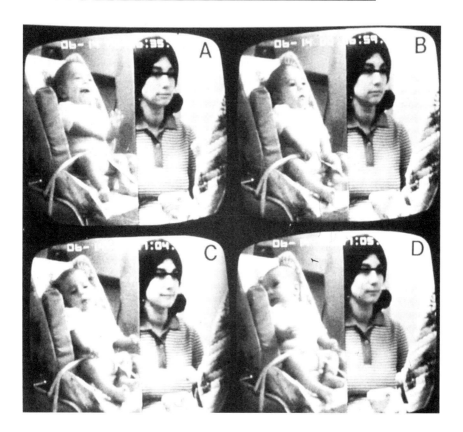

monitoring her with peripheral vision, and then looking back toward her, again with a bright face, only to look away again. This elicitation sequence was repeated a varying number of times, but eventually the infant would turn and remain away, often engaging in self-comforting behaviors. There were three phases in the infant's reactions. The first was the normal greeting, the second an elicitation phase, and the third a withdrawal and averting phase.

The interpretation follows the model of interactive rules. The infant and mother appear initially to share a goal for mutual playful interaction. The mother apparently is enacting the goal by seating herself in an en face position. The infant responds with the normal greeting on his side and with the prediction that she will go on to the next stage of play. When she fails to move on, the infant, still holding to the goal of mutual play, attempts to reelicit the expected interaction. When that fails, the infant changes goals, withdraws, and turns to self-comforting behaviors. It is a strong emotional reaction.

Brazelton, Koslowski, and Main (1974), Stern (1971), and Massie (1975) have observed similar phenomena and have seen more long-lasting conse- quences. Brazelton et al. (1974), in their studies of face-to-face play of moth- ers and infants, and of infants with objects, uncovered a crucial pattern of inter- action. Using frame-by-frame analysis, they found that a mother, by not pausing during an interaction and allowing the infant to respond, produced turning away by the infant. They interpreted this pattern as a violation by the mother of the basic cyclic pattern of reciprocity. Most significantly, mothers who habit- ually engaged in this pattern had infants who, as they developed, deployed less and less visual attention to the mother.

Field (1977) has found this to be a more general phenomenon than we pre- viously thought. She has looked at the interactions of mothers with 3-month- old infants who were either premature or postmature. She found that mothers of these infants did not give their infants enough pause time, and the infants responded by turning away. When she had the mothers imitate their infants— a maneuver that changes the mother's rate of behavior and thus gives the infant more time to take his turn, the infants looked at their mothers more and had more positive expressions.

Stern (1977), in his observational study of the interaction of a mother and her twins, also found a rule-violating pattern. With one twin, the pattern was one that repeatedly resulted in his turning away and, one might suggest, being turned off. The sequence is shown in Figure 18.4. As the mother would approach the infant, he would begin to turn away and then, as the infant would start to turn toward the mother, she would begin to turn away. Thus, there was a vicious cycle. The cycle was time consuming, so that the mother and this twin interacted for longer periods of time than the mother and the other twin did, but it was an unsatisfying interaction.

This pattern is important because it constituted an important adaptive expe- rience for the infant. Further, it seemed to become a pattern with which the infant began to approach other situations. At 15 months, this twin was more fearful and dependent than his brother. He refused prolonged eye contact and regularly performed gaze aversion in social situations. This pattern was clearly consistent with the earlier pattern.

Massie (1975), in an ingenious study, did frame-by-frame analysis of home movies parents had taken of their infants prior to the diagnosis of autistic-like psychosis. In some sense, the films serve as prospective account of the early natural history of psychosis. Massie found a pattern of interaction in which positive approach by the infant produced turning away by the mother, followed by turning away of the infant and then turning toward the infant by the mother (Figure 18.5). He felt that their interaction violated a basic biological rule of mothers and infants seeking eye-to-eye contact. Moreover, he suggested that the pattern was paradoxical, with the mother signaling through her holding and touching of the infant the message, "Respond warmly to me but don't look at me." At 3 years, when this infant was brought into a therapeutic setting, she

FIGURE 18.4. Pattern of approach withdrawal between mother and one of her twins. (From Stern, 1971)

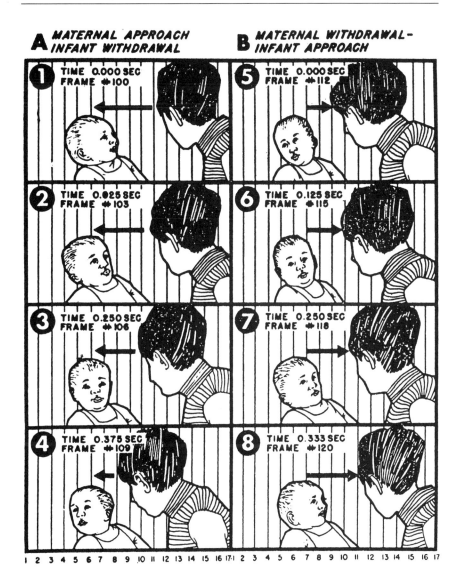

no longer engaged in eye-to-eye contact with anyone and clearly behaved in an autistic-like fashion. Except for some flaccidity in infancy, this child showed normal developmental milestones during the first year, and Massie was understandably tempted to attribute her aberrant outcome to this pattern of interaction.

FIGURE 18.5. Pattern of interaction between mother and child analyzed from home movies. (From Massie, 1975)

a

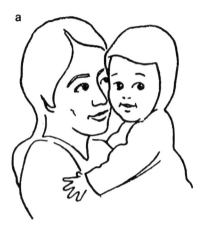

Mother and child are relaxed. Mother touches baby's check.

b

Child turns her head and eyes toward mother's face. Mother's expression tenses and her eyes shift away from child's face. Child tenses.

c

Mother shifts her head backward and to the side of the child's face, blocking child's facial approach and obstructing eye contact. Mother relaxes. Child appears dejected.

d

Mother and baby resume original postures, not in eye contact. Child's expression shifts from dejection to pleasure and drooling appears when mother pats child's head.

These observations suggest a more general definition for what is mean *appropriate* in an interaction. *Appropriate* is the mutual following of interactive rules that have a format which specifies who does what and when to do it. It is a rule of joint activity. "I act this way and I predict that you act that way." In the well-coordinated interaction, a participant's communicative act conforms to his or her partner's prediction about his or her act. In these observations, mother and infant did not follow the same rule at the same time. In each case, as in the Beatles' song, one said "hello" as the other said "goodbye."

Although these rules are elaborated, I do not think they are learned. Learning would allow for the mixing and matching of any of a diverse set of combinations to become appropriate. But these observations demonstrate that only certain patterns are permissible. First, to violate such rules is to violate a constraint inherent in the organism. Second, even in the earliest of social interactions this same pattern is found. The burst-pause pattern of sucking is reciprocal to the pause-act pattern of maternal behavior, as Kaye and Brazelton (Kaye, 1977a) have shown. Third, as has been argued for language learning, it is hard to imagine how an infant would learn the complicated and uniquely ordered sequences seen at 3 and 4 months in face-to-face interaction without some built-in constraints and capabilities. Rather, I think these latter patterns are elaborations of the basic format of one partner "on," the other partner "off."

CONSEQUENCES OF DISRUPTIONS
ON INFANT DEVELOPMENT

To understand the developmental impact of these interactive rule-violating experiences on the infant, they must be placed in an evolutionary perspective. Bowlby (1969) has suggested that attachment arises out of an adaptation to predation. I think that the significance of the interactive system goes beyond so singular a cause.

All species develop a system of mutuality—a set of mechanisms for sharing a territory, signaling to defend against predators, signaling in dominance relations, signaling in courtship, and so forth. Thus, adaptation from an evolutionary perspective and learning from an ontogenetic perspective can be seen as the development of mutual relations with the animate and inanimate environment. This notion holds true to the extent that the environment provides constraints that have significance for the organism (Ashby, 1956; Mayr, 1963).

The system of mutuality most central to human adaptation is that of reciprocal obligations (Mead, 1934). For the human, as for the gorilla, chimp, and baboon, the species' most characteristic feature is that the group is the context for subsistence activities—reproduction, protection, and socialization of the young (Fishbein, 1976). What competencies make reciprocal obligations possible? In answering this question, there is an interesting concurrence of answers that makes it possible to analyze how meanings are exchanged, how interactions are structured, and what skills re required for these tasks.

Reciprocal obligations involve the capabilities of self-awareness and empathy. Self-awareness is the ability to take another's point of view, while empathy is the ability to accurately perceive the emotional experience of another. In Piaget's framework, these abilities are slowly constructed during the child's first 2 years of life. To be reciprocally obligated, one must be aware of the effects of one's behavior on others and to act in ways that would be satisfying to yourself, were you to be in the other's place.

The philosopher Habermas (1969), in analyzing communication and the exchange of meaning, has said that the communicator's primary task is to understand the message-carrying displays of the other and to modify his own actions in accordance with the other's expressed intent while fulfilling his own intentions. Communication is not monologic but dyadic. Thus, communicative competence allows the interlacing of perspectives between communicators (Tronick, Als, & Adamson, 1979).

As Ryan (1974) noted, these analyses of reciprocal obligations and meaning emphasize the fundamental nature of the mutual recognition of particular kinds of intention by the speaker and the listener. And if one does not want to talk of intentions, one can substitute a mutual recognition function. However, the fundamental aspect is that something, some function, must be shared between two interactants that results in a mutual recognition of the other's ongoing intentionality or direction in behavior as it relates to one's own. The sharing is the intersubjective structure.

This way of characterizing the process or coordination makes the analysis of interactions a problem of the analysis of the components of skilled performance or what has been called communicative competence.

When interaction is looked on as a problem of the joint organization of serially ordered behavior, connections are again made with the concept of reciprocal obligations and the exchange of meaning.

Lashley (1951) analyzed skill performances and argued that three conditions must be fulfilled. First, there must be the arousal of an intention or goal in the presence of an appropriate object. Second, there must be a set of organized units of behavior or adaptive acts. Third, a syntax or set of rules for organizing these acts is required. For example, when presented with an object within reach, an infant extends his arm, opens his hand, and then closes it on the object. The skillful infant does not, although the younger infant does, open his hand and then close it and then extend his hand only to bat at the object. A syntax aroused by an intention organizes the sequencing of the components for achieving the goal. Cybernetic systems made up of a control element, a comparator for input and goal, and a corrective response have been used to model these performances.

In joint interaction, these same conditions must be fulfilled but, in addition, as we have seen, the two communicators must share goals, interactive rules, and communicative behaviors, and then use these rules to generate their own communicative behavior as well as a prediction of their partner's behavior. Thus, the reasons why I see communicative skills as being the basis for other skilled performances are that first, by 3 months of age, long before the infant is skillful with objects, he is able to skillfully regulate social interaction with organized social behaviors. Second, the regulation of joint activity is, in fact, more complicated than interaction with objects, since objects after all do not change goals or switch rules. Interaction requires shared functions. Third, from an evolutionary perspective and from work I have done with older infants, it is evident that objects are incorporated into social interaction and not social interaction into object play. In these ways, I think skillful performance with objects borrows its competencies from the competence for the joint regulation of behavior.

Bruner (1970, 1975b) has argued that language has many isomorphic relations to joint action and to skilled performances in general—and it is easy to see why. Skilled performances involve syntax, components, and goals. Language, as Lashley (1951) noted, is a form of serially ordered behavior. But the skillful regulation of joint activity is more complicated than performances with objects and possibly as complicated as language, since it, too, requires the sharing of the rules that govern it. Objects do not require such rule sharing and, although language does, the organism, prior to language, already has one shared system of rules. How much easier now to learn a second set. In this sense, I think it can be said that skillful performances with objects and language borrow their competencies from the capacity for the joint regulation of behavior.

But our understanding cannot simply be one of the attainment of competencies. In disturbed interactions the infant expresses a strong emotional reaction, a reaction of hopelessness, that eventually becomes a highly disturbed pattern of withdrawal; on the other hand, when the interaction is appropriate, as Stern (1971) pointed out, joy is the result. The rules of social interchange and the communicative acts that enact those rules can be viewed as the infant's initial and biologically primary adaptive system, in much the same way as later cognitive abilities are an adaptive system. This adaptive system is the basis for ontogenetic adaptation.

When these rules are not followed, a helplessness is learned by the infant that goes beyond the learned helplessness of infants with objects that they have learned they cannot control. The infant is caught in a biological double bind. The infant is adapted to act to achieve reciprocity, for his dependency makes this a biological imperative. When reciprocity is not achieved, the infant can try to continue to elicit the normal reaction and in disturbed situations continue to fail, or, just as disastrously, the infant can give up. In either case, the infant learns that his actions have no effect and that the situation requires a giving up of the goals of mutuality. The infant develops a pattern of behavior that precludes human interchange, and in such withdrawal a denial of the child's self is produced. Where confirmation of intersubjective goals occurs, patterns of greater and greater complexity are elaborated and a confirmation of self takes place. Such self-evaluations are learned in the context of social interactions and then become the patterns that the infant takes into all of his or her environmental transactions.

The Infant's Response to Entrapment Between Contradictory Messages in Face-to-Face Interaction

In face-to-face interactions, young infants begin to learn and define the rules of social interaction. In these early affective interchanges with caregivers, they learn: (1) the meaning of their own expressive behavior; (2) the characteristics of people who are important to them; and (3) cognitive and affective information that allows them to fit into their culture, to identify with their caregivers, and to identify themselves. Obviously, this communication system is an important source of nurturance for their cognitive and affective development (Stern, 1974a).

In our studies of face-to-face interactions between mothers and 2- to 20-week-old infants, we have characterized the hierarchy of goals of such interactions (Tronick, Als, & Adamson, 1979; Brazelton, Koslowski, & Main, 1974). These goals, which can be thought of as phases of an interaction, include initiation of the interaction, mutual orientation of the partners, greetings, cyclical exchange of affective information as in play dialogues and games, and mutual disengagement. The process of achieving these goals requires that the system be mutually regulated, that is, that both participants reciprocally modify their actions based on the feedback they receive from their partner.

To examine the infant's capacity for such regulation and the importance of interactional reciprocity for him or her, we experimentally distorted the feedback that the infant normally receives from the mother. The mother is asked to sit in front of her seated infant, remaining unresponsive and maintaining an expressionless face. The infant's intense reaction to this distortion demonstrates not only the importance of interactional reciprocity but also his impressive ability to regulate his affective displays to achieve the goals of the interaction.

METHODOLOGY

Subjects

Seven mothers and their healthy full-term infants ranging in age from 1 to 4 months were seen for a total of 20 sessions. Two pairs were seen longitudinally for 6 sessions, each at approximately 2-week intervals. The other five pairs were seen cross-sectionally; three were seen for 2 sessions each, and two for 1 session each.

Procedure

In each session, the mother either first interacted normally with her infant for 3 minutes, or remained still faced for 3 minutes and then after a 30-second break, during which the infant remained in his seat, she returned for the other condition. The order of condition was determined ahead of time, so that order effects could be assessed. In the normal interaction condition, the mother was instructed to "play" with her baby. In the still-face condition, she was instructed to look at her infant with a neutral face.

Our laboratory is set up to videotape the face-to-face interaction of a mother and her infant. The infant is seated in an infant seat placed on a table surrounded by an alcove of curtains. The mother comes from behind the curtains to seat herself in front of the infant (Figure 19.1). One video camera is focused

FIGURE 19.1. Schema of laboratory during observation of mother-infant interaction. A schematic drawing of the video laboratory illustrating the placement of infant and adult and their respective cameras.

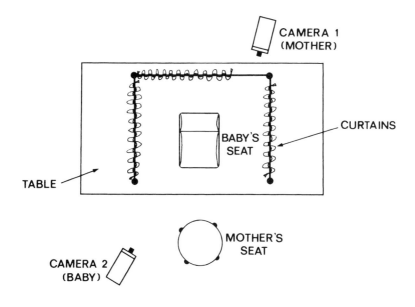

FIGURE 19.2. Schema of picture on TV monitor.

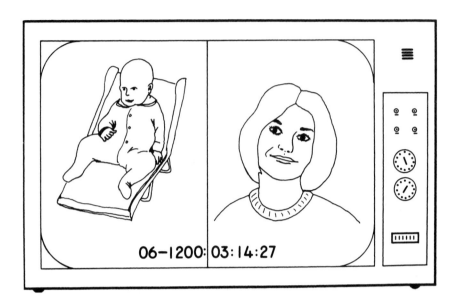

on the infant, the other on the mother. Their two pictures are fed through a digital timer and a split-screen generator into a single videotape recorder. The resulting split-screen image provides a frontal view of mother and infant, each on one side of the image along with a digital time display (Figure 19.2).

From this video recording, we categorize and score the infant's vocalizations, direction of gaze, head and body position, facial expression, and movement; and the mother's vocalizations, head position, body position, direction of gaze, facial expression, and handling of the infant. Table 19.1 shows the categories used. This scoring is done by two trained observers for each 1-second time interval as the tape runs at 1/7th normal speed. Interscorer reliability on each category is checked consistently and is maintained above .85.

RESULTS

The effect of the violation of reciprocity in the still-face condition can be seen clearly in the contrast between the infant's behavior during a normal interaction and the same infant's behavior during the experimental condition. The following is an abbreviated description of a 2-month-old infant's behavior in a normal face-to-face interaction with his mother.

Baby is looking off to side where mother will come in. He sits completely quiet, back in his baby seat, face serious, cheeks droopy, mouth half open, corners down, but there is an expectant look in his eyes as if he were waiting. His

TABLE 19.1   Behavior Scored for Mother and Infant

Infant	Mother
(1) *Vocalization:* 1. none; 2. isolated sound; 3. grunt; 4. coo; 5. cry; 6. fuss; 7. laugh	(1) *Vocalizing:* 1. abrupt shout; 2. stern, adult narrative; 3. rapid tense voice; 4. whispering; 5. little or no vocalizing; 6. rhythmic sounds with little modulation: 7. burst-pause talking; 8. single bursts in rapid succession with wide pitch range; 9. burst of sound that peaks with much change of modulation and pitch
(2) *Direction of gaze:* 1. toward mother's face; 2. away from mother's face; 3. follows mother; 4. looking at toy or hand mother is using as part of interaction	(2) *Head position:* 1. toward and down; 2. toward and up; 3. toward and level; 4. part side and down; 5. part side and up; 6. part side level; 7. toward and level; 8. toward and up; 9. toward and down; 10. thrusting; 11. nodding; 12. nuzzling; 13. cocked head
(3) *Head orientation:* 1. head toward, nose level; 2. head toward, nose down; 3. head toward, nose up; 4. head part side, nose level; 5. head part side, nose down; 6. head part side, nose up; 7. head complete side, nose level; 8. head complete side, nose down; 9. head complete side, nose up	(3) *Body position:* I. turns body full away; 2. sits back and still; 3. slumping; 4. neutral, slightly forward; 5. sideways shifts; 6. slight rocking; 7. large sideways shifts into line of vision; 8. medium-close forward; 9. going close and staying close; 10. large shifts forward and back
(4) *Head position:* 1. left; 2. right	(4) *Specific handling of the infant:* 1. abrupt shift of baby's position; 2. abrupt but no shift; 3. jerky movement of limbs; 4. no contact; 5. gently containing; 6. small rhythmic backing: 7. rhythmic movements of limbs; 8. intensive movement, fast rhythm
(5) *Facial expression:* 1. cry face; 2. grimace; 3. pout; 4. wary/sober; 5. lidding; 6. yawn; 7. neutral; 8. sneeze; 9. softening; 10. brightening; 11. simple smile; 12. coo face; 13. broad smile	(5) *direction of gaze:* 1. toward infant's face; 2. toward infant's body; 3. away from infant but related to interaction; 4. away from infant and not related to interaction

TABLE 19.1 *Continued*

Infant	Mother
(6) *Amount of movement:* 1. 3/4 limbs, large movement; 2. 1/2 limbs, large movement; 3. 3/4 limbs, medium movement; 4. 1/2 limbs, medium movement; 5. 3/4 limbs, small movement; 6. 1/2 limbs, small movement; 7. no movement; 8. mother moving infant	(6) *Facial expression:* 1. angry; 2. frown; 3. serious, sad, sober; 4. lidded; 5. neutral flat; 6. brightening; 7. animated; 8. simple smile; 9. imitative play face; 10. kisses; 11. exaggerated play face; 12. broad full smile; 13. "ooh" face
(7) *Blinks:* 1. yes; 2. no	
(8) *Specific hand movements:* 1. eye-wiping; 2. hand to mouth; 3. swipe; 4. fidgets; 5. all lower limbs extended forward	
(9) *Specific foot movements:* 1. kick; 2. startle	
(10) *Tongue placement:* 1. tongue slightly exposed; 2. tongue maximally exposed	

face and hands reach out in the same direction. As his mother comes in, saying, "Hello" in a high-pitched but gentle voice, he follows her with his head and eyes as she approaches him. His body builds up with tension, his face and eyes open up with a real greeting that ends with a smile. His mouth opens wide and his whole body orients toward her. He subsides, mouths his tongue twice, his smile dies, and he looks down briefly, while she continues to talk in an increasingly eliciting voice. During this, his voice and face are still, but all parts of his body point toward her. After he looks down, she reaches for and begins to move his hips and legs in a gentle, containing movement. He looks up again, smiles widely, narrows his eyes, brings one hand up to his mouth, grunting, vocalizing, and begins to cycle his arms and legs out toward her. With this increasing activity, she begins to grin more widely, to talk more loudly and with higher-pitched accents, accentuating his vocalizations with hers and his activity with her movements of his legs. The grunting vocalizations and smiles as well as the cycling activity of his arms and legs come and go in 2-second bursts—making up small cycles of movement and attention toward her. She contains his hips with her hands as if to contain the peaks of his excitement.

Meanwhile, with her voice and her face as well as with her hands, she both subsides with and accentuates his behavior with her own. He looks down again, gets sober at 40 seconds, makes a pouting face. She looks down at his feet at this point, then comes back to look into his face as he returns to look up at her. She lets go of his legs, and they draw up into his body. He bursts out with a broad smile and a staccato-like vocalization for three repetitions. Each time, his face broadens and opens wide, his legs and arms thrust out toward her. She seems to get caught up in his bursts and smiles broadly, her voice also getting brighter. After each burst, he subsides to a serious face, limbs quiet, and her quieting response follows his.

At 70 seconds, he subsides completely, and looks down at his feet with a darkly serious face. She gets very still, her face becomes serious, her voice slows down and almost stops, the pitch becomes low. Her mouth is drawn down, reflecting his serious mouth. After 3 seconds, he begins to brighten again into a wide, tonguing smile. This time he is more self-contained, holding back on the movement of his extremities and his excitement. She responds immediately, cocks her head coyly, smiles gently, and her voice gently begins to build up again. He builds up to two more staccato vocalizations with smiles and jerky, cycling movements of his legs out toward her. She contains his hips, and this time her voice does not build up to a peak of excitement with him. She looks down after 6 seconds to pick up his arms with her hands as if to keep control over his buildup. He follows her downward look about 10 seconds later, by looking down as well. His movements subside and his face becomes serious. She also is quite serious at 90 seconds.

He sneezes. She responds with a staccato "God bless you!" and a brighter face, head nodding toward him. She begins to talk more insistently as he looks serious, studying her face. He finally brightens to a smile, and with it, she throws back her head to smile broadly and excitedly. After this broad smile, they both subside. He continues to look at her seriously and quietly. She talks seriously to him, holding his buttocks and legs between her hands. At prolonged intervals, he gives her two rather brief, tentative, but encouraging smiles. After each, he returns to a quiet serious face, body entirely motionless. She smiles to his smiles but does not get more insistent and continues to talk quietly. At 135 seconds, he looks down at his feet, then comes in with a longer smile—tongue showing at his lips. His legs also cycle out toward her. She looks down when he does, then begins to move his legs in cycles. As he smiles at her, she looks up, brightens, moves his legs more rapidly, and her voice builds up. This smile decreases after 5 seconds and he looks away again. Then, they begin another period of serious looks, alternating with brief smiles in short cycles. She builds up with each of his cues, pumping his legs, smiling and vocalizing more herself, building up to a final peak. Each partner produces wide smiles, her voice becomes high-pitched, her hands pump his legs together. He subsides first to look down and serious. She loses her broad smile, gets up to leave, letting his legs go. At this, he looks beseechingly up into her face, his mouth turns down, his eyebrows arch, his legs and arms quiet, and he follows her with his eyes and head as she moves away.

This description illustrates the pattern of normal face-to-face interaction. It can be conceptualized as a sequence of phases, each representing different states of the partner's mutual attentional and affective involvement. The dyadic phases in an interaction of a typical 2-month-old infant and his mother are: (1) initiation, (2) mutual orientation, (3) greeting, (4) play-dialogue, and (5) disengagement. The phases are not defined by a single piece of behavior. Initiation may occur when the mother brightens and baby-talks to a sober baby, or a baby vocalizes and smiles to a caretaker who has paused too long. Mutual orientation may take place with neutral or bright faces, with the caretaker talking or the infant making single utterances. Greetings occur with smiles and "ooh" faces, and play-dialogues with mother talking in a burst-pause pattern and the baby making grunts or continuous vocalizations. Disengagement may occur when the caretaker goes from neutral face to sober face, or keeps the neutral face but starts to talk to the infant in adult conversational terms, or starts looking away from the baby. In each case, behaviors can be substituted for one another.

By contrast, the interaction pattern is dramatically different in the still-face condition.

The infant is looking contemplatively down at his hands, fingering the fingers of one hand with the other. As the mother enters, his hand movements stop. He looks up at her, makes eye-to-eye contact, and smiles. Her masklike face does not change. He looks away quickly to one side and remains quiet, his facial expression serious. He remains this way for 20 seconds. Then he looks back at her face, his eyebrows and lids raised, his hands and arms startling slightly out toward her. He quickly looks down at his hands, stills for 8 seconds, and then checks her face once more. This look is cut short by a yawn, with his eyes and face turning upward. His fingers pull at the fingers of his other hand; the rest of his body is motionless. The yawn and neck stretches last 5 seconds. He throws out one arm in a slight startle and looks briefly at her face. Arm movements are jerky, his mouth curves downward, his eyes narrow and partially lid. He turns his face to the side, but he keeps his mother in peripheral vision. He fingers his hand again, his legs stretch toward her and rapidly jerk back again. He arches forward, slumps over, tucks his chin down on one shoulder, but he looks up at her face from under his lowered eyebrows. This position lasts for over a minute, with brief checking looks at the mother occurring almost every 10 seconds. He grimaces briefly and his facial expression becomes more serious, his eyebrows furrowing. Finally, he completely withdraws, his body curled over, his head down. He does not look again at his mother. He begins to finger his mouth, sucking on one finger and rocking his head, looking at his feet. He looks wary, helpless, and withdrawn. As the mother exits at the end of the 3 minutes, he looks halfway up in her direction, but his sober facial expression and his curled body position do not change.

This description illustrates the typical pattern of an infant's response to his mother remaining still faced. As in the normal interaction, the infant orients toward the mother and greets her. But when she fails to respond, he sobers and looks wary. He stares at her, gives her a brief smile, and then looks away from her. He then alternates brief glances toward her with glances away from her,

FIGURE 19.3. A time series of photos taken from the recorded video image of a still-face condition. Infant, 74 days old.

thus monitoring her behavior. He occasionally smiles briefly, yet warily, in less and less convinced attempts to get the interaction back on track. As these attempts fail, the infant eventually withdraws, orients his face and body away from his mother with hopeless expression, and stays turned away from her. None of the infants cried, however.

Figures 19.3 and 19.4 illustrate this pattern with a time-sequence photograph of two different babies. Figure 19.3a shows the infant greeting. Then, in 19.3b and 19.3c, he warily looks away and then checks back toward her again. In 19.3d he withdraws with a sober facial expression, eyes averted, head turned fully away. This baby was 74 days old.

The baby in Figure 19.4a looks serious and wary. In 19.4b and 19.4c he is leaning further to the right, monitoring the mother peripherally, and briefly glances back at her. His arms and legs are pulled in toward his body. In 19.4d he is completely turned away and curled up into himself. This baby was 100 days old.

A time series of photos taken from the recorded video image of a still-Infant, 100 days old.

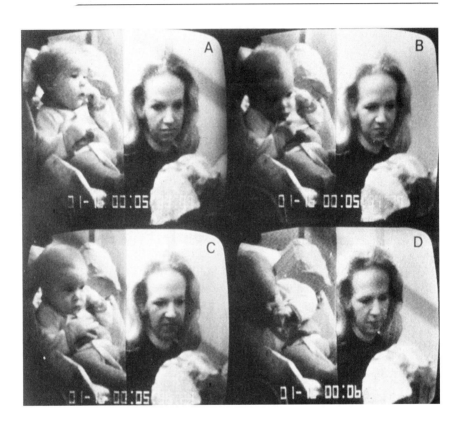

The sequence of initial greeting, realization of the distortion, wariness, checking, repeated attempts to bring the mother out of her immobility, and eventual withdrawal was observed in all babies from the earliest age studied, that is, from 1 month through 4 months. The order of presentation did not affect the infants' reaction in the still-face condition. It did affect the normal interaction if the normal interaction followed the still-face condition. Under those circumstances, the infant generally showed an initial period of wary monitoring of the mother when she came in. Occasionally he would arch away from the mother as if he had not forgiven her the previous insult. Mothers generally would apologize to their infants and say things like: "I am real again. It's all right. You can trust me again. Come back to me." After less than 30 seconds, all infants gave in to the normal interaction sequence.

Statistical analyses fully support these descriptions. Given the small sample size and repeated measures on some of the Ss, sign tests were used to evaluate the data. The test was performed on the paired ranking of each S's percentage score in the two conditions for each behavioral category. The N was set equal to the total number of sessions. The differences for gaze direction and vocalization between the two conditions were not significant. However, the other measures indicated the infant's ability to differentiate between the two conditions. In the still-face condition, infants smiled significantly less than in the normal condition ($p = .03$). In the still-face condition, the infants' head orientation was toward the mother less of the time than in the normal ($p = .02$), and they slumped down in their seats more of the time than in the normal ($p = .01$). Examination of the joint occurrence of particular behaviors showed that in the still-face condition infants had their gaze and head oriented toward their mothers less of the time than in the normal condition ($p = .04$) and there was a tendency for the infants to turn their heads in profile and gaze away from their mothers more during the still-face conditions than during the normal ($p = .11$).

Mothers reported that they found it very difficult to sit still-faced in front of the infant and resist his powerful sallies and bids to interaction. They found it at the same time very reassuring that the infant trusted his own powers to engage them in interaction. They well understood the infant's anger at reunion and were flattered by his demonstration of their importance to him.

DISCUSSION

The differential observations made in the still-face and the normal face-to-face interaction support our conceptualization of mother-infant interaction as a goal-oriented, reciprocal system in which the infant plays a major active role, constantly modifying his own communicative displays in response to the feedback provided by his partner. If the system is violated by a partner's nonreciprocity, the infant will respond in an appropriate manner, which indicates how powerfully he is affected by the disturbance.

Social interaction is a rule-governed, goal-oriented system in which both partners actively share from the very beginning. The still face violates the rules of this system by simultaneously conveying contradictory information about one partner's goal or intent. The mother by her entrance and en face position is initiating and setting the stage for an interaction, but then her lack of response indicates a disengagement or withdrawal. She is communicating "hello" and "good-bye" simultaneously. The infant, because of his capacity to apprehend this display of intent, is trapped in the contradiction: He initiates and greets but then turns away, temporarily withdraws, only to initiate again. If the infant's efforts fail to get the interaction back on track and to establish reciprocity, eventual complete withdrawal results.

We see the emotional displays of the infant and adult as message-carrying displays. Language is not yet a part of the interaction, but there appears to be a lexicon of expression that conveys information to each about the partner's inner emotional state and serves to regulate the interaction. These messages have two aspects—a content aspect and a regulatory aspect. The content of the message may refer to any event or object. It is conveyed in interactions primarily by language. The regulatory aspect of a signal contains information about a communicant's acceptance, rejection, or modification of the current state of the interaction. It is expressed through the behavioral displays of each communicant with their subtlety of emotional qualities. The content portion is similar to what Watzlawick, Beavin, & Jackson (1967) called the report aspect of a message, and the regulatory aspect of behavioral signals is a metacommunication: a communication about a communication. In the still-face condition, the infant responds to the mother's contradictory messages by trying to signal that mutual regulation should be reestablished. We believe that this same process of mutual regulation occurs in the normal interaction. Moreover, the messages exchanged via behavioral displays are almost purely regulatory in character in that they refer only to the ongoing state of the interaction and not to objects or events, so that prior to the incorporation of language into the interaction the infant has developed and practiced the ability to regulate the pragmatic aspects of an interchange.

The infant's response to the still-faced mother resembles a pattern described in the animal literature by Altmann (1952) and Chance (1962) that occurs in other primates when they establish dominance relationships. As two conspecifics meet, the partner establishing or testing his dominant position initiates eye-to-eye contact but with little facial movement. The subordinate partner quickly assumes an appeasing role, turning partly away, but glancing back repeatedly, constantly changing his facial expressions in an attempt to draw the dominant partner into a more equal, reciprocal interaction. With the first partner's continued nonreciprocal reactions, the still face becomes an aggressive signal. This is brought about by the contradictory message of the face-to-face orientation but nonreciprocal behavior. The second partner, like the human infant, attempts to deal with these mixed messages by a repeated approach-withdrawal pattern, and finally submits.

An infant's recognition of the mother's violation of reciprocity in the still-face condition begins very early. Along with Stechler and Latz (1966) and Carpenter (1974), we have seen anecdotal evidence of it as early as 2 to 3 weeks. The pattern described above is clearly established by 4 weeks and becomes increasingly complex. For instance, a 5-month-old infant began reacting to the still face by showing the characteristic wary pattern of behavior. About a minute and a half into the interaction, he looked at his mother and laughed briefly. After this brief tense laugh, he paused, looked at her soberly, and then laughed again, loud and long, throwing his head back as he did so. At this point, the mother became unable to maintain an unresponsive still face, broke into laughter, and proceeded to engage in normal interactional behavior. The intentions and emotions of the older infant are similar to those of a younger infant. The richness and skill in reestablishing a reciprocal interaction, however, are greater.

The strategies the infant employs to bring his mother out of her immobility demonstrate his growing confidence in his effectiveness as a social partner;

the seriousness of the infant's reaction when the mother remains unresponsive despite his efforts demonstrates how critical reciprocity is to him. The final withdrawing of the young infant when he no longer seeks to pull his mother into the interaction reminds us of the withdrawn behavior and huddled postures of isolated monkeys (Harlow & Zimmerman, 1959) and of Bowlby's (1969) description of the withdrawn behavior of children separated from their caretakers.

The still-face mothers in our study remained unresponsive for only 3 minutes, yet their infants found even such a temporary violation greatly disturbing. This suggests that reciprocity and mutual achievement of the goals of social interaction form a necessary basis for the growth of affective well-being in early infancy.

CHAPTER 20

Depressed Mothers and Infants:
The Failure to Form Dyadic
States of Consciousness

The primary aim of this chapter is to present a model of the process of infant emotional functioning and experience—the model of mutual regulation—that in part accounts for the toxic effects of maternal depression on a child's social emotional functioning and development. A consequence of successful mutual regulation, the creation of dyadic states of consciousness, is presented as an attempt to explain why humans so strongly seek states of intersubjectivity. To accomplish these aims, we will summarize our work on microanalytic studies of normal interactions and our experimental perturbations of interactions in the face-to-face still-face paradigm. We will not review the literature on maternal depressive effects, normal interactions, or intersubjectivity, much of which is available in other chapters of this volume.

Our research focuses on understanding normal interactions, including interactive errors and repairs, deviations and disruptions. It also provides an understanding of the different emotional and social regulatory styles observed in the sons and daughters of depressed as well as normal mothers. Our hope is to understand why some children of depressed mothers develop behavioral disorders or even a pathology that is similar to their mother's pathology. We also recognize that many of these children develop normally. Thus an accounting of the development of children of depressed mothers must ipso facto account for a wide variety of outcomes including normalcy. A daunting task.

THE MUTUAL REGULATION MODEL

The mutual regulation model (MRM) takes a particular focus on development—a focus on the joint or interactive nature of development. A critical assumption of the MRM is that the infant is motivated to communicate with people or, as we originally formulated, to establish intersubjective states (Blumberg, 1980; Tronick, 1989). This motivation is assumed to be a biological characteristic of our species (but see below; Bruner, 1990; Trevarthen, 1979, 1989a, 1990; Tronick, 1980). The child also is inherently motivated to act on the world of objects. The accomplishment of motivated action on the inanimate world, however, is dependent on the establishment of intersubjective relationships. As is the case for *Homo sapiens*, children can only create meanings in collaboration with others. Their understanding of the world of objects, no matter how primitive, is dependent on establishing intersubjective states with others and the mutual construction of meaning. Thus the establishment of social relationships is the primary process of development and the understanding of the inanimate world is secondary to it. When the child successfully accomplishes communication with others, normal development occurs. A child who does not engage the world in a culturally appropriate manner does not develop normally no matter what causes the failure—chronic or acute illness, congenital malformations, poor parenting, toxic exposures, or parental psychopathology.

Success or failure in accomplishing motivated intentions is dependent on at least three critical processes, among others. The first is the integrity and capacity of the child's physiological systems and central nervous system to organize and control the child's physiological states and behavior. The second is the integrity of the infant's communicative system, including the central nervous system centers that control and generate messages and meanings and the motor system that makes the messages manifest. The earliest and continuing function of the communicative system is to express the child's intention for action to the caregiver and to communicate the extent to which the infant is succeeding or failing in fulfilling his or her intentions or goals. The third process, reciprocal to the second, is the caretaker's capacity to appropriately read the child's communications and willingness to take appropriate action. Therefore, successful engagement with the world of people and things depends on the status and the effectiveness of the child-caretaker communicative system in facilitating the child's motivated intentions. These processes make up the process of mutual regulation—the capacity of each of the interactants, child and adult, to express their motivated intentions, to appreciate the intentions of the partner, and to scaffold their partner's actions so that their partner can achieve their goals.

How does the mutual regulatory process work? We will focus on its workings from the child's perspective, but it should be obvious that the model applies to the adult as well. When an infant is not in homeostatic balance (e.g., she is cold) or is emotionally dysregulated (e.g., she is distressed), she is at the mercy of these states. Until these states are brought under control, the infant must devote all of her regulatory resources to reorganizing them. While she is doing that, she can do nothing else. Her engagement with people or things is preempted by her internal discordance and by the singular devotion of her capacities to overcome it. On the other hand, when her internal states are controlled, the infant is free to take agency and act on the world. Her internal states become an organized background for foreground actions with people and things (Sander, 1983b).

This account sounds like the precept of Claude Bernard—the maintenance of milieu interior is the organism's primary task. Bernard, however, failed to appreciate a critical feature of the homeostatic regulatory process for humans (and, one might note, many other species as well). For humans, the maintenance of homeostasis is a dyadic collaborative process. Humans evolved in such a manner that they must collaborate with others to regulate their physiological states, emotional states, and external engagements with people and objects. Obviously, the infant is a bounded organism and the adult is external to that boundary. Nonetheless, the adult is a part of the infant's regulatory system; as much a part as any internal regulatory process.

What is meant by this? Start with an example of Bernard's classic case of temperature regulation. While Bernard did not see it, the regulation of the infant's core body temperature is a dyadic process. The infant may regulate her temperature by changing her posture and increasing her activity level. She may also be held against the caretaker's body. These processes, internal and external, are functionally equivalent processes for regulating the infant's temperature. Moreover, these regulatory processes involve communication among different components of the infant's regulatory system. Changes in metabolism are guided by central and peripheral mechanisms that respond to signals from central and peripheral sites. Changes in the holding patterns of caretakers are guided by active (e.g., crying) and passive (e.g., color changes) signals from the infant. Thus, the infant's physiological state is dyadically regulated with the caregiver functioning as an external regulatory component of the infant's regulatory system. As we shall see, infant emotions are also regulated dyadically. The principal components are the infant's central nervous system (e.g., primarily the limbic system) and the behaviors it controls (e.g., facial and vocal emotional displays) and the caregiver's regulatory input (e.g., facial expressions). This dyadic collaborative regulatory system is guided by communication between internal and external components, that is, infant and caregiver.

The idea of caregiver behavior as an external regulator of the infant's states is supported by the animal as well as the human literature. Hofer (1981, 1984) has demonstrated that specific maternal stimuli modify a host of the immature offspring's physiological systems. Maternal body warmth affects the infant's neuroendocrine system; maternal touch affects growth hormone production; and maternal milk affects heart rate beta-adrenergic systems, responsiveness to touch, and the production of growth hormone. Importantly, it is not just the body that is affected by caretaker behavior, but the brain as well (Lester & Tronick, 1994). What we now know about brain development is a radical shift from the perspective that saw interactive experience as modifying only what an already formed brain learns or stores. We now know that the quality of caretaking affects the function, structure, and neurochemical architecture of the brain. For example, maternal touch affects hippocampal cell production and the production of neurotransmitters (Gunzenhauser, Lester, & Tronick, 1987; Spinelli, 1987).

In the following passage, pediatric neurologist Heinz Prechtl clearly expresses this view:

> The effects of the selective pressure on the pre-programmed maturation of the nervous system [and related changes in behavior] should not be considered without taking into account the influence of the caregiver. There is an inevitable process of matching between the offspring and caregiver through mutual influences. Put differently, the young will only survive and grow and develop properly if the mothering and nursing repertory of the caregiver is precisely adapted to the properties of the young and vice versa . . . [Thus] [w]ithin limits, during normal development a biologically different brain may be formed given the mutual influence of maturation of the infant's nervous system and the mothering repertory of the caregiver (adapted from Prechtl). (Connelly & Prechtl, 1981)

Prechtl's position is broad; nonetheless, he is very specific that nonneurological factors such as the "mothering and nursing repertory" and caregiver's and infant's behavioral characteristics are among the primary forces shaping the organization of the infant's brain. These effects have lifetime consequences. For example, the increase in the proliferation of hippocampal cells associated with maternal touch in infancy have an effect on memory during senescence (Gunzenhauser et al., 1987; Schore, 1994). Thus the critical nature of mutual regulation is clear—it shapes the behavior, the body, and the brain (Tronick & Morelli, 1991).

THE MUTUAL REGULATION OF INFANT-MOTHER (AND OTHER) SOCIAL INTERACTIONS

The study of social interactions between infants and parents began with Brazelton's pioneering study (Brazelton, Koslowski, & Main, 1974). Brazelton filmed the face-to-face interactions of mothers and infants and then coded the mothers' and infants' behavior on a second-by-second time base. Brazelton characterized the interaction as reciprocal (i.e., infant and mother moving in synchrony from positive through negative behavioral states). The cycle was analogized to a sinusoid wave with "synchrony" requiring the matching of both positive and negative emotions. At about the same time, Condon and Sander (1974a) described a phenomenon of microsynchrony between infant movement and the phoneme boundaries of the adult partner's speech. They professed that infant movements of a variety of limbs were coincident with the phoneme boundaries of speech. This coordination was too fast to take place on a contingent basis because movements take longer to organize than the duration of phoneme boundaries. Thus Condon and Sander argued that there was a coordination of the biorhythms of speech and movement that accounted for the observed synchrony.

These two terms—synchrony and reciprocity—became the primary descriptors for normal mother-infant interactions. Synchrony was argued to be the optimal state of the interaction and to be nearly perfect over the course of the interaction (Condon & Sander, 1974a). Additionally, in the synchrony model, the interaction was seen as having high levels of positive emotions, and little anger, sadness, or distress. Thus "optimal" mother-infant interactions were typically in sync and emotionally positive. Other features of the synchrony model included the characterization of the infant as diffusely organized. Therefore the infant's behavior was unrelated to specific stimulation expressed by the adult. From this perspective, the infant did not appreciate or respond to the mother's social affective behavior. Rather, the mother was the active interactant and she created the structure of the interaction. Thus the interaction was seen as a "pseudo-dialogue" (Kaye, 1977b; Schaffer, 1977a). The mother structured the interaction and made the infant appear "as if" he was active. The optimal interaction was analogized to a synchronous dance with one partner fully in control; it was a unilaterally regulated system.

Based on the synchrony model, clinical assessment scales were developed that rated the interaction on a dimension of synchrony, attunement, or contingency (Massie, 1982). Underlying these scales was the widely accepted assumption that the more synchronous and contingent the interaction, the more positive the affect, the better the interaction, the more optimal the outcome of the child. The synchrony model was a prototypical model and allowed for little variation, and like other categorical models saw deviation from the prototype as (potentially) pathological.

Using the temporal microanalytic coding systems (Cohn & Tronick, 1987, 1988, 1989; Dowd & Tronick, 1986; Mayer & Tronick, 1985; Tronick, 1985; Tronick & Cohn, 1989; Weinberg & Tronick, 1989, 1992, 1994, 1996), we found that the synchrony model needed radical revision. We, along with others, found that infants, mothers, and their interactions did not fit the model. We found that infants' communicative behavior was well organized and contingently related to maternal communicative behaviors (Tronick & Cohn, 1989; Weinberg & Tronick, 1994). Furthermore, we found little evidence for the synchrony described by Condon and Sander (1974a). We did find that infants as well as their mothers adjusted their behavior in relation to the behavior of their partner with some measurable temporal delay (Cohn & Tronick, 1988). Moreover, we found that the interactions of normal mothers and their infants were characterized by at most moderate levels of positive affect, some negative affect, and only moderate levels of synchrony (Cohn & Tronick, 1987; Tronick & Cohn, 1989).

Infant communicative behavior is hardly diffuse. Weinberg and Tronick (1994) found that infant affective behavior is organized into configurations of face, voice, gesture, and gaze. In one configuration, which we have labeled social engagement, the infant looks at the mother, positively vocalizes, and smiles. Importantly, crying, looking away, and withdrawal behaviors are less likely to occur. In another configuration, active protest, the infant looks away from the mother, engages in active withdrawal behaviors, cries, and displays a facial expression of anger. In this configuration, smiles, positive gestures, and vocalizations are inhibited. There are two other configurations, object engagement and passive withdrawal, that also involve distinct combinations of expressive modalities. From our perspective, each of these configurations reflects a different state of brain organization that assembles distinctly different configurations of face, voice, and body. Such expressive configurations and brain organization shatter the idea that the infant is diffusely organized.

Each configuration clearly communicates the infant's affective state and evaluation of the interaction. The social engagement configuration functions to convey the message, "I like what we are doing"; the active protest configuration tells the caregiver that "I don't like what is happening and I want it to change now"; the configuration communicates messages such as, "I don't like what is happening but I don't know what to do"; and the passive withdrawal configuration conveys the message, "Let's continue what we are doing. I like looking at this object." Thus the configurations serve to regulate the behavior of the partner during the interaction by conveying information to the partner about the infant's immediate intentions, and the infant's evaluation of the current state of the interaction. Nonetheless, as clearly defined as these configurations are, the interaction is neither always positive nor synchronous.

In our studies of normal mother-infant face-to-face interactions, expressions of positive affect by either the mother or the infant occur, respectively, about 42% for the mother and 15% for the infant (Cohn & Tronick, 1987; Tronick & Cohn, 1989). A dramatic instance of normal variation are Weinberg's (Weinberg & Tronick, 1992; Weinberg, 1992) findings of gender differences in the affective and regulatory behaviors of normal 6-month-old infants as well as differences in interactive coherence between mothers and sons and mothers and daughters (Tronick & Cohn, 1989). Infant boys are more emotionally reactive than girls. They display more positive as well as negative affect, focus more on the mother, and display more signals expressing escape and distress and demands for contact than girls. Girls show more interest in objects, a greater constancy of interest, and better self-regulation of emotional states. Girls also evidence greater stability of sadness over time than boys. Sex differences in interactive coherence (i.e., synchrony) have also been demonstrated, with mother-son dyads evidencing more coherence than mother-daughter dyads (Tronick & Cohn, 1989). These gender differences reflect normal variants and highlight the range of affective expressiveness, regulatory behavior, and synchrony that occurs during normal interactions.

These findings speak strongly against hypotheses, such as the synchrony model, that assert that there is a single optimal form of interaction, unless one is willing to assert that the interaction of boys (girls) is more appropriate than the interaction of girls (boys). The findings on differences in interactions in different communities also speak against optimization models of the mother-infant interaction. The structure of the interaction varies in different community settings where there are different emotional and interactive socialization goals for children. For example, Tronick and his colleagues (Keefer, Tronick, Dixon, & Brazleton, 1982) found that among the Gusii, an agricultural community in western Kenya, mothers turn away from their infants just when their infants become most affectively positive and excited. Among the Gusii, this maternal behavior presages the socialization of later restrictions on the expression of positive affect among different individuals (e.g., younger individuals do not look directly at older individuals, especially when expressing strong affect). This looking-away pattern is normative for the Gusii, but is quite different from that seen in the United States. American middle-income mothers respond to the infant's affective excitement with continued intense looking and heightened positive arousal.

Thus there is no singular universal optimal form of mother-child interaction in which deviations are considered pathological as implied by the synchrony model (but for an alternative view, see Trevarthen, 1990; Trevarthen & Hadley, 1978). Rather, interactions vary among individuals and across communities in regular and culturally meaningful ways. On a daily basis, infants repeatedly participate in an interactive routine—a routine with a beginning, middle, and end—that socializes the infant to eventually incorporate culturally accepted social-emotional interactive practices. This interactive routine can be thought of as having a narrative structure, even though it is a narrative of communicative action and not words (Bruner, 1983). Like a narrative, this interactive routine serves as a meaning system for the child based on the sequencing of affective messages in the flow of social interaction. The child comes to "know" that "this is what is happening; this is what will happen; and this is how it will feel" (Bruner, 1990). This meaning system is established long before the child can engage in a narrative of words. In fact, we agree with Bruner (1983) that participation in this narrative of affective routines is a prerequisite for learning language. However, the unit of meaning is not primarily sensorimotor, although sensorimotor action in the form of affective communicative displays (e.g., facial expressions) are its manifest components (Cohen, 1988). The units of meaning (morphemes or, better yet, the sentences, if you wish) are affective experiences (states of brain organization), and their sequencing in relation to external events, usually the communicative displays of others.

The analogy to narrative is limited. The interaction as well as the affective meaning system are jointly regulated and socially constructed by both the infant and the adult. Both partners appreciate and adjust their behavior in relation to their partner's behavior and the state of the interaction. In a series of papers, we have explored the contingencies and the structure of the interaction (Cohn & Tronick, 1987, 1988, 1989; Tronick, 1980; Tronick & Cohn, 1989). For example, infant averts from the mother are prolonged by maternal elicitation and shortened when the mother watches and waits for the infant to look back at her (Cohn & Tronick, 1987).

We have demonstrated this bidirectionality using time series analyses of interactions at 3, 6, and 9 months of age (Cohn & Tronick, 1987; Mayer &

Tronick, 1985; Tronick & Cohn, 1989). In these analyses, we found that the infant's and mother's behavior are explained by two factors. The first is the infant's and mother's own behavior as measured by their autocorrelation. The autocorrelation measures how much of an individual's behavior can be accounted for by his or her own preceding behavior. The second component, as measured by the cross-correlation of the mothers' and infants' behaviors after removal of the autocorrelation, indexes the degree of influence each partner has on the other. At 3 months of age, more than 50% of the mothers' and 39% of the infants' behaviors were influenced by their partner's behaviors. This research indicates that a large proportion of mother-infant pairs are responding to and adjusting their affective behavior to the behavior of their partner. It is also of interest that the proportion of bidirectional pairs does not increase with infant age. Infants as young as 3 months appear to be as capable of making adjustments as are older infants. Perhaps this is a characteristic of the infant or of the dyad. Unfortunately, no research looking at the stability of bidirectionality has been carried out.

Despite the finding of bidirectionality, when we examined the proportion of time that mother and infant were in synchronous states, we found that synchrony occurred only a moderate proportion of the time (Tronick, Als, & Brazelton, 1980b). For example, matching of infant and mother social affective states occurred only 24% of the time. In an alternative analysis of synchrony using time series analyses, the coherence of the interaction accounted for only 17% of the variance of the interactions. Thus, interactions are not as synchronous as predicted by the synchrony model. Rather, interactions move between matching/synchronous states and nonmatching/nonshared states then back again to matching/synchronous states (Tronick & Cohn, 1989; see Figure 20.1).

Based on these findings, we (Tronick & Cohn, 1989) have characterized the typical mother-infant interaction as one that moves from coordinated (or synchronous) to miscoordinated states and back again over a wide affective range (see Figure 20.2). The miscoordinated state is referred to as a normal interactive communicative error. The interactive transition from a miscoordinated state to a coordinated state is referred to as an interactive repair. The process of reparation, like the dynamics of regulating homeostatic states, is mutually regulated. The partners, infant and adult, signal their evaluation of the state of the interaction through their affective configurations. In turn, in response to their partner's signals, each partner attempts to adjust his or her behavior to maintain a coordinated state or to repair an interactive error. Critically, successful reparations and the experience of coordinated states are associated with positive affective states, whereas interactive errors generate negative affective states. Thus the infant's affective experience is determined by a dyadic regulatory process.

In normal dyads, interactive errors are quickly repaired. In studies of face-to-face interaction at 6 months of age, repairs occur at a rate of once every 3 to 5 seconds, and more than one third of all repairs occur by the next step in

FIGURE 20.1. Movement of a 6-month-old mother-infant dyad among dyadically defined states of matching (e.g., mother and infant doing the same social-emotional actions at the same time), conjoint (e.g., mother and infant doing similar but not identical social-emotional actions at the same time), and disjoint (e.g., mother and infant engaging in different social-emotional activities at the same time). Adjust is what is referred to in this paper as reparation (i.e., moving from less similar dyadic states to more similar states), whereas diverge is what is referred to here as an interactive error.

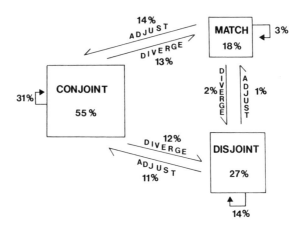

the interaction (Tronick & Gianino, 1980). Observations by Beebe (Beebe & Lachmann, 1994) and Isabella and Belsky (1991) replicate these findings and support the hypothesis that the normal interaction is a process of reparation. They found that maternal sensitivity in the midrange, rather than at the low or high end, typifies normal interactions. Midrange sensitivity is characterized by

FIGURE 20.2. A schematic of the regulatory structure of the interaction. Matched or regulated states when misregulated change to mismatched states, but reparation re-achieves matched states. Matched states and reparation are associated with positive affect whereas mismatched states and interactive errors are associated with negative affect. Matching can either be purely social or focused on objects. (From Tronick, 1992)

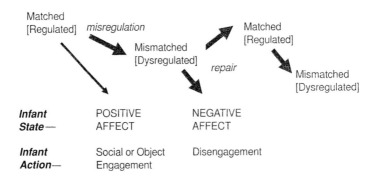

errors and repairs as contrasted to interactions in which the mother is "always never sensitive or always sensitive." These researchers also found that midlevel sensitivity was associated with security of attachment.

It is our hypothesis that reparation of interactive errors is the critical process of normal interactions that is related to developmental outcome rather than synchrony or positive affect per se. That is, reparation, its experience and extent, is the "social-interactive mechanism" that affects the infant's development. In interactions characterized by normal rates of reparation, the infant learns which communicative and coping strategies are effective in producing reparation and when to use them. This experience leads to the elaboration of communicative and coping skills, and the development of an understanding of interactive rules and conventions. With the experiential accumulation of successful reparations, and the attendant transformation of negative affect into positive affect, the infant establishes a positive affective core (Emde, Kligman, Reich, & Wade, 1978; Gianino & Tronick, 1988). The infant also learns that he or she has control over social interactions. Specifically, the infant develops a representation of himself or herself as effective, of his or her interactions as positive and reparable, and of the caretaker as reliable and trustworthy. These representations are crucial for the development of a sense of self that has coherence, continuity, and agency and for the development of stable and secure relationships (Tronick, 1980; Tronick, Cohn, & Shea, 1986).

The functional consequences of reparation from the perspective of mutual regulation suggest that when there is a prolonged failure to repair communicative errors, infants will initially attempt to reestablish the expected interaction but when these reparatory efforts fail they will experience negative affect. To evaluate this hypothesis, we created a prolonged mismatch by having the mother hold a still face and remain unresponsive to the infant (Tronick, Als, Adamson, Wise, & Brazelton, 1978). The mother fails to engage in her normal interactive behavior and regulatory role. The effect on the infant is dramatic. Infants almost immediately detect the change and attempt to solicit the mother's attention. Failing to elicit a response, most infants turn away only to look back at the mother again (see Figure 20.3A, a–d). This solicitation cycle may be repeated several times. But when the infants' attempts fail to repair the interaction, infants often lose postural control, withdraw, and self comfort (see Figure 20.3B, a–d). The disengagement is profound even with this short disruption of the mutual regulatory process and break of intersubjectivity. The infant's reaction is reminiscent of the withdrawal of Harlow's isolated monkeys or of the infants in institutions observed by Bowlby and Spitz (Bowlby, 1951, 1982; Spitz, 1965). The still-faced mother is a short-lived, experimentally produced form of neglect.

To examine the process of reparatory failure in natural settings, we examined the interaction of infants with depressed mothers. We hypothesized that maternal depression, like the still face, disrupts the mutual regulatory process and constitutes a break in intersubjectivity. The break is brought about by the effects of depression on maternal affect and responsiveness. Depression compromises the

1.3. Sequences of two infants reacting to the mother holding a still face in face-to-face still-face paradigm.

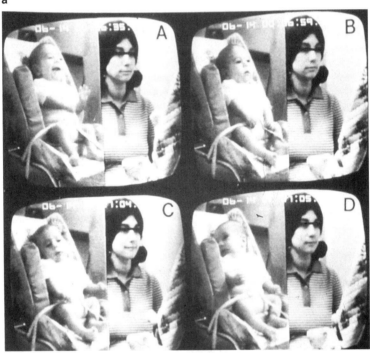

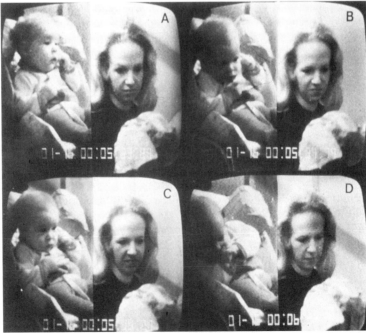

mother's and eventually the dyad's capacity to mutually regulate the
(Cohn & Tronick, 1989; Gianino & Tronick, 1988; Tronick & I
Weinberg & Tronick, 1994). However, we found that not all depressed moṃ̇ᵢ̣ₓ
disrupt the interaction in the same fashion, and that depressed mothers with
similar levels of depressive symptoms do not engage in the same interactive style
(Cohn, Matias, Tronick, Connell, & Lyons-Ruth, 1986; Tronick, 1989). There
are at least two interactive patterns (intrusive and withdrawal), and each disrupts
the regulatory process. Importantly, each form has a different effect on the
infant.

    We found that intrusive mothers engaged in rough handling, spoke in an
angry tone of voice, poked at their babies, and actively interfered with their
infants' activities. Withdrawn mothers, by contrast, were disengaged, unresponsive, affectively flat, and did little to support their infants' activities. As a
striking demonstration of the sensitivity of the infant to affective displays, we
found that infants of intrusive mothers (re)acted one way whereas infants of
withdrawn mothers (re)acted another way. Infants of intrusive mothers spent
most of their time looking away from the mother and seldom looked at objects.
They infrequently cried. Infants of withdrawn mothers were more likely to
protest and to be distressed than the infants of the intrusive mothers, suggesting that maternal withdrawal may be particularly aversive to young infants.

    These differential infant reactions are expectable. The infants are reacting
to and acting on different kinds of input; that is, the affective reality they are
regulating is different. Infants of withdrawn mothers are failing to achieve social
connectedness because of the mothers' lack of response and their inability to
repair the interaction. Initially, they may become angry. However, since they
are unable to successfully cope or self-regulate this heightened negative state,
they become dysregulated, fuss, and cry. This dysregulation, similar to the dysregulation associated with homeostatic failures, compels them to devote much
of their coping resources to controlling their dysregulated state. With chronic
exposure, they develop a disengaged and self-directed regulatory style characterized by self-comforting, self-regulatory behaviors (e.g., looking away, sucking
on their thumb), passivity, and withdrawal as a way of coping with their state.
To the extent that this coping style is successful in stabilizing their affective
state, it is deployed automatically and becomes defensive. This self-directed
style of coping is used in an effort to preclude anticipated negative emotions
even in situations in which negative affect may not occur. This interpretation
explains Tiffany Field's finding that infants of depressed mothers have less
engaged and more negative interactions with a friendly stranger than do infants
of nondepressed mothers (Field et al., 1988). The infants of the depressed
mothers are utilizing this strategy automatically without evaluating whether or
not it is warranted. Eventually, with the reiteration and accumulation of failure, these infants develop a negative affective core primarily characterized by
sadness and anger, a representation of the mother as untrustworthy and unresponsive, and of themselves as ineffective and helpless.

The infants of hostile intrusive mothers must cope with a different regulatory problem. The mother's behavior prevents reparation of the interaction because she consistently disrupts the infant's activities. These infants initially experience anger, turn away from the mother, push her away, or screen her out. However, unlike the failure experience of the infants of withdrawn mothers, these coping behaviors are occasionally successful in limiting the mother's intrusiveness. Thus these infants erratically experience reparation, that is, a transformation of their anger into a more positive state. To the extent that these coping behaviors are successful in fending off the mother, these infants eventually internalize an angry and protective style of coping that is deployed defensively in anticipation of the mother's intrusiveness. We believe that infants are easily angered when interacting with their mother and others, and more easily frustrated when acting on objects.

More speculatively, these differences in infant reactions to maternal withdrawal and intrusiveness suggest an interpretation of differential effects associated with parental neglect and abuse. Infant failure to thrive, withdrawal, and lack of motivation seen in situations of parental neglect probably result from the constant demands forced on the infant to self-regulate. The infant is continuously required to control his or her own physiological and affective states. This self-directed coping style compromises the infant's interchanges with the environment and motivation to engage with the world. By contrast, in the abusive situation, parental abuse leads to chronic physical defensiveness and anger as well as heightened vigilance and fear.

These observations need to take into account gender differences in infant regulatory and affective styles (Weinberg, 1992; Weinberg & Tronick, 1992). Boys are more affectively reactive and less able to self-regulate their affective states. We hypothesize that they may be particularly susceptible to the withdrawn style associated with depression because maternal withdrawal denies them the regulatory support that they need. On the other hand, girls, who at 6 months are significantly more focused on objects than boys, may be more vulnerable to the intrusive style of depression, which interferes with their activities. Combined with the findings that girls show more stability of sadness than boys, and boys show more stability of distancing and escape behaviors than girls, we think these gender differences in regulatory styles may be the first signs presaging the differential proportion of depression in girls and hyperactivity and aggressiveness in boys. Note that it is not that girls are inherently depressed and boys inherently hyperactive. Each has different regulatory styles that in interaction with different caregiving styles make one or another outcome more likely.

This perspective also has implications for the higher rates of conduct and delinquency disorders in boys. We know from the literature on juvenile delinquency that boys commit many more crimes than girls. However, there is not a very good explanation for this phenomenon. Our research indicates that gender differences in infancy may already set the stage for this differential rate. The explanation, however, is not simply that boys are more aggressive than girls.

Rather, boys have greater difficulty controlling their emotional reactions. Because of this difficulty, they are more likely than girls to fail to accomplish their goals. This failure generates frustration and anger and may lead to aggression. This may be exacerbated in those situations where parenting behavior is also compromised by, for example, depression.

The argument is as follows: boys are more demanding than girls, more reactive, and have a harder time controlling their negative as well as their positive emotional states. This makes it more difficult for parents to interact with them and sets the stage for later struggles and conflicts. There is also strong evidence indicating that boys continue to be more demanding and emotionally reactive as they grow up (Weinberg, 1992). During the preschool period, boys are more aggressive than girls and parents report having more difficulty disciplining them. It is also during the preschool period that we begin to see a surge in the number of boys seen in clinical settings who have conduct disorders. Children with conduct disorders, both during the school-age period and in adolescence, are characterized by acting-out behavior, destructiveness, impulsiveness, and an inability to control their emotions. Our hypothesis is that they have problems regulating their affective states and are therefore easily frustrated and angry. Failure to control emotional states interferes with the accomplishment of goals. During infancy these goals revolve around the exploration of objects and social interaction. During adolescence, these goals include successful performance in school and interaction with peers. Failure to accomplish these goals leads to frustration, anger, and in some cases aggression, which may result in conduct disorders or delinquency. Thus it is not aggression per se that distinguishes boys from girls but their emotional regulatory differences.

There is a parental piece to the argument as well. During infancy and at later ages, parents help children modulate their emotional states. Parents play a crucial role in teaching their children how to talk about and cope with failure, anger, and frustration. They also teach their children how to channel these emotions into productive activities. If a parent is unable to provide the guidance children need because they are depressed, fatigued, physically ill, or simply not present in their children's lives, the stage is set for conflict and struggle with the child.

During infancy, parental unresponsiveness or inappropriate parenting serve to dysregulate the infant, which prevents the infant from achieving his or her goals of social interaction and object exploration. This leads to anger and a decrease in enjoyment, and teaches the infant that the parent is unreliable and unavailable. Most important, it also has the effect of interfering with the infant's development of a sense of mastery and control over events. That is, the infant fails to learn that he or she has the power to change things. Instead the infant develops a sense of helplessness and hopelessness. These developments may be more likely in boys because of their greater need for parental regulatory support.

These early processes may become more problematic during adolescence. Adolescence is a time of turmoil and change for both adolescents and parents.

nally, adolescence is a difficult time for boys, girls, and parents alike. An
adolescent who has been chronically deprived of parental guidance, support,
and involvement during infancy and childhood will not have had the opportunity to master the coping strategies necessary to successfully cope with the
normal changes and pressures of adolescence. The child also will not have
developed a sense of effectance or a sense that he or she has the power to
change events in his or her life. Similarly, parents who have been chronically
uninvolved with their child will not have learned how to help that child cope
with the normal vicissitudes of life. Therefore, it is very unlikely that these parents will suddenly be able to help the child cope with the normal tasks of adolescence. Again, failure to master the tasks of adolescence will lead to frustration, anger, low self-esteem, and sometimes aggression. This aggression may
lead to an affiliation with other children who have similar problems and
propensities. Again, boys may experience these problems more acutely because
of their early regulatory problems and the subsequent parenting they received.

In general, just as in the case of conduct disorders, the model of mutual regulation must be modified as the child gets older because of developmental
changes. For example, around the end of the first year infants begin to develop
an awareness of their own and their partners' intentions and affective states. This
awareness was originally named intersubjectivity by Tronick (Tronick, Als, &
Adamson, 1979) and has been adapted and elaborated by Trevarthen as secondary intersubjectivity and by Stern as attunement (Stern, 1977; Trevarthen,
1980, 1993b). The developmental accomplishment of secondary intersubjectivity has important implications for the effects of maternal depression on the child.

THE FORMATION OF DYADIC STATES
OF CONSCIOUSNESS

With the development of secondary intersubjectivity in the older infant, infants
of depressed mothers become increasingly aware that their mothers are angry,
hostile, or sad. They no longer simply react to what the mother does; rather,
they are becoming aware of and react to her state of mind. This awareness is
not necessarily conscious but takes the form of an apprehension of her mental
state even when that state is not directly manifest in her behavior. However, it
is also not a "magical nonmaterial" apprehension but one generated by the
child's newly developed capacities for integrating past experiences. At this age,
infants also become aware of their own feelings of sadness, helplessness, and
anger. The awareness of their own negative feelings must be especially intolerable because it is associated with their mother and demands an enormous regulatory effort to control. It is our expectation that older infants become hyper-
vigilant of their mother's emotional state in order to protect themselves from her
state. They also monitor their own emotional reactions, especially their anger,
and attempt to control them, to not express them to their mother. An additional
cost to this vigilance is that they need to limit their excited positive feelings since

a high level of arousal, even if it is positive, might threaten their capacity to control their affective states. Thus they may become emotionally constricted. Osofsky (1992) presented findings that support this argument. She found that by the end of the first year, infants of depressed mothers express less intense affective reactions to stressful situations and are less emotionally responsive than infants of nondepressed mothers.

A serious implication of the development of secondary intersubjectivity is that it may "enable" the infant to develop psychopathological states. With the development of secondary intersubjectivity, the infant's reaction is no longer determined simply by what he or she directly experiences in interaction with the mother. The infant's reaction increasingly becomes an integration of immediate events with self-reflective representational processes. With these developmental changes, distortions of reality become possible. For example, we would expect that when children become aware of their depressed mother's affective state (e.g., her anger and sadness apparently directed at them) and their own intolerable feelings of rage directed at her, children may develop a pathological form of coping—denial, detachment, repression, projection—in an attempt to control their awareness of these overwhelming feelings.

Representations take time to develop. Early in development these representations are instantiated in patterns of action and emotion before they become representations incorporating elements of the self, cognition, and history. Critically, these representations are not simply stored information in a preformed or predetermined universal brain. Mutual regulatory experience is not simply the storage of material (e.g., the filing of information in some area of the brain dedicated to the storage of information) that can be accessed for present use, but is one of the processes that shapes the brain itself, as noted by Prechtl. Thus the brain, like emotional experience, is jointly created. Or to invert the idea, the human brain is inherently dyadic and is created through interactive interchanges.

Up until now we, like others (Emde et al., 1978; Trevarthen, 1993b; Tronick, 1980), have assumed that the motivation for intersubjectivity is an inherent, biological given characteristic of our species. This assumption has its rationale in the evolution of our species as a social species, in our use of language, the collaborative nature of meaning making, and in relational theories of the formation of attachments and the self (Bowlby, 1982; Stern, 1985; Trevarthen, 1989b; Tronick, 1980; Tronick, Morelli, & Winn, 1987). However, while the assumption is reasonable, it is a de facto assumption, making it less satisfying. It assumes the phenomenon we want to explain: Why do we seek (choose the term) connectedness, social contact, intersubjectivity, attunement, emotional synchrony? We would like to advance a hypothesis, the dyadic consciousness (DC) hypothesis, that may offer a way out of this conundrum. The DC hypothesis explains the centrality of intersubjectivity in terms of principles borrowed from systems theory. Furthermore, the DC hypothesis moves away from the strictly behavioral account offered above to a more mindful account of social-emotional development that provides a richer understanding of depression and its effects.

A principle of systems theory is that open biological systems, such as humans, function to incorporate and integrate information into increasingly coherent and complex states. This incorporative process is paradoxical. On the one hand, more information is integrated into the system, making it more complex, while on the other hand, to the extent that a more coherent state is formed, then to that extent the new organization with its greater amount of information is simpler. This process is often thought of as a self-generated characteristic of open systems. However, it can also be a dyadic process—a process involving two minds.

The infant is able to endogenously (self-) organize a coherent affective state. This state can be thought of as a state of consciousness or, if one prefers, a state of brain organization. The state of consciousness is isomorphically manifest in the infant's affective configurations of face, body, voice, gaze and gesture. The state incorporates a certain amount of information—perceptual input, motor output, representations, information feedback and feed forward, plans, intentions, reentry information, and much, much more (Edelman, 1987; Stern, 1985; Weinberg & Tronick, 1994). Constraints on the complexity of this self-generated state are determined by the limits of the infant's central nervous system (e.g., speed of information processing, channel capacities of different sensory modalities, motor control limitations, etc.; Aronson & Tronick, 1971). However, the complexity of the infant's state of consciousness is not solely dependent on processes endogenous to the infant. As an open system, the complexity of the infant's state is expandable with input from an external source—the caregiver.

The caregiver provides the infant with regulatory input that can expand the complexity and coherence of the infant's state of consciousness. This expansion of consciousness is an emergent property of the mutual microexchange of affective information. During an interaction, information about the infant's state of consciousness (e.g., intentions, affective states, arousal level) is conveyed through affective configurations that are apprehended by the mother. In response to this information about the infant's state of consciousness, the mother provides the infant with regulatory support that permits the infant to achieve a more complex state of organization. For example, the caregiver, by giving the infant postural support in response to the infant's frustration vocalizations because he can't free his arms and control his posture at the same time, facilitates the infant's ability to employ gestural communication during social interaction, a complex action beyond the infant's own ability. At the same time, the infant's state of consciousness gains coherence and complexity beyond the infant's endogenous capacities. Bullowa (1979) emphasized this phenomenon when she documented the greater complexity of the infant's behavior in the presence of others compared to the infant alone.

There is a critical and emergent property of this collaboration—the creation of a single dyadic state of consciousness. This dyadic state organization is bounded and has more components—the infant and the mother—than the infant's (or mother's) own state of consciousness. Thus this dyadic system contains more information, is more complex and coherent than either the infant's (or the mother's) endogenous state of consciousness alone. When infant and mother mutually create this dyadic state, they fulfill the system's principle of gaining greater complexity and coherence. Thus the mother-held infant performs an action, gesturing, and experiences the state of consciousness associated with gesturing that is an emergent property of the dyadic system. Both the behavior and the state of consciousness occur because the infant and mother are related to the other as components of a dyadic mutually regulated system.

Creation of this dyadic system necessitates that the infant and mother apprehend elements of the other's state of consciousness. If they did not, it would not be possible to create a dyadic state. For example, if the mother's apprehension of the infant's state of consciousness is that the infant intends to reach for a ball when in fact the infant intends to stroke her face, a dyadic state will not be created. The two systems—infant and mother—will remain separate and uncoordinated. Thus a principle governing the human dyadic system is that successful mutual regulation of social interactions requires a mutual mapping of (some of) the elements of the partner's state of consciousness into each partner's brain. This mutual mapping process may be a way of defining intersubjectivity. In the young infant, the process is one of emotional apprehension of the other's state, referred to as primary intersubjectivity (Campos, Barrett, Lamb, Goldsmith, & Stenberg, 1983; Tronick, Als, & Brazelton, 1980a). In the older infant, the process is one of secondary intersubjectivity because the infant becomes aware of his or her apprehension of the other's state. In older children and adults, the process may be what is called empathy—a state which contains an awareness of the other's state, and a paradoxical awareness of the differentiation between one's state and the state of the other.

To restate the DC hypothesis, each individual is a self-organizing system that creates its own states of consciousness—states of brain organization—which can be expanded into more coherent and complex states in collaboration with another self-organizing system. When the collaboration of two brains is successful, each fulfills the system principle of increasing its coherence and complexity. The states of consciousness of the infant, and the mother, are more inclusive and coherent at the moment that they form a dyadic state that incorporates the state of the other.

Thus to return to the original question: What is it about intersubjectivity that makes it so critical to human experience and to infants' development? The answer suggested by the DC hypothesis is that the "fulfilling" of the principle of systems theory for increased complexity and coherence is the motivation of social engagement. Fulfillment of this principle is what gives social interaction its critical experiential value. At the moment the dyadic system is created, both partners experience an expansion of their own state of consciousness. The boundary surrounding their own system expands to incorporate elements of consciousness of the other in a new and more coherent form. In this moment of dyadic formation, and for the duration of its existence, there must be something akin to a powerful experience of fulfillment as one paradoxically becomes larger than oneself.

An important consequence of the DC hypothesis relates to how the toxic effects on the infant of maternal depression, whichever its manifest style, come about. As we have demonstrated, maternal depression disrupts the establishment of a dyadic infant-mother system. The infant is deprived of the experience of expanding his or her states of consciousness in collaboration with the mother. This deprivation limits the infant's experience and forces the infant into self-regulatory patterns that eventually compromise the child's development. The DC hypothesis suggests another more insidious possibility. Given that the infant's system functions to expand its complexity, one way open to the infant of the depressed mother to accomplish this expansion is to take on elements of the mother's state of consciousness. These elements are likely to be negative—sad and hostile affect, withdrawal, disengagement—however, by taking them on, the infant and the mother form a larger dyadic system. Intersubjectivity is established and with it the infant's state is expanded. Thus in the service of becoming more complex and coherent, the infant incorporates a state of consciousness that mimics the depressive elements of the mother. That this intersubjective state contains painful elements does not override the need for expansion. Critically, when the infant comes to other relationships, the only way he or she has learned and has available to expand the complexity of his or her states is by establishing intersubjective states around the depressive features of consciousness that were first established with the mother. Thus the reiterated and often debilitating attachment to and seeking of negative relation experiences seen in some individuals.

In sum, the process of mutual regulation, whether at the level of social-emotional exchanges or at the level of states of consciousness and intersubjectivity, determines much of the emotional, social, and representational course of the infant, including the formation of the infant's brain. When regulation goes well, development proceeds apace. Increasingly complex tasks are approached and resolved, not by the child alone but by the child in collaboration with others. The child, as a system and as a component of a dyadic system, expands and becomes more coherent. When failures take place, development gets derailed and the child's complexity (and we expect the complexity of the child's partners as well) is limited or even reduced. The effect is in the child, but the failure is a joint failure. With continued, chronic failure, and the structuring that goes on around that failure, affective disorders and pathology may result.

CHAPTER 21

Specificity of Infants' Response to Mothers' Affective Behavior

Face-to-face interaction with parents (or other primary caregivers) is centrally important to infants' development. Face-to-face interaction is a context for early socialization experience (Brazelton et al., 1974; Kaye, 1982; Malatesta & Haviland, 1982) and is particularly important for the baby's developing sense of identity (Escalona, 1968; Winnicott, 1967). Individual differences in patterns of mother-infant adaptation are believed to influence profoundly the security of the baby's attachment to his or her mother and other aspects of the baby's socioemotional development (Ainsworth, Blehar, Waters, & Wall, 1978; Belsky, Rovine, & Taylor, 1984; Kaye, 1982; Schaffer, 1984). Until recently, however, little has been known about the mechanisms that mediate the mother's influence. In particular, what aspects of the mother's behavior impact on the baby's behavior, and how closely do mother's and baby's behavior correspond?

In this study, the authors review findings from a series of laboratory studies that suggest that the major functional components of the mother's behavior are its affective quality and its contingent relationship to the baby's behavior. They then show that these functional components accounted for individual differences in the behavior of 7-month-old babies living in multiproblem families. The families were characterized by high rates of factors related to childhood behavior disorder and psychopathology, including low socioeconomic status (SES), single-parent family, depressive symptoms or history of psychopathology in the mother, and child abuse or neglect (Robins, 1974; Rutter et al., 1974). In this group, face-to-face interactions in the families' homes were observed and close correspondences between individual differences in mothers' affect and (lack of) contingent responsiveness and infants' behavior were found.

PREVIOUS LABORATORY STUDIES
OF MOTHER-INFANT DYADS

To evaluate whether babies have specific responses to the quality of their mother's affect and its relationship to their own, Cohn and Tronick (1987) used a cross-sectional design to study mother-infant face-to-face interactions at 3, 6, and 9 months of age. Mothers were asked to play with their babies as they normally would. At each age, mothers used positive affective expressions about half the time and almost never looked away from their infants. The percentage of mothers' gaze away from the baby was consistently less than 1%. Depending on the age, between 12% and 25% of the infant's expressions were positive. Babies also had high proportions of interest in objects (object attend), especially at 6 months.

Within mother-infant pairs, the affective behaviors of each partner were highly related for 52 of the 54 dyads. In particular, babies were almost never positive in affective expression when their mothers were not also.

When Cohn and Tronick (1987) looked at how babies became positive, they found further support for the functional importance of both the affective quality and the organization of the mother's behavior. Babies at each age were far more likely to become positive after their mother did so. At 3 and 6 months, the probability of the baby becoming positive following the mother was 0.33; the probability of the infant becoming positive before the mother was only 0.03. Not until 9 months did babies begin to initiate joint positive engagement, but even then the mother was more likely to do so. Thus, the normal pattern is for the mother's positive expressions to provide a frame within which the infant cycles between neutral and positive expression (Cohn & Tronick, 1987; Kaye & Fogel, 1980). These findings suggest that the mother's positive affective expressions are essential to the quality and organization of the infant's behavior.

This idea was tested in a more rigorous way in an earlier study by Cohn and Tronick (1983) by asking how infants would respond were their mother to act depressed. Thirty mothers were instructed either to simulate depression or behave normally while interacting with their babies. Infants responded dramatically to simulated depression.

Figure 21.1 shows the difference in the infant's behavior between the simulated depression and a normal control condition. The size of the circles represents the proportion of time spent in each state. The arrows represent the probability of transitions among states. The thickness of the arrows represents the size of the transition probability. For clarity, only transition probabilities greater than 0.20 are shown.

In the depressed condition, the proportion of play was far less than in a normal, control condition. Extreme reductions in the mother's positive affect resulted in extreme reductions in the positive affect of the baby. Indeed, if infants in the simulated depressed condition became positive, it was only briefly (brief positive).

FIGURE 21.1. State transition diagram for the normal and depressed conditions. The relative proportion of time spent in each state is indicated by the size of the circle representing that state. Arrows represent transition probabilities among states. The thickness of arrows represents the size of transition probabilities. Striped arrows indicate those transition probabilities for which conditional and unconditional probabilities significantly differ, $p < .05$. Only transition probabilities greater than .20 are shown.

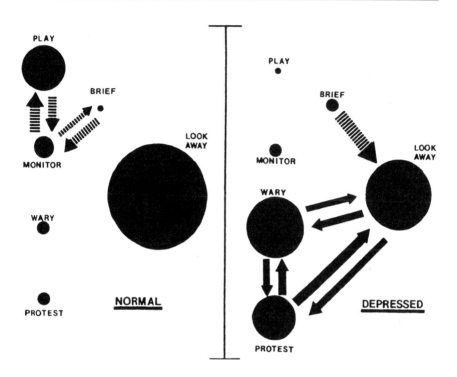

When mothers simulated depression, the organization as well as the distribution of the infant's behavior was affected. Not only were the infants less positive and more negative, they organized their behavior in a totally different way. They no longer cycled between monitor (neutral expression and gaze directed at the mother) and play. Instead, they cycled between negative affective states and look away.

To rigorously test whether the timing as well as the quality of the mother's affect influences the infant's behavior, Cohn and Elmore (1988) modified Tronick, Als, Adamson, Wise, & Brazelton's (1978) still face procedure. In the original study, Tronick et al. asked mothers to hold a still face and remain unresponsive while seated en face with their babies. They found that babies tried to elicit their mother's normal behavior; when they failed, their affect became negative and they turned to self-directed regulatory behaviors.

Despite these dramatic effects, because the still face is continuous one cannot assess whether changes in babies' behavior are contingent on the mothers'. To do so, Cohn and Elmore asked mothers of 3-month-old babies to become still faced for 5 seconds contingent on their infant becoming positive. This perturbation of the usual relation between mothers' and infants' affect provided a test of how closely infants monitor changes in the mothers' behavior. If infants are sensitive to the mothers' signals, they should show less positive affect following the mothers' becoming still faced. Specifically, they should show an increased frequency of transitions from positive to neutral expression.

Consistent with earlier research, mothers were always in a positive state when their infants became positive. But when mothers became briefly still faced contingent on infants' positive expression, the infants became less likely to cycle between positive and neutral expression and more likely to turn away. This study demonstrated that babies have an exquisite sensitivity to the quality and reciprocity of mothers' emotional response.

CLINICAL STUDY

The studies reviewed in the preceding section all involved mother-infant pairs from working- or middle-class, well-functioning families. In those studies, distortions of maternal affect and responsiveness, such as simulated depression, were achieved through experimental instructions. The mothers did not ordinarily distort the quality of their affect or its contingent relationship to the baby's behavior. To determine whether these characteristics could account for individual differences in naturally occurring environments, we studied 13 mother-infant pairs from multiproblem families.

Method

Subjects

The mothers and infants were all participants in a large intervention project conducted in Cambridge, Massachusetts; they were referred to the project by health service providers because of concerns about the mothers' caregiving ability. All the mothers were of low SES; only two had had more than a high school education; seven were single parents; four were under the supervision of the Department of Social Services because of documented child abuse or neglect; and three had had a prior psychiatric hospitalization. They had high rates of self-reported depressive symptoms, as assessed at intake with the Center for Epidemiologic Studies Depression-Scale (CES-D; Radloff, 1977). The mean CES-D score was 27 (SD = 11), which was well within the range for outpatient depressed patients (Myers & Weissman, 1980). Thus, these mothers were identified as needing intervention; they had high rates of factors associated with risk of childhood behavior disorder (Robins, 1974; Rutter et al.,

1974; Rutter & Garmezy, 1983). For these reasons, the authors believed that these mothers would show the wide variability in interactive behavior we were seeking.

Procedure

Two staff members, at least one of whom was known to the families, videotaped the mothers and their babies at home when the babies were 6 to 7 months old. The staff explained what was wanted to the mothers; 3 minutes of face-to-face play preceded by a typical, 40-minute segment when they were free to relate to their baby as they wished (naturalistic observation).

During the face-to-face interaction, the babies sat in an infant seat placed on a table, and their mothers sat on a facing chair. The distance between mothers and babies was similar to that found in the studies reviewed before, about 1 to 2 feet. A mirror placed to the side of the baby enabled us to videotape frontal views of both partners with a single camera.

For the naturalistic interaction, mothers were asked to behave as they normally would and interact with their babies as they wished. The naturalistic interaction allowed the mothers to become comfortable with the videotaping and provided us with the opportunity to assess the generalizability of the behavior and emotions observed in the face-to-face play session.

Coding

Mother's and baby's behavior during the face-to-face interactions was coded using behavioral descriptors and a 1-second scoring interval. Coded for the mother were *anger/poke*, *disengage*, *elicit*, and *play*. *Anger/poke* refers to facial or vocal expressions of anger or irritation or rough, intrusive handling, such as forcing the baby's face into alignment with the mother's. *Elicit* refers to attempts to elicit the baby's attention, such as repeatedly calling his name or making repetitive noises, combined with neutral affective expressions. *Play* referred to positive facial expressions with or without vocalizations.

Coded for the baby were *protest*, *avert*, *attend*, *object*, and *play*. *Protest* refers to strong negative expressions (fuss/cry or grimace); *avert* refers to neutral to slightly negative facial expressions with gaze directed away from the mother. *Object* refers to gaze directed at an object; *attend* refers to gaze directed at the mother and neutral facial expression (*attend* corresponds to Cohn & Tronick's, 1983, *monitor*). *Play* was coded as for the mothers. Interobserver agreement across descriptors was assessed with Cohen's kappa, which corrects for chance levels of agreement. Kappa coefficients were .62 for mothers' codes and .66 for babies'.

Mothers' and babies' behavior during the naturalistic observation was later described with 5-point rating scales and one timed variable. The rating scales included maternal Warmth, Sensitivity, and Flatness of Affect, and baby's Positive and Negative Affect. The timed variable was the amount of time that mothers spent in another room away from their baby. Interobserver agreement within one scaled point averaged .77 to .98 across scales for the mothers' ratings (Tinsley-Weiss coefficients, which correct for chance agreement, averaged from .60 to .98) and .84 to .99 for the babies' ratings (Tinsley-Weiss coefficients across scales averaged from .75 to .96).

Results

Face-to-Face Interactions

Taken as group, during the face-to-face interactions, the mothers' behavior was unlike that of mothers from families without multiple problems. Mothers in well-functioning families typically display positive affect about half the time and do not show expressions of angry or rough behavior. The mothers in this clinical group were withdrawn or interacted in an aggressive, intrusive way with few positive affective expressions (Table 21.1). Nevertheless, variation in their interactive style was pronounced ($\chi^2 = 491$, $p < .001$), requiring that the group be broken down into subgroups based on the quality of their affective expression and degree of intrusiveness (Figure 21.2). At the extreme of disengagement, two mothers (M-Disengaged) showed a pattern similar to some clinical descriptions of depressed mothers (Weissman & Paykel, 1974) and what Cohn and Tronick (1983) had modeled in the simulated depression study. These mothers were disengaged more than 75% of the time. They slouched back in their chairs, often turned away, and spoke in an expressionless voice. They were responsive only to active infant distress.

TABLE 21.1   **Means and Standard Deviations for the Percentage of Mothers' and Babies' Times in Each Behavioral State**

	Percentage of Time*	
	X	SD
Mothers		
Anger/poke	23	24
Disengage	39	24
Elicit	18	14
Play	21	21
Babies		
Protest	7	11
Avert	57	17
Object attend	12	11
Social attend	19	14
Play	6	6

Because of rounding error, percentages do not sum to 100.

FIGURE 21.2. Individual differences among mothers in the percentage of time spent in behavioral states during face-to-face interaction with their babies.

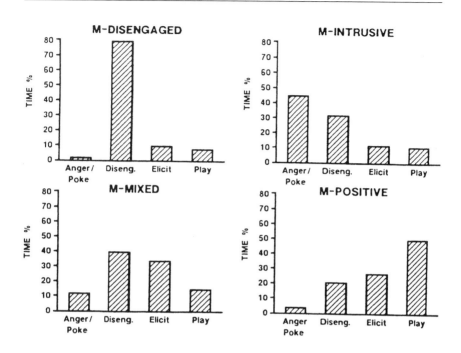

At the other extreme was the largest group (M-Intrusive): six mothers with high proportions of angry or intrusive behaviors, such as rough handling, poking at their babies, and speaking in an angry tone. Two others (M-Mixed) also showed *anger/poke*, although less so, together with some *play*, and much *elicit*. A small group of three mothers (M-Positive) showed high rates of positive expression, comparable to that found in laboratory studies of normal development (Cohn & Tronick, 1987; Kaye & Fogel, 1980).

With the exception of the small M-Positive group, these patterns were unlike those in studies of mothers without risk factors (e.g., Cohn & Tronick, 1987; Kaye & Fogel, 1980). The mothers showed a wider range of variation in behavior and affect than has been previously reported, from extremes of withdrawal to negativity. The majority were not disengaged, but highly engaged, albeit intrusively.

The babies were consistent in showing little positive expression (*play*), but otherwise their behavior, too, was highly variable ($\chi^2 = 1507$, $p < .001$). Whereas the means for babies' positive expressions in prior research with low-risk families ranged from 15% to over 25% (Cohn & Tronick, 1987; Kaye & Fogel, 1980), only one infant in this clinical study had a proportion within this range. A significant reduction was also found in the proportion of *object attend*,

FIGURE 21.3. Individual differences among babies in the percentage of time spent in behavioral states during face-to-face interaction with their mothers.

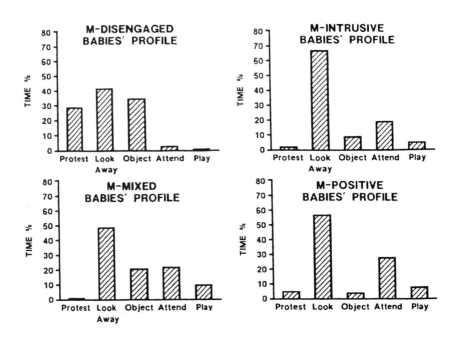

which suggested that they were compromised not only in the affective domain but in the domain of objects (things), as well.

When we analyzed the babies' data by grouping them into their maternal subgroups (Figure 21.3), we found differences corresponding to those among the mothers. Babies of disengaged mothers had the highest proportions of *protest*, which suggests that the most distressing behavior for infants may be the pattern of maternal disengagement (see below). Infants of intrusive mothers had the highest proportions of *look away*, which was consistent with previous work indicating that increases in maternal intensity are unsuccessful in reestablishing mutual interaction when infants are looking away (Cohn & Tronick, 1987; Hirshfeld & Beebe, 1987; Kaye & Fogel, 1980). The infants in the M-Mixed group showed higher rates of *look away* but little *protest*. The infants of the more positive mothers showed the most positive expression but also a greater proportion of *look away* than found among infants of mothers from low-risk families. These findings indicate that infants' behavior is specifically related to the mothers' behavior.

In the interactions of mothers and infants from families without multiple problems, the matching of positive expressions is a highly consistent finding. Mothers and infants tend to be in positive states simultaneously (Cohn & Tronick, 1987). To evaluate whether this matching occurred, the percentage of mutual positive expression in each group was computed first. The percentages were low: 0% to only 3%, which is far less than that reported in comparable studies of mothers and babies from families without multiple problems (Cohn & Tronick, 1987, e.g., found mutual positive engagement occurring 12–25%). The low percentage of mutual positive expressions suggests that these dyads were seldom able to coordinate their behavior to achieve mutually positive engagement.

The relative absence of matching positive states was part of a more general pattern of nonresponsiveness. While watching the videotapes, we were continually struck with the lack of contingent turn-taking, or reciprocity, in these interactions. Reciprocity is a characteristic feature of normal interactions (Brazelton et al., 1974): Contingent responsiveness is found in one half to two thirds of mothers and one third or more of babies (Cohn & Tronick, 1988). To evaluate the impression of its absence in this study, time series analysis was used (see Cohn & Tronick, 1988, for details of this methodology) to test whether or not either partner was responsive to the other. Only four mothers and two babies showed evidence of contingent responding. This low percentage was consistent with the analysis of mutual positive expression in indicating little coordination of affective expression.

To see whether these individual differences in mothers' and infants' behavior were related to variability in risk factors, the distribution of each within each of the four groups was examined. Mean CES-D scores appeared unrelated to mother-infant functioning. CES-D scores were higher in the M-Disengaged group ($\bar{X} = 40$) than in the M-Positive group ($\bar{X} = 26$), but the latter were comparable to those of the M-Intrusive group ($\bar{X} = 23$). Abuse or neglect was documented in all but the M-Disengaged group. Prior psychiatric hospitalization was documented in all but the M-Mixed group. Absence of the father from the home was equally likely in each group. The only factor possibly related to better outcome was mother's education. The two mothers with a college degree showed no intrusive behavior: One was in M-Disengaged; the other was in M-Positive. With the possible exception of mothers' education, then, variability in the quality of face-to-face interaction appeared to be unrelated to any particular risk factor. Of course, since all the mothers were of low SES, we were unable to investigate its influence.

Overall, these interactions differed dramatically from what has been found in studies of families with multiple problems. Most of the mothers in this study either failed to express positive affect or else combined it with negative or intrusive behavior. Most were unable to respond contingently to their babies. Their babies showed high percentages of disengagement. When they did become positive, they did so only briefly. Even their engagement with objects was attenuated.

Naturalistic Observations

Maternal affective expression during the face-to-face interactions was consistent with that observed during the naturalistic interactions. *Anger/poke* during the face-to-face interactions was inversely correlated with Sensitivity ($r = -.42, p <$ .10) and with Warmth ($r = -.56, p < .05$) and positively correlated with Flatness of Affect ($r = .54$). Play was positively correlated with Warmth ($r = .45, p < .10$) and inversely correlated with Flatness of Affect ($r = -.50, p < .05$). The correlation with Sensitivity was positive but not significant. This continuity across situations suggests that the individual differences we found were not limited to the face-to-face interaction.

Mothers, especially those who seem most irritable and negative, may have ways of coping that buffer their babies. The naturalistic observations, as contrasted to the face-to-face interactions, did not require that mothers interact with their infants. Thus, it presented them with the opportunity to minimize contact, which they did. Mothers who had high scores for *anger/poke* during the face-to-face interaction spent more time out of the room during the 40 minutes of naturalistic interaction.

No continuity was found between babies' behavior in the two contexts. The low proportions of positive expression in both contexts may have attenuated any associations.

Discussion

The results of this study converge with those from studies of mothers and infants from families without multiple problems to suggest the following model: Infants respond to the affective quality of their mother's behavior in a way that is specific to that affect. In particular, infants' cycles of neutral to positive affect occur primarily within the mothers' periods of positive expression. When mothers are unable to provide such periods, infants' affective expression is limited to neutral to negative displays and they become less involved with both persons and objects. In an experimental situation these effects are short-lived, whereas in a clinical group the effect is chronic, carries over between situations, and has a more profound effect.

Consistent with the present authors' clinical experience, the mothers in this study were not uniformly withdrawn and sad or lacking in affective expression. The largest proportion was rough, insensitive, intrusive, and, on occasion, angry.

These individual differences among mothers had striking effects on their babies: Infants of disengaged mothers were distressed and unsuccessfully sought engagement; infants of intrusive mothers looked away; whereas infants of mixed and positive mothers had a greater breadth of behavior and affect. These individual differences were unrelated to variability in risk factors. Depressive symptoms and other risk factors did not predict maladaptive interaction patterns in a simple one-to-one fashion. These findings make it clear that infants' affective behavior and experience are specific to the affective quality and reciprocity of mothers' behavior.

The findings of this study have important implications for both developmental psychopathology and clinical practice. Mothers with similar combinations of risk factors may behave dissimilarly with their babies. Risk factors may be predictive only weakly of interactive behavior. To adequately assess an infant's risk status, behavioral assessment of mother-infant interaction is necessary.

Mother-infant interaction assessment can provide the clinician with valuable information about how symptomatology is related to caregiving behavior and infants' response. Although treatment efforts typically focus on the individual patient, a broader focus may be warranted when the patient is a woman with an infant or young child. The present data suggest that depressive symptoms in combination with other risk factors have dramatic effects on infants. Medication or other treatment may successfully eliminate symptomatology, but it is unknown whether successful treatment also remedies the kinds of maternal behaviors studied here. Maladaptive patterns of interaction may continue even after symptoms remit. In this regard, the experimental data suggest that infants may continue to be withdrawn and negative even after mothers resume normal behavior. Thus, clinicians should be alert to the possible need to direct intervention efforts to the mother-infant dyad, as well as the mother herself.

It is interesting to speculate on the psychological processes underlying the different patterns of infants' behavior. The infants of the withdrawn mothers were the most distressed. Their mothers may have failed to provide them with the necessary regulatory support to control the negative affect generated in response to the mothers' withdrawn behavior. The infants thus were forced to self-regulate their own negative affect. Unsuccessful, they become even more distressed. The infants of the intrusive mothers, by contrast, may have experienced less distress because they were able to regulate their experience by turning away from their mothers and disengaging.

If this perspective is accurate, one might hypothesize that infants of the withdrawn mothers are at greater risk than those of the intrusive mothers because the former never experience success at regulating either themselves or the interaction (Tronick, Ricks, & Cohn, 1982). Infants of the more positive mothers are likely to experience a wider range of affect and some successful periods of self-regulation, although on an inconsistent basis, which suggests that they might be developmentally at less risk. Normal interactions have been characterized as ones in which the infant regularly experiences affective disruptions that are quickly resolved, experiences that may have positive developmental effects (Tronick & Cohn, 1989).

Engagement with objects was reduced for all the infants. We propose that a common experience was the need to devote excessive resources to regulating the negative affect occasioned by their interactive experience, which resulted in fewer resources available for regulating exchanges with the inanimate environment. Thus the experience of relating to a mother whose affect and responsiveness are atypical disrupts both social and object engagement. In this regard, Sameroff, Seifer, & Zax (1982) found cognitive deficits at 4 and 18 months.

To summarize the present findings: In families characterized by multiple risk factors, mothers disrupted the normal interaction in one of several ways, all of which forced the infants both to self-regulate their own negative affect and to try to reduce the effects of their mothers' inappropriate behavior. The infants' response was specific to the type of affective expression mothers displayed, but in each case positive affective experience was compromised. It is expected that the accumulation of such interactive experience has a structuring effect on infants such that a self-directed regulatory style comes to dominate all interpersonal exchanges. Thus, the increased rate of affective disturbance seen in at-risk infants may result from the infants' normal capacities for internal and external regulation becoming increasingly narrowly deployed in the service of self-regulation.

CHAPTER 22

The Impact of Maternal Psychiatric Illness on Infant Development

Maternal depression and anxiety are related to compromises in maternal emotional responsivity and infant socioemotional functioning. In this chapter, we briefly review the research on this topic. The studies have been carried out primarily in the tradition of developmental psychology and focus largely on maternal depression, since this is the maternal psychiatric illness that has received most attention in this literature. We also discuss some of the methodological shortcomings and unanswered questions of this research. These questions include: (1) How do mothers in treatment describe their affective and psychological functioning on self-report measures? and (2) Do these self-descriptions fit the emotional quality of their interactions with their infants? This is a critical question, because mothers' self-reports are often used as key indicators of their functioning, including their ability to parent. To address this and other issues, we present preliminary findings on the socioemotional functioning of a group of infants and their mothers who are in treatment for major depressive disorder, panic disorder, or obsessive-compulsive disorder. The results suggest that although mothers report feeling well, their affective responsiveness as well as their infants' socioemotional development are compromised in significant ways.

The chapter is guided by the thesis that maternal depression and anxiety interfere with infants' active engagement with people and objects and that exposure to compromised parenting may predispose children to develop socioemotional, cognitive, and psychiatric difficulties. This interpretation is not complete or exclusive of other perspectives. For instance, there is evidence that mood and anxiety disorders have a genetic basis (Tsuang & Faraone, 1990), that prenatal physiological mechanisms associated with maternal psychiatric illness may alter neonatal outcome (Fride & Weinstock, 1989), and that a lower threshold of limbic arousal in response to novelty may underlie the development of psychopathology in some individuals (Mullen, Snidman, & Kagan, 1993; Rosenbaum et al., 1988). The interaction of these processes is complex, and it is likely that there are multiple pathways to psychopathology. Understanding these pathways requires consideration of a broad range of physiological, genetic, and environmental factors.

EFFECTS OF MATERNAL PSYCHIATRIC ILLNESS ON INFANT FUNCTIONING

Infant Sensitivity to Maternal Affect

It is now well established that infants are exquisitely sensitive to the emotional states of their mother and other caregivers (Tronick & Weinberg, 1997). This sensitivity, in the earliest months of life, is fundamental to understanding the impact of maternal psychiatric illness, such as depression and anxiety, on infant development (Tronick, 1989). For example, Cohn and Tronick (1983) asked nondepressed mothers of 3-month-old infants to simulate depression for 3 minutes. The mothers were asked to speak in a monotone, to keep their faces flat and expressionless, to slouch back in their chair, to minimize touch, and to imagine that they felt tired and blue. The infants exposed to this brief simulation of depression reacted strongly. Compared with their normal interactions with their mother, the infants expressed little positive affect, looked away from the mother, and became wary and distressed during the simulation. Their affective behavior was restricted, cycling among states of wariness, disengagement, and distress with brief bids to their mother to resume her normal affective state. Importantly, the infants continued to be distressed and disengaged from the mother even after the mother resumed normal interactive behavior. This research suggested that infants as young as 3 months can detect even short-lived changes in their mothers' affective behavior and that they react with affective states of their own that are specifically related to the affect expressed by their mother. The research also raised questions as to what happens when infants are exposed to more prolonged periods of maternal social and emotional unavailability. On the basis of these findings and others like them (Field, 1984), it was hypothesized that exposure to maternal depression and anxiety might be associated with affective and interactive disturbances in the infant.

Depression and Maternal and Infant Functioning

Weinberg and Tronick (1997; Tronick & Weinberg, 1997) have reviewed the literature on the effects of maternal depression on maternal and infant functioning (Downey & Coyne, 1990; Field, 1995; Murray & Cooper, 1997). The research indicates that in each communicative domain—face, voice, and touch—the quantity, quality, and timing of depressed mothers' social and affective behavior are distorted in ways that contrast sharply with the behavior of nondepressed mothers. In turn, distortions of maternal affect and behavior are related to compromises in infant social, emotional, and cognitive functioning (Cohn, Campbell, Matias, & Hopkins, 1990; Field, Healy, Goldstein, & Gutherz, 1990).

Much of the research that evaluates the behavior and affect of depressed mothers has treated these mothers as if they form a homogeneous group. The picture, however, is more complicated. Research suggests that the behavior of depressed mothers is heterogeneous and that maternal depression does not have a singular compromising effect on the infant. Several researchers have found that some depressed mothers' behavior and affect appear quite normal, whereas the behavior and affect of other mothers with similar levels of depressive symptomatology are compromised (Cohn, Matias, Tronick, Connell, & Lyons-Ruth, 1986; Cohn & Tronick, 1989; Field et al., 1990; Lyons-Ruth et al., 1986; Radke-Yarrow, 1987). Cohn and Tronick (1989), for example, describe depressed mothers who are disengaged and withdrawn when interacting with their infants. These withdrawn mothers engage in little play, talk only rarely to their infants using motherese, and show flat and sad affect. Other mothers are more intrusive. They express anger directed at their infants and interfere with their infants' activities. Still other mothers are able to mobilize sufficiently to interact positively with their infants. This research indicates that not all depressed women function poorly as parents. The research, however, does not indicate whether the "positive" depressed mothers represent a subgroup of mothers with less severe and chronic depression. These women may not experience an impairment in interactional skills, whereas women with more severe and chronic depression may be unable to compensate for a worsening in their mood. It is also unclear whether the positive depressed mothers have infants who are temperamentally more easygoing and better able to elicit a positive interaction from the mother. Further research is necessary to determine the role of the infant and to establish whether the inability to mobilize and to derive pleasure from interchanges with the infant is a predictor of risk for chronic depression.

Maternal depression is associated with adverse effects on infant functioning (Tronick & Weinberg, 1997; Weinberg & Tronick, 1997). Infants of depressed mothers have difficulties engaging in social and object interactions as early as 2 months of age (Campbell & Cohn, 1991). These infants look less at the mother, engage less with objects, show less positive and more negative affect, lower activity levels, and greater physiological reactivity as indexed by higher heart rate and cortisol levels than the infants of nondepressed control mothers (Field, 1995). They show compromised ability to regulate their affective and behavioral states. These regulatory dysfunctions are present as early as the newborn period (often in the form of irritability and inconsolable crying; Zuckerman, Bauchner, Parker, & Cabral, 1990), which suggests that prenatal factors (e.g., neuroendocrine changes associated with the mothers' depression) may have had an impact on the infants' behavior.

The infants' affective states are specifically related to their mothers' style of interaction. Cohn and Tronick (1989) found that the infants of withdrawn depressed mothers spend most of their time fussing and crying, whereas the infants of the intrusive depressed mothers rarely cry but avoid looking at and interacting with their mother. The infants of the positive depressed mothers behave similarly to control infants. These findings emphasize how sensitive infants are to maternal affect and suggest that mothers' affective style is a critical factor that needs to be considered in clinical and research work in addition to the mothers' diagnostic status. The data also suggest that there is a need to tailor interventions, since the interactional difficulties of mothers within the same diagnostic category vary and are associated with different maternal and infant outcomes.

Male infants may be more vulnerable to maternal depression than female infants. Weinberg, Tronick, Cohn, and Olson (1998) found that 6-month-old male infants of nondepressed mothers have greater difficulty regulating affective states on their own and need to rely more on maternal support than girls to help them maintain affective regulation. Mother-son, as compared to mother-daughter, pairs also take longer to repair interactive errors (e.g., misreading of cues) that typically occur during mother-infant interactions. To facilitate well-modulated interactions, mothers' and sons' affective behaviors are tightly synchronized. This careful tracking of each other's behavior may function to help boys maintain affective regulation. In other research, Weinberg (1996) described similar gender differences in mother-infant dyads when the mother is depressed. Preliminary data suggest that male infants are more demanding social partners than female infants and that depressed mothers have difficulties providing their sons with the regulatory help that they need. A cycle of mutual interactive problems between mothers and sons becomes established, with the mothers showing more anger to their sons than their daughters and the sons showing less positive affect and greater difficulty maintaining affective regulation.

At 1 year of age, many infants of depressed mothers show poorer performance on developmental tests, such as the Bayley Scales of Infant Development and Piagetian object tasks (Lyons-Roth, Connell, & Grunebaum, 1990; Murray, 1992). These findings suggest that the children of depressed mothers are at risk for cognitive compromises at an early age (Lyons-Ruth et al., 1990; Murray, 1990; Murray, Kempton, Woolgar, & Hooper, 1993). Furthermore, there is some indication that these infants have an insecure attachment to the mother, especially if the mother's illness is severe and chronic (Teti, Gelfand, Messinger, & Isabella, 1995). Insecure attachment has been related to a number of difficulties, including conduct disorders and behavior problems during the preschool and later school periods, and has been suggested as an environmental mechanism for the occurrence of familial psychopathology (Crowell, O'Connor, Wollmers, et al., 1991; Greenberg, Speltz, Deklyen, et al., 1991; Hubbs-Tait et al., 1996; Mrazek, Casey, & Anderson, 1987).

Anxiety and Maternal and Infant Functioning

Little is known about the effects of anxiety on infant functioning. Most of the literature has focused on older children and on panic disorder to the exclusion of other anxiety disorders. Despite the paucity of findings, the available research suggests that maternal anxiety, like depression, may have a powerful developmental effect on children.

Increased rates of psychiatric difficulties have been reported in the children of mothers with anxiety disorders. Weissman et al., (1984) for example, found that 6- to 7-year-old children with a parent who has panic disorder were three times more likely than control children to experience anxiety disorders. Several studies have also reported higher rates of behavioral inhibition in the children of mothers with panic disorder (Biederman et al., 1990, 1993; Manassis, Bradley, Goldberg, Hood, & Swinson, 1995; Rosenbaum, Biederman, Hirshfeld, Bolduc, & Chaloff, 1991; Rosenbaum et al., 1988). Behavioral inhibition is defined by Kagan, Mullen, Reznick, and colleagues (Kagan, Reznick, & Snidman, 1987; Mullen et al., 1993; Reznick, Kagan, Snidman, et al., 1986) as a temperamental tendency to withdraw from novelty and unfamiliar situations. Research by Mullen et al. (1993) indicates that 10% to 15% of American children are inhibited and predisposed to be irritable as infants and shy, fearful, quiet, and introverted at older ages. Rosenbaum et al. (1988, 1991) found that 85% of the children (ages 2–7) of parents with panic disorder, with or without agoraphobia, were rated as behaviorally inhibited, compared with 50% of the children of parents with depression and 15% of the children whose parents had neither panic disorder nor depression. Biederman et al. (1990) further found higher rates of multiple anxiety disorders (two or more anxiety disorders per child) in children described as behaviorally inhibited. These rates increased markedly over a period of 3 years when the children were reassessed (Biederman et al., 1993). However, as Biederman et al. (1993) cautioned, the majority (approximately 70%) of inhibited children do not develop an anxiety disorder. Thus, behavioral inhibition may be one of several risk factors contributing to the ontogeny of later psychopathology.

Children of mothers with panic disorder may also have a higher rate of insecure attachment to the mother (Manassis, Bradley, Goldberg, Hood, & Swinson, 1994; Manassis et al., 1995). In a study by Manassis et al. (1994), 80% of the preschool children were classified as insecurely attached to the mother. This study, however, was based on a small sample and the findings must be considered with some caution until they are replicated.

Thus, the research indicates that the children of mothers with panic disorder are at risk for developing anxiety disorders themselves and that inhibited temperamental characteristics or attachment difficulties may be early risk factors. More extended longitudinal observational studies are needed to confirm initial findings and evaluate the importance of these risk factors in the development of psychopathology.

Methodological Issues and Unanswered Questions

Several of the studies that examine the impact of maternal psychiatric illness on infant functioning have suffered from methodological problems, including small sample sizes, lack of appropriate comparison groups, and absence of blindness in respect to maternal psychiatric status. Many studies have not been replicated, making it difficult to ascertain the robustness of findings. Several of the studies have also relied on maternal reports of child psychopathology, either parental interviews or parental ratings on measures such as the Child Behavior Checklist (CBCL). The extent to which these reports are biased by the parental disorder is unknown, but there is some evidence that depressed mothers may perceive their infants more negatively than asymptomatic mothers (Field, Morrow, & Adlestein, 1993).

Most of the studies that evaluate the impact of depression or anxiety on maternal and infant functioning have not explored the potential effect of treatment on maternal behavior. Many studies have used community-based samples of women who have symptoms but who have not typically sought treatment. Although self-reported symptoms are common during the postpartum period, treatment utilization is low (Campbell, Cohn, & Meyers, 1995; O'Hara, Zekoski, Phillips, & Wright, 1990). Women who seek treatment may represent a more ill group than women who do not seek treatment. These women may also possess characteristics (e.g., higher IQ, more education, higher income) that make it more likely that they will receive treatment. Exclusive evaluation of untreated women from community-based samples, however, fails to delineate the extent to which treatment affects maternal and infant functioning. Thus, there is a need for observational studies to evaluate the functioning of women with a psychiatric illness who are in treatment as well as the functioning of their infants.

Few studies have evaluated the relation between mothers' self-report of their own functioning, the mothers' interactive behavior with their infants, and the infants' functioning. Research on this topic has yielded contradictory findings. Teti et al. (Teti & Gelfand, 1991; Teti, Gelfand, & Pompa, 1990), found that the quality of depressed mothers' caretaking behavior was related to the mothers' perceptions of their maternal competence. The poorer the mothers' feelings of self-efficacy in the mothering role, the poorer their interactions with their infants. Frankel and Harmon (1996), however, found discontinuity between maternal self-report and maternal interactive behavior. Although depressed mothers' self-evaluations of their affective state and ability to parent were primarily negative, their interactions and attachment relationships with their children were no more impaired than those of controls. Discontinuity between parent report and behavior has also been reported by Weissman and Paykel (1974) but in the opposite direction. Weissman and Paykel found that, even after an acute psychiatric episode is over, mothers continue to show parenting difficulties with their children. This research indicates that there is a need to ask mothers how they are feeling, assess their psychiatric status with objective measures based on structured clinical interviews, and observe their interactions with their infants if we are to understand the relation between maternal psychiatric illness, maternal behavior, and infant development.

PRELIMINARY RESULTS

As part of an ongoing collaboration between the Child Development Unit at Boston's Children's Hospital and the Perinatal Psychiatry Clinical Research Program at the Massachusetts General Hospital, we are currently studying a group of mothers with a pregravid history of psychiatric illness. One of the primary goals of the study is to evaluate the relations between maternal self-reported psychiatric functioning and direct observations of mother-infant interactions and socioemotional functioning.

Characteristics of the Mothers and Infants

The study included two groups of mothers and infants. The proband group consisted of 30 mothers with a pregravid clinical diagnosis of panic disorder (37% of sample), major depressive disorder (43% of sample), or obsessive-compulsive disorder (20% of sample). Mothers were diagnosed using the Structured Clinical Interview for DSM-III-R Axis I Disorders (SCID; Spitzer et al., 1988) and were recruited from and treated at the Perinatal Psychiatry Clinical Research Program. The majority of the mothers were treated with psychotropic medications, the most common of which were clonazepam, tricyclic antidepressants (i.e., nortriptyline, desipramine, and imipramine), and fluoxetine. Sixty-eight percent of the mothers were maintained on medication during some part of their pregnancy. During the postpartum period, 48% of the mothers were treated with psychotropic medication and an additional 40% with psychotropic medication and therapy. Furthermore, 40% of the sample breastfed while taking medication. Thus a majority of the infants were exposed to psychotropic medication during pregnancy or the postpartum period.

The second group of mothers was a control group drawn from the community. These mothers were recruited from the maternity wards of Boston area hospitals. The group consisted of 30 mothers with no documented depressive symptomatology on the Center for Epidemiologic Studies Depression Scale (CES-D; Radloff, 1977) or clinical diagnosis on the Diagnostic Interview Schedule-Version-III-R (DIS-III-R; Robins, Cottler, & Keating, 1991).

Mothers and infants in both groups met a set of low-risk social and medical criteria (e.g., age over 21 years, living with the infant's father, at least a high school education, healthy mother and infant). Many developmental studies have included high-risk samples of mothers and infants. Risk factors (e.g., teen parenthood, poverty, illness), however, are known to affect maternal and infant functioning and to obscure the effects of psychiatric status. The use of medical and social selection criteria makes it easier to disentangle the effects of psychiatric illness per se from other factors.

The study is ongoing, and it is important to note that the current proband group is comprised of a heterogeneous cohort of mothers with different diagnoses. Following the completion of the study, the major depressive disorder, panic disorder, and obsessive-compulsive disorder groups will be disaggregated in order to determine if there is a differential effect of diagnosis on maternal and infant functioning. Although specificity is one of the most important issues in the field of high-risk research (Seifer, 1995), few studies have evaluated what outcomes are unique to a specific diagnostic group. Furthermore, the sample is complete; the effects of different kinds of treatment on maternal and infant functioning, as issues of chronicity, remission, and severity of maternal disorder, will be assessed.

Observations of the Mothers and Infants

Mothers completed self-report measures designed to assess their level of depressive symptomatology—using the CES-D—and psychiatric symptoms—using the Symptom Checklist-90, Revised (SCL-90R; Derogatis, 1983). Mothers and infants were also videotaped in the laboratory of the Child Development Unit at Boston's Children's Hospital at 3 months postpartum. The infants were videotaped with their mother in the face-to-face still-face paradigm developed by Tronick, Als, Adamson, Wise, and Brazelton (1978). This paradigm includes a 2-minute face-to-face play interaction with the mother, a 2-minute still-face episode during which the mother is unresponsive to the infant, and a second 2-minute face-to-face play interaction with the mother. In addition, the infants were videotaped during a 2-minute face-to-face play interaction with an unfamiliar female research assistant.

Contrasted to face-to-face play (during which mothers are instructed to play with the baby as they would at home), the still face perturbs the mothers' behavior. During this episode, mothers are asked to look at their infants but not to touch, smile, or talk to them. The mothers' en face position and eye contact signal the infants that social interaction is forthcoming, while their expressionless face and lack of response communicate the opposite. The mothers are saying "hello" and "good-bye" at the same time and remain expressionless even after attempts by the infants to reinstate the interaction.

The still face has been used extensively to evaluate young infants' communicative abilities, sensitivity to changes in maternal behavior, ability to cope with interpersonal disturbances, and capacity to regulate affective states (Tronick & Cohn, 1989; Weinberg & Tronick, 1996). For example, Gianino and Tronick (1988) found that infants who experienced frequent repairs of minor interactive errors (e.g., misreading of cues) during mother-infant face-to-face play were likely to elicit their mothers' attention using smiles and vocalizations during the still face. Infants who experienced fewer repairs were more likely to become distressed. Gianino and Tronick concluded that infants who routinely experience repairs have a representation of themselves as effective and of their mother as responsive and sensitive. These data on the still face, like the data on the simulation of depression reported above, have implications for the infants of psychiatrically ill mothers who may be exposed to periods of maternal unavailability. Infants of mothers with a psychiatric illness would be expected to react with more negative affect to the still face than the infants of well mothers.

The infants were also videotaped interacting with an unfamiliar female research assistant (or stranger). This episode was included because of work by Field et al. (1988) suggesting that negative interactive patterns of infants of depressed mothers generalize to the infants' interactions with an unfamiliar adult. Specifically, Field et al. found that infants of depressed mothers showed similar compromises whether they were interacting with their mother or a stranger and that the stranger performed less optimally with these infants than with the infants of control mothers. These findings suggest that infant affect and behavior are not simply immediate by-products of the adult partner's interactive style but reflect the infants' representations of their interactions with the mother and other social partners.

The infants' and mothers' behaviors and facial expressions were coded microanalytically second by second from videotapes using Tronick and Weinberg's Infant and Maternal Regulatory Scoring Systems (IRSS and MRSS) and Izard's AFFEX system (Izard & Dougherty, 1980). (The IRSS and MRSS are available from the authors on request. The systems are described in Weinberg & Tronick, 1994). These systems have been very effective at documenting subtle changes in infant and maternal behavior. Coders were masked to maternal group membership.

Maternal Self-Reported Functioning and Mother/Stranger-Infant Interactions

The findings from the study are counterintuitive. On the one hand, proband mothers reported feeling as well as control mothers on the questionnaires assessing depressive symptomatology and other psychiatric symptoms. An exception was a slightly higher level of anxiety reported by the proband mothers. However, even though the proband mothers perceived themselves as functioning and feeling well overall, they evidenced a number of difficulties when interacting with their infants.

During the mother-infant play interactions, mothers in the proband group were more disengaged than control mothers. Proband mothers talked less to their infants, showed fewer facial expressions of interest, were less likely to share the infants' attention to objects, and touched their infants less than control mothers. In addition, in the reunion play, during which mothers and infants must renegotiate the interaction after it has been stressed by the still face, proband mothers were more likely to perceive the interaction negatively (as reflected in comments such as, "You don't like me," "I bore you," or "You don't want to play with me") and had a tendency to show more anger to their infants than control mothers. These findings suggest that the proband mothers found it difficult to repair the interaction after it had been disrupted by the still face.

The proband infants also showed compromises in their interactive behavior. Although there were few notable differences in the infants' affect and behavior during the first play interaction, the proband infants had more negative interactions with their mothers than controls after having experienced the stress of the still face. The proband infants showed less interest, more anger and sadness, and a greater tendency to fuss and cry than controls during the reunion face-to-face play. These findings indicate that they, like their mothers, had difficulties regulating their emotional states and repairing the interaction after it had been disrupted. This is consistent with previous work by Weinberg and Tronick (1996), who found that the reunion episode is often the most challenging episode of the face-to-face still-face paradigm to mothers and infants.

The proband infants also showed more negative affect in response to the still face and the interaction with the stranger. During both situations, the proband infants showed less interest, more anger and sadness, and had a tendency to fuss and cry more than control infants. In addition, the proband infants were less likely than control infants to engage the stranger in an interaction by vocalizing. These results indicate that the proband infants reacted with a decrease in interest and an increase in anger, sadness, fussiness, and crying to the episodes of the face-to-face still-face paradigm that presented them with a challenge or stress.

The strangers' reactions to the infants in the proband and control groups were also evaluated. The stranger interaction is interesting because the strangers were unbiased. The strangers had never seen the baby before, had not watched the preceding mother-infant interactions, and were masked to the infants' and mothers' background. Thus the strangers were influenced by the infants' ongoing behavior during the interaction and not by prior knowledge of the mother and infant.

The strangers were more disengaged with the infants of the proband mothers than with the infants of control mothers. Of particular interest was the minimal amount of time the strangers touched these infants. They especially avoided using touches such as tickles that are arousing and intrusive. The strangers also maintained a greater physical distance from these infants than from control infants and used behaviors (e.g., hand waves, calling the infant's name) to try to elicit the proband infants' attention. The strangers may have behaved in a disengaged manner because they were picking up cues from the infants that the infants did not want to play with them (e.g., these infants were less likely to invite interaction by vocalizing). The strangers may also have perceived these infants as more emotionally vulnerable than controls (e.g., these infants expressed higher levels of negative affect) and more likely than controls to become overwhelmed or overstimulated if they played with them in a more animated manner. Both alternative explanations suggest that the infants in the proband group exhibited an affective-behavioral organization that affected their interactions with the strangers in significant ways.

COMMENTS

Mothers in treatment with a pregravid history of panic disorder, major depressive disorder, or obsessive-compulsive disorder consistently perceived themselves as doing well when asked to complete self-report measures assessing psychiatric symptoms. They reported levels of depression and other psychiatric symptoms that were comparable to those of control mothers. An exception was a slightly higher level of self-reported anxiety. Surprisingly, how well the proband mothers said they were doing did not accurately reflect their interactions with their infants. The proband mothers were significantly more disengaged than control mothers when interacting with their infants. This disengagement extended to the communicative domains of face, voice, and touch. They also had a more difficult time regulating their affect and coping with the disruption generated by the still face than control mothers. These interactional difficulties are similar to those reported in prior research with depressed untreated mothers.

These results indicate that psychiatrically ill mothers' self-evaluations are not always concordant with the emotional quality of their interactions with their infants. A similar discordance has been reported by Weissman and Paykel (1974). They found that, even after an acute psychiatric episode is over, mothers continue to show interactive and emotional difficulties with their children.

The findings suggest that some areas of maternal functioning may change more easily than others. Self-perceptions may be the first area to improve as a result of treatment or remission of the disorder. Changes in interactive behavior and intimate relationships, on the other hand, may be less easily amenable to treatment or remission. Mother-infant relationships develop stable characteristics based on the mothers' and infants' interactive history. As a result, both mothers and infants interact with each other following predictable patterns. For a change to occur in the mother-infant relationship, the mother's perceptions of her infant and of herself as a parent as well as her interactive behavior with the infant must change. The infant's interactive representations and behavior must also change, given the reciprocal nature of interactions and the infant's active role in shaping relationships (Tronick, 1989). Thus change takes place at different levels and is often a slow and difficult process.

The infants of the proband mothers showed compromises in their socioemotional functioning. Compared with controls, the proband infants reacted with more anger, sadness, fussiness, and crying and less interest to the episodes of the face-to-face still-face paradigm that presented them with a challenge or stress. Thus they reacted with negative affect to the still face, the stranger, and the reunion episode during which the mothers and infants had to repair the interaction following the disruption of the still face. Furthermore, the infants' behavior affected the unfamiliar adults' interactions. The strangers were more disengaged with the proband infants than with the control infants. The disengagement apparent in both the mothers' and strangers' interactions is worrisome and raises the question of whether these infants receive adequate levels of social and emotional stimulation necessary for optimal development.

The findings in this study are consistent with the mutual regulation model (MRM) developed by Tronick et al. (Tronick, 1989; Tronick & Weinberg, 1997). The MRM focuses on the interactive nature of development and argues that mothers and infants jointly regulate interactions by responding to each other's affective displays. Parental unresponsiveness dysregulates infants' affective states, which prevents the infants from achieving their goals of social connectedness and object exploration. This inability leads to sadness and anger and compels the infants to devote much of their coping resources to control negative affect. With chronic failure to change their mothers' behavior, the infants' sense of mastery and agency may become compromised. They develop a representation of the parent as unreliable and unavailable and of themselves as ineffective and helpless. In addition, they may develop a self-directed style of coping that is deployed defensively and automatically in an effort to preclude anticipated negative emotions even in situations in which negative affect may not occur. This interpretation may explain the findings of Field et al. (1988) and this study that the infants of psychiatrically ill mothers were affectively negative even with people who were not depressed or anxious.

The process of mutual regulation is not a complete or exclusive explanation. A large body of literature supports a genetic basis for mood and anxiety disorders. Family studies have demonstrated that relatives of depressed probands are at greater risk of mood disorders than the general population (see Tsuang & Faraone, 1990, for a review). Higher concordance rates of anxiety disorders have been found in monozygotic as compared with dizygotic twins (Torgeson, 1983). This genetic diathesis is likely to influence infants' behavior independently of their interactive experiences. There is also some evidence that prenatal maternal habits influence infants' later behavior. Depressed women are more likely than nondepressed women to use alcohol, cigarettes, and drugs during pregnancy, and each of these factors has been associated with compromises in infant outcome (Zuckerman, Amaro, Bauchnes, & Cabral, 1989). Physiological mechanisms associated with depression may also alter neonatal outcome. These factors include hypercortisolemia and increased serum catecholamines that alter uterine blood flow and induce uterine irritability (Lederman, 1995). Animal studies also indicate that significant changes in offsprings' neurotransmitter systems and regulation of the hypothalamic-pituitary axis can be induced by prenatal maternal stress (Fride & Weinstock, 1989; Peters, 1988, 1990; Smythe, McCormick, & Meaney, 1996; Weinstock, Fride, & Hertzberg, 1988). These studies suggest that physiological changes induced by prenatal stress may undermine the ability of offspring to cope with anxiety-provoking situations (Fride & Weinstock, 1989).

The finding of greater irritability (i.e., anger, sadness, fussiness, and crying) in the proband infants in this study is also reminiscent of the descriptions of inhibited infants in Mullen et al. (1993), who found that 4-month-old infants who later become inhibited are motorically active and irritable when confronted with novelty. In this study, the still face and the stranger were novel to the infants, and both situations elicited anger, sadness, fussiness, and crying in the proband infants. Rosenbaum et al. (1988, 1991) and Biederman et al. (1990, 1993) have argued in a series of papers that inhibition may reflect a temperamental predisposition to the development of anxiety disorders. They hypothesize that a lower threshold of limbic arousal in response to novelty and challenge is a basic process underlying the development of psychopathology in some individuals.

The present study does not allow us to distinguish genetic from environmental effects. It is clear, however, that the developmental process leading to psychopathology is complex. It is likely that there are multiple pathways to both similar and dissimilar developmental outcomes. Thus an inhibited child with an asymptomatic mother and a normal child with a mother with panic disorder may develop similar forms of disturbances. Or the child of a depressed intrusive mother may experience a different outcome from the child with a withdrawn depressed mother. Understanding these pathways requires consideration of a broad range of biological, genetic, and environmental factors.

The findings from this study highlight several difficult therapeutic issues. The disjunction of maternal self-report and observed interactive behavior indicates that descriptions of how good mothers are feeling do not fully capture the quality of their functioning. This is a significant issue, because maternal self-report is often a primary method of evaluating the effects of therapy and medication. Are mothers unaware of interactional problems with their infants? Are they denying these difficulties? Has the therapeutic process transformed only some aspects of the mothers' functioning and not others? Do the mothers need more therapy or a different kind of therapeutic intervention? These are difficult questions to which there are no easy answers.

A related issue is how clinicians should handle the effects of the mothers' disorder on the infants' development. The primary question here is whether it is enough to treat the mother alone or whether the dyad should also be a focus of the therapeutic intervention. In many cases, the infant is the "forgotten patient." By excluding the infant from the therapeutic process, clinicians may miss the opportunity to address developmental difficulties that may lead to later psychiatric problems in a child who may already be genetically vulnerable to psychiatric illness. Furthermore, clinicians may not fully address the potential exacerbating effect of the birth of a child on the mother's psychiatric status.

Clinicians need to be aware of mother-infant interactional difficulties and to be alert to the fact that these difficulties emerge early in the child's life. The research suggests that it is important to evaluate how well mothers are doing with their infants. One technique may be to ask mothers direct questions about their relationship with their infant (e.g., "How connected do you feel to your baby?" "Do you enjoy holding and playing with the baby?" "What do you and the baby do together?"). Another technique may be to observe mothers' interactions with their infant.

The inclusion of a mother-infant interaction component in the therapeutic process may have several benefits. It may help alleviate mothers' concerns about their infant's development and feelings of guilt and worry that they are not doing everything they should to foster the child's development. It allows clinicians to directly address mother-infant interactional difficulties with the mother, which in turn may improve the mother-child relationship and enhance the infant's development. Finally, the infant who functions well can be used as a therapeutic ally to increase a mother's sense of competence as a parent. Discussion of mothers' and infants' strengths may be an invaluable and self-affirming experience for these mothers.

The current study has a number of limitations. The findings are preliminary and not based on the final sample of mothers and infants. The current proband group is comprised of a heterogeneous cohort of infants and mothers with different diagnoses. It is possible that the effects observed in this study are primarily accounted for by a particular diagnostic group. Following the completion of the study, the major depressive disorder, panic disorder, and obsessive-compulsive disorder groups will be disaggregated in order to determine if there is a differential effect of diagnosis on maternal and infant functioning. Furthermore, issues of chronicity and severity of maternal illness were not taken into account in this preliminary data set. It will be important to determine whether mothers in remission or in episode show dissimilar responses on self-report measures and patterns of interaction with their infants and whether their infants' socioemotional functioning differs. Finally, it is unclear what role exposure to prenatal psychotropics plays in the outcome of the proband infants. When the sample is complete, the effects of different kinds of treatment on maternal and infant functioning, as well as issues of chronicity, remission, and severity of maternal disorder, will be addressed.

Despite these limitations, the findings of this study add to the literature indicating that the infants of mothers with mood and anxiety disorders are at risk for socioemotional difficulties early in life. The recognition of the importance of mother-infant interactional problems as a risk factor in the development of later psychopathology may facilitate the early identification of infants at greatest risk. Early intervention with both the mothers and infants may limit or prevent the development of psychopathology in these children. More extended longitudinal follow-up studies are needed to observe the evolution of early difficulties into manifest disorder and to determine the importance of protective and risk factors in the ontogeny of psychopathology.

CHAPTER 23

Making Up Is Hard to Do, Especially for Mothers With High Levels of Depressive Symptoms and Their Infant Sons

The goal of this chapter is to describe the interactions of mothers with normative or high levels of depressive symptoms and their 3-month-old infants. The study focuses on maternal and infant affective expressiveness as well as on the dyadic processes that link both partners' affect together. These processes have been seen in the literature as reflecting interactive qualities such as the mutuality, attunement, or harmony of the mothers' and infants' interactions (Brazelton, Koslowski, & Main, 1974; Stern, Hofer, Haft, & Dore, 1985). Although successful mutual regulation of affect is critical to children's socioemotional development (Shore, 1994; Tronick, 1989), little is known about the factors that influence these processes during early infancy. Therefore, this study evaluates the effects of maternal depressive symptom status, infant gender, and variations in interactional context on mother-infant affective expressiveness and the dyadic features of their interactions.

The study is guided by the mutual regulation model (MRM), which provides a theoretical framework for understanding how mothers and infants shape their interactions moment by moment (Tronick, 1989; Tronick & Weinberg, 1997). The MRM stipulates that mothers and infants form a dyadic system in which they jointly and actively regulate their interactions by responding to each other's affective and behavioral displays. The success or failure of this mutual regulation process depends on the infants' and the mothers' ability to regulate their own homeostatic, affective, and behavioral states and their capacity to interpret and respond to each other's affect and behavior. These abilities are often limited in the young infant, and a caregiver's sensitive scaffolding is required for the infant to successfully modulate arousal and emotional states. Specifically, the caregiver's ability to interpret and respond appropriately and sensitively to the infant's communications facilitates the infant's regulation, achievement of goals, and interpersonal functioning.

Relatively few studies have evaluated dyadic features in mother-infant interactions. While evaluation of infant and maternal affect provides a picture of each partner's affective expressiveness, dyadic measures refer to the degree to which the mother and infant coordinate their affective or behavioral states and reflect what the mother and baby are doing together. Dyadic processes have been defined in a number of different ways in the literature. Studies have focused on mothers' and infants' ability to change affective or behavioral states in temporal coordination with one another (synchrony), to share the lead in the interaction (bidirectionality), and to share joint affective or behavioral states at the same moment in time (matching; Beebe & Lachmann, 1994; Cohn & Tronick, 1987; Feldman, Greenbaum, & Yirmiya, 1999; Jaffe, Beebe, Feldstein, Crown, & Jasnow, 2001; Malatesta & Haviland, 1982; Tronick & Cohn, 1989; Weinberg, Tronick, Cohn, & Olson, 1999).

Research using nonclinical samples indicates that infant affective expressiveness and mother-infant dyadic processes vary as a function of gender. Weinberg et al. (1999) found that male infants have more difficulty maintaining affective regulation than female infants and that female infants use looking at objects as an effective means of self-regulation. In addition, mother-son dyads are more likely than mother-daughter dyads to match positive affective states, whereas mothers and daughters are more likely than mothers and sons to share a focus on objects (Weinberg, Olson, Beeghly, & Tronick, in press). These differences may have important consequences for the infants' emotional responsiveness and formation of the self (Carter, Mayes, & Pajer, 1990; Chodorow, 1978; Robinson, Little, & Biringen, 1993; Tronick & Cohn, 1989). For instance, Kindlon and Thompson (1999) have argued that parents provide a different emotional education to their sons and daughters, which has profound influences on boys' and girls' inner emotional lives and emotional literacy.

Studies also demonstrate that maternal depression has an effect on maternal and infant socioemotional functioning (Downey & Coyne, 1990; Field, 1995; Tronick & Weinberg, 1997; Weinberg & Tronick, 1998a) and on the interactive dialogue that takes place between mothers and infants (Jaffe et al., 2001). Maternal depression compromises mothers' ability to read and respond to infant signals and to facilitate interactions with their young infants. For example, depressed mothers compared to nondepressed mothers engage in less play, use less motherese, show less positive affect, and are more disengaged, intrusive, and negative during social interaction with their infant (Bettes, 1988; Cohn & Tronick, 1989; Kaplan, Bachorowski, & Zarlengo-Strouse, 1999; Malphurs et al., 1996; Murray & Cooper, 1997; Murray, Fiori-Cowley, & Hooper, 1996; Murray, Kempton, Woolgar, & Hooper, 1993). In turn, infants of depressed mothers have difficulties engaging in sustained social and object engagement and show less ability to regulate affective states than infants of nondepressed mothers (Campbell, Cohn, & Meyers, 1995; Cohn & Tronick, 1989; Hart, Field, Del Valle, & Pelaez-Nogueras, 1998; Murray & Cooper, 1997; Pickens & Field, 1993). These effects of depression appear most pronounced if the mother's illness is severe and chronic (Campbell & Cohn, 1997; Teti, Gelfand, Messinger, & Isabella, 1995) or if the mother is from an economically disadvantaged or high-risk background (Carter, Garrity-Rokous, Chazan-Cohen, Little, & Briggs-Gowan, 2001; Lovejoy, Graczyk, O'Hare, & Neuman, 2000).

Only a handful of studies have evaluated dyadic variables in the interactions of depressed mothers and their young infants. Cohn, Campbell, Matias, and Hopkins (1990) found no difference in bidirectional influence in the interactions of depressed and nondepressed mother-infant dyads but found that depressed mothers' and their infants' negative affect were strongly related. Field, Healy, Goldstein, and Guthertz (1990) observed that depressed mothers and their 3-month-old infants shared negative behavior states more often and positive behavior states less often than nondepressed mothers and their infants. Jaffe et al. (2001) and Beebe et al. (2000) found that midrange levels of coordination between maternal and infant vocal exchanges were associated with security of attachment, whereas either very low or very high levels of coordination were associated with insecure attachment.

Male infants of depressed mothers may be particularly vulnerable to the socioemotional effects of maternal depression. Murray et al. (1993) found that male infants of depressed mothers had lower Bayley developmental quotient scores than female infants of depressed mothers. Carter et al. (2001) reported greater regulatory problems in male than female infants of depressed mothers at 4 months of age. Tronick and Weinberg (2000) found that the 6-month-old male infants of clinically depressed mothers were significantly less likely to express positive affect and to use self-comforting strategies to regulate affective states than the female infants of these mothers. The depressed mothers were also more affectively negative with their sons than their daughters. Thus maternal depression appeared to have a differential effect on the early interactive behavior of boys and girls, with the boys displaying less pleasure during the interaction and the depressed mothers in turn being more affectively negative with their sons than their daughters.

The definition of depression is an issue that must be considered in any study evaluating the effects of maternal depression. Maternal depression has typically been defined either in terms of a clinical diagnosis of depression or in terms of levels of depressive symptomatology on well-known self-report measures, such as the Center for Epidemiologic Studies-Depression Scale (CES-D; Radloff, 1977), the Beck Depression Inventory (BDI; Beck, Ward, Mendelson, Mock, & Erbaugh, 1961), or the Edinburgh Postnatal Depression Scale (EPDS; Cox, Holden, & Sagovsky, 1987). In this study, maternal self-report of depressive symptomatology on the CES-D was used to define groups. Recent research suggests that there is considerable stability in CES-D scores over the first year postpartum and that CES-D scores are related to mothers' diagnostic status, even in community samples (Beeghly et al., 2002, 2003). Research also shows that mothers with elevated CES-D scores report poorer psychosocial functioning and show greater impairment in emotional communication with their infant than control mothers with normative depression scores (Lyons-Ruth, Connell, & Grunebaum, 1990; Pelaez-Nogueras, Field, Hossain, & Pickens, 1996; Weinberg et al., 2001). Furthermore, Lovejoy et al. (2000), in a meta-analysis of depression studies, found that studies using either diagnostic interviews or self-report measures yielded similar effects. Thus the literature indicates that self-report measures can be successfully used to evaluate the effects of maternal depression on mother-infant interaction, although it will be important in future studies to empirically evaluate the distinction between diagnosed and self-reported depression.

The goals of this study were to evaluate maternal and infant affect and dyadic interactive processes in mothers with normative or high levels of depressive symptomatology on the CES-D during the face-to-face still-face (FFSF) paradigm. The FFSF was chosen because it permits the observation of maternal and infant affect and dyadic processes in both a baseline face-to-face play and in a more challenging reunion play episode, which follows the interactive stress of the still face during which mothers are instructed to maintain a still poker face and not to respond to the infant. Research indicates that both infants and mothers react to the reunion play following the still face with more negative affect than during the baseline play episode (Kogan & Carter, 1996; Rosenblum, McDonough, Muzik, Miller, & Sameroff, 2002; Weinberg et al., in press; Weinberg & Tronick, 1996). Weinberg and Tronick (1996) have suggested that the reunion episode provides an excellent opportunity to observe mothers' and infants' ability to make up or renegotiate the interaction following the stress of the still face. Thus, the inclusion of both play episodes permits the evaluation of whether infant and maternal affect and the dyadic features of their interactions change as a function of the nature of the interactional context.

It was expected that mothers and infants in the high-symptom group as compared to mothers and infants in the mid-symptom normative control group would show more negative and less positive affect, less matching and greater mismatching of affective states, less bidirectionality, and less synchronous interactions. It was also expected that these effects would be more evident in the male infants as compared to the female infants in the high-symptom group; and that these effects would be the most pronounced during the stressful reunion play of the FFSF paradigm, during which the mother and baby have to make up and repair the interaction following the perturbation of the still face.

METHODS

Sample Characteristics

The study was based on 133 first-time mothers and their healthy full-term infants (52% male) who were participants in a longitudinal study on infant-maternal regulatory processes and maternal depressive symptomatology during the first 12 months postpartum. All mothers met a set of low-risk sociodemo-graphic and medical inclusion criteria in order to minimize the confounding influence of factors (e.g., teen or single parenting) known to affect maternal and infant outcome. Mothers were recruited into the study during the new-born period if they were 21 to 40 years of age, healthy with no serious med-ical conditions, living with the infant's father, and had at least a high school level education. Multiparas and mothers who had returned to work prior to their infant's 3-month birthday were excluded to minimize differences in mater-nal caregiving experience. The infants also met low-risk inclusion criteria. All infants were born at term (37 to 42 weeks gestational age) and were healthy as determined by pediatric examination.

Subject Recruitment and Depression Screening

Recruitment of study mothers and infants took place in the maternity wards of two Harvard-affiliated teaching hospitals. A research assistant approached moth-ers in the maternity ward with the permission of the nursing staff. The research assistant briefly described the research protocol to the mother and, if the mother was interested, invited her to complete a brief demographic question-naire and to provide signed permission to be contacted again by telephone at 2 months of infant age. Seventy-eight percent of the mothers approached in the hospital agreed to be contacted for the telephone interview.

At 2 months, consenting mothers were contacted by phone and given a detailed description of the study. In addition, mothers were interviewed about their pregnancy and delivery experiences, their health, and the infant's eating, sleeping, and social behavior. At the end of the interview, after a comfortable rapport had been established, the CES-D was administered to assess the moth-ers' current level of depressive symptoms. The CES-D is a 20-item self-report scale designed to measure depressive symptomatology in the general popula-tion (Radloff, 1977). The symptoms assessed include depressed mood, feelings of guilt and worthlessness, feelings of helplessness and hopelessness, psy-chomotor retardation, loss of appetite, and sleep disturbance. Possible scores range from 0 to 60, with a cutoff score of 16 used as indicative of high levels of depressive symptomatology. The CES-D has been shown to have internal, concurrent, and predictive validity and has been used in numerous studies eval-uating the effects of maternal depressive symptomatology on maternal and infant functioning (Beeghly et al., 2002, 2003; Boyd, Weissman, Thompson, & Myers, 1982; Campbell et al., 1995; Husaini, Neff, Harrington, Hughes, & Segal, 1980; Radloff, 1977; Weinberg et al., 2001).

Eight percent of the mothers interviewed had an intake CES-D score at or above the cutoff of 16. This percentage is at the low end of the rates reported for postpartum depressive symptoms in the literature, probably because of the low-risk nature of the sample. In community samples, the rate of elevated depressive symptoms beyond the immediate postpartum period is approximately

8–18% (Boyd et al., 1982; Campbell, Cohn, Flanagan, Popper, & Meyers, 1992; Cooper, Campbell, Day, & Kennerley, 1988; O'Hara, Zekoski, Phillips, & Wright, 1990). For mothers with high sociodemographic risk profiles, the rates are substantially higher (Beeghly et al., 2003; Hobfoll, Ritter, Lavin, Hulsizer, & Cameron, 1995). Of the remaining mothers in this study, 14% had an intake CES-D score of 0–1, 72% had an intake CES-D score of 2–12, and 6% had an intake CES-D score of 13–15.

All eligible mothers with a 2-month intake CES-D score of 16 or higher were invited to participate in the study. Mothers with an intake CES-D score of 0 or 1 were also recruited because of contradictory reports in the literature that these mothers may be either very highly functioning (Tronick, Beeghly, Weinberg, & Olson, 1997) or resemble mothers with high levels of depressive symptoms (Pickens & Field, 1993). Immediately following the recruitment of a low- or high-scoring mother, a mid-scoring control with an intake CES-D score of 2–12 was recruited. Mothers scoring 13–15 on the intake CES-D were excluded from the study in order to more clearly differentiate the control and high-symptom groups. This latter criterion applied only at the initial recruitment at 2 months of infant age and the scores were free to vary at the 3-month visit.

In total, 144 mothers and infants were recruited to the study. Of these, 133 mothers met the inclusion criteria, agreed to participate in the study, and had complete data at 3 months of infant age. These mothers were classified into three groups on the basis of their 2-month intake CES-D score. Of the 133 mothers, 45 mothers had an intake CES-D score of 16 or higher (26 with a male infant and 19 with a female infant) and were classified into the high-symptom group; 46 mothers (20 with a male infant and 26 with a female infant) had an intake CES-D score of 0 or 1 and were classified into the low-symptom group; and 42 mothers had an intake CES-D score between 2 and 12 (23 with a male infant and 19 with a female infant) and were classified into the normative symptom group or control group. These 133 dyads did not differ on any infant, maternal, or demographic variable from the dyads ($n = 11$) that were recruited but did not participate in this study (e.g., those that did not meet inclusion criteria, $n = 7$; had incomplete 3-month data, $n = 2$; or did not show for the 3-month visit, $n = 2$).

Subjects in the three groups did not differ significantly on any demographic, maternal, or infant variable. Mothers ranged in socioeconomic status from working to upper-middle class (average Hollingshead Four Factor Index = 54.99, range: 28.00–66.00), had an average of 16 years of education (range: 12–23 years), were on average 32 years of age, and primarily Caucasian (98%). The infants were full term and healthy.

Table 23.1 presents the mothers' average CES-D scores in the three groups at 2 and 3 months of infant age. A 3 (group) × 2 (age) ANOVA indicated that there was a significant main effect for maternal symptom groups at both infant ages. At 2 months, differences between groups were expected because of the study's recruitment criteria. However, at 3 months, the mothers in the high-symptom

Table 23.1 CES-D Scores by Intake Depressive Symptom Group at 2 (Intake) and 3 Months of Infant Age

Age	Group	N	Mean	SD	Min	Max	F (for group) df = 2,130
Intake	Low CES-D	46	1[a]	1	0	1	316.99***
	Control	42	7[b]	3	2	12	$\omega^2 = .83$
	High CES-D	45	21[c]	6	16	48	
3 months	Low CES-D	46	2[a]	3	0	12	53.57***
	Control	42	6[b]	4	0	16	$\omega^2 = .44$
	High CES-D	45	16[c]	10	4	44	

Note. Means with different superscripts are significantly different from each other.
*** $p < .0001$.

group continued to have significantly higher CES-D scores than mothers in the other two groups and mothers in the low-symptom group continued to report significantly lower scores than mothers in the control or high-symptom groups. There was no significant interaction between group and age. A Pearson product-moment correlation between the mothers' CES-D scores at 2 and 3 months indicated that the CES-D scores at both ages were highly correlated, $r (133) = .75$, $p < .0001$. This finding indicates that mothers retained their relative rank ordering in level of depressive symptomatology from 2 to 3 months of infant age, which is consistent with prior research (Beeghly et al., 2002, 2003).

Laboratory Procedures and Setting at 3 Months

Mothers and infants were videotaped in Tronick's FFSF paradigm when the infants were 3 months of age (Tronick, Als, Adamson, Wise, & Brazelton, 1978). The paradigm included three episodes: (1) a 2-minute face-to-face baseline interaction for which the mother was instructed to play with the infant; (2) a 2-minute still-face interaction for which the mother was instructed to keep a still or poker face, to look at the infant but not to smile, talk, or touch the infant; and (3) a 2-minute reunion interaction during which the mother was again free to play, talk, and touch the infant. Each of these episodes was separated by 15-second intervals during which the mother turned her back to the infant. At the end of the 3-month visit, mothers completed the CES-D. The Institutional Review Board (IRB) at Boston's Children's Hospital approved all study procedures and all mothers provided written informed consent prior to participating.

The laboratory setting and procedures were based on those originally developed by Tronick et al. (1978). The observation room was equipped with an infant seat mounted on a table, an adjustable swivel stool for the mother, two cameras (one focused on the infant, the other on the mother), a microphone, and an intercom through which mothers were given procedural instructions. The signals from the two cameras were transmitted through a digital timer and split-screen generator into a video recorder to produce a single image with a simultaneous frontal view of the adult's face, hands, and torso and the infant's entire body.

Coding of Data

All coders were masked to maternal group status and the study's hypotheses. Coders scored the infants' and mothers' facial expressions independently second by second using Izard's AFFEX system (Izard & Dougherty, 1980). The AFFEX system identifies 10 facial expressions (i.e., joy, interest, sadness, anger, surprise, contempt, fear, shame/shyness/guilt, distress, and disgust) as well as blends of facial expressions. Coders were trained to reliability using Izard's training tapes and manuals.

A digital time display on the videotape was used to track time intervals. This produced an absolute frequency count of the facial expressions and maintained their temporal sequence to within a 1-second interval. Each coder used the same onset time for starting the coding of each episode of the FFSF. Tapes were run at normal speed although they were frequently stopped or run in slow motion to accurately determine the beginning and end of shifts in infant and maternal facial expressions.

To assess interobserver reliability, 20% of the first play, still-face, and reunion play episodes were selected randomly and recoded independently by different coders. The mean kappa (Cicchetti & Feinstein, 1990; Cohen, 1960) for infant AFFEX facial expressions was .76. The mean kappa for maternal AFFEX codes was .82. These kappas are similar to those reported in previous studies (Toda & Fogel, 1993; Weinberg et al., 1999).

Data Reduction, Dependent Variables, and Creation of Mutual Regulation Variables

For both the mother and the infant, AFFEX codes were first combined to form three larger categories: positive affect (facial expressions of joy, surprise, and blends involving joy or surprise), interest (facial expressions of interest), and negative affect (facial expressions of sadness, anger, shame, fear, disgust, distress, contempt, and blends involving these affect expressions). For both the infant and the mother, the facial expressions of surprise, fear, disgust, distress, and contempt either did not occur or occurred less than 1% of the time. However, if they did occur, they were included in the larger categories, as described above, because they were needed to maintain continuity in the time series analysis evaluating synchrony (described below).

The dependent variables for the mother, infant, and dyad were the adjusted proportion of time infants or mothers displayed positive, neutral, and negative affect. In addition, four dyadic measures were generated, following Tronick and Cohn (1989) and Weinberg et al. (1999).

Matching was defined as the extent to which mothers and infants shared joint affective states at the same moment in time (i.e., in the same second). A positive affect match involved both partners showing positive affect at the same time; an interest affect match involved both showing interest simultaneously, and a negative affect match indicated that both mother and infant displayed negative affect at the same time.

Mismatching was defined as any nonshared dyadic affective state occurring in the same moment of time (e.g., infant positive and mother negative). *Synchrony* referred to the extent to which mothers and infants changed their affect in temporal coordination with respect to the other. Synchrony was defined as the proportion of shared variance at lag 0, as indexed by the cross-correlation between each mother's and infant's time series. In preparation for the synchrony analyses, maternal and infant AFFEX data were scaled from 1 to 3 with an engagement scale score of 1 representing negative engagement and an engagement scale score of 3 representing positive engagement. To deal with missing data, a replacement strategy was used that involved joining the data points before and after the missing data point and rounding the value at the missing data point to the nearest integer.

Bidirectionality referred to the extent to which each partner's affect influenced the other partner's affect or, more specifically, the extent to which infant engagement scale scores were predicted from maternal engagement scale scores and maternal engagement scale scores were predicted from infant engagement scale scores.

Analytic Plan

An ANOVA model was used to assess the effects of depressive symptom status, infant gender, and interactional context on maternal and infant affect and on the dyadic variables. Data were analyzed using 2 (episode: play 1 and reunion play) × 2 (gender) × 3 (group: control, low-, and high-symptom groups) repeated measures ANOVAs with episode as the repeated measure. Simple effect tests were used to interpret significant two-way interactions. Significant three-way interactions were evaluated using Tukey Kramer post hoc test. Effect size was calculated using omega squared (ω^2). Interactional context was included as an independent variable in the analyses because prior research indicates that the reunion play following the still face is more challenging to both the mother and the infant than the first play (Kogan & Carter, 1996; Weinberg & Tronick, 1996). The still face was excluded from the analyses since all mothers in that episode had been instructed to act in the same manner and the evaluation of maternal affect and the dyadic measures was therefore not possible.

For infant and maternal affect and the matching/mismatching data, the dependent variables were the adjusted proportion of time the infants and the mothers displayed each affect or were in each matching or nonmatching state during the videotaped interaction. Adjusted proportions were calculated by dividing the total time each infant and maternal affect and matching or nonmatching state occurred by the number of seconds during the episode for which there was valid, nonmissing data. The adjusted or relative percentage of each affect, match, or mismatch variable was used in the analyses to account for missing data and differences in the base rates of the different types of affects, matches, and mismatches. For the synchrony data, the cross-correlation between each mother's and infant's time series was analyzed. To assess bidirectionality, time series regression was used to predict the infant engagement scale score from the mother's and the mother's engagement scale score from the infant's. After removing the effects of autocorrelation from the time series of the infant and mother engagement scale scores, the two series were cross-correlated to predict the scores of one from the lagged values of the other. The R^2 of this regression was used as the dependent variable in the ANOVA.

RESULTS

Infant and Maternal Affect

For the sample as a whole, the most common infant affect was interest (mean = 61%, SD = 28) followed by positive (mean = 21%, SD = 22) and negative affect (mean = 18%, SD = 27). The most common maternal affect was positive affect (mean = 67%, SD = 19) followed by interest (mean = 27%, SD = 16) and negative affect (mean = 6%, SD = 10).* Table 23.2 presents the means and standard deviations for infant and maternal affect stratified by episode, gender, and group. Figures 23.1 and 23.2 present the means of significant two and three-way interactions.

Analyses indicated that there were no significant main or interaction effects for infant positive affect. However, there were significant main and interaction effects for infant interest and negative affect. For infant interest, there was a main effect for episode, $F(df = 1,127) = 12.44$, $p < .001$, $\omega^2 = .08$, indicating that infants were more likely to show interest in the first play compared to the reunion play. There was also a significant main effect for gender, $F(df = 1,127) = 4.88$, $p < .05$, $\omega^2 = .03$, indicating that female infants exhibited more interest than

*Replicating earlier studies (Adamson & Frick, 2003), main effects of episode indicated that both male and female infants in the three groups reacted negatively to the still face. There was a significant decrease in positive affect, $F(df = 1,126) = 37.13$, $p < .0001$, $\omega^2 = .36$, and increase in negative affect, $F(df = 2,126) = 15.54$, $p < .0001$, $\omega^2 = .18$, during the still face as compared to the first play. There was also a main effect of episode for interest, $F(df = 2,126) = 20.42$, $p < .0001$, $\omega^2 = .23$. Although the level of interest remained the same in the first play and the still face, interest dropped significantly in the reunion play. No other significant effects were observed in the still face.

Table 23.2 Means and Standard Deviations for Maternal and Infant Affect Stratified by Episode, Gender, and Group

| | Episode | | | | Gender | | | | Group | | | | | |
| | Play 1 | | Reunion | | Male | | Female | | 0–1 | | 2–12 | | 16+ | |
Affect	Mean	SD	Mean	SD	Mean	SD	Mean	SD	Mean	SD	Mean	SD	Mean	SD
Infant														
Positive	22.91	22.44	19.62	20.95	23.83	23.56	18.55	19.29	21.86	20.56	18.32	19.95	23.40	24.28
Interest	65.13	26.60	56.03	28.53	56.72	29.88	64.90	25.00	56.70	27.69	66.25	25.93	59.64	29.28
Negative	11.96	20.07	24.34	30.70	19.45	28.91	16.55	23.74	21.44	29.90	15.42	22.99	16.96	25.78
Mother														
Positive	70.78	17.48	62.51	20.46	67.50	18.74	65.86	20.47	64.87	19.10	64.85	18.21	70.30	20.48
Interest	25.10	15.35	29.47	15.49	26.58	15.21	27.97	15.93	28.95	14.97	28.81	15.33	24.07	15.99
Negative	4.12	6.61	8.02	11.58	5.92	8.52	6.17	10.64	6.18	8.76	6.34	11.34	5.63	8.73

FIGURE 23.1. Means for significant two-way interactions for male and female infants in the low (0–1), mid (2–12), and high (16+) symptom groups.

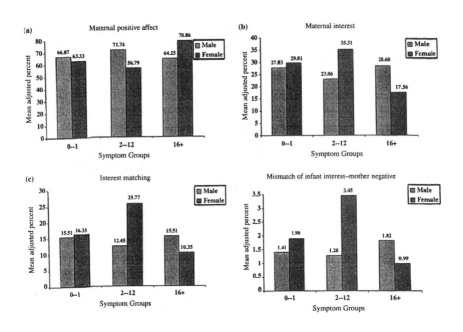

male infants. These findings were qualified by a three-way interaction, $F(df = 2,127) = 3.40$, $p < .05$, $\omega^2 = .04$. Examination of the means (see Figure 23.2a) indicated that female infants in the control group showed the most interest in both the first and the reunion play episodes and that male infants in the high-symptom group displayed the least interest in the reunion play. Post hoc tests comparing differences in means indicated that female infants in the control group in the first play showed significantly more interest than male infants in the high-symptom group in the reunion play ($p < .003$) and that male infants in the high-symptom group showed a significant drop in interest from the first to the reunion play ($p < .02$).

For infant negative affect, there was a main effect for episode, $F(df = 1,127) = 21.70$, $p < .001$, $\omega^2 = .14$, indicating that the infants showed significantly more negative affect during the reunion play than the first play. This result was qualified by a three-way interaction, $F(df = 2,127) = 4.17$, $p < .05$, $\omega^2 = .05$. Examination of the means (see Figure 23.2b) indicated that female infants in the control group showed the least amount of negative affect in the first play, and that male infants in the high-symptom group, followed by the female infants in the low-symptom group, exhibited the most negative affect in the reunion play. Post hoc tests comparing differences in the means indicated that the male infants in the high-symptom group during the reunion displayed significantly

FIGURE 23.2. Means for significant three-way interactions for male and female infants in the low (0–1), mid (2–12), and high (16+) symptom groups in the first play and reunion play.

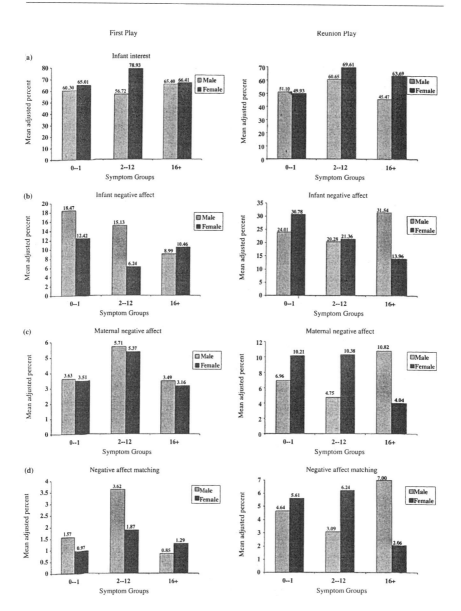

more negative affect than the female infants in the control group during the first play ($p < .003$). Furthermore, the male infants in the high-symptom group showed a significant increase in negative affect from the first to the reunion play ($p < .003$), as did the female infants in the low-symptom group ($p < .05$).

There was a main effect for episode for maternal positive affect, $F(df = 1,127) = 19.36, p < .0001, \omega^2 = .12$, indicating that mothers showed less positive affect in the reunion play compared to the first play. There was also a group $\times$ gender interaction for positive maternal affect, $F(df = 2,127) = 10.06, p < .0001, \omega^2 = .12$. Mothers of female infants in the control group showed significantly less positive affect than mothers of female infants in the high-symptom group (see Figure 23.1a).

There was a main effect for episode for maternal interest indicating that mothers showed more interest in the reunion than the first play, $F(df = 1,127) = 8.86, p < .05, \omega^2 = .06$. There was also a group $\times$ gender interaction for maternal interest, $F(df = 2,127) = 8.91, p < .001, \omega^2 = .11$. Mothers of female infants in the control group showed significantly more interest than mothers of female infants in the high-symptom group (see Figure 23.1b).

There was a main effect for episode for maternal negative affect, $F(df = 1,127) = 13.95, p < .0001, \omega^2 = .09$, indicating that mothers showed significantly more negative affect in the reunion than the first play. This finding was qualified by a significant three-way interaction, $F(df = 2,127) = 3.59, p < .05, \omega^2 = .04$. Post hoc tests comparing differences in means (see Figure 23.2c) indicated that mothers in the high-symptom group showed more negative affect to their boys in the reunion compared to the first play ($p < .04$).

Affective Matching

Three matching variables were evaluated. For the sample as a whole, positive and interest matches occurred equally often with a mean of 16% ($SD = 16$ and 14, respectively) whereas negative matching occurred on average 3% ($SD = 8$) of the time. Table 23.3 lists the means and standard deviations of the matching variables stratified by episode, gender, and group.

For positive matching, there was a main effect for gender indicating that mothers were more likely to share moments of positive affect with their male than their female infants, $F(df = 1,127) = 3.90, p < .05, \omega^2 = .02$.

For interest matching, there was a main effect for group, $F(df = 2,127) = 3.40, p < .05, \omega^2 = .04$, indicating that moments of mother-infant shared interest were more common in the control group than the high-symptom group. This result was qualified by a group $\times$ gender interaction, $F(df = 2,127) = 7.86, p < .001, \omega^2 = .10$, indicating that, within the control group, mothers and their female infants were more likely to experience moments of shared interest than mothers and their male infants (see Figure 23.1c).

For negative matching, there was a main effect for episode indicating that mothers and infants were more likely to share negative affect in the reunion

Table 23.3 Means and Standard Deviations for Mutual Regulation Variables Stratified by Episode, Gender, and Group

	Episode				Gender				Group					
	Play 1		Reunion		Male		Female		0–1		2–12		16+	
Variable	Mean	SD	Mean	SD	Mean	SD	Mean	SD	Mean	SD	Mean	SD	Mean	SD
Matching														
Positive	16.66	16.49	14.37	16.01	17.71	17.81	13.18	14.11	16.00	16.57	13.54	14.13	16.87	17.71
Interest	16.39	13.91	15.47	13.25	14.52	12.76	17.46	14.29	15.97	13.45	18.67	14.21	13.41	12.74
Negative	1.67	4.57	4.81	9.56	3.38	7.58	3.04	7.67	3.21	6.71	3.46	8.76	2.99	7.43
Mismatching														
I. Positive–M. Interest	2.68	4.13	2.15	3.15	2.60	4.31	2.23	2.86	2.47	2.93	2.05	3.62	2.70	4.39
I. Positive–M. Negative	.36	.90	.31	.87	.37	.91	.30	.87	.43	1.06	.18	.63	.38	.88
I. Interest–M. Positive	40.46	20.61	32.62	19.75	34.24	21.00	39.14	19.78	33.03	19.26	38.24	18.03	38.80	23.45
I. Interest–M. Negative	1.58	3.18	2.01	3.55	1.52	2.72	2.09	3.93	1.69	2.41	2.28	4.44	1.47	3.05
I. Negative–M. Positive	5.83	9.87	8.44	11.20	7.75	12.13	6.43	8.66	8.36	12.14	6.04	9.82	6.82	9.53
I. Negative–M. Interest	3.12	6.70	8.75	13.16	6.32	11.49	5.43	9.92	7.63	13.27	5.00	8.14	4.91	9.77
Synchrony	.07	.15	.06	.18	.08	.16	.05	.17	.09	.18	.05	.14	.04	.17
Bidirectionality	.03	.04	.03	.09	.03	.09	.03	.05	.04	.11	.02	.03	.03	.04

compared to the first play, $F(df = 1,127) = 15.88$, $p < .0001$, $\omega^2 = .10$. This finding was qualified by a significant three-way interaction, $F(df = 2,127) = 3.77$, $p < .05$, $\omega^2 = .04$. Examination of the means (see Figure 23.2d) indicated that mother-son dyads in the high-symptom group rarely shared moments of negative affect in the first play but were the most likely of all the groups to share negative affect in the reunion play. Post hoc comparisons of the means indicated that mother-son dyads in the high-symptom group experienced a significant increase in shared negative affect from the first play to the reunion play ($p < .02$).

Affective Mismatches

Table 23.3 presents the mean and standard deviations for the affective mismatch variables stratified by episode, gender, and group. There were several main effects of episode for the mismatch variables. The data indicated that mismatches involving the infant showing interest when the mother showed positive affect were more likely to occur in the first play compared to the reunion play, $F(df = 1,127) = 19.13$, $p < .001$, $\omega^2 = .12$. However, mismatches involving the infant showing negative affect and the mother positive affect, $F(df = 2,127) = 6.48$, $p < .05$, $\omega^2 = .04$, and the infant showing negative affect and the mother interest affect, $F(df = 2,127) = 21.23$, $p < .0001$, $\omega^2 = .14$, were more likely to occur in the reunion play than the first play. There was also a group $\times$ gender interaction for the mismatch of infant interest and mother negative affect, $F(df = 2,127) = 3.38$, $p < .05$, $\omega^2 = .04$. This type of mismatch was more likely to occur in the control group between mothers and their female infants than between mothers and their male infants (see Figure 23.1d).

Synchrony

Table 23.3 presents the means and standard deviations for the synchrony and bidirectionality variables stratified by episode, gender, and group. There was no main effect for synchrony. However, a significant group $\times$ gender interaction, $F(df = 2,126) = 3.23$, $p < .05$, $\omega^2 = .03$, indicated that mother-son dyads in the low-symptom group had higher synchrony scores than mother-daughter dyads.

Bidirectionality

No significant finding was revealed for the mutual regulation variable of bidirectionality. All groups showed equivalent amounts of bidirectionality in their interactions. The lack of group differences is consistent with the research by Cohn et al. (1990).

DISCUSSION

The findings from this study emphasize the complexity of how maternal and infant affective processes are affected by maternal depressive symptoms, infant gender, and interactional stress. As expected, the results indicated that mother-son dyads in the high-symptom group had more negative interactions than other dyads in the reunion episode of the FFSF. Thus mothers in the high-symptom group showed significantly more negative affect to their boys than their girls in the reunion play; male infants in the high-symptom group showed the most negative affect and the least interest in the reunion play; and although mothers and male infants in the high-symptom group rarely shared moments of negative affect in the first play, they were much more likely to do so in the reunion play. Furthermore, male infants in the high-symptom group showed a significant increase in negative affect and a drop in interest from the first play to the reunion play, and mother-son dyads in the high-symptom group experienced a significant increase in shared negative affect from the first play to the reunion play. These patterns were not observed among the infants and mothers in the control group and suggest that making up following an interactive stress like the still face is hard to do, especially for mothers with high levels of depressive symptoms and their infant sons.

The data suggest that male as compared to female infants may be more vulnerable to high levels of maternal depressive symptoms but only in the reunion episode when both infants and mothers were stressed. When they were not stressed, neither the mothers nor the infants were more negative than control mothers and infants. These data add to a growing literature indicating that male infants may be less resilient to maternal depression than female infants (Carter et al., 2001; Murray et al., 1993; Tronick & Weinberg, 2000), particularly in situations that involve interactional stress or challenge. The data are also consistent with the work of Tronick and Weinberg (2000) that used a sample of mothers with a clinical diagnosis of major depression and that showed similar interactional difficulties in the mother-son dyads.

From the perspective of the MRM, these findings suggest that a cycle of regulatory problems may become established early between high-symptom mothers and their sons (Tronick & Weinberg, 2000). Male infants' greater negativity during stressful social interactions may make them difficult interactive partners, which may further challenge high-symptom mothers' ability to provide their sons with the scaffolding needed for them to maintain the interaction within comfortable bounds. This in turn is likely to generate even more negative affect and regulatory problems and may raise mothers' concerns about their effectiveness as parents and ability to meet their infants' needs. Although these moment-by-moment disruptions may seem relatively small, Tronick and Gianino (1986a) have argued that their cumulative effect over time may have long-term compromising effects.

Even though the male infants in the high-symptom group were more negative in the reunion play than the infants in the low- and mid-symptom groups, several main effects of episode indicated that all infants, including those in the high-symptom group, showed the classic reunion effect that has been reported in previous studies using the FFSF paradigm (Kogan & Carter, 1996;

Rosenblum et al., 2002; Weinberg & Tronick, 1996). Regardless of group membership and gender, infants showed a significant increase in negative affect and interest in the reunion play compared to the first play, suggesting that they were sensitive to the changes in their mother's affect and that they reacted to the stress that carried over from the still face into the reunion play. Thus infants' capacity to detect, process, and respond to variations in maternal interactive behavior was not compromised by high levels of maternal depressive symptoms even though the infants in the high-symptom group had a more difficult time than the other infants in down-regulating negative affect during the reunion play.

The data also indicate that the mothers displayed a decrease in positive affect and an increase in interest and negative affect in the reunion play compared to the first play. Furthermore, the amount of shared negative affect increased in the reunion play compared to the first play, as did the incidence of mismatches involving the infant being negative and the mother being either positive or interested. These data reflect the interactional difficulties that characterize the reunion play. This episode presents the mother and the infant with a difficult regulatory challenge during which they must repair the interaction following the stressful interruption of the still face, and the mother must often cajole the infant out of a negative affective state. Taken together, the data indicate that making up is not easy either for mothers or infants.

Surprisingly, mothers of female infants in the high-symptom group showed significantly more positive affect than mothers of female infants in the control group. This result was not expected. It is possible that mothers with high levels of depressive symptoms identify with their daughters and attempt to compensate for their symptoms of depression (Chodorow, 1978). It may be useful in future work to evaluate the mothers' positive affect even more precisely than was done in this study to determine whether these mothers may have appeared false or ungenuine in the positive affect expressed to their infants. Regardless of the explanation, mothers' greater expression of positive affect is likely to have a positive effect on their infant. The mothers' positive affect may have a protective role that buffers the infant against stress, facilitates the infant's coping and regulatory efforts, and may be one of the reasons why the female infants in this study appeared less vulnerable to maternal depressive symptoms than the male infants.

Consistent with prior research, mothers and boys were more likely than mothers and girls to share moments of positive affect. In contrast, female infants were more likely than male infants to show interest (Weinberg et al., 1999, in press). The data also indicated that moments of mother-infant shared interest were more common in the control group than the high-symptom group, although this finding was qualified by an interaction indicating that, within the control group, mothers and their female infants were more likely than mothers and their male infants to share moments of interest. These findings are consistent with the research by Weinberg et al. (1999) and Tronick and Cohn (1989) with 6-month-old infants and the work by Malatesta and Haviland (1982) documenting girls' greater interest in the exploration of objects during social interactions. Interestingly, mismatches involving infant interest and mother negative affect were also more likely to occur in the control group between mothers and their female infants than between mothers and their male infants. This finding is difficult to interpret and needs further evaluation and replication in future studies.

There was little evidence suggesting that mothers who reported very low scores on the CES-D had a qualitatively different pattern of functioning than mothers with normative scores. Although female infants in the low-scoring group displayed somewhat more negative affect than controls in the reunion play, mothers and boys in the low-symptom group had higher synchrony scores than mothers and girls, suggesting that these mothers and infants were sensitive to changes in each other's affect. Shedler, Mayman, and Manis (1993) have argued that mothers who score very low on self-report depression scales may be denying symptoms and therefore present an illusion of mental health. Pickens and Field (1993) found that infants of both high- and low-scoring mothers on the BDI showed more sadness and anger and less interest during face-to-face play with their mother than the infants of control mothers. By contrast, Tronick et al. (1997) found that low-scoring mothers were comparable to mid-symptom control mothers in the level of self-reported positive emotions and that these mothers reported higher maternal self-esteem and satisfaction with and adaptation to motherhood than mothers with normative CES-D scores. More research is needed to evaluate the nature of this subgroup of mothers and infants.

There are several limitations to this study. Similar to many projects in the literature, this study did not include a validating measure for the CES-D, such as a clinical diagnosis of major depression. At this point, it remains unclear whether subclinical levels of depression and a clinical diagnosis of major depression are associated with similar effects on maternal and infant interactive behavior (Campbell & Cohn, 1997; Weinberg et al., 2001). However, a meta-analysis of depression studies by Lovejoy et al. (2000) indicates that the effects of depression are similar whether assessed by clinical interview or self-report. Future research should focus on clarifying the distinction between diagnosed and self-reported depression.

Another limitation is that the mothers' 2-month, and not their 3-month, CES-D score was used to define groups. Although the mothers' average level of depression declined somewhat between 2 and 3 months, at 3 months, the mothers in the high-symptom group continued to have significantly higher CES-D scores than mothers in the other two groups, and mothers in the low-symptom group continued to report significantly lower scores than mothers in the control or high-symptom groups. A Pearson product-moment correlation between the mothers' CES-D scores at 2 and 3 months also indicated that the CES-D scores at both ages were highly correlated, indicating that mothers retained their relative rank ordering in level of depressive symptomatology from 2 to 3 months of infant age. This is consistent with research by Beeghly et al. (2002, 2003), which indicates that mothers who had a high CES-D score at 2 months postpartum were significantly more likely to have a high CES-D score again over the first 18 months postpartum, that mothers retained their initial rank ordering in level of depressive symptomatology over time, and that mothers' most recent CES-D score contributed unique variance in predicting their subsequent CES-D score at later ages.

Another limitation was that the entire range of CES-D scores obtained at 2 months were not used. Mothers with a CES-D score between 13 and 15 were excluded at intake to more clearly demarcate the defined groups. In future work, the entire range of CES-D scores should be included in analyses. In future research, the dyadic interactive variables must also be externally validated by relating them to independent outcome measures, either within the interaction or later in development (e.g., attachment). This is an area of research that is currently receiving some attention as exemplified by the work of Feldman (Feldman et al., 1999) and Jaffe and Beebe (Jaffe et al., 2001). Relating these dyadic variables to later developmental outcomes will allow researchers to determine if and how mutual regulatory processes in infancy lay the foundation for later socioemotional development, as has been suggested in the literature (Shore, 1994; Tronick, 1989). In future work, it will also be important to determine the long-term outcome of the children of mothers with high levels of depressive symptoms.

It is also important to note that all the variables (facial expressiveness and dyadic variables) were dependent upon the mother-infant dyad, making it difficult to know if the results are specific to the mother-infant interaction or to social interactions with other interactive partners. Finally, because the sample was primarily Caucasian and at low medical and social risk status, generalizability of the data to other ethnic groups and to dyads at higher risk may be limited. In future studies, it will be important to replicate this research in non-white and higher-risk samples.

CONCLUSION

The results from this study have implications for both researchers and clinicians. The findings suggest that it is important to evaluate mothers with high levels of depressive symptoms and their infants in different interactive contexts varying in degree of interactive challenge to obtain a complete picture of the mother-infant relationship. Looking at them only in nonstressful situations may not sufficiently highlight difficulties in the relationship. The data also suggest that infant gender is of great importance. Male infants appear more vulnerable to maternal depressive symptoms and mothers with depressive symptoms have more difficulty interacting with their sons than with their daughters, particularly in challenging social contexts. The long-term consequences of this early vulnerability in terms of attachment and later developmental and psychological problems need to be further investigated.

CHAPTER 24

Gender Differences and Their Relation to Maternal Depression

Our research is beginning to uncover gender differences in the socioemotional reactions and behavior of infant sons and daughters of mothers with a history of depression. These findings are arising out of our work on the effects of maternal depression on infant development and our work on gender differences in the behavior of sons and daughters of well mothers (Weinberg & Tronick, 1998b; Weinberg, Tronick, Cohn, & Olson, 1999). These two lines of research naturally converged on the question of whether or not infant sons and daughters of depressed mothers might be differentially affected by the socioemotional behavior of their depressed mothers. Gender differences in infant reactions to depressed affect is a critical question to evaluate if we are to understand differences in the forms of psychopathology manifested by boys and girls. Given our findings on the effects of depression and the affective and regulatory differences of boys and girls, we hypothesized that boys would be more vulnerable to the effects of maternal depression than girls would be (Tronick & Weinberg, 1997). To put it differently, boys would be more reactive to maternal depression than would girls. Indeed, these are the differences that we seem to be finding in these studies of the infant sons and daughters of depressed mothers, which were supported by grants from the Prevention and Intervention programs at the National Institutes of Mental Health (NIMH).

Maternal depression is a common postpartum problem shown to compromise maternal and infant socioaffective functioning (see Downey & Coyne, 1990; Field, 1995; Weinberg & Tronick, 1997, for reviews). Several studies have found that during social interaction with their infants, depressed mothers, when compared to nondepressed mothers, are more affectively negative and more disengaged. For example, depressed mothers engage in less play, use less motherese, and express more sad affect. However, depressed mothers behave in more specific and heterogeneous ways. Some depressed mothers are intrusive and show angry facial expressions, whereas other depressed mothers express sadness and are withdrawn (Cohn & Tronick, 1989).

In general, infants of depressed mothers have difficulties engaging in sustained social and object engagement and show less ability to regulate affective states. Thus, they look less at their mother and they show less positive affect and more negative affect. Their reactions are specific, however, to their mothers' interactive style; the infants of the intrusive, depressed mothers act in a more avoidant fashion compared to the infants of withdrawn mothers, who are more distressed. At 1 year of age, many of these infants show poorer performance on developmental tests (e.g., the Bayley Scales of Infant Development) and higher levels of insecure attachment to the mother (Lyons-Ruth, Connell, & Grunebaum, 1990; Murray & Cooper, 1997). Thus, exposure to maternal postpartum depression appears to compromise infant social, emotional, and cognitive functioning.

In previous research, Tronick and Weinberg (Tronick & Cohn, 1989; Weinberg et al., 1999) found gender differences in 6-month-old infants of nondepressed mothers. For example, Weinberg and her colleagues found that boys were more emotionally reactive than were girls during face-to-face social interactions with their mothers. Boys were more likely than were girls to show facial expressions of anger, to fuss and cry, to want to be picked up, and to attempt to get away or distance themselves from their mothers by arching their backs and turning and twisting in their infant seats. Boys were also more oriented toward their mothers than were girls. Boys were more likely than were girls to display facial expressions of joy and to communicate with their mothers using neutral or positive vocalizations and gestures. By contrast, girls were more object oriented than were boys. They were more likely than were boys to look at and explore objects and to display facial expressions of interest. Furthermore, girls showed more self-regulatory behaviors than did boys.

Our interpretation of these gender differences focused on differences in boys' and girls' self-regulation of affect. Boys' greater emotional reactivity suggested that boys have greater difficulty self-regulating their affective states and that they need to rely more on maternal regulatory input than do girls. To the extent that boys are more dependent than are girls on their mothers to regulate their affective states, they then must communicate their needs more explicitly and frequently than do girls. The boys' greater dependence on external regulation might explain the greater variability and intensity of their expressions and the finding that much of their affective behavior was directed toward their mothers. This interpretation of the differences between boys and girls is based on the mutual regulation model (MRM) developed by Tronick (1989), in which the affective state of the infant is dependent on the capacity to regulate his or her affect and the adult partner's ability to provide regulatory input.

The MRM sees the mother (or any adult interactant) as an exogenous, but functionally integral, component of the infant's capacity for regulation (Hofer,

1981, 1984). The mother's capacity to effectively regulate the infant's affective state is affected by many factors, including her affective state, her representation of the infant, her history of parenting, the state of her other intimate relationships, and during the interaction, by her apprehension of the infant's affective messages. Thus, the infant's capacity to organize his or her affective communications is critical to the quality of the mutual regulation of the interaction.

Weinberg and Tronick (1994) found that infant affective behavior is organized into configurations of face, voice, gesture, and gaze. In one configuration, labeled social engagement, the infant looks at the mother, positively vocalizes, and smiles. Importantly, crying, looking away, and withdrawal behaviors are less likely to co-occur with the displays making up social engagement. In another configuration, active protest, the infant looks away from the mother, engages in active withdrawal behaviors, cries, and displays a facial expression of anger. In this configuration, smiles, positive gestures, and vocalizations are inhibited. Two other configurations, object engagement and passive withdrawal, also involve distinct combinations of expressive modalities. From our perspective, each of these configurations reflects a different state of brain organization that assembles distinctly different configurations of face, voice, and body (Tronick et al., 1998).

Each configuration clearly communicates the infant's affective state and evaluation of the interaction. The social engagement configuration conveys the message, "I like what we are doing together; let's continue doing it"; the active protest configuration tells the caregiver that "I don't like what is happening and I want it to change now"; the passive withdrawal configuration communicates messages such as, "I don't like what is happening but I don't know what to do"; and the object engagement configuration conveys the message, "I want to continue looking at this object and not playing with you." Thus, the configurations serve to regulate the behavior of the infant's partner during the interaction by conveying information to the partner about the infant's immediate intentions and evaluation of the current state of the interaction. Nonetheless, as clearly defined as these configurations are, the interaction is neither always positive nor synchronous.

In our studies of normal mother-infant face-to-face interactions, expressions of positive affect by either the mother or the infant occur about 42% of the time for the mother and 15% for the infant (Cohn & Tronick, 1987; Tronick & Cohn, 1989). A dramatic instance of normal variation is Tronick and Weinberg's (Tronick & Cohn, 1989; Weinberg et al., 1999) findings of gender differences in affect and interactive coherence. These gender differences reflect normal variants and highlight the range of affective expressiveness, regulatory behavior, and synchrony that occurs during normal interactions.

Tronick (Tronick & Cohn, 1989; Tronick, 1989) has characterized the typical mother-infant interaction as one that moves from coordinated (or synchronous) to miscoordinated states and back again over a wide affective range. The miscoordinated state is referred to as a normal interactive communicative error or misregulation. The interactive transition from a miscoordinated state to a coordinated state is referred to as an interactive repair. The process of reparation is mutually regulated. The partners—infant and adult—signal their evaluation of the state of the interaction through their affective configurations. In turn, in response to their partner's signals, each partner attempts to adjust his or her behavior to maintain a coordinated state or to repair an interactive error. Critically, successful reparations and the experience of coordinated states are associated with positive affective states, whereas unrepaired interactive errors generate negative affective states. Thus, the infant's affective experience is determined by a dyadic regulatory process.

In normal dyads, interactive errors are quickly repaired. In studies of face-to-face interaction at 6 months of age, repairs occur at a rate of once every 3 to 5 seconds, and more than one third of all repairs occur by the next step in the interaction (Tronick & Gianino, 1980). Observations by Beebe and Lachmann (1994) and Isabella and Belsky (1991) replicated these findings and support the hypothesis that the normal interaction is a process of reparation. They found that maternal sensitivity in the midrange, rather than at the low or high end, typify normal interactions. Midrange sensitivity is characterized by errors and repairs as contrasted to interactions in which the mother is "never sensitive or always sensitive." These researchers also found that midlevel sensitivity was associated with security of attachment.

It is our hypothesis that reparation of interactive errors or miscommunications is the critical process of normal interactions that is related to developmental outcome rather than sensitivity, synchrony, or positive affect per se. That is, reparation, its experience and extent, is the social interactive mechanism that affects the infant's development. In interactions characterized by normal rates of reparation, the infant learns which affective, communicative, and coping strategies are effective in producing reparation and when to use them. This experience leads to the elaboration of communicative and coping skills and the development of an implicit procedural understanding of interactive rules and conventions (Tronick, 1998). With the experiential accumulation of successful reparations, and the attendant transformation of negative affect into positive affect, the infant establishes a positive affective core (Emde, Kligman, Reich, & Wade, 1978; Gianino & Tronick, 1988). The infant also learns that he or she has control over social interactions. Specifically, the infant develops a representation of himself or herself as effective, of his or her interactions as positive and reparable, and of the caretaker as reliable and trustworthy. These representations are crucial for the development of a sense of self that has coherence, continuity, and agency and for the development of stable and secure relationships (Tronick, 1980; Tronick, Cohn, & Shea, 1986).

From the perspective of mutual regulation, the functional consequences of reparation suggest that when there is a prolonged failure to repair communicative errors, infants will initially attempt to reestablish the expected interaction and experience negative affect when these reparatory efforts fail. To evaluate this hypothesis, Tronick created a prolonged mismatch with the face-to-face still-face paradigm (Tronick, Als, Adamson, Wise, & Brazelton, 1978). In this paradigm, the mother engages in normal face-to-face interaction until a mismatch is created by having the mother hold a still face and remain unresponsive to the infant. The mother fails to engage in her normal interactive behavior and regulatory role. Infants almost immediately detect the change and attempt to solicit the mother's attention. Failing to elicit a response, most infants turn away, only to look back at the mother again. This solicitation cycle may be repeated several times. When the infants' attempts fail to repair the interaction, however, infants often lose postural control, withdraw, and self-comfort. Disengagement is profound even with this short disruption of the mutual regulatory process and break of intersubjectivity. The infant's reaction, although much less severe, is reminiscent of the withdrawal of Harlow's isolated monkeys or of the infants in institutions observed by Bowlby and Spitz (Bowlby, 1951, 1982; Spitz, 1965). The still-faced mother is a short-lived, experimentally produced mild form of neglect that precludes the establishment of a shared interaction and the dyadic expansion of consciousness (Tronick, 1998).

These findings have implications for the infants of depressed mothers, given the effects of depression on maternal affect and caregiving (Murray & Cooper, 1997; Weinberg & Tronick, 1998b). We hypothesized that infant boys would be more vulnerable to maternal depressive status than would infant girls because boys appear to require more regulatory support than do girls. Thus, we expected that the interactions of depressed mothers and their sons would have longer and more chronic failures of reparation than would the interactions of mothers and daughters. We also expected that sons of depressed mothers would become more affectively reactive than would daughters of depressed mothers.

In a preliminary study, we examined 23 infants (12 girls and 11 boys) and their mothers. All mothers and infants were recruited from the maternity wards of Boston-area hospitals. The infants and mothers met a set of low-risk criteria to minimize the confounding effects of variables (e.g., poverty and prematurity) known to compromise parenting and infant outcome. Mothers were between the ages of 21 and 39, healthy, living with the infants' fathers, and had at least a high school education. Infants were healthy, full-term, and clinically normal at delivery as determined by pediatric examination. All infants were first born. Mothers of boys and mothers of girls did not differ on these demographic or medical variables. Thus, this sample of mothers and infants was low risk in social and medical status. This low-risk status allowed us to more effectively assess the effects of depression unconfounded by other high-risk factors.

All mothers met criteria for a lifetime diagnosis of major depression using the *Diagnostic Interview Schedule, Version III–Revised* (DIS–III–R). The DIS–III–R is a well-established, structured instrument developed by NIMH to assess psychiatric status using both research diagnostic criteria and *DSM–III–R* criteria. All mothers received a clinical diagnosis of major depression prior to having the baby, and approximately 20% of them met diagnostic criteria for depression during the first 6 months postpartum.

At 3 months and 6 months of infant age, mothers and infants were video-taped in Tronick's face-to-face still-face paradigm (Tronick, Als, et al., 1978; Weinberg & Tronick, 1996, 1997). The infants' and mothers' facial expressions and behaviors were coded second by second from videotapes. Infants' and mothers' facial expressions were coded with Izard's system for identifying affect expressions by holistic judgments (AFFEX) system. The infants' behavior was coded with Tronick and Weinberg's Infant Regulatory Scoring System (IRSS), which codes six dimensions of infant behavior, including the infants' direction of gaze, vocalizations, gestures, self-comforting, distancing or withdrawal, and autonomic stress indicators. The mothers' behavior was coded with Tronick and Weinberg's Maternal Regulatory Scoring System (MRSS), which codes six dimensions of maternal behavior, including direction of gaze, proximity to infant, caregiving activities, types of touch, vocalizations, and eliciting behaviors.

Although the coders were blind to maternal group (i.e., depressed and nonde-pressed) membership, maintaining coders' blindness to gender is difficult. Mothers refer to the infants by name and often dress them in a manner suggestive of gender. Asking mothers to modify their normal routines with their infant may produce reactive effects in the mothers. To overcome these problems, we adopted the procedures we used in our previous study of gender differences. Mothers and coders were not told that one objective of the study was to evaluate gender issues, but that the study was concerned with infant interactive and communicative behavior with mothers. Thus, neither mothers nor coders knew that the study was concerned with issues of gender. Furthermore, coding was done by several independent coders. For example, one coder coded infant gaze, whereas another coded infant vocalizations. As noted by Melson and Fogel (1982), the independent multiple coder approach is unlikely to result in consistent bias. Moreover, frequent interrater reliability checks ensured that coders remained unbiased and reliable. Interrater reliability was calculated on 20% of the data. Mean kappas ranged from .77 to .85.

To determine the effect of infant gender, *t* tests were performed on (a) maternal MRSS behavior and AFFEX facial expressions, and (b) infant IRSS behavior and AFFEX facial expressions across the episodes of the face-to-face still-face paradigm. Preliminary analyses of 3-month observations indicate that depressed mothers were nearly twice as likely to express neutral affect to their sons than to their daughters. They also tended to show more facial expressions of anger when interacting with their sons than with their daughters. Analyses of 6-month observations indicate that these mothers continued to show significantly more facial expressions of anger directed toward their sons than their daughters.

No significant gender differences were apparent in the infants' behavior at 3 months of age. At 6 months of age, however, boys as compared to girls appeared more vulnerable to their mothers' depressive status. Male infants, as compared to female infants, were two times less likely to express facial expressions of joy. They were also more likely to gesture, suggesting that they were more agitated or that they were attempting to communicate their needs to their mother. In addition, male infants, as compared to female infants, were three times less likely to use self-comforting strategies such as sucking on a thumb to self-regulate emotional states.

The data indicate that mothers with a history of major depression were more affectively negative with their sons than their daughters. In addition, male infants, as compared to female infants, were less emotionally positive and less likely to use self-comforting strategies to regulate affective states on their own. Thus, maternal depression seemed to have a differential effect on the early interactive behavior of sons and daughters; the sons of depressed mothers appeared more disrupted and dysregulated by maternal behavior than did the daughters of depressed mothers.

The research on gender differences in children of nondepressed mothers and the MRM suggest an interpretation of these findings (Tronick & Cohn, 1989; Weinberg et al., 1999). Boys, compared to girls, are more demanding social partners, have more difficult times regulating their affective states, and may need more of their mothers' support to help them regulate affect. This increased demandingness would affect the infant boys' interactive partner.

In this study, mothers with a history of depression appeared to have difficulties giving their sons the regulatory scaffolding that they needed. For example, mothers displayed more angry and neutral facial expressions to their sons than to their daughters. The mothers' behavior alone, however, does not account for the effects. Infant sons of depressed mothers expressed less joy and were more agitated. These affective regulatory difficulties most likely reflect the interplay of the son's behavior, the mother's neutral and angry affect, and the ongoing interplay and self-reinforcing quality of the dyad's greater negativity. Thus, the negativity observed in the mother-son dyads is a mutually produced effect.

One can speculate on the long-term consequences of this early interaction pattern. For example, we would predict, although it has not been reported, that infant sons may be more likely to be insecurely attached to their depressed mothers than would be infant daughters. Furthermore, boys may be more likely to express negative affect, particularly anger, as they get older because of the frustrations experienced during social interactions. At the same time, depressed mothers would be more likely to express anger to their sons than to their daughters. The daughters' ability to self-regulate may induce more sadness in mothers, however, because daughters may seem disconnected from their mothers, leading to a mutual withdrawal on both their parts. These differentially mutually regulated pathways may increase the likelihood that as boys get older, they will express their disconnection in the form of angry interactions and behavioral disturbances such as conduct disorders, whereas girls will express their interactive problems in the form of withdrawal and depressive behavior.

Other developmental changes powerfully affect the emotional development of these infants. Toward the end of the first year of life, the infants develop a sense of intersubjectivity, or capacity to attribute a state of mind to the other and to oneself. Tronick and his colleagues (1998) have hypothesized that a serious outcome of the development of secondary intersubjectivity is that it may enable the infant to develop psychopathological states. With the development of secondary intersubjectivity, the infant's reaction is no longer determined simply by what he or she directly experiences in interaction with the mother. The infant's reaction is increasingly based on an integration of immediate events with self-reflective representational processes. With these developmental changes, distortions of reality become possible. For example, when children become aware of their depressed mother's affective state (e.g., her anger and sadness, which is apparently directed at themselves) and their own intolerable feelings of rage directed at her, children may develop a pathological form of coping—denial, detachment, repression, or projection—in an attempt to control their awareness of these overwhelming feelings.

Representations of these experiences take time to develop. Early in development, these experiences are instantiated in patterns of action and emotion, what Tronick referred to as procedural knowledge, before they become representations incorporating elements of the self, cognition, and history (Tronick, 1998). Critically, these representations are not simply stored information in a preformed or predetermined universal brain (e.g., the filing of information in some area of the brain dedicated to the storage of information) that can be accessed for present use. Rather, these representations are one of the processes that shapes the brain itself. Thus, the brain, like emotional experience, is jointly created. To invert the idea, the human brain is inherently dyadic and is created through interactive interchanges.

Tronick further hypothesized that there is a critical and emergent property of this collaboration—the creation of single dyadic states of consciousness (see Tronick et al., 1998, for details). This dyadic state organization is bound and has more components than the infant's (or mother's) own state of consciousness. Thus, this dyadic system contains more information and is more complex and coherent than either the infant's (or the mother's) endogenous state of consciousness alone. When infant and mother mutually create this dyadic state, they fulfill the system principle of gaining greater complexity and coherence. For example, the infant who is held and supported by the mother—the mother-held infant—is able to perform an action such as gesturing that he or she would not be able to perform alone without the maternal scaffolding. Most important, the mother-held infant, as contrasted to the alone infant, experiences a state of consciousness associated with gesturing that emerges from his or her participation in a dyadic system.

Creation of this dyadic system necessitates that the infant and mother apprehend elements of the other's state of consciousness. If they did not, it would not be possible to create a dyadic state. For example, if the mother's apprehension of the infant's state of consciousness is that the infant intends to reach for a ball when in fact the infant intended to stroke her face, a dyadic state will not be created. In this case, the two systems—infant and mother—will remain separate and uncoordinated. Thus, a principle governing the human dyadic system is that successful mutual regulation of social interactions requires a mutual mapping of (some of) the elements of the partner's state of consciousness into the partner's brain. This mutual mapping process may be a way of defining intersubjectivity. In the young infant, the process is one of emotional apprehension of the other's state, referred to as primary intersubjectivity (Campos, Barrett, Lamb, Goldsmith, & Stenberg, 1983; Tronick, Als, & Brazelton, 1980a). In the older infant, the process is one of secondary intersubjectivity because the infant becomes aware of his or her apprehension of the other's state. In older children and adults, the process may be what is called empathy—a state that contains an awareness of the other's state and a paradoxical awareness of the differentiation between one's state and the state of the other.

The dyadic consciousness hypothesis suggests that each individual is a self-organizing system that creates its own states of consciousness—states of brain organization—that can be expanded into more coherent and complex states in collaboration with another self-organizing system. When the collaboration of two brains is successful, each fulfills the system principle of increasing its coherence and complexity. The states of consciousness of the infant and the mother are more inclusive and coherent the moment they form a dyadic state that incorporates the state of the other.

An important consequence of the dyadic consciousness hypothesis relates to the toxic effects on the infant of maternal depression. Maternal depression disrupts the establishment of a dyadic infant-mother system. The infant is deprived of experiencing dyadically expanded states of consciousness (see Tronick, 1998, for details). This deprivation forces the infant into a self-regulatory pattern of coping that further constricts his or her experience. Yet an even more insidious possibility is suggested by the dyadic consciousness hypothesis. Given that the infant's system functions to expand its complexity and coherence, the infant of the depressed mother may be able to accomplish this expansion by taking on elements of the mother's state of consciousness. These elements, however, are likely to be negative (e.g., sad and hostile affect, withdrawal, and disengagement). Intersubjectivity is established and with it, the infant's state is expanded. Thus, in the service of becoming more complex and coherent, the infant incorporates a state of consciousness that mimics the depressive elements of the mother. That this intersubjective state contains painful elements does not override the need for expansion. From the perspective of dyadic states of consciousness, neither boys nor girls are more vulnerable to the effects of maternal depression because for both sons and daughters, their interactive and subjective states are constricted and restricted. Both experience a failure to achieve dyadic states and, for both, the consequence is a limitation of the affective development of their mind.

Infant Moods and the Chronicity of Depressive Symptoms: The Cocreation of Unique Ways of Being Together for Good or Ill, Paper 1: The Normal Process of Development and the Formation of Moods

Mood states are central phenomena to adult psychopathology and normal functioning. Mood disorders such as depression and anxiety are some of the most prevalent forms of pathology. And though there is a clear recognition that moods are feeling states, much of the work on mood disorders has focused on ideational or cognitive processes as the key mechanisms underlying the disorders, with the affective state a product of these processes. Depressed individuals are seen as having negative thoughts or not appreciating positive events to the same extent as nondepressed individuals. Their depressed mood state is secondary to their cognitive, representational, or ideational processes. Oddly, there is little consideration that the mood states may come first, such that a depressed mood may bias the cognitive process or the meaning of experience. However, in clinical situations we know that is true: The patient simply seems stuck in a negative mood and all the meaning of experience is toned by the mood. Of course it is more reasonable to think that there is an interplay of mood and cognition, with each amplifying and regulating the other such that understanding which process came first is rather moot.

However, what I think is not appreciated about moods is that they can function in the way that cognitions or representations function. They can be states of consciousness, that is, the explicit, implicit, or unconscious sense the individual makes of the world. For many the world feels scary. For example, the meaning we place in being alone in a dark, shadow-filled unknown city is fear, anxiety, and creepiness. Cognition is of course required: One needs to perceive the buildings and shadows, recall other similar cities, and know that one is alone; but even when one is assured by friends and tourist guides that the city is safe at night, the feeling is still one of danger and fear. Why do we get stuck in this primary-process meaning rather than in the secondary-process meaning?

In this chapter, I want to address the question of the ontogenesis of moods and the process that establishes them. Moods arise out of normal developmental processes at both macro- and microdevelopmental levels. Moods are part of normal development, but as we shall see they are also a component of pathological processes. They are a ubiquitous presence and give meaning to experience in daily life and therapy. In this first part of a two-part essay I will address the normal development of moods; in the second part I want to address issues related to psychopathology and therapy, especially depression and the intergenerational transfer of mood. As will become obvious, I will argue that moods are dyadic phenomena—a long-lasting affective state that develops out of the interaction of two individuals. It is not solely an intrapsychic process. I will also argue, especially when one considers the development of moods in infants, that moods make sense of the world as components of states of consciousness that give unique meaning to the individual's engagement with the world. Moreover, I will try to show how moods function to bring the past into the present.

THE DEVELOPMENT OF MOODS

Despite parents' attribution of moods to their infant ("He was just out of sorts all day. I stood on my head but nothing pleased him."), there has been little or no research on the establishment of infant moods or the mechanisms underlying them. A reason for this failure is the difficulty of having to adjust our thinking to the radical idea that long-lasting emotional states, no less than short-lived affective states, can be organizing processes that structure behavior rather than functioning as primary processes that disorganize and disrupt behavior (Beebe & Stern, 1977; Fogel, Diamond, Langhorst, & Demos, 1983; Tronick, 1989; Weinberg & Tronick, 1994). Furthermore, as Downing has persuasively argued, at their core moods have something to do with the body, and the body is out of favor in the current context of neuroscientists' focus on the brain and the psychoanalytic focus on the self and relationships.

My model of moods is that infants have long-lasting (e.g., hours, days, and even longer), dynamically changing yet distinct, assemblages of affective behaviors and affective states. Most critically, mood creation (control) processes are modified by affective input from others. Mood states function to organize behavior and experience over time. Critically, they serve an anticipatory function by providing directionality to the infant's behavior as he moves into the future. Mood states are also implicitly and often explicitly known to the infant's caregivers or partners. As communications, moods function to give the caregiver a sense of what the infant will be like in the ongoing current moment as it moves into the future. Importantly, I also believe that moods are generated out of the chronic interplay of active self-organized biorhythmic affective control processes in the infant and the effect of the emotions expressed by others during routine social-emotional exchanges on the infant's mood control processes. Thus while we attribute moods to the individual—the infant is *in* a mood and the mood is *in* her—I will argue that moods are related to others. Furthermore, moods are cocreated as part of a sloppy process of creating dyadic states of consciousness—dyadic states of shared meaning—with other people in which moods are a component of meaning of the state of consciousness.

MACRO DEVELOPMENT

An understanding of the processes generating moods requires a model of the macroprocesses governing development. A somewhat simplified view is that there are three primary forces for development (Figure 25.1): maturation, external regulatory processes, and internal self-organized regulatory processes (Brazelton, Tronick, & Als, 1979; Hofer, 1994a; Tronick, 1989). Maturation and our evolutionary history constantly push development through a series of changes that are regulated by processes internal to the infant as well as external processes in the (social) environment. As an open self-organizing system, the developing organism is attempting to garner resources from the environment to increase its coherence (Tronick, 2004; Weinberg, Tronick, et al., 2003). However, development is not smooth. It is characterized by periods of stable organization in one domain (e.g., motor capacities) followed by periods of

FIGURE 25.1. Processes regulating development. (From Brazelton, 1994)

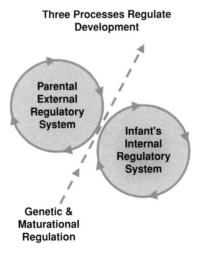

**Three Processes Regulate
Development**

**Parental
External
Regulatory
System**

**Infant's
Internal
Regulatory
System**

**Genetic &
Maturational
Regulation**

FIGURE 25.2. Disorganization in one system can disorganize others. (From Tronick, 2002)

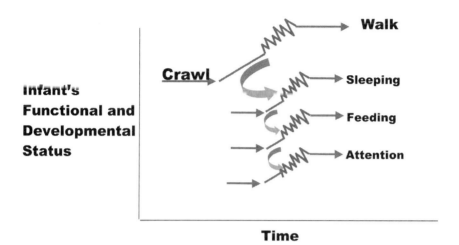

disorganization followed by a reorganization into a new more coherent form of organization (Brazelton, 1992; Rijt-Plooij & Plooij, 1993). Periods of disorganization are an inherent characteristic of self-organizing systems and can be thought of as the avalanches of Per Bak's sand pile model from which new organization emerges from self-organizing processes. Adding to the complexity, the disorganization of one system disorganizes other systems (Figure 25.2). For example, the infant who is beginning to change from crawling to walking becomes motorically, emotionally, and sleep disorganized. The task of regulating this disorganization falls to the internal self-organizing resources of the infant. However, in many instances the infant's resources are inadequate to the task and must be supplemented by external regulation. Without additional external regulation, regulatory resources development would be derailed (Figure 25.3).

Under normal circumstances, the combination of internal and external processes is adequate to the regulatory demands and development moves forward. However, when the internal and external resources are inadequate, development may be seriously disrupted. Disorganization increases and coherence and complexity are lost. It is at this time that the entry of a clinician into the parent-infant system can further scaffold it and reorient or even prevent derailment. Note however, a critical feature of the model is that disorganization is part of the normal process. Disorganization is necessary for development to move forward. Thus the clinician should not aim to shut off disorganization, but rather the clinician can help to contain it such that it does not exceed the capacities of the dyad to regulate it and as such let new development emerge from the disorganization (Figure 25.4). Another way to put this idea is that a lack of disorganization does not allow for change, developmental or therapeutic. Fixed systems do not change. Disorganization is the wellspring of change and the new.

FIGURE 25.3. Inability to regulate disorganization can lead to developmental derailment. (From Tronick, 2002)

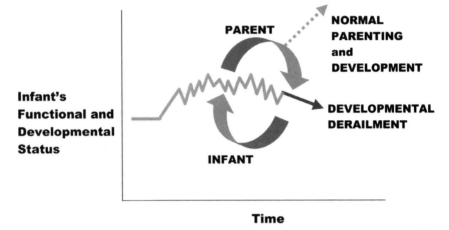

MICRODEVELOPMENTAL PROCESSES

The macroprocess of organization-disorganization is effectively regulated by microtemporal communicative processes that regulate the moment-by-moment exchanges of the infant and the adult. For example, the disorganization that comes with the disassembling of crawling is worked on day after day, moment after moment by the infant and the caregiver. The regulatory process is referred to as the mutual regulation model (MRM; Brazelton, Koslowski, & Main, 1974; Tronick & Cohn 1989; Tronick & Weinberg, 1997; see also Fogel's theory of coregulation, Fogel, 1993; Hofer, 1978, 1994a). The model stipulates that mothers and infants are linked subsystems of a dyadic system. Each component, infant and mother, regulates their relational intentions and the state of the interaction by apprehending and responding to the moment-by-moment meaning of each other's affective and behavioral displays. In the MRM, both interactants are active in the regulatory process. For example, in my still-face manipulation mothers are asked to sit and face their infant but not to respond to their infant. Infants react strongly to this display. After detecting their mother's failure to respond, infants often turn away from their mother but then turn back toward her and try to elicit her response. Infants utilize abbreviated smiles and even fake

FIGURE 25.4. The clinician's work can prevent or overcome derailment but not the disorganization of the system. (From Tronick, 2002)

Clinican's Work Can Prevent or Overcome Derailment But NOT the Disorganization of the System

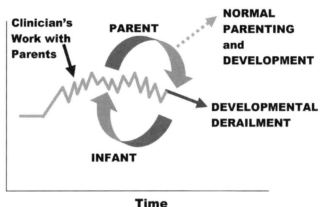

coughs. When these maneuvers fail, the infant may lose postural control and collapse into sad affect (Figure 25.5).

Until they give up, the infants are active detectors and elicitors of their mother's behavior during the still face. Moreover, as conveyed by the infants' compelling and organized response to their mother's lack of response, the meaning of the still face to the infant is that the mother is disconnected, that she no longer wants to love them, and possibly as Modell has suggested, that she is dead to them. Of course we cannot validly know what the display means to the infant, but the quality, sequencing, and specifics of the infants' response tell us that the display has an impelling meaning for them, that the meaning is primarily affective, and that they organize their behavior around the affective meaning.

Let us elaborate a bit more. A simple but core way to think of the infant is as an "emotion detector." The idea of emotion detection is not simply suggesting that infants see or discriminate affective displays differently from one another, as novel or interesting. Nothing could be further from the reality. Infants see affective displays as carrying meaning about what a person is doing in relation to them and what the meaning of an event or action is. Meaning in this case is not the dictionary meaning of words, categories, and symbols.

FIGURE 25.5. The infant in response to the still-faced mother loses postural control.

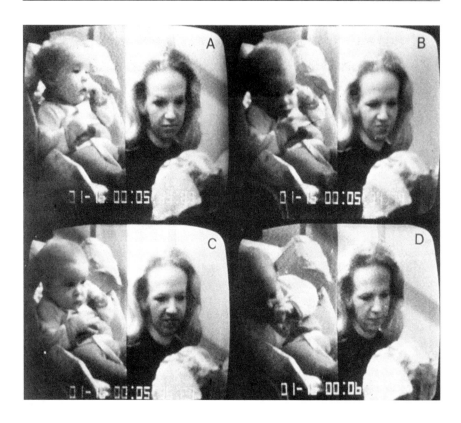

Meaning to the infant is more like the sensorimotor meaning that Piaget talked about (e.g., this thing—a spoon to a toddler—is bangable or suckable). I also think that affects convey sensory-affective and body-affective meanings about people and events. For example, when seeing a virtual image driven at them on a collision course (something adults see as an approaching object), infants as young as 11 weeks of age put their hands up in front of their faces and try to duck down in their infant seats (Tronick, 1982). They experience the display as dangerous and they try to protect themselves. They do not see it as an interesting changing display with no meaning. Just as Piaget's spoon has the meaning bangable, the looming image has the meaning danger, collision. The optical display has significance to them and we can find the meaning they make of it by looking at the organized complexity of their response. We believe that the organization of this response is as good as having the infant say, "Duck, look out!" But this response does not mean that they know about the physics of objects such as solidity. What they know is that this display means—feels—dangerous.

In the social domain, we have seen similar meaning-conveying reactions by infants. For example, we have seen an infant react to an angry facial display by his mother as she attempts to get him to let go of her hair. The maternal angry facial expression and vocalization lasts less than half a second, but the infant detects it and immediately brings his hands up in front of his face, partially turns away in the chair, and looks at her from under his raised hands (Figure 25.6). Her angry face, perhaps the first he has ever seen, is not just interesting or novel. He apprehends it as a threat. Something dangerous is about to occur and he organizes a reaction to protect himself from what seems about to happen. The infant does not know what the danger may be, only that the angry face makes him feel vulnerable to what may be coming. Again, it is the infant's organized event-related behaviors that convey the meaning of the angry facial expression to the infant.

Thus mutual regulation depends on the exchange of meaningful affective information. Its success or failure between the mother and the infant depends on the infant's and the mother's collaborative ability to regulate the infant's homeostatic, affective, and behavioral states. The infant's regulatory abilities include physiological mechanisms (e.g., stress control systems), coping behaviors (e.g., acts of self-comforting, withdrawal, approach), attentional mechanisms (e.g., direction of gaze), and gestural, facial, and vocal communicative capacities (e.g., reaching for the mother, facial expressions, crying; Braungart-Reiker & Stifter, 1996; Kopp, 1989; Rothbart & Derryberry, 1981; Stifter & Braungart, 1995). In the mother-infant interaction, the regulation of the infant's homeostatic, attentional, behavioral, and emotional state is primarily accomplished using the infant's and adult's communicative capacities. In interaction, each partner communicates their affective evaluation of three things that are going on simultaneously: the interaction (e.g., enjoyment of the current activity), relational affect (e.g., feeling apart from, feeling in synch; Foscha, 2000), and their relational intention (e.g., let's continue, let's stop, let's be connected; Weinberg & Tronick, 1994). These communications are simultaneously expressed with what we have called affective configural communications.

Similar to macro-level regulatory capacities of the infant, the micro-interactive regulatory abilities of the young infant are limited and a caregiver's scaffolding is required for the infant to achieve its regulatory and interactive goals. The caregiver's ability to interpret and respond appropriately to the infant's communications facilitates the infant's regulation, successful achievement of goals, and interpersonal functioning. Further, in a micro form, similar in form to the macro form of disorganization, there is disorganization in the interaction. The moment-by-moment interaction between the infant and an adult is neither continuously smooth nor synchronous. Rather, the interaction is characterized by disruptions and mismatches of affective states and relational goals. In essence, the interaction is sloppy. However, in successful interactions the sloppiness, mismatches, miscommunications, and misattunements are quickly repaired. In time, of course, matches again become miscoordinated and again they are repaired, and so on.

FIGURE 25.6. Infant defensive reaction (b) to maternal anger display (a).

a

b

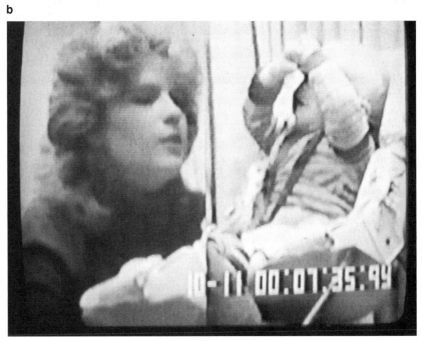

Thus the typical mother-infant interaction can be characterized as one that moves from coordinated (or synchronous) to miscoordinated states and back again over a wide affective range (Figure 25.7). A miscoordinated state is referred to as a normal interactive communicative error. The interactive transition from a miscoordinated state to a coordinated state is referred to as an interactive repair.

The process of reparation, like the dynamics of regulating macrodevelopmental change, is mutually regulated. The infant and adult communicate their evaluation of the state of the interaction with their meaningful affective configurations. In response to their partner's signals, each partner attempts to adjust his or her behavior to maintain a coordinated state or to repair an interactive error to a new, more coherent state. Critically, successful reparations and the experience of coordinated states are associated with positive affective states, whereas interactive errors generate negative affective states. Thus the infant's affective experience is determined by a dyadic regulatory process.

In normal dyads, interactive disorganization is quickly repaired. In studies of face-to-face interaction at 6 months of age, repairs occur at a rate of once every 3–5 seconds and more than one third of all repairs occur by the next step in the interaction (Figure 25.8; Tronick & Gianino, 1980). Observations by Beebe and Lachmann (1994) and Isabella and Belsky (1991) replicated these findings and support the hypothesis that the normal interaction is a process of reparation. They found that maternal sensitivity in the midrange, rather than at the low or high end, typify normal interactions. Midrange sensitivity is characterized by errors and repairs as contrasted to interactions in which the mother is never sensitive or always sensitive. These researchers also found that midlevel sensitivity was associated with security of attachment. But a critical feature of reparations is that in going from a match to a mismatch and back to a match, the subsequent match is not identical to the previous match. It is not a return to a prior state but a dynamic movement to a new way of being together.

It is my hypothesis that reparation of interactive errors is the critical process of normal interactions that is related to developmental outcome rather than synchrony or positive affect per se. That is, the extent and quality of reparatory experience is the social-interactive mechanism that affects the infant's development. In interactions characterized by normal rates of reparation, the infant learns which communicative and coping strategies are effective in producing reparation and when to use them. This experience leads to the elaboration of communicative and coping skills, and the development of an understanding of interactive rules and conventions. The infant also learns that he or she has control over social interactions. Specifically, the infant develops a representation of himself or herself as effective, of his or her interactions as positive and reparable, and of the caretaker as reliable and trustworthy. These representations are crucial for the development of a sense of self that will have coherence, continuity, and agency, and for the development of stable and secure relationships (Tronick, 1980; Tronick & Weinberg, 1980; Tronick, Cohn, & Shea, 1986).

FIGURE 25.7. (a) Infant and mother in matching affective state; (b) infant and mother in mismatching affective state; (c) infant and mother repair mismatching to matching state.

a

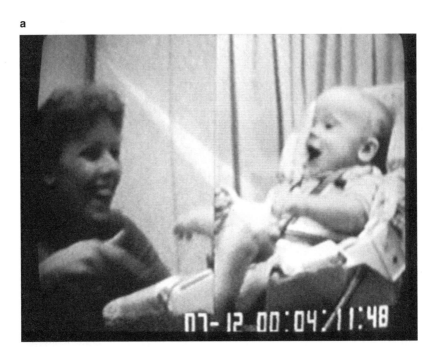

b

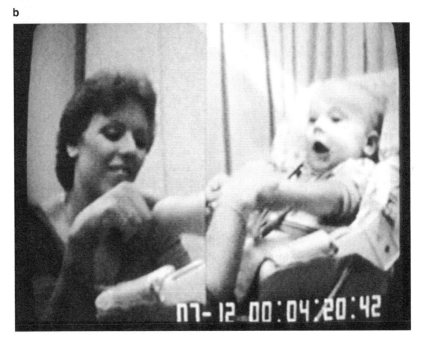

c

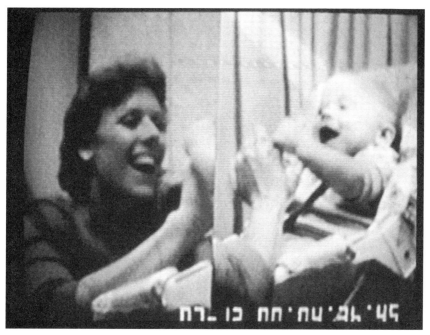

There are critical effects in the affective domain associated with the reparatory process. Among the most critical is that with the experiential accumulation of successful reparations, the infant learns that negative affect generated during a mismatch can be transformed into a positive affect. With chronic successful reparatory experience the infant begins to establish what Emde refers to as a positive affective core (Emde, Kligman, Reich, & Wade, 1978; Gianino & Tronick, 1988) or what I see as a mood. A mood is established out of the chronic moment-by-moment generation of positive affect experienced in match, mismatch, and reparation experience. Of course, the mood could be negative as well when reparation fails.

But what are moods? There is no good definition, but one way to think of moods is as longer lasting affective states. In some ways moods are like waking up from a nap. The sleep state is "sticky"; you seem to come out of it and then go back into it, and getting out of it takes time. Again, like behavioral sleep and awake states, moods last over time and have critical temporal features such as stickiness, momentum, and ebb and flow. What are some of the effects or functions of moods? A mood acts to bias the infant's experience of events. For example, an infant in a positive mood is more likely to experience playing with a stranger as positive because the infant's processing of the stranger's play

FIGURE 25.8. Match and mismatch effects on infant action and affect (quick repairs, short mismatches). (From Tronick, 2000)

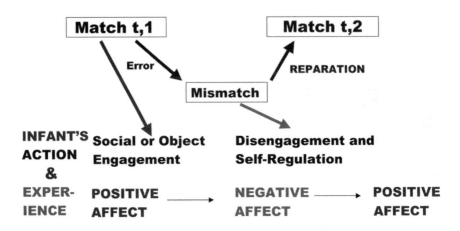

is positively biased by the infant's positive mood. There is no need to compare the stranger to some form of template or expectation such that, if the stranger matches the template, he is experienced as positive. Rather, the input from the stranger as it is processed by the infant's mood state becomes positive.

What does it mean to say that moods are sticky? Stickiness is the idea that once an infant (and likely adults as well) is in a mood, it is hard to move the infant out of it, and when the infant does get out of it, he readily falls back into it. "She woke up in a cranky mood and she just wouldn't get out of it. Even when she smiled to her teddy, she just went back to fussing." Moreover, moods ebb and flow and have stronger effects at one time than another. This ebb and flow, like the ebb and flow of sleep states, is both self-organized and affected by input. However, the dominance of a mood is not fixed and another mood may replace it, although the changeover to another mood occurs slowly. Last, moods have momentum because they continue to be manifest even after the triggering event has ended. "She smiled to the rabbit and then just kept on smiling even when it was gone. Playing with it just put her into a great mood."

Momentum is also generated by self-organizing internal processes. As a consequence of their momentum, ongoing affective inputs may have little role in maintaining a mood state. Moods may simply go on and on on their own momentum. Over longer time spans they seem to be present for some period of time (e.g., a month or so) and then dissipate. "She used to be so cranky after her nap but now she is just a joy." The wavelike biorhythmic ebb and flow is a self-organized process that organizes affective states over time and into the future.

Parents also know that moods are different than what might be thought of as temperament. Moods are modified by input, though change may come only slowly. Moods grow out of the recurrence of the infant's affective experience, whereas temperament is an organismic characteristic. However, organismic features of an infant may predispose an infant toward establishing one mood or another. "You could see she was easily overstimulated as a newborn and now too much of even good things get to her." Most important, moods' long duration, flow, stickiness, momentum, and temporal features make them different than fleeting affects that are briefly present and then dissipate. Nonetheless, because both are affective states, many of their behavioral components and likely central nervous system and physiological components are similar.

Thus though moods were established in interaction with the mother, and they grew out of the reparatory experience, as self-organizing processes moods have a life of their own and they fulfill the Janus principle of bringing the past into the present. For example, a short-lived mood of negative affect generated during the infant's confrontation with the still-faced mother is carried forward into the reunion play episode when she is acting normally. The carryover of negative affect functions to bias the infant's responses and affect, making the infant more negative in the reunion play than he was in the first play. More dramatically, we can think of the infants reared in orphanages that were studied by Spitz and Bowlby, or Harlow's isolation-reared monkeys as having had disastrous negative experiences, with no reparations. Eventually they established sticky negative moods. The moods brought the past into the present, biased their experience of the present and their reactions to it.

To conclude this first essay on normal processes and before moving on to the second essay on problems of maternal depression and its effects on infants, I want to emphasize several key points. Normal development is not a smooth process, either at the macro level where it gains much of its coherence from maturational forces or at the micro level where it gains much of its coherence from the effectiveness of mutual regulation of affect between the active infant and caregiver. At both the macro and micro level, there is disorganization, error, and sloppiness, which is the wellspring out of which new things are created in the infant by processes that repair the sloppiness. Critically, reparation is not going back to what was present before. It is not a homeostatic process but a process of moving toward a new way of doing or being together. Moods grow out of the chronic reparatory and affective experience of the infant with others. They are a critical force and constraint on the interactive reparatory process. Positive moods are known to make individuals more flexible and more creative, whereas negative moods restrict their creativity. We will examine this kind of constraint in the second essay on the effects of maternal depression on infant development, especially the transfer of mood.

Infant Moods and the Chronicity of Depressive Symptoms: The Cocreation of Unique Ways of Being Together for Good or Ill, Paper 2: The Formation of Negative Moods in Infants and Children of Depressed Mothers

In this second part of this two-part essay, I want to address how infant mood is related to psychopathology, especially depression and the formation of negative mood in the child of a depressed mother. It is an issue of understanding the active processes required to have an intergenerational transfer of mood. This essay is not a general review but focuses on some of the work in my laboratory and thinking about mood (see reviews by Downey & Coyne, 1990; Murray & Cooper, 1997; Weinberg & Tronick, 1997).

In the first part of this essay, I addressed the question of the ontogenesis of moods (see also, Tronick, 2002a). Though little attention is paid to moods in infants and children, moods are ubiquitous and powerfully affect how they experience the world. From my perspective, moods make sense of the world as the content of states of consciousness that give unique meaning to the infant in the world. Further, because of temporal characteristics such as stickiness and momentum that allow moods to move into the future, moods function to bring the past into the present. Most important, I argued in Part 1 that moods are dyadic phenomena—long-lasting affective states that develop out of the interaction of two individuals—rather than solely being generated intrapsychically.

Several points from the model I developed in Part 1 need to be kept in mind. First, as Brazelton (1994) has argued in his touchpoints model, the development of moods is not a smooth process. At the macro level there are periods of stability that are interspersed with periods of disorganization which must be regulated by self-organizing processes and external regulatory processes provisioned by others. However, mutual regulatory processes at the microtemporal level also are far from smooth. There is disorganization, mismatches of affect and intention, error, and sloppiness. This messiness may be repaired by the mutual regulation of the infant and partner in the interaction. Critically, messiness—affective mismatches—is associated with the experience of negative affect, whereas reparation to a matching state is associated with the experience of positive affect.

Moods are an outcome of the infant's chronic reparatory experience. In an ongoing and reiterated chronic interactive experience in which interactive affective mismatches are short lived and reparation happens quickly, the infant experiences the rapid transformation of negative to positive affect. With the accumulation of this positive affective transformation the infant establishes a positive mood state or affective core. This mood is brought by the child into situations and makes him more likely to react positively than negatively. By contrast, when interactive mismatches are not repaired the infant has repeated and ongoing negative experiences that lead to accumulation of negative affect and the development of a negative mood. The infant who has experienced repeated reparatory experience carries this negative mood into new situations and is more likely to experience and react to them negatively. Thus moods function to bias the individual's ongoing experience of the moment. As such, moods function as a noncognitive mechanism for bringing the past into the present.

In our work on understanding the establishment of moods in infants, we have examined the interactions of infants and depressed mothers (Tronick, 1989, 1996; Tronick & Field, 1986; Tronick & Weinberg, 1997; Weinberg & Tronick, 1994). Our view was that depressed mothers are likely to have problems in reading their infants' affective communications and responding appropriately (see Figure 26.1). As a consequence, the infant (and the mother) chronically experience negative affect because of a failure to repair negative affective mismatches, and over time the infant develops a negative mood. Further, once the negative mood is established the infant also would become a poorer interactive partner and further compromise his own and his mother's experience. That is, there would be a mutual amplification of their negative moods and their interactive problems.

In our initial work, we first established that maternal depression in the postpartum period is a chronic state that is associated with compromised maternal psychosocial functioning. In one study (Beeghly et al., 2003), one of several that had similar findings, we evaluated stability and change in the level of maternal depressive symptomatology over the course of the first postpartum year. The sample was a community cohort of 106 first-time mothers of full-term, healthy infants. The mothers were healthy and at low social risk except for depression. Our goal with this sample was to minimize the effects of factors such as prematurity or poverty that are known to affect infant and mother functioning. Though our primary focus was on levels of depressive symptoms, we also evaluated if there were effects of a woman having a diagnosed depression on her

FIGURE 26.1. The effects of maternal depression on mutual regulation and infant affect. Matching states are of short duration, whereas mismatching states are of long duration and associated with negative affect. See Figure 25.8 for the complementary depiction of the flow of normal interaction matches, mismatches, and repairs. (From Tronick, 1998)

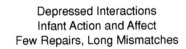

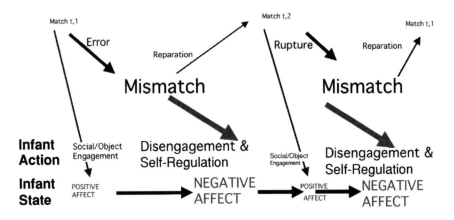

symptom level and its stability. Further, because we have found infant gender effects in normal and depressed samples, we investigated gender effects on stability and change of maternal symptoms.

At 2 months postpartum (intake), mothers were classified into one of two symptom groups on the basis of their total score on the Center for Epidemiological Studies–Depression Scale (CES-D): high (CES-D score ≥16, 46%) or normative (CES-D score = 2–12, 54%). Mothers completed the CES-D again at 3, 6, and 12 months postpartum. At 12 months, maternal diagnostic status for major depression and related disorders was evaluated using the Diagnostic Interview Schedule–III–Revised for the postpartum year and for lifetime history.

We found that mothers in the high-symptom group at intake continued to have significantly higher CES-D scores at 3, 6, and 12 months than mothers in the normative symptom group at intake (see Figure 26.2). In addition, more than a third of the mothers in the high-symptom group at intake had a subsequent CES-D score that was above the clinical cutoff (≥16). There was a striking stability of maternal CES-D scores over the first year. Maternal CES-D scores were significantly correlated across all visits. The average of the correlations was $r = .52$, from intake at 2 months to 3 months, $r = .61$; intake to 6 months, $r = .46$;

FIGURE 26.2. Maternal depressive symptoms from 2 to 12 months.

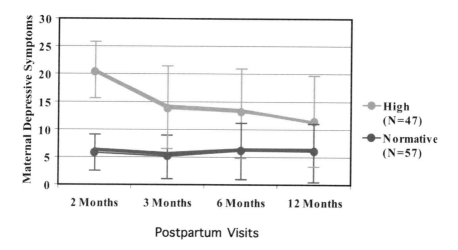

intake to 12 months, $r = .38$; 3–6 months, $r = .65$; 3–12 months, $r = .48$; and 6–12 months, $r = .46$ (all p's $< .0001$). These correlations indicate that individual mothers retained their relative rank ordering in level of depressive symptomatology over the course of the first postpartum year. Using regression analyses to evaluate diagnostic status and gender effects on maternal CES-D scores at 3, 6, and 12 months, we found that the most recent prior assessment contributed significant unique variance to mothers' CES-D score at each subsequent assessment. For example, the 6-month CES-D score was more strongly related to the 12-month CES-D score than was the 3-month CES-D score. Interestingly, CES-D scores were higher at 3 months if mothers had a diagnosed depression and were parenting a son.

Taken together, these findings indicate that the high levels of depressive symptomatology experienced by some first-time mothers early in the postpartum period are not transient. Rather, these mothers are likely to continue to experience high levels of distress and depressed mood throughout the first postpartum year. This appears to be the case even when the mothers' scores are below the cutoff. These findings suggest that whether or not a mother has symptoms above the cutoff, that higher symptom mothers continue to have higher symptoms over the first year of life than lower symptom mothers. Having a diagnosis further exacerbates their symptomatology. Further, mothers with diagnosed depression who were parenting an infant son had a higher CES-D score than the mothers who had daughters. Although the reason for this gender-related finding is not well understood, this result corroborates findings from prior studies that depressed mothers exhibit poorer psychosocial adaptation if they are parenting a son (Murray, 1992; Tronick & Weinberg, 2000). These findings clearly demonstrate that an infant of a high-symptom mother compared to a low-symptom mother will be chronically exposed to a more depressive affective climate than an infant whose mother has low symptom levels. This chronic exposure occurs over the entire range of symptoms. Further, the findings suggest that when a mother's symptoms are no longer above the cutoff (i.e., she is clinically normal) that she likely is not yet "well" because she continues to experience levels of symptoms that are higher than those of mothers who have lower levels of symptoms.

Exacerbating this depressive effect are our findings that the nature of the compromise extends to other areas of maternal functioning as well. In another study with a similar sample of mothers, we found that many aspects of their psychosocial functioning were compromised (see Figure 26.3a–c). High-symptom-group mothers compared to controls reported more anxiety and a greater total number of psychiatric symptoms, experienced more negative affect and less positive affect, and had poorer maternal self-esteem and confidence in their role as mothers. When we compared the high-symptom mothers to a group of mothers with a diagnosed major depression pre- or postbirth and high levels of depressive symptomatology, the psychosocial functioning of the mothers in both groups was similar in all domains of functioning (Weinberg et al., 2001). The only exception was that the total number of psychiatric symptoms was higher

FIGURE 26.3. Psychosocial functioning of women with high levels of depressive symptoms, a diagnosed depression with high levels of symptoms, and a nonclinical control.

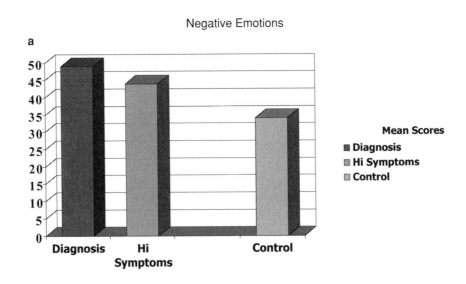

FIGURE 26.3. *Continued*

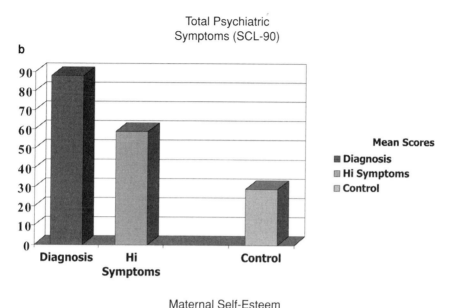

Total Psychiatric
Symptoms (SCL-90)

Mean Scores
■ Diagnosis
▩ Hi Symptoms
▢ Control

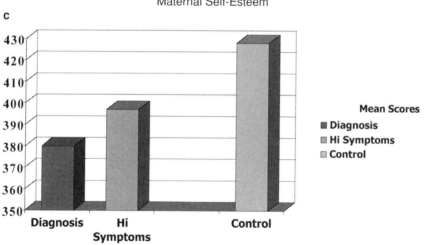

Maternal Self-Esteem

Mean Scores
■ Diagnosis
▩ Hi Symptoms
▢ Control

in the group with a major depression. Thus high symptom levels may be as compromising of psychosocial functioning as having a diagnosed depression with high symptom levels.

The findings on the somewhat unchanging and stable nature of depressive symptoms and the related compromise of aspects of psychosocial functioning in the depressed women indicates that these mothers' infants are chronically exposed to a negative "affective climate." In this affective climate, our expectation was that there would be a compromise of the mother-infant relationship and a failure of reparation that over time would generate a negative mood state in the infant and compromise other aspects of the infant's functioning.

To first evaluate this question of how maternal depression might compromise infant development, we created an experimental model of depression—the simulated depression paradigm (Cohn & Tronick, 1983). The simulated depression paradigm mimicked the still-face paradigm except that we asked mothers to interact with their infants in an affectively flat manner. The mothers kept their faces neutral or even sad and talked to their infants with a flat voice. They slowed down their movements. Thus while there was contingent responsiveness on the part of the mother, her affect was depressed, and reparation to positive affect matching states was not possible. The infants reacted very strongly to this simulation of depression. Compared to the normal interaction, the infants in the simulated depression cycled their affective reactions through protest, wary, and look away (see Figure 26.4). They hardly looked at

FIGURE 26.4. Flow of infant behaviors in normal interaction and in simulated depressed interaction. The size of the circles represents the proportion of time the infant was in each state and the arrows indicate the transitions among states. The absence of arrows indicates that movement between states without arrows was rare.

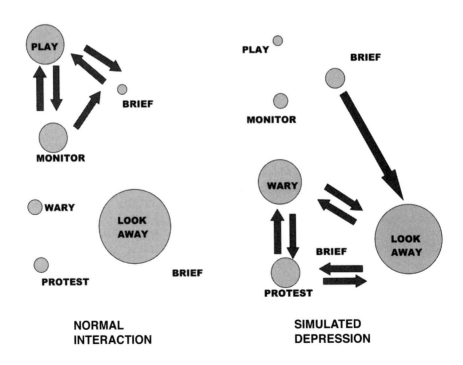

NORMAL
INTERACTION

SIMULATED
DEPRESSION

the mother and hardly ever became affectively positive. The results strongly supported the hypothesis that depression would have a negative affective effect on the infants.

Armed with the findings from the simulated depression paradigm, we looked at the interactions of mothers and their infants who had high levels of depressive symptoms but were otherwise healthy and at low social risk (Tronick & Field, 1986; Tronick & Weinberg, 1997; Weinberg & Tronick, 1994). The findings were much as we expected. Depressed mothers were less emotionally positive with their infants than nondepressed mothers (see Figure 26.5a and b). They looked away from their infants and were generally unresponsive. The infants of the depressed mothers also looked away from the mothers more than infants of non-depressed mothers and they expressed more anger and negative affect. These results strongly supported our expectations.

The infants could be seen as developing a sad and angry mood out of their chronic exposure to the reparatory failure with the mother. This negative mood state explains Field's (1995) findings that infants of depressed mothers have more negative interactions with unfamiliar adults. They bring their negative mood into their interaction with a new person and their mood makes them more difficult interactive partners and negatively biases their interaction. In our laboratory we have observed the same phenomenon and have found that the infant of a depressed mother has a powerful effect on the unfamiliar but expe-rienced partner. We find that the adult touches and smiles less, and stays more distant from the infants of depressed mothers. Of course the adult is blind to the status of the infant. The findings show just how much effect the infant can have on the interaction. My interpretation is that for the infant the history of interaction with the mother generated a negative detached mood that com-promised his interactions with others. It can be seen as a kind of problematic protodefense, a reaction to the other even before the infant knows what the other person will be like. Unfortunately the effect is to further compromise the infant's experience with others, experiences that might have a palliative effect.

We also found something that was quite surprising and yet fit with our ideas that the infant detects the meaning of emotions. The finding was that depressed mothers with equivalent levels of depression were not a homogeneous group in the ways they interacted with their infants. Rather there were at least two groups: one intrusive and the other disengaged and withdrawn (see Figure 26.6a–d; Cohn, Matias, Tronick, Connell, & Lyons-Ruth, 1986; Tronick, 1989). Importantly, each form of interaction had a different effect on the infant. We found that intrusive mothers engaged in rough handling, spoke in an angry tone of voice, poked at their babies, and actively interfered with their infants' activities. Disengaged and withdrawn mothers, by contrast, were unresponsive, affectively flat, and did little to support their infants' activities. As a striking demonstration of the sensitivity of the infant to affective displays, we found that infants of intrusive mothers reacted one way, whereas infants of disengaged and withdrawn mothers reacted another way. Infants of intrusive mothers spent most

Figure 26.5. Depressed mothers and controls and their infants.

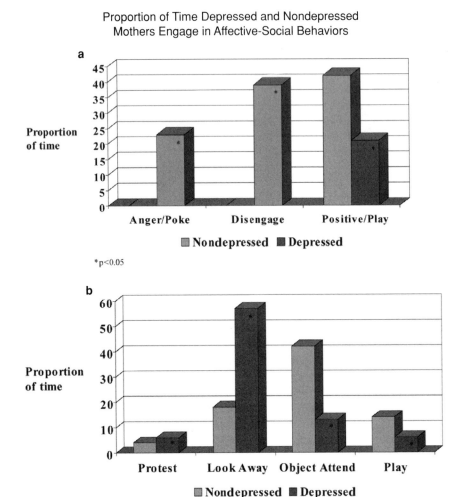

Proportion of Time Depressed and Nondepressed
Mothers Engage in Affective-Social Behaviors

of their time looking away from the mother and seldom looked at objects. They infrequently cried though they did express anger. Infants of disengaged and withdrawn mothers were more likely to protest, to be distressed and sad than the infants of the intrusive mothers, suggesting that maternal withdrawal may be particularly aversive to young infants.

FIGURE 26.6. Behavioral and affective profiles of intrusive and disengaged depressed mothers and their infants.

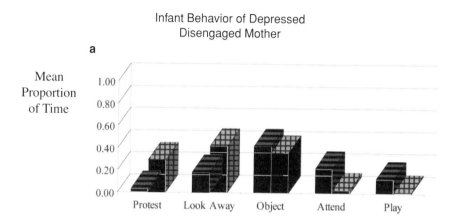

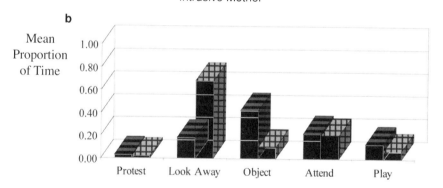

FIGURE 26.6. *Continued*

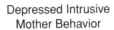

Depressed Intrusive
Mother Behavior

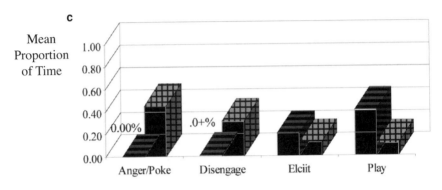

Depressed Disengaged Mother
Behavior

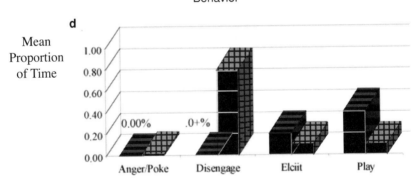

These differential emotional reactions are expectable when one thinks of the infant as an emotion detector in conjunction with the idea that chronic exposure to interactive disruption affects the infant's affect and mood in a specific manner. The infants of intrusive compared to disengaged and withdrawn mothers are reacting to and acting on different kinds of input—their affective reality is different. Infants of disengaged and withdrawn mothers are failing to achieve social connectedness because of the mother's lack of affective responsiveness, their inability to repair the interaction, and their failure to achieve dyadically positive affective matching states. The regulatory effect of the mother's withdrawal is that the infant has to self-regulate his affective states without any external regulatory input from her. However, infants are unable to successfully cope or self-regulate their affective state on their own and they become dysregulated, fuss, and cry. This failure of self-regulation, not unlike failures to regulate homeostatic states, compels them to devote much of their coping resources to controlling their own affective organization. As a consequence of this chronic experience with the withdrawal of the depressed mother, they develop a disengaged, sad, and withdrawn mood and self-directed regulatory style characterized by self-comforting and self-regulatory behaviors, and passivity.

Thus the infants of the disengaged and withdrawn mothers look depressed. However, it is not simply because the mother transferred her depression to them or because they imitated or mirrored her affect. Rather, the transfer comes out of a more active process. These infants simultaneously attempt to regulate the interaction as well as their own affective states, but they fail. As a consequence of the failure they become sad and withdrawn, and utilize self-regulation to control their negative states. The effect is that they develop a depressed turning away from the world. Further, this sad withdrawn mood is used in an effort to preclude anticipated negative emotions even in situations in which negative affect may or may not occur. Eventually with the reiteration and accumulation of failure, these infants develop mood primarily characterized by sadness, a representation of the mother as untrustworthy and unresponsive, and of themselves as ineffective and helpless.

The infants of hostile intrusive mothers must cope with a different regulatory pattern and affective climate than the infants of the disengaged and withdrawn mothers. The intrusive mother's behavior prevents reparation of the interaction because she consistently disrupts the infants' activities. These infants initially experience anger because of her thwarting of their agency and intentions. They turn away from the mother, push her away, or screen her out. However, unlike the failure experience of the infants of disengaged and withdrawn mothers, these coping behaviors are occasionally successful in limiting the mother's intrusiveness. Thus these infants erratically experience reparation—a transformation of anger into a more positive state. Nonetheless, given the experience of reiterated anger, these infants eventually internalize an angry and protective style of coping that is deployed defensively in anticipation of the mother's intrusiveness. We believe that these infants are easily angered when interacting with their mother and others, and more easily frustrated when acting on objects.

These differences in infant reactions to maternal withdrawal and intrusiveness suggest an interpretation of differential effects associated with parental neglect and abuse. Infants who experience neglect suffer under the constant demand to self-regulate. Their withdrawal can be extreme and they may even fail to grow, as occurs for children in orphanages. The infant is continuously required to control his or her own physiological and affective states without regulatory scaffolding from the mother. This self-directed coping style compromises the infant's interchanges with the environment and even his or her motivation to engage with the world. By contrast, in the abusive situation, parental abuse leads to chronic physical defensiveness and anger as well as heightened vigilance and fear. Nonetheless, their affect and regulatory style are active, and these children do engage with others. Thus I expect that the effects of chronic neglect may be more compromising because it limits the capacity of the child to engage with others and to be an active participant in a therapeutic process.

We have now followed up these laboratory observations with observations of depressed mothers with their infants at home (Bell, Weinberg, Yergeau, & Tronick, 2004). The sample consisted of 111 first-time healthy mothers and their healthy infants. Mothers were contacted by phone by a female research assistant when the infant was 2 months of age. The CES-D (Radloff, 1977) was administered to assess the mothers' current level of depressive symptomatology. All eligible mothers who scored 16 or more on the CES-D were recruited for the study and the next mother contacted whose score was below 12 was recruited for the comparison group. Participating mothers' mean age was 31.6 years ($SD = 3.4$) and a majority were Caucasian (97.1%). These mothers were living with the infant's father and had at least a high school level education. The infants were at low medical risk. They were full-term infants and the sample was 48.6% female.

Two hours of naturalistic observations of the mothers and their infants at home were videotaped at 3, 6, and 12 months. Here we will report for the first time on the 3-months-postpartum results. Using the Home Affect Coding Scale, 30 minutes of the observations were coded in 5-second intervals. Infant's affect was coded as positive, neutral, negative, cry, or unscorable. Mother's affect was coded as exaggerated positive, positive, neutral, withdrawn, hostile, or unscorable. Affective matching, a measure of the proportion of time the infant and mother were in the same affective state, was also evaluated (e.g., positive/positive). There were no significant differences in the expression of positive or negative affect by mothers by depression status, but these 3-month-old infants of depressed mothers expressed less positive affect than infants of nondepressed mothers. The infants of depressed mothers also cried significantly less than infants of nondepressed mothers. The depressed dyads also had less positive affective matching than their nondepressed counterparts.

The findings from these home observations demonstrate that infants of depressed mothers are in a less positive and less positively contingent social environment. The lower amount of crying in the infants of depressed mothers suggests that they have developed their self-regulatory capacities for controlling their own negative affect. The lower rates of positive affective matching is a sign of reparatory failure. These findings are similar to laboratory studies and support the validity of those observations. More important, the findings suggest that infants of depressed mothers are chronically exposed to less positive and well-regulated interactions, which even at 3 months is having an effect on infants' affective regulatory style. In particular, the 3-month-olds are developing a mood that is characterized by less positive affect. Our expectation is that at 6 months they will have more fully established a negative affective mood if their mothers' affective state does not change.

These observations on the interactions of depressed mothers and their infants need to take into account gender differences in infant regulatory and affective styles (Tronick & Cohn, 1989; Weinberg, 1992; Weinberg & Tronick, 1992). We have found that boys are more affectively reactive and less able to self-regulate their affective states. I think that they may be particularly susceptible to the disengaged and withdrawn style associated with depression because maternal withdrawal denies them the regulatory support that they need. On the other hand, girls, who at 6 months are significantly more focused on objects than boys and more effectively self-regulate, may be more vulnerable to the intrusive style of depression because it interferes with their own agency and regulation. There are differences in the dyadic organization of interactions of boys and girls. There are higher levels of synchrony in mother-son than in mother-daughter dyads. Though synchrony is often thought to measure a good quality of the mother-child attunement, we are now starting to think that it measures greater vigilance by the mother of her son because of his greater regulatory needs and emotional reactivity. Thus synchrony, as contrasted to positive affective matching, may actually be an index of problems in the interaction.

Tronick and Weinberg (2000), in a small study of mothers with a diagnosis of major depression, found that the 6-month-old male infants of these mothers were significantly less likely to express positive affect or to use self-comforting strategies to regulate affective states than the female infants. The depressed mothers were also more affectively negative with their sons than their daughters. Thus maternal depression appeared to have a differential effect on the early interactive behavior of boys and girls, with the boys showing more dysregulated behavior than girls and the mothers in turn being more affectively negative with their sons than their daughters. In a recent study with 3-month-olds, we have found that sons of depressed mothers in a stressful interaction had the lowest levels of social play and interest and the highest level of negative affect. In addition, depressed mothers of sons engaged in the lowest level of social play. These findings are consistent with previous research by Murray (Murray, Kempton, Woolgar, & Hooper, 1993), who found compromises on the Bayley scales in the 18-month-old male infants of depressed mothers, and Tronick and Weinberg (2000), who found greater effects of maternal depression on both 6-month-old male infants' and their mothers' socioemotional functioning. Taken together, these data support the conclusion that male infants are more vulnerable to maternal depression than female infants and that depressed mothers have more trouble interacting with their male than female infants.

This view fits with the work of Gottman (Levenson & Gottman, 1983), who found that couples with the most problematic marital relationship paradoxically show the highest degree of physiological concordance.

In terms of the mutual regulation model, these findings suggest that a cycle of regulatory problems may become established between depressed mothers and their sons. Male infants' greater negativity, less interest, and less social play during social interactions makes them difficult interactive partners. These difficulties challenge depressed mothers' ability to provide their sons with the regulatory scaffolding needed for them to maintain regulation, which in turn further dysregulates the infants' interactive behavior. As a consequence, there is a self-amplification of their interactive problems.

Combined with the findings that girls show more stability of sadness than boys, and boys show more stability of distancing and escape behaviors than girls, we think these gender differences in regulatory styles may presage the well-documented different development of problems in boys compared to girls. Girls show more internalizing problems, sadness, and withdrawal than boys, a form of early pathology that may be related to their greater capacity for self-regulation. Boys show more externalizing problems, more acting out and aggression that may be related to their greater emotional reactivity. Thus it is not that girls are inherently depressed and boys inherently hyperactive. Rather it is that each has different regulatory styles that over months and years of regulating themselves and interactions in particular ways makes one outcome more likely.

This perspective has implications for the higher rates of conduct and delinquency disorders in boys. We know from the literature on juvenile delinquency that boys commit many more crimes than girls. However, there is not a very good explanation for this phenomenon. Our research indicates that gender differences in infancy may already set the stage for this differential rate. The explanation, however, is not simply that boys are more aggressive than girls. Rather, because boys have greater difficulty controlling their emotional reactions and because of this difficulty, they are more likely than girls to fail to accomplish their goals. This failure generates frustration and anger and may lead to aggression. These effects will be exacerbated when parenting behavior is compromised by an affective disorder, especially if it is intrusive.

In this and the preceding chapter I have discussed the question of the ontogenesis of moods and the process that establishes them. Whether looking at normal interactions or disturbed interactions, the chronic quality of the process of mutual regulation generates moods in infants and children that have ongoing consequences for the way they function and approach the world. I think with infants and children we have not taken sufficient account of the child's mood. Though this oversimplifies, the child of the intrusive mother is likely to have a mood of anger whereas the child of a disengaged and withdrawn mother is likely to have a sad and depressed mood. These moods function to organize the child's sense of a situation in a way that can be unrelated to what is going on in the situation. One child may be angry or another child may be withdrawn, but there is no obvious reason why they are reacting that way until we begin to consider the mood that each child brings with him.

Clinically I think we need to carefully consider the child's experience with mutual regulation in order to try to figure out the mood that the child's regulatory experience might have generated. First, we need to figure out what mood the child is in. We need to make this assessment because moods have long-term consequences. Moods are continuously present and continuously organizing behavior. The most insidious of these effects is one of circular causality in which the operation of a negative mood further compromises the child's functioning and makes the mood even more negative. The angry child elicits anger and gets angrier. The sad child elicits withdrawal and gets sadder. The mood is self-amplifying and self-compromising. Of course, positive moods function in just the opposite fashion; they self-amplify and aid the child's coping with stress. Second, we need to see that moods give meaning to the world even though they are not cognitive, and we need to try to understand that meaning. The angry child has a state of consciousness in which his impelling certitude is that the world is threatening and angry, and the sad child is certain that the world is unavailable and sad. For infants and young children, moods are a primary and powerful way of making meaning, but moods also make meaning of the world for adolescents and adults. Third, we need to treat moods and engage in practices to shift it. Though I do not know what mood therapy might look like, I know that it will have to be a chronic process that over time will lead to the establishment of a new and more positive mood. Likely the therapeutic process can take advantage of the self-amplifying effects of mood in which a small shift can amplify further shifts. Whatever such mood therapy will look like, from my research on normal and abnormal development I have come to see moods as central to infants' and children's functioning, which makes it necessary to develop mood-focused therapies and to better understand development of moods.

The Stress of Normal Development and Interaction Leads to the Development of Resilience and Variation in Resilience

Michael Rutter (2006) has defined resilience as individual variation in the relative resistance to environmental risk experiences. Though many factors affect the development of resilience, I want to advance the hypothesis that behavioral and physiological resilience develops in part from the infant's and young child's experience coping with the inherent normal stress of social interaction. This hypothesis—let us call it the normal stress resilience hypothesis—is framed by a dynamic systems perspective on development of behavior and the brain and the processes that regulate development, in particular the interactive communicative engagements between infants/children and caretakers that regulate stressful experiences. In this chapter, I will present a dynamic systems perspective on development, the mutual regulation model (MRM) of child-caregiver communicative exchanges, and recent behavioral and physiological data from my laboratory on the nature of the interactive process. The normal stress resilience hypothesis begins with the idea from a dynamic systems perspective and supported by empirical evidence that stress inevitably and ubiquitously travels with normal developmental change and paradoxically stress also travels with the interactive regulatory processes that regulate the stress of developmental change (Tronick, 2003a, 2004). Second, based on developmental theory and empirical evidence, it argues that as a consequence of coping with normal developmental and regulatory stresses, children develop both new coping capacities and increase the effectiveness of their capacities for resisting normal and even nonnormal (traumatic) levels of stress. Furthermore, individual variation in children's relative resistance to stress, their resilience, is in part determined by the unique experience of success or failure of each child in coping with normal stressors (Tronick, 2003b).

Fortunately, everyday life provides plenty of small stressors. The mature organism has to cope with the stresses of garnering specifically fitted energy to maintain its current level of complexity and coherence. Finding and acquiring resources is one source of stress. In normal environments the stress is not overwhelming. In the developing young human, even more energy has to be obtained to permit growth. Development itself is messy and unpredictable and a source of stress. In normal development, the stress is not overwhelming and to meet these demands, humans have evolved a highly effective dyadic (and larger) mutually regulated system for garnering energy for both maintenance and growth and for coping with stress. It is a system that is effective in garnering more resources than individuals can gain on their own and for regulating stresses individuals would not be able to regulate on their own. Paradoxically, the interactive system in and of itself is inherently stressful but normally is not overwhelming. As a consequence of coping with these normal stressors, all individuals develop and grow their coping capacities, and their unique experience with stressors makes for differences in resilience.

COMPLEXITY AND DISSIPATION IN OPEN SYSTEMS

Prigogine (Stengers & Prigogine, 1997) stated that a primary principle governing the activities of open biological systems is that they must acquire energy from the environment to maintain and increase their coherence and complexity, their distance from entropy. The energy must have a particular form to be useful (i.e., what Sander, 1995, called fittedness for the organism). For example, though the food that prey eat has plenty of energy, if predators eat it, they cannot utilize the energy—it has no metabolic fittedness, no "meaning" for the animal. Complex systems are systems that have a hierarchical organization operating at multiple size and temporal scales, and they are information-rich with local contextual interactions. Complex systems exhibit emergent properties at different levels that are neither fixed nor chaotic. Self-organizing processes generate these emergent properties and lead to an increase in the complexity of the system, but there are always limits on a system's maximum complexity. Mature and healthy open biological systems are in a dynamic state of organization that approaches these limits, such that the mature organism attempts to garner energy to maintain and optimize its level of coherence and complexity. However, in mature systems emergence of new properties is limited and variation in the relative complexity among individuals is primarily related to their success or failure in gaining fitted energy. Further, for mature organisms, self-organized maintenance of complexity becomes increasingly demanding energetically and when there is a failure to achieve sufficient amounts of energy, the system begins to dissipate and lose complexity. In the extreme, there is a shift to a less complex state or phase. Baltes, (Lindenberger, and Staudinger 1998), for example, argue that aging is a losing fight against the dissipation of complexity within an already achieved state of organization and an inevitable shifting into a lower state of organization, such as death.

In contrast to the mature system, the developing organism is in a time-limited period in which the second law of thermodynamics is locally violated. For a developing organism, the developmental process is aimed at increasing and optimizing complexity. This aim has high energetic demands because the organism must garner sufficient energy to maintain its level of complexity and to make state and phase shifts to higher levels of complexity and coherence. Successful developing systems manifest emergent properties as well as directionality, that is, movement optimization of complexity and coherence. However, making stage and phase shifts is unpredictable and the shifts are potentially dissipative. Dissipation is possible because of how a complex system is organized and changes. The organism exists as a coherent assemblage of many interacting elements with both constitutive and integrative levels. At the point when a system is about to shift into a new emergent phase, it is close to a chaotic edge and the transition is inherently unstable. Failure to make the shift is dissipative, that is, there is loss of complexity and increase in entropy. In a typically developing system in a typical environment failure is unlikely, yet even in systems that are successfully increasing their complexity there is the necessity of disorganizing the extant state and assembling a new state. The disorganization of the extant state during a transforming transition is always associated with a loss of complexity and coherence. Thus there is a paradox of the emergence of the new: It is at one and the same time fulfilling the first principle of increasing complexity and at the same time threatening dissipation. The system is both optimizing and imperfecting itself and the outcome is unpredictable until it coalesces. As we shall see, these changes at both the macro level of development and the microregulatory level are stressful (Tronick, 2004).

Humans have developed an exceptional (though hardly unique) way to garner more energy from the environment and avoid dissipation by forming a dyadic regulatory system. The MRM attempts to describe the operation of this dyadic system (Gianino & Tronick, 1988). In the MRM there is a working together of two individuals such that they form an integrated dyadic system for acquiring energy. Though a dyadic system of course has limits, it is able to garner more resources and become more complex than either individual would be able to garner or to achieve on their own. As a component in a dyadic system, each individual can appropriate energy to itself and consequently increase its own complexity. The disorganization that comes with increasing complexity and associated dissipation is dyadically regulated by the microtemporal interplay of the child's self-organizing capacities and external organizing input provided by an adult (caretaker) system. The interplay of internal and external organizing capacities is regulated by a bidirectional communicative system that can be conceptualized as an interchange of signals and receptors, but for humans both the child and adult simultaneously and sequentially play both roles. This simultaneous and sequential shifting of roles makes the workings of this dyadic system astonishingly complicated. When the interplay or coordination of signaling and reception is adequate, the infant/child and adult/caretaker form a more complex dyadic system made up of two major component systems from which each appropriates fitted energy and as a consequence gains in complexity. But even when successful the process is stressful because there is a loss of complexity as the old organization is disassembled and because of the unpredictability of the outcome. Of course the stress is even greater when the system is unsuccessful and complexity is lost.

DEVELOPMENT AND ITS REGULATION

Development is one source of stress because it does not proceed smoothly but is characterized by periods of disorganization in one domain to new more coherent forms of organization within that domain (e.g., changes in motor systems for mobility; Brazelton, 1992; Heimann, 2003, see in particular chapters by Plooij and Trevarthen). Periods of disorganization are an inherent characteristic of developing self-organizing systems. They can be thought of as the "avalanches" of Per Bak's (1996) sand pile model from which new organization emerges from self-organizing processes at the edge of chaos. Adding to the complexity, the disorganization of one system disorganizes other systems. For example, the infant who is beginning to change from crawling to walking not only becomes disorganized motorically, but other systems such as sleep/activity cycling, emotions and mood, and even perception become disorganized as well. As with temperature regulation, a portion of the task of regulating this disorganization falls to the internal self-organizing resources of the infant. However, the infant's resources are inadequate to the task and must be supplemented by external regulation. Without external caretaker-provisioned regulation, regulatory resources development would be derailed (Figure 27.1). Under normal circumstances the formation of a dyadic regulatory system, a combination of

FIGURE 27.1. Inability to regulate disorganization can lead to developmental derailment. (From Tronick, 1996)

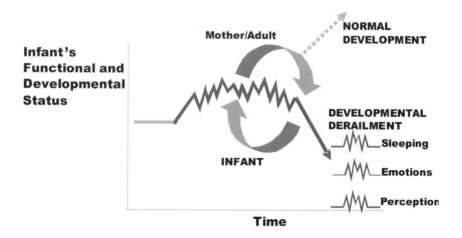

internal and external processes, is adequate to meet the regulatory demands and development moves forward. However, when the dyadic system fails, when internal and external resources are inadequate, development may be seriously disrupted. Disorganization increases and coherence and complexity are lost. Note, however, a critical feature of the model is that disorganization is part of the normal process. It is necessary for the emergence of something new and for an increase of complexity and coherence — disorganization is the wellspring of change and the new. But again, change is costly.

DYADIC REGULATION: THE WORKINGS OF THE MICROTEMPORAL REGULATORY PROCESS

What is the structure of the microtemporal communicative processes that in the accumulation of moment-by-moment interchanges regulate development and lead to the growth of complexity? The development of walking takes months, but it is worked on during millions of moment-by-moment exchanges. To understand mutual regulation, I want to start with an example far from macrodevelopmental processes as well as the issue of resilience — infant temperature regulation. I choose this example because it illustrates the dyadic regulatory process for a psychobiological state that is most typically seen solely as a self-organized process.

Temperature regulation is a process governed by a simple rule: Maintain homeothermic status and it leads to complex system behavior (Freeman, 2000). Fulfilling the rule is complicated and this regulatory system is hierarchically organized with a multitude of subsystems from metabolic processes to behavioral systems. It is a system that operates to maintain equilibrium, and though it changes with development (e.g., the loss of brown fat) and is influenced by environmental factors (e.g., the increase in capillary networks in the hand in cold environments) its change and development is limited compared to other psychobiological systems (e.g., respiratory systems, motor systems, or coping systems). Infants have self-organizing capacities to upregulate a below-normal temperature, such as increasing their activity level, preferentially metabolizing high-energy brown fat, or moving into less energetic behavioral states (e.g., sleep). But these self-organized capacities are limited and immature and will eventually fail, an especially quick event for infants with their high surface-to-volume ratio. Such failure is obviously stressful. However, though Claude Bernard saw temperature regulation as a within-individual process, it is not. It is a dyadic process.

Infants' self-organized regulatory capacities for operating on temperature control are supplemented by external regulatory input by caregivers that is specifically fitted to overcome the infant's limitations (Hofer, 1984). For example, caregivers place infants against their chests and share their body heat with their infants, which in turn reduces their infants' surface heat loss. This dyadic regulatory process itself is guided by communicative signals from the infant. These communicative signals convey the state of the infant to a receptive caregiver.

When done successfully, the input provided by the adult is fitted (meaningful) to the infant's temperature regulatory system and the system becomes dyadic and more coherently organized than the infant would be on his or her own.

A major consequence for the developing organism of the formation of a dyadic system is that the capacity or effectiveness of its self-organized regulatory capacities actually will increase such that later in development the infant will be able to self-regulate temperature without as much external regulatory scaffolding. One reason for the increase is because the energetic demands on the infant are reduced and the saved energy can be channeled into the growth of regulatory capacity. This increase in the self-organizing capacity of the individual by its participation in a dyadic regulatory system is not unlike Vygotsky's (1967) concept of the zone of proximal development. By contrast, were the formation of a dyadic system to fail, the infant would lose control of his temperature, and his homeostatic state would dissipate. When the failure is chronic, the infant's self-regulatory capacities might maintain themselves at a cost to other systems, but there would be no energy for growth of regulatory capacity. The system would lose complexity and coherence and eventually move to a less complex state of organization. Keeping this dyadic model of temperature in mind, let's examine the process of development and the microtemporal dyadic communicative system that regulates it.

The perspective is derived based on the MRM and empirical work examining the organization of the regulatory process (Beebe & Lachmann, 1998; Beeghly & Tronick, 1994; Gianino & Tronick, 1988). The MRM stipulates that caregivers/mothers and infants/children are linked subsystems of a dyadic system and each component, infant and caregiver/mother, regulates disorganization and its costs by a bidirectional process of behavioral and expressive signaling and receiving. However, the communicative process between the developing human and the adult is inherently imperfect, unstable, and unpredictable. The infant's signals to the caregiver may vary from one day to another. The caregiver's reception of them and of course the caregiver's input to the infant also varies. Moreover, the infant signals that worked one time may not work the next time, and the same is true for the caregiver's response. Thus the mutual regulatory process is "messy" and energetically costly. Nonetheless, over time it is likely that the activities that work more often will become more and more a part of the workings of the dyadic regulatory process. The process will become less costly and energy will be freed up for growing self-organized regulatory processes and increasing self-system complexity.

THE FACE-TO-FACE STILL-FACE PARADIGM: A SOCIAL STRESSOR ON BEHAVIOR AND PHYSIOLOGY

To study the dyadic microregulatory process, I developed the the face-to-face still-face paradigm (FFSF; Tronick, Als, Adamson, Wise, & Brazelton, 1978).

The FFSF confronts the young infant with three interactive contexts: (1) an episode of "normal" face-to-face social interaction with a caregiver (typically the mother), during which the caregiver is asked to play with the infant; followed by (2) a still-face (SF) episode, during which the caregiver is instructed to keep an unresponsive poker face and not smile, touch, or talk to the baby; followed by (3) a reunion episode, during which the caregiver and infant resume face-to-face social interaction. Each episode typically lasts 2 minutes. The paradigm has primarily been used with infants ranging in age from 2 to 15 months, with a mean age of 5.2 months (Adamson & Frick, 2003), but a modified form has also been used with 30-month-olds and even with adults.

The FFSF paradigm demonstrates the costliness of the stress of an experimental disruption of the mutual regulatory process, and as I will show it serves as model for the stress inherent in normal interactions. The FFSF exposes infants to a unique social-emotional stressor (maternal SF) that differs from inanimate stressors as well as typical forms of social interaction and elicits well-documented emotional reactions and stress in infants. Over the past 25 years, hundreds of infants have been videotaped in the FFSF paradigm (Tronick, Als, et al., 1978). The FFSF has proven to be a fruitful methodological tool for evaluating young infants' ability to cope with an interactive perturbation and emotional stressor (caregiver SF; Adamson & Frick, 2003; Cole, Martin, & Dennis, 2004; Stack & Muir, 1990; Tronick, 1989, 2001; Tronick, Als, et al., 1978; Weinberg & Tronick, 1996).

Infants typically respond to the SF with what Adamson and Frick have labeled the still-face effect (Adamson & Frick, 2003). In study after study, infants respond with a signature decrease in positive affect and an increase in negative affect and gaze aversion (Figure 27.2; Stack & Muir, 1990; Toda & Fogel, 1993; Weinberg & Tronick, 1996). In studies using microanalytic signal scoring systems, infants have additionally been shown to react to the SF with an increase in visual scanning, pick-me-up gestures, distancing behavior such as twisting and turning in their seat, and autonomic stress indicators such as spitting up (Kogan & Carter, 1996; Rosenblum, McDonough, Muzik, Miller, & Sameroff, 2002; Toda & Fogel, 1993; Weinberg & Tronick, 1996; Weinberg, Tronick, Cohn, & Olson, 1999). The still-face effect is seen with infants and toddlers over a wide age range. Gender differences have been found in young infants' reactions to the FFSF. For instance, in a study from our lab (Weinberg et al., 1999), 6-month-old male infants had more difficulty than female infants in maintaining affective regulation during the FFSF.

Infants' neurophysiological reactions also index the stressfulness of the FFSF. Whereas heart rate reflects degree of physiological arousal, respiratory sinus arrhythmia (RSA) reflects neural regulation of the heart via the vagal nerve and is measured in terms of an index of cardiac activity related to respiratory function that is mediated by the parasympathetic nervous system (Moore & Calkins, 2004). Changes in RSA reflect a functional relation between the central nervous system and the heart as mediated by the vagus

FIGURE 27.2. Infants respond to the still-face with gaze aversion, self-co in this case, a loss of postural control.

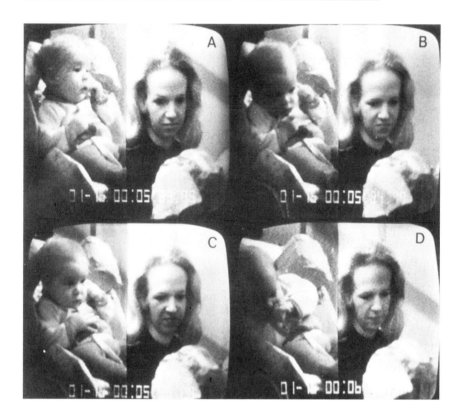

(Berntson, Hart, & Sarter, 1997; Porges, 1995) and are thought to serve an important regulatory function in human social engagement (Porges, 1995, 2001). The regulation of vagal control of the heart is associated with the ability to engage and disengage with people and objects in one's environment. High RSA measured at rest reflects a baseline of neural integrity and a readiness to respond to social engagement or the environment. Prior research (Calkins, 1997; Donzella, Gunnar, Krueger, & Alwin, 2000; Doussard-Roosevelt, Montgomery, & Porges, 2003; Porges, Doussard-Roosevelt, Portales, & Suess, 1994) has shown that higher RSA measured at rest is related to less negative behavior and less difficult temperament in infants and preschoolers (Calkins, 1997; Huffman et al., 1998; Porges et al., 1994). Moreover, a decrease in RSA is thought to reflect an individual's active coping in reaction to stressors or an increase in attention to (or engagement with) the environment. For instance, greater suppression of RSA during challenging situations is related to better state regulation, greater self-soothing, more attentional control, and greater capacity for social engagement (Calkins, 1997). In contrast, a deficit in the ability to suppress RSA in challenging contexts may be related to a lack of behavioral and emotional control (DeGangi, DiPietro, Porges, & Greenspan, 1991; Porges, Doussard-Roosevelt, Portales, & Greenspan, 1996). In general, the research is consistent with a view that RSA is an index of the manner in which an individual actively engages with the environment and regulates emotion and behavior in the face of environmental challenge (Bornstein & Suess, 2000; Porges, 1995, 2003; Richards, 1987).

Only a few studies have evaluated changes in infants' RSA during the FFSF. In a prior study in our lab using the FFSF with 6-month-olds (Weinberg & Tronick, 1996), infants' RSA dropped significantly during the SF episode compared to the first play episode, and recovered to baseline levels in the reunion episode. In my laboratory, Ham (Ham & Tronick, 2006) has recently replicated these findings of a suppression of RSA to the stress of the SF. Similar findings were reported in a study evaluating stranger-infant interaction using a modified version of the FFSF (Bazhenova, Plonskaia, & Porges, 2001). Using a version of the FFSF paradigm, Haley and Stansbury, (2003) found an increase in infants' heart rate during each SF episode (RSA was not evaluated). In a study of 3-month-olds, Moore and Calkins (2004; Moore, Cohn, & Campbell, 2001) investigated changes in infants' RSA, heart rate, and behavioral reactivity during the FFSF and found that infants exhibited decreased RSA and increased heart rate and negative affect during the SF episode, indicating physiological regulation of distress. Of note, individual differences in RSA reactivity were also observed. Infants who did not suppress RSA in the SF evidenced less positive affect, higher reactivity, and lower RSA during the play and reunion episodes with their mothers.

In an innovative and unique aspect of his study, Ham (Ham & Tronick, 2006) has successfully utilized skin conductance with infants as a measure of the activation of the sympathetic nervous system to the FFSF paradigm. This measure had long been thought not to be usable with infants. Ham developed sensors for use with infants that could be bound to the soles of their feet, eliminating much of the movement artifact, and with modern computer technology and programming was able to get clean and stimulus-responsive measures. The development of this technique is an important contribution because it provides a pure measure of sympathetic nervous system control and another window into the functioning of the infant nervous system. Ham found that skin conductance increased from the first play episode to the SF episode and that it further increased in the reunion play episode. These findings substantiate the arousing and stressful effect of the SF as well as the cost of recovering from it in the subsequent normal play episode. These findings parallel behavioral findings indicating that infants' arousal (e.g., levels of negative affect) is higher in the reunion episode than in the first play episode.

In another methodological advance, Ham was also able to simultaneously record RSA and skin conductance from the mothers during the FFSF episode.

As was the case for the infants, the mothers' reactions demonstrated the ٥٤ ful nature of the SF to them. Furthermore, in results similar to the relations found between the behavioral signals of infants and mothers during the FFSF, there were relations between infant and maternal physiological reactions. For example, there were significant positive relations between infant and mother skin conductance, and positive relations between infant heart rate and maternal skin conductance, and infant RSA and maternal heart rate. These results are suggestive of mutual regulation of physiology by infants and mothers not unlike the relations seen in their behavior or the relations seen in animal studies.

The reactivity of the hypothalamic-pituitary axis (HPA) as measured by the level of glucocorticoids also has been examined using the FFSF paradigm (Haley & Stansbury, 2003; Lewis & Ramsay, 2005). As is the view based on animal work (de Quervain, Roozendaal, & McGaugh, 1998; Lupien et al., 2005; McEwen & Sapolsky, 1995), HPA activity in humans is viewed as a measure of the stress response as well as a regulator of emotional and social behavior. For example, Gunnar et al. (Stansbury & Gunnar, 1994; White, Gunnar, Larson, Donzella, & Barr, 2000) utilized pre- and postsalivary cortisol reactions as a measure of infant stress and found that stressful events such as inoculations lead to an elevation in infants' cortisol levels. Though the relation between cortisol response and stress is now viewed as more complicated than originally thought, peak cortisol response is still seen as an indicator of physiological reactivity (Goldberg et al., 2003). In a review of the relation between acute stress and cortisol reactivity in adults and older children, Dickerson and Kemeny (2004) concluded that perceived uncontrollable social threats to the self are strongly predictive of cortisol reactivity. Although this interpretation is based on the adult and older child literature, it theoretically could be applied to infants confronting the SF, which is an uncontrollable and possibly threatening event.

Several recent studies have examined infants' cortisol reactivity during the FFSF. Ramsey and Lewis (Lewis & Ramsay, 2005; Ramsay & Lewis, 2003) found a significant but modest increase in cortisol level in 6-month-old infants following exposure to the SF. However, they found no significant association between peak cortisol response and response dampening or behavioral reactivity. In a second study, Lewis and Ramsey (2005) found that peak cortisol response was related to infants' expressions of sadness but not anger. Haley and Stansbury (2003) evaluated 5- to 6-month-olds' behavior, heart rate, and cortisol reactivity during a modified FFSF, in which infants were exposed to two SF and two reunion episodes to increase the stress level and likelihood of a cortisol response. Infants exhibited a significant increase in heart rate and cortisol response. The different measures of reactivity were not highly correlated, although higher baseline cortisol was positively correlated with more infant negative affect during the SF. Others have also reported a lack of tight coupling among behavioral and physiological reactivity measures during infancy (Buss et al., 2003; Gunnar, Mangelsdorf, Larson, & Hertsgaard, 1989; Lewis & Ramsay, 2005). Moreover, the level of cortisol change reported in these studies was relatively modest, especially in comparison to the cortisol changes observed in the animal literature, which shows an inverted U-shaped relation between cortisol and memory (McGaugh, 2004; Roozendaal, Quirarte, & McGaugh, 1997). In sum, the SF demonstrates that breaking the mutual regulatory process is a powerful psychobiological and behavioral stressor and that the infant has self-organized capacities for coping with it.

THE EFFECTS OF REPARATION
ON DEVELOPMENT

The SF is an experimental paradigm and though it may be thought of as unnatural, a lack of regulatory reception signaling between mother and child often occurs (e.g., a lack of response to the infant when the adult is driving in a car, talking on a phone, or being out of proximity to the child), suggesting that the infant is often exposed to stressful experience. More important, the FFSF paradigm actually serves as a model for normal interactions and the stress that accompanies them. The FFSF paradigm has an experimentally induced miscoordination or mismatch in the interaction of the mother/adult and infant (i.e., the infant attempting to interact and the mother "refusing") and their reestablishment of coordination in the reunion play. The mismatch and match of the FFSF has a time course of minutes but in our research on normal face-to-face and play interactions we have a pattern of matching and mismatching of behavior, affect, and communicative expressions at the microtemporal level (10ths of a second) of the mutual regulatory process. These mismatches are inherent to the interaction because of: (1) the speed at which signals are emitted (three or four times per second); (2) the demands on infants' and adults' receptor apparatus to detect and decode the signals; (3) the response time demands, again on the order of 10ths of a second; (4) the occurrence of miscues; (5) the likelihood of missed signals given their rate of occurrence; and (6) the mismatching of intentions between the interactants and changes in their intentions as affected by their ongoing interactive state (Cohn & Elmore, 1988; Cohn, Krafchuk, Ricks, Winn, & Tronick, 1985; Cohn & Tronick, 1987, 1988; Tronick, Krafchuk, Ricks, Cohn, & Winn, 1985). Add to these reasons the fact that the child has limited and immature regulatory, behavioral, and attentional capacities and the likelihood of mismatches and miscoordinations becomes quite high. In our studies we have found that periods of mismatching make up as much as 70% or 80% of the interaction (Tronick & Gianino, 1986a).

Importantly, using the SF as a model, the microtemporal mismatches are microstressors and are associated with negative affect. By contrast, matching states are associated with positive affect, though at high intensity they too can be stressful. The level of stress associated with mismatches is of course small compared to the stress induced by the SF and it is also of shorter duration. However, these mismatches and microstressors occur frequently, on the order of 4 to 10 times per minute. The interaction moves from matching to mismatching states and

FIGURE 27.3. Moving from matching to mismatching states generates stress that is resolved by the reparation back to matching states. (From Tronick, 2006)

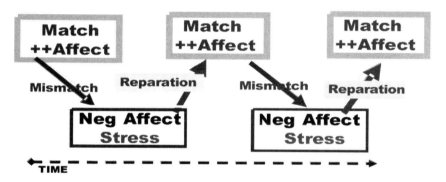

PROCESS OF REPARATION
IN RESOLVING STRESS OF NORMAL
INTERACTIONS

back again; that is, from positive affect nonstressful microstates to negative affect stressful microstates at a very high rate. I have labeled the change from a mismatching to a matching state a repair and the process one of reparation, because it leads to a change of negative to positive affect and a reduction in stress (Figure 27.3; Tronick & Cohn, 1989). A metaphor is to think of dancing with lots of miscoordinations such as stepping on toes, but the dancers are wearing socks and they quickly get off each other's feet. The interaction is stressful, but in successful interactions the stress from mismatches, miscommunications, and misattunements are quickly repaired and over time matches again become miscoordinated and stressful, and again they are repaired. Critically, the process of mismatch and stress, reparation and the reduction of stress literally occurs thousands of times in the course of a day and millions of times over the course of the year such that as the microeffects of matches, mismatches, and reparation accumulate, they have profound effects.

THE INDUCTION OF RESILIENCE
AND INDIVIDUAL DIFFERENCES

How does the experience in normal interactions of matching and mismatching and reparation lead to resilience? And how is individual variation in resilience induced? The normal interactive stress hypothesis is that the reparation of interactive mismatches and associated stress has a powerful effect on inducing effect on resilience (capacity to regulate or resist stress) and that the reparation process helps shape individual differences in resilience (Tronick &

Weinberg, 1997). In interactions characterized by normal rates of reparation, the infant learns which communicative strategies are effective in producing reparation and consequently effective in reducing stress. The infant also learns new self-organized ways of coping that are effective in reducing that stress, for example, averting gaze from a stressor or engaging in self-comforting behaviors. With the experiential accumulation of successful reparations, and the attendant transformation of negative affect and stress into positive affect, the infant establishes a robust positive affective core (Emde, Kligman, Reich, & Wade, 1978; Gianino & Tronick, 1988). A positive affective core biases experience by increasing the likelihood that an event is experienced as positive rather than as negative and stressful; in other words, an optimistic implicit attitude about events. Importantly, the infant also learns that he or she has control over social interactions. Specifically, the infant develops a representation of himself or herself as effective, and of his or her interactions as positive and reparable. He or she also learns that the caretaker is a reliable and trustworthy regulatory partner. These representations are crucial for the development of a sense of self that has coherence, continuity, and agency and for the development of stable and secure relationships, all of which add to resilience (Tronick, 1980; Tronick, Cohn, & Shea, 1986). Thus a child who has a normal range of interactive experience develops robust resources and resilience for confronting stressors and effectively coping with them. By contrast, we know that infant animals and humans who have confronted overwhelming stress early in development fail to develop normally. And while we refer to these situations with a single word such as *deprivation*, the effect actually emerges from millions of reiterated moments in which reparation fails to resolve the stress.

Research supports the hypothesis that individual differences in resilience in part emerge from different experiences with stress and reparation at the microtemporal level. Research has demonstrated short- and long-term stability in infants' reactions to the SF. Tronick and Gianino (1986a) found significant stability across a 10-day period in infant signaling, attention, and self-comforting at 6 months of age. More recently, Tronick, Weinberg, Beeghly, and Olson (2003) found short-term stability in 6-month-old infants' behavior between the administrations of the FFSF 2 weeks apart. The proportion of time infants spent averting from the mother, looking at objects, socially attending to the mother, and playing with the mother were significantly correlated over time. Moore et al. (2001) evaluated stability and change in infants' negative and positive affect and gaze away from the mother in response to the FFSF at 2, 4, and 6 months. Although there was no stability in infant positive affect, there were stable individual differences in negative affect from 4 to 6 months and in gazing away from 2 to 4 months and from 4 to 6 months. Similarly, Shapiro, Fagen, Prigot, Carroll, and Shalan (1998) evaluated stability and change in the FFSF from 3 to 6 months. They found cross-time stability in infants' expression of interest and joy and in prepointing behaviors. In addition, Rosenblum and Muzik

(2004) reported stability in infants' positive and negative affective responses during the SF from 7 to 15 months of age.

Neurophysiological measures have been found to be stable and related to interactive experiences. In typically developing children, measures of vagal tone (VT) exhibit small to moderate levels of stability across contexts and over time during infancy and early childhood (Bazhenova et al., 2001; Bornstein & Suess, 2000; Doussard-Roosevelt et al., 2003; Doussard-Roosevelt, McClenny, & Porges, 2001; El-Sheikh, 2005; Gunnar, Porter, Wolf, Rigatuso, & Larson, 1995; Porges, 1992; Porges, Doussard-Roosevelt, Stifter, McClenny, & Riniolo, 1999; Stifter & Fox, 1990; Stifter, Fox, & Porges, 1989). Individual differences in RSA have been reported, which are associated with observations of infants' negative behavior during challenging tasks, although the correlations between infants' physiological and behavioral responses are typically not high (Calkins, Dedmon, Gill, Lomax, & Johnson, 2002; Calkins & Keane, 2004; El-Sheikh, 2005). In a study of 3-month-olds, Moore and Calkins (2004; Moore et al., 2001) investigated changes in infants' VT, heart rate, and behavioral reactivity during the FFSF. They found individual differences in RSA reactivity. Infants who did not suppress RSA in the SF evidenced less positive affect, higher reactivity, and lower RSA during the play and reunion episodes with their mothers. Calkins and Keane (2004) found that children who displayed a pattern of stable and high RSA suppression during challenging tasks from 2 to 4 years of age were less emotionally negative and had fewer behavior problems and better social skills than other children. Investigators have also observed that children also exhibit decreased RSA during attention-demanding activities indexing individual differences in how an individual actively engages with the environment and regulates emotion and behavior in the face of environmental challenge (Bornstein & Suess, 2000; Porges, 1995, 2003; Richards, 1987). Gunnar et al. (1995) found that newborns' RSA measures were related to their distress at limitations (frustration) at 6 months of age, as assessed via maternal report. In a study examining the relation between RSA and later compliance in 5-, 10-, and 18- month-old infants, Stifter et al. (1989; Stifter & Jain, 1996) found that the younger infants' RSA was related to their later noncompliance at 18 months. In a second study using a modified stranger-infant FFSF procedure with 5- to 6-month-olds (Bazhenova et al., 2001), infants' VT and behavioral responses were correlated across different episodes of the FFSF.

There are also individual differences in cortisol reactivity. Ramsey and Lewis (2003) collected saliva samples from 33 infants at 2, 4, 6, and 18 months of age before, immediately after, and 20 minutes after routine inoculations. When infants were divided into low, moderate, and high reactor groups, significant correlations were found, indicating that infants within groups retained their relative rank ordering in reactivity from 6 to 18 months of age. Nachmias and colleagues (Nachmias, Gunnar, Mangelsdorf, Parritz, & Buss, 1996) observed 18-month-olds in two moderately stressful procedures administered one week apart. Significant cross-age correlations were found between the baseline levels

and the peak responses. Goldberg et al. (2003) examined the stability of cortisol reactivity 1 week apart in 12- to 18-month-old infants. The stressors used
were Ainsworth's strange situation and a coping task in which three novel
events were presented to the infant (e.g., a noisy clown). Baseline levels of cortisol were collected at home, and in the lab, cortisol was assessed repeatedly
(20 to 40 minutes) after exposure to the stressors. Significant stability was found
for the cortisol measures made within each stressful context. In a study of low-
income preschoolers (Blair, Granger, & Razza, 2005), multiple measures of
cortisol made on the same day were significantly correlated. Taken together,
these findings indicate that infants' cortisol response to stressors shows moderate short-term stability.

These findings of stability in infants' behavioral and physiological reaction to
the SF help us to understand the findings on the development of infants of
depressed mothers and how a lack of reparation affects resilience (Tronick &
Field, 1986). Infants of depressed mothers experience fewer interactive reparations and can be under chronic stress. These infants develop self-organized patterns of coping that include looking away during interactions and higher levels
of self-comforting to help reduce stress, but the cost is evident in higher levels
of negative affect and less engagement with the inanimate environment. Their
negative mood and disengagement compromise their interactions with others
and their cognitive development with the consequence of compromising their
development and making them less resilient. Further, we have found that infant
sons of depressed mothers are more stressed by their interactions with their
mothers than are infant daughters (Weinberg & Olson, 1995). These findings
make sense given our studies showing that infant boys of clinically normal mothers are more stressed by the SF than are infant girls. Thus the coping of all
infants is affected by the chronic moment-by-moment stress of their interactions
with their depressed mothers and a lack of reparation, with the boys being more
stressed because they have less ability in general to self-regulate stress compared
to girls. We believe that this inability to self-regulate continues to compromise
boys' as contrasted to girls' experience with reparation, which results in more
disorganized behavior and coping by boys throughout development.

There is a well-established relation between infants' early experience and
their coping and resilience to challenges. Much of this literature is about the
quality of infants' and young children's attachment relationship. The attachment relation, whether secure, ambivalent, avoidant, or disorganized, can be
viewed as indicating the ways in which young children cope with stress, in particular the stress of separation from their primary caregiver (i.e., mother). The
secure child, for example, has multiple strategies for dealing with stress, whereas
the disorganized child is overwhelmed by stress. In clinically normative studies, infants' reactions to the SF as well as to the normal FF interactions are
predictive of infants' security of attachment. The infants' reactions to the SF
are thought to index infants' accumulated experience with their mothers. For
example, infants who repeatedly solicit their mother's attention during the SF

and are positive during the normal interaction have learned to trust their mother and to expect positive interactions with her. Supporting this interpretation, Fuertes et al. (2006) found that the quality of the mothers' reactions to their infants during play as well as the infants' reactions to the SF were predictive of infants' attachment security. There is also a large literature demonstrating the relation between early maternal sensitivity in caretaking and infants' coping with separation from the mother. Indeed it is widely accepted that sensitive caretaking is a primary factor affecting the quality of an infant's attachment to the mother. Importantly, research by Beebe and colleagues (Jaffe, Beebe, Feldstein, Crown, & Jasnow, 2001) and by Belsky (1999) and his colleagues demonstrates that sensitivity in the midrange is most predictive of infant secure attachments. Midrange sensitivity is characterized by a pattern of mismatching and reparation back to matching. In contrast, high and low sensitivity index a lack of reparation albeit in different ways: low sensitivity reflects a lack of reparation of long-duration mismatches, and high sensitivity reflects vigilance, matching that is too long with little opportunity for reparation. Infants' experience of midrange sensitivity develops ways of coping with the stress of separation, whereas infants experiencing low sensitivity are constantly overwhelmed by stress and fail to develop ways of coping, and the high-sensitivity infants do not confront a sufficient amount of stress to develop their own resources, but end up relying on parental regulation to cope with stress. Thus normal interactive experience with mismatching, reparation, and stress have a strong relation to individual variation in the quality of infants' capacity for coping with stress and their resilience in the face of stress. Of course, when the infant is resilient the mother has a better chance to find the midrange because it is wider than that of a vulnerable infant whose midrange is narrow, forcing the mother into one extreme or the other.

CONCLUDING POINTS

The mutual regulation model and the normal interactive stress hypothesis argue that normal and typical experience with reparation, matching, and mismatching has a profound effect on the development of coping and individual differences in resilience in the face of stress. The effects are not only behavioral but neurophysiological, as indicated by the research on the sympathetic, parasympathetic, and HPA systems. These systems are not tightly linked, which allows for adaptive flexibility in the face of stress (e.g., gaze aversion is a fast and less costly way of coping with stress than is a sympathetic nervous system activation), but all of these systems are affected by moment-to-moment events and experience. Though the literature is far too great to be summarized here, this normal interactive stress hypothesis is strongly supported by the animal research on the effects of stress on the development of brain and behavior (see Lupien & McEwen, 1997; McGaugh, 2000; Roozendaal et al., 1997; Smythe, McCormick, & Meaney, 1996).

I believe that taking a normal interactive stress perspective on many animal experiments that manipulate the environment (e.g., avoidance conditioning, handling, environmental impoverishment or enrichment) can give us a better understanding of how stress has its long-term effects. Like the SF, many of the manipulations used in animal work serve to highlight the stress that is inherent, normal, and typical in the animal's environment. The SF in humans highlights the match-mismatch-reparation process of normal interactions. Rats that are handled more by humans develop coping capacities, not because handling by humans is special but because the normal contact they have with other conspecifics, which is mimicked by human handling, is the way they normally develop coping and resilience. When the dominance hierarchy of a monkey troop is manipulated, individual animals have to cope with the change, but it has its effects not because it is a dramatic manipulation but because the manipulation mimics the daily moment-by-moment experience of animals coping with dominance, and that experience is one way in which they develop coping and resilience.

By contrast to normal stress manipulations, manipulations that are traumatic, ones that exceed the individual's capacity for coping, highlight the limits of the system. Such traumatic experiences do not lead to resilience. Indeed, such trauma can overwhelm and debilitate the system, similar to the way in which the normally protective shock response to a physical injury can go out of control and lead to death. However, individuals vary in what is or is not experienced as traumatic based on their experience with levels of stress that they have been able to cope with. The adage that what doesn't kill you makes you stronger likely is not true. Rather, more likely is the hypothesis that a whole lot of small well-coped-with stressors makes you more resilient and leads to growth in coping and variations in resilience. Such is the value of the normal stressful messiness of life.

PART V

DYADIC EXPANSION OF CONSCIOUSNESS AND MEANING MAKING

CHAPTER 28

Infant Responses to Impending Collision: Optical and Real

The perception of an approaching object is of obvious significance to an organism. The approach is a complex spatiotemporal event. To apprehend its significance, the organism must detect object qualities, including relative distance and direction of approach, within a brief period of time. Moreover, if this apprehension is to occur more than once, the organism must act in a fashion appropriate to the event. T. G. R. Bower (personal communication, 1971) found that infants respond to symmetrically looming shadows or to real approaching objects with an integrated response that consists of an initial widening of the eyes, a head withdrawal, and a raising of the arms. In addition, the stimulus presentation, particularly in the case of the real object, often produces upset and crying in the infants. Just as other species avoid looming shadows (Schiff, 1965) or the deep side of a visual cliff (Gibson & Walk, 1960), the infant's response reflects a capacity to respond appropriately to the distal stimulus.

The purpose of this research was to specify further the infant's initial perceptual capacities. The displacement of an object is specified optically by the transformation of a bounded segment of the optic array (Gibson, 1961). The solidity and shape of the object are specified by the closed contour and by transformations of it that produce kinetic depth (Gibson, 1961; Wallach & O'Connell, 1953). The path of approach is specified by the symmetrics or asymmetrics of an expanding bounded segment, and withdrawal is specified by its minification. In addition, collision is specified when the bounded segment fills 180° of the frontal visual field. The psychophysics of the infant's capacities requires the assessment of its response to these higher order, event-specifying stimuli.

Supported by Grant 12623 from the National Institutes of Mental Health and Grant 03049 from the National Institute of Child Health and Human Development to Harvard University, Center for Cognitive Studies.

FIGURE 28.1. Shadow-casting apparatus.

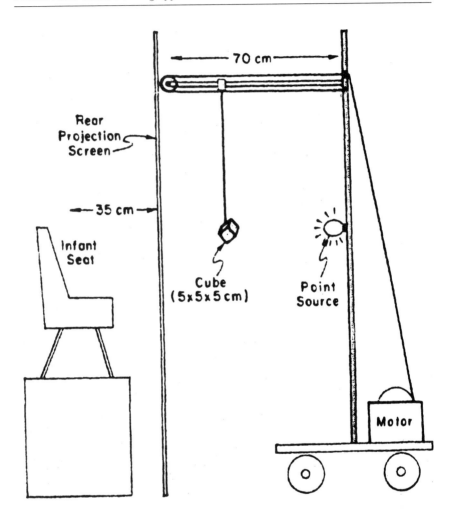

To make this assessment with shadow-casting techniques, 24 infants (8 infants, 2 to 5 weeks of age; 8 infants, 5 to 8 weeks of age; and 8 infants, 8 to 11 weeks of age) served as subjects. The apparatus (see Figure 28.1) consisted of a 100-watt concentrated point-source lamp mounted at the end and below a 70-cm track. A Styrofoam cube (5 × 5 × 5 cm) was attached to a 51-cm rod suspended from the track. A motor-operated pulley system moved the rod along the track at a constant speed of 12 cm per second. A second motor permitted rotation of the rod at a speed of one-half revolution per second. In addition, the point source could be displaced laterally relative to the track, so that the object moved either directly toward it or off to one side.

The shadow caster was placed on one side of a rear projection screen (1.8 × 1.8 m). The infant was seated approximately 35 cm away from the opposite side of the screen in an infant chair. The chair had no head support or waistband and thus allowed free head, arm, and leg movements; but the infant was supported by an adult holding him around the waist. To the left of the infant, a television camera and microphone recorded the infant's responses to the various displays. The room itself was darkened except for the light from the point source, light from an overhead bulb, and light from a lamp on the floor to the infant's left. This combination of lights was intense enough for efficient operation of the television camera but was dim enough not to interfere with the clarity of the shadow transformations.

Movement of the static cube toward the point source (flat hit) produced a symmetrical growth in the shadow and the visual experience of an approaching object for an adult observer. Shifting the point source laterally produced an asymmetrically growing shadow that appeared to be an object coming toward an observer but on a miss path (flat miss). Movement of the cube away from the point source after an approach appeared to be an object moving away from the observer (flat recession). Rotation of the cube in front of the point source prior to and during its movement along the track resulted in the visual experience of a solid object. The rotating cube went through the same sequence as the static cube; that is, it was driven directly toward the point source (solid hit), toward the laterally shifted point source (solid miss), and away from the point source (solid recession).

A trial consisted of an approach followed by a withdrawal of the object from the point source. Two of the infants in each age group started with one of the four possible conditions. After three trials, if they were still alert and attentive, they continued through the other three conditions in a predetermined Latin square order.

In a second experiment, seven infants 3 to 6 weeks of age were exposed to a 30 × 30 cm object approaching on a collision or miss path (Figure 28.2). Its rate of approach was 17 cm per second. The object was hung from the shadow-casting apparatus and displayed in a three-sided visual corridor made of bamboo curtains. Its run was 75 cm in length and ended about 15 cm in front of the infant. The object was not rotated but remained frontal parallel to the infant seated at the end of the run, in the same fashion as in the shadow-casting procedure. Infants started with either hit or miss sequences in a balanced design across subjects. Three trials of each sequence were again attempted, and a videotape recording was made of the sessions.

Because the form of the infant's response is fundamental to the experiment, a qualitative description will be given before the quantitative results. Infants generally began the session slumped in the chair with their arms down. During a hit sequence, the infant moved his head back and away from the screen and brought his arms toward his face. This was the full avoidance response. Sometimes the infant finished by facing toward the ceiling. The coming back

FIGURE 28.2. Real object apparatus.

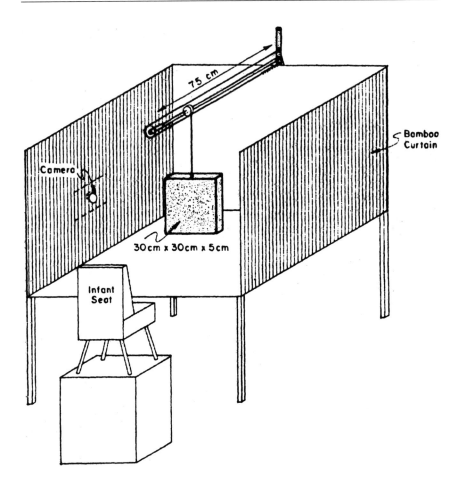

of the head was usually observed only after the shadow had begun to fill the field or when the object came close. It was never observed before the transformation began. The person holding the infant often reported a stiffening of the infant's body during looming phases, followed by a relaxation during the recession phase. The response during the miss trials was dramatically different. There was commonly a slow turning of the head and eyes along the path of the shadow or object. The arms tended to come up, but the head did not come back as it did in hit trials, nor did the infant stiffen. Strikingly, visitors with no knowledge of the stimulus conditions, who observed the tapes, commented that the baby seemed to be either avoiding or following something in the respective conditions.

For the quantitative analysis, counts were made of the movement of the head backward, of the arms upward, and of the head tracking to the side; counts were also made of fussing (primarily vocalizations, from low cries to wailing). Each of these events was scored and analyzed separately, and a combined measure of two out of three components produced a tracking or upset index. The qualitative results support the qualitative descriptions.

In the shadow-casting experiment, hit and miss trials were significantly different ($x^2 = 16.8$, $df = 1$, $p < .001$) for the combined upset measure. The difference was accounted for by a significant difference between the movement of the head (movement backward versus tracking) in the two conditions ($x^2 = 82$, $df = 1$, $p < .001$). There were no differences in any of the measures for the different age groups or for the solid as compared with the flat sequences. The recession trials did not produce the above components at all. The results in the case of the real object were similar. Hit versus miss was significantly different on the combined upset measures (Fisher exact test, $p = .003$), and the difference was accounted for by the head movement measure.

The qualitative and quantitative results support the interpretation that infants can detect object qualities of direction and relative depth of approach and collision for both real objects and their optical equivalent. Neither kinetic depth in the optical displays nor the real display appeared to produce a stronger response than the simple expansion pattern. It may be that the infants are unable to process all the information available simultaneously or that expansion alone is a sufficient elicitor of the response with or without additional information. The lack of age differences over the age range studied indicates that learning (either to detect the event or, in the shadow-casting case, to detect that it is not a real object) does not play a major role in the phenomenon.

CHAPTER 29

Dyadically Expanded States of Consciousness and the Process of Therapeutic Change

Why do humans so strongly seek states of emotional connectedness and intersubjectivity and why does the failure to achieve connectedness have such a damaging effect on the mental health of the infant? The primary aim of this chapter is to offer a hypothesis, the dyadic expansion of consciousness hypothesis, as an attempt to explain these phenomena. The dyadic consciousness hypothesis states that each individual, in this case the infant and mother or the patient and the therapist, is a self-organizing system that creates his or her own states of consciousness (states of brain organization), which can be expanded into more coherent and complex states in collaboration with another self-organizing system. This hypothesis is based on my mutual regulation model (MRM) of infant-adult interaction (Tronick, 1989). The MRM describes the microregulatory social-emotional process (from "moving along" to "now moments" to "moments of meeting"; see Stern et al., 1998) of communication which generates (or fails to generate) dyadic states of consciousness.

Critically, understanding how the mutual regulation of affect functions to create dyadic states of consciousness also can help us understand what produces change in the therapeutic process. Like many others, I believe that the therapeutic process involves "something more" than interpretation as the sole modality of therapeutic change (see Lyons-Ruth et al., 1998). It is my view that by understanding the mother-infant interaction we can gain insight into what this something more may be in the therapeutic interaction. The issue of therapeutic change will be dealt with after first presenting the theory of mutual regulation and the hypothesis of dyadic states of consciousness.

To highlight the critical importance of social connectedness and mutual regulation, let us begin by asking what happens when infant-mother social connectedness is broken and the process of mutual regulation is disrupted. To evaluate this hypothesis, I created the face-to-face still-face paradigm (Tronick, Als, Adamson, Wise, & Brazelton, 1978; see also Carpenter, Tecce, Stechler, & Freidman, 1973). In this experiment, the mother is instructed not to engage in her normal interactive behavior. She faces the infant but remains unresponsive. The effect on the infant is dramatic. Infants almost immediately detect the change and attempt to solicit the mother's attention. Failing to elicit her response, most infants turn away only to look back at her again. This solicitation cycle may be repeated many times. But when the attempts fail, infants withdraw, lose postural control, and self-comfort in response to their failure to repair the interaction. The disengagement is profound even with this short break of intersubjectivity. The response of infants reminds one of the withdrawal of Harlow's isolated monkeys or of the infants in institutions observed by Spitz and Bowlby, and what we have now seen in Romania. The still-faced mother is an experimental model of emotional neglect and the denial of intersubjectivity, what Green (1986) has referred to as the "dead mother syndrome" (i.e., it precludes the creation of a dyadic state of consciousness).

What accounts for this dramatic effect? Up until now I, like others, simply assumed that the motivation to establish emotional connectedness or intersubjectivity was an inherent characteristic of all humans. The rationale advanced referred to the evolution of our species as a social species, to our use of language and the collaborative nature of meaning making, and to (object) relational theories of the formation of attachments and the self. However, while these rationales (i.e., we seek connectedness because we are built that way) are reasonable, they assume the very phenomenon that begs for explanation. What experience makes connection so powerful a force in our lives? (Note: the reader may actually choose a favorite term because there is a vast vagueness associated with many terms—connectedness, intersubjectivity, social contact, attunement, emotional synchrony, reciprocity, attachment—that for the moment need not be dealt with.) The dyadic expansion of consciousness offers a way out of this conundrum of assuming what we really would like to explain by invoking concepts from systems theory.

Before presenting this hypothesis, let me develop an analogy between affective regulation and the infant's regulation of homeostatic states. Homeostatic states are a long way from states of consciousness, but the processes of regulating homeostatic states and of creating dyadic states of consciousness share one critical feature—both kinds of states are regulated dyadically. Claude Bernard's first precept was that the maintenance of milieu interior was the organism's primary task. When an infant is not in homeostatic balance (e.g., her core body temperature is low), she must devote all of her temperature regulatory capacity to try to reinstate normal homeostatic balance. However, Bernard failed to appreciate a critical feature of the homeostatic regulatory process for humans. For humans, the maintenance of homeostasis is a dyadic collaborative process. Infants must collaborate with others to successfully regulate their physiological homeostatic states. Of course, the infant is a bounded organism and obviously the adult is external to the infant's (anatomical) bound-aries. Nonetheless, the adult is part of the infant's homeostatic regulatory sys-tem, as much a part as any internal regulatory process.

What is meant by the idea that temperature regulation is a dyadic process? While Bernard did not see it, successful regulation of the core body tempera-ture cannot be accomplished solely by the infant. While the infant has mech-anisms to regulate temperature on her own by, for example, changing her pos-ture and increasing her activity level, these processes will eventually fail depending on the surrounding conditions. But her temperature can also be reg-ulated externally by her caretaker, for example, by being held in ventral con-tact with the caretaker's body. These processes, internal and external, are func-tionally equivalent processes for regulating the infant's temperature. The internal and external mechanisms form a single system made up of two com-ponent systems (i.e., infant and mother)—a dyadic system. Moreover, these reg-ulatory processes involve communication among different components of this dyadic system. Internally generated adjustments are guided by central and peripheral nervous system mechanisms, which respond to signals from central and peripheral sites. Changes in the holding patterns of caretakers are guided by active (e.g., crying) and passive (e.g., color changes) signals from the infant. Thus the infant's physiological state is always in some part dyadically regulated with the caregiver, an external component of the infant's regulatory system.

Moving on to the question of the regulation of emotional states of the infant, we find that the infant's emotional states are also regulated dyadically. The principal components are the infant's central nervous system (e.g., limbic sites) and the behaviors it organizes and controls (e.g., facial and vocal emotional dis-plays) and the caregiver's regulatory input (e.g., facial expressions, touches, ges-tures). The dyadic emotional regulatory system is guided by communication between internal and external components (i.e., infant and caregiver). The fol-lowing interactive sequence illustrates this emotional regulatory process.

A 6-month-old infant and his mother are playing a game and the mother leans in to nuzzle the baby. The infant takes hold of the mother's hair and when she pulls away he does not let go. In pain, the mother responds with an angry facial expression and vocalization. The infant immediately sobers and brings his hand up to his face in a defensive move. The mother pulls back, pauses, and then slowly approaches the infant again. The infant drops his hands and they resume their normal exchange.

This interaction illustrates several critical features of mother-infant interac-tion. First, the infant appreciates the meaning of the affective displays of the mother. The infant does not simply imitate the maternal response but reacts in a manner that is appropriate to the implicit meaning of the display (e.g., maternal expressions of anger mean "duck, something bad is about to happen" versus maternal joy, "smile back and stay connected"). Second, these differen-tial infant reactions communicate to the mother his evaluation of the state of the interaction with well-organized emotional displays of his own. Unlike more

FIGURE 29.1. The normal interaction moves from matching to mismatching states that affect the infant's affective state and activity.

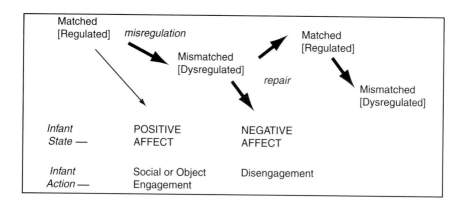

classical assumptions about emotions, the infant's emotions are in no way "disorganized" or "disorganizing." Rather, they are exquisite configurations of face, voice, gaze, posture, and gesture (Weinberg & Tronick, 1994). Moreover, as contrasted to the view that the infant has only a functioning reptilian brain (limbic system), which is only arousing, the infant's affective behavior makes it obvious that whatever brain mechanisms (limbic or cortical) the infant does have operating, they are adequate to organize and inhibit responsiveness. Third, the mother and the infant are active participants in the interaction. It is a mutually regulated process. Thus the infant's emotional reaction is determined by maternal emotional displays and the infant's implicit understanding of those emotional displays. This is the process of mutual regulation—the capacity of each of the interactants to appreciate the meaning of the affective displays of their partner and to scaffold their partner's actions so that they can achieve their goals.

I have argued that a critical event or unit of analysis for understanding mutual regulation is the process of reparation (see Figure 29.1). The typical mother-infant interaction moves from coordinated (or synchronous) to miscoordinated states and back again over a wide affective range. The miscoordinated state is referred to as a miscommunication. Miscommunications are normal events. They occur when one of the partners fails to accurately appreciate the meaning of the other's emotional display and in turn reacts inappropriately. The interactive transition from a miscoordinated state to a coordinated state is an interactive repair. Given that the infant and mother are active regulators of the other's behavior, the process of reparation also is a mutually regulated process. Both partners, infant and adult, signal their evaluation of the state of the interaction through their affective configurations. In turn, in response to their partner's signals, both partners attempt to adjust their behavior to maintain a coordinated state or to repair a miscoordination (e.g., in the above example, the mother's anger display and the infant's defensive display are dyadically repaired as the mother pauses and the infant lowers his hand and looks at her). This process can be likened to the process of moving along in therapy (see Stern, 1998). Critically, successful reparations and the experience of coordinated states are associated with positive affective states, whereas interactive errors generate negative affective states (Tronick, in press). Thus, the infant's affective experience is determined by a dyadic regulatory process.

Let me emphasize one aspect of the homeostatic and emotional examples before focusing on dyadic states of consciousness: In both examples, each participant must "come to know" the current state of the other if the regulation is to succeed. In the homeostatic example, the mother must come to know that the infant is in a state of temperature imbalance. If she sees the cold infant as merely irritable, she may disregard the infant's communicative signals and leave the infant on her own, only to get even colder and more dysregulated. In the emotional example of the mother with an angry display, the mother must come to know that the infant's emotional state is protective. If she sees the infant covering his eyes as playful, she might move in closer to the infant and produce even a greater upset. In either example, when one or the other interactants fails to accurately appreciate the state of the other—homeostatic or emotional—reparation of the state will fail.

What is so experientially powerful about the achievement or failure to achieve these affective dyadic states? It is my hypothesis that the social-emotional exchanges of mothers and infants (and of all humans) have the potential for expanding each individual's state of consciousness with powerful experiential and developmental consequences. The hypothesis of the dyadic expansion of consciousness is derived from systems theory. A first principle of systems theory is that open biological systems, such as humans, function to incorporate and integrate increasing amounts of meaningful information into more coherent states. This process is paradoxical. On the one hand, more information is integrated into the system, making it more complex, while on the other hand, the increase in coherence results in a more organized state. This process is often thought of as a self-generated characteristic of open systems; that is, all systems are self-organizing. Indeed, systems are self-organizing, but in humans this process is just as importantly dyadic. It is a process involving two minds.

For example, take a 6-month-old in interaction with his mother. As we have seen, the infant is able to endogenously (self-)organize a coherent affective state. This state can be thought of as a state of consciousness (or for the materialists among you, a state of brain organization). This affective state of consciousness is manifest in the infant's affective configurations of face, body, gaze, and gesture. A self-organized state of consciousness incorporates a certain amount of information—perceptual input, motor output, representations, information feedback and feed forward, plans, intentions, reentry information, and much, much more. The limits of the infant's nervous system (e.g., speed of information processing, channel capacities of different sensory modalities, motor control limitations, etc.) place a constraint on the complexity of the state that the infant can self-generate. However, the complexity of the infant's state of consciousness is not solely dependent on processes endogenous to the infant. As an open system, the complexity of the infant's state is expandable with input from an external source—the caregiver.

The caregiver provides the infant with regulatory input, *scaffolding* in Bruner's (1975a) terminology, but unlike Bruner, the scaffolding in this case is emotional not cognitive, which can expand the complexity and coherence of the infant's state of brain organization. Thus the expansion of the infant's state of consciousness emerges from the process of the mutual regulation of emotion. During an interaction, information about the infant's state of consciousness (e.g., intentions, affects, and arousal level) is conveyed through affective configurations that are apprehended—come to be known—by the mother. In response, the mother provides the infant with regulatory support that permits the infant to achieve a more complex level of brain organization.

Consider a somewhat concrete example. Gestural communication is a complex action somewhat beyond the non-self-sitting young infant's ability because the infant is not yet able to control his posture to free his arms for communicative purposes. However, the caregiver, by giving the infant postural support in response to the infant's communicative expressions of frustration, scaffolds the infant's ability to use gestural communication. The scaffolding "controls" the infant's head and frees the infant to control her arms and hands. Through this process of providing the regulatory input, the now-sitting infant's brain organization takes on a new and different organization with greater coherence and complexity, which is much beyond the infant's endogenous capacities to organize.

There is a critical and emergent property of this collaboration—the creation of a singular dyadic state of organization. This dyadic state organization has more components—the infant and the mother—than the infant's (or mother's) own self-organized state. Thus, this dyadic system contains more information and is more complex and coherent than either the infant's (or the mother's) endogenous state of consciousness alone. When infant and mother mutually create this dyadic state—when they become components of a dyadic system— both fulfill the first principle of systems theory of gaining greater complexity and coherence. The gesturing mother-held-infant performs an action—gesturing— that is an emergent property of the dyadic system that would not and could not occur unless the infant and mother were related to each other as components of a single dyadic system.

Creation of this dyadic system necessitates that the infant and mother apprehend elements of each other's state of consciousness. If they did not, it would not be possible to create a dyadic state. For example, if the mother's apprehension of an infant's state of consciousness is that the infant intends to reach for a ball when in fact the infant intended to stroke her face, a dyadic system will not be created. The two systems—infant and mother—will remain separate, uncoordinated, and disconnected. Thus, a principle governing the human dyadic system is that successful mutual regulation of social interactions requires a mutual mapping of (some of) the elements of each partner's state of consciousness into the other partner's brain.

To restate the dyadic consciousness hypothesis, it is that each individual is a self-organizing system that creates its own states of consciousness—states of brain organization—which can be expanded into more coherent and complex states in collaboration with another self-organizing system. When the collaboration of two brains is successful, each fulfills the system principle of increasing its coherence and complexity. The states of consciousness of the infant and of the mother are more inclusive and coherent at the moment when they form a dyadic state (a moment of meeting; see Stern, 1998) because it incorporates elements of the state of consciousness of the other.

Thus, to return to the original question: What is it about connectedness that makes it so critical to human experience and to development? The answer suggested by the dyadic consciousness hypothesis is that the "fulfilling" of the first principle of systems theory is the unintended and unconscious force driving social engagement and with this fulfillment travels a powerful subjective effect on the interactants. At the moment when the dyadic system is created, both partners experience an expansion of their own state of consciousness (brain organization). Their states of consciousness become dyadic and expand to incorporate elements of consciousness of the other in a new and more coherent form. At this moment of forming a dyadic state of consciousness, and for the duration of its existence, there must be something akin to a powerful experience of fulfillment as one paradoxically becomes larger than oneself. To rephrase Descartes, I interact, therefore I am.

Let me give another example of the experimental impact of breaking this dyadic consciousness. It is another still-face experiment, but this time with a girl 30 months of age. At the start of the experiment, we (Tronick, 2004) had the mother playing normally with the little girl. After a few minutes of normal play, we asked the mother to hold a still face and not respond to the little girl. As with 6-month-olds, the effect was dramatic. The little girl detected the change in the mother's state almost immediately. She begged the mother with an emotionally laden voice to play with her, to respond to her. She threw things and eventually hit the mother in an attempt to get her to respond. When the mother did resume her normal responding, the little girl was still distressed, and only with the most gentle and soothing approach by the mother was the interaction repaired. Thus, at 30 months we see again how powerful the effect of breaking and preventing the establishment of joint states of consciousness is on the child. These effects of preventing and breaking states of consciousness may play out in many typical situations. For example, the dyadic state of consciousness hypothesis suggests that the anxiety and fear at separation that emerges in the second half year of life is produced by an experience of diminution—literally, a sense of becoming less coherently organized—when the caregiver leaves and is no longer present. A similar effect may account for the emergence of a fear of strangers.

What happens to children when the establishment of dyadic states of consciousness is chronically denied? The effect of chronic denial is that the infant's normal development is arrested and distorted. The infant is deprived of the experience of expanding his or her state of consciousness in collaboration with the mother (or others). An example of the many possible ways that dyadic states might fail to be formed is our work (Weinberg & Tronick, 1998b) on the toxic effects of maternal depression on the infant's social, emotional, and cognitive functioning. From the perspective of mutual regulation, maternal depression disrupts the establishment of a dyadic infant-mother system and the normal experience of emotional reparation. But the dyadic consciousness hypothesis suggests a more venomous possibility.

Given that the infant's system functions to expand its complexity and coherence, one way open for the infant of the depressed mother to accomplish this expansion is to take on elements of the mother's state of consciousness. These elements will be negative—sad and hostile affect, withdrawal, and disengagement. However, by taking them on the infant and the mother may form a dyadic state of consciousness, but one that is negative at its core. Thus, in the service of becoming more complex and coherent, the infant incorporates depressive elements from the mother's state of consciousness. This dyadic state of consciousness contains painful elements, but its painfulness does not override the need for expansion. Critically, when the infant of the depressed mother comes to other relationships, the only way he or she is available for expanding the complexity and coherence of his or her states is by establishing dyadic states of consciousness around the depressive features that were first established with the mother. Thus one consequence of early dyadic history is often a debilitating attachment to negative relational experiences.

Thus, it is my hypothesis that the process of mutual regulation, at the level of social-emotional exchanges and more critically at the level of states of consciousness, determines much of the emotional, social, and representational course of the infant. When the affective regulation of interactions goes well, development proceeds apace. Increasingly, complex tasks are approached, resolved, and incorporated, not by the child alone, but by the child in collaboration with others. But as a consequence of their resolution, the child expands and becomes more coherent. When failure occurs, development gets derailed and the child's complexity is limited or even reduced (i.e., the child may regress). The effect is in the child, but the failure is a joint failure. With continued failure and the structuring that goes on around that failure, affective disorders and pathology may result.

To return to the question of therapeutic change, there are several reasons for my belief that the process of mother-infant regulation can shed light on the process of change. First, the infant and young child are changing at an incredibly fast rate. And while some of the forces of change such as maturational forces are no longer available in the adult therapeutic setting, a major force leading to change is available: the social exchange that takes place between the patient and therapist. Second, the infant-mother exchange does not contain semantic knowledge or any elements of interpretation. It is made up only of emotional communication—procedural knowledge (see Lyons-Ruth et al., 1998)—between the mother and the infant. This emotional communication may be the "something more" we are searching for in the therapeutic process. Of course, I recognize that the mother-infant interaction is asymmetrical, but so is the interaction of the therapist and the patient (Morgan et al., 1998). Moreover, the mother brings her past into the interaction, whereas the infant is developing his or her past.

Thus, I believe that some guidance for understanding what brings about change in the therapeutic process can be found in the mother-infant interaction. For the infant, connectedness with the mother permits the infant to expand his or her state of consciousness. Dyadic expansion of consciousness is a powerful force for change. The infant's mind becomes more coherent and incorporates more information. And when a dyadic state of consciousness is achieved, there is a restructuring and change of the infant's present and past mental organization. Analogously, in the therapeutic setting my hypothesis is that the therapist and patient can also achieve these dyadic states. Dyadic states of consciousness between the patient and the therapist do not involve interpretation, although interpretation may aid in their creation. They are purely emotional and procedural (implicit). As such, they are a force for change in the mental organization of the patient, that is, the "something more" in therapy.

More specifically, the hypothesis is that the patient and the therapist create dyadic states of consciousness. These states of consciousness emerge from the mutual regulation of affect between the patient and the therapist. When these dyadic states are achieved, the state of consciousness of the patient expands and changes. The patient has the experience of a unique shared dyadic state with the therapist. The state is specific and singular to their relationship, but its elements are incorporated into the patient's state of consciousness. The future relationship between the patient and the therapist will be changed from what it was because this new experience will be part of their connection (their moving along; see Stern, 1998) in the future. Thus, the patient becomes capable of a qualitatively unique relationship with the therapist. From a subjective perspective, the patient experiences "something new, something expanded, and something singular" with the therapist, and this experience is incorporated into the patient's future exchanges with the therapist. (Note that because the process is achieved through mutual regulation, these moments will have the same effect on the therapist.)

Were the changes restricted to the patient-therapist relationship, these changes would be of only limited importance. However, they are not restricted. The patient-therapist dyadic state of consciousness reorganizes aspects of the patient's state of consciousness of other relationships (i.e., the patient's implicit knowledge of how to relate; see Lyons-Ruth et al,. 1998, and the cases by Harrison et al., 1998). This restructuring again follows from the principles of systems theory. With the achievement by the patient (and therapist) of a more coherently organized and complex state of dyadic consciousness, old elements of consciousness need to be reintegrated into this new state of consciousness. The "something else with the therapist" becomes part of the patient's having to (re-experience something else (or the lack of something else, or a different something else) specific to his or her consciousness of past and current relationships with others. Thus, out of the change with the therapist, a therapeutic change is assembled in the patient.

In sum, this view of therapeutic change is based on the hypothesis that all humans are able to achieve dyadic states of consciousness, which emerge from affective mutual regulation. This process is most clearly seen in the mother-infant affective interchange. In the infant-parent interchange, achievement of dyadic states is a force for developmental change and for the development of states of consciousness in the infant that will become his or her implicit procedural knowledge of relationships that guide present ways of relating and representing the past. The process of mutual regulation also characterizes the therapeutic relationship. It is hypothesized that the achievement of dyadic states of consciousness between the therapist and the patient is "something more" that accounts for therapeutic change. However, in therapy, as contrasted to the creation of the past in the infant, the change occurs primarily in the reintegration and reconfiguring of already extant states of consciousness for the patient. These changes are a consequence of the mutual creation by the therapist and the patient of new and unique dyadic states.

Indeed, to close with an additional speculative notion, I would hypothesize that the capacity to create dyadic states of consciousness with another, and the quality of those states, depends in part on the history the individual had in creating these states early in development with his or her mother (and others). Thus, it is not simply the content (e.g., my mother always did x) of the past that (in part) determines current functioning, but the procedures of past mutual regulations (e.g., we always interacted this way) that affect current emotional and relational functioning. Moreover, this idea clarifies why therapy must contain "something more" other than interpretation. Interpretation was neither possible nor part of the earliest developmental stages of relationships. However, the early experience of mutual regulation nonetheless shapes much of the how the individual goes about currently relating (i.e., his or her implicit procedural knowledge). Thus, therapy must contain something more because only through experiencing and exploring this something more can one access patients' implicit knowledge about their earliest relationships in relation to their current relationships, that is, the specific and unique creative process of the mutual regulation of affect dyadic state creation. Thus, new therapeutic techniques for exploring and changing this implicit domain of representation need to be developed to modify and expand individual states of consciousness.

Implicit Relational Knowing: Its Role in Development and Psychoanalytic Treatment

There has long been a consensus that "something more" than interpretation is needed in psychoanalytic therapies to bring about change. Interpretation, in the sense of making repressed impulses and fantasies conscious, may not in itself be sufficient. So how *do* psychoanalytic therapies bring about change? The Process of Change Study Group, began meeting early in 1995 to consider how to develop a language and a set of constructs to begin to elaborate on the something more that is needed in therapeutic encounters to catalyze change. This set of symposium papers is the first presentation of our attempt to bring together the joint strengths of developmental research, systems theory, and close observation of clinical process. We consider the framework presented here as a work in progress, with both additional elaboration and revisions needed. We present it here in hopes of stimulating the dialogue needed in the field to achieve an interdisciplinary synthesis of scientific research and clinical theory and observation.

Early in our discussions, our attention was drawn to the observation that most patients remember "special moments" of authentic person-to-person connection with their therapist, moments that altered their relationship with him or her and thereby their sense of themselves. We believe that these moments of intersubjective meeting constitute a pivotal part of the change process. We also find that the role of such moments in therapeutic change can best be understood in relation to concepts drawn from recent infant research and from current systems theories.

As we struggled with the problem of change using the traditional constructs of psychoanalytic theory, it became clear that two kinds of representational processes needed to be separately conceptualized. The first kind of representation we will call semantic in that it relies on symbolic representation in language.

The second kind we will call procedural representation. We are drawing on distinctions made by Kihlstrom and Cantor (1983) and other cognitive psychologists but are adapting them to our own needs. Procedural representations are rule-based representations of how to proceed, of how to do things. Such procedures may never become symbolically coded, as, for example, knowledge of how to ride a bicycle. More important to us than bicycle riding, however, is the domain of knowing how to do things with others. Much of this kind of knowledge is also procedural, such as knowing how to joke around, express affection, or get attention in childhood. This procedural knowledge of how to do things with others we have termed *implicit relational knowing.* In using this term, we want to differentiate implicit relational knowing from other forms of procedural knowledge and to emphasize that such "knowings" are as much affective and interactive as they are cognitive. This implicit relational knowing begins to be represented in some yet-to-be-known form long before the availability of language and continues to operate implicitly throughout life. Implicit relational knowing typically operates outside focal attention and conscious experience, without benefit of translation into language. Language is used in the service of this knowing, but the implicit knowings governing intimate interactions are not language based and are not routinely translated into semantic form.

Recognition of such a nonsymbolically based representational system has been one central contribution of infant research (e.g., Ainsworth, Blehar, Waters, & Wall, 1978; Beebe & Lachman, 1994; Tronick, 1989). In our thinking, implicit relational knowing subsumes what has been termed *internalized object relations.* The older term, internalized object relations, has connotations of taking in from the outside, rather than of coconstruction, and of taking in another person, rather than of representing a mutually constructed regulatory pattern (Tronick, 1989). The older term is also more identified with the literature on pathological rather than adaptive relatedness and is more often used to refer to past relationships and their activation in the transference rather than with more general representational models that are constantly accessed and updated in day-to-day encounters.

Therefore, we view implicit relational knowing as a construct that raises internal object relations to a more general representational systems conception. In this conception, implicit relational knowing encompasses normal and pathological knowings and integrates affect, fantasy, behavioral, and cognitive dimensions. Implicit procedural representations will become more articulated, integrated, flexible, and complex under favorable developmental conditions because implicit relational knowing is constantly being updated and "re-cognized" as it is accessed in day-to-day interaction (as articulated at the level of neuronal group selection by Edelman, 1987).

In a therapeutic context, some small areas of the patient's implicit relational knowing may become the subject of verbal articulation or transference interpretation. However, the areas that become consciously articulated will be only a small part of the totality of the patient's (or therapist's) implicit operating procedures in relationships. Although these knowings are often not symbolically represented, they are also not necessarily dynamically unconscious in the sense of being defensively excluded from awareness. Implicit relational knowing, then, operates largely outside the realm of verbal consciousness and the dynamic unconscious. However, though we use the term throughout these papers, we see it as a working term and one that will need further revision (for a fuller and more developmentally grounded discussion, see Lyons-Ruth, (1999).

In addition to implicit relational knowing, we needed two more constructs to talk about therapeutic change that is not based on interpretation. The second construct was that of the "real relationship" (another term that too must be seen as a work in progress; see Morgan, 1998). The third construct was the notion of "moments of meeting."

We will define the "real relationship" as the intersubjective field constituted by the intersection of the patient's and the therapist's implicit relational knowing. This field extends beyond the transference-countertransference domain to include authentic personal engagement and reasonably accurate sensings of each person's current "ways of being with." Labeling this intersubjective field the *real relationship* also serves to differentiate it from the psychoanalytic components of the relationship in which semantic representations are elaborated via verbal interpretations.

In contrast to more traditional views, we feel that the real relationship is also subject to therapeutic change by processes that alter the intersubjective field directly. In traditional theory, interpretation is viewed as the semantic event that rearranges the patient's understanding. We propose that a moment of meeting is the transactional event that rearranges the patient's implicit relational knowing by rearranging the intersubjective field between patient and therapist, what Tronick (1998) refers to as their dyadic state of consciousness.

What do we mean by a moment of meeting? A moment of meeting occurs when the dual goals of complementary fitted actions and intersubjective recognition are suddenly realized. Moments of meeting are jointly constructed, and they require the provision of something unique from each partner. Sander (1995) has pointed out that the essential characteristic of these moments is that there is a specific recognition of the other's subjective reality. Each partner grasps and ratifies a similar version of "what is happening now, between us."

Moments of meeting catalyze change in parent-infant interaction as well as in psychotherapy. In the process of infant development, the baby's implicit relational knowing encompasses the recurrent patterning of mutual regulatory moves between infant and caregiver (Tronick, 1989, 1998). These regulatory moves shift to negotiate a series of adaptive challenges emerging over the early years of life, as delineated by theorists such as Sander (1962) and Stern (1985). In the course of this ongoing mutually constructed regulation, the interactive field between infant and caregiver becomes more complex and well articulated, giving rise to emergent possibilities of new forms of interaction. For example, once recurrent expectations regarding each partner's moves in a peekaboo game are established, the stage is set for both partners to "play with" that form by violating established expectations. This mutual sense of the emerging possibility of new forms of interaction occurring between the two participants creates heightened affect. Beebe and Lachman (1994) have called attention to the importance of "heightened affective moments" as one of three principles of salience in early development and psychoanalytic treatment. We would further elaborate this concept by tying the heightened affect to a sense of emergent new possibilities in the interactive field. In the positive case, these new interactive possibilities would create more complex and coherent intersubjective regulation because they integrate new developmental capacities of the infant or achieve a fuller and more satisfying adaptation to the infant's current capacities and affective potentials.

The transition to a more inclusive and hence coherent mutual regulatory system hinges on a moment of meeting between parent and child. These moments of changed intersubjective recognition ratify a change in the range of regulation achievable between the two partners. They signal an opening for the elaboration of new initiatives. New forms of shared experience can now be elaborated around previously unrecognized forms of agency. The implicit relational knowing of the two partners will also of necessity be altered. New potential is not only enacted but also represented as a future possibility. Tronick (1998) will further elaborate on the more inclusive and coherent regulation inherent in an intersubjective moment of meeting in his discussion of dyadically expanded states of consciousness.

These concepts can be illustrated in the developmental domain with the description of a brief observation of a young mother with her 18-month-old baby. As an extensive attachment literature demonstrates, the infant's strategies for negotiating comforting contact with caregivers are constructed in a series of mutually regulated negotiations with parents and are one of the best-documented forms of implicit relational knowing displayed during the first 2 years of life (for review, see Bretherton, 1988; Lyons-Ruth & Zeanah, 1993). As part of the standard Ainsworth assessment of the infant's strategies for approaching the parent, mother and baby were observed reuniting with one another after the mild stress of two brief 3-minute separations in an unfamiliar laboratory playroom. As recent evidence confirms, infants are physiologically aroused during these brief separations, even in the absence of obvious distress. However, the fluidity of the physical and affective dialogue between mother and infant at such moments of stress can mitigate the onset of longer term stress responses mediated by the hypothalamic-pituitary-adrenal axis (Hertsgaard, Gunnar, Erickson, & Nachmias, 1995; Spangler & Grossmann, 1993).

The mother and her 18-month-old daughter, whom I will call Tracy, had been receiving therapeutic home visits for 9 months, both to help the mother stabilize her life situation and to help her become more consistently emotionally available to her infant. Over this period of home visiting, Tracy and her mother had both been struggling to find ways of making satisfying physical and emotional contact with one another. This mutual struggle to negotiate more satisfying moments of contact was also obvious in the laboratory observation session. As you will see from the following account, however, this particular session led to a subtle shift between them, to a moment of meeting, that surprised us all.

After arriving at the laboratory playroom, Tracy explored the toys in the room for several minutes while her mother chatted with the female research assistant. When her mother left the playroom for the first time, Tracy did not appear visibly upset. She continued to play with the toys and ignored the research assistant. However, when the assistant got up to leave, Tracy quickly alerted and looked at the door. When she caught sight of her mother entering, she immediately averted her eyes and turned away. Her mother said, "Hey!" and stood in front of Tracy. Still looking away, Tracy said, "Mummy!" with a pleased tone and then turned toward her mother and took several tentative steps toward her as though to join her. Her mother said, "What are you doing?" but did not step forward or kneel down toward Tracy. Tracy sidled past her mother's legs with a blank look, went around her mother, and pushed hard to open the door to leave the room. Her mother forcibly removed her hand from the door, saying, "Come here, look what Mama's got." Tracy pulled her hand away, turned away from her mother, and threw the toy she was holding hard onto the floor. She then continued to turn her back to her mother and push on the door while ignoring her mother's invitations to play. Finally her mother pulled her by the arm and she allowed herself to be drawn over to the toy her mother was holding. Still she ignored the toy, instead stepping with her head averted and without apparent purpose closer to her mother's body and then past her, where she squatted briefly beside her mother with her back turned. Then she stood and returned to the door. Finally, after wandering around the room aimlessly for several more seconds, she sat down facing her mother and played with the toy between them while her mother watched and praised her warmly and appropriately.

In contrast to her avoidant and conflicted behavior when her mother was present, Tracy was quite distressed when her mother left again and could not be comforted by the assistant who came in and tried to engage her. When she caught sight of her mother at the door the second time, she exclaimed "Mummy!" with a delighted squeal and began to run toward her. Rather than responding with similar delight, her mother said, "Hi! What have you been doin'?" In response, Tracy started to fuss loudly as she ran toward her mother. Perhaps because of this protest on Tracy's part, her mother held out her hands and kneeled as Tracy approached, saying again, "What are you doing?" Tracy lifted her arms up and her mother first grasped her under the arms but then put her arms fully around her as Tracy pushed up against her body. After only a brief squeeze, however, her mother released her, drew back to look at her, and said, "Did you miss me?" Tracy sobered as her mother drew back, then fussed again and tried to move back into her mother's arms. Her mother gave her another awkward squeeze, saying, "All right, all right, all right." Then she picked her up, moved to the toys, and kneeled with Tracy on her knee, directing her attention to a toy on the floor. Tracy looked at the toys impassively for a few minutes, sitting stiffly on her mother's knee. Then she stared off into space with a dazed look, began to fuss, slid off her mother's knee, and stood facing her again with her arms outstretched. Her mother responded by opening her own arms. For a long minute they stood frozen with open arms, facing each other silently. Then Tracy gave a little laugh of relief and sank fully into her mother's arms, letting her whole body relax on her mother's shoulder. Her mother was able to give an open delighted smile in return and hold her daughter close while rocking and hugging her. Her mother then specifically recognized and ratified this moment of meeting by murmuring, "I know, I know" to her daughter as she hugged and rocked her.

In our view, mother and child had negotiated a more fitted and inclusive way of being together and had achieved in the final moment of meeting the dual goals of complementary fitted actions and specific intersubjective recognition—a moment of meeting and a dyadic state of consciousness. Recent studies of cortisol metabolism and attachment behaviors confirm that the fuller emotional sharing achieved by Tracy and her mother by the end of the observation constitutes a regulatory system of more inclusive fittedness in that open and responsive communication between mother and infant is associated with reduced cortisol secretion to mild stressors (Hertsgaard et al., 1995; Spangler & Grossmann, 1993).

We would argue that such moments of meeting shift the implicit relational expectations of each partner and signal an opening for the elaboration of new initiatives between mother and child. Such moments of meeting create the potential for the elaboration of new forms of shared experience and for a new range of more mutual and responsive regulation between them.

In summary, these moments of intersubjective meeting are experienced and represented in the implicit relational knowing of infant with caregiver. They are also experienced in the patient-therapist interaction, with similar resulting changes in the patient's implicit relational knowing. These moments of meeting between patient and therapist may or may not become the subject of interpretation. Nevertheless, these moments of meeting open the way to the elaboration of a more complex and coherent way of being together, with associated change in how relational possibilities are represented in each participant's implicit relational knowing.

Noninterpretive Mechanisms in Psychoanalytic Therapy: The "Something More" Than Interpretation

How do psychoanalytic therapies bring about change? There has long been a consensus that *something more* than interpretation, in the sense of making the unconscious conscious, is needed. The discussion of what is the something more comes from many perspectives, involving different polarities, where the something more has taken the form of psychological acts versus psychological words; of change in psychological structures versus undoing repression and rendering conscious; of a mutative relationship with the therapist versus mutative information for the patient. Many psychoanalytic writers, beginning early in the psychoanalytic movement and accelerating up to the present, have directly or indirectly addressed these issues (Fenichel, 1941; Ferenczi & Rank, 1924/1986; Greenson, 1967; Loewald, 1971; Sterba, 1940; Strachey, 1934; Winnicott; 1957; Zetzel, 1956). More recently, the same issues have been reconsidered by Ehrenberg (1992), Gill (1994), Greenberg (1996), Lachmann and Beebe (1996), Mitchell (1993), Sandler (1987), Schwaber (1998) and Stolorow, Atwood, and Brandchaft (1994).

This chapter will present a new understanding of the something more, and attempt to show where in the therapeutic relationship it acts, and how. We will do this by applying a developmental perspective to clinical material.

Anecdotal evidence suggests that after most patients have completed a successful treatment, they tend to remember two kinds of nodal events that they believe changed them. One concerns the key interpretations that rearranged their intrapsychic landscape. The other concerns special moments of authentic person-to-person connection (defined below) with the therapist that altered the relationship with him or her and thereby the patient's sense of himself.

These reports suggest that many therapies fail or are terminated, not because of incorrect or unaccepted interpretations, but because of missed opportunities for a meaningful connection between two people. Although we cannot claim that there is a one-to-one correlation between the quality of what one remembers and the nature of the therapeutic outcome, we also cannot dismiss the fact that both the moments of authentic meeting and the failures of such meetings are often recalled with great clarity as pivotal events in the treatment.

The present chapter will differentiate these two mutative phenomena: the interpretation and the moment of meeting. It will also ask in what domain of the therapeutic relationship these two mutative events occur. While interpretations and moments of meeting may act together to make possible the emergence or reinforcement of each other, one is not explicable in terms of the other. Nor does one occupy a privileged place as an explanation of change. They remain separable phenomena.

Even those analysts who believe in the mutative primacy of interpretation will readily agree that as a rule, good interpretations require preparation and carry along with them something more. A problem with this inclusive view of interpretation is that it leaves unexplored what part of the enlarged interpretive activity is actually the something more, and what part is purely insight via interpretation. Without a clear distinction, it becomes impossible to explore whether the two are conceptually related or quite different.

Nonetheless, we do not wish to set up a false competition between these two mutative events. They are complementary. Rather, we wish to explore the something more, as it is less well understood.

We will present a conceptual framework for understanding the something more and will describe where and how it works (see also Tronick, 1998). First, we make a distinction between therapeutic changes in two domains: the declarative, or conscious verbal, domain; and the implicit procedural or relational domain (see Clyman, 1991; Lyons-Ruth, 1999). Then we will apply a theoretical perspective derived from a dynamic systems model of developmental change to the process of therapeutic change. This model is well suited to an exploration of the implicit, procedural processes occurring between partners in a relationship.

AN APPROACH TO THE PROBLEM

Our approach is based on ideas from developmental studies of mother-infant interaction and from studies of nonlinear dynamic systems, and their relation to mental events. These perspectives will be brought to bear as we elaborate our view on the something more of psychoanalytic therapy, which involves grappling with notions such as moments of meeting, the real relationship, and authenticity. We present here a conceptual overview for the sections on developmental and therapeutic processes.

The something more must be differentiated from other processes in psychoanalysis. At least two kinds of knowledge, two kinds of representations, and two kinds of memory are constructed and reorganized in dynamic psychotherapies. One is explicit (declarative) and the other is implicit (procedural). Whether they are in fact two distinct mental phenomena remains to be determined. At this stage, however, we believe that further enquiry demands that they be considered separately.

Declarative knowledge is explicit and conscious or readily made conscious. It is represented symbolically in imagistic or verbal form. It is the content matter of interpretations that alter the conscious understanding of the patient's intrapsychic organization. Historically, interpretation has been tied to intrapsychic dynamics rather than to the implicit rules governing one's transactions with others. This emphasis is currently shifting.

Procedural knowledge of relationships, on the other hand, is implicit, operating outside both focal attention and conscious verbal experience. This knowledge is represented nonsymbolically in the form of what we will call *implicit relational knowing*. Most of the literature on procedural knowledge concerns knowing about interactions between our own body and the inanimate world (e.g., riding a bicycle). There is another kind that concerns knowing about interpersonal and intersubjective relations, that is, how "to be with" someone (Stern, 1985, 1995). For instance, the infant comes to know early in life what forms of affectionate approaches the parent will welcome or turn away, as described in the attachment literature (Lyons-Ruth, 1991). It is this second kind that we are calling implicit relational knowing. Such knowings integrate affect, cognition, and behavioral/interactive dimensions. They can remain out of awareness as Bollas's (1987) "unthought known," or Sandler's "past unconscious" (Sandler & Fonagy, 1997) but can also form a basis for much of what may later become symbolically represented.

In summary, declarative knowledge is gained or acquired through verbal interpretations that alter the patient's intrapsychic understanding within the context of the "psychoanalytic," and usually transferential, relationship. Implicit relational knowing, on the other hand, occurs through "interactional, intersubjective processes" that alter the relational field within the context of what we will call the shared implicit relationship.

The Nature of Implicit Relational Knowing

Implicit relational knowing has been an essential concept in the developmental psychology of preverbal infants. Observations and experiments strongly suggest that infants interact with caregivers on the basis of a great deal of relational knowledge. They show anticipations and expectations and manifest surprise or upset at violations of the expected (Sander, 1988; Trevarthen, 1979; Tronick, Als, Adamson, Wise, & Brazelton, 1978). Furthermore, this implicit knowing is registered in representations of interpersonal events in a nonsymbolic form, beginning in the first year of life. This is evident not only in their expectations but also in the generalization of certain interactive patterns (Beebe & Lachmann, 1988; Lyons-Ruth, 1991; Stern, 1985).

Studies of development by several of the authors (Lyons-Ruth & Jacobvitz, 1999; Sander, 1962, 1988; Stern, 1985, 1995; Tronick & Cohn, 1989) have emphasized an ongoing process of negotiation over the early years of life involving a sequence of adaptive tasks between infant and caregiving environment. The unique configuration of adaptive strategies that emerges from this sequence in each individual constitutes the initial organization of his or her domain of implicit relational knowing. Several different terms and conceptual variations have been proposed, each accounting for somewhat different relational phenomena. These include Bowlby's (1973) "internal working models" of attachment, Stern's (1995) "proto-narrative envelopes" and "schemas of being-with," Sander's (1997) "themes of organization," and Trevarthen's (1993a) "relational scripts," among others. A formal description of how these strategies are represented remains an active field of enquiry.

Implicit relational knowing is hardly unique to the presymbolic infant. A vast array of implicit knowings concerning the many ways of being with others continues throughout life, including many of the ways of being with the therapist that we call transference. These knowings are often not symbolically represented but are not necessarily dynamically unconscious in the sense of being defensively excluded from awareness. We believe much of transference interpretation may avail itself of data gathered by the analyst about the patient's relational knowings. A prototypical example is that reported by Guntrip (1975) from the end of his first session with Winnicott. Winnicott said, "I don't have anything to say, but I'm afraid if I don't say something, you will think I am not here."

How Changes in Implicit Relational Knowing Are Experienced

A feature of dynamic systems theory relevant to our study is the self-organizing principle. Applying the self-organizing principle to human mental organization, we would claim that, in the absence of an opposing dynamic, the mind will tend to use all the shifts and changes in the intersubjective environment to create progressively more coherent implicit relational knowledge. In treatment, this will include what each member understands to be his own and the other's experience of the relationship, even if the intersubjective relationship itself does not come under therapeutic scrutiny; that is, it remains implicit. Just as an interpretation is the therapeutic event that rearranges the patient's conscious declarative knowledge, we propose that what we will call a moment of meeting is the event that rearranges implicit relational knowing for patient and analyst alike. It is in this sense that the moment takes on cardinal importance as the basic unit of subjective change in the domain of implicit relational knowing. When a change occurs in the intersubjective environment, a moment of meeting will have precipitated it. The change will be sensed and the newly altered environment then acts as the new effective context in which subsequent mental actions occur and are shaped and past events are reorganized. The relationship as implicitly known has been altered, thus changing mental actions and behaviors that assemble in this different context.

The concept that new contexts lead to new assemblies of a system's constitutive elements is a tenet of general systems theory. An illustration of the same principle from the neurosciences is that of Freeman (1994). He describes the way that in the rabbit brain the neural firings activated by different odors create a different spatial pattern. When a new odor is encountered, not only does it establish its own unique pattern, but the patterns for all of the previously established odors become altered. There is a new olfactory context, and each preexisting element undergoes a change.

The idea of a moment of meeting grew out of the study of the adaptive process in development (Sander, 1962, 1977, 1987; Nahum, 1994). Such moments were seen to be key to state shifts and organismic reorganization. We believe the idea of the well-timed interpretation is also an attempt to grasp aspects of this idea.

A major subjective feature of a shift in implicit relational knowing is that it will feel like a sudden qualitative change. This is why the moment is so important in our thinking. The moment as a notion captures the subjective experience of a sudden shift in implicit relational knowing for both analyst and patient. We will discuss this in greater detail below.

Clinically, the most interesting aspect of the intersubjective environment between patient and analyst is the mutual knowing of what is in the other's mind, as it concerns the current nature and state of their relationship. It may include states of activation, affect, feeling, arousal, desire, belief, motive, or content of thought, in any combination. These states can be transient or enduring, as mutual context. A prevailing intersubjective environment is shared. The sharing can further be mutually validated and ratified. However, the shared knowing about the relationship may remain implicit.

DEVELOPMENTAL PERSPECTIVES ON THE PROCESS OF CHANGE

Since infants are the most rapidly changing human beings, it is natural to wish to understand change processes in development for their relevance to therapeutic change. Of particular relevance is the widely accepted view that despite neurological maturation, new capacities require an interactive intersubjective environment to be optimally realized. In this environment, most of the infant and parent's time together is spent in active mutual regulation of their own and each other's states, in the service of some aim or goal. For further explication of the mutual regulation model and the concepts that underpin it, see Tronick (1989) and Gianino and Tronick (1988). The key notions that elaborate this general view follow.

Mutual Regulation of State
Is the Central Joint Activity

State is a concept that captures the semistable organization of the organism as a whole at a given moment. As Tronick (1989) has argued, dyadic state regulation between two people is based on the microexchange of information through perceptual systems and affective displays as they are appreciated and responded to by mother and infant over time. The states that need to be regulated initially are hunger, sleep, activity cycling, arousal, and social contact; soon thereafter (the level of) joy or other affect states, (the level of) activation or excitation, exploration, attachment, and attribution of meanings; and eventually almost any form of state organization, including mental, physiological, and motivational. Regulation includes amplifying, downregulating, elaborating, repairing, and scaffolding, as well as returning to some preset equilibrium. How well the caretaker apprehends the state of the infant, the specificity of his or her recognition, will, among other factors, determine the nature and degree of coherence of the infant's experience. Fittedness gives shared direction and helps determine the nature and qualities of the properties that emerge. Mutual regulation implies no symmetry between the interactants, only that influence is bidirectional. Each of the actors brings his or her history to the interaction, thus shaping what adaptive maneuvers are possible for each. Current concepts from development studies suggest that what the infant internalizes is the process of mutual regulation, not the object itself or part objects (Beebe & Lachmann, 1988, 1994; Stern, 1985, 1995; Tronick & Weinberg, 1997). Ongoing regulation involves the repetition of sequenced experiences giving rise to expectancies and thus becomes the basis of implicit relational knowing (Lyons-Ruth, 1991; Nahum, 1994; Sander, 1962, 1983a; Stern, 1985, 1995; Tronick, 1989).

Regulation Is Goal-Directed

The processes of mutual regulation moving toward a goal are neither simple nor straightforward most of the time and do not run smoothly (Tronick, 1989). Nor would we expect or want them to, ideally. Rather, they demand a constant struggling, negotiating, missing and repairing, midcourse correcting, and scaffolding to remain within or return to a range of equilibrium. This requires both persistence and tolerance of failures on both partners' part. (Of course the work is asymmetrical, with the caregiver in most situations doing the lion's share.) This trial-and-error temporal process of moving in the general direction of goals, and also identifying and agreeing on these goals, we will call *moving along*, to capture the ongoing ordinariness of the process as well as its divergence from a narrow and direct path to the goal. Sometimes the goal is clear and the dyad can move along briskly, as when hunger requires feeding. Sometimes an unclear goal must be discovered or uncovered in the moving-along process, as in free play or most play with objects.

Mutual Regulation Also Involves an
Intersubjective Goal

The moving-along process is oriented toward two goals simultaneously. The first is physical or physiological, and is achieved through actions that bring about a behavioral fittedness between the two partners, such as positioning and holding of the baby for a feeding by the caregiver, coupled with sucking and drinking by the baby; or high-level facial and vocal stimulation during face-to-face play by the caregiver, coupled with a high level of pleasurable activation and facial expressivity in the baby. The second, parallel goal is the experience of a mutual recognition of each other's motives, desires, and implicit aims that direct actions, and the feelings that accompany this process (Tronick, Als, et al., 1979). This is the intersubjective goal. In addition to a mutual sensing of each other's motives or desires, the intersubjective goal also implies a signaling or ratifying to one another of this sharing. There must be some act assuring consensuality. Affect attunement provides an example (Stern, 1985).

It is not possible to determine which goal is primary, the physical or intersubjective. At times one of them seems to take precedence, and a shifting back and forth occurs between what is foreground or background. In any event, both are always present. Our central interest here, however, remains the intersubjective goal.

The Regulatory Process Gives Rise to
Emergent Properties

In moving along much of the time, one does not know exactly what will happen, or when, even if general estimates can be made. This indeterminacy is due not only to the nature of dynamic systems but to the shifting of local and even intermediate goals, as well as the fact that so much of moving along is ad-libbed. Even frequently repeated interactions are almost never repeated in exactly the same way. Themes of interaction are always in the process of evolving variations, quite evident in certain activities such as free play, where part of the nature of the activity is to constantly introduce variations so as to avoid habituation (Stern, 1977). But even a more tightly structured activity, such as feeding or changing, is never repeated exactly.

The improvisational nature of these interactions has led us to find guidance in the recent theoretical work on nonlinear, dynamic systems that produce emergent properties (Fivaz-Depeursinge & Corboz-Warnery, 1995; Maturana & Varela, 1980; Prigogine & Stengers, 1984; and as applied to early development, Thelen & Smith, 1994). These concepts seem to provide the best models to capture the process of moving along and the nature of specific moments of meeting (see below), which are emergent properties of moving along. In the course of moving along, the dual goals of complementary fitted actions and intersubjective meeting about that fittedness can be suddenly realized in a moment of meeting, one that has inevitably been well prepared for, but not determined, over a longer period of time. Such moments are jointly constructed, requiring the provision of something unique from each party. It is in this sense that meeting hinges on a specificity of recognition as conceptualized by Sander (1991).

Examples of moments of meeting are such events as the moment when the parent's behavioral input fits with the baby's movement toward sleep so as to trigger a shift in the infant from awake to asleep; or the moment when a bout of free play evolves into an explosion of mutual laughter; or the moment that the baby learns, with much teaching and scaffolding by the parent, that the word to use for that barking thing is *dog*. In the latter two examples, the meeting is also intersubjective in the sense that each partner recognizes that there has been a mutual fittedness. Each has captured an essential feature of the other's goal-oriented motive structure. To state it colloquially, each grasps a similar version of "what is happening, now, here, between us."

We assume that intersubjective meetings have goal status in humans. They are the mental version of the aim of object relatedness. In systems terms, such meetings involve linking between organism and context, inside and outside, giving rise to a state that is more inclusive than what either system alone can create. Tronick has termed this *more expansion of consciousness*.

A Moment of Meeting Can Create a New Intersubjective Environment and an Altered Domain of Implicit Relational Knowing

An example provides the best illustration. If in the course of playing a mother and infant unexpectedly achieve a new and higher level of activation and intensity of joy, the infant's capacity to tolerate higher levels of mutually created positive excitement has been expanded for future interactions. Once an expansion of the range has occurred, and there is the mutual recognition that the two partners have successfully interacted together in a higher orbit of joy, their subsequent interactions will be conducted within this altered intersubjective environment. It is not the simple fact of each having done it before, but the sense that the two have been here before. The domain of implicit relational knowing has been altered.

As another example, imagine a young child visiting a new playground with his father. The child rushes over to the slide and climbs the ladder. As he gets near the top, he feels a little anxious about the height and the limits of his newly emerging skill. In a smoothly functioning dyadic system, he will look to his father as a guide to help him regulate his affective state. His father responds with a warm smile and a nod, perhaps moving a little closer to the child. The child goes up and over the top, gaining a new sense of mastery and fun. They have shared, intersubjectively, the affective sequence tied to the act. Such moments will occur again in support of the child's confident engagement with the world.

Immediate Consequences of Moments of Meeting That Alter the Intersubjective Environment

When a moment of meeting occurs in a sequence of mutual regulation, an equilibrium occurs that allows for a "disjoin" between the interactants and a détente in the dyadic agenda (Nahum, 1994). Sander (1983a) has called this disjoin an "open space" in which the infant can be alone, briefly, in the presence of the other, as they share the new context (Winnicott, 1957). Here an opening exists in which a new initiative is possible, one freed from the imperative of regulation to restore equilibrium. The constraint of the usual implicit relational knowledge is loosened and creativity becomes possible. The infant will recontextualize his new experience.

During the open space, mutual regulation is momentarily suspended. Then the dyad reinitiates the process of moving along. However, the moving along will now be different because it starts from the terrain of the newly established intersubjective environment, from an altered implicit relational knowing.

APPLICATION TO THERAPEUTIC CHANGE

We shall now provide a descriptive terminology and conceptual base for the something more, showing how it operates as a vehicle for change in psychoanalytic therapies.

The key concept, the moment of meeting, is the emergent property of the moving-along process that alters the intersubjective environment and thus the implicit relational knowing. In brief, moving along is comprised of a string of present moments, which are the subjective units marking the slight shifts in direction while proceeding forward. At times, a present moment becomes "hot" affectively, and full of portent for the therapeutic process. These moments are called *now moments*. When a now moment is seized, that is, responded to with an authentic, specific, personal response from each partner, it becomes a moment of meeting. This is the emergent property that alters the subjective context. We will now discuss each element in this process.

The Preparatory Process: Moving Along and Present Moments

In many ways, the therapeutic process of moving along is similar to the moving-along process in the parent-infant dyad. The form is different. One is mainly verbal while the other is nonverbal, but the underlying functions of the moving-along process share much in common. Moving along involves movement in the direction of the goals of the therapy, however they may be explicitly or implicitly defined by the participants. It subsumes all of the usual components of a psychoanalytic therapy, such as interpretation, clarification, and so on. In any therapeutic session, as in any parent-infant interaction, the dyad moves toward an intermediate goal. One intermediate goal in a session is defining the topics they will take up together, such as lateness to a session, whether the patient was properly heard yesterday, the upcoming vacation, whether therapy is helping the feeling of emptiness, whether the therapist likes the patient, and so forth. The participants do not have to agree. They must only negotiate the interactive flow so as to move it forward to grasp what is happening between them and what each member perceives, believes, and says in the particular context, and what each member believes the other member perceives, feels, and believes. They are working on defining the intersubjective environment, moving along. The events in the conscious foreground that propel the movement are free associations, clarifications, questions, silences, interpretations, and so on. Unlike the largely nonverbal behaviors that make up the background of the parent-infant environment, the verbal content usually occupies the foreground in the consciousness of both partners. In the background, however, the movement is toward intersubjective sharing and understanding. The verbal content should not blind us to the parallel process of moving along toward an implicit intersubjective goal.

Analogous to the physical fittedness goal in the nonverbal parent-infant interactions, we see the moving-along process in an adult therapy session as consisting of two parallel goals. One is a reordering of conscious verbal knowledge. This would include discovering topics to work on, clarify, elaborate, interpret, and understand. The second goal is the mutual definition and understanding of the intersubjective environment that captures the implicit relational knowing and defines the shared implicit relationship. A set of smaller local goals are needed to microregulate the moving-along process. Local goals perform almost constant course corrections that act to redirect, repair, test, probe, or verify the direction of the interactive flow toward the intermediate goal.

As will be seen, the intersubjective environment is part of what we shall call the shared implicit relationship. The negotiating and defining of the intersubjective environment occurs in parallel with the explicit examination of the patient's life and the examination of the transference. It is a process that is conducted out of awareness most of the time. Yet it is going on with every therapeutic maneuver. Moving along carries the interactants toward a clearer sense of where they are in their shared implicit relationship.

We conceive of moving along as a process that subjectively is divided into moments of different quality and function that we call present moments. Among clinicians the notion of a present moment is intuitively evident and has proved invaluable in our discussions. The duration of a present moment is usually short, because as a subjective unit it is the duration of time needed to grasp the sense of "what is happening now, here, between us." Accordingly, it lasts from microseconds to many seconds. It is constructed around intentions or wishes and their enactment, and traces a dramatic line of tension as it moves toward its goal (see Stern, 1995). A present moment is a unit of dialogic exchange that is relatively coherent in content, homogeneous in feeling, and oriented in the same direction toward a goal. A shift in any of the above ushers in a new, the next, present moment. For example, if the therapist says, "Do you realize that you have been late to the last three sessions? That's unusual for you," the patient responds, "Yes, I do," and the analyst adds, "What are your thoughts about that?," this exchange constitutes a present moment.

The patient replies, "I think I've been angry at you." Silence. "Yes I have been." Silence. This is a second present moment.

The patient then says, "Last week you said something that really got me ticked off . . ." This is the third present moment.

These present moments are the steps of the moving-along process. Between each there is a discontinuity of a kind, but strung together they progress, though not evenly, toward a goal. They proceed in a fashion that is rarely linear.

In brief, we are speaking of a bounded envelope of subjective time in which a motive is enacted to microregulate the content of what is being talked about and to adjust the intersubjective environment.

The fairly tight cyclicity of infant activities (sleep, activity, hunger, play, etc.) ensures a high level of repetition, creating a repertoire of present moments. In therapy too, present moments repeat variations on the theme of habitual moves that constitute the unique way any therapeutic dyad will move along. Present moments will of course be constrained by the nature of the therapeutic technique, the personalities of the interactants, and the pathology at issue.

Because present moments are so often repeated with only minor variations, they become extremely familiar, canons of what moments of life with that other person are expected to be like. Present moments become represented as "schemas of ways of being with another" (Stern, 1995) in the domain of implicit relational knowing. The pair evolves a set of microinteractive patterns in which steps include errors, disruptions, and repairs (Lachmann & Beebe, 1996; Tronick, 1989). These recurrent sequences tell us about the patient's unthought known (Bollas, 1987) or the prereflective unconscious of Stolorow and Atwood (1992). They are the building blocks of Bowlby's working models and of most internalization. They are not in awareness but are intrapsychically distinct from that which is repressed.

In sum, present moments strung together make up the moving-along process. But the units, present moments, and direction of this moving along occur within a framework that is familiar to and characteristic of each dyad.

Now Moments

In our conceptualization, now moments are a special kind of present moment, one that gets lit up subjectively and affectively, pulling one more fully into the present.* They take on this subjective quality because the habitual framework—the known, familiar intersubjective environment of the therapist-patient

---

*We borrow the term *now moment* from Walter Freeman.

relationship—has all of a sudden been altered or risks alteration. The current state of the shared implicit relationship is called into the open. This potential breach in the established proceedings happens at various moments. It does not have to threaten the therapeutic framework, but requires a response that is too specific and personal to be a known technical maneuver.

Now moments are not part of the set of characteristic present moments that make up the usual way of being together and moving along. They demand an intensified attention and some kind of choice of whether or not to remain in the established habitual framework. And if not, what to do? They force the therapist into some kind of action, be it an interpretation or a response that is novel relative to the habitual framework, or a silence. In this sense, now moments are like the ancient Greek concept of *kairos*, a unique moment of opportunity that must be seized, because your fate will turn on whether you seize it and how.

Clinically and subjectively, the way the therapist and patient know that they have entered a now moment and that it is distinct from the usual present moments is that these moments are unfamiliar, unexpected in their exact form and timing, unsettling or weird. They are often confusing as to what is happening or what to do. These moments are pregnant with an unknown future that can feel like an impasse or an opportunity. The present becomes very dense subjectively, as in a moment of truth. These now moments are often accompanied by expectancy or anxiety because the necessity of choice is pressing, yet there is no immediately available prior plan of action or explanation. The application of habitual technical moves will not suffice. The analyst intuitively recognizes that a window of opportunity for some kind of therapeutic reorganization or derailment is present, and the patient may recognize that he has arrived at a watershed in the therapeutic relationship.

Now moments can be described as evolving subjectively in three phases. There is a pregnancy phase that is filled with the feeling of imminence. There is the weird phase when it is realized that one has entered an unknown and unexpected intersubjective space. And there is the decision phase when the now moment is to be seized or not. If it is seized, it will lead to a moment of meeting, if all goes well, or to a failed now moment if it does not.

A now moment is an announcement of a potential emergent property of a complex dynamic system. Although the history of its emergence may be untraceable, it is prepared for with fleeting or pale prior apparitions, something like a motif in music that quietly and progressively prepares for its transformation into the major theme. Still the exact instant and form of its appearance remain unpredictable.

The paths toward the now moment are many. The patient may identify an event during a session and immediately realize that the intersubjective environment has just shifted, but not share and ratify this shift during the session. Or the patient might have let the event pass without much notice and later rework it to discover its importance in signaling a possible shift in the intersubjective environment. These events are forms of hidden or potential now moments that are part of the preparatory process. They will perhaps, one day, reach a state of readiness to enter into the mutual dialogue and become now moments as we have described.

Now moments may occur when the traditional therapeutic frame risks being, or is, or should be, broken, for example:

- If an analytic patient stops the exchange and asks, "Do you love me?"
- When the patient has succeeded in getting the therapist to do something out of the (therapeutic) ordinary, as when the patient says something very funny and both break into a sustained belly laugh.
- When by chance patient and therapist meet unexpectedly in a different context, such as in a queue at the theater, and a novel interactive and intersubjective move is fashioned, or fails to be.
- When something momentous, good or bad, has happened in the real life of the patient such that common decency demands that it be acknowledged and responded to somehow.

Recall that we are dealing with a complex dynamic process where only one of several components may be changing in a slow and progressive fashion during the preparatory phase, which may be hardly perceptible, until reaching a certain threshold when it suddenly threatens to change the context for the functioning of other components. Conceptually, now moments are the threshold to an emergent property of the interaction, namely, the moment of meeting.

The most intriguing now moments arise when the patient does something that is difficult to categorize, something that demands a different and new kind of response with a personal signature that shares the analyst's subjective state (affect, fantasy, real experience, etc.) with the patient. If this happens, they will enter an authentic moment of meeting. During the moment of meeting a novel intersubjective contact between them will become established, new in the sense that an alteration in the shared implicit relationship is created.

The Moment of Meeting

A now moment that is therapeutically seized and mutually realized is a moment of meeting. As in the parent-infant situation, a moment of meeting is highly specific; each partner has actively contributed something unique and authentic of himself or herself as an individual (not unique to their theory or technique of therapeutics) in the construction of the moment of meeting. When the therapist (especially), but also the patient, grapples with the now moment, explores and experiences it, it can become a moment of meeting. There are essential elements that go into creating a moment of meeting. The therapist must use a specific aspect of his or her individuality that carries a personal signature. The two are meeting as persons relatively unhidden by their usual therapeutic roles, for that moment. Also, the actions that make up the moment of meeting cannot be routine, habitual, or technical; they must be novel and fashioned to meet the singularity of the moment.

Of course, this implies a measure of empathy, an openness to affective and cognitive reappraisal, a signaled affect attunement, a viewpoint that reflects and ratifies that what is happening is occurring in the domain of the shared implicit relationship, that is, a newly created dyadic state specific to the participants.

The moment of meeting is the nodal event in this process because it is the point at which the intersubjective context gets altered, thus changing the implicit relational knowing about the patient-therapist relationship.

That the moment plays such a key mutative role has been recognized by others as well. Lachmann and Beebe (1996) have emphasized it, and Ehrenberg (1992) has described her mutative therapeutic work as taking place precisely during intimate subjective moments.

An example is instructive at this point. Molly, a married woman in her midthirties, entered analysis because of poor self-esteem that was focused on her body, her inability to lose weight, and her severe anxiety about losing the people most dear to her. She was a second daughter. Because her older sister had been crippled by polio as an infant, Molly's parents cherished her healthy body. When she was a child, they would ask her to dance for them while they watched admiringly.

She began the session talking about "body things" and associated having feelings of sexual excitement and a flash of anger at the analyst on her way to the session. "I have the image of your sitting back . . . and watching me from some superior position." Later in the session she recalled her parents watching her dance and wondered if there were some sexual excitement in it for them, too, "if they wanted it, too." There followed a long discussion of her body experience, including physical examinations, fears there was something wrong with her body, and body sensations. Then, after a prolonged silence, Molly said, "Now I wonder if you're looking at me." (The now moment began here.)

The analyst felt taken aback, put on the spot. Her first thought was whether to remain silent or say something. If she were silent, would Molly feel abandoned? Repeating Molly's statement—"You wonder if I'm looking at you"—seemed awkward and distancing. The analyst's responding with a remark of her own, however, felt risky. The sexual implications were so intense that to speak them seemed to bring them too close to action. Noting her own discomfort and trying to understand its source, the analyst identified the related issue of dominance and realized that she felt as if she were being invited either to take the superior position or to submit to Molly. At this point in her considerations, she suddenly felt free to be spontaneous and communicate to Molly her actual experience.

"It kind of feels as if you're trying to pull my eyes to you," she said. "Yes," Molly agreed, with avidity. (These two sentences made up the moment of meeting.) "It's a mixed thing," said the analyst. "There's nothing wrong with the longings," Molly replied. "Right," the analyst agreed. "The thing is, it takes two to manage," Molly said. "Certainly at first," the analyst replied. "That's what I was thinking. . . . It's nice thinking about this now . . . and I actually am able to feel some compassion." "For yourself?" the analyst asked. "Yes," Molly answered. "I'm glad," the analyst responded.

In this vignette, an intersubjective meeting took place because the analyst used her own inner struggle to apprehend the patient and seize the now moment by responding specifically and honestly, "It kind of feels [to me as a specific individual, is implied] as if you are trying to pull my eyes to you." This turned the now moment into a "moment of meeting." This is quite different from the various possible, technically adequate, responses that leave the specificity of the analyst as person, at that moment, out of the picture, such as, "Is this the way it was with your parents?" or "Tell me what you imagined," and so forth.

Interpretations in Relation to Moments of Meeting

Now moments can also lead directly to an interpretation. And interpretations can lead to moments of meeting or the other way around. A successful traditional interpretation allows the patient to see himself, his life, and his past differently. This realization will invariably be accompanied by affect. If the interpretation is made in a way that conveys the affective participation of the analyst, a moment of meeting may also have occurred. "Matched specificities between two systems in resonance, attuned to each other" (Sander, 1997) will have happened. This is akin to the affect attunement seen in parent-infant interactions (Stern, 1985).

Suppose that the analyst makes an excellent interpretation with exquisite timing. It will have an effect on the patient, which may be a silence, or an "aha," or most often something like, "Yes, it really is like that." If the analyst fails to convey his or her affective participation (even with a response as simple as, "Yes, it has been, for you," but said with a signature born of his own life experience), the patient could assume or imagine that the analyst was only applying technique, and there will have been a failure to permit an important new experience to alter the known intersubjective environment. In consequence, the interpretation will be much less potent.

Strictly speaking, an interpretation can close out a now moment by explaining it further or elaborating or generalizing it. However, unless the therapist does something more than the strict interpretation, something to make clear his or her response and recognition of the patient's experience of a shift in the relationship, then no new intersubjective context will be created. A sterile interpretation may have been correctly or well formulated but it will most likely not have landed and taken root. Most gifted psychoanalysts know this and do the something more, even considering it part of the interpretation. But it is not. And that is exactly the theoretical problem we are grappling with. If the scope of what is considered an interpretation becomes too large and ill defined, the theoretical problems become impossibly confused.

A distinction must be made here. A now moment can, and often does, arise around charged transferential material, and gets resolved with a traditional interpretation. If this interpretation is given in an authentic manner, how is that different from a moment of meeting? It is different for this reason. During a traditional interpretation involving transferential material, the therapist as a person, as he exists in his own mind, is not called into the open and put into play. Nor is the shared implicit relationship called into the open for review. Rather, the therapeutic understanding and response occurring within the analytic role is called into play. What authentic means in this context is difficult to define. During an authentic transference interpretation, there should not be a moment of meeting of two people more or less denuded of their therapeutic roles. If there were, the act of the therapist, in response to the transference act of the patient, would have the character of countertransference. In contradistinction, the transference and countertransference aspects are at a minimum in a moment of meeting and the personhood of the interactants, relatively denuded of role trappings, is put into play. Assessing the relative lack of transference-countertransference, and the relative presence of two people experiencing one another outside of their professionally prescribed roles, is, of course, not easy, but we are all aware of such moments, provided that the very concept is accepted. We will return to this point below.

The Open Space

As in the developmental sequence, we assume that in the therapeutic situation moments of meeting leave in their wake an open space in which a shift in the intersubjective environment creates a new equilibrium, a disjoin with an alteration in or rearrangement of defensive processes. Individual creativity, agency emerging within the individual's configuration of open space, becomes possible, as the patient's implicit relational knowing has been freed of constraints imposed by the habitual (Winnicott, 1957).

Other Fates of the Now Moment

The other various fates of the now moment, if it is not seized to become a moment of meeting or an interpretation are as follows.

A Missed Now Moment

A missed now moment is a lost opportunity. Gill provides a graphic example: "In one of my own analyses . . . I was once bold enough to say, 'I'll bet I will make more of a contribution to analysis than you have.' I almost rolled off the couch when the analyst replied, 'I wouldn't be a bit surprised.' I must also regretfully report that the exchange was not further analyzed, not in that analysis at any rate" (1994, pp. 105–106). We take him to mean there was no further discussion of this exchange. Here a moment had been allowed to pass by, never to be returned to.

A Failed Now Moment

In a failed now moment, something potentially destructive happens to the treatment. When a now moment has been recognized but there is a failure to meet intersubjectively, the course of therapy can be put in jeopardy. If the failure is left unrepaired, the two gravest consequences are that either a part of the intersubjective terrain gets closed off to the therapy, as if one had said "we cannot go there," or even worse, a basic sense of the fundamental nature of the therapeutic relationship is put into such serious question that therapy can no longer continue (whether or not therapy actually stops).

David, a young man, had begun an analysis. In a session after several months had elapsed, he was talking about a severe burn covering much of his chest that he had sustained as a toddler and musing about its influence on his subsequent development. It had left him with a disfiguring scar, easily seen when he was in a bathing suit or shorts, which had caused him much self-consciousness and acted as the focus for various issues concerning his body. Without thinking, David reached down and started to pull back his shirt, saying, "Here, let me show you. You will understand better." Abruptly, before he had uncovered the scar, his analyst broke in, "No! Stop, you needn't do that!" Both were left surprised by the analyst's response.

Both David and his analyst later agreed that what had transpired had not been helpful. David felt, however, and told his analyst, that the analyst's subsequent response had compounded the failure because, instead of saying that he felt badly for having reacted as he had to David, he said only that he had not performed to his own standards.

A Repaired Now Moment

Failed now moments can be repaired, by staying with them or by returning to them. Reparation, in itself, can be positive. Almost by definition, the repair of a failed now moment will lead the dyad into one or more new now moments.

A Flagged Now Moment

A now moment can be labeled. These labels are not easy to come by because the dyadic states concerned do not, in fact, have names and are extremely subtle and complex entities. They usually acquire names like, "the time when you ... and I ...." Flagging them with a label is extremely important, not only because it facilitates their recall and use, but it also adds another layer to the jointness of this interpersonal creation. Flagging may also serve the purpose of dealing with a now moment only partially at the time of its first emergence without running the risk of missing or failing the moment. In this way it can buy the therapy needed time.

An Enduring Now Moment

Sometimes a now moment emerges that cannot be immediately resolved, disclosed, or shared, but it does not go away. It remains and hangs in the air for many sessions, even weeks. Nothing else can happen until its fate is determined.

These enduring now moments are not necessarily failures. They may result from conditions that do not permit the usual solutions because the timing or readiness is not ripe or because the intersubjective meeting required is too complex to be contained in a single transaction. In this sense, they also may buy needed time. Usually they are resolved with a different now moment that encompasses the enduring now moment. We will discuss this further below.

THE SHARED IMPLICIT RELATIONSHIP AS THE LOCUS OF MUTATIVE ACTION IN THERAPY

We return now to the question posed at the beginning of this chapter, namely, in what domain of the relationship between therapist and patient does the moment of meeting occur and implicit knowledge get altered? We suggest that it takes place in the shared implicit relationship.

The notion of any relationship in analysis that is not predominantly transferential-countertransferential has always been troublesome. Many analysts claim that all relatedness in this clinical situation is permeated with transference and countertransference feelings and interpretations, including those intermediary phenomena such as the therapeutic alliance and its related concepts. Yet others insist that a more authentic sense of relatedness is the necessary experiential background without which transference is not perceivable, let alone alterable (Thoma & Kachele, 1987).

The shared implicit relationship consists of shared implicit knowledge about a relationship that exists apart from but parallel to both the transference-countertransference relationship and the assigned psychoanalytic roles. While each partner's implicit knowledge about the relationship is unique to him, the area of overlap between them is what we mean by the shared implicit relationship. (This shared implicit relationship is never symmetrical.)

The emphasis on the importance of the shared implicit relationship was for us unexpected, a conclusion that we came to after realizing the nature of a moment of meeting. Since a moment of meeting could only occur when something happened that was personal, shared, outside, or in addition to technique, and subjectively novel to habitual functioning, we were forced to reconsider the entire domain of the shared implicit relationship.

In our view, infant research has simplified consideration of the shared implicit relationship by highlighting the fact of affective communication and intersubjectivity virtually from the outset of postnatal life (Lachmann & Beebe, 1996; Tronick, 1989). Infant and caretaker are both seen to be capable of expressing affect and comprehending the affective expressions of the other. This first communication system continues to operate throughout life and has attracted ever more interest in our field under the rubric of the nonverbal. We agree with Stechler (1996) that although our professional responsibility enjoins us from sharing the same life space as the patient, it is misguided to assume that the complex emotional being of the analyst can be (or should be) kept from the sensings of the patient, sensings based on the operation of a highly complex system that is always functioning. Our position is that the operation of this system constructs the shared implicit relationship, which consists of a personal engagement between the two, constructed progressively in the domain of intersubjectivity and implicit knowledge. This personal engagement is constructed over time and acquires its own history. It involves basic issues that exist beyond and endure longer than the more therapeutically labile distortions of the transference-countertransference prism, because it includes more or less accurate sensings of the therapist's and patient's person.

When we speak of an authentic meeting, we mean communications that reveal a personal aspect of the self that has been evoked in an affective response to another. In turn, it reveals to the other a personal signature, so as to create a new dyadic state specific to the two participants.

It is these stable, implicit knowings between analyst and analysand, their mutual sensings and apprehendings of one another, that we are calling their shared implicit relationship. Such knowings endure over the fluctuations in the transference relationship and could even be detected with a microanalysis, much of the time, by a third party observing them, in which case it could be an objective event.

We have been forced by our reflections upon the moment of meeting and its role in altering implicit knowledge to focus on and examine this shared implicit relationship. This is so because of several characteristics of a moment of meeting:

1. It is marked by a sense of departure from the habitual way of proceeding in the therapy. It is a novel happening that the ongoing framework can neither account for nor encompass. It is the opposite of business as usual.
2. It cannot be sustained or fulfilled if the analyst resorts to a response that feels merely technical to the patient. The analyst must respond with something that is experienced as specific to the relationship with the patient and that is expressive of her own experience and personhood, and carries her signature.
3. A moment of meeting cannot be realized with a transference interpretation. Other aspects of the relationship must be accessed.
4. It is a dealing with "what is happening here and now between us." The strongest emphasis is on the *now*, because of the affective immediacy. It requires spontaneous responses and is actualized in the sense that analyst and patient become contemporaneous objects for one another.
5. The moment of meeting, with its engagement of "what is happening here and now between us" need never be verbally explicated, but can be, after the fact.

All these considerations push the moment of meeting into a domain that transcends but does not abrogate the professional relationship and becomes partially freed of transferential-countertransferential overtones.

Although it is beyond the scope of this chapter, we believe that a further exploration of this shared implicit relationship is badly needed.

SUMMARY AND DISCUSSION

Whereas interpretation is traditionally viewed as the nodal event acting within and upon the transferential relationship and changing it by altering the intrapsychic environment, we view moments of meeting as the nodal event acting within and upon the shared implicit relationship and changing it by altering implicit knowledge that is both intrapsychic and interpersonal. Both of these complementary processes are mutative. However, they use different change mechanisms in different domains of experience.

With the aim of furthering clinical enquiry and research, we have attempted to provide a descriptive terminology for the phenomenology of these moments that create the shared implicit relationship.

It should be noted that change in implicit relational knowledge and change in conscious verbal knowledge through interpretation are sometimes hard to distinguish from each other in the actual interactive process of the therapeutic situation. The shared implicit relationship and the transferential relationship flow in parallel, intertwined, one or the other taking its turn in the foreground. However, it is a necessary condition for relatedness that processing of implicit knowing be ongoing. Interpretation, on the other hand, is a punctate event.

We locate the foundations of the shared implicit relationship in the primordial process of affective communication, with its roots in the earliest relationships. We suggest it consists largely of implicit knowledge and that changes in this relationship may result in long-lasting therapeutic effects. In the course of an analysis, some of the implicit relational knowledge will get slowly and painstakingly transcribed into conscious explicit knowledge. How much is an open question. This, however, is not the same as making the unconscious conscious, as psychoanalysis has always asserted. The difference is that implicit knowing is not rendered unconscious by repression and is not made available to consciousness by lifting repression. The process of rendering repressed knowledge conscious is quite different from that of rendering implicit knowing conscious. They require different conceptualizations. They may also require different clinical procedures, which has important technical implications.

The proposed model is centered on processes rather than structure and is derived from observing infant-caretaker interaction and from dynamic systems theory. In this model, there is a reciprocal process in which change takes place in the implicit relationship at moments of meeting through alterations in "ways of being with." It does not correct past empathic failures through the analytic empathic activity. It does not replace a past deficit. Rather, something new is created in the relationship that alters the intersubjective environment. Past experience is recontextualized in the present such that a person operates from within a different mental landscape, resulting in new behaviors and experiences in the present and future.

Our position on mutual regulation in the therapy situation is akin to one described by Lachmann and Beebe (1996). Our idea of a now moment potentially becoming a moment of meeting differs from their idea of heightened affective moments in that we have tried to provide a terminology and a detailed sequential description of the process that leads up to and follows these privileged moments.

We agree with many contemporary thinkers that a dyadic state shift is fundamental, but we locate its emergence in the moment of meeting of the interactants. Our position is similar to those taken by Mitchell and Stolorow and Atwood. We add to these authors, however, in considering most of the intersubjective environment as belonging to implicit relational knowing, which gets built into the shared implicit relationship in the course of therapy. The process of change, thus, takes place in the shared implicit relationship. Finally, we anticipate that this view of altering implicit relational knowing during moments of meeting will open up new and useful perspectives that consider therapeutic change.

CHAPTER 32

Emotional Connections and Dyadic Consciousness in Infant-Mother and Patient-Therapist Interactions: Commentary on a Paper by Frank Lachmann

Allow me to begin with something of a digression before getting to the ideas provoked by Lachmann's (2001) paper. At a fundamental level, I have thought that work with infants and work with patients are connected by core feelings. We who do infancy research always have thought of ourselves as blessed to work with these little beings who elicit exuberant emotions, deep forms of connectedness, a sense of awe at their astonishing growth and change, and the promise of their and our own future. Of course when they fail our sense of desperation is great. The future seems lost. I believe that these also are the feelings provoked in the therapist working with a patient. It too is work filled with possibility, change, the future. And it too provokes feelings of caring and desperation. Nonetheless these core feelings, in contrast to the obvious and important theoretical and empirical connections between developmental and therapeutic work, are seldom appreciated. Yet I believe that these feelings connect us—researchers and therapists—just as they connect us to our 'subjects' and our patients.

I make this digression (an association) because it was what I felt and experienced in reading Lachmann's paper. The paper is infused with a sense of connectedness: His connectedness to (and respect for) his patients, his colleagues, his field, the research on infants, and theory. Of course, much of my sense of this is inferred, but inference, whether based on language or behavior, is always part of the recognition process. And though this digression may be just that (or worse, a distraction), I believe that these feelings are critical to our— researchers, clinicians, theorists—effort to coconstruct new procedures for our work with infants, patients, theory, and practice. Indeed, Lachmann is demonstrating how important these feelings of connectedness can be to our understanding, especially when they scaffold thoughtfulness such as Lachmann's.

Let me give an example of the importance of these feelings. In recent meetings with clinical colleagues, I have been struck by the gap between the language and ways of thinking of researchers and therapists. In a recent encounter, I described in microanalytic terms an infant's reaction to a depressed mother to a clinical colleague. She immediately incorporated my description into a theoretical language. She saw her language as descriptive and I saw it as abstruse and overdone. Upon my remarking upon these differences in our language, she responded that I was interested in description (did she mean *mere* description?) whereas she was interested in meaning (*real* understanding).

This interchange was distressing, not only because I lost my baby (after all, this was my description of one of my subjects) but because the gap in the way we saw things was so great. But there was a mutuality of feeling between us that allowed us to move along and to struggle to establish a common direction. I came to see that researchers often do "merely" want to see what is going on with development. How does the infant change? What is the process that produces change? By contrast, clinicians want to help their patients to change. Their interpretative language provides them with guideposts for action. Clinicians want to know how what I am saying will help them work with their patients, and for my part I want to know how what they see will help me see things about my infants. We are both impatient in different ways. Development is complicated. I want to understand it now. But (really, except when the grants are due) I have lots of time. Therapeutic change is complicated. Clinicians want to know how to do it now. They don't have time. At the end of our discussion, we both had gained some insight about each other. However, what made our mutual insight possible was our sense of connectedness because of a shared set of core feelings and our implicit knowledge about procedures for being together.

I connected to Lachmann through his paper. It produced many thoughts for me, which I want to discuss. One of Lachmann's points that I like in particular is that we must not blame the baby for the pathology we see in the adult. Babies were never like pathological adults. They never went through a normal stage that resembles pathological states. Lachmann, like Beebe (Beebe & Lachmann, 1994) and Stern (1985) and others, again saves the baby from all sorts of slurs accumulated over years of incorrect thinking about virtual infants.

To invert this idea, as an adult, I also want to thank Lachmann because if pathology is not infantile, then patients cannot be thought of as babies. Pathology develops in an individual who has been experiencing the world longer than the infant. But the difference is not just time and the accumulation of the past brought into the present. The adult is a being who once had infant capacities, but no longer has (or no longer only has) infant, toddler, or child capacities. The adult has developed (an endless list of) capacities that were never present in the infant (e.g., perspective taking, conscious and unconscious abstract reasoning, time perspectives, representational processes) or capacities that were present in less complex forms (dynamic processes, a repertoire of implicit procedures for being with others, specific relational knowings, and a variety of relational moves that regulate intersubjective distance, direction, and emergent states of consciousness). It is with these fundamentally and qualitatively different capacities that adults experience, even reexperience (interpret), their experiences. Thus pathology can occur at any point in development and it will be different given the capacities at the time it developed and it will be transformed as later developing processes come into place. Thus thinking that pathology is a linear outcome of an infantile/child experience is, as Kagan (1998) puts it, a seductive idea but one that is incorrect. Adults are not infants and pathology is not infantile; it is "adultile."

To extend these points a bit further, it also means that we must not apply models of mother-infant/child interaction to the therapeutic situation in a simple-minded, noncritical fashion. Infants are not patients. Mothers are not therapists. Although Wolff (1996) suggests that the two (infant research and psychoanalysis) are unrelated, it seems to me that we can learn a great deal about both by comparing and contrasting them to each other (Tronick, 1998). Contrasting them may be especially useful for understanding processes that lead to change when language is not at the center of the process. Nonetheless, we should not confuse and confabulate mothers and infants, patients and therapists. For example, though it is a dearly loved analogy, "holding" is not what goes on in mother-child interaction. We know that the infant, no less the mother, is far too active for holding to capture more than some part of what is going on. As Lachmann says, mother and infant are coconstructing meanings. Similarly, the patient and the therapist are far too active, even if only through implicit procedures, to be captured by the concept of holding.

Lachmann provides us with an extremely interesting case to illustrate other critical ideas. In his discussion of his patient, a 39-year-old woman, he speaks to her early childhood experiences with her father and her mother that affected her subsequent relationships. The events are clear, powerful, and nuanced: As a girl it was not only that she was raised to high excitement with her father but that it was flattened when she returned home to her mother. Lachmann refers to this as the "model scene." Model scenes, like Stern's (1985) RIGS, (Representations, Interactions, Generalized) are abstracted, depersonified ways of having expectations about being with others. The model scene for this patient was experienced initially with the father and was (re)experienced in her relationships with others for 30 or so years. Lachmann does not see its effects as linear ("I did this with my father as a girl, and now I do it with my partner"). Rather, Lachmann recognizes it was also changed by those relationships. It is no longer the model scene of her childhood.

It also seems to me that this model scene is now changed again by their (the patient and Lachmann's) relationship. I think Lachmann would agree. He does not see her as simply coming to a therapeutic insight. From his knowledge of infancy research and therapy, he recognizes that the model scene is (now) their coconstruction. It has been coconstructed by what they bring from their own past and from their ongoing and past active engagement with each other during therapy. He recognizes that he and his patient came to their version of her model scene together. Obstacles were in both of them and their success came from their mutual engagement (Beebe & Lachmann, 1994; Tronick, 1989). Thus Lachmann can say that what they have done is to coconstruct the model scene. It is different than the childhood scene, and all the scenes inbetween, because of their mutual engagement.

Lachmann goes on to suggest that what also has been coconstructed is their transference. Certainly this may be what has happened, but as an infancy researcher I see something additional. I believe Lachmann and his patient, like a mother and child, have coconstructed an implicit interactional procedure between them (Stern et al., 1998; Tronick, 1998). The procedure gives them a new way of being together. The procedure did not exist before. It uniquely arose out of their present and past interactions with each other in the therapeutic setting. It is a form of relational knowing (Lyons-Ruth et al., 1998). It is still implicit between them. It is not conscious (nor is it an insight) and it may or may not become conscious over the course of the therapy. In Lachmann's terms, they may or may not develop a model scene about it. Thus, I do not think they have only (re)coconstructed the transference, as wonderful as that may be. To me, they have done something far more wonderful: They have cocreated a truly new and unique implicit procedure for being together. Of course it is based on their individual pasts, but critically it is also based on their own ongoing and past interactions with each other. At the time that Lachmann is writing it seems that this procedure is not likely to occur outside of their ongoing interactions. Nonetheless, the therapeutic effect is that it (may) eventually give her a new way of being with others (and give Lachmann a new way as well).

I think that the ideas of uniqueness and cocreation demand that distinctions be made about the conceptualization of the model scene or Stern's RIGS, as abstracted and depersonified generalizations of how to be with others. Model scenes arise out of reiterated interactions with another person, often the mother. The child learns what the procedural rules are for interactions and uses them as an initial format or guide for interactions with others. In a way it is like the child learning a game of peekaboo ("I do this; the other person does this"). The child also learns that the procedure can be used with lots of people. However, the polar opposite also occurs during development. Infants interact with mothers, fathers, and others in unique ways that are mutually created as the infant and the individual engage with each other (Tronick, 1989). These interactions and relational knowing are not generalized but remain specific to specific relationships. To me, the actions of the infant and a particular other are specifically fitted to each other and become increasingly differentiated and specific with ongoing engagement. ("I do this with my mother." "I do this with my father." "I don't do what I do with my mother with my father.") The fittedness and singularity of interactions and the experience of them is a fabulous cocreation that remains unique. They are not only reduced to a generalized model scene. Thus on one side the reiteration of interactions with others leads to learning general ways of being with others (e.g., "baby small talk"), but on the other side it leads to increasingly specific and particular ways to be with different individuals ("Only we do this together."). Indeed, I think what distinguishes relationships from mere interactions are their degree of specificity, singularity, and the richness and coherence of their implicit knowings.

One comment on another related point. Model scenes, RIGS, interactional schemes, and such are things that are extremely useful in therapy. In therapy, discussions about interactions become narrations. They take on what Bruner (1990) called a canonical form, perhaps what Lachmann means by model scenes. Such canonization seems to be extremely effective in helping the patient and the therapist elaborate an understanding of how the patient was and is with others. They help to provide insight into the patient's relational successes and failures. However, these canonical forms must not be confused with actual interactions or the interactional procedures and implicit relational knowings that the patient cocreates with specific others. Model scenes and such must not be instantiated. They are not the equivalent of the lived experience with others. Lachmann's patient with her father was uniquely related to him and experienced their relationship in unique ways. This was also the case for each of her subsequent relationships with others. However, if we as researchers and therapists can gain an understanding of the polarities of the generalized model (e.g., model scene) and the singular (e.g., specific relationship), I think our understanding of the development of interactions and relationships outside in the patient's world as well as inside in the therapeutic setting will be enhanced, as will our understanding of each other.

Lachmann has also suggested a set of basic motivations. I find these to be powerful concepts. These motives help us to understand the therapeutic process as well as what is changing during therapy. However, they are for the most part motivations "within the individual." But I believe that there is also a motivation that is related to the conceptualization of the mother-infant or the therapist-patient as a dyadic system. The dyadic motivation arises out of the interaction and interactional processes (e.g., reparation, ongoing regulation, moving along; see Gianino & Tronick, 1988). I have referred to this dyadic motivation as the dyadic expansion of consciousness (DEC) hypothesis (Tronick et al., 1998; Tronick & Weinberg, 1997).

Briefly, the DEC hypothesis is that each individual is a self-organizing system that creates its own states of consciousness—states of brain organization, if you will—which can be expanded into more coherent and complex states in collaboration with another self-organizing system, another person. When the collaboration of two individuals (two brains) is successful, each fulfills the fundamental system principle of increasing their coherence and complexity. For example, during the mutual exuberant smiling and cooing of an infant and mother, their states of consciousness are expanded because they have incorporated elements of the state of consciousness of the other into their own state. There is some form of recognition that "we know each other's minds." I believe similar expansions of consciousness occur between patient and therapist, perhaps at the moment when they have cocreated an insight or at the moment when they mutually recognize that they are having the same experience.

I believe that DEC is fundamental to developmental change in the infant and to change in the therapeutic setting. The infant, mother, patient, and therapist all change when such dyadic states are formed. Critically, at the moment of its forming and for the duration of its existence, there must be something akin to a powerful experience of fulfillment as one paradoxically becomes larger than oneself. I believe that this experience is the proximal reason for our seeking connection with others. Dyadic consciousness is a motivation in Lachmann's sense, but it is a motivation that is only available to individuals as they engage each other and form dyadic systems.

Lachmann has addressed issues based on systems theory and coconstruction, infant research, and the therapeutic process. He provides us with ideas that demand our attention—our joint attention and mutual elaboration. Most important, he creates ways for therapists and researchers to coconstruct new understanding, to expand their consciousness and to develop ways of being together.

CHAPTER 33

A Model of Infant Mood States and Sandarian Affective Waves

Despite parents' attribution of moods to their infants ("He was just out of sorts all day. I stood on my head but nothing pleased him."), there has been little research on the establishment of infant moods or the mechanisms underlying them. Researchers like myself have not tackled this problem of long-lasting affective states but, rather, have almost exclusively focused on specific, short-lived affective expressions. Pragmatically, short-lived expressions are easier to study and have been used either as measures of the meaning of an event to the infant (e.g., the sad and negative reaction to the still-faced mother) or as communicative signals that regulate interactions (e.g., infant smiles signal the mother to "continue what she is doing"; Tronick, Als, Adamson, Wise, & Brazelton, 1978; Tronick, 1980; Weinberg & Tronick, 1994). But there are conceptual challenges to the study of moods that go beyond pragmatics. One challenge may be related to the only recent recognition that infants have affects at all and that those affects are organized and not disruptive. Another, greater difficulty is having to adjust our thinking to the radical idea that emotions are organizing processes that structure behavior (Beebe & Stern, 1977; Fogel, Diamond, Langhorst, & Demos, 1983; Tronick, 1989; Weinberg & Tronick, 1994). If these challenges to our thinking are difficult, it may be an even greater mind stretch to entertain the idea that infants have affective processes that have long-lasting organizing continuous effects. It is this possibility that I want to consider. I want to do some thinking on what moods are, how they are created, and what some of their functions are. I want to present a model of moods.

My model of moods is that infants have long-lasting (e.g., hours-long, days-long, and even longer) mood states. Mood states are dynamically changing yet distinct assemblages of affective behaviors, and their control processes are modified by affective input from others. Mood states organize behavior and experience over time, and they critically serve an anticipatory representational function by providing directionality to infants' behavior as they move into the future. Moods states are also implicitly, and often explicitly, known to the infants' caregivers or partners and as a consequence give them a sense of what the infants will be like in the present and in the future. I also believe that moods are cocreated by the interplay of active, self-organized biorhythmic affective control processes in the infant and the effect of the emotions expressed by others during routine social-emotional exchanges on mood-control processes. Thus, although we attribute moods to an individual—the infant is *in* a mood, and the mood is *in* her—I argue that moods are cocreated by the infant interacting with others and that they organize the infant and communicate that organization to others.

SANDER'S SLEEP RESEARCH AS A BASIS FOR THINKING ABOUT MOODS

The theory of moods that I am presenting is derived from Sander's (1976, 1977) pioneering thinking and research on the organization of sleep and wake cycles in newborns and how they come to be organized by caretaking input. Thus when Sander (2002) asked where the field of parent-infant research is going, he left out a possibility that I have seized—the possibility of looking back to his own work as a way of moving forward. Clearly moods are not sleep cycles. Both, however, are phenomena that organize behavior and experience over time. I believe that, by seeing the relations between sleep states and mood states, we can begin to understand what mood states are and how they come about. Indeed, in recognition of the central importance of Sander's thinking to my thinking about moods, I have named one of the critical mood control processes the Sanderian activation wave (SAW).

To understand how the biological is transformed into the psychological, Sander investigated how sleep states come to be organized. He found and argued that, although there are critical self-organizing processes that control sleep, the organization of sleep is not simply a maturational phenomenon. To the contrary, it is powerfully influenced by the temporal and social-emotional features of caretaking. Sander carried out a series of foundational studies on the effects of caretaking on the organization of behavioral states during the newborn period. He found that infants have ongoing self-generated, biorhythmically organized patterns of sleep and awake states, but, critically, he also found that many features of sleep and awake states are modified by the quality and timing of caretaking. His interpretation was that sleep organization is the outcome of an interaction of endogenous and exogenous processes. Sleep organization is not just "in" the infant, it is "in" the interaction of the infant and the other.

The actual experiment was complex (see Sander 1976, 1977, for a complete description), but its most important experimental manipulation was that there was one nursery caretaking routine for newborns that was contingent on state behaviors (e.g., crying, eyes open) and another routine that was on a fixed schedule independent of the infants' state. Sander's hypothesis was that the different caretaking routines would modify the temporal organization of the infants' behavioral states. This hypothesis was strongly supported. Initially the sleep-wake activity cycles of the infants were monitored. It was found that each infant had an endogenous "diurnal" organization of awake, REM, and non-REM sleep states. Although the diurnal organization was still immature (e.g., non-REM and REM sleep states had varying durations; transitions among states were irregular), Sander found that there were individual differences and that each infant had its own self-organized pattern. Most important, Sander demonstrated that the coherence of the organization of the different states and their diurnal cycling was much more rapidly established by the state-contingent caretaking routine than by noncontingently scheduled caretaking routine.

This finding was stunning. Sleep organization did not just mature. Its organization (its maturation) was modified by the temporal quality of the caretaking the infant received in relation to the self-organized state cycles of the infant. The finding is fundamental because it demonstrated that the organization came exclusively neither from the inside nor from the outside. Rather, there were two processes, one in the infant and the other in the environment, that, in their interaction over time, led to the emergence of a more coherent state organization. State organization was no longer an internal maturational process but a mutually regulated process. Thus Sander's thinking on sleep was not a one-person but a two-person model of a dynamic social exchange process cocreating organization. At the time, as it is today, this was a profound insight about the organization and development of human behavior.

Several other findings from this study are also interesting in the current context. Sander found that female and male infants reacted differently, suggesting that female infants establish diurnal cycles more quickly. This difference speaks to differences in the self-organizational capacities of male and female infants and, more broadly, to the pervasiveness of individual differences in endogenous organization and receptivity to the environment (Weinberg, Cohn, & Olson, 1999). He also found that two different caretakers carrying out the same contingent regime nonetheless were differentially successful in establishing diurnal rhythmicity in their infants. This finding emphasizes that the process of establishing sleep rhythmicity is a mutually regulated process affected and modulated by both participants. Unfortunately, Sander was not able to specify what it was that the two caretakers did differently nor how those differences were regulated by the different caretakers and infants. Nonetheless, the finding demonstrates the specific fittedness that takes place between caretaker and infant. Sander also showed that if infants were shifted from one routine to the other, their sleep cycles persisted for a time in the face of the new routine, but after several days they shifted in response to the new routine. This indicated that something had been internalized by the infant that was not inside the infant already. Critically, he also found that a perturbation of the normal behavior of the caretaker—having the caretaker wear a mask during a feeding—disrupted the subsequent cycling of the infant. This masking experiment demonstrates the receptivity of the cycles to specific inputs, their mutability, and the active process of exchange that takes place between the infant and the caretaker.

Despite the differences between moods and sleep states, I see them as related because both are long-lasting states, one behavioral, the other affective. Thus Sander's work on sleep has scaffolded my thinking about moods. But what are moods?

THE QUESTION OF MOODS

I believe that understanding the establishment of moods is central to our understanding of infant as well as adult functioning. Spitz (1965) believed that affective processes (e.g., the social smile, stranger anxiety) were the organizers of the psychic life of the infant. Emde (1983) argued that infants develop an affective core, which provides continuity for the self over the life span. Certainly clinicians believe that affects are central to an adult's psychic life and have a continuity from infancy. Like Spitz and Emde, I believe that moods provide continuity to infants' experiential life and that they are organized and organizing processes of infants' affective and social behavior. Furthermore, I believe that an affective organization for understanding the continuity and "expectancy" of behavior can stand in stark contrast to cognitive and information-processing models of infant functioning. These models overestimate infants' cognitive abilities and underestimate infants' affective capacities and the adaptive possibilities and functions of affects. For example, I hypothesize that moods fulfill the Janus principle of bringing the past into the future for the infant but as a noncognitive/symbolic/linguistic—that is, purely affective—memorial process.*
It is typical for parents to note with much affect of their own that "he was angry yesterday when we didn't go out and he is still that way." I also believe that consideration of the development of moods opens the way for thinking about dynamic conflictual processes in infants (Anni Bergman, personal communication). Again, parents implicitly know this too when they observe, "Now he is always upset with her since she made him cry by leaving, though they were having such fun together." And, of course, while I am for the most part focused on infants, I hope that thinking about infant moods will provoke thoughts about therapist-patient interactions ("Is he going to be in that mood again in this session?") and about the interactive basis for the development of psychopathology.

Although there is no accepted definition of mood, and the concept of mood is vague and murky, parents have a good deal of knowledge about moods.

---

*The Janus principle states that we use the past to anticipate the future; that we look backward in order to look forward. Looking back requires that there be some form of representation that carries the past into the present and the future in a meaningful way to guide thought, action, and emotions.

Papousek and Papousek (1983) would call this a form of intuitive knowledge. For example, a mother and father in my laboratory were discussing their 4-month-old infant in response to my question, "What is he like and how was he today?" We asked this question to find out if anything unusual was going on for the infant. The mother responded, "He was in a tough mood this morning when he got up. I tried everything but nothing worked. Well, when I gave him his mobile he seemed okay, but after a few minutes he was really unhappy again. He would-n't even look at me. But we got through it, and I finally got him to nap around noon. And after his nap, he was in a great mood even though I was pretty tired and flat. It's funny because a month ago he used to wake up in a great mood, but hated his nap and got really cranky after it. But I figured out that if I just crooned to him for 20 minutes, he would calm down and after a while he got up like now, in a better mood." The father added with concern and caring, "I thought he would always be tough in the morning. He really was tough on her, but now it seems to have switched around. She figured out this crooning thing, and it changed him. She was just great. In lots of ways I think he is easier than he used to be. My sister had a baby who made you nervous because she would suddenly fuss and cry for no reason at all. Drove her crazy. He is really wonderful."

What are some of the characteristics of mood states that these intuitive observations point toward? Like the distinct states of sleep and wakefulness (REM, non-REM, alert, and distress), mood states are a set of mutually exclusive states made up of a distinct set (assemblage) of affective behaviors. In our research, we have found that during social interactions infants are most often in one of four highly organized short-lived affective states (Tronick, Beeghly, Fetters, & Weinberg, 1991; Weinberg & Tronick, 1994). One is a sad/withdrawn config-uration, which assembles a sad facial expression, looking away, slumping, and whimpering. A second is social engagement, a distinctly different assemblage of a smile face, looking toward the partner, open-handed gestures, and positive vocalizations. A third is an angry configuration, and the fourth is an inter-ested/curious configuration. But mood states are not just fleeting affective states. Like behavioral states of sleep and awake, moods last over time with such critical temporal features as stickiness, momentum, and ebb and flow.

Stickiness means that once an infant (and likely for adults as well) is in a mood, it is hard to move the infant out of it; and when the infant does get out of it, she readily falls back into it. "She woke up in a cranky mood, and she just wouldn't get out of it, even when she smiled to her teddy. She just went back to fussing." Moods are sticky because of the self-organizing processes in the central nervous system (CNS) and the body that generate moods. Acting synergistically with these self-organizing processes, receptive processes bias the infant's response to affective input even when the mood itself is not fully man-ifest. "She looked OK, not really happy, and then—bang!—she was screaming. I had no clue why. I sang her favorite song and it even made her worse. Everything annoyed her." The biasing of affective input by receptive mood processes makes one or another mood both more likely to occur and more stable. The dominance of a mood is not, however, fixed, and another mood may replace it, although the changeover to another mood may occur slowly: "So I just took her as she came, and little by little with a lot of cuddling she slowly came out of it."

Mood states also evidence what I call momentum because they continue to be manifest even after the triggering event has ended. "She smiled to the rabbit and then just kept on smiling even when it was gone. Playing with it just put her into a great mood." Momentum is also generated by self-organizing internal processes. As a consequence of these processes, even though affective input is critical initially to generating a mood, affective input may paradoxically have little role in maintaining a mood state. Mood states may simply "go on and on" under their own momentum. Moods also have other short and long-term temporal qualities. In the short run, moods ebb and flow over the course of the day, often with a predictable regularity, although sometimes without any apparent regularity: "She was really fussy for a while, but then she was better, but when it came back it was with a vengeance." Over longer time spans, moods seem to be present for some period of time (e.g., a month or so) and then dissipate: "She used to be so cranky after her nap, but now she is just a joy." The wavelike biorhythmic ebb and flow is a self-organized process that organizes affective states over time and into the future.

Moods are different from what might be thought of as temperament. Moods grow out of the recurrence of an infant's affective experience, whereas temperament is an organismic characteristic. However, organismic features of an infant may predispose the infant to establishing one or another mood: "You could see she was easily overstimulated as a newborn, and now too much of even good things get to her." Most important, the long duration of moods, their flow, stickiness, and momentum make them different from fleeting affects, which are briefly present and then dissipate. Yet because both are affective states, many of their behavioral components and likely CNS and physiological components are shared.

One of the shared features of mood states and shorter lived affective states is that, during social exchanges, different affective states are receptive (have specific fittedness) to specific emotional input that exceeds an activation threshold. We have found specific contingencies between infant affective expressions and maternal expressed affect (Cohn & Tronick, 1988, 1989). For example, we have found high correlations and contingencies between sad maternal affective expressions and infant sadness, and between maternal positive emotional expressions and infant social engagement. Again, as with states of sleep and wakefulness where the infant is in one or another state but not both, we see little if any "cross-talk" among affective states (i.e., the infant is in one or another of these states): "He just shifted between being happy and being upset." Although specific receptiveness to specific affective input may be adequate for understanding the triggering of brief affective states, it is inadequate for understanding the generation of a mood. Such a situation would invoke a simple stimulus-response model in which affective states would be activated in the presence of a specific affective stimulus that exceeds a threshold and would be absent when the stimulus is below threshold or absent. As a consequence, infants would be at the mercy of stimulus input and their affective states would be under stimulus control. Obviously, such a model fails to account for a mood's chronicity, stickiness, and momentum, its organizing of behavior over time, or the infant's self-organized activity.

To overcome these problems in my model of moods, I hypothesize that (1) moods are controlled in part by self-organized affective control processes and (2) affective input induces as well as stabilizes changes in the settings of the affective control processes. Thus, like the variation induced by caretaking input in the temporal flow of sleep and awake states and the establishment of an infant's diurnal cycle, moods arise out of the interaction of external affective input from others and the infant's internal self-organized affective processes (Sander, 1977) but then develop their own stability. In this model of moods, the infant is neither void of affective processes and simply under the control of external regulators nor completely under the internal control of self-generated emotional processes independent of input. Indeed, I hypothesize that the introduction of an interaction between another's affective input and the infant's self-organized processes as a source of variation of the control parameters of mood states helps account for the development and establishment of moods. Moreover, with variation of control parameters as a key element of this model of moods, the explanation for the continuity of infant experience remains within the affective domain without the need to introduce cognitive processes as a kind of deus ex machina.

MOOD CONTROL PROCESSES: SANDERIAN ACTIVATION WAVES

What might the internal self-organized processes look like that regulate the activation of moods? Let me begin with a caveat. My goal in presenting this model of moods is to provoke thinking about how affective control processes might operate. The model should not be reified but used only to challenge our usual (often cognitive) models about moods. Given this caveat, let us focus on how the sensitivity for activating a mood state is set. Again, following from the work on behavioral states of sleep and wakefulness, it is my hypothesis that self-organizing CNS and bodily processes (e.g., biological clocks) generate a biorhythmic, wavelike pattern of the sensitivity of the mood to activating affective input over time. I refer to this sensitivity, or activation curve, as a SAW.

The amplitude of the SAW at any one moment in time specifies the likelihood (the sensitivity) that affective input will activate a mood state at that point in time. When the amplitude is high, the likelihood of activation is high; whereas when the amplitude is low, the sensitivity is low. The wavelike ebb and flow over time (e.g., over hours) of the amplitude of a SAW specifies the change of a mood state's likelihood of activation. For example, the effect of the variation in a SAW can be seen when affective input from a partner (e.g., a lulling voice) can trigger an infant's affective state (e.g., a big smile and gesture) at one point in time, when the SAW's amplitude is high, but is ineffective at another point in time, when the amplitude has ebbed and is low. Thus a mood state is activated not by stimulation alone nor by stimulation mistimed or at the "wrong" place on the SAW. Activation is dependent on the interaction of the self-organized amplitude features of the SAW and the occurrence of input in relation to the parameters of the SAW. With the introduction of the SAW, the infant is no longer simply under stimulus control. Internal processes in relation to external events have an effect on the infant's affective state. For example, the variation of the SAW in relation to affective input is one mechanism that underlies the waxing and waning of moods. When the SAW associated with a positive affective state (posSAW) is high, the infant is more likely to be in a positive mood; but as the amplitude of the SAW decreases, the positive mood is likely to wane.

Clearly, to understand moods it is critical to understand how the sensitivity of the self-organized affective control processes of the SAW are set or modified. Most of the changes are associated with affective input. Affective input that exceeds the threshold of activation has two effects. First, when affective input exceeds the threshold of the SAW, it triggers an affective state. Second, it also transiently increases the sensitivity (raises the amplitude) of the SAW. For example, a smile from the caretaker that triggers a positive state in the infant also will increment the sensitivity (raise the amplitude) of the infant's posSAW. This increment in sensitivity has the effect of increasing the likelihood that the infant will be in a positive mood because, even if the caretaker's next smile is less intense than the first smile, it is more likely to exceed the posSAW's threshold. As a consequence of this modifiability of the SAW, affective input can increase (or the absence of affective input can decrease) the likelihood that a mood state is triggered by affective input and the likelihood of a mood state becoming established.

The size of the increment in the sensitivity of the SAW and its duration (rate of dissipation) are unknown. However, I can suggest several factors that affect the size of the increment and its duration. More intense and longer duration affective input will produce a larger and more lasting increment of sensitivity than will less intense or short-duration emotional input. Indeed, very powerful singular traumatic events (e.g., violent anger) will have a larger, possibly even a permanent effect on the sensitivity of a SAW. Furthermore, rapidly repeated affective events will have a greater effect on a SAW's sensitivity than events that occur more slowly. This effect is the result of self-amplification. Self-amplification occurs when the prior increment in sensitivity associated with a single affective event has not yet dissipated at the time the next input occurs. As a consequence, the changes in sensitivity begin to "pile up one on top of the other" and there is an accumulation—a self-amplification—of the increase in sensitivity of the SAW. I also expect that a SAW is more likely to be shifted by chronically recurrent events, especially ones that occur at the same point in time (i.e., at the same place on the SAW), for example, the excitement an infant begins to experience around the time when his father usually comes home from work. The effect of chronically recurrent, "well-timed" events is based on the assumption that the SAW, like other biorhythmic processes (e.g., sleep and awake states), is both open to input from the environment and has a stable temporal (e.g., ultradian and diurnal) organization that can function to anticipate the event that is yet to happen.

THE MOOD IN THE MORNING

Let me present an example of how my model describes how mood states and SAWs generate and establish long-lasting affective states with stickiness, momentum, ebb and flow, and other temporal features. The example is called the Mood in the Morning and begins with a transient event during one morning.

As the infant awakens, she is in a neutral mood, and the amplitudes of her negSAW and posSAW are close to, but still below, their activation thresholds (i.e., their sensitivity to triggering affective input is about the same). The mother approaches, does not smile, and comments angrily on the messy diaper and sheets. The occurrence of this negative affective input increases the amplitude of the infant's negSAW. It goes above the activation threshold, and the infant goes into a negative affective state. She has a pouty facial expression, whimpers, turns her head into the bedding, and starts to suck on her thumb. Within moments, more negative affective elements are recruited to this negative affective state. She starts to wail. The mother shifts her behavior and starts to comfort her. However, despite this change in the mother's affective behavior, the infant stays in her negative state. But the mother persists, and the negative mood starts to weaken. The amplitude of the negSAW has begun to dissipate because it is not receptive to (activated by) soothing input. Simultaneously the soothing input raises the amplitude of the posSAW above its activation threshold, and the infant moves into a positive affective state. She looks at the mother with big wide eyes, smiles, reaches up to her to be picked up. But the mother gets distracted and looks away, lost in thought. The baby almost immediately goes back into her negative affective state in response to this "still face" by her mother, and she is mostly in a negative mood for much of the morning until her nap. The mother says to her husband, "Boy, was she in a mood this morning. Nothing I tried seemed to make a difference."

How did the infant get into this mood on this morning? Given the amplitude of her negSAW when she first awakened, her mother's negative affect activated the negative affective state. One can imagine that, had the amplitude been lower or the mother's input less intense, the threshold might not have been exceeded. But the amplitude was high enough and the input was intense enough. The effect was to trigger a negative affective state (i.e., a large number of negative behaviors were assembled). But why was wailing added to the state

after a few moments? This adding on is one of the most interesting features of
moods. Mood states self-amplify; they feed on themselves. Being in a state further raises its amplitude and leads to the recruitment of additional related behaviors. The recruitment is a self-organized process that does not require external
input, but is in a sense (self-)triggered by the infant's own negative affective
behavior. But why does the infant stay in the negative state despite the mother's
soothing? States are sticky and not fully controlled by input. With the activation
of the state, there is a cascade of affective processes. The amplitude of the negSAW
is raised. Less intense and even internal events can now activate the state. It is
more coherently organized. Effectively there is an ongoing self-amplification of
these changes that generates the mood's momentum, and it keeps on going on
its own.

But why doesn't the infant simply stay in the negative affective state for the
whole morning? The infant shifts from a negative to a positive affective state
because the soothing no longer activates the negative state and its sensitivity
dissipates below threshold. Simultaneously the soothing input activates the positive affective state. But then why does the mother's looking away trigger the
negative affective state again? Such triggering is a critical feature of moods, as
opposed to more fleeting affects. It is also related to the dissipation of the SAW.
In this case, although the amplitude of the negSAW has dissipated below the
activation threshold, it has not returned to its earlier, lower level. It remains at
a heightened level close to the threshold. Now less intense input is able to activate it, even though the input would not be a sufficient trigger at other times.
By considering this movement between the negative mood state and positive
affects, we can see that other, briefer affects can be manifest as the negative
mood's threshold is crossed or as the SAW dissipates. These affects, however,
are vulnerable to preemption by the coherently organized, negative mood lurk-
ing just below the surface. Thus over the course of the morning other affective
states come and go in relation to the waxing and waning of the infant's mood.
But they have short durations because the negative mood is so readily activated
by external affect input or even internal processes. Of course, there is likely to
be a reciprocal effect on the mother. Her positive affective state is likely to dissipate in the face of her frustration in dealing with her baby's mood. Perhaps
she thinks to herself, "I just got more and more frustrated. I couldn't figure
what pleased her." Her reactions become part of an external social amplification of the infant's own internal self-amplification processes.

But how can this one-day morning mood become a stable affective state that
lasts for days for this baby? As Sander (1977, 1983a) has argued, the key to
understanding how psychological processes become established is the recurrence of events, and establishing a mood—an affective state that may last for
days—also takes recurrence. Let me extend the example to a longer period of
time, a month. The mother of our 4-month-old, recurrently, rather than just
occasionally, greets her in the morning with a negative affective display—lack
of eye contact, flat or angry facial expressions, veiled but hostile vocal tone, and

delayed comforting. At first the baby moves into a negative affective state, but she often can be comforted. After a few days of this recurrent pattern, however, she will become affectively negative when the mother performs even a slight behavior that expresses negative affect. For example, if the mother's voice is flat, the baby will go into a negative affective state, even though "flat-voiced mother" was not initially able to trigger her negative affective state. The infant is sensitized to the mother's negative affective displays. The duration of the state increases, even in response to the most comforting input from her mother. Everyone comments on how "tough she is to deal with in the mornings," and the mother begins to feel that "she doesn't know her anymore." Social amplification becomes more likely and regular.

How did the baby become so tough? Again, as in the one-day morning mood, the central events are the self-organizing and self-amplifying processes of affective states as they are repeatedly triggered. Essentially, with the daily recurrence of the daughter-mother negative interaction at waking, the increments in the sensitivity induced in the SAW are preserved over days. The ultradian and diurnal organizations of the negSAW are modified. Stabiization of these ultradian and diurnal changes is especially likely to occur when the recurrent event occurs at about the same time every day (i.e., at the same place on the SAW). As a consequence, the SAW of the elicited mood is shifted upward, and the amplitudes of unelicited moods are shifted downward. To stabilize the changes further, a self-reinforcing cascade of processes amplifies the shifts. In the example, with chronic exposure to the mother's negative affective state, the infant wakes up in the morning with the negSAW already approaching threshold. The baby is now very easily provoked. Moreover, the amplitude of her posSAW is low because it has recurrently not been triggered and has become difficult to provoke. As a consequence, there is an increase in the likelihood that the negative state is activated, which further induces and self-amplifies incremental changes in the sensitivity of the negSAW. These modifications, in turn, increase the likelihood that the negative state will occur the next day. The Mood in the Morning is established. All these processes are further amplified by the mother's social-affective behavior. Indeed, moods come to characterize, and be embodied in, the cocreated patterns of interpersonal relationships.

MOODS AND POLYMORPHIC REPRESENTATIONS

What are some of the implications of this model of moods? I expect, or perhaps I should better say feel, that we can now see how the characteristics of moods and the underlying SAW process fulfill the Janus principle. Edleman (1987) refers to an internal mapping process of an unlabeled world that can organize action. Though typically our first thoughts are to think of representations as cognitive, in fact, for adults, representations take on many forms: linguistic, symbolic, imagic, motoric, olfactory, visual, bodily. Any of these forms of representation may be in or out of awareness, conscious or unconscious, explicit or implicit. Given these polymorphs, it is critical to realize that representations do not have be a one-to-one mapping to the object, event, or experience, and they do not have to correspond in a one-to-one fashion to each other. A linguistic representation of an object is hardly the object, and it is hardly the same as an imagic representation. The transformation rules from the "real" event to its representation may be complex, but that complexity in no way diminishes that the past has been mapped into the present.

To explore this complexity, let me present an imprecise but revealing example. It is the idea that the representation we rely on when riding a bicycle does not correspond to the bicycle itself. Instead it captures the interaction between the rider, the object, and the riding environment. More specifically, the dynamic form of our body movements in riding a bicycle is an isomorphic representation of the bicycle, just as the word *bicycle* is a representation of the bicycle. Certainly, one would be hard pressed to figure out what a bicycle actually looked like simply by looking at riding movements. Riding movements have a self-generated and constrained organization that is modified by the forces acting on the body and the brain as they engage the bicycle as it engages the features of the terrain. The transformation functions of these constraints and forces to the movements that are actually made are complex. Nonetheless, the movements are fitted to the shape of the bicycle in unique ways. They would not be confused with the movements associated with riding a scooter or rowing a boat. Thus, the movements isomorphically represent the bicycle, just as does a picture or a blueprint. Importantly, once this bodily representation is established, once the bicycle and terrain become mapped into the body and the brain, these movements will shape movements in the future. If the bicycle is changed, the movements initially will be like the ones made on the original bicycle. However, over time the movements will change and take on a form unique to the new bicycle. Thus, the movements as representations are open and modifiable by input. If they were not, we would always deploy tricycle-riding movements with bicycles, a past we would not want to maintain into the present and the future.

I believe moods are another member of this polymorphic set of representational forms, but one with a special centrality in infancy. Moods and the interplay among them are representations of the emotional experience, especially the chronic emotional experience of the infant. Mood processes and the parameters of their control processes, such as the level and temporal flow of their SAW, are affected by affective input. The induced changes in the control processes bias how new affective input is processed and which affective behaviors will be assembled and activated. Thus, the settings of these parameters encode the history of the infant's affective experience. Were the experience different, the settings would be different. In turn, the affective state's stickiness organizes the infant's social-affective behavior in the present moment. Its momentum moves that social-affective behavior into the future.

In the example of the Mood in the Morning, the infant awakens in a mood that organizes a negative affective state and negatively biases how she will react to her mother's affective input. Her mood is sticky, and it has momentum. It got that way because her recurrent negative experience with her mother at waking was isomorphically mapped into her mood. Her Mood in the Morning is stable (though changeable). For now it organizes her actions in the present, the immediate future, and even tomorrow's future. The ebb and flow of the mood's SAW, as a representation, allows her to anticipate what she "expects" to happen and organizes her response. However, while her mood is a mapping, a representation that functions as a memorial anticipatory process, it has no schemes, language, or symbols. It is purely affective.

MOODS AND AFFECTIVE DISTURBANCES

Moods are normal affective processes, but the same processes that generate them can produce affective disturbances in the infant. Such disturbances are associated with a limitation or even a failure of the mood state to be affected by input. In the Mood in the Morning example, after a month of negative maternal greetings with their repeated activation of her negative affective state, things "get worse"—the infant wakes up in a negative affective state. Her SAW has a flow, but the whole SAW has been elevated and acutely entrained to her waking in the morning. Thus she does not look at her mother when she enters but, rather, looks at an object, fusses, sucks on her thumb, and cries without reaching up to her mother to be picked up. Whatever the mother does makes no difference. Indeed, even some soothing actions only intensify the state (the negSAW is so sensitive that the soothing is experienced as intrusive). She is in a negative mood pretty much regardless of what the mother is doing. Her mother says, "She just wakes up in a bad mood."

What has occurred is that the reiterated activations of her negative affective state around the same time each day have led to a self-organized and stable level of her negative affect state's SAW such that it can be above its activation threshold "on its own." It has become independent of input. Or, if independent is too strong a word, the negative state can be activated by an extremely wide variety of very low-intensity internal or external stimuli. Much of the SAW's specific fit to affective input is lost. The mood is, or at least seems to be, activated for no apparent reason. It is very sticky, has a lot of momentum, and is amplified and stabilized by the infant's self-organizing processes. In a sense, it is disconnected from reality. Indeed, the infant now engages in coping behaviors, such as looking away, that exacerbate this disconnection. These coping behaviors, which normally limit the disruptive effect of negative events, are now deployed in anticipation of affective events. However, since these events may not be forthcoming, the behaviors are in some ways defensive (i.e., affective actions deployed in anticipation of events that may not occur but that preclude processing the real event; see Gianino & Tronick, 1988). Thus the infant's self-organizing affective processes and self-regulatory processes increasingly conspire with each other to detach the infant from reality. The infant's mood, functioning as an affective representation of the past, distorts the future. The infant has developed an affective problem.

I do not know if such an affective problem can be thought of as an affective disorder or if we could reify it into a diagnosis. It is, in fact, a diagnosis in clinical infant work. At times I am tempted to make such a diagnosis, for instance, when I think about infants exposed to traumatic events. These events may drive the threshold so high that the affective state is often activated, especially if the traumatic event almost always occurs in the context of recurrent chronic stress and distortion. Or I think of affective disorder when an infant uses internal coping processes in an attempt to segregate the trauma-induced affective state from other affective states and experiences. This affective segregation of one affective state from other states may be analogous to cognitive dissociation or splitting, as, for example, in the infant who interacts positively with her mother but is unable to express any anger toward her mother even though her mother has left her repeatedly in stressful situations. The infant's reaction may be seen as adaptive, but it does not integrate her positive and negative affective states in relation to her mother. The negative affect is split off. This segregation is an affective process, not a cognitive process. In fact, given my experience it seems to me almost unimaginable for the young infant to have any sort of cognitive processes (e.g., working models) that would be capable of splitting off experience. By contrast, affective and regulatory processes would seem able to isolate affective states and split them off from other states and distort the infant's functioning. Of course, we have not identified such phenomena in infants, but we also have not looked for them. I believe they exist, and this thinking would help us to observe and identify them.

Another situation that tempts me to think of affective disorders involves infants who are chronically exposed to low levels of negative input. For example, we have found that maternal depressed affect is extremely stable and unchanging over the first year of life even if the mother fails to meet diagnostic criteria (Beeghly et al., 2002). In these situations, though the exposure to negative affect is constant, it is not intense enough always to generate a negative affective state. This low-intensity affective input, a kind of low-level affective radioactive contamination, nonetheless insidiously raises the sensitivity of the negative affective state. Over time the infant is forced to deploy self-directed coping behaviors to restrict the experience of this chronically oppressive state. As a consequence, the infant's affective experience is dramatically compressed and shifts toward an aberrant pathway of development. But whether or not we use terms like *disorder* or even diagnostic terms, my hypothesis is that these sorts of chronic affective problems are signaled by the dominance of a single affect, a restricted range of affect (e.g., no heightened positive or negative emotions), an anticipatory deployment of self-directed coping behaviors that produce a detachment from people and things, and expressions of affect that are not connected to affective reality. Unfortunately, because we do not know the range and variation of affective states in normal infants, it is difficult to identify a restricted range or dominance of a single affect. Of course, we can identify the extreme cases, but we must also be concerned for those infants in low-level chronic situations who are experiencing affective problems that are currently completely unrecognized, cases that I refer to as the "Oh, don't worry, he will grow out of it" cases, which are not grown out of but grown into.

MOODS AS A TWO-PERSON MODEL OF COCREATION

This discussion of affective problems—of moods deployed independent of ongoing input—raises the conceptual danger of thinking about this model of moods as locating mood processes only in the infant. But the affective processes that generate moods are not simply located in the infant; the model is not a one-person model. It is a model of two (or more) persons engaging in affective regulation. It is a two-sided model. On the infant's side, the model sees the infant as neither void of organized processes nor passive in the face of affective input. Infants have self-organizing processes that generate affective states that have short- and long-run temporal features. The model also sees infants as self-regulating their affective states with coping behaviors (e.g., self-comforting, looking away, disengaging). In the Mood in the Morning example, had the infant initially been able to comfort herself by sucking on her thumb and turning away from the mother when the mother first came into the room, her SAW might have stayed below threshold and allowed for a better morning. Thus in no sense are infants simply at the mercy of input.

As I have argued in my mutual regulation model (MRM; Gianino & Tronick, 1988; Tronick, 1989; see also Beebe, Jaffe, & Lachmann, 1992; Hofer, 1994b; Stern, 1976) and as others have noted (Cramer & Stern, 1988; Field, 1995; Fogel et al., 1983), despite an infant's affective and self-regulatory capacities, the affective and regulatory input from the caregiver affects the infant's affective states and regulatory success. The underlying processes of mood are open to input, and they change as the affective input from another person interacts with these processes. Thus other persons are external regulators (Hofer, 1994b) of the infant's affective state, making affective processes dyadic, not monadic. In the Mood in the Morning example, it is clear how the mother's affective state affects the infant's state. It is also clear how her regulatory actions scaffold the infant's own regulatory actions (e.g., the mother's persistent soothing of the infant despite her infant's upset). Thus affective regulation is not only within the infant or only within the caretaker. It is dyadic. From my perspective, as a consequence of these dyadic processes, the infant and the caregiver cocreate infant moods. A hypothesis about an individual's mood being cocreated may seem odd, but I do not see how it could be otherwise (see Tronick, 2003b, for an elaboration of this perspective).

REPRESENTATIONAL INFUSIONS AND
INTERGENERATIONAL TRANSFER

Given this view of the mutuality of the processes that create moods, it is important to consider, at least briefly, the mother's (caretaker's) role in this process. My
hypothesis is that mutual regulatory processes make possible the transfer of maternal moods to the infant. Once the infant detects the mother's expressed affect
(and if infants are anything, they are mood detectors), the infant actively processes
the mother's affect to generate his or her own affective state. This is not simply
a passive mirroring by the infant. Moreover, in this mutually regulated process,
the caretaker's affective state is affected by the infant's affective state. In the Mood
in the Morning example, the mother's mood becomes more negative as the infant
becomes more and more distressed. Thus the infant and the mother create their
moods together. But because there is an asymmetry in the dyad, what the infant
and the mother carry into this creative process is different.

A mother's mood states are more complexly, or perhaps it is better to say differently, governed than are the processes governing infant moods. In particular, mothers have dynamic representational processes (Fraiberg, Adelson, &
Shapiro, 1975; Seligman, 1994). The mother may have said to the father that
she "just wakes up in a bad mood," but the mother may have consciously, or
more likely unconsciously, thought, "The baby is just like my mother. I could-
n't please her because I didn't really know her, either." The mother's affective
state is not simply a pure affective state (a state connected only to the moment),
or a mood based only on her emotional experience with her infant (which is
more likely to characterize infants' affective states). Rather, the mother's affective state is in part determined by dynamic representations (representations the
infant has not yet developed). These representational processes typically (but
not always) unconsciously affect the mother's affective state. The effect of
maternal dynamic representations is to bring unconscious meanings and memories of the mother's past into her present affective state. Thus, infants have to
process an affective state that contains unconscious and implicit meanings,
what I refer to as representational infusions.

There is evidence that infants are affected by these representational infusions, clinical cases in which infants take on the symptoms of the mother (e.g.,
the infant of a once-but-no-longer anorexic mother and who fails to thrive).
There is also therapeutic research on how changing maternal representations
changes her engagement with her infant and, in turn, her infant's state
(Bruschweiler-Stern & Stern, 1989; Cramer, 1997; Seligman, 1999; Stern,
1985). More difficult is understanding how representational infusions, which
are largely unconscious, can be conveyed in ways that affect the infant. One
way is that they might add something specific to the mother's behavioral and
affective displays. For a toddler or a child, one might think about how words
are used or about the concordance of words and actions. The mother might
use sweet words with a hostile voice and gesture. Another possibility is that the

mother's affective infusions affect how she responds to her infant's affective displays in ways that are distorted. For example, the mother responds with affective displays that do not match the infant's affective state (e.g., maternal sadness or anger in response to infant positive affective displays, or maternal turning away from infant solicitations of eye-to-eye contact). Massie (1982), Stern (1976), and others have described the profoundly derailing developmental effects of affective mismatching on infants who chronically experience them. They have also shown how the mismatching is founded on and generated by unconscious representational infusions (see also Tronick & Weinberg, 1997).

Yet another possibility is that maternal affective processes are distorted by representational infusions in particular contexts such that they distort specific infant emotional and behavioral processes. For example, anorexic mothers disrupt the feeding of their infants (Stein, Woolley, Cooper, & Fairburn, 1994). The disruption is not so much in their feeding technique but is more related to the affective states they express during feeding. These states result in a lack of pleasure in feeding for the infant, and as a consequence feeding-related problems develop in the infant, including failure to thrive. Such context-specific disruptions hold out the possibility of generating distortions of an infant's affect and behavior that are specifically related to the maternal representations. But, whatever the process, I do not think that this process is (yet) one in which the infant is generating cognitive models (e.g., working models) of its own. Rather, I think we need to seek out an explanation in how representational infusions affect the affective processes of the mother-infant dyad and, in turn, the infant's mood states.

NEUROPHYSIOLOGICAL MECHANISMS

I have not addressed the question of which underlying neurophysiological processes might account for the establishment of moods and processes such as the SAW. There are several reasons for this omission. First, although we are "infatuated" with the brain, some of the processes may not be in the brain. I think they may be in the body. Downing (2001) has suggested that we need to think about the infant's developing implicit motor procedures that go along with moods. These bodily processes would be stable ways of being in a mood and expressing it. They would be ways in which we as well as others come to know our moods. Given that we are talking primarily of infants, I think our disregard of the body at the very least undermines our attempt to understand affect and moods. Second, I do not want to tie the model to a particular model of the brain or a particular set of functions in the brain. Nonetheless, a number of neurophysiological processes are compatible with this model of moods. One is that there might be chronic changes in the brain's neurotransmitters. I like this idea because one can think of neurotransmitters as a soup that affects brain processes. Think of pea soup. Adding one carrot sends waves of flavor through the soup, but if it is the only carrot, then its effect dissipates over time.

Adding a lot of carrots may permanently change the soup's flavor. Indeed, enough carrots may change it into carrot soup. Affective input may change the neurotransmitter soup action in similar ways. The neurotransmitter soup may generate a sad mood but, with enough positive input, there could be a dynamic shift into another state, such as joy. There are other processes, such as the stabilization of neural nets, electrophysiological changes analogous to kindling, changes in attractor states of brain processes, shifting central timing mechanisms, modifying the synchronicities among different regions of the brain, and neuronal selection (Edelman, 1987; Schore, 1994). All these processes and others have been linked to affective states and are modifiable by input. Choosing among them, despite my preference for the soup idea, is not possible at the current time, and it is not necessary for understanding moods.

SOME FUTURE ISSUES

A number of other issues might be pursued further. One is how moods may modify infant-parent therapeutic work. This is a critical issue and requires fuller treatment, but it will have to be taken up elsewhere. I would note only that moods are dissipative states that change slowly. Getting them to shift requires the induction of chronic changes in the affective experience of the infant. Moreover, the work must be dyadic, and it must work with the dyad's creative processes. Another issue to pursue is that the model is not restricted to infants. I think it applies to children and adults as well. Thus it has implications for the role of moods in adult mental states and psychopathology and for adult therapeutic work. In my work with the Boston Change Process Study Group (2002) we have not talked much about moods but rather about the processes of moving along and relational moves (affective moves) that provoke change. I believe that, when mood states are an issue for a patient, as they often are, relational affective processes in the therapeutic setting will be critical for inducing change. This is not to deny the importance of other dynamic processes, such as insight or analyzing the transference. My point is simply that moods are likely to be more open and "shiftable" through affective input than through cognitive processes, because, as implicit isomorphic representational processes, they are not readily transformed into a narrative structure (Beebe et al., 1992; Emde, 1983; Fonagy & Target, 1998; Fosha, 2000; Schore, 1994; Tronick, 1998, 2001).

Last, there has been little elaboration of the interplay among moods. Their interplay is a complex process. But one of the possibilities is that, by seeing mood states as central to the organization of the infant, one can begin to consider that they come into dynamic conflict with one another (also see Seligman, 1999, for a related discussion). For example, when one mood is manifest but another mood is moving toward activation, the infant may find itself in a dynamic internal conflict. This kind of dynamic conflict would not be a conflict of unconscious, adultlike representational processes (which, once again, the infant does not yet have) but a conflict of implicit affective representational processes. It is interesting to think, following Downing (2001), that the conflict may be felt most keenly in the body. Another instance where there would likely be dynamic conflict concerns the segregating of an affective state from other affective states. Thus, thinking about affective dynamics might provide a deeper understanding of the disregulation and disorganization seen in infants and even in adults. But this and other issues will have to be pursued in other papers.

Allow me one last thought. If infant moods have even some of the centrality I have argued they have, why haven't we attended to them more than we have? I believe that this may be the case because we (researchers and clinicians) want to deny that infants have moods. Were we to accept the phenomenon of infant moods, it would shatter our often romanticized images of infants as affectively curious and happy and emotionally flexible (Tronick, 1989). But, if we did bring the mood idea into consciousness, we would have to examine the possibility that "infants with moods" might also experience affective problems and disorders. Such a possibility is a very painful and disquieting thought, but it has unexplored implications for our research and clinical work with children and adults.

CHAPTER 34

"Of Course All Relationships Are Unique": How Cocreative Processes Generate Unique Mother-Infant and Patient-Therapist Relationships and Change Other Relationships

UNIQUENESS, THERAPY, AND COCREATION

Other than lip service reiteration of an overly general and featureless belief that "of course relationships are unique," little thought has been devoted to questions related to the uniqueness of relationships: How do relationships come to be unique? What are some of the features of their uniqueness? It is a striking oversight because in our work with patients we always work with the unique. Many models that attempt to explain these questions, especially the question of how one relationship has a unique effect on another, unknowingly limit and constrain change processes and forms of uniqueness. These models invoke notions of scripts, rule-governed structures, canonical forms, narrative structures, schemes, and schemas. These forms generate plenty of orderliness but little uniqueness. In an extreme but typical example, a narrative structure leaves little room for change or the emergence of something new. It has order, a shape, and a form, a beginning, middle, and end, but it is much the same every time. Moreover, these models fail to see that all relationships would look alike were they influenced by a single preeminent model (e.g., the mother-infant relationship).

Much of what I present emerges from my long collaboration with T. Berry Brazelton, Katherine Weinberg, and Marjorie Beeghly at the Child Development Unit and from my early work with the Boston Change Process Study Group (Boston CPSG). In this chapter, I focus on the uniqueness of several relational processes that express relational affect and intentions (i.e., affective configurations or relational moves), past knowing about how to be together (e.g., implicit relational knowing), and the contexts that partners have regulated together (what I will call thickness). These characteristics emerge from the past history of the relationship, but I will try to show how these features add specificity to aspects of what we generally lump into the term *past history*. Thus, I hope that examining these characteristics of relationships can help us to disaggregate how the past affects the present and the future. For example, these features will help in understanding the difference between relationships and "mere" interactions. A fundamental point I want to make is that uniqueness emerges out of mutual regulatory recurrent cocreative interactive processes between the infant and another person from the microtemporal level to more macrolevels of the interaction (Tronick, 2001, 2002b; Tronick, Als, & Adamson, 1979; Tronick, Als, & Brazelton, 1980a).

THE MUTUAL REGULATION MODEL

Uniqueness arises out of microregulatory socioemotional processes. My mutual regulation model (MRM) is an attempt to understand the microregulatory socioemotional processes that generate the unique features of the relationship (Brazelton, 1992; Brazelton, Koslowski, & Main, 1974; Brazelton & Yogman, 1986; Gianino & Tronick, 1988; Tronick, 1989; see also Beebe, Jaffe, & Lachmann, 1992; Beebe & Lachmann, 1994; Belsky & Nezworski, 1998; Fogel, Diamond, Langhorst, & Demos, 1983;). Briefly, in the mother-infant interaction, each partner communicates his or her affective evaluation of the state of what is going on in the interaction, what Foscha (2000) refers to as relational affects (e.g., feeling apart from, feeling in sync), and their relational intention (e.g., continue, stop, be connected; Weinberg & Tronick, 1994). These communications are simultaneously expressed with what I and my colleagues call affective configurations or relational moves (Weinberg & Tronick, 1994). In response to the partner's relational moves, each individual attempts to adjust his or her behavior to maintain a coordinated dyadic state or to repair a mismatch (Tronick & Cohn, 1989).

When mutual regulation is particularly successful—that is, when the age-appropriate forms of meaning (e.g., affects, relational intentions, representations; see Tronick, 2002d, 2002e) from one individual's state of consciousness are coordinated with the meanings of another's state of consciousness—I have hypothesized that a dyadic state of consciousness emerges (Tronick et al., 1998; Tronick, 2002d). Though it shares characteristics with intersubjective states, a dyadic state of consciousness is not merely an intersubjective experience (Tronick, Als, et al., 1980a). A dyadic state of consciousness has dynamic effects. It increases the coherence of the infant's state of consciousness and expands the infant's (and the partner's) state of consciousness (Tronick, 2002b, 2002e; Tronick et al., 1998). Thus, dyadic states of consciousness are critical, perhaps even necessary for development (Tronick & Weinberg, 1997).

An experiential effect of the achievement of a dyadic state of consciousness is that it leads to feeling larger than oneself. Thus, infants' experience of the world and states of consciousness is determined not only by their own self-organizing processes, but also by dyadic regulatory processes that affect their state of consciousness (Tronick et al., 1998; see also Tronick, 2002a, for a dyadic account of the generation of moods).

COCREATION AND THE INCREASING DIFFERENTIATION OF RELATIONSHIPS

A fundamental principle of the MRM is that the form of the interaction and the meaning of the relational affects and intentions that regulate the exchange emerge from a cocreative process. Cocreative processes produce unique forms of being together, not only in the mother-infant relationship but in all relationships. Cocreation emphasizes dynamic and unpredictable changes of relationships that underlie their uniqueness. I want to emphasize that I am not using the term *cocreative* as a reformulated substitute for the more commonly used term *coconstruction*. Coconstruction contains a metaphor of a blueprint that implies a set of steps for getting to an end state. Cocreativity implies neither a set of steps nor an end state. Rather, it implies that when two individuals mutually engage in a communicative exchange, how they will be together, their dynamics and direction, are unknown and only emerge from their mutual regulation. Thus, while we can look at an exchange that has taken place and make a narrative account of it, we must realize that there was no narrative or blueprint structuring the exchange before or even as it was happening. Seeing this difference—that what has happened can be narrated, but what is happening cannot be narrated—and holding onto the distinction have critical implications for understanding what goes on in relationships, including the therapeutic relationship (Boston CPSG, 2002; Tronick, 2002b).

A primary implication of the principle of cocreation is my relationship differentiation hypothesis: Relationships increasingly differentiate from one another over time. That is, relationships become more and more unique from one another over time as new forms of being together are cocreated. The development of relationships contrasts sharply with the development of cognition. Cognition becomes increasingly abstract, decontextualized, schematized, and transferable. By contrast, relationships do not become increasingly general, but become more detailed; they do not become more abstract, but become concrete; they do not become increasingly decontextualized (i.e., depersonified), but become increasingly personified, tied to an individual; they do not become more schematized, but become increasingly specific; and they do not become more universally applicable, but become less and less transferable. This view of the differentiation of relationships contrasts to notions of RIGS (Stern, 1985) or model scenes (Beebe & Lachmann, 1994), which see interactive regulatory patterns as abstracted, depersonified ways of having expectations about being with others. Though the issue is complex, for me these concepts actually refer to a narrative of what happened and not to the process of their cocreation at the time of their happening.

Another implication of cocreativity is that unlike many other accounts of relational processes which see interactive "misses" (e.g., mismatches, misattunements, dissynchronies, miscoordinations) as indicating something is wrong with an interaction, these misses are the interactive and affective stuff from which cocreative reparations generate new ways of being together (Cohn & Tronick, 1989; Tronick, 1989). Instead there are only relationships that are inherently sloppy, messy, and ragged and individuals in relationships that are better able, or less able, to cocreate new ways of being together (Tronick, 2002d, 2002e). Thus, there is no perfect or perfectible form of a relationship (e.g., the ideal mother-infant relationship) nor would one want one, because it would not change.

COCREATION AND NONTRANSFERABILITY

Cocreation leads to unique features of the interaction at several levels, and because they are unique I think that they are not transferable to other relationships. Uniqueness first emerges at the microtemporal level of relational moves, but the uniqueness of relationships does not reside only at the microbehavioral level of relational moves (Boston CPSG, 2002; Stern et al., 1998; Tronick, 1998). The cocreation of relational intentions and affects and the recurrence of relational moves generate implicit relational knowing about how to be together (Lyons-Ruth, 1999; Lyons-Ruth et al., 1998). Implicit relational knowing is a form of implicit knowledge about how we do things together. Implicit relational knowing comes in several forms. One is as an integration of the recurrent microinteractions of the dyad (Lyons-Ruth et al., 1998). These microinteractive knowings are found in the details of different unique games played by the infant, for example, with the mother, with the father, or with others. Even when the same behaviors occur in several dyads, the meanings of the behavior in each relationship may be unique. For example, mutual looks away by the mother and the infant mean "we are teasing," whereas with the father and infant the same manifest behavior carries the meaning "we need to pause and switch to something new." Moreover, the difference in the meaning of a piece of behavior between individuals in a relationship is cryptic to other individuals. As a consequence, I have hypothesized that much of the knowing in one relationship may be nontransferable to other relationships (Tronick, 2002e). As we shall see, nontransferability has significance for how relationships influence other relationships.

A second kind of unique implicit knowledge is knowing how we are able to work together (e.g., how we repair misses) no matter what the content of the errors (Tronick, 2002d). Though I find the terminology awkward, it is something like a metaprocedural knowing. For example, out of the recurrence of reparations, the infant and another person come to share the implicit knowledge that "we can move into a mutual positive state even when we have been in a mutual negative state." Or "We can transform negative into positive affect." Clearly this is a very powerful piece of implicit knowing. This kind of knowing develops regardless of the particular behaviors or relational moves that generated the mismatches and the reparations. Thus, one form of implicit relational knowing has to do with the specific things done in the interaction (e.g., idiosyncratic forms of common baby games such as peekaboo or click games), whereas the metaprocedural kind is a more general way of working together (e.g., "we repair mismatches this way").

Nonetheless, both pieces of knowing are specific to a particular relationship. They will not be found in the same way in other relationships. However, my sense is that the metaprocedural ("how we work together") has an effect on the infant (and the other person) that the microinteractive form does not. The metaprocedural knowing generates ways of feeling about one's self in relationships (e.g., "I feel effective," "I feel trustful"). Importantly, while implicit relational knowing may not be transferable to other relationships, the feelings of self-in-relationships that emerge from metaprocedural knowing are brought by the infant into other relationships. These feelings can be seen in the infant who robustly approaches new people bravely and openly compared to the infant who is wary and fearful. Brazelton (personal communication, 1995) has talked about these feelings of self-in-relationship in describing 9-month-olds who already have developed a sense of their mastery ("Yes, I can!") or a feeling of failure ("No, I won't try") in a relationship. So, these feelings of self-in-relationship do affect how the infant is with others and these forms will be critical when we consider how one relationship can influence another (Brazelton & Cramer, 1990).

COCREATION OF THICKNESS

Another unique characteristic of relationships emerges from recurrent experiences in different time-activity contexts shared by a dyad. I refer to this kind of uniqueness as thickness. Thickness refers to the variety of time-activity contexts that are coexperienced and mutually regulated by the infant and another. Time-activity contexts include feedings, diaper changing, putting to bed, playing with toys, and almost all other infant activities. Each of these time-activity contexts will develop particular meanings, temporal organization, and sequential relations compared to other time-activity contexts (Hofer, 1994b; Tronick, 2002a). Thus, the thickness of the cocreated experience of each dyad is unique.

For example, mothers (most typically) experience and coregulate sleep and awake states with their infant. Many of these activities are not experienced with others by the infant, or if they are they have a very different regulatory organization. Furthermore, mothers most often feed the infant, change the infant, play with the infant, and move through the day with the infant with a regulatory pattern that is not shared by the infant and another. The infant and the mother coregulate an especially varied set of time-activity contexts and they develop unique implicit knowledge of how they are together in each of these contexts. Moreover, for them the implicit knowledge from one context affects how other contexts are experienced. For example, the mother implicitly knows when the infant will be awakening and how he wakes up ("his mood in the morning"; see Tronick, 2002a). She also knows what he likes to do when he wakes up. Together they know how to be together at waking. Thus, the mother-infant relationship is not only very thick, it is singularly thick compared to other relationships. More generally, all relationships have some unique qualities because of the thickness of the time-activity contexts they share and the meanings cocreated in those contexts.

An objection raised to the concept of thickness by one somewhat (forgive me) "thick" colleague was that thickness was simply another term for the past. Certainly thickness refers to the past and is but one dimension of the past. However, I think it adds precision to the broad concept of the past by focusing on the microregulatory process of cocreating meanings in different time-activity contexts and their reciprocal effects on one another. For me, the concept of thickness makes it possible to disaggregate the past into different kinds of events (time-activity contexts) that can be identified and described, and at least theoretically can be counted. Put another way, all relationships have different pasts and what the concept of thickness does is to give us a way of seeing one aspect of each relationship's different past and enabling us to characterize them as differing in their degree of thickness.

RELATIONSHIPS AND "MERE" INTERACTIONS

The uniqueness of the meaning of relational moves, micro- and metaknowings, and thickness helps us to sort out the difference between interactions and relationships. Simply put, relationships have unique forms of these features whereas interactions lack them. For example, when an infant interacts with a stranger, the interaction is characterized by what Marilyn Davillier (personal communication, April 1999) calls baby small talk (BST). BST is a somewhat scripted form of interaction and it lacks cocreativity. For example, though the infant and the stranger are able to interact with one another, their implicit relational knowing is severely limited and there is no thickness to their interaction. Our research (Dixon et al., 1981) shows that the initial segment of an infant-stranger interaction is characterized by BST. A 5-month-old infant initially smiles at the stranger and the stranger responds with a smile. The interaction looks "good" for a brief time. There may be a second set of mutual smiles. But then the interaction seems to run down. The infant or the stranger tries something like a touching game but one or the other fails to pick up on it. The interaction does not move on. Often it ends up with the stranger at a loss as to what to do and the infant looking away. They are not able to cocreate a direction for the interaction. As Davillier's BST implies, this sequence is much like what happens when two people meet at a cocktail party and find they have nothing in common ("Hello." "Hello." "What do you do? Oh." "What do you do? Oh. . . ." "Oh." "I think I'll get another drink," said simultaneously).

The common feature between Davillier's BST and adult small talk is that both are scripted interchanges. They are limited, formal, canonical, and fixed. They lack cocreativity. It will take more interchanges for the infant and the stranger to cocreate ways to be together before they begin to generate thickness and specificity, if they ever can. They may not succeed. Interacting with another many times is no guarantee that a relationship will develop. Some interactions (e.g., interactions with neighbors) can occur often and have a long history, yet never get beyond small talk. Of course, other interactions can be brief and nonetheless generate uniqueness (e.g., falling in love). Thus, thinking in terms of the cocreation of implicit relational knowing and thickness moves beyond the general idea of having a history together to a delineation of what happens and what is cocreated when the pair is together. These qualities begin to help us separate relationships from mere interactions and to think about how relationships differ.

THE INCREASING DIFFERENTIATION OF RELATIONSHIPS AND SOME IMPLICATIONS FOR THE MUTUAL INFLUENCE OF ONE RELATIONSHIP ON ANOTHER RELATIONSHIP

The ongoing cocreation of the unique features of relationships leads to relationships becoming increasingly differentiated from each other. For example, what the infant does with the mother, how many different things they do together, and the meaning of what they do together are increasingly specific and thick and differentiated from what is done with the father. Moreover, though the differentiation of infant-adult relationships is only implicitly representational in the usual sense of that word (Emde, 1983; but see Tronick, 2002a, and below), as the infant develops cognitive, linguistic, symbolic, reflective, and explicit representational capacities, further differentiation among relationships occurs in these developmental forms of meaning (Tronick, 2002d). Additionally, this developmental emergence of these different forms of meanings makes relationships at every stage of development uniquely different from what they were or will be at other stages of development. As a consequence of differentiation, more and more of what is done in one relationship becomes increasingly nontransferable to other relationships. For example, mutual looks between the mother and infant may mean "we are ready for doing something special," whereas with others, looking away may mean "let's take a break" (Brazelton et al., 1974).

Seeing this differentiation and resulting nontransferability of cocreated ways of being together raises the question of how one relationship affects another relationship. Taking possibly the most important example, how does the mother-infant relationship, most likely the most differentiated relationship, affect other relationships?

The answer offered by attachment theory is that the mother-infant relationship is the prototype of other late-developing relationships (Ainsworth, 1993; Bowlby, 1969, 1982; Cassidy, 1994; Main, 1995, 1999; Sroufe, 1998). In contrast to the concerns focused on by the model of cocreation of relationships, attachment theory shows less concern for the dynamics of change in the mother-child relationship over time even in the face of developmental changes in the child's emotional and cognitive capacities. It also is less concerned with the issue of uniqueness of the mother-child relationship and how it is influenced by other relationships. But, if not by prototypical processes, how might the mother-infant relationship, which does seem to have an undeniable influence on other relationships, influence other relationships? Or, to reformulate the question, how might a hypothesis of a cocreated and growing differentiation of relationships permit the singular influence of specific features of the mother-infant relationship on the child's and adult's later relationships, and how might other relationships influence it? (For a fuller discussion of the these issues, including the question of how relationships are sought after for their own sake and not as a counterpoint for exploration, see Brazelton, 1992; Tronick, 2002c.)

DYNAMIC RELATIONSHIP EFFECTS IN AN EXPERIENTIAL RELATIONAL SPACE

For me an initial starting point is not to give up the ideas that each relationship is singular and dynamically changing and that as each is experienced and reexperienced it influences the other. Holding to cocreativity and change, we can turn to the work of Freeman (1994) for guidance.

Relational Activation Processes in an Experiential Relational Space

Freeman (1994) has shown that the EEG activation pattern for an odor in the olfactory cortex of the rabbit is different each time it is experienced. Second, different odors nonetheless produce activation patterns and responses that are differentiated from one another. Third, when a new odor is introduced, the organization of all of the individual EEG patterns of the previously experienced odors and the overall olfactory cortical pattern are changed. Though there are constraints on the possible patterns, Freeman found no fixed patterns or prototypes. Nonetheless, the responses to the odors were veridical. Freeman's interpretation is that there is a dynamic array of odor activation patterns that reciprocally influence one another. This array of patterns is contextualized in a changing overall gestalt of the olfactory space that allows for the recognition of different odors. Though not part of Freeman's account, an assembling of odor activation patterns from different odors could be thought of as the rabbit's more integrated implicit knowledge of that assemblage.

Applying Freeman's thinking to relationships, I would first hypothesize that there are relational activation patterns (RAPs) that are activated by different relational experiences. RAPs are analogous to the activation patterns of different odors. Second, RAPs are dynamically assembled in an experiential relational space (ERS) in an analogous fashion to the assembling of odor activation patterns in the olfactory cortex. The ERS may reside in the cingulate and other limbic structures (Schore, 2001). Third, as with the assembling of many activation patterns of odors from different odors in the olfactory space, the thickness of the accumulated RAPs from the different time-activity contexts experienced in a relationship is assembled in the ERS. Furthermore, RAPs are contextualized by the overall gestalt of RAPs in the ERS, just as individual and assembled activation patterns of odors are contextualized by the gestalt of the activation patterns in the olfactory cortex.

The Dynamic Specific Influence of Relationships on Other Relationships

This conceptualization of RAPs in an ERS is both dynamic and specific. Dynamically, each time the infant interacts with a particular other, the infant's RAPs and assemblage of RAPs of the relationship change. This change in RAPs is analogous to the change in the activation pattern of the reexperienced odor. Critically, as with the odors, the change of RAPs also affects the RAPs and the assemblages of RAPs of other relationships. As a consequence, "all" the infant's ways of being are changed. Importantly, when a RAP is reinvoked by an interactive experience, the change is not divorced from its past. Rather, it is influenced by the integrated assembling of the relationship's already existing RAPs and the gestalt of the RAPs in the ERS. Thus, RAPs are subject to a host of changes that make each relationship dynamically singular (unique but not static) and capable of influencing other relationships in unique ways. But how might different relationships influence other relationships? I think that processes related to the recurrence and the intensity of experience are critical to the effect of one relationship's RAPs on another's RAPs. Returning to the infant-mother relationship, it is the more often experienced relationship. Its assemblage of RAPs is singularly thick and because of its thickness it is likely to take up more ERS. The mother-infant relationship may be analogous to an intense odor that the rabbit is exposed to far more times than it is exposed to other odors.

Much of the change arising out of recurrent infant-mother interactions is likely to be small in magnitude and is likely to have only a small effect on its RAPs and the RAPs of other relationships. However, occasionally the assemblage of RAPs in the infant-mother relationship has a coherence that generates a dyadic state of consciousness and a radical shift in the relationship takes place (Tronick, 2001, 2002e). This dyadic state of consciousness will generate a shift of the gestalt of the RAPs pattern in the ERS, which will more powerfully affect the RAPs of the other relationships in the ERS. Importantly, the effect is specific to the implicit knowing of how the infant and mother are together. It is not some general form of Davillier's BST. Of course, it should be obvious that other relationships can have similar small and large effects on other relationships, including the infant-mother relationship.

However, this influence does not require that the mother-infant relationship (or any other relationship) have a fixed form. Again, building on Freeman, the recurrent experience of the mother-infant relationship and recurrent elicitation of its RAPs ensures that its RAPs continue to change. Each (re)experiencing of the relationship by the infant and mother changes its characteristics. The mother and infant in their recurrent exchanges are continuously cocreating new ways of being together. Their RAPs are changing. Thus, the mother-infant relationship changes because of its recurrent elicitation and the effect of other relationships on it. But it still can have a powerful influence on other relationships because of its thickness and size of its assemblage of RAPs in the ERS. But most critically, the kind of influence it has on other relationships is constantly changing because it is changing. Thus, a cocreative model of relationships can explain how the mother-infant relationship (and other relationships) can influence other relationships without the infant-mother relationship or any other relationship becoming fixed or the form of its influence becoming fixed. Thus, the dynamics of cocreated relationships and their influence are quite different from the notions of influence embedded in prototypes, RIGS, schemata, and model scenes.

INFANT PSYCHODYNAMICS?

Let me make two more points before concluding. An emergent possibility from the concept of an ERS being formed in infancy is that there could be infant psychodynamic processes (Tronick, 2002a). There are many ways that these psychodynamics might play out. For me, the implicit relational knowing of different relationships may come into conflict. "I do this with my mother, and never with my aunt. But I want to." In this situation, there may be a dynamic conflict such as the loss or threat of loss of one or the other relationship. Controlling the cost of this conflict might limit the infant's possible actions, restrict the creativity of the relationship, or even lead to a defensive turning away from the other (Gianino & Tronick, 1988). For the most part, we have neither seen evidence of this sort of process nor have we looked for it, but see Brazelton's pioneering description of such a case (Brazelton, Young, & Bullowa, 1971; see also Massie, 1982; Tronick, 2001). More generally, it is important to see that the concept of an ERS could incorporate psychodynamics and unconscious processes. Thus, it is unlike many of the neuroscience models that are essentially linear because they tend not to deal with a dynamic unconscious and dynamic conflict.

STUCK IN INFANCY

The ~~~ ~ative process of change presented here suggests that in therapy with adults a focus needs to be on changing the patient's and therapist's way of being together, what the Boston CPSG has referred to as the "something more than insight process" of analysis (Tronick, 1998). However, a problem in the group's thinking about psychodynamic processes was that it was "stuck in infancy." What I have come to understand now, and what I mean by "stuck in infancy," is that the group paid insufficient attention to dealing with the changes and differences of infant and adult emotional and cognitive capacities, states of consciousness (states of making sense of the world), and age-possible meanings over the course of development.

The locus of change in the infant seems to be the terrain of implicit relational intentions, knowings, and affect, which are the primary elements and age-possible meanings of the infant's states of consciousness (Tronick, 2002e). Were these the only forms of meaning available to the adult patient and the therapist to work with, the "something more" process of changing "infantile" ways of making sense of the world would be *the* process of adult therapeutic change, for changing the adult's sense of the world. But the idea is "silly." The adult patient and the therapist have forms of age-possible meanings and ways of being together that are qualitatively different from those of the infant (child, adolescent). Adult states of consciousness include language, explicit knowing, different forms of representation, self-regulation, analytic capacities, and much, much more. Some of these are explicit, and many of them are implicit. Relational intentions and affect may be the stuff of infant-adult interaction, and certainly they are part of the therapist-patient interaction, but they are not the only part, and they may not even be the most important part. Words, symbols, representations, and insight do count for adults. Not everything in adult therapy is the "something more than insight process," which becomes obvious once one begins to incorporate developmental change into one's account.

As I see it, the patient and therapist cocreate dyadic states of consciousness of mature minds. Though their dyadic states of consciousness may contain some elements of dyadic states of consciousness cocreated by an infant and an adult, their dyadic states of consciousness contain things that are fundamentally different. Thus, we need to understand how these mature elements work during therapy if we are to understand the change process of mature minds; that is, our thinking about therapeutic change processes needs to grow up (Fonagy & Target, 1998; Tronick, 2002d, 2002e).

CONCLUSION

My goal has been to move beyond the aphorism that "of course all relationships are unique." Uniqueness is generated by cocreative regulatory processes. At the base of relational uniqueness are inherently sloppy microtemporal communicative processes expressing relational intentions, affects, and knowings that are then further elaborated, repaired, and apprehended by cocreative processes. Intentions and relational affects are on the border of the objective and the subjective. On the one hand, they are observable in behavior. On the other hand, their meaning is only (at best) subjectively known to individuals. From the cocreative workings at the microlevel, other unique qualities emerge such as meta-implicit knowings and thickness. These qualities distinguish relationships from mere interactions and they can be used to distinguish one relationship from another.

The growing differentiation of relationships, including their differentiation in the domains of emerging developmental capacities, their ongoing dynamics, and the nontransferability of ways of being together, raises a question about how any relationship could serve as a model for other relationships. Specifically, it makes it unlikely that the mother-infant relationship could serve as the prototype for other relationships. However, by holding to the assumptions that each relationship is unique and dynamically changing, it becomes possible to conceptualize a process of mutual influence among relationships, with a changing mother-infant relationship having a greater influence, but not the only and not a unidirectional influence, on other relationships. To help account for this process view of reciprocal influences among relationships, I have turned toward Freeman's (1994) work on the olfactory cortex. I have proposed a conceptualization of an ERS containing RAPs of relationships residing in the right limbic system. RAPs of relationships dynamically maintain their identity and mutually influence one another.

The conceptualization of cocreative regulatory processes suggests that there are many ways to induce change in therapy and that change can come through many domains. Infants may only live in the implicit but children and adults do not. The uniqueness of child-adult therapeutic relationships, their relational affects and intentions, implicit relational knowings, and thickness, come in many forms, and these polymorphs of how to be together are part of what therapy needs to change. However, no one process, be it implicit or explicit, will be sufficient to induce change. The possible forms of change processes must be determined and explored along with the interplay of explicit insight-oriented work and work on implicit relational affects and intentions. We have made some headway in understanding developmental change and therapeutic change at the implicit level. Now we need to move along to understanding how to change other forms of knowing how to be together.

To accomplish this work, I believe we must give up the ideas that things are preformed and formed only inside the individual. Instead we need to see that most change emerges from cocreative processes constrained by background processes, though as Modell (personal communication, 2001) has emphasized to me, not everything is dyadic; some things do happen within the privacy of the self. Most important, we must come to see that dyadic states of consciousness—states of age-possible meaning—are the fundamental terrain of therapeutic and developmental change and the uniqueness of relationships.

Why Is Connection With Others So Critical? The Formation of Dyadic States of Consciousness and the Expansion of Individuals' States of Consciousness

Why do infants, indeed all people, so strongly seek states of interpersonal connectedness, and why does the failure to achieve connectedness wreak such damage on their mental and physical health? When the break in connection is chronic, as occurs in some orphanages, infants and children become distressed, depressed, listless, and fail to develop. In less extreme situations, where caregivers are withdrawn and emotionally unavailable, infants go into sad withdrawn mood states. Even in experimental manipulations that briefly break the interactive connection between infants or children and others, such as the face-to-face still-face paradigm or the strange situation procedure, infants and children become angry, distressed, frustrated, or withdrawn and apathetic. No less dramatic are the exuberant smiles and giggles of infants and children when they are connected to others, a phenomenon that also needs explanation. Furthermore, the contrast between the subjective experiences of connection and disconnection is vivid. When connection is made with another person, there is an experience of growth and exuberance, a sense of continuity, and a feeling of being in sync along with a sense of knowing the other's sense of the world. With disconnection there is an experience of shrinking, a loss of continuity, a senselessness of the other. Feeling disconnected is painful, and in the extreme there may be terrifying feelings of annihilation. However, what makes this contrast between connection and disconnection so objectively and phe- nomenologically powerful? Why does connection have such a profound effect on the body, brain, behavior, and experience in the moment and over time? Indeed, what do we mean by connection? What is being connected, and how is connection made?

DYADIC STATES OF CONSCIOUSNESS MODEL

The hypothesis I want to explore is the dyadic states of consciousness model (DSCM). The DSCM assumes that humans are complex and open psychobi- ological systems. As open systems, humans must garner energy from the envi- ronment to maintain and increase their organization and complexity—that is, to reduce their entropy. At the top of the human hierarchy of the complexly assembled multitude of psychobiological subsystems are emergent psychobio- logical states of consciousness (SOCs). The content of an SOC is the individ- ual's age-possible implicit and explicit sense of the world, and his or her rela- tion to it. An SOC is also an anticipation of how to move into the future. SOCs are linked and dependent on all the psychobiological levels below them (e.g., physiological, neuronal, neuronal group, whole brain processes), and in a cir- cular (downward) causal manner SOCs affect the lower levels. SOCs are gen- erated with the purpose of making as coherent and complex a sense of the world as possible at every moment by garnering meaning from the world. However, as we shall see, the sense made of the world is at best messily coher- ent and continuously changing.

Though SOCs are in the individual and individuals have self-organizing meaning-making capacities for creating them, these capacities are limited com- pared with dyadic meaning-making regulatory processes. Thus, as with many other psychobiological states (e.g., states of hunger, sleep, moods, temperature, metabolism), SOCs are created by a dyadic regulatory system that operates to make meaning within and between individuals. The successful regulation of meaning leads to the emergence of a mutually induced dyadic state of mean- ing, what I call a dyadic state of consciousness (DSC). When a DSC is formed, new meanings are created, and these meanings are incorporated into the SOCs of both (or more) individuals. As a consequence, the coherence and complex- ity of each individual's sense of the world increases, a process I refer to as the dyadic expansion of consciousness model (DECM). Thus, the successful cre- ation of SOCs fulfills the open system principle of garnering energy and increasing complexity. Connection, then, is the dyadic regulation of meaning to form a DSC, and the creation and incorporation of meaning with its con- sequent increase in the coherence and complexity of the individual's SOC. An unfortunate implication of the DECM derived from open systems theory is that when individuals chronically fail to create DSCs, there is a dissipation (loss) of their coherence and complexity; they move closer to entropy (i.e., death). Disconnection is the failure of the dyadic meaning-making system. Meaning is not created, exchanged, and incorporated, and consequently the coherence of the individual's SOC incrementally dissipates.

At the outset, I want to acknowledge that this chapter draws heavily on the work of Bruner (1970, 1972, 1990) on meaning making and my discussions with him on cocreative processes; Freeman (1994, 2000) for his ideas on the purposive functioning of the brain; Prigogine (Stengers & Prigogine, 1997) and Per Bak (1996) for their descriptions of open and complex systems; Edelman (1987) for his ideas on neuronal selection; and my collaborator Brazelton (Brazelton, 1992; Brazelton, Koslowski, & Main, 1974) for his perspective on development and dyadic processes. Of further importance to the conceptualizations in this chapter are the works and thinking of Hofer (1994a, 1994b), Trevarthen (1980, 1990, 1993b), Kagan (1998), Fogel (1993), LeVine (1977; Levine & Coe, 1985; LeVine & Leiderman, 1994), and my work with Sander (1976, 1977, 1988, 1995) and the Process of Change Group (Stern et al., 1998; Tronick, 1998).

WHAT IS A STATE OF CONSCIOUSNESS?

What is an SOC? The literature is filled with varying definitions and meanings about consciousness, and it is foolhardy to try and make coherent sense of them. As used here, an SOC is seen as a psychobiological state, which is derived from the medical and developmental literature, and not from the typical dictionary definition that often equates consciousness with the sole characteristic of awareness. The dictionary definition is somewhat all-or-none, and once consciousness is attained it is seen as much the same even with development. In fact, although there may be different levels or kinds of consciousness, this unchanging adevelopmental quality permeates much of neuroscience models of consciousness. By contrast, a psychobiological definition encourages the examination of components and elements of states, their coherence and complexity, their linkage and organization, and most important, their development. Thus, an SOC is a psychobiological state with a distinct complex organization of body, brain, behavior, and experience. It is a distinct assemblage of implicit and explicit meanings, intentions, and procedures. SOCs are individuals' private, continuously changing knowledge of the world and their relationship to it.

SOCs are purposive and organize internal and external actions toward some end. Freeman (2000) sees individuals as operating with intentionality, but what the individual intends and does is only sensible in the context of the individual's SOC—sense of the world at that moment. There is no necessity for awareness in an SOC, as demonstrated by the fact that most daily activities are purposive and carried out without awareness. With or without awareness, SOCs have an impelling certitude about the way the world is (Harrison, personal communication, 2003). What is meant by an impelling certitude? Freeman refers to our "brains and bodies [as being] committed to the action of projecting ourselves corporeally into the world" (2000, p. 18). Impelling certitude is that sort of commitment, an empowering of intentions and actions. Like the air we breathe, it is likely to be out of awareness, but it is always present with greater or lesser intensity. However, when an impelling certitude is violated, it comes into awareness. Think of the impelling certitude about the reality of wholeness that is violated when a magician makes a body separate from a head, or a New Englander's discomfort when confronted by a Californian's desire for sharing personal stories, or an adolescent's insistence that it is realistic to achieve peace by everyone just agreeing to it. Thus, SOCs might be thought of as unique gestalts of meaning that have an impelling certitude about the way things are for the individual. They are the meaning the individual has for being in and acting on the world in the present as he or she moves into the future.

AGE-POSSIBLE SOCs

A critical feature of SOCs is that they can only be "age-possible," though as we shall see, age-possible is hardly the only constraint on SOCs. The concept of age-possible SOCs is needed to take into account the developmentally possible sense individuals are capable of making, given their meaning-making processes. For example, the sense of the world that is in a baseball player's muscles (sometimes referred to as muscle memory) when he catches a ball is qualitatively different from the knowing that is in a toddler's body when she catches a ball. Yet both of their SOCs make coherent sense of what they are doing. Furthermore, the concept of age possibility makes explicit that the interpersonal connection, the DSC made between an infant and adult versus a child and adult, will be qualitatively different. Thus, SOCs and connectedness are not fixed, but dynamically changing with development.

Young infants' SOCs are psychobiological assemblages of affect, actions, and experience. The meaning is in what their body and brain do, and their subjective experience. It is of and in the moment, although the moment soon integrates personal experience and lengthens with development. For example, the alert newborn has an SOC that might be something like "there are things to look at." This SOC of the world is an integration of the circadian rhythms of their bodily (i.e., the biorhythmic flow of sleep and awake states) and brain processes (i.e., occipital processing of visual input), and their perceptual activity (e.g., visual exploration of the world) for gaining meaning. Of course, a "look for things" SOC is difficult for young infants to maintain given their self-organizing capacities (e.g., head movements go in a different direction than eye movements, their intention switches, their bowels act up), and it deteriorates into distress and crying, a rather different SOC.

For older infants, Piaget (1954) described how the meaning of an object is what infants can do with it—an object is "graspable" or "bangable"—and their action and intention of repetitive banging make sense once we appreciate their SOC. The Piagetian infant's SOC is qualitatively different, if she can reach and grasp an object with one hand and explore it with the other while sitting, from the SOC of an infant who has to hold objects with two hands while lying on his back, because the meaning is in the action. Take another example: Infants' SOC about a (virtual) looming object is that it is "dangerous" and ducking out of its way makes sense given their meaning making. If this ascription of meaning to the infant's actions seems over the top, realize that the infant could apprehend the looming event in other ways—it might be interesting, novel, or make no sense at all. Moving into the domain of social interactions, but still holding to Piaget's ideas, infants smiling back at a smiling adult apprehend that there is a general affordance for connection, but infants have more specific and different SOCs for different people. Forgive the grammar, but for the infant the SOC of one "liked-familiar-person" is simultaneously "huggable," "communicable-with," "synchronizable-with," "happy- and cryable-with," and "sing-songable-with," whereas a different liked-familiar person is "exciting," "not-to-be-irritable-with," "too-arousing-with," "bouncable-with," and "peeka-boo-able-with."

Infant SOCs also have an impelling certitude. Observe the young infant who fails to search for a hidden object to see that she is "absolutely certain" that it is gone. Another example is the total distress of the infant separated from the mother—the certitude that not only is she gone forever, but the certitude that he will be annihilated, or the absolute thrill an infant experiences being tossed into the air by an older sibling (and the parents' impelling certitude that the infant will be dropped). Of course, I recognize that we are inferring infants' SOCs about the world, and we cannot truly know them. However, in different contexts we can see what infants do, as well as what they do not do, which gives our inference power, but our inference does not tell us if they are conscious or not, self-aware or self-reflective, which is a different problem than our inferring their SOCs. If this still seems difficult, we must realize that, if infants did not have age-possible SOCs about themselves in the world, they could not function in it. Their actions would be incoherent and unpredictable, a veritable Jamesian "blooming buzzing confusion," a view that is no longer tenable given the past 50 years of research on infant competencies.

The toddler and young child have qualitatively different SOCs from those of the infant. Their meaning-making tools include language and symbols, and complex body skills (e.g., from finger movements to running) and body micropractices (e.g., false coyness). In pretend play, toddlers assemble fantasy, reality, and their age-possible memories into new SOCs. Not only they are in the moment, but their meanings are disjunctive assemblages of illogical narratives. The SOCs of toddlers are complex, and have an "and _____, and _____, and _____, . . ." organization of apprehension that places no demand for the possible or the logical. Think only of a toddler's impelling certitude when he loudly demands to have the identical berries that fell from a branch back on the tree the way they were, and his utter distress when he says a different branch is bad and he does not want it . . . ever! (A. Bergman, personal communication).

There is little need to further elaborate the idea that SOCs are different for older children, adolescents, and adults. Nonetheless, it is worth noting, because developmental and neuroscientists tend not to attend to it; at some point in development, SOCs assemble meanings from psychodynamic processes, including a psychodynamic unconscious. These dynamic processes are not equivalent to the passionless nonconscious or implicit processes invoked by developmental psychologists, cognitive neuroscientists, or even some psycho-analytic writers. I believe that unconscious dynamic processes are inherent to the SOCs of children and adults. Dynamic unconscious processes make some-one's knowing what is in another person's SOC cryptic and as problematic as knowing the SOC of an infant, yet somehow we do come to apprehend the SOC of another. How we come to have that apprehension is based on under-standing how SOCs are formed and what principles govern their formation.

DYADIC REGULATION

Open Systems and Complexity

The coherence of an individual's sense of the world is both regulated and increased by internal self-organizing and dyadic regulatory processes. Prigogine (Stengers & Prigogine, 1997) states that a primary principle gov-erning the activities of open biological systems is that they must acquire energy from the environment to maintain and increase their coherence, com-plexity, and distance from entropy. The energy for a biological system must have a particular form to be useful (i.e., have meaning, or what Sander, 1988, calls fittedness for the organism). For example, although the food that prey eats has plenty of energy, if predators eat what their prey eats, they cannot utilize that energy—it has no "meaning" for them. Complexity refers to a hierarchical system exhibiting emergent systems properties. It is neither fixed nor chaotic. It is information rich with local contextual interactions. Self-organizing processes that increase complexity have limits that put a ceiling on a system's maximum complexity. These limitations of self-organization are an inherent characteristic of all open systems. Humans have developed an exceptional (though hardly unique) way to overcome these limits by forming synergistic relationships with others, what I refer to as a dyadic regulatory sys-tem. Though dyadic regulation also has limits, this dyadic system is able to garner more resources than each individual's self-organizing processes could on its own. As a consequence, the complexity of each individual as a com-plex psychobiological system is increased.

Psychobiological States

To understand mutual regulation, I want to start with an example far from the regulation of SOCs—infant temperature regulation. I choose this example because it illustrates the dyadic regulatory process for a psychobiological state that is most typically seen as a self-organized process. Temperature regulation is a complex system with a singular purpose: maintaining homeothermic status. This regulatory system is hierarchically organized with a multitude of subsystems, from metabolic processes to behavioral systems. It is a system that operates to maintain equilibrium, and although it changes with development (e.g., the loss of brown fat) and is influenced by environmental factors (e.g., the increase in capillary networks in the hand in cold environments), its change and development is limited compared with other psychobiological systems (e.g., respiratory systems, motor systems, or SOCs). Infants have self-organizing capacities to regulate below-normal temperature, such as increasing their activity level, preferentially metabolizing high-energy brown fat, or moving into less energetic behavioral states. However, these self-organized capacities are limited and immature, and will eventually fail, an especially quick event for infants with their high surface-to-volume ratio. However, although Claude Bernard saw temperature regulation as a within-individual process, it is not. It is a dyadic process.

Infants' self-organized regulatory capacities for operating on temperature control are supplemented by external regulatory input by caregivers that is specifically fitted to overcome the infant's limitations (Hofer, 1984). For example, caregivers place infants against their chests, sharing their body heat with their infants, which in turn reduces their infants' surface heat loss. This dyadic regulatory process itself is guided by communicative signals from the infant. These communicative signals induce the implicit purpose and intentions of the infant into the caregiver's sense of what is going on with the infant. "I'm cold. Help me." Adult; "Got it!" When done successfully, the input provided is fitted (meaningful) to the infant's temperature regulatory system and the system becomes more coherently organized than it would be on its own.

Additionally, the capacities for self-regulation actually grow with the acquisition of meaningful input from the caregiver, such that later in development, the infant will be able to self-regulate temperature without as much external regulatory scaffolding, an idea not unlike Vygotsky's (1978) concept of the zone of proximal development. Alternatively, were the formation of a dyadic state to fail, the infant would lose control of his temperature and his homeostatic state would dissipate. When the failure is chronic, the infant's self-regulatory capacities would not grow. Furthermore, even this equilibrium system is not fully predictable. The infant actions that induced the infant's intent into the caregiver may have one form one day and another form another day. The caregiver's apprehension of it and the caregiver's input to the infant might also vary. Moreover, the infant signal that worked one time may not work the next time, and the same is true for the caregiver's response, as most parents have experienced. Nonetheless, it is likely that the activities that work more often will become more and more a part of the workings of the dyadic regulatory process.

SOCs and Actions in the World

Dyadic processes more effectively regulate the infant's SOCs than the infant can do on his or her own, even when the infant is doing something that seems to be an individual task. Take, for example, a not-yet-independently-reaching infant who tries to reach an object. The infant has an intent that is beyond his own self-regulatory capacities. At first, his SOC is organized, and his looking and intent are coherently organized. However, once he attempts to get his hands to the object, he is unable to coherently organize his actions, looking, and intent. The organization of his SOC is decreased. He becomes distressed, loses what motor control he has, but does not necessarily give up the intent. In a way, the infant can no longer make sense of the world and his relation to it. His SOC loses some coherence and complexity. By contrast, as part of a dyadic system with a caregiver who, by apprehending the infant's intent, provides postural support, the infant is able to free up his arms, control his posture, and bat at the object. The infant engages in a more complex action than he would be capable of on his own.

Individual SOCs and the Emergence of DSCs

Bullowa (1979) described this phenomenon when she documented the greater complexity of the infant's behavior in the presence of others compared with the infant alone. In the example given, had the mother's apprehension of the infant's SOC been that the infant intended to reach for the object when, in fact, he intended to stroke her face, the infant and mother would remain separate and uncoordinated. Then again, when there is a successful mutual mapping of (some of) the constituent meanings in each individual's SOC into the other's SOC, there is the emergence of a dyadic state of shared meaning, a DSC. This DSC is more complex and information rich than individual SOCs. It is more complex because it is made up of more systems, the infant's and the mother's, and their hierarchically arranged subsystems, and it is information rich because it contains meanings from both the infant's and the mother's SOCs. Critically, the effect of being subcomponents of a DSC is that the infant and the mother can appropriate information from it into their own SOCs. A critical consequence of this appropriation is the expansion of their individual SOCs. Namely, by being connected, their sense of themselves in the world expands and becomes more coherent and complex.

SOCs, DSCs, and Social Interactions

Infant-adult interaction, or for that matter any dyadic human interaction, is perhaps the quintessential example of dyadic regulation of meaning making (Fogel, 1993). In interaction each individual attempts to increase the coherence of their sense of themselves, the other, and what they are doing together. When an interaction is dyadically well regulated, there is an emergence of a more coherent and complex sense of the world. For example, in an infant-mother interaction, each individual communicates their affective evaluation of the state of what is going on in the interaction: relational affects (e.g., feeling apart from, feeling in sync with; Foscha, 2000) and their relational intention (e.g., continue, stop, change; Weinberg & Tronick, 1994). These communications simultaneously express what they are experiencing in the moment and what they intend to do. In response to the induction of meaning in the other, infants and mothers attempt to adjust their behavior to maintain a coordinated dyadic state. When the mutual induction is successful, a DSC is formed, meanings from the other's SOC are incorporated, and their SOCs gain coherence and complexity.

Figure 35.1a–f illustrates the process of mutual regulation, formation, and breaking of dyadic DSCs. A 6-month-old infant and his mother are playing a game, and the mother leans in to nuzzle the baby. The infant takes hold of the mother's hair and they are both joyful. The infant's age-possible SOC is in his actions and his affect. He has yet to make sense of the game as a game,

FIGURE 35.1. Sequence of infant responding to mother's anger facial expression. In the first images, the infant is pulling on the mother's hair. She then takes his hands and disengages, and then makes an angry face and vocalization. The infant brings his hands and arms up to his face in a defensive maneuver, and then looks at her from under his arms. The mother backs away and then attempts to elicit his attention by touching his legs. In the last frame, they have resumed their playful interaction.

a

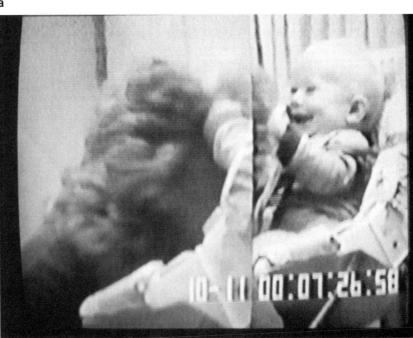

FIGURE 35.1. *Continued*

b

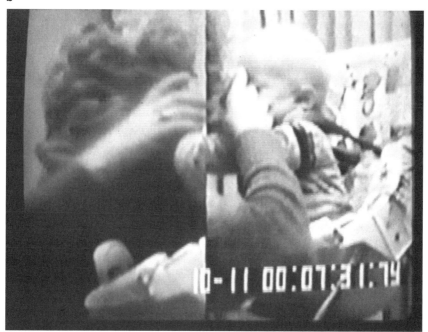

c

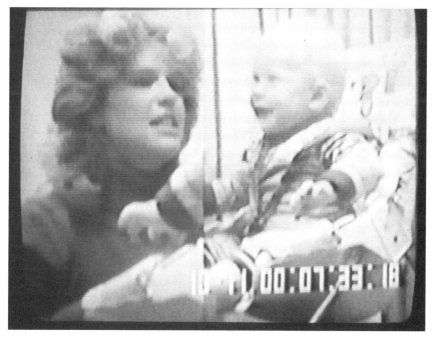

FIGURE 35.1. *Continued*

d

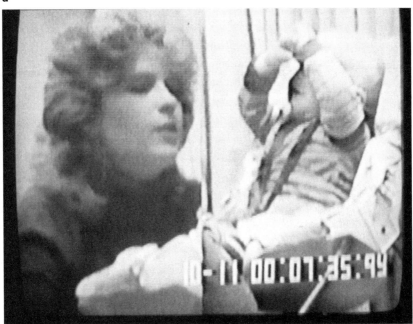

e

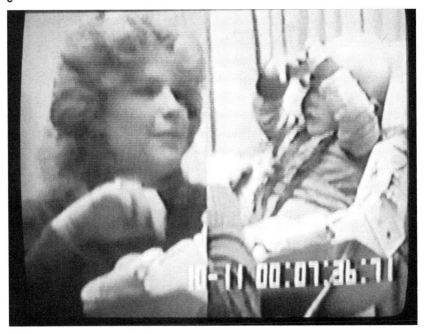

FIGURE 35.1. *Continued*

f

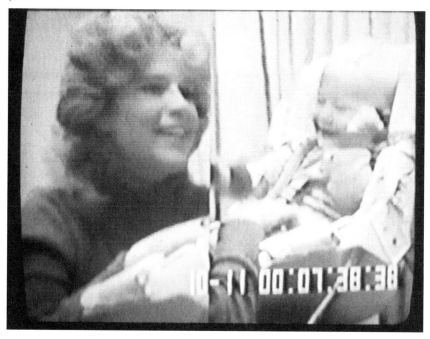

echoing Piaget's argument that objects are not yet objects for infants, but only what they do to them. His impelling certitude is something like, "This is the greatest thing I have ever done!" The mother's more complex SOC includes a similar age-possible feeling (i.e., "the joy of him!"), as well as her greater knowledge of the game, how to make it work, their other games, and many other implicit and unconscious things. Collaborating together, they create a DSC by inducing some of each one's meanings into the SOC of the other person.

When she pulls away, he does not let go. In pain, the mother responds with a bare-toothed angry facial expression and angry vocalizations—"Ouch, ouch!" The infant immediately sobers and brings his hand up to his face in a defensive move. His SOC changes to something like "this is threatening" and he defensively ducks behind his hands. The meaning is in the ducking and the feeling of threat. The mother almost immediately pulls back. The mother's own mentalization (Fonagy & Target, 1998) of her action (an age-possible knowing that the infant is not yet able to do), and the infant's induction of meaning into her SOC, changes her SOC. They disconnect, the hair-pulling DSC is broken, and each is left to self-organize their SOCs. The infant's SOC is now in his sober wary face and his looking away from behind his hands. His impelling certitude perhaps is something like, "I'm confused. This doesn't happen!"

Likely the mother is feeling something like "concern" or "apology," and age-possible meanings such as "I scared him. I messed up our good time," and maybe meanings out of her own past ("I always felt apologetic to my mother"). The mother pauses and then slowly approaches the infant again. The infant drops his hands with a number of coy moves that convey his intent to cautiously reengage. The mother, too, makes a slow approach and they reconnect with joyful smiles. A DSC is restored: "Whew!" They again induce meaningful elements of each SOC in the other. Specifically, the infant's emotional reaction is determined by his own meaning-making capacities, his capacities for effectively apprehending his mother's affective displays and reactions.

HUMAN CONNECTION

DSCs and the Expansion of SOCs

We can now return to the opening question: Why do infants, indeed all people, so strongly seek states of connectedness, and why does the failure to achieve connectedness wreak such damage on their mental and physical health? Connection is the formation of a DSC, and it is critical because it expands the coherence and complexity of individuals' SOCs. Normal interactions are examples of the creation of DSCs. The mutual smiling and cooing of mother and infant in face-to-face interactions is an example of a DSC. So, too, is the pretend play of the toddler with another person and the all-night conversations of adolescents. Social referencing by infants, children, and adults is a way to gain meaning about ambiguous events that leads to a new impelling certitude about their meaning (Campos & Lucariello, 1999). The 12-month-old who backs away from the visual cliff in apprehension of the mother's expression of fear has used her expressed meaning to form his sense of the event. Similarly, the 2-year-old's laughing at the mother who makes a fear face in the visual cliff reflects his certitude about the situation and her actions—this is pretend! By being in a DSC, individuals experience a growth in the coherence and complexity of their SOCs. Thus, forming DSCs is not an exotic state or an exceptional moment in time, but very much the chronic experience of normal development (but see below as regards their intensity).

The Still Face as a Breaking of Connection

The still face (SF) is an example of a failure to create a DSC and dissipation of the individuals' SOCs (Adamson & Frick, 2003; Tronick, Als, & Adamson, 1979; Tronick, Als, Adamson, Wise, & Brazelton, 1978; Vygotsky, 1978). The still-faced mother precludes the formation of a DSC because there is no exchange or creation of meaning. The recipient of the SF has to make meaning with his or her own self-organizing abilities. In response to the SF, infants act to acquire and reinstate their exchange of meaning, but with the mother's

Why Is Connection With Others So Critical?

continued lack of response they engage in self-organized regulatory behav ___
to maintain their coherence and complexity, to avoid the dissipation of their
SOCs. Figure 35.2 shows how an infant during the SF literally loses postural
control, turns away, has a sad facial expression, and is self-comforting with his
hands in his mouth. The age-possible impelling certitude of the infant's SOC
is something like, "This is threatening." This certitude is both in and expressed
by his posture and actions. As the SF continues, the infant's SOC is likely to
change to something like, "I must try to hold myself together." This certitude
is similar to the earlier examples—the infant's apprehension of the looming
object or the mother's anger expression as dangerous. If one doubts these or
similar interpretations, simply consider that the infant could apprehend the
still-faced mother in other ways—as boring, playful, or novel—all of which
would result in different behaviors by infants, none of which happen in the SF.

More recent work on the SF with young children and adults makes it even
clearer how the SF is failing to form DSCs. In my laboratory, we have developed

FIGURE 35.2. An infant losing postural control and turning to self-comforting behaviors
in response to the mother being still faced.

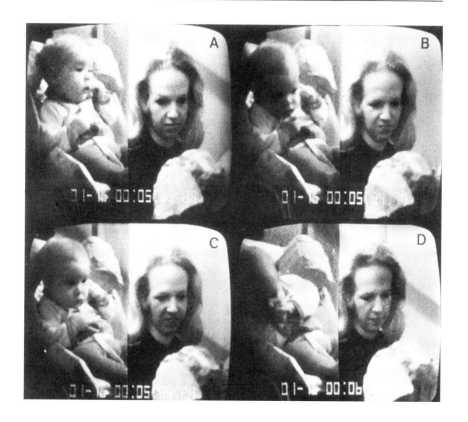

a procedure for using the SF with children 18 to 54 months of age (Weinberg et al., 2002). In the first episode of this procedure, the child and the adult engage in floor play with toys. This episode is followed by an SF episode in which the mother freezes and does not respond to the infant. In a third episode, the mother resumes her normal play. The findings are as striking as our original SF findings with infants. Young children respond to the maternal SF with heightened negative affect, expressions of confusion, and demands for change. The toddlers ask, "Why don't you talk to me?" or command, "Talk to me!" while soliciting the mother's interactive behavior (e.g., pointing at her eyes, tapping or almost hitting the mother, making repeated louder and louder requests), and then distancing themselves from her. Importantly, and in keeping with their greater age-possible meaning-making capacities, preschoolers may attribute states of mind to the mother (e.g., "Are you sleeping? Wake up!" or "Don't be afraid of the alligator [toy]!"). Thus, there is meaning in their affect and actions (similar to the age-possible meanings of the infant), but also in their age-possible capacities for pretend play, cognitions, language, mentalization, and complex affects. Their impelling certitude is one of confusion and fearfulness at the break in connection. When play is resumed, the child asks questions that attempt to make coherent sense of what happened (e.g., "Why didn't you talk to me?") even though it brings back the painfulness of the experience.

In further extension of the SF to adults, a research assistant, Lisa Bohne, interviewed college sophomores after they participated in an experimental role-play of an adult version of the SF. One student role-played an unresponsive mother and the other simulated being in the mind of an infant. The infant-persons who experienced the SF reported feeling anxious and vulnerable, angry, frustrated, sad, afraid, confused, even panicky. The students who acted out the SF mother reported feeling guilty, distressed, anxious, depressed, shamed, vulnerable, and confused. One reported, "It felt terrible to be so closed off from the infant. It made me feel depressed and I'm sure the infant did too after our interaction." Preventing an exchange of meanings and the formation of a DSC disorganized each adult's own SOC and generated a fearful, confused, and less coherent sense of the world. Importantly, these adults did not try to step away from their negative experience, but in more sophisticated ways than the toddlers, continued to try to make coherent sense of what they had experienced after the procedure was terminated. Some of them actually apologized for what they had done. It is unfortunate that we cannot know what sense the infant makes of the SF sometime after it is terminated.

The Chronic Breaking of Connection and Downward Causation

An extreme example of the failure to form DSCs is the chronic deprivation of infants in orphanages described by Spitz (Spitz & Cobliner, 1965). For these infants, I believe that the complexity of their SOCs actually dissipated. Perhaps, still more compromising, their self-organizing and dyadic capacities were stunted such that they could hardly make coherent sense of their place in the world. Of note is the general finding of their apathy, an extremely pathological state for infants in which there is a reduction of attempts to acquire meaningful input from others or the environment to expand their SOCs. Nonetheless, the apathy may be a protective state in which the infants self-organized themselves to maintain whatever remnant of a coherent sense of the world they had. However, I believe the compromise is so great that there was an ongoing dissipation of their SOCs and further diminishment of their self-organizing abilities.

It is easy to think that compromising the food intake of Spitz's infants would lead to their kind of "malnourished" body, brain, and SOC. However, in many cases we know that the nutrition and other necessities were adequate, and that the necessity that was unavailable was connection with others, namely the establishment and maintenance of DSCs. These infants were not able to exchange meanings with others. This deprivation of meaning led not only to the failure to maintain and expand their SOCs, but also to the disorganization of many of the lower level psychobiological states, such as metabolic systems and immune system. This "downward causation," what Freeman (2000) calls circular causality, is a characteristic of complex systems.

Downward causation occurs when the operation of the emergent properties at higher levels (e.g., SOCs) in the hierarchical assembling of subsystems constrains and impacts the actions of the lower level systems (e.g., motor systems). For Spitz's infants, the downward causal effect of being unable to form DSCs was to downwardly cause systems such as their immune system to dissipate, for many resulting in death by opportunistic infections. In the infants who were physiological survivors of the deprivation of meaning, their capacity for acquiring resources was so damaged that they failed to grow and develop. We also see damaged self-organizing capacities for acquiring resources in the reports on Romanian orphans who as older children are not able to engage in forms of normal exchange. Thus, Spitz's infants are an example of a failing open system—human systems that were deprived of connection and could not increase the complexity of their SOCs and could not maintain their complexity. In a sense, these infants as systems lost much of their capacity to generate the most human of characteristics.

The Distortion of Connection

Distortion of DSCs can help us understand the effects of parental affective disorders on infants and children in two ways. First, a mother with an affective disorder (e.g., a depressed mother) is often an inadequate external regulator of the infant. Her responsiveness and her apprehension of communications are limited; her communications are harder for the infant to apprehend; and her responses are less likely to fit the infant's regulatory needs. Forming a DSC with her is difficult and it is self-amplifying—the initial difficulties increase the effects of later exchanges. Second, despite these dyadic regulatory problems, the mothers' and infants' capacities are not so compromised that they cannot form a DSC, but the formation of a DSC insidiously compromises the infant.

The DSC between a depressed mother and her infant contains sad and angry affect, melancholic feelings, and gloomy meanings. Were this depressed DSC restricted to the connection between the child and the mother, its toxicity might be restricted as well, but lamentably it is not. Field (Field et al., 1988) found that the interactions of infants of depressed mothers with others were sadder.

My hypothesis is that the impelling certitude of children of depressed mothers is that connection can only be made in sadness, and their self-organizing capacities for creating DSCs aim to create or reinstate this kind of DSC with others. For example, in our laboratory, infants of depressed mothers have more dysregulated interactions with our experienced research assistants (RAs) who are blind to the depressive status. The RAs feel that the infant induces an experience of "stay away, don't connect," and the RAs touch the infant less and maintain a greater distance from the infant. In the interactions with their mothers, there is a growth of complexity and coherence of these infants' SOC, but their impelling certitude limits the child's acquiring of resources from nondepressed others.

The Blind Selective Operation of Coherence on Messy Meaning Systems

The SOCs of infants of depressed mothers clearly are not growth promoting in the long run, but the alternative would be to not form a DSC at all. From the perspective of open systems, what the infant does is to choose the lesser of two evils: either grow complexity now or dissipate now. As a consequence, the child's experience of expansion becomes focused on sharing depressed states. Thus, the more general question is, how is an individual's sense of the world put together? My proposal is that SOCs emerge from selective processes operating to increase the coherence and complexity of the individual's age-possible sense of the world. However, we must first understand that selection has to repetitively activate SOCs and DSCs—meanings, as well as meaning-making processes—that are messy.

This argument is analogous to the argument made by neuroscientists that initially disordered arrays of neurons are selected to form Hebbian circuits or cell groups because of repetitive co-occurring activation. Edelman (1987) sees selection operating on neurons to form neuronal groups. Cells that fire together in relation to sensory input, motor output, and all the other forms of input and output in the brain and its subsystems (e.g., reafferent signals) come to form coherent cell groups. More specifically, selection operates to maximize the coherence of the relations among brain and bodily processes, and structures from the level of neurons to neuronal groups to activation patterns in different areas of the brain to the autonomic nervous system to homeostatic physiological systems to endocrine systems, to metabolic processes, to bodily movements and behavior, in order to make these systems into a functioning whole in an environmental context. Coherence means that there is a growth of relations (correlations) among previously unrelated internal and external variables. These new relations can be thought of as a pattern in space or time (e.g., unrelated neurons become a cell group by having a coordinated pattern of firing) which may have greater complexity and emergent properties.

LEARNING PEEKABOO: SELECTIVE COHERENCE AND MESSY SYSTEMS

Let me begin with an example of selection from messiness: the infant learning to play peekaboo. The learning of peekaboo emerges through the repetitive operation of coherence on the messiness of the infant's actions, intentions, and apprehensions in an incremental bit-by-bit and moment-by-moment manner. Initially, the infant makes a large number and variety of behaviors and has lots of varying intentions and apprehension of what is going on. Most of these actions are unrelated to each other or to the adult's game-playing actions. The infant looks away when he should be looking toward, or he raises his shoe, or he wants the light and reaches for it. What he is doing is messy—variable, unstable, disorganized. There is no coherence in what he is doing in relation to the game, though, of course, he is making some sort of sense of what is going on. Nonetheless, over time and with repetition, some of the infant's behaviors, intentions, and apprehensions of the adult's actions and intentions come to be related to one another. The infant looks at the same time the adult places her hands over her eyes or looks back at her after the adult says "boo." Furthermore, the adult makes adjustments (e.g., holding positions longer) in what she does in relation to the infant's actions and her apprehension of his intent to increase the likelihood and maintenance of the coordination.

The selective assembling of these co-occurrences of the infant's self-organized actions and intentions and his apprehension of the adult's intentions and actions becomes incrementally more coherent than what was assembled in prior moments. There is still lots of messiness to the actions and intentions of his sense making, but without belaboring the process, with an enormous number of repetitions the messiness is pared away over weeks and months, and finally the game is put together. The infant's SOC and his DSC of the game become more coherent (see Thelen, 1995, for a similar example as regards reaching).

The example can help us to understand that selection of new meanings about the world cannot increase the coherence of SOCs with too little messiness or too much messiness. A low-coherence state of meanings is unpredictable, and constantly randomly changing and self-organizing, and external processes are unable to generate order. The peekaboo infant's actions are messy, but not random. By contrast, a highly coherent organization of meanings is predictable and static, but the infant's initial actions are hardly fixed. Perhaps when the game is learned they do become fixed and unchanging (do we all play peekaboo the way we did when we were 15 months old?), but by then the infant will have new intentions.

THE UBIQUITOUSNESS OF MESSINESS

Fortunately, messiness is ubiquitous in development. The expression of meaning and intent does not have fixed forms. Infants have sets of affective configurations for expressing meanings, but they are expressed by a variable assembling of expressive modalities. "Stop" is expressed by turning away one time, or pushing away another time, or with cries and flailing arms another time. For toddlers, the same word can express different intents. *Ball* means "there is the ball," or "give me the ball," or "you have the ball," or "ball?" Older children and adults seem to express meaning more clearly, but there is much that is cryptic. Also, whatever the age of the individuals, meanings are missed or misread, responses are inappropriate, do not fit to the expressed meaning, or are mistimed. Importantly, meanings and intentions are not fully formed; they change from one moment to the next and, of course, there are differences in the intent of the two individuals, and intention often exceeds capacities. Even without these difficulties that create messiness, the expression of meaning operates at 10ths of seconds or faster, a rate that cannot be maintained for sustained periods. Furthermore, because SOCs are age appropriate and are assemblages of implicit, nonconscious, and dynamically unconscious meanings, the individuals have a problem of fathoming intent across age and "explicitness" gaps. Indeed, one can wonder how infants can induce meaning in adults when their meaning-making systems are qualitatively different. This accounting leaves out the meanings that are purely personal and individually historical. Messiness, indeed!

For SOCs, when an individual is engaged with things, there is a selective assembling of intentions, information garnered by exploratory behaviors and from the effects of instrumental behaviors on the environment that enhances their coherence. When the individual is with another person, there is more stuff to work on and more relations to bring together for incrementing coherence. In a dyad, coherence comes with the apprehension of mutual intentions, and the coordination of their behaviors and their mutual effects on each other. When one of the individuals is an infant or child and the other individual an adult, coordination can be easier because the adult adjusts his or her activities to better fit to the child's SOCs. With mutual apprehension, the SOCs of each individual become increasingly well fitted together. When the coherence of their intentionalizing, talking, looking, touching, and moving is increased sufficiently, a DSC is formed. In this DSC, age-possible meanings that are expressed with their bodies, movements, and intentions can be appropriated by the two individuals to increase the coherence of their own SOCs.

BLIND SELECTION AND COMPROMISES OF DEVELOPMENT

From the moment-to-moment of the SF to the chronic failure to form DSCs in Spitz's orphans to the derailment of normal SOCs in children of depressed mothers, selection operates to make more coherent meaning of infants' or children's place in the world. When the SF is done, children and adults struggle to find a coherent sense of what happened to them to overcome their confused and disjointed (i.e., incoherent) SOCs. In the depressed dyads, increasing the coherence of the meaning being made in the moment, requires selecting an assemblage of meanings from those available that are the most coherent: "We can be sad together (or not make sense of things at all)." These SOCs are more coherent now, but in the long run they will become increasingly problematic as they limit the resources available to the infant or child. However, that is the rub of maximizing the coherence of meaning moment by moment. Selecting meanings to increase coherence is blind to the meaning assembled in an SOC and blind to its long-term impact. It simply operates to maximize what better fits together from what is available now. It operates even if the long-run costs are extremely high, not only because the long run is unknowable but also because in the moment the alternative is to dissipate, to lose coherence and complexity about the world, a loss that must be avoided by open systems.

BLIND SELECTION AND THE COCREATION OF THE VARIETIES OF NORMAL DEVELOPMENT

Blind as it is, selection to increase coherence of the individual's sense making is not the only generator of pathology. It is ubiquitously normal. I have observed a surprising example of how coherence governed selection operating in the face-to-face interactions of Gusii mothers and their infants. This example also illustrates how what emerges from selective processes is a cocreation of the two individuals. It also shows how different age-possible SOCs, in this example the acultural infant and the acculturated adult, as well as other constraints interplay with one another to affect development. The Gusii are agriculturalists in the western highlands in Kenya (LeVine & Leiderman, 1994). Although face-to-face play is a rare activity, when asked to engage in it, the Gusii infants and mothers do it much like we observe in our Boston studies. However, what was surprising in their interaction was that at the moment when the Gusii infants were getting most excited and about to express a big greeting with a smile and a hand wave, the mothers looked away. In response, the infant greeting dissolved midstream. The infant looked away and actually looked deflated. It is as if the mother made an SF. The infant's SOC dissipated because his intent and actions were assembled to greet the mother, but the mother's intention was to not engage in mutual excited affective greeting. There was a lack of coherence between the infant's and the mother's SOCs, but over time a coherent way of greeting emerged. How does the infant come to know her intention and get his intention coordinated with hers?

My sense is that in the next exchange as they move into play and the infant greets her again, the mother turns away and they remain disconnected, but bit by bit the infant no longer goes into a big gaping smile, as well as doing a lot of other messy things (e.g., squirming, looking at his feet). At one point he may look at her briefly and soberly. The mother responds in a reciprocal manner — soberly. Their intentions and actions have relations that were not there previously. From this small increment in coherence, they select mutual actions and intentions so that they develop a different way of how to greet — a kind of somber looking at each other that has greater coherence and complexity.

Making sense of this cocreation requires knowing that the mother's SOC was constrained by a cultural rule about who can look at whom and with what affect. Women, for example, do not share heightened affect with others and, although this rule is relaxed with infants, it still operates. The mother's impelling certitude of what makes sense guides her actions. On the infant side, after repetitions of the interaction he too comes to know in an age-possible way — perhaps with a body micropractice — what gaze and affect to assemble to maximize the coherence he experiences with the mother. This way of greeting takes on an age-possible or more completely, an age-possible cultural impelling certitude.

This example is very surprising when we think of the mutually exuberant smiles that mothers and infants in communities in the West assemble with one another into DSCs. To make sense of Western mothers' and infants' mutual greeting, we need to know that the Western mother's sense of her infant is that he is a social partner who needs to express emotions. Consequently, bit by bit with repetition of interactions, they assemble a heightened way of being together. On the Boston infants' side, they come to know this meaning in an age-possible (cultural) form of affect, behavior, and expectation. Despite these stunning differences, both the Western shared exuberant dyadic greetings and the Gusii sober greetings, are assembled through a reiterated selective process of increasing the coherence of the sense of what their shared greeting is. Thus, despite claims to the contrary, neither greeting is natural in the sense of being innate and neither pattern, or for that matter the thousands of other greeting patterns seen in other cultures, is universal. They are cocreated by individuals. The Gusii and Western greetings are distinct SOCs cocreated by Gusii mothers and infants, and Western mothers and infants. Neither infant came into the world armed with a Gusii or Western greeting. The greetings had to be cocreated.

COCREATION AND PRIOR CONSTRAINTS

It is critical to note that the greetings created are not simply de novo creations. One of the powerful constraints is the adult's cultural meaning. It affects what the mothers do and what will feel natural and be coherently assembled with their infants. As cultural forms, they are an example of Tomasello's (2001) view that culture is created over historical time spans in a bit-by-bit bootstrapping process. Another constraint is mood. The depressed mothers' mood operates as a constraint on how the infant and the mother can form DSCs in the same manner as nondepressed mothers' joyful mood acts as a constraint.

It is beyond the scope of this chapter to elaborate on the issue of constraints, but there are numerous constraints including age-possible meanings, personal history and experience, temperament, and personality. However, even with constraints, coherence-governed selection out of messiness and the cocreation of meaning emphasize the dynamic and unpredictable changes of meaning making. Meaning making is always in process, taking form, and changing. It is not simply an exchange of preformed meanings from one brain to another brain, a common but false view in fields from linguistics to brain sciences. Instead, there is a mutual induction of not yet fully formed constituents of meaning from each individual's SOC into the other's SOC. These not-so-well-formed meanings are then selectively assembled to increase the coherence of the meaning being created. Elements that do not increase the coherence of meaning are not selected (neurons that do not fire together do not get linked together). Furthermore, cocreation also is not a process of coconstruction of meaning. Coconstruction implies a preexisting plan or, more specifically, preformed meanings that are put together to build a larger and shared meaning. Cocreation, in contrast, emphasizes that the meaning made is a process in which each individual's meaning is changed and created into a new meaning. The still-in-process eventual shared meaning that is created by both of them is also new. However, the concept of cocreation does not question that meaning making is also private (Modell, 1993). Private meaning making is undeniable and when brought into dyadic processes it affects the meanings that are cocreated.

CONCLUSION

I would like to cautiously assert the possibility that many psychobiological states are SOCs because it may give us a more unified way to think about development. It is easy to see SOCs as ways of making implicit sense of the world and for organizing action to gain meaning from the world when there is awareness or even when there is no awareness. Although perhaps more difficult to conceptualize, other psychobiological states, such as sleep and hunger, may also be thought of as SOCs or at least as somewhat similar. These states are not regulating meaning, but they too organize brain, body, behavior, and experience. Actions in these states are purposive and operate to maintain the organization of the state, change it, or change the world. Furthermore, in these states individuals garner specific (meaningful) input from the world, leading to an increase in the coherence of the organization of the state. For example, when core body temperature drops, infants adjust their posture to minimize surface heat loss, switch to metabolizing brown fat, and may fall asleep to minimize energy consumption. Thus, even at the mechanical psychobiological level,

purposive, have an implicit intended end state, organize behavior and
ce, and require meaningful input to operate. This way of thinking
sychobiological states as SOCs is not unlike the ethnologists' term
Umwelt, the way the world is to an animal in its niche.

I make this suggestion because an advantage of even weakly accepting this
argument is that development from infancy through adulthood can be viewed
as the development of specific characteristics of SOCs, and the specifics of their
self and dyadic regulatory processes. Moreover, regulatory processes, especially
dyadic regulatory processes for these more mechanical psychobiological states,
can aid us in thinking about the dyadic regulation of SOCs. Nonetheless, a key
difference between psychobiological SOCs and other psychobiological states is
that SOCs are nonequilibrium states that are often in a state of criticality. They
go through qualitative developmental changes, whereas many other psychobiological states are equilibrium states that tend not to qualitatively change.

Over the past 50 years of infancy research, we have demonstrated the competencies of the infant. The implication is that the subjective experience of the
infant is orderly as well. However, understanding that meaning is made out of
messiness and while coherence is increased it is never perfect, I would hypothesize that the infant's experience of the world is messy as well. It is not a
Jamesian confusion, but I think that it can be disjointed, contradictory, and
confusing. For example, remembering that infant meanings are in their bodies, actions, intents, and affects, what is the not-yet-reaching infant's sense of
the world when he falls over as he reaches toward an object with both hands
and throws his head back? "Where did it all go? What is happening?"

Simply put, I think we have overestimated the continuity and orderliness of
experience, and the experience of states such as dissociation may be more common and normal than we have previously thought (as suggested by Fisher; see
Noam, 1996), but there can be abnormal effects as well. Incoherent SOCs will
lack impelling certitude and because of their incoherence will be experienced
as threatening to the integrity of the individual. Both of these experiential
aspects will have profound effects, including the sudden total distress of the
infant or the toddler in a situation that, to adults, appears to be a normal event
(e.g., the berries falling off a branch), similar to what we used to call nervous
breakdowns, decompensation, and perhaps some psychoses.

Another point and one that contrasts with some of the work I have done in
the past that emphasized high experiential moments—now moments and
moments of meeting—is that in this chapter I have emphasized that the formation of DSCs is a common phenomenon (Tronick, 1998). I think the ordinariness of dyadic meaning making is obvious, but equally obvious is that not
all DSCs are experienced the same way; they do not have the same incremental
effect on the coherence and complexity of SOCs. Rather, it seems that DSCs
and SOCs have an intensity and force. The emotion brought into an SOC may
be one variable affecting intensity. Another may be differences in the meanings being worked on. Based on the idea of coherence-governed selection, I

would suggest that the DSCs with greater force and intensity are ones that assemble more private meanings from each individual into shared meanings. Such assemblages are most likely to lead to an increase in complexity of each individual's SOC, an emergence of something new and unexpected. For example, when an infant and a mother both engage in simultaneous huge gaping smiles, everything about them and between them—actions, intentions, apprehensions—is coherently organized. They both experience expansion and connectedness. Another example of an intense and forceful DSC is a psychodynamic interpretation. Its effect is to bring together into a single coherent insight a vast variety of explicit and implicit and dynamically unconscious meanings in the patient's SOC that will generate a powerful feeling of connection to the therapist (transference) and an experience of expansion.

Connection is the regulation and cocreation of the age-possible meanings individuals make of the world and their place in it. The making of meanings is dyadic and continuous. The meaning emerges out of the messiness of individuals' SOC and the DSC that is created. Neither SOC nor the DSC are perfectly coherent. At best in the moment, and with development they become increasingly coherent and complex. Perhaps more important, the experience itself has to be seen as messily coherent. Even more important is to recognize that no connection between individuals is ever perfect, but out of all this imperfection unique meanings and connections emerge. Such is the wonder of the human condition—the emergence of the new out of messiness.

ACKNOWLEDGMENT

I would like to acknowledge the invaluable work on this paper by Jacob Ham and my discussion with my colleagues Marilyn Davillier, George Downing, and Alexandre Harrison.

CHAPTER 36

Contributions to Understanding Therapeutic Change: Now We Have a Playground

Many concepts can contribute to an understanding of how people change in psychoanalysis and psychoanalytic psychotherapy. This chapter attempts to contribute to an understanding of therapeutic change in two ways, both of which draw on insights from infant/developmental research. First, we provide a model of change that emphasizes the expanded opportunities for change in the moment-by-moment interactions between therapist and patient in an individual session, interactions similar but not identical to those between mothers and infants that generate change. For shorthand, we refer to this model—the dyadic expansion of consciousness model—as the dyadic expansion model or simply expansion. Second, we provide detailed information on change drawn from a videotape of a child analyst's first session with a 3-year old girl ("Kate") to illustrate how this model of dyadic expansion can be helpful in understanding therapeutic change.

Kate, who had witnessed the World Trade Center attack on television, in the absence of her mother, suffered from severe separation anxiety disorder and sleep disturbance. In the reported session with Kate, change can be appreciated first in Kate's enhanced capacity to play freely and to represent symbolically in her play the traumatic image of people jumping, and then by her creation with the analyst of a "safe playground"—where children can jump "safely" and "softly."

Videotape information has long been used by infant researchers to explore interactions between mothers and infants (Stern, 1985; Tronick, 1980, 1989). Here, we intend to show how the dyadic expansion model of the moment-to-moment change process, and the related videotape analysis, can supplement psychoanalytic tools used to understand therapeutic change. Many important elements of the psychoanalytic process cannot be observed in videotape and can be usefully explained by previously existing theories. For example, videotape cannot record the private, inner world of the patient or the analyst (Modell, 1993), nor can videotape record meanings in the intersubjective space that is mutually created (Aron, 1996; Mitchell, 1997; Ogden, 1994; Winnicott, 1971). Nevertheless, modeling and examining the microexchanges that take place between the therapist and the patient as revealed in videotapes can provide important insights into the nature of their therapeutic interchange and into how change occurs.

This chapter has several sections. We will begin with an overview of the clinical material from the videotaped session. This material is derived from seven 3- to 4-minute clips captured from the videotape of the entire session and consists of the verbal transcript, as well as descriptions of some of the nonverbal behaviors of the child and analyst. Next we will present the model of dyadic expansion of consciousness. Then we will demonstrate how this conceptual model can be used to better understand some of the change processes illustrated in the videotaped clinical material. We conclude with some thoughts about how theory and observation of clinical material continue to evolve in a mutually enhancing interaction to offer us new opportunities to understand the process of therapeutic change.

THE CLINICAL SESSION

Introduction to the Clinical Session

Kate, 2 years and 9 months old, viewed the September 11 attacks on television. She saw planes crashing into buildings and people jumping out of windows. Kate developed symptoms of panic attacks and flashbacks. She told her mother, "Get those planes out of my head!" She also suffered from stammering, a severe sleep disorder, and separation anxiety. The context of the events of that morning included the absence of Kate's mother, who had gone to the hospital for a minor medical emergency, the absence of her father, who was taking her older brother to his first day of school, and the absence of her grandmother, who was taking her mother to the hospital. Her grandfather was the adult taking care of Kate. Kate's immediate family consisted of her mother, father, and 4- and-a-half-year-old brother.

Summary of the Clinical Session Derived From Reviewing the Videotape of the Session

Kate begins this first session by avoiding the airplane and dolls' house, turning her back on the analyst (AMH), and playing a pretend game of filling up cars with gas from the gas pump of a toy garage. She is taking both roles—that of the driver in need of gas and that of the gas station attendant, the supplier of gas, and she is using different pretend voices to represent them. AMH attempts to enter Kate's gas station play, using a pretend voice similar to hers and asking, "Excuse me, excuse me, can I have some gas?" Through a repetitive sequence of small exchanges about asking for and receiving gasoline for different cars by different pretend owners, Kate and AMH make a connection that leads to a movement in the play to a more active car race with small dolls. Kate pronounces one car the winner. AMH refers to the other car, saying, "It isn't much fun to lose," and makes a pretend crying sound for the loser car. Immediately after this, Kate tells AMH's dolls, "We're going to the circus. Would you like to come with us?"

Kate pronounces a dolls' house to be "the circus" and explains that there are people "lookin' out the windows." This is the first image that could be recognized as the World Trade Center. AMH brings three dolls to the circus. In another sequence of repetitive play moves, Kate and AMH elaborate three kinds of jumping down—"jump," "slide," and "slide-jump."

The dolls' house play leads to a greater freedom of movement and use of space in the playroom, and to Kate's suggestion of building a "playground." Together Kate and AMH build a playground, into which the doll children jump. When AMH introduces the theme of hurt by making one of her dolls say "Ow!" after his jump, Kate leans over close to the doll and says, "Do you know why you said 'Ow'? You said 'Ow' because you took too big a jump. You were supposed to take a little jump." Kate and AMH repetitively practice little jumps with their doll children, and Kate declares the playground to be a place where people are free to jump safely: "You can do [even] big jumps when you're inside the playground," she says.

The session thus ends with Kate able to open up her rigid meanings of what happens when little girls are separated from their mothers—perhaps something like "their mothers jump down from big buildings and are gone forever"—and create with AMH new, more adaptive meanings about separations—children can find a safe playground where "you can do even big jumps." How did this shift come about?

Tronick's Model of Dyadic Expansion of Consciousness

The dyadic expansion of consciousness model conceptualizes growth, in normal development as well as in psychotherapy, as occurring when two individuals interact in a way that results in the disorganization of old meanings and the emergence of new meaning (Tronick, 1998, 2004). Whereas the psychoanalytic model offers perhaps the best insight into the private world of the individual, the dyadic expansion of consciousness model offers an additional way of understanding how the private worlds of the patient and analyst interact to create change. The expansion model defines general principles of meaning making that are isomorphic for psychoanalytic treatment and infant-caregiver exchange. This is not to say that all or even most of the observations made by infant researchers can be applied to psychoanalysis; indeed, they cannot. Instead, this model identifies general principles of growth and development based on dynamic systems theory that can be used in these two different domains in which change is central. The evidence, the two sets of data to which these principles can be applied, is obtained by different means—by psychoanalytic or psychotherapeutic practice and by direct observation. Hence, dyadic expansion offers a way of understanding data about the psychoanalytic change process collected in a different way, through applying the same overarching organizing principles derived from dynamic systems theory.

Dyadic expansion states that new meanings are cocreated during ongoing messy exchanges of age-possible meanings from each individual's sense of the world (Tronick, 2004). The exchanges are messy because whatever the form of the meanings—words, actions, gestures—they are neither fully formed nor fixed, and because the meaning-making process is difficult, demanding, and messy. Nevertheless, when the meanings come together, a dyadic state of consciousness emerges, in which both individuals' meanings are mutually apprehended and coordinated.

In this model, humans are understood as open systems that cocreate meanings either internally (in their private world) or with others (in their relational world) to modify their own states of consciousness. These states are not necessarily in awareness but are the moment-by-moment states of being and acting in the world. The cocreation of meaning is a bit-by-bit, continuously occurring process. This ongoing evolution of states of consciousness is necessary in order to fulfill the basic theoretical requirement of open systems—to continue to exist, open systems must maintain or even increase their coherence and complexity. When new meanings are cocreated, the individual's state of consciousness is expanded, and the individual's sense of the world becomes more whole and complex.

The mind is a complex system, hierarchically organized, with both upward and downward influences connecting its multiple levels, each with unique emergent properties. Dyadic expansion holds that nonstatic, changing meanings exist in each level—in the body, in actions, in the dynamic unconscious, in the nonconscious, and in the conscious. These meanings are implicit and explicit, and each of these forms of meaning brings the past into the present, makes sense of the individual's place in the world, and guides future actions and sense making. As meanings emerge from one level to the other, they take on new emergent properties. No level is fully privileged. Thus, even if one were to assume that fixed, fully formed unconscious meaning exists (an assumption we do not make because meanings are mainly fuzzy and messy), as the meaning is brought into consciousness it takes on emergent properties associated with the conscious level of the mind. These new properties, such as symbolic forms, represent a change from its unconscious form. In turn, the meaning is immediately acted upon by the patient-analyst dyad and changes further.

Finally, the now dynamically changing conscious meaning transforms the still-in-flux unconscious meaning by downward causality (Freeman, 1994, 2000).

But not all new meanings lead to expansion. Some new meanings constrict and rigidify the individual's sense of the world, and the person's state of consciousness loses coherence and complexity. In the language of open systems, the state of consciousness dissipates (Stengers & Prigogene, 1997). There is a violation of the first principle of open systems theory—to maintain organization and grow. As a consequence, the individual experiences a subjective sense of loss of freedom, of chaos and anxiety. The person anticipates loss of organization and the perception of impending annihilation. However, there is another origin of anxiety predicted by open systems theory, and this origin is in change itself. The process of cocreating new meaning out of messiness always threatens dissipation of the level of coherence and complexity previously achieved, with a consequent—at least temporary—loss of organization. Thus there is an experiential conflict between expansion and shrinkage that accompanies the psychodynamic conflicts that are also part of the meaning making, and these domains of conflict influence each other.

In the case of trauma, the event may be beyond the capacity of the individual to make sense of in a manner that expands his or her state of consciousness. But since the individual must always attempt to make sense of his experience, the sense may be rigid, impossible to integrate into an ongoing state of consciousness, and closed to the meaningful input of others—what clinicians would call a dissociated meaning. In order to maintain this defensive isolation— to maintain as much coherence and complexity as possible—the individual further limits communication that might allow access to the dissociated meaning and other disorganizing meanings. The result is further deterioration of the individual's meaning making.

Although the subjective sense of the world accompanying a state of consciousness is that of stability—it has certitude—states of consciousness are inherently unstable and changing. They are at "criticality," the state of a system that is highly complex and coherent yet inherently unstable (Bak, 1996). Criticality requires energetic input and constraint to maintain itself. Some of the input is self-organized and much of it must come from others. By contrast, states of consciousness made up of rigid meanings are far from criticality, more stable and highly coherent, less complex, and less open to input.

How the Dyadic Expansion of Consciousness Model Is Useful to the Psychoanalyst and Psychotherapist

According to dyadic expansion, the goal of the psychoanalyst is to help the patient move his state of consciousness toward criticality so that new states of consciousness can be formed and the patient's impelling certitude can be changed. The work of the analyst of a traumatized patient is to initiate the cocreative process of meaning making in order to change the patient's less complex, rigidly coherent state of consciousness. Since meaning exists at many levels—bodily processes and actions, affect, the dynamic unconscious, and conscious thought—implementing this change begins with establishing domains of communication where the cocreation of meaning can take place. Then the cocreating of new meanings of the trauma can occur by bringing elements of meaning from the analyst's own states of consciousness and from the patient to the meaning-making process.

The connection is accomplished through the use of age-possible means of communication. The concept of "age-possible" is key because it takes into account the developmentally available competencies each partner brings to the meaning-making process.* For example, body movements, including facial expressions and vocalizations, are the communicative tools of infants, and the meanings shared are intentions and affects. Language and pretend play are the communicative tools of the preschool child, and the meanings that are shared are symbolic, often action-based representations and illogical thematic play narratives. Adolescents and adults communicate with the analyst primarily in language with abstract symbols. This communication is mostly in narrative form and has, especially for adolescents, few constraints. The establishment of a domain of communication about meaning is not specific to content, but rather to what is age-possible.

Then the analyst brings her own meanings into the mix as she tries to understand her patient's communications. This step is explicitly conceptualized in the dyadic expansion model where it is seen as a universal feature of the psychoanalytic process. At the higher organizational level of spoken language the meaning making is explicit, conscious, in awareness. Much of the meaning making—especially from moment to moment—is implicit, unconscious, out of awareness. A prolonged silence, a body position, an averted gaze, a shift in the rhythm of vocal turn taking, and many other non verbal communications have meaning and become elements of the meanings that the dyad makes together (Beebe & Lachmann, 2002; Fivaz-Depeursinge & Corboz-Warnery, 1999). In this cocreative process, both partners bring the meanings from all the multiple levels that make up states of consciousness into the interaction that opens up old meanings and transforms them into new ones. The new states of consciousness are not planned nor predictable. Instead, they emerge from repetitive exchanges of meanings that have the immediate goal of creating and maintaining a connection through making meaning (Bruner, 1990).

Repetition and rhythm are key mechanisms in changing states of consciousness (Beebe et al., 2000; Sander, 1983b). At the higher level of meaning making, repetition is necessary to ensure explicit understanding, because the meanings individuals have for words are neither identical nor fully known even to the

---

*Valenstein wrote, "in the earliest phase of development, object representation and self representation coalesce more around the affective correlates of experience than around its cognitive potential" (1973, p. 374).

speaker. At the moment-to-moment level of meaning making, change in mean-ing may emerge from small variations, when the state of consciousness has reached criticality (Bak, 1996). Bak, in fact, demonstrates that in complex sys-tems such as dyadically interacting minds, repetition of apparently identical forms inevitably generates change in the system (Bak, 1996). The rhythmic turn tak-ing functions as a carrier wave that maintains the momentum of the meaning-making process, and in doing so it also conveys meaning, such as, "We are work-ing together to find a directionality to our meaning making." Once established, directionality self-amplifies and leads toward a greater coherence and complexity of shared meaning. In the moment-to-moment process of a psychoanalytic ses-sion, repetitive patterns are a common event. In the expansion model, they are given a central role in the change process. In the videotape microanalysis of the treatment of a young child, the repetitiveness becomes observable, with its sub-tle shifts and eventual transformation into something new.

The cocreating of meaning is inherently messy but the messiness is not error; rather, it is the wellspring of new meanings (Tronick, 2004). In the illustrated case—observable in the videotape—AMH and Kate interact at many levels that convey meaning, from the nonverbal domains of body movement and facial expression to the age-possible meanings communicated in language, symbolic play, and prosodic elements of speech. Each of these domains conveys behav-ioral and relational intentions, motivations, and affects as well as unconscious, including dynamically unconscious, meanings. In this interplay, there is a vari-ability of coordination of the meanings communicated between the two part-ners. The variability diminishes over time as the new meanings are cocreated and shared, but messiness is always present, because the rate of the exchange at the local level is so fast and complex that accurate apprehension and expres-sion cannot be maintained and because the newly emerging meanings become the stuff of the continuously ongoing meaning-making process.

The Change of Kate's State of Consciousness From the Perspective of the Dyadic Expansion of Consciousness Model

The meaning Kate made of the images on television was a traumatic meaning. Yet her state of consciousness includes far more than just her viewing of the images on television. At not yet 3 years old, Kate has a large vocabulary, skill-ful actions, concern about bodily integrity, a robust memory, preoperational thinking, and some reflectivity and self-awareness. Her sense of what has hap-pened emerges from these age-possible meaning-making processes, as well as from the crucial context of her family experiences, and also from other private meanings such as fantasies and developing psychodynamic processes. All these factors contribute to the state of consciousness and the "impelling certitude" Kate generates in response to these images. How does she come to have this impelling certitude that makes her symptomatic?

Kate's normal sense-making capacities work to create a coherent and complex sense of what she experienced, but they are not able to generate a nontoxic way of understanding the events. Her capacities have faltered under the stress of the event—the viewing, including the context in which it occurred, in other words, the whole experience—given her normal but still limited 2-year-old capacity. She cannot let her mind operate in its preoperational, unconstrained mode, because to do so would engage her overwhelming feelings. Fonagy (Fonagy, Gergely, Jurist, & Target, 2003; Fonagy & Target, 1998) would argue that her mentalization, the capacity for reflective mental activity—at this point an emerging capacity—has been disrupted. At the same time, if she were not able to make any sense of her experience, the disorganization would be overwhelming. Thus the trauma includes not only the viewing but also her diminished but still operating age-possible sense-making capacity, amplifying the negative effect.

Without the help of her mother to scaffold or contain her, Kate is unprotected from thoughts such as, "Even grownups can fall down from tall buildings and get hurt and lose their mommies forever!" With her emerging capacity to mentalize, she is reflecting on the feelings and thoughts of others. Perhaps she is terrified by beginning to imagine how frightened those people are to be falling down so far and to know that they will get so badly hurt. Unable to integrate her frightening sense of this experience into her usual sense of the world, she dissociates the experience in order to keep its disruptive effects isolated, which also serves to protect her from the anxiety that would come with its disorganizing effects. For similar reasons she cannot talk freely about it, further limiting opportunities for help from others.

It is important to appreciate that the event occurred within a rich context that further amplifies its effects. The state of her grandfather during the television broadcast is not fully known. We do know that he was frightened and unable to be adequately responsive to her; she had to confront his anxiety. Furthermore, her mother's going to the hospital may have evoked Kate's experience of her mother's vulnerability, as well as images of hospitals as big buildings, provoking the threat of loss of her mother. Also, her brother—an object of admiration and envy—was being taken to his first day of "big boy school" by their father. Finally, in addition to what was going on at the time of the viewing, her current and past relationships with her family members and their characteristic ways of managing stress in general and whatever meaning the 9/11 attack had for them in particular form a crucial part of the context.

Kate must try to make meaning of this assemblage of events and previously created elements of meaning, connecting her experience of the external world with her inner world to create her state of consciousness. If she does not, her state dissipates, and there would be overwhelming anxiety. In her inner world, symbolic representations are continually being put together with other elements of meaning in the local context—affective configurations, memories, and body sensations. Or they are moved from one level of the mind to another, in an evolving synthesis, by implicit mental processes. All these elements of meaning, and the mental processes that act to create the meanings, are influenced by these multiple factors—Kate's developmental capacities, her unique personal capacities, her past experience with others and of events, her culture, and her fantasies. And all are governed by the inescapable requirement to maintain and expand complexity and coherence.

Fantasy, as well as other meaning, is cocreated in a continuously evolving communicative/interactive process. Cocreation of meaning with another, and also one's own meanings, function as operators on (modifiers of) meaning. Both self-awareness and communication alter an individual's state of consciousness. It is only those fantasies that are fixed—because they have become isolated from self-organized processes or from the communicative process—that result in distortions of reality and symptom formation. These fixed fantasies, both the meanings that are the symbolic elements of fantasy and the ways of putting together those meanings, normally part of the cocreative process, end up causing problems.

Kate may be able to put the frightening events of September 11 behind her and carry on with her everyday life. Yet images of airplanes, or the unresponsiveness of an important adult, for example, could trigger the set of old images and affective reactions, as well as the old illogical brain operations. For example, one important triggering context was bedtime, not only because of the intrinsic theme of separation in the experience, but also because the different mental processes during the state changes involved in going to sleep likely had a role in the re-creation of the frightening meanings.

Whatever Kate's state of consciousness, we can appreciate the complexity of her meaning making. Kate's meaning is not that of an infant or an older child, but it is also not that of another child of her same age. It is unique, much of it unknown and unknowable, messy, illogical, and constantly changing. However, because of her traumatic experience, elements of her meaning are relatively more fixed, less messy, and isolated from her own meaning-making processes and from the meaning she makes with others. Using this formulation derived from dyadic expansion to complement her psychoanalytic formulations, and without knowing what the future will bring, how does AMH understand what happened in the first session with Kate?

The Analyst's Use of the Dyadic Expansion of Consciousness Model to Understand the Videotape

At the beginning of the session, the video demonstrates the first step in the implementation of change—the establishment of domains of communication where the cocreation of meaning can take place. In three steps Kate and AMH make a connection, using their bodies, language, pretend, and affect.* The first

---

*Whereas many analysts consider these analytic behaviors to be part of their repertoires, they are rarely part of an analyst's clinical theory; new concepts and techniques are required to bring them within a coherent theoretical model.

step is Kate's, and it is implicit: a slight turn of her body in AMH's direction, and a pause in her activity, as if to ask, "Would you like a turn?" These nonverbal communications of meaning directly precede AMH's initial verbal communication to her, but were not in AMH's conscious awareness at the time. It was only in viewing the videotape after the session that AMH could see them, but in the moment she acted on them, they were in her implicit awareness, much like the intuitive knowing parents have for the infant's communication (Papousek & Papousek, 1986). After AMH's first request for gas, Kate turns toward her without a smile and silently gives her car some gas. In the second step, AMH repeats her request, this time with a different car and with a different pretend voice. Kate turns toward her with a small smile, says "Yes?" quietly, and gives her some gas. In the third step, Kate turns toward AMH and Kate herself initiates the question, "Do you want some gas?" The turn taking and rhythm convey the message that they were doing something together. But what were they doing together?

The second step in the implementation of change is bringing elements from AMH's own experience and from Kate's to a cocreative meaning-making process, with the goal of changing Kate's traumatic meaning. What meanings are conveyed by each of the steps in the gas station play? Though communicated by nonverbal displays, the first step has meaning. The meaning might be something like, "I must pretend the powerless (out of gas) and the powerful (supplier of gas) all by myself. I have no one." Yet Kate still has the capacity to imagine that AMH might be a good partner. She turns toward her and pauses in invitation. By step three, the meaning might be understood as, "Together we can create new ways to deal with not-having, or loss. We can use symbolic play to represent a situation in which a powerless person asks for what she needs and gets what she needs from the powerful person." This expanded meaning allows both Kate and AMH to play with the affective experiences of powerlessness and powerfulness.

AMH repeats the same request for gas with one car after another, each time giving another reason for needing gas. The cocreative process is facilitated by repetition; each repetition is both the same and contains something new. The new part is unpredictable, perhaps unknown. Not only does AMH vary her question slightly each time, offering unpredictability to Kate, but also Kate is unpredictable in her response. For example, she might have said, "No," or "You can have a little bit." She actually responds by giving the gas each time, but each time with different affective communication, body movement, and speech. Kate and AMH have engaged in a cocreative process, and Kate has been able, through the regulating connection with AMH, to deal with the stress of the unpredictability and the messiness of the meaning-making process.

When Kate initiates a car race between a girl doll and the "mommy," AMH uses her analytic experience with little girls Kate's age, particularly her knowledge of the fantasy meanings they typically use to make sense of their worlds. AMH thinks about the Oedipal competition between Kate and her mother, but she does not know how or even if this will play out. Using the dyadic expansion model, she does not privilege Oedipal—or any other—symbolic material, but she keeps it in mind. AMH does not worry that she might choose the wrong intervention, because she imagines an infinite number of alternative ways the meaning making could proceed. Instead, she focuses on the flow of the cocreative meaning-making process and on supporting Kate's initiative both to introduce new elements and to accept or decline elements introduced by AMH into the play. The therapeutic technique is to open up the messiness of meaning making and allow Kate to tolerate that messiness, even if the content is not the content of her trauma.

After the race, Kate reiterates the "winner" and "loser" positions, and AMH expresses her acceptance of "loser" feelings. Kate responds with her invitation to the circus. This is a further elaboration of "doing something together," something special like the circus. AMH recalls that "going to the circus" was one of the explanations she had given for a driver needing gas at Kate's gas station, and she recognizes that Kate is choosing to use one of the motifs AMH had introduced earlier in their play together in a new context, a form of repetition of an assimilated element of meaning from AMH by Kate. Kate then takes the initiative to introduce a new theme into the play. It is a risk because she cannot predict where it will go, but it conveys her sense that they will go there together. She invites AMH's dolls to join her dolls inside the building, where they are "lookin' out the window." It is here that AMH recognizes an image that resembles the traumatic images of the World Trade Center in the play, but she does not know what Kate is really thinking. Dyadic expansion might see this as a bifurcation point, something similar to a "now moment," a moment that says something is about to happen (Stengers & Prigogine, 1997; Stern et al., 1998). This is a point in the therapeutic activity when there is a choice between a direction that leads toward a new state of consciousness and one that maintains the old. While it seems obvious that the path toward a new state of consciousness is preferable, the actual choice is made up of multiple responses to complex issues including therapeutic perspective, technique, clinical experience, AMH's evaluation of where Kate is at that moment, and the anxiety that always comes with moving toward the unknown. In addition, even if the path toward the new state of consciousness is taken, there is no assurance that the opportunity will be realized, due to the messiness of the moment-by-moment creative process and its threat of dissipation.

AMH recognizes that something more than her moment-to-moment responsiveness is needed to scaffold Kate in her meaning making at this critical point in the session. She draws on her analytic theory and clinical experience. She also uses dyadic expansion, because Kate is offering her play elements to use in what might result in cocreating a new meaning for her traumatic experience. In order to prepare for this type of play, AMH takes three dolls to the circus. The choice of three dolls is an explicit choice by AMH, whereas other actions—such as the initiation of the gas station game—are more implicit, though all become part of the meaning making. AMH wants to use the technique of repetition to prepare for opening up Kate's traumatic meanings. Even if she does not yet know how or when her dolls will take action in the play, she knows that three dolls will not obey the constraints of the all-or-nothing pattern of a traumatic meaning.

Kate invites AMH's dolls to join hers inside the dolls' house, saying, "We're up here!" AMH asks, "How should I come up?" She wonders whether Kate will elaborate the traumatic image of jumping, but she does not know whether or not she will—and if she does, when or how she will do it. Kate responds, "You could jump up." AMH now has in mind the idea of opening up a rigid, all-or-nothing pattern organized around the meaning of jumping. She would like to create something other than the two extremes, which could be represented by *losing mommy forever and therefore self-annihilation*, or *clinging to mommy and refusing to separate from her*. Based on dyadic expansion and on AMH's experience with the technique of repetition, she consciously prepares to scaffold Kate's opening up the meaning of *jump*. She wants to be able to put into action multiple possibilities of jumping, so that they will be able to introduce at least some tiny change in the meaning of jumping and in that way cocreate a new meaning together. Although AMH has as her goal cocreating a more adaptive meaning of *jump*, she does not know what that new meaning will be or when it will emerge in the play.

AMH makes one doll jump up ("Jump!"), the second doll jump up ("Jump!"), and the third doll jump up ("Jump!"). Repetition is an important technique of this model. It maintains the exchange, the messiness of the exchange, and opens up possibilities for something new. In this case, the something new is the presence of three dolls who have jumped up and now are in a position to jump down. Maybe Kate will choose to make them jump down, and maybe she will not. The model's concepts of unpredictability and messiness support AMH's not knowing what will happen in this clinical situation.

At Kate's invitation to join her dolls on the first floor, a modest distance from the second-floor location of AMH's dolls, AMH detects another bifurcation point, a point where something new may happen. When AMH asks whether this means another jump, Kate suggests, "You could jump . . . or you could slide." AMH is pleased at what she sees as a sign of the potential opening up of the meaning of *jump* that is introduced by the new alternative of *slide*, an alternative generated by Kate. AMH makes one of her three dolls jump down, the second doll slide down, and—in collaboration with Kate—the third doll jump-slide. At the articulation of "jump-slide," both Kate and AMH laugh. There is a warm sense of connection that marks a successful expansion of shared meaning. The new meaning is more complex. The experiences of affect, connection, and expanded meaning are inseparable. Kate took a chance by initiating a new possibility and trusting AMH with it. And yet there is nothing certain about where Kate and AMH will go with this expanded meaning of *jump*. The new, cocreated meaning of *jump* may bring them too close to the traumatic meaning of *jump*, and Kate could withdraw. Or AMH may discover that Kate's meaning has less to do with jumping than she had initially thought. The path they take will only become manifest in the next moments of engagement.

Kate suggests that she and AMH build a playground, expressing agency in a new way as she states cheerfully, "Follow me!" and scampers across the floor to a new part of the room. Here, AMH consciously attempts to establish a turn-taking rhythm with Kate in choosing blocks and laying them in a line, by following each move of Kate's with a comparable move and placing each block with a definitive gesture to accent the end of her turn. As the rhythmic turn-taking proceeds, the blocks are laid in a line, establishing both a physical and psychical direction. The rhythmic turn taking establishes a directionality, moving the meaning making of the interactants forward (Sander, 1983a). The momentum of rhythmic turn taking helps prevent the process from being derailed by mismatches and stumbles.

Unpredictability is again illustrated in the fact that Kate and AMH both know something will be created over time—a playground made of blocks—but the size and shape it will take are unknown, how elaborated the meanings will become is unknown, and when they will have to "back off" is also unknown. As the two lines of blocks approach each other, Kate says, "We're getting closer to each other." In this statement, she brings together elements of meaning in language, body movement, affect, and intention. AMH repeats, in a softer voice, "We're getting closer to each other," and waits for Kate to lay the last block that completes the connection. After the circle is completed, Kate stands up and surveys their creation. "Now we have a playground," she remarks.

Kate indicates that the dolls should enter the playground, declaring, "Another jump!" Here, AMH decides to take the risk of linking hurt and potentially the traumatic affect to jumping for the first time. She makes her doll say "Ow!" after jumping into the playground. This contribution by AMH might be considered by more traditional models to close off other alternatives. Yet the expansion model understands this introduction of an element of meaning by the analyst as leading to messiness, and this messiness makes possible an enhancement of alternatives in the meaning-making process. Remaining silent would have contributed another element of meaning to the process. AMH is watching for Kate's reaction, and when Kate hesitates, she wonders if she has gone too far. She decides to make the second and third doll jump into the playground without the "Ow." After her hesitation, however, Kate walks over and crouches down beside the doll who said "Ow," asking, "Do you know why you said 'Ow'? Because you took too big a jump. You're supposed to take a little jump." AMH makes her doll ask Kate if he should "practice little jumps," and she nods in assent. AMH makes him do so, and Kate repeats the practicing with another doll. AMH is delighted to recognize that now she and Kate have accumulated a large repertoire of jumps—big, terrible jumps down (from the World Trade Center), jumps up, modest jumps down (from the second floor of the dolls' house), slides down, jump-slides, and now little jumps. Finally,

Kate tells her, "But you can jump big when you're inside the playground!" "Oh," AMH says, "because it's safer inside the playground?" "Yes," Kate says. "And softer." AMH repeats, "And softer."

IMPLICATIONS FOR FUTURE INVESTIGATIONS OF THERAPEUTIC CHANGE

Considering how to integrate theory and observation in order to provide insights to clinicians is itself an interactive process. Conceptual formulations allow one to view clinical material in a new light, and the detailed analysis made possible by videotape allows one to see new interactions, both in turn leading to enrichments in the theory. The session with Kate provides an example of this mutually reinforcing process.

The dyadic expansion of consciousness model has two features that support the integration of knowledge from infant research and psychoanalysis and make this knowledge useful to the clinician. The first is the inclusiveness that derives from the model's adherence to the general principles of open systems theory. The second is the factor of specificity—in terms of age-possible meaning-making capacities and uniquely cocreated meanings. Both features of the model—the inclusiveness and the specificity—are realized in the concept of state of consciousness. States of consciousness constitute the result of the meaning-making activity and encompass a multitude of meanings—from sensory, perceptual, and motoric to affective systems, and from meanings of the dynamic unconscious to conscious thoughts. As such, the model does not privilege one or another form of meaning making. Rather it recognizes that meanings come in many forms and are made in many ways at many levels.

Despite the potential complementarity of psychoanalysis and dyadic expansion, it is evident that integrating theories that derive from different kinds of data—psychoanalytic practice and direct observation of infant and caregiver—remains a challenge. The dyadic expansion model supplements the analyst's tools by offering the means to understand the moment-to-moment interactive process, but what about the intrapsychic? Is there a place for analytic concepts such as insight, conflict, and working through in dyadic expansion? One answer is obtained by referring to dynamic systems theory's general principle of levels of organization; accordingly, the cocreative activities of change occur at different levels of organization within a complex system. That system may be comprised of two individuals, or it may consist of two parts of the same individual. Dyadic expansion includes the idea of cocreating meaning between the conscious mind and the dynamic unconscious, such as with insight. In this cocreative process, there can also be conflict between conscious and unconscious meanings. Kate experiences anxiety from two sources related to the traumatic event—the anxiety from unconscious conflict about aggression (psychoanalytic theory), and also the fear of dissipation of her psychic organization through opening it up to change (dyadic expansion). The expansion model also sees conflicts between the messy meanings within one level as well as the meanings between levels. Similarly, what psychoanalysis describes as working through could be seen as a more macroscopic version of the microscopic repetitive interactions we have stressed as a central part of the meaning-making process.

However, the concepts from these two theoretical sources cannot be integrated without shared overarching principles governing the process of change. Referring to the general principles of open systems theory, dyadic expansion sees change as taking place in a continuously evolving interactive process of messy, disorganizing meaning making, in which no meanings are ever fixed or fully formed, but only in process. To the extent that contemporary psychoanalytic theories are in agreement with this perspective, the two conceptual models may be integrated. Still, a comprehensive integration is a project for the future.

AMH used both psychoanalytic theory and dyadic expansion in complementary ways to make sense of her clinical experience with Kate. Two-and-three-quarter-year-old Kate's conflicts about her hostility and aggression in the dependent relationship with her mother were catapulted into a new category of traumatic meaning when she witnessed the World Trade Center attack on television in her mother's absence. Without the comforting presence of her mother, the sense she made of the television images terrified her and resulted in symptoms of trauma. In the first session with AMH, months after the traumatic event, no real insight into her intrapsychic conflicts could be achieved, nor could these conflicts be worked through. However, the dyadic expansion model gives us a way to understand the microscopic process of change, because it was that local-level process that brought about an emergence of creative play and even significant symptomatic relief after the session. Nevertheless, the local-level process was at all times inseparable from meaning-making processes at other levels of organization; it was essential for this microscopic process to always be framed in the background and in the foreground by an analytic sense of what meanings were possible and available to work on.

In the case, new meaning is created as a shared state of consciousness for Kate and AMH, and from this dyadic state of consciousness a changed state of consciousness for each of them emerges. Their new states of consciousness will carry a different impelling certitude about the world. In the old world, 3-year-olds have to cling to mother and resist sleep for fear of terrible jumps. In the new world, there are places where children are free to jump safely and softly. In the old world, the danger of dissipation is too great. In the new world, danger is modulated by dyadic meaning making. At the time of the session, AMH had focused on Kate's remark about being able to jump "big" when you are "inside the playground." To her, Kate's remark had meant hope for the future, changing the terrifying meaning of *jump* in order to grow into more flexible, adaptive approaches to life. Yet in looking back, her attention was caught by Kate's use of the word *softer*. In response to AMH's remark, "Oh, I guess it [the playground] is safer," Kate says, "Yes, and softer." With dyadic expansion, AMH can now appreciate the cocreative process of making meaning with Kate in a different way. At 3 years old, Kate's sense of "safer" is expressed well by the word *softer*. *Softer* captures the sense of a soft landing. Of course, if one is jumping from a great height, no "softer" will make the landing safe, but Kate's thinking is age-appropriately illogical on this point. In contributing her word *softer*, Kate is actively participating in opening up her problematic but familiar meaning, and her limited but familiar way of making meaning, to an uncertain process between AMH and herself. *Softer* as safer is a new meaning. Both contributors find value in it, though neither exactly understands the other's contribution. This new meaning is a work in progress, a step out of one position and toward a future position yet unknown.

Thus the dyadic expansion model holds that change occurs in psychoanalysis, as it does in development, when states of consciousness are communicated and shared, causing the states of consciousness in each individual to open up to the messy and unpredictable process of making new meaning and increasing each individual's coherence and complexity. The challenge for the expansion model is to make its terms psychologically meaningful and the framework technically useful in the psychoanalytic setting. As we make progress toward these goals, we will be creating the connections necessary for a more effective integration of the two models.

Credits

PART I: NEUROBEHAVIOR

Chapter 1. Tronick, E. (1987). The neonatal behavioral assessment scale as a biomarker of the effects of environmental agents on the newborn. *Environmental Health Perspectives*, 74: 185–189. Reproduced with permission from *Environmental Health Perspectives*.

Chapter 2. Lester, B. & Tronick, E. (2001). Behavioral assessment scales: The NICU Network Neurobehavioral Scale, the Neonatal Behavioral Assessment Scale, and the Assessment of the Preterm Infant's Behavior. In P. S. Zeskind & L. T. Singer (Eds.), *Biobehavioral assessment of the infant* (pp. 363–380). New York: Guilford.

Chapter 3. Reprinted from *Human Movement Science*, 22(6). Fetters, L., Chen, Y., Jonsdottir, J., & Tronick, E. Z. (2004). Kicking coordination captures differences between full-term and premature infants with white matter disorder, pp. 729–748. Copyright 2004 with permission from Elsevier.

Chapter 4. Tronick, E. (1996). Late dose-response effects of prenatal cocaine exposure on newborn neurobehavioral performance. Reproduced with permission from *Pediatrics*, 98, 76–83. Copyright © 1996 by the AAP.

Chapter 5. Chen, Y., Fetters, L., Olson, K., & Tronick, E. (2004). Similar and functionally typical kinematic reaching parameters in 7- and 15-month-old in utero cocaine-exposed and unexposed infants. *Developmental Psychobiology*, 44, 168–175. Reprinted with permission of Wiley-Liss, Inc., a subsidiary of John Wiley & Sons, Inc.

PART II: CULTURE

Chapter 6. Tronick E. (1992). Cross-cultural studies of development, *Developmental Psychology*, 28, 566–567. Copyright © 1992 by the American Psychological Association. Reprinted with permission.

Chapter 7. Morelli, G. & Tronick, E. (1991). The role of culture in brain organization, child development, and parenting. In T. Brazelton, B. Lester, & J. Nugent (Eds.), *The cultural context of infancy, Volume 2: Multicultural and interdisciplinary approaches to parent–infant relations* (pp. ix–xiii). Norwood, NJ: Ablex. Copyright 1991 by Ablex Publishing Corporation. Reproduced with permission of Greenwood Publishing Group, Inc., Westport, CT.

Chapter 8. Reprinted from *The psychobiology of attachment*, Field, T. & Reite, M. (Eds.), Multiple caretaking in the context of human evolution: Why don't the Efé know the Western prescription for child care? by Tronick, E., Morelli, G., & Winn, S. (pp. 293–322). Copyright 1984 with permission from Elsevier.

Chapter 9. Tronick, E. (1994). The Manta pouch: A regulatory system for Peruvian infants at high altitude. This article was originally published in *Children's Environments*, *11*(2), 142–146. *Children's Environments* is currently published under the title *Children, Youth, and Environments* and is accessible online at www.colorado.edu/journals/cye/index.htm.

Chapter 10. Brazelton, T., Dixon, S., Keefer, C., & Tronick, E. (1981). Mother-infant interaction among the Gusii of Kenya. In T. Field, P. Leiderman, A. Sostek, & P. Vietze (Eds.), *Culture and early interactions* (pp. 149–168). New York: Academic Press. Reproduced with permission of Edward Z. Tronick and Lawrence Erlbaum Associates/The Analytic Press.

PART III: INFANT SOCIAL-EMOTIONAL INTERACTION

Chapter 11. Tronick, E. & Gianino, A. (1986). Interactive mismatch and repair: Challenges to the coping infant. *Zero to Three*, *3*: 1–6. Copyright 1986 ZERO TO THREE. Reproduced with permission of the copyright holder, www.zerotothree.org.

Chapter 12. Tronick, E. (1989). Emotions and emotional communication in infants. *American Psychologist*, *44*: 112–119. Copyright 1989 by the American Psychological Association. Reprinted with permission.

Chapter 13. Gianino A. & Tronick E. (1988). The mutual regulation model: The infant's self and interactive regulation and coping and defense capacities. In T. Field, P. McCabe, & N. Schneiderman (Eds.), *Stress and coping* (pp. 47–68). Mahwah, NJ: Erlbaum. Reproduced with permission of Edward Z. Tronick and Lawrence Erlbaum Associates/The Analytic Press.

Chapter 14. Cohn, J. & Tronick E. (1989). Infant-mother face-to-face interaction: Age and gender differences in coordination and the occurrence of miscoordination. *Child Development*, *60*: 85–92. Reprinted with permission of Edward Z. Tronick and Jeffrey Cohn.

Chapter 15. Cohn, J., Shea, E., & Tronick, E. (1986). The transfer of affect between mothers and infants. In T. B. Brazelton & M. W. Yogman (Eds.), *Affective development in infancy* (pp. 11–25). Norwood, NJ: Ablex. Copyright 1986 by Ablex Publishing Corporation. Reproduced with permission of Greenwood Publishing Group, Inc., Westport, CT.

Chapter 16. Cohn, J. & Tronick, E. (1988). Mother-infant face-to-face interaction: Influence is bidirectional and unrelated to periodic cycles in either partner's behavior. *Developmental Psychology*, *24*: 386–392. Copyright 1988 by the American Psychological Association. Reprinted with permission.

Chapter 17. Tronick, E. & Weinberg, M. (1994). Beyond the face: An empirical study of infant affective configurations of facial, vocal, gestural, and regulatory behaviors. *Child Development*, *65*: 1495–1507. Reprinted with permission of Blackwell Publishing.

PART IV: PERTURBATIONS: NATURAL AND EXPERIMENTAL

Chapter 18. Tronick, E. (1980). The primacy of social skills in infancy. Copyright 1980 from *Exceptional Infant, 4*, by Sawin, D., Hawkins, R., Walker, L., & Penticuff, J. (Eds.). Reproduced by permission of Taylor & Francis Group, LLC., www.taylorandfrancis.com.

Chapter 19. Adamson, L., Als, H., Brazelton, T., Tronick, E., & Wise, S. (1978). The infant's response to entrapment between contradictory messages in face-to-face interaction. *American Academy of Child Psychiatry, 17*: 1–13. Reprinted with permission of Lippincott Williams & Wilkins.

Chapter 20. Tronick, E. & Weinberg, M. (1997). Depressed mothers and infants: The failure to form dyadic states of consciousness. In L. Murray & P. Cooper (Eds.), *Postpartum depression and child development* (pp. 54–81). New York: Guilford. Reprinted with permission of Guilford Publications, Inc.

Chapter 21. Cohn, J. & Tronick, E. (1989). Specificity of infants' response to mothers' affective behavior. *Journal of the American Academy of Child Adolescent Psychiatry, 28*: 242–248. Reprinted with permission of Lippincott Williams & Wilkins.

Chapter 22. Tronick, E. & Weinberg, M. (1996). The impact of maternal psychiatric illness on infant development. Paper presented (May, 1996, New Orleans) at *Mood & Anxiety: Disorders in the Childrearing Years*, American Psychiatric Association. Reprinted with permission of M. Katherine Weinberg and Edward Z. Tronick.

Chapter 23. Weinberg, M., Olson, M., Beeghly, M., Tronick, E.Z. (2006). Making Up Is Hard to Do, Especially for Mothers with High Levels of Depressive Symptoms and Their Infant Sons. *Journal of Child Psychology & Psychiatry, 47*(7): 670–683. Reprinted with permission of Blackwell Publishing.

Chapter 24. Tronick, E. & Weinberg, M. (2000). Gender differences and their relation to maternal depression. In S. Johnson, A. Hayes, T. Field, N. Schneiderman, & P. McCabe (Eds.), *Stress, coping, and depression* (pp. 23–34). Mahwah, NJ: Lawrence Erlbaum Associates. Reprinted with permission of Edward Z. Tronick, M. Katherine Weinberg, and Lawrence Erlbaum Associates/The Analytic Press.

Chapter 25. Tronick, E. (2003). Infant moods and the chronicity of depressive symptoms: The cocreation of unique ways of being together for good or ill, Paper 1: The normal process of development and the formation of moods. *Zeitschrift für Psychosomatische Medizin und Psychotherapie, 4*: 408–425. Reprinted with permission of Edward Z. Tronick.

Chapter 26. Tronick, E. (2004). Infant moods and the chronicity of depressive symptoms: The cocreation of unique ways of being together for good or ill, Paper 2: The formation of negative moods in infants and children of depressed mothers. *Zeitschrift für Psychosomatische Medizin und Psychotherapie, 1*: 153–171. Reprinted with permission of Edward Z. Tronick.

Chapter 27. Tronick, E. (2006). The stress of normal development and interaction leads to the development of resilience and variation. In *Resilience*. B. Lester, A. Masten, &

B. McEwen (Eds.), *Resilience in children, Annals of New York Academy of Sciences,* 1094: 83–104.

PART V: DYADIC EXPANSION OF CONSCIOUSNESS AND MEANING MAKING

Chapter 28. Ball, W. & Tronick, E. (1971). Infant responses to impending collision: Optical and real. *Science,* 171: 818–920. Copyright 1971 AAAS. Reprinted with permission from AAAS.

Chapter 29. Tronick, E., Brushweller-Stern, N., Harrison, A., Lyons-Ruth, K., Morgan, A., Nahum, J., Sander, L., & Stern, D. (1998). Dyadically expanded states of consciousness and the process of therapeutic change. *Infant Mental Health Journal,* 19: 290–299. Reprinted with permission from Michigan Association for Infant Mental Health.

Chapter 30. Lyons-Ruth, K., Brushweller-Stern, N., Harrison, A., Morgan, A., Nahum, J., Sander, L., Stern, D., & Tronick, E. (1998). Implicit relational knowing: Its role in development and psychoanalytic treatment. *Infant Mental Health Journal,* 19: 282–289. Reprinted with permission from Michigan Association for Infant Mental Health.

Chapter 31. Stern, D., Bruschweiler, N., Harrison, A., Lyons-Ruth, K., Morgan, A., Nahum, J., Sander, L., & Tronick, E. (1998). Noninterpretive mechanisms in psychoanalytic therapy: The "something more" than interpretation. *The International Journal of Psycho-Analysis,* 79: 903–921. © Institute of Psychoanalysis, London, UK.

Chapter 32. Tronick, E. (2001). Emotional connections and dyadic consciousness in infant-mother and patient-therapist interactions: Commentary on a paper by Frank Lachmann, *Psychoanalytic Dialogues,* 11: 187–194.

Chapter 33. Tronick, E. (2002). A model of infant mood states and sandarian affective waves. *Psychoanalytic Dialogues,* 12: 73–99.

Chapter 34. Tronick, E. (2003). "Of course all relationships are unique": How cocreative processes generate unique mother-infant and patient-therapist relationships and change other relationships. *Psychological Inquiry,* 23: 473–491. Reprinted with permission of Edward Z. Tronick and Lawrence Erlbaum Associates/The Analytic Press.

Chapter 35. Tronick, E. (2004). Why is connection with others so critical? The formation of dyadic states of consciousness and the expansion of individuals' states of consciousness: Coherence-governed selection and the cocreation of meaning out of messy meaning making. In J. Nadel & D. Muir (Eds), *Emotional development: Recent research advances* (pp. 293–315). Reproduced by permission of Oxford University Press.

Chapter 36. Harrison, A. & Tronick, E. (in press). Contributions to understanding therapeutic change: Now we have a playground. *Journal of the American Psychoanalytic Association.*

References

Abend, W., Bizzi, E., & Morasso, P. (1982). Human arm trajectory formation. *Brain*, *105*, 331–348.

Adamson, L., Als, H., Tronick, E., & Brazelton, T. B. (1977). The development of social reciprocity between a sighted infant and her blind parents. *Journal of the American Academy of Child Psychology*, *16*, 194-207.

Adamson, L., & Frick, J. (2003). The still-face: A history of a shared experimental paradigm. *Infancy*, *4*, 451–473.

Ainsworth, M. D. S. (1993). Attachment as related to mother-infant interaction. *Advanced Infancy Research*, *8*, 1–50.

Ainsworth, M., Bell, S., & Stayton, D. (1974). Infant-mother attachment and social development: "Socialization" as a product of reciprocal responsiveness to signals. In M. P. M. Richards (Ed.), *The integration of a child into a social world*. London: Cambridge University Press.

Ainsworth, M. D., Blehar, M. C., Waters, E., & Wall, S. (1978). *Patterns of attachment: A psychological study of the strange situation*. Hillsdale, NJ: Erlbaum.

Alexander, R. D. (1977). Natural selection and the analysis of human sociality. In C. E. Goulden (Ed.), *Changing scenes in the natural sciences, 1776–1976* (pp. 283–337). Philadelphia: Academy.

Almroth, S. G. (1978). Water requirements of breast-fed infants in a hot climate. *American Journal of Clinical Nutrition*, *31*, 1154–1157.

Als, H. (1977). The newborn communicates. *Journal of Communication*, *27*(2), 66–73.

Als, H. (1994). Individualized developmental care for the very low birthweight preterm infant: Medical and neurofunctional effects. *Journal of the American Medical Association*, *272*, 853.

Als, H. (1997). Neurobehavioral development of the preterm infant. In A. A. Fanaroff & R. J. Martin (Eds.), *Neonatal–perinatal medicine* (pp. 964–989). St. Louis: Mosby.

Als, H., Lester, B. M., Tronick, E. C., & Brazelton, T. B. (1982). Towards a research instrument for the assessment of preterm infants' behavior (A. P. I. B.). In H. E. Fitzgerald, B. M. Lester, & M. W. Yogman (Eds.), *Theory and research in behavioral pedintrics* (pp. 85–132). New York: Plenum.

Als, H., Tronick, E., Adamson, L., & Brazelton, T. B. (1976). The behavior of the full-term yet underweight newborn infant. *Developmental Medicine and Child Neurology, 18,* 590–602.

Als, H., Tronick, E., & Brazelton, T. B. (1979). Analysis of face-to-face interaction in infant-adult dyads. In M. E. Lamb, S. J. Suomi, & G. R. Stephenson (Eds.), *Social interaction analysis: Methodological issues* (pp. 33–76). Madison: University of Wisconsin.

Als, H., Tronick, E., Lester, B. M., & Brazelton, T. B. (1977). Specific neonatal measures: The Brazelton Neonatal Behavioral Assessment Scale. In J. D. Osofsky (Ed.), *Handbook of infant development* (pp. 185–215). New York: John Wiley.

Altmann, S. A. (1952). A field of study of the sociobiology of Rhesus monkey. *Annals of the New York Academy of Science, 102,* 338–435.

Anderson, B. J., Vietze, P., & Dokechi, P. R. (1977). Reciprocity in vocal interaction of mothers and infants. *Child Development, 48,* 1676-1681.

Andre-Thomas, C. Y. (1960). *The neurological examination of the infant: Little Club Clinics in developmental medicine.* London: National Spastics Society.

Amiel-Tison, C. (1968). Neurological evaluation of the maturity of newborn infants. *Archives of Disease in Childhood, 43,* 89–93.

Amiel-Tison, C., Barrier, G., & Schnider, S. M. (1982). A new neurologic and adaptive capacity scoring system for evaluation obstetric medications in full-term newborns. *Anesthesiology, 56,* 340–350.

Anday, E. K., Cohen, M. E., Kelley, N. E., & Leitner, D. S. (1989). Effect of in utero cocaine exposure on startle and its modification. *Development in Pharmacology Therapy, 12,* 137–145.

Anders, T. F., & Weinstein, P. (1972). Sleep and its disorders in infants and children: A review. *Pediatrics, 50,* 312–324.

Anokhin, P. K. (1964). Systemogenesis as a general regulation of brain development. *Progress in Brain Research, 9,* 54–86.

Argyle, M., & Cook, M. (1976). *Gaze and mutual gaze.* Cambridge, UK: Cambridge University Press.

Armelagos, G. J., & McArdle, A. (1975). Population, disease and evolution. In A. C. Swedlund (Ed.), *Population studies in archaeology and biological anthropology: A symposium* (No. 30, pp. 1–10). Washington, DC: Society for American Archaeology.

Aron, L. (1996). *A meeting of minds: Mutuality in psychoanalysis.* Hillsdale, NJ: Analytic Press.

Aronson, E., & Tronick, E. Z. (1971). Perceptual capacities in early infancy. In J. Eliot (Ed.). *Human development and cognitive processes* (pp. 216–224). New York: Holt, Rinehart and Winston.

Ashby, W. R. (1956). *An introduction to cybernetics.* London: University Paperbacks.

Atkinson, J., & Braddwick, D. (1982). Sensory and perceptual capacities of the neonate. In P. Stratton (Ed.), *Psychobiology of the newborn* (pp. 191–220). New York: Wiley.

Atwood, G., & Stolorow, R. (1984). *Structures of subjectivity.* Hillsdale, NJ: Analytic Press.

Bailey, R. C., & Peacock, N. R. (1982). *Sex differences in subsistence patterns among Efe Pygmies in the Ituri Forest Zaire.* Paper presented at the Conference on Uncertainty in Food Supply, Bad Homberg, Germany.

Bailey, R. C., & Peacock, N. R. (1988). Efe Pygmies of northeast Zaire: Subsistence strategies in the Ituri Forest. In I. de Garine & G. A. Harrison (Eds.), *Coping with uncertainty in food supply.* London: Oxford University Press.

Bak, P. (1996). *How nature works.* New York: Springer-Verlag.

Bakeman, R., & Brown, J. V. (1977). Behavioral dialogues: An approach to the assessment of mother-infant interaction. *Child Development, 48,* 195-203.

Balint, M. (1966). *Primary love and psychoanalytic technique.* London: Tavistock.

Baltes, P., Lindenberger, U., & Staudinger, M. (Eds.). (1998). *Life-span theory in developmental psychology, Vol. 1*. New York: John Wiley.

Barrett, K. C., & Campos, J. J. (1987). Perspectives on emotional development: II. A functionalist approach to emotions. In J. D. Osofsky (Ed.), *Handbook of infant development* (2nd ed., pp. 555–578). New York: Wiley.

Bateman, D., Ng, S. K. C., Hansen, C., & Heagerty, M. (1993). The effects of intrauterine cocaine exposure in newborns. *American Journal of Public Health, 83,* 190–193.

Bazhenova, O. V., Plonskaia, O., & Porges, S. W. (2001). Vagal reactivity and affective adjustment in infants during interaction challenges. *Child Development, 72,* 1314–1326.

Beck, A. T., Ward, C. H., Mendelson, M., Mock, J., & Erbaugh, J. (1961). An inventory for measuring depression. *Archives of General Psychiatry, 4,* 561–569.

Beebe, B. (1975). *The regulation of interpersonal space through the creation of visual spatial boundaries, and implications for defensive processes: One case study at 4 months.* Unpublished manuscript, Albert Einstein University Psychiatric Institute.

Beebe, B. (1982). Micro-timing in mother-infant communication. In M. Key (Ed.), *Nonverbal communication today: Current research* (pp. 169–195). New York: Mouton.

Beebe, B., & Gerstman, L. J. (1980). The "packaging" of maternal stimulation in relation to infant facial-visual engagement: A case study at four months. *Merrill-Palmer Quarterly, 26,* 321–338.

Beebe, B., Jaffe, J., Feldstein, S., Mays, K., & Alson, D. (1985). Interpersonal timing: The application of an adult dialogue model to mother–infant vocal and kinesic interactions. In T. M. Field & N. A. Fox (Eds.), *Social perception in infants* (pp. 217–248). Norwood, NJ: Ablex.

Beebe, B., Jaffe, J., & Lachmann, F. (1992). A dyadic systems view of communication. In N. Skolnick & S. Warshaw (Eds.), *Relational perspectives in psychoanalysis* (pp. 61–81). Hillsdale, NJ: Analytic Press.

Beebe, B., Jaffe, J., Lachmann, F., Feldstein, S., Crown, C., & Jasnow, M. (2000). Systems models in development and psychoanalysis: The case of vocal rhythm coordination and attachment. *Infant Mental Health Journal, 21*(1–2), 99–122.

Beebe, B., & Lachmann, F. (1988). The contribution of mother-infant mutual influence to the origins of self and object representations. *Psychoanalytic Psychology, 5,* 305–337.

Beebe, B., & Lachmann, F. (1994). Representation and internalization in infancy: Three principles of salience. *Psychoanalytic Psychology, 11,* 127–165.

Beebe, B., & Lachmann, F. (1998). Co-constructing inner and relational process: Self and mutual regulation in infant research and adult treatment. *Psychoanalytic Psychology, 15,* 1–37.

Beebe, B., & Lachmann, F. (2002). *Infant research and adult treatment: Co-constructing interactions*. Hillsdale, NJ: Analytic Press.

Beebe, R., & Stern, D. N. (1977). Engagement-disengagement and early object experiences. In N. Freedman & S. Grand (Eds.), *Communicative structures and psychic structures* (pp. 35–55). New York: Plenum.

Beeghly, M., Olson, K. L., Weinberg, M. K., Pierre, S. C., Downey, N., & Tronick, E. Z. (2003). Prevalence, stability, and socio-demographic correlates of depressive symptoms in black mothers during the first 18 months postpartum. *Maternal and Child Health Journal, 7*(3), 157–168.

Beeghly, M., & Tronick, E. Z. (1994). Effects of prenatal exposure to cocaine in early infancy: Toxic effects on the process of mutual regulation. *Infant Mental Health Journal 15*(2), 158–175.

Beeghly, M., Weinberg, M. K., Olson, K. L., Kernan, H., Riley, J., & Tronick, E. Z. (2002). Stability and change in level of maternal depressive symptomatology during the first postpartum year. *Journal of Affective Disorders, 71*, 169–180.

Bell, L. H. J., Weinberg, M. K., Yergeau, E., & Tronick, T. (2004). In naturalistic home observations depressed mothers have a less positive and contingent relationship with their infants. Paper presented at International Conference on Infant Studies, Chicago.

Bell, R. Q. (1971). Stimulus control of parent or caretaker behavior by offspring. *Developmental Psychology, 4*, 63–72.

Belsky, J. (1999). Interactional and contextual determinants of attachment security. In C. J. Shaver & P. R. Shaver (Eds.), *Handbook of attachment: Theory, research, and clinical applications* (pp. 249–264). New York: Guilford.

Belsky, J., & Nezworski, T. (1998). *Clinical implications of attachment.* Mahwah, NJ: Erlbaum.

Belsky, J., Rovine, M., & Taylor, D. G. (1984). Pennsylvania infant and family development project III: The origins of individual differences in infant-mother attachment. *Child Development, 55*, 718–728.

Benedek, T. (1949). The psychosomatic implications of the primary unit, mother-child. *American Journal of Orthopsychiatry, 19*, 642–649.

Ben Shaul, D. M. (1962). Notes on hand-rearing various species of mammals. *International Zoological Year Book, 4*, 300–332.

Berntson, G. G., Hart, S., & Sarter, M. (1997). The cardiovascular startle response: Anxiety and the benzodiazepine receptor complex. *Psychophysiology, 34*(3), 348–357.

Bertram, B. C. R. (1976). Kin selection in lions and evolution. In P. P. G. Bateson & R. A. Hinde (Eds.), *Growing points in ethology* (pp. 281–301). New York: Cambridge University Press.

Bettelheim, B. (1969). *The children of the dream.* New York: Macmillan.

Bettes, B. A. (1988). Maternal depression and motherese: Temporal and intonational features. *Child Development, 59*, 1089–1096.

Bibring, E. M. (1959). Some considerations of the psychological processes in pregnancy. *Psychoanalytical Study of the Child, 14*, 113–121.

Biederman, J., Rosenbaum, J. F., Bolduc-Murphy, E. A., Faraone, S. V., Chaloff, J., Hirschfeld, D. R., et al. (1993). A 3-year follow-up of children with and without behavioral inhibition. *Journal of the American Academy of Child and Adolescent Psychiatry, 32*, 814–821.

Biederman, J., Rosenbaum, J. F., Hirshfeld, D. R., Faraone, S. V., Bolduc, E. A., Gersten, M., et al. (1990). Psychiatric correlates of behavioral inhibition in young children of parents with and without psychiatric disorders. *Archives of General Psychiatry, 47*, 21–26.

Billman, D., Nemeth, P., Heimler, R., & Sasidharan, P. (1996). Prenatal cocaine/polydrug exposure: Effect of race on outcome. *Perinatology, 16*, 366–369.

Blair, C., Granger, D., & Razza, R. P. (2005). Cortisol reactivity is positively related to executive function in preschool children attending Head Start. *Child Development, 76*(3), 554–567.

Blau, A., Slaff, B., Easton, R., Welowitz, J., Spingain, J., & Cohen, J. (1963). The psychogenic etiology of premature births, a preliminary report. *Psychosomatic Medicine, 25*, 201–211.

Bloom, K. (1977). Operant baseline procedures suppress infant social behavior. *Journal of Experimental Child Psychology, 33*, 138–132.

Blumberg, N. J. (1980). Effects of neonatal risk, maternal attitude, and cognitive style on earlypostpartum adjustment. *Journal of Abnormal Psychology, 89*, 139–150.

Blurton Jones, N. (1972). Comparative aspects of mother-child contact. In N. Blurton Jones (Ed.), *Ethological studies of child behavior* (pp. 315–328). New York: Cambridge University Press.

Bollas, C. (1987). *The shadow of the object: Psychoanalysis of the unthought known.* New York: Columbia University Press.

Bornstein, M. H., & Suess, P. E. (2000). Child and mother cardiac vagal tone: Continuity, stability, and concordance across the first 5 years. *Developmental Psychology, 36,* 54–65.

Bornstein, M. H., Tal, J., Rahn, C, Galperin, C. Z., Pêcheux, M.-G., Lamour, M., et al. (1992). Functional analysis of the contents of maternal speech to infants of 5 and 13 months in four cultures: Argentina, France, Japan, and the United States. *Developmental Psychology, 28,* 593–603.

Boston Change Process Study Group. (2002). Explicating the implicit: The local level and the microprocess of change in the analytic situation. *International Journal of Psychoanalysis, 83,* 1051–1062.

Bowlby, J. (1951). *Maternal care and mental health* (2nd ed.). World Health Organization. Monograph Series, No. 2.

Bowlby, J. (1958). The nature of the child's tie to his mother. *International Journal Psycho-Analysis, 39,* 350–373.

Bowlby, J. (1969). *Attachment and loss: Vol. 1. Attachment.* New York: Basic Books.

Bowlby, J. (1973). *Attachment and Loss: Vol. II. Separation.* New York: Basic Books.

Bowlby, J. (1982). *Attachment and loss: Vol. 1. Attachment* (2nd ed.). New York: Basic Books.

Boyd, J. H., Weissman, M. M., Thompson, W. D., & Myers, J. K. (1982). Screening for depression in a community sample: Understanding the discrepancies between depression symptoms and diagnostic scales. *Archives of General Psychiatry, 39,* 1195–1200.

Brakbill, Y. (1976). Obstetric medication and infant behavior. In J. E. Osofsky (Ed.), *Handbook of infant development* (pp. 76–125). New York: John Wiley.

Braungart-Reiker, J. M., & Stifter, C. A. (1996). Infants' responses to frustrating situations: Continuity and change in reactivity and regulation. *Child Development, 67,* 1767–1779.

Brazelton, T. B. (1971). Influence of perinatal drugs on the behavior of the neonate. In J. Helmuth (Ed.), *The exceptional infant: II. Abnormalities* (pp. 419–432). New York: Brunner-Mazel.

Brazelton, T. B. (1973). *Neonatal behavioral assessment scale.* Clinics in Developmental Medicine, No. 50. Philadelphia: J. B. Lippincott.

Brazelton, T. B. (1974). Does the neonate shape his environment? *Birth defects. The Infant at Risk, 10,* 131–140.

Brazelton, T. B. (1982). Joint regulation of neonate-parent behavior. In E. Tronick (Ed.), *Social interchanges in infancy: Affect, cognition, and communication.* Baltimore, MD: University Park Press.

Brazelton, T. B. (1984). *Neonatal Behavioral Assessment Scale.* Philadelphia: Lippincott.

Brazelton, T. B. (1992). *Touchpoints: Your child's emotional and behavioral development.* Reading, MA: Addison-Wesley.

Brazelton, T. B. (1994). Touchpoints: Opportunities for preventing problems in the parent-child relationship. *Acta Paediatrica, 394*(Supplement), 35–39.

Brazelton, T. B., & Cramer, B. G. (1990). *The earliest relationship.* Reading, MA: Addison-Wesley.

Brazelton, T. B., Koslowski, B., & Main, M. (1974). The origins of reciprocity: The early mother-infant interaction. In M. Lewis & M. Rosenblum (Eds.), *The effect of the infant on its caretaker: The origins of behavior* (pp. 49–76). New York: Wiley.

Brazelton, T. B., Tronick, E., Adamson, L., Als, H., & Wise, S. (1975). Early mother-infant reciprocity. In *Parent-infant interaction* (pp. 137–154). Ciba Foundation Symposium 33. Amsterdam: Elsevier.

Brazelton, T. B., Tronick, E., & Als, H. (1979). Early development of neonatal and infant behavior. In F. Faulkner & J. M. Tanner (Eds.), *Human growth: A comprehensive treatise* (pp. 305–328). New York: Plenum.

Brazelton, T. B., & Yogman, M. W. (1986). *Affective development in infancy.* Norwood, NJ: Ablex.

Brazelton, T. B., Young, G. G., & Bullowa, M. (1971). Inception and resolution of early developmental pathology: A case history. *Journal of the American Academy of Child Psychiatry, 10,* 124–135.

Bretherton, I. (1988). Open communication and internal working models: Their role in the development of attachment relationships. In R. A. Thompson (Ed.), *Nebraska symposium on motivation: Socio-emotional development* (pp. 57–113). Lincoln, NE: University of Nebraska Press.

Bronfenbrenner, U. (1970). *Two worlds of childhood.* New York: Sage.

Brooks, V. B. (1974). Some examples of programmed limb movements. *Brain Research, 71,* 299–308.

Bruner, J. S. (1970). The growth and structure of skill. In K. J. Connolly (Ed.), *Mechanisms of motor skill development* (pp. 63–94). London: Academic Press.

Bruner, J. S. (1972). Nature and uses of immaturity. *American Psychologist, 27,* 687–702.

Bruner, J. (1975a). From communication to language—a psychological perspective. *Cognition, 3,* 255–287.

Bruner, J. (1975b). The ontogenesis of speech acts. *Journal of Child Language, 2,* 1–19.

Bruner, J. (1983). *Child's talk.* New York: Norton.

Bruner, J. (1990). *Acts of meaning.* Cambridge, MA: Harvard University Press.

Bruschweiler-Stern, N., & Stern, D. N. (1989). A model for conceptualizing the role of the mother's representational world in various mother-infant therapies. *Infant Mental Health Journal, 10,* 142–156.

Bullowa, M. (1975). When infant and adults communicate, how do they synchronize their behavior? In A. Keodon, R. M. Harris, & M. R. Key (Eds.), *The organization of behavior in face-to-face interaction.* The Hague: Mouton.

Bullowa, M. (1979). Prelinguistic communication: A field for scientific research. In M. Bullowa (Ed.), *Before speech: The beginning of interpersonal communication* (pp. 1–62). Cambridge: Cambridge University Press.

Buss, K. A., Schumacher, J. R. M., Dolski, I., Kalin, N. H., Goldsmith, H. H., & Davidson, R. J. (2003). Right frontal brain activity, cortisol, and withdrawal behavior in 6-month-old infants. *Behavioral Neuroscience, 117*(1), 11–20.

Calkins, S. D. (1997). Cardiac vagal tone indices of temperamental reactivity and behavioral regulation in young children. *Developmental Psychobiology, 31*(2), 125–135.

Calkins, S., Dedmon, S. E., Gill, K. L., Lomax, L. E., & Johnson, L. M. (2002). Frustration in infancy: Implications for emotion regulation, physiological processes, and temperament. *Infancy, 3*(2), 175–197.

Calkins, S., & Keane, S. (2004). Cardiac vagal regulation across the preschool period: Stability, continuity, and implications for childhood adjustment. *Developmental Psychobiology, 45,* 101–112.

Campbell, S. B., & Cohn, J. F. (1991). Prevalence and correlates of postpartum depression in first-time mothers. *Journal of Abnormal Psychology, 100,* 594–599.

Campbell, S. B., & Cohn, J. F. (1997). The timing and chronicity of postpartum depression: Implications for infant development. In L. Murray & P. J. Cooper (Eds.), *Postpartum depression and child development.* New York: Guilford.

Campbell, S. B., Cohn, J. F., Flanagan, C., Popper, S., & Meyers, T. (1992). Course and correlates of postpartum depression during the transition to parenthood. *Development and Psychopathology, 4,* 29–47.

Campbell, S. B., Cohn, J. F., & Meyers, T. (1995). Depression in first-time mothers: Mother-infant interaction and depression chronicity. *Developmental Psychology, 31,* 349–357.

Campos, J. J., & Barrett, K. C. (1984). Toward a new understanding of emotions and their development. In C. E. Izard, J. Kagan, & R. B. Zajonc (Eds.), *Emotions, cognition, and behavior* (pp. 229–263). Cambridge, UK: Cambridge University Press.

Campos, J., Barrett, K., Lamb, M., Goldsmith, H., & Stenberg, C. (1983). Socioemotional development. In M. Haith & J. J. Campos (Vol. Eds.) & P. H. Mussen (Series Ed.), *Handbook of child psychology: Vol. 2. Infancy and developmental psychology* (pp. 783–915). New York: Wiley.

Campos, J. J., & Lucariello, J. (1999). *Origins and consequences of social signaling.* Paper presented at the National Conference on Child and Human Development, Rockville, MD.

Camras, L. A., Oster, H., Campos, J. J., Miyake, K., & Bradshaw, D. (1992). Japanese and American infants' responses to arm restraint. *Developmental Psychology, 28,* 578–583.

Carpenter, G. C. (1974). Visual regard of moving and stationary faces in early infancy. *Merrill-Palmer Quarterly, 20,* 181–195.

Carpenter, G. C., Tecce, J. J., Stechler, G., & Freidman, S. (1973). Differential visual behavior to human and humanoid faces in early infancy. *Merrill Palmer Quarterly, 16,* 91–108.

Carter, A. S., Garrity-Rokous, F. E., Chazan-Cohen, R., Little, C., & Briggs-Gowan, M. J. (2001). Maternal depression and comorbidity: Predicting early parentting, attachment security, and toddler social-emotional problems and competencies. *Journal of the American Academy of Child and Adolescent Psychiatry, 40,* 18–26.

Carter, A. S., Mayes, L. C., & Pajer, K. A. (1990). The role of dyadic affect in play and infant sex in predicting infant response to the still-face situation. *Child Development, 61,* 764–773.

Casaer, P. (1979). *Postural behaviour in newborn infants.* Lavenham, UK: Spastics International Medical Publications.

Cassidy, J. (1994). Emotion regulation: Influences of attachment relationships. In N. A. Fox (Ed.), *The development of emotion regulation* (Vol. 59, pp. 228–249). Chicago: University of Chicago Press.

Caudill, W., & Weinstein, H. (1969). Maternal care and infant behavior in Japan and America. *Psychiatry, 32,* 12–43.

Chance, M. R. A. (1962). An interpretation of some agonistic postures. *Symposium in Zoology of the Society of London, 8,* 71–90.

Chasnoff, I. J., Burns, W. J., Schnoll, S. H., & Burns, K. A. (1985). Cocaine use in pregnancy. *New England Journal of Medicine, 313,* 666–669.

Chasnoff, I. J., Griffith, D. R., Freier, C., & Murray, J. (1992). Cocaine/polydrug use in pregnancy: Two year follow-up. *Pediatrics, 89,* 284–289.

Chatfield, C. (1980). *The analysis of time series: An introduction.* London: Chapman and Hall.

Chen, Y. P., & Fetters, L. (2004). *The development of exploratory behaviors in poly-drug-exposed and control infants from 7 to 15 months.* Unpublished manuscript.

Chen, Y., Fetters, L., Holt, K. G., & Saltzman, E. (2002). Making the mobile move: Constraining task and environment. *Infant Behavior and Development, 25,* 195–220.

Chiriboga, C. A., Bateman, D. A., Brust, J. C. M., & Hauser, W. A. (1993). Neurologic findings in neonates with intrauterine cocaine exposure. *Pediatric Neurology, 9,* 115–119.

Chodorow, N. (1978). *The reproduction of mothering.* Los Angeles: University of California Press.

Cicchetti, D., & Feinstein, A. (1990). High agreement but low kappa: I. The problems of two paradoxes. *Journal of Clinical Epidemiology, 43,* 543–549.

Cioni, G., Ferrari, F., & Prechtl, H. F. R. (1992). Early motor assessment in brain-damaged preterm infants. *Medicine and Sport Science, 36,* 72–79.

Claman, D. L., & Zeffiro, T. A. (1986). Motor consequences of posterior parietal lobe injury. *Neuroscience Abstracts, 12,* 972.

Clarke-Stewart, A. (1973). Interactions between mothers and their young children: Characteristics and consequences. *Monographs of the Society for Research in Child Development* (No. 6 & 7).

Clyman, R. (1991). The procedural organisation of emotions: A contribution from cognitive science to the psychoanalytic theory of therapeutic action. *Journal of the American Psychoanalytic Association, 39,* 349–381.

Cohen, J. (1960). A coefficient of agreement for nominal scales. *Educational and Psychological Measurement, 20,* 37–46.

Cohen, J. (1988). *Statistical power analysis for the behavioral sciences.* Hillsdale, NJ: Erlbaum.

Cohler, B., Weiss, J., & Grunebaum, H. (1970). Child care attitudes and emotional disturbance among mothers of young children. *Genetic Psychological Monographs, 82,* 3–47.

Cohn, J. F., Campbell, S. B., Matias, R., & Hopkins, J. (1990). Face-to-face interactions of postpartum depressed and nondepressed mother-infant pairs at 2 months. *Developmental Psychology, 26,* 15–23.

Cohn, J. F., Connell, D., & Lyons-Ruth, K. (1984, April). *Face to face interactions of high risk infant pairs.* Paper presented at International Conference on Infant Studies, New York.

Cohn, J. F., & Elmore, M. (1987). [Three-month-old infants' response to 5 s of mother's still face contingent on their becoming positive]. Unpublished raw data.

Cohn, J. F., & Elmore, M. (1988). Effect of contingent changes in mothers' affective expression on the organization of behavior in 3-month-old infants. *Infant Behavior and Development, 11,* 493–505.

Cohn, J. F., Matias, R., Tronick, E. Z., Connell, D., & Lyons-Ruth, K. (1986). Face-to-face interactions of depressed mothers and their infants. In E. Z. Tronick & T. Field (Eds.), *Maternal depression and infant disturbance* (pp. 31–46). San Francisco: Jossey-Bass.

Cohn, J. F., & Tronick, E. Z. (1987). Mother-infant face-to-face interaction: The sequence of dyadic states at 3, 6, and 9 months. *Developmental Psychology, 23,* 68–77.

Cohn, J. F., & Tronick, E. (1988). Mother-infant face-to-face interaction: Influence is bidirectional and unrelated to periodic cycles in either partner's behavior. *Developmental Psychology, 24,* 386–392.

Cohn, J. F., & Tronick, E. Z. (1989). Specificity of infants' response to mothers' affective behavior. *Journal of the American Academy of Child and Adolescent Psychiatry, 28,* 242–248.

Cole, P. M., Martin, S. E., & Dennis, T. A. (2004). Emotion regulation as a scientific construct: Methodological challenges and directions for child development research. *Child Development, 75,* 317–333.

Coles, C. D. (1993). Saying "goodbye" to the "crack baby." *Neurotoxicology and Teratology, 15,* 290–292.

Coles, C. D., Platzman, K. A., Smith, I., James, M. E., & Falek, A. (1992). Effects of cocaine and alcohol use in pregnancy on neonatal growth and neurobehavioral status. *Neurotoxicology and Teratology, 14,* 23–33.

Condon, W. S. (1979). Multiple response to sound in dysfunctional children. *Journal of Autism and Childhood Schizophrenia, 5,* 37–56.

Condon, W. S., & Ogston, W. D. (1967). A segmentation of behavior. *Journal of Psychiatric Research, 5,* 221–235.

Condon, W. S., & Sander, L. W. (1974a). Neonate movement is synchronized with adult speech: Interactional participation and language acquistion. *Science, 183,* 99–101.

Condon, W. S., & Sander, L. W. (1974b). Synchrony demonstrated between movements of the neonate and adult speech. *Child Development, 45,* 456–462.

Connelly, K. J., & Prechtl, H. F. R. (Eds.). (1981). *Maturation and development: Biological and psychological perspectives* (Clinics in Developmental Medicine No. 77/78, Spastics International Medical Publications). London: William Heinemann Medical Books.

Cooke, R. W. L. (1987). Early and late cranial ultrasonographic appearances and outcome in very low birth weight infants. *Acta Physiologica Scandinavica, 62,* 931–937.

Cooper, P. J., Campbell, E. A., Day, A., & Kennerley, H. (1988). Non-psychotic psychiatric disorder after childbirth: A prospective study of prevalence, incidence, course and nature. *British Journal of Psychiatry, 152,* 799–806.

Corwin, M. J., Lester, B. M., Sepkoski, C., McLaughlin, S., Kayne, H., & Golub, H. L. (1992). Effects of in utero cocaine exposure on newborn acoustical cry characteristics. *Pediatrics, 89,* 1199–1203.

Cox, J. L., Holden, J. M., & Sagovsky, R. (1987). Detection of postnatal depression: Development of the Edinburgh Postnatal Depression Scale. *British Journal of Psychiatry, 150,* 782–786.

Cramer, B. (1997). Psychodynamic perspectives on the treatment of postpartum depression. In L. Murray & P. J. Cooper (Eds.), *Postpartum depression and child development* (pp. 237–261). New York: Guilford.

Cramer, B., & Stern, D. N. (1988). Evaluation of changes in mother-infant brief psychotherapy. *Infant Mental Health Journal, 9,* 20–45.

Crowell, J. A., O'Connor, E., Wollmers, G., et al. (1991). Mothers' conceptualizations of parent-child relationships: Relation to mother-child interaction and child behavior problems. Attachment and developmental psychopathology. *Developmental Psychopathology, 3,* 431–444.

DeGangi, G., DiPietro, J., Porges, S. W., & Greenspan, S. (1991). Psychophysiological characteristics of the regulatory disordered infant. *Infant Behavior and Development, 14,* 37–50.

Dempsey, D. A., Hajnal, B. L., Partridge, J. C., Jacobson, S., Good, W., Jones, R. T., et al. (2000). Tone abnormalities are associated with maternal cigarette smoking during pregnancy in utero cocaine exposed infants. *Pediatrics, 106,* 79–85.

de Quervain, D. J., Roozendaal, B., & McGaugh, J. L. (1998). Stress and glucocorticoids impair retrieval of long-term spatial memory. *Nature, 394,* 787–790.

Derogatis, L. R. (1983). *Symptom Checklist-90 (Revised): Administration, scoring, and procedures manual, II.* Towson, MD: Clinical Psychometric Research.

Derryberry, D., & Rothbart, M. (1984). Emotion, attention, and temperament. In C. Izard, J. Kogen, & R. Zejoc (Eds.), *Emotion, cognition and behavior.* New York Cambridge University Press.

Dickerson, S. S., & Kemeny, M. E. (2004). Acute stressors and cortisol responses: A theoretical integration and synthesis of laboratory research. *Psychological Bulletin, 130*(3), 355–391.

Dixon, S. D. (1994). Neurological consequences of prenatal stimulant drug exposure. *Infant Mental Health Journal, 15,* 134–145.

Dixon, S. D., Yogman, M., Tronick, E., Adamson, L., Als, H., & Brazelton, T. B. (1981). Early infant social interaction with parents and strangers. *Journal of American Academy of Child Psychiatry, 20,* 32–52.

Donzella, B., Gunnar, M. R., Krueger, W. K., & Alwin, J. (2000). Cortisol and vagal tone responses to competitive challenge in preschoolers: Associations with temperament. *Developmental Psychobiology, 37*(4), 209–220.

Doussard-Roosevelt, J., Montgomery, L., & Porges, S. (2003). Short-term stability of physiological measures in kindergarten children: Respiratory sinus arrhythmia, heart period and cortisol. *Developmental Psychobiology, 43,* 230–242.

Doussard-Roosevelt, J. A., McClenny, B. D., & Porges, S. W. (2001). Neonatal cardiac vagal tone and school-age developmental outcome in very low birth weight infants. *Developmental Psychobiology, 38,* 56–66.

Dowd, J., & Tronick, E. Z. (1986). Temporal coordination of arm movements in early infancy: Do infants move in synchrony with adult speech? *Child Development, 57,* 762–776.

Dow-Edwards, D. (1988). Developmental effects of cocaine. *NIDA Research Monographs, 88,* 290–303.

Dow-Edwards, D. L. (1991). Cocaine effects on fetal development: A comparison of clinical and animal research findings. *Neurotoxicology and Teratology, 13,* 347–352.

Dow-Edwards, D. (1993). The puzzle of cocaine's effects following maternal use during pregnancy: Still unsolved. *Neurotoxicology and Teratology, 15,* 295–296.

Downey, G., & Coyne, J. C. (1990). Children of depressed parents: An integrative review. *Psychological Bulletin, 108,* 50–76.

Downing, G. (2001). Emotion theory reconsidered. In M. Wrathall & J. Malpas (Eds.), *Heidegger, coping, and cognitive science.* Cambridge, MA: MIT Press.

Draper, P. (1976). Social and economic constraints on child life among the !Kung. In R. B. Lee & I. DeVore (Eds.), *Kalahari hunter-gatherers: Studies of the !Kung San and their neighbors* (pp. 199–217). Cambridge, MA: Harvard University Press.

Droit, S., Boldrini, A., & Cioni, G. (1996). Rhythmical leg movements in low-risk and brain-damaged preterm infants. *Early Human Development, 44,* 201–213.

Dubowitz, L., Dubowitz, A., & Goldberg, C. (1970). Clinical assessment of gestational age in the newborn infant. *Journal of Pediatrics, 77,* 110.

Dunn, F. L. (1968). Epidemiological factors: Health and disease in hunter-gatherers. In R. B. Lee & I. DeVore (Eds.), *Man the hunter* (pp. 221–228). New York: Aldine.

Durand, D. J., Espinoza, A. M., & Nickerson, B. G. (1990). Association between prenatal cocaine exposure and sudden infant death syndrome. *Journal of Pediatrics, 117,* 909–911.

Edelman, G. M. (1987). *Neural Darwinism: The theory of neuronal group selection.* New York: Basic.

Ehrenberg, D. B. (1992). *The intimate edge.* New York: Norton.

Eimas, P. D. (1975). Speech perception in early infancy. In L. B. Cohen & P. Salapalek (Eds.), *Infant perception: from sensation to cognition.* New York: Academic.

Eimas, P. D., & Miller, J. L. (1980). Contextual effects in infant speech perception. *Science, 209,* 1140–1141.

Eimas, P. D., Siqueland, E. R., Jusczyk, P., & Vigorito, J. (1971). Speech perception in infants. *Science, 171,* 303–306.

Eisen, L. N., Field, T. M., Bandstra, E. S., Roberts, J. P., Morrow, C., Larson, S. K., et al. (1991). Perinatal cocaine effects on neonatal stress behavior and performance on the Brazelton Scale. *Pediatrics, 88,* 477–480.

Ekman, P. (1980). Biological and culture contributions to body and facial movement in the expression of emotions. In A. Rossy (Ed.), *Explaining emotion.* Berkeley: University of California Press.

Ekman, P., & Oster, H. (1979). Facial expressions of emotions. *Annual Review of Psychology, 30,* 527–554.

El-Sheikh, M. (2005). Stability of respiratory sinus arrhythmia in children and young adolescents: A longitudinal examination. *Developmental Psychobiology, 46,* 66–74.

Emde, R. (1983). The prerepresentational self and its affective core. *Psychoanalytic Study of the Child, 38,* 165–192.

Emde, R. N., Kligman, D. H., Reich, J. H., & Wade, T. D. (1978). Emotional expression in infancy: I. Initial studies of social signaling and an emergent model. In M. Lewis & L. A. Rosenblum (Eds.), *The development of affect* (pp. 125–148). New York: Plenum.

Engen, T., Lipsitt, L. P., & Kaye, H. (1963). Olfactory responses and adaptation in the human neonate. *Journal of Comparative and Physiological Psychology, 56*, 73–77.

Escalona, S. K. (1968). *The roots of individuality: Normal patterns of development in infancy.* Chicago: Aldine.

Eyler, F. D., & Behnke, M. (1999). Early development of infants exposed to drugs prenatally. *Clinics in Perinatology, 26*, 107–151.

Eyre, J. A., Miller, S., Clowry, G. J., Conway, E., & Watts, C. (2000). Functional corticospinal projections are established prenatally in the human foetus permitting involvement in the development of spinal motor centres. *Brain, 123*, 51–64.

Eyre, J. A., Taylor, J. P., Villagra, F. M. S., & Miller, S. (2001). Evidence of activity-dependent withdrawal of corticospinal projections during human development. *Developmental Neuroscience, 57*, 1543–1554.

Fafouti-Milenkovic, M., & Uzgiris, I. C. (1979). The mother-infant communication system. *New Directions for Child Development, 4*, 41–56.

Fantz, R. (1961). The origin of form perception. *Scientific American, 204*, 66–72.

Fantz, R. L., Fagan, J. F., & Miranda, S. B. (1975). Early visual selectivity. In L. B. Cohen & P. Salapatek (Eds.), *Infant perception: from sensation to cognition.* New York: Basic Visual Processes.

Fawer, C. L., & Calame, A. (1991). Significance of ultrasound appearances in the neurological development and cognitive abilities of preterm infants at 5 years. *European Journal of Pediatrics, 150*, 515–520.

Fedrizzi, E., Inverno, M., Bruzzone, M., Botteon, G., Saletti, V., & Farinotti, M. (1996). MRI features of cerebral lesions and cognitive functions in preterm spastic diplegic children. *Pediatric Neurology, 15*, 207–212.

Fein, G. G., Schwartz, P. M., Jacobson, S. W., & Jacobson, J. L. (1983). Environmental toxins and behavioral development: A new role from psychological research. *American Psychologist, 38*, 1188–1197.

Feldman, J., Minkoff, H. L., McCalla, S., & Salwen, M. (1992). A cohort study of the impact of perinatal drug use on prematurity in an inner-city population. *American Journal of Public Health, 82*, 726–728.

Feldman, R., Greenbaum, C. W., & Yirmiya, N. (1999). Mother-infant affect synchrony as an antecedent of the emergence of self-control. *Developmental Psychology, 35*, 223–231.

Fenichel, O. (1941). *Problems of psychoanalytic technique.* New York: Psychoanalytic Quarterly.

Ferenczi, S., & Rank, O. (1986). *The development of psychoanalysis.* Madison, CT: International Universities Press. (Original work published 1924)

Fetters, L., & Todd, J. (1987). Quantitative assessment of infant reaching movements. *Journal of Motor Behavior, 19*, 147–166.

Fetters, L., & Tronick, E. (1994). *Kinematic analysis of the movements of in utero cocaine-exposed 1-month-old infants in different movement elicitation conditions.* Paper presented at the annual meeting of the Society for Pediatric Research.

Fetters, L., & Tronick, E. Z. (1996). Neuromotor development of cocaine exposed and control infants from birth through 15 months: Poor and poorer performance. *Pediatrics, 98*, 938–943.

Fetters, L., & Tronick, E. (2000). Discriminate power of the Alberta Infant Motor Scale and the movement assessment of infants for infants exposed to cocaine. *Pediatric Physical Therapy, 12*, 16–23.

Field, T. M. (1977). Effects of early separation, interactive deficits, and experimental manipulation on infant-mother face-to-face interaction. *Child Development, 48*, 763–771.

Field, T. (1982). Social perception and responsivity in early infancy. In T. Field, A. Huston, H. Quay, L. Troll, & G. Finley (Eds.), *Review of human development* (pp. 20–31). New York: Wiley.

Field, T. (1983). Child abuse in monkeys and humans: A comparative perspective. In M. Reite & N. Caine (Eds.), *Child abuse: The non-human primate data*. New York: Liss.

Field, T. (1984). Early interactions between infants and their postpartum depressed mothers. *Infant Behaviour and Development, 7,* 517–522.

Field, T. (1995). Infants of depressed mothers. *Infant Behavior and Development, 18,* 1–13.

Field, T., Healy, B., Goldstein, S., & Guthertz, M. (1990). Behavior-state matching and synchrony in mother-infant interactions of nondepressed versus depressed dyads. *Developmental Psychology, 26,* 7–14.

Field, T., Healy, B., Goldstein, S., Perry, S., Bendell, D., Schanberg, S., et al. (1988). Infants of depressed mothers show "depressed" behavior even with nondepressed adults. *Child Development, 59,* 1569–1579.

Field, T., Morrow, C., & Adlestein, D. (1993). Depressed mothers' perceptions of infant behavior. *Infant Behavior and Development, 16,* 99–108.

Field, T., Woodson, R., Cohen, D., Garcia, R., & Greenberg, R. (1983). Discrimination and imitation of facial expressions by term and pre-term neonates. *Infant Behavior and Development, 6,* 485–490.

Field, T. M., Woodson, R., Greenberg, R., & Cohen, D. (1982). Discrimination and imitation of facial expressions by neonates. *Science, 218,* 179–181.

Finnegan, L. (1981). Evaluation on parenting, depression, and violence profiles in methadone-maintained women. *Child Abuse and Neglect, 5,* 267.

Finnegan, L. P. (1986). Neonatal abstinence syndrome: Assessment and pharmacotherapy. In F. F. Rubatelli & B. Granati (Eds.), *Neonatal therapy and update*. New York: Experta Medica.

Fishbein, H. D. (1976). *Evolution, development, and children's learning*. Santa Monica, CA: Goodyear.

Fisk, J. D., & Goodale, M. A. (1988). The effects of unilateral brain damage on visually guided reaching: Hemispheric differences in the nature of the deficit. *Experimental Brain Research, 72,* 425–435.

Fivaz-Depeursinge, E., & Corboz-Warnery, A. (1995). Triangulation in relationships. *The Signal, 3*(2), 1–6.

Fivaz-Depeursinge, E., & Corboz-Warnery, A. (1999). *The primary triangle: A developmental systems view of mothers, fathers, and infants*. New York: Basic Books.

Fogel, A. (1977). Temporal organization in mother-infant, face-to-face interaction. In H. R. Schaffer (Ed.), *Studies in mother-infant interaction* (pp. 119–151). London: Academic Press.

Fogel, A. (1982). Early adult-infant interaction: Expectable sequences of behavior. *Pediatric Psychology, 7,* 1–22.

Fogel, A. (1993). Two principles of communication: Co-regulation and framing. In J. Nadel & L. Camaioni (Eds.), *New perspectives in early communicative development*. London: Routledge and Kegan Paul.

Fogel, A., Diamond, G. R., Langhorst, B. H., & Demos, V. (1983). Affective and cognitive aspects of the 2-month-old's participation in face-to-face interaction with the mother. In E. Z. Tronick (Ed.), *Social interchange in infancy: Affect, cognition, and communication* (pp. 37–57). Baltimore, MD: University Park Press.

Fogel, A., & Hannan, E. T. (1985). Manual actions of nine- to fifteen-week-old human infants during face-to-face interaction with their mothers. *Child Development, 56,* 1271–1279.

Fogel, A., Nwokah, E., Dedo, J. Y., Messinger, D., Dickson, K. L., Matusov, E., et al. (1992). Social process theory of emotion: A dynamic systems approach. *Social Development, 1,* 122–142.

Folio, M. R., & Fewell, R. R. (1983). *Peabody developmental motor scales and activity cards manual*. Allen, TX: DLM Teaching Resources.

Fonagy, P., Gergely, G., Jurist, E., & Target, M. (2002). *Affect regulation, mentalization, and the development of the self*. New York: Other Press.

Fonagy, P., & Target, M. (1998). Mentalization and the changing aims of child psychoanalysis. *Psychoanalytic Dialogues, 8,* 87–114.

Foscha, D. (2000). *The transforming power of affect*. New York: Basic Books.

Fraiberg, S., Adelson, E., & Shapiro, V. (1975). Ghosts in the nursery: A psychoanalytic approach to the problem of impaired infant-mother relationships. *Journal of the American Academy of Child Psychiatry, 14,* 387–422.

Frank, D. A., Bresnahan, K., & Zuckerman, B. S. (1993). Maternal cocaine use: Impact on child health and development. *Advances in Pediatrics, 40,* 65–99.

Frank, D., Zuckerman, B., Amaro, H., Aboagye, A., Bauchner, H., Cabral, H., et al. (1988). Cocaine use during pregnancy: Prevalence and correlates. *Pediatrics, 82,* 888–895.

Frankel, K. A., & Harmon, R. J. (1996). Depressed mothers: They don't always look as bad as they feel. *Journal of the American Academy of Child and Adolescent Psychiatry, 35,* 289–298.

Freeman, W. (1994). *Societies of brains*. Hillsdale, NJ: Erlbaum.

Freeman, W. J. (2000). *How brains make up their mind*. New York: Columbia University Press.

French, E. (1981). *Re-establishing equilibrium: A study of the ontogeny of transition strategies*. Unpublished manuscript, Amherst College.

Freud, A. (1937). *The ego and its mechanisms of defense*. London: Hogarth.

Fride, E., & Weinstock, M. (1989). Alterations in behavioral and striatal dopamine asymmetries induced by prenatal stress. *Pharmacology, Biochemistry, and Behavior, 32,* 425–430.

Fuertes, M., Dos Santos, P. L., Beeghly, M., & Tronick, E. (2006) More than maternal sensitivity shapes attachment: Infant coping and temperament. In B. Lester, A. Masten, & B. McEwen (Eds.), *Resilience in children. Annals of New York Academy of Sciences, 1094:* 292–296.

Fulroth, R. F., Phillips, B., & Durant, D. J. (1989). Perinatal outcome of infants exposed to cocaine and/or heroin in utero. *American Journal of Diseases of Children, 143,* 905–910.

Gaensbauer, T. J., Mrazek, D., & Emde, R. N. (1979). Patterning of emotional response in a playroom laboratory setting. *Infant Behavior and Development, 2,* 163–178.

Geerdink, J. J., Hopkins, B., Beek, W. J., & Heriza, C. B. (1996). The organization of leg movements in preterm and full-term infants after term age. *Developmental Psychobiology, 29,* 335–351.

Gianino, A. (1982). *The ontogeny of coping responses in infancy*. Unpublished manuscript, University of Massachusetts.

Gianino, A. (1985). *The stability of infant coping with interpersonal stress*. Unpublished doctoral dissertation, University of Massachusetts.

Gianino, A., & Tronick, E. Z. (1988). The mutual regulation model: The infant's self and interactive regulation, coping, and defensive capacities. In T. Field, P. McCabe, & N. Schneiderman (Eds.), *Stress and coping* (pp. 47–68). Hillsdale, NJ: Erlbaum.

Gibson, E. J., & Walk, R. (1960). The visual cliff. *Scientific American, 202,* 64-71.

Gibson, H. (1961). Vision research. *Ecological Optics, 1*(3/4), 253–262.

Gill, M. (1994). *Psychoanalysis in transition*. Hillsdale, NJ: Analytic Press.

Goeman, J. M. (1979). Detecting cyclicity in social interaction. *Psychological Bulletin, 86,* 338-348.

Goldberg, S. (1972). Infant care and growth in urban Zambia. *Human Development, 15,* 77–89.

Goldberg, S., Levitan, R., Emans, J. B., Leung, E., Masellis, M., Basile, V., et al. (2003). Cortisol concentrations in 12- and 18-month-old infants: Stability over time, location and stressor. *Biological Psychiatry, 54,* 719–726.

Gottman, J. M. (1977). Detecting cyclicity in social interaction. *Psychological Bulletin, 86,* 338–348.

Gottman, J. M. (1981). *Time series analysis: A comprehensive introduction for social scientists.* New York: Cambridge University Press.

Gottman, J. M., & Ringland, J. T. (1981). The analysis of dominance and bidirectionality in social development. *Child Development, 52,* 393–412.

Graham, F. K., Matarazzo, R. C., & Caldwell, B. M. (1956). Behavioral differences between normal and traumatized newborns. II. Standardization, reliability, and validity. *Psychology Monographs 70*(21), Serial No. 428: 1–16.

Green, A. (1998). The dead mother. In _____ (Ed.), *On private madness* (pp. 142–173). Madison, CT: International Universities Press.

Greenberg, J. (1996). Psychoanalytic words and psychoanalytic acts. *Contemporary Psychoanalysis, 32,* 195–203.

Greenberg, M. T., Speltz, M. L., Deklyen, M., et al. (1991). Attachment security in preschoolers with and without externalizing behavior problems: A replication. Attachment and developmental psychopathology. *Developmental Psychopathology, 3,* 413–430.

Greenberg, N. H., & Hurley, J. (1971). The maternal personality inventory. In J. Hellmuth (Ed.), *Exceptional infant: Vol. 2. Studies in abnormalities.* New York: Brunner/Mazel.

Greenson, R. R. (1967). *The technique and practice of psychoanalysis, Vol. 1.* New York: International Universities Press.

Greenspan, S. (1982). *Psychopathology and adaptation in infancy and early childhood: Principles of clinical diagnosis and preventive intervention.* New York: International University Press.

Gunnar, M. R., Mangelsdorf, S., Larson, M., & Hertsgaard, L. (1989). Attachment, temperament, and adrenocortical activity in infancy: A study of psychoendocrine regulation. *Developmental Psychology, 25,* 355–363.

Gunnar, M. R., Porter, F. L., Wolf, C. M., Rigatuso, J., & Larson, M. C. (1995). Neonatal stress reactivity: Predictions to later emotional temperament. *Child Development, 66,* 1–13.

Guntrip, H. (1971). *Psychoanalytic theory, therapy, and the self.* New York: Basic Books.

Guntrip, H. (1975). My experience of analysis with Fairbairn and Winnicott. *International Review of Psycho-Analysis, 2,* 145–156.

Gunzenhauser, N., Lester, B. M., & Tronick, E. Z. (1987). *Infant stimulation: For whom, what kind, when, and how much?* Pediatric Round Table Series; 13 Skillman, NJ: Johnson & Johnson.

Gyorgy, P. (1953). A hitherto unrecognized biochemical difference between human milk and cow's milk. *Pediatrics, 11,* 98–111.

Habermas, J. (1969). *Knowledge and human interests.* Boston: Boston Press.

Haley, D. W., & Stansbury, K. (2003). Infant stress and parent responsiveness: Regulation of physiology and behavior during still-face and reunion. *Child Development, 74,* 1534–1546.

Ham, J., & Tronick, E. (2006). Infant resilience to the stress of the still-face: Infant and maternal psychophysiology are related. In B. Lester, A. Masten, & B. McEwen (Eds.), *Resilience in children. Annals of New York Academy of Sciences, 1094:* 297–302.

Hamburg, D. A. (1968). Evolution of emotional responses: Evidence from recent research on nonhuman primates. *Science and Psychoanalysis, 12,* 39–54.

Hamilton, P. (1989). *The interaction of depressed mothers and their 3 month old infants.* Unpublished doctoral dissertation, Boston University.

Handler, A., Kistin, N., Davis, F., & Ferre, C. (1991). Cocaine use during pregnancy: Perinatal outcomes. *American Journal of Epidemiology, 133,* 818–825.

Harlow, H. F., & Harlow, M. K. (1965). The affectional systems. In A. M. Schrier, H. F. Harlow, & F. Stollnitz (Eds.), *Behavior of nonhuman primates* (Vol. 2, pp. 287–334). New York: Academic Press.

Harlow, H. F., & Harlow, M. K. (1969). Effects of various mother-infant relationships on Rhesus monkey behaviors. In B. M. Foss (Ed.), *Determinants of infant behavior* (Vol. 4, pp. 15–40). London: Methuen.

Harlow, H. F., & Zimmerman, R. R. (1959). Affectional responses in infant monkeys. *Science, 130*, 421–432.

Harrison, A. M. (2003). Change in psychoanalysis: Getting from A to B. *Journal of the American Psychoanalytic Association, 51*, 221–257.

Harrison, A. M., Brushweller-Stern, N., Lyons-Ruth, K., Morgan, A. C., Nahum, J. P., Sander, L., Stern, D. N., & Tronick, E. Z. (1998). The case of Sophie: Interventions that effect change in psychotherapy. *Infant Mental Health Journal, (19)*, 309–314.

Hart, S., Field, T., Del Valle, C., & Pelaez-Nogueras, M. (1998). Depressed mothers' interactions with their one-year-old infants. *Infant Behavior and Development, 21*, 519–525.

Haviland, J. (1977). Sex-related pragmatics in infants. *Journal of Communication, 27*, 80–84.

Hayes, A. (1984). Interaction, engagement, and the origins and growth of communication: Some constructive concerns. In L. Feagans, C. Garvey, & R. Golinkoff (Eds.), *The origins and growth of communication* (pp. 136–161). Norwood, NJ: Ablex.

Head, J. R., & Beer, A. E. (1978). The immunologic role of viable leukocytic in mammary exosecretions. In B. L. Larson (Ed.), *Lactation, Vol. IV. Mammary gland/human lactation/milk synthesis* (pp. 337–366). New York: Academic Press.

Heimann, M. (2003). *Regression periods in human infancy.* London: Erlbaum.

Heriza, C. B. (1988). Organization of leg movements in preterm infants. *Physical Therapy, 68*, 1340–1346.

Heriza, C. B. (1991). Qualitative changes in joint coordination with age in preterm infants with documented hemorrhages. *Pediatric Physical Therapy, 3*, 209.

Hertsgaard, L., Gunnar, M., Erickson, M., & Nachmias, M. (1995). Adrenocortical response to the strange situation in infants with disorganized/disoriented attachment relationships. *Child Development, 66*, 1100–1106.

Hinde, R. A. (1979). *Towards understanding relationships.* London: Academic Press.

Hinde, R. A. (1983). *Biological bases of the mother-child relationship.* Unpublished manuscript.

Hirschfeld, N., & Beebe, B. (1987, April). *Maternal intensity and infant disengagement in face-to-face play.* Paper presented at the Society for Research in Child Development, Baltimore.

Hitchcock, J. (1979). *Infant holding.* Unpublished manuscript, Harvard University.

Hobel, C., Youkeles, L., & Forsythe, A. (1979). Prenatal and intrapartum high-risk screening: II. Risk factors reassessed. *American Journal of Obstetrics and Gynecology, 135*, 1051–1056.

Hobfoll, S. E., Ritter, C., Lavin, J., Hulsizer, M. R., & Cameron, R. P. (1995). Depression prevalence and incidence among inner-city pregnant and postpartum women. *Journal of Consulting and Clinical Psychology, 63*, 445–453.

Hodapp, R. M., & Mueller, E. (1982). Early social development. In B. B. Wolman (Ed.), *Handbook of developmental psychology* (pp. 284–300). Englewood Cliffs, NJ: Prentice-Hall.

Hofer, M. (1978). Regulatory processes in early social relationships. In P. P. G. Bateson & P. H. Klopfer (Eds.), *Perspectives in ethology, Vol. 3.* New York: Plenum.

Hofer, M. (1981). Parental contributions to the development of their offspring. In D. Gubernick & P. Klopfer (Eds.), *Parental care in mammals* (pp. 77–111).

Hofer, M. A. (1984). Relationships as regulators: A psychobiologic perspective on bereavement. *Psychosomatic Medicine, 46*, 183–197.

Hofer, M. A. (1994a). The development of emotion regulation: Biological and behavioural considerations. *Monographs of the Society for Research in Child Development, 59*, 192–207.

Hofer, M. A. (1994b). Hidden regulation in attachment, separation, and loss. In N. A. Fox (Ed.), *The development of emotion regulation: Biological and behavioural considerations* (pp. 192–207). Chicago: University of Chicago Press.

Hollingshead, A. (1979). *Four-factor index of social status.* New Haven, CT: Yale University.

Horowitz, F. D., & Linn, P. L. (1984). Use of the NBAS in research. In T. B. Brazelton (Ed.). *Neonatal Behavioral Assessment Scale* (pp. 97–104). Philadelphia: Spastics International Medical Publications.

Hrdy, S. B. (1976). Care and exploitation of nonhuman primate infants by conspecifics other than the mother. In J. Rosenblatt, R. Hinde, E. Shaw, & C. Beer (Eds.), *Advances in the study of behavior, Vol. 6.* New York: Academic Press.

Hubbs-Tait, L., Hughes, K. P., Culp, A. M., Osofsky, J. D., Hann, D. M., Eberhart-Wright, A., et al. (1996). Children of adolescent mothers: Attachment representation, maternal depression, and later behavior problems. *American Journal of Orthopsychiatry,* 66, 416–426.

Huffman, L. G. M., Bryan, Y. E., del Carmen, R., Pedersen, F. A., Doussard-Roosevelt, J. A., & Porges, S. W. (1998). Infant temperament and cardiac vagal tone: Assessments at twelve weeks of age. *Child Development,* 69, 624–635.

Hughes, J. G., Ehemann, B., & Brown, V. A. (1948). Electroencephalography of the newborn: III. Brain potentials of babies born of mothers given "second sodium." *American Journal of Diseases of the Child,* 76, 626–633.

Hurt, H., Brodsky, N., Betancourt, L., Braitman, L., Malmud, E., & Giannetta, J. (1995). Cocaine-exposed children: Follow-up through 30 months. *Journal of Developmental and Behavioral Pediatrics,* 16, 29–35.

Husaini, B. A., Neff, D. A., Harrington, J. B., Hughes, M. D., & Segal, D. (1980). Depression in rural communities. Validating the CES-D scale. *Journal of Community Psychology,* 8, 20–27.

Hutchings, D. E. (1978). Behavioral teratology: Embryopathic and behavioral effects of drugs during pregnancy. In G. Gottlieb (Ed.), *Early influences* (Vol. 4, pp. 7–34). New York: Academic Press.

Hutchings, D. E. (1993a). The puzzle of cocaine's effects following maternal use during pregnancy: Are there reconcilable differences? *Neurotoxicology and Teratology,* 15, 281–286.

Hutchings, D. E. (1993b). Response to commentaries. *Neurotoxicology and Teratology,* 15, 311–312.

Isabella, R., & Belsky, J. (1991). Interactional synchrony and the origins of mother-infant attachment: A replication study. *Child Development,* 62, 373–384.

Izard, C. E. (1977). *Human emotions.* New York: Plenum.

Izard, C. (1978a). Emotions as motivations: An evolutionary-developmental perspective. In H. E. Howe Jr. (Ed.), *Nebraska Symposium on Motivation* (Vol. 26, pp. 163–199). Lincoln: University of Nebraska Press.

Izard, C. E. (1978b). On the ontogenesis of emotions and emotion-cognition relationships in infancy. In M. Lewis & L. Rosenblum (Eds.), *The development of affect.* New York: Plenum.

Izard, C. E., & Dougherty, L. (1980). *A system for identifying affect expressions by holistic judgments* (AFFEX). Newark, DE: University of Delaware, Instructional Resources Center.

Izard, C. E., Huebner, R. R., Risser, D., McCinnes, G., & Dougherty, L. (1980). The young infant's ability to produce discrete emotion expressions. *Developmental Psychology,* 16, 132–140.

Izard, C. E., & Malatesta, C. Z. (1987). Perspectives on emotional development: I. Differential emotions theory of early emotional development In J. D. Osofsky (Ed.), *Handbook of infant development* (2nd ed., pp. 494–554). New York: Wiley.

Jacobson, J. L., & Jacobson, S. W. (1996). Methodological considerations in behavioral toxicology in infants and children. *Developmental Psychology,* 32, 390–403.

Jacobson, J. L., Jacobson, S. W., Schwartz, P. M., Fein, G. G., & Dowler, J. K. (1984). Prenatal exposure to an environmental toxin: A test of the multiple effects model. *Developmental Psychology, 20,* 523–532.

Jaffe, J., Beebe, B., Feldstein, S., Crown, C., & Jasnow, M. (2001). Rhythms of dialogue in infancy: Coordinated timing in development. *Monographs of the Society for Research in Child Development, 66*(2, Serial No. 265).

Jaffe, J., Stern, D., & Peery, C. (1973). "Conversational" coupling of gaze behavior in prelinguistic human development. *Journal of Psycholinguistic Research, 2,* 321–329.

Jasnow, M., & Feldstein, S. (1986). Adult-like temporal characteristics of mother-infant vocal interactions. *Child Development, 57,* 754–761.

Jeng, S.-F., Chen, L.-C., & Yau, K.-I. T. (2002). Kinematic analysis of kicking movements in preterm infants with very low birth weight and full-term infants. *Physical Therapy, 82,* 148–159.

Jeng, S., Yau, K. T., & Teng, R. (1998). Neurobehavioral development at term in very low-birth weight infants and normal term infants in Taiwan. *Early Human Development, 51,* 235–245.

Jensen, J. L., Ulrich, B. D., Thelen, E., Schneider, K., & Zernicke, R. F. (1994). Adaptive dynamics of the leg movement patterns of human infants: I. The effects of posture on spontaneous kicking. *Journal of Motor Behavior, 26,* 303–312.

Johnson, M. (1975). Fathers, mothers and sex-typing. *Sociological Inquiry, 45*(1), 15–26.

Kagan, J. (1984). The idea of emotion in human development In C. E. Izard, J. Kagan, & R. B. Zajonc (Eds.), *Emotions, cognition, and behavior* (pp. 38–72). New York: Cambridge University Press.

Kagan, J. (1998). *Three seductive ideas.* Cambridge, MA: Harvard University Press.

Kagan, J., Kearsley, R. B., & Zelazo, P. R. (1975). The emergence of initial apprehension to unfamiliar peers. In M. Lewis & L. Rosenblum (Eds.), *Friendship and peer relations* (pp. 187–203). New York: Wiley.

Kagan, J., Reznick, J. S., & Snidman, N. (1987). The physiology and psychology of behavioral inhibition in children. *Child Development, 58,* 1459–1473.

Kaltenbach, K., & Finnegan, L. P. (1988). The influence of the neonatal abstinence syndrome on mother-infant interaction. In E. J. Anthony & C. Chiland (Eds.), *The child in his family. Perilous development: Child raising and identity formation under stress* (pp. 223–230). New York: Wiley Interscience.

Kaplan, P. S., Bachorowski, J., & Zarlengo-Strouse, P. (1999). Child-directed speech produced by mothers with symptoms of depression fails to promote associative learning in 4-month-old infants. *Child Development, 70,* 560–570.

Kaye, K. (1977a). The maternal role in developing communication and language. In M. Bullowa (Ed.), *Before speech: The beginnings of human communication.* Cambridge, UK: Cambridge University Press.

Kaye, K. (1977b). Toward the origin of dialogue. In H. R. Schaffer (Ed.), *Studies in mother-infant interaction* (pp. 89–118). New York: Academic Press.

Kaye, K. (1982). *The mental and social life of babies.* Chicago: University of Chicago Press.

Kaye, K., & Fogel, A. (1980). The temporal structure of face-to-face communication between mothers and infants. *Developmental Psychology, 16,* 454–464.

Kearsley, R. B. (1973). The newborn's response to auditory stimulation: A demonstration of orienting and defensive behavior. *Child Development, 44,* 582–590.

Keefer, C. (1977, March). *A cross-cultural study of face-to-face interaction: Gusii infants and mothers.* Paper presented at the Society for Research in Child Development, New Orleans.

Keefer, C. H., Tronick, E. Z., Dixon, S., & Brazleton, T. (1982). Specific differences in motor performance between Gusii and American newborns and a modification of the Neonatal Behavioral Assesment Scale. *Child Development, 53,* 754–759.

Kellerman, H. (1981). *Group cohesion: Theoretical and clinical perspectives.* New York: Grune & Stratton.

Kessen, W. (Ed.). (1975). *Childhood in China.* New Haven: Yale University Press.

Kihlstrom, J., & Cantor, N. (1983). Mental representations of the self. In L. Berkowitz (Ed.). *Advances in experimental social psychology* (Vol. 17, pp. 1–47). San Diego, CA: Academic Press.

Kindlon, D., & Thompson, M. (1999). *Raising Cain: Protecting the emotional life of boys.* New York: Ballantine.

Klaus, M. H., & Kennell, J. H. (1976). *Maternal-infant bonding.* Saint Louis, MO: Mosby.

Kluzik, J., Fetters, L., & Coryell, J. (1990). Quantification of control: A preliminary study of effects of neurodevelopmental treatment on reaching in children with spastic cerebral palsy. *Physical Therapy, 70,* 65–76.

Kogan, N., & Carter, A. S. (1996). Mother-infant reengagement following the still-face: The role of maternal emotional availability in infant affect regulation. *Infant Behavior and Development, 19,* 359–370.

Kohut, H. (1971). *The analysis of the self.* New York: International Universities Press.

Konner, M. J. (1976). Maternal care, infant behavior, and development among the !Kung. In R. B. Lee & I. Devore (Eds.), *Kalahari hunter gatherers* (pp. 218–245). Cambridge, MA: Harvard University Press.

Konner, M. (1977a). Evolution of human behavior development. In R. H. Munroe, R. L. Munroe, & B. B. Whiting (Eds.), *Handbook of cross-cultural human development* (pp. 3–51). New York: Garland STPM.

Konner, M. (1977b). Infancy among the Kalahari Desert San. In P. H. Leiderman, S. Turkin, & A. Rosenthal (Eds.), *Culture and infancy: Variations in the human experience.* New York: Academic Press.

Konner, M., & Worthman, C. (1980). Nursing frequency, gonadal function and birth spacing among !Kung hunter-gatherers. *Science, 207,* 788–791.

Kopp, C. B. (1989). Regulation of distress and negative emotions: A developmental view. *Developmental Psychology, 25,* 343–354.

Koren, G., Graham, K., Shear, H., & Einarson, T. (1989). Bias against the null hypothesis: The reproductive hazards of cocaine. *Lancet, 334,* 1440–1442.

Korner, A. F., & Thom, V. A. (1990). *Neurobehavioral assessment of the preterm infant.* New York: Psychological Corporation.

Korner, A. F., & Thoman, E. (1970). Visual alertness in neonates as evoked by maternal care. *Journal of Experimental Child Psychology, 10,* 67–78.

Kosofsky, B. E. (1998). Cocaine-induced alterations in neuro-development. *Seminars in Speech and Language, 19,* 109–121.

Kosofsky, B. E., & Wilkins, A. S. (1998). A mouse model of transplacental cocaine exposure: Clinical implications for exposed infants and children. *Annals of the New York Academy of Sciences, 24,* 248–261.

Kron, R. E., Stein, M., & Goddard, K. E. (1966). Newborn sucking behavior affected by obstetric sedation. *Pediatrics, 37,* 1012–1016.

Kuban, K., & Levitan, A. (1994). Cerebral palsy. *New England Journal of Medicine, 330,* 188–195.

Kuban, K., Leviton, A. E. A., Pagano, M., & Dammann, O. (1997). Developmental epidemiology network investigators BM: Intraventricular hemorrage, ventriculomegaly, and white matter disease of prematurity. *Annals of Neurology, 42,* 493.

Kurland, J. A. (1979). Paternity, mother's brother, and human sociality. In N. A. Chagnon & W. Irons (Eds.), *Evolutionary biology and human social behavior* (pp. 145–180). North Scituate, MA: Duxbury Press.

Lachmann, F. Some contributions of empiriical infant research to adult psychoanlysis: What have we learned? How can we apply it? *Psychoanalytic Dialogues, 11*(2), 167–187.

Lachmann, F., & Beebe, B. (1996). Three principles of salience in the patient-analyst interaction *Psychoanalytic Psychology, 13*, 1–22.

Lamb, M. E., & Hwang, C. P. (1982). Maternal attachment and mother-neonate bonding: A critical review. In M. E. Lamb & A. L. Brown (Eds.), *Advances in Developmental Psychology* (Vol. 2, pp. 1–39). Hillsdale, NJ: Erlbaum.

Lancaster, J. B. (1971). Play-mothering: The relations between juvenile females and young infants among free-ranging vervet monkeys (*Cercopithecus aethiops*). *Folia Primatologica, 15*, 161–182.

Lancaster, J. B. (1976). Primate sex roles and the evolution of the division of labor in humans. In M. S. Teilelbaum (Ed.), *Sex differences: Social and biological perspectives* (pp. 22–62). Garden City, NY: Anchor Press/Doubleday.

Lashley, K. S. (1951). The problem of serial order in behavior. In L. A. Jeffrees (Ed.), *Cerebral mechanisms in behavior: The Hixon Symposium* (pp. 112–146). New York: Wiley.

Lawrence, R. A. (1980). *Breast feeding: A guide for the medical profession.* London: Mosby.

Lederman, R. P. (1995). Relationship of anxiety, stress, and psychosocial development to reproductive health. *Behavioral Medicine, 21*, 101–112.

Lee, R. B., & Devore, I. (1968). *Man the hunter.* New York: Aldine.

Legerstee, M., Corter, C., & Kienapple, K. (1990). Hand, arm, and facial actions of young infants to a social and nonsocial stimulus. *Child Development, 61*, 774–784.

Leifer, M. (1977). Psychological changes accompanying pregnancy and motherhood. *Genetic Psychology Monographs, 89*, 55–96.

Lelwica, M., & Haviland, J. (1983, April). *Ten-week-old infants' reactions to mothers' emotional expressions.* Paper presented at the biennial meeting of the Society for Research in Child Development, Detroit.

Lester, B. M. (1979). Behavioral assessment of the neonate. In E. J. Sell (Ed.), *Follow-up of the high-risk newborn—A practical approach* (pp. 50–74). Springfield, IL: Charles C. Thomas.

Lester, B. M. (1984). Data analysis and prediction. In T. B. Brazelton (Ed.), *Neonatal Behavioral Assessment Scale* (pp. 85–96). Philadelphia: Lippincott, Spastics International Medical Publication.

Lester, B. M. (1994). Introduction. *Infant Mental Health Journal, 15*, 104–106.

Lester, B. M. (1998). The Maternal Lifestyles study. *Annals of the New York Academy of Science, 846*, 296–306.

Lester, B. M. (1999). *Clinics in perinatology: Prenatal drug exposure and child outcome* (26th ed.) Philadelphia: Saunders.

Lester, B. M., Als, H., & Brazelton, T. B. (1982). Regional obstetric anesthesia and newborn behavior: A reanalysis toward synergistic effects. *Child Development, 53*, 687–692.

Lester, B. M., Corwin, M. J., Sepkoski, C., McLaughlin, S., Kayne, H., & Golub, H. L. (1991). Neurobehavioral syndromes in cocaine exposed newborn infants. *Child Development, 57*, 11–19.

Lester, B. M., & Dreher, M. C. (1987). Effects of marijuana smoking during pregnancy on newborn cry analysis. *Society for Pediatric Research, Annual Meeting Abstracts* (Serial No. 18454).

Lester, B., Hoffman, J., & Brazelton, T. B. (1985). The rhythmic structure of mother-infant interaction in term and preterm infants. *Child Development, 56*, 15–27.

Lester, B. M., LaGasse, L. L., & Bigsby, R. (1998). Prenatal cocaine exposure and child development: What do we know and what do we do? *Seminars in Speech and Language, 19*, 123–146.

Lester, B. M., & Tronick, E. Z. (1994). The effects of prenatal cocaine exposure and child outcome. *Infant Mental Health Journal, 15*, 107–120.

Lester, B. M., & Tronick, E. Z. In press. Newborn Behavioral Assessment Scale and NNNS. In P. S. Zeskind & C. Singer (Eds.), *Biobehavioral assessment of the newborn and young infant: Developmental models and implications for the infant at risk.* New York: Guilford.

Levenson, R. W., & Gottman, J. M. (1983). Marital interaction: Physiologic concordance and affective exchange. *Journal of Personality and Social Psychology, 45,* 587–597.

LeVine, R. A. (1963). Witchcraft and sorcery in the Gusii community. In J. Middleton & E. Winter (Eds.), *Witchcraft and sorcery in East Africa.* London: Routledge & Kegan Paul.

LeVine, R. A. (1973). *Culture, behavior and personality.* Chicago: Aldine.

LeVine, R. A. (1977). Child rearing as cultural adaptation. In P. H. Leiderman, S. R. Tulkin, & A. Rosenfeld (Eds.), *Culture and infancy: Variations in the human experience* (pp. 15–27). New York: Academic Press.

LeVine, R. A. (1979). *Gaze in an African society: Looking and being looked at.* Preliminary report.

LeVine, R. A. (1980a). The self and its development in an African society: A preliminary analysis. In B. Lee (Ed.), *New approaches to the self.* Norwood, NJ: Ablex.

LeVine, R. A. (1980b). Adulthood among the Gusii of Kenya. In N. Smelser & E. Erickson (Eds.), *Themes of love and work in adulthood.* Cambridge, MA: Harvard University Press.

LeVine, R. A., & Leiderman, P. H. (1994). *Child care and culture: lessons from Africa.* New York: Cambridge University Press.

LeVine, R. A., & LeVine, B. (1966). *Nyansongo: A Gusii community in Kenya.* New York: Wiley.

LeVine, S. (1979). *Mothers and wives: Gusii women of East Africa.* Chicago: University of Chicago Press.

Levine, S., & Coe, C. L. (1985). The use and abuse of cortisol as a measure of stress. In T. Field, P. McCabe, & N. Schneiderman (Eds.), *Stress and coping* (pp. 19–23). Mahwah, NJ: Erlbaum.

Leviton, A., & Paneth, N. (1990). White matter damage in preterm newborns: An epidemiologic perspective. *Early Human Development, 24,* 1–22.

Lewis, M. (1987). Social development in infancy and early childhood. In J. D. Osofsky (Ed.), *Handbook of infant development* (2nd ed., pp. 419–555). New York: Wiley.

Lewis, M., & Michalson, L. (1982). The measurement of emotional state. In C. E. Izard (Ed.), *Measuring emotions in infants and children* (pp. 178–207). Cambridge, UK: Cambridge University Press.

Lewis, M., & Ramsay, D. (2005). Infant emotional and cortisol responses to goal blockage. *Child Development, 76,* 518–530.

Lipsitt, L. P. (1977). The study of sensory and learning processes of the newborn. *Clinics in Perinatology, 4,* 163–186.

Livesay, S., Ehrlich, S., & Finnegan, L. P. (1987). Cocaine and pregnancy: Maternal and infant outcome. *Pediatric Research, 21,* 238.

Loevinger, J. (1976). *Ego development conceptions and theories.* San Francisco: Jossey-Bass.

Loewald, H. W. (1971). The transference neurosis: Comments on the concept and the phenomenon. *Journal of the American Psychoanalytic Association, 19,* 54–66.

Lough, S., Wing, A. M., Fraser, C., & Jenner, J. (1984). Measurement of recovery of function in the hemiparetic upper limb following stroke: A preliminary report. *Human Movement Science, 3,* 247–256.

Lovejoy, M. C., Graczyk, P. A., O'Hare, E., & Neuman, G. (2000). Maternal depression and parenting behavior: A meta-analytic review. *Clinical Psychology Review, 20,* 561–592.

Loyd, B. H., & Abiden, R. R. (1985). Revision of the Parenting Stress Index. *Journal of Pediatric Psychology, 10,* 169–177.

Lozoff, B., Brittenham, G. M., Trause, M. A., Kennell, J. H., & Klaus, M. H. (1977). The mother-newborn relationship: Limits of adaptability. *Journal of Pediatrics*, 91(1), 1–12.

Lupien, S. J., Fiocco, A., Wan, N., Maheu, F., Lord, C., Schramek, T., et al. (2005). Stress hormones and human memory function across the lifespan. *Psychoneuroendocrinology*, 30, 225–242.

Lupien, S. J., & McEwen, B. S. (1997). The acute effects of corticosteroids on cognition: Integration of animal and human model studies. *Brain Research Reviews*, 24(1), 1–27.

Lyons-Ruth, K. (1991). Rapprochement or approchement: Mahler's theory reconsidered from the vantage point of recent research on early attachment relationships. *Psychoanalytic Psychology*, 8, 1–23.

Lyons-Ruth, K. (1999). The two-person unconscious: Intersubjective dialogue, enactive relational representation, and the emergence of new forms of relational organization. *Psychoanalytic Inquiry*, 19, 576–617.

Lyons-Ruth, K., Bruschweiler-Stern, N., Harrison, A. M., Nahum, J. P., Sander, L., Stern, D. N., et al. (1998). Implicit relational knowing: Its role in development and psychoanalytic treatment. *Infant Mental Health Journal*, 19, 282–289.

Lyons-Ruth, K., Connell, D. B., & Grunebaum, H. U. (1990). Infants at social risk: Maternal depression and family support services as mediators of infant development and security of attachment. *Child Development*, 61, 85–98.

Lyons-Ruth, K., & Jacobvitz, D. (1999). Attachment disorganization: Unresolved loss, relational violence, and lapses in behavioural and attentional strategies (pp. 520-554). In J. Cassidy & P. Shaver (Eds.), *Handbook of attachment theory and research*. New York: Guilford.

Lyons-Ruth, K., & Zeanah, C. (1993). The family context of infant mental health: part I. Affective development in the primary caregiving relationship. In C. Zeanah (Ed.), *Handbook of infant mental health* (pp. 14–37). New York: Guilford.

Lyons-Ruth, K., Zoll, D., Connell, D., et al. (1986). The depressed mother and her one-year-old infant: Environment, interaction, attachment, and infant development. *New Directions for Child Development*, 34, 61–82.

MacFarlane, J. A. (1975). Olfaction in the development of social preferences in the human neonate. In M. Hoffer (Ed.), *Parent-infant interaction* (pp. 103–113). Ciba Foundation Symposium 33 (New Series). New York: Elsevier.

MacGregor, S. N., Keith, L. G., Chasnoff, I. J., Rosner, M. A., Chisum, G. M., Shaw, P., et al. (1987). Cocaine use during pregnancy: Adverse perinatal outcome. *American Journal of Obstetrics and Gynecology*, 157, 686–690.

Mahler, M. S., Pine, F., & Bergman, A. (1975). *The psychological birth of the human infant*. New York: Basic Books.

Main, M. (1981). Avoidance in the service of attachment: A working paper. In K. Immelmann, G. Barlow, M. Main, & L. Petrinovich (Eds.), *Behavioral development: The Bielfield Interdisciplinary Project* (pp. 651–693). New York: Cambridge University Press.

Main, M. (1995). Attachment theory: Social, developmental and clinical perspectives. In S. Goldberg, R. Muir, & J. Kerr (Eds.), *Recent studies in attachment* (pp. 407–472). Hillsdale, NJ: Analytic Press.

Main, M. (1999). Epilogue. Attachment theory: Eighteen points with suggestions for future studies. In J. Cassidy & P. R. Shaver (Eds.), *Handbook of attachment* (pp. 249–264). New York: Guilford Press.

Malanga, C. J., & Kosofsky, B. E. (1999). Mechanisms of action of drugs of abuse on the developing fetal brain. In B. M. Lester (Ed.), *Clinics in perinology* (pp. 17–38). Philadelphia: Saunders.

Malatesta, C. Z. (1981). Infant emotions and the vocal affect lexicon. *Motivation and Emotion*, 5, 1–22.

Malatesta, C. Z., & Haviland, J. M. (1982). Learning display rules: The socialization of emotional expression in infancy. *Child Development*, 53, 991–1003.

Malatesta, C. A., & Izard, C. E. (1984). The ontogenesis of human social signals: From biological imperative to symbol utilization. In N. A. Fox & R. J. Davidson (Eds.), *The psychobiology of effective development* (pp. 161–206). Hillsdale, NJ: Erlbaum.

Malphurs, J. E., Raag, T., Field, T., Pickens, J., Yando, R., Bendell, D., et al. (1996). Touch by intrusive and withdrawn mothers with depressive symptoms. *Early Development and Parenting, 5*, 111–115.

Manassis, K., Bradley, S., Goldberg, S., Hood, J., & Swinson, R. P. (1994). Attachment in mothers with anxiety disorders and their children. *Journal of the American Academy of Child and Adolescent Psychiatry, 33*, 1106–1113.

Manassis, K., Bradley, S., Goldberg, S., Hood, J., & Swinson, R. P. (1995). Behavioral inhibition, attachment and anxiety in children of mothers with anxiety disorders. *Canadian Journal of Psychiatry, 40*, 87–92.

Marin-Padilla, M. (1997). Developmental neuropathology and impact of perinatal brain damage: II. White matter lesions of the neocortex. *Journal of Neuropathology and Experimental Neurology, 56*, 219–235.

Martin, J. (1981). A longitudinal study of the consequences of early mother-infant interaction: A microanalytic approach. *Monographs of the Society for Research in Child Development, 46*(Serial No. 190).

Massie, H. N. (1975). The early natural history of childhood psychosis. *Journal of the American Academy of Child Psychiatry, 14*, 683–707.

Massie, H. N. (1977). Patterns of mother-infant behavior and subsequent childhood psychosis. *Child Psychiatry and Human Development, 7*, 211-230.

Massie, H. M. (1978). The early natural history of childhood psychosis. *Journal of American Academy of Child Psychiatry, 17*, 29–45.

Massie, H. N. (1982). Affective development and the organization of mother-infant behavior from the perspective of psychopathology. In E. Tronick (Ed.), *Social interchange infancy: Affect, cognition and communication* (pp. 161–182). Baltimore, MD: University Park Press.

Matas, L., Arend, R., & Sroufe, L. A. (1978). Continuity of adaptation in the second year: The relationship between quality of attachment and later competence. *Child Development, 49*, 547–556.

Matias, R., Cohn, J. F., & Ross, S. (1989). A comparison of two systems to code infants' affective expression. *Developmental Psychology, 25*, 483–489.

Maturana, H., & Varela, F. (1980). *The tree of knowledge.* Boston: Shambhala.

Mayer, N., & Tronick, E. (1985). Mother turn-giving signals and infant turn-taking in mother-infant interaction. In T. Field & N. Fox (Eds.), *Social perception in infants.* Norwood, NJ: Ablex.

Mayer, P. (1951). *Two studies in applied anthropology in Kenya.* Colonial Research Studies No. 3. London: His Majesty's Stationery Office.

Mayes, L. C. (1994). Neurobiology of prenatal cocaine exposure effect on developing monamine systems. *Infant Mental Health Journal, 15*, 121–130.

Mayes, L. C., Granger, R. H., Frank, M., Schottenfeld, R., & Bornstein, M. H. (1993). Neurobehavioral profiles of neonates exposed to cocaine prenatally. *Pediatrics, 91*, 778–783.

Mayr, E. (1963). *Animal species and evolution.* Cambridge, MA: Harvard University Press.

McCall, R. B., & McGhee, P. E. (1977). The discrepancy hypothesis of attention and affect in infant. In E. C. Uzgiris & F. Weismann (Eds.), *The structuring of experience.* New York: Plenum.

McCleary, R., & Hay, R. A. (1980). *Applied time series analysis for the social sciences.* Beverly Hills, CA: Sage.

McEwen, B. S., & Sapolsky, R. M. (1995). Stress and cognitive function. *Current Opinion in Neurobiology, 5*, 205–216.

McGaugh, J. L. (2000). Memory: A century of consolidation. *Science, 287,* 248–251.

McGaugh, J. L. (2004). The amygdala modulates the consolidation of memories of emotionally arousing experiences. *Annual Review of Neuroscience, 27,* 1–28.

Mead, G. H. (1934). *Mind, self and society.* Chicago: University of Chicago Press.

Melson, G. F., & Fogel, A. (1982). Young children's interests in unfamiliar infants. *Child Development, 53,* 693–700.

Meltzoff, A. N., & Moore, M. K. (1977). Imitation of facial and manual gestures by human neonates. *Science, 198,* 75–78.

Merimee, T. J., Zapf, J., & Froesch, E. R. (1981). Dwarfism in the Pygmy: An isolated deficiency of insulin-like growth factor I. *New England Journal of Medicine, 305,* 965–968.

Michel, G. F., Camras, L. A., & Sullivan, J. (1992). Infant interest expressions as coordinative motor structures. *Infant Behavior and Development, 15,* 347–358.

Mirochnick, M., Meyer, J., Cole, J., Herren, T., & Zuckerman, B. (1991). Circulating catecholamine concentrations in cocaine-exposed neonates: A pilot study. *Pediatrics, 88,* 481–485.

Mitchell, G. D. (1968). Persistent behavior pathology in rhesus monkeys following early social isolation. *Folia Primatology, 8,* 132–147.

Mitchell, S. (1993). *Hope and dread in psychoanalysis.* New York: Basic Books.

Mitchell, S. (1997). *Influence and autonomy in psychoanalysis.* Hillsdale, NJ: Analytic Press.

Modell, A. (1993). *The private self.* Cambridge, MA: Harvard University Press.

Monset-Couchard, M., de Bethmann, O., Radvanyi-Bouvet, M. F., Rapin, C., Bordarier, C., & Relier, J. P. (1988). Neurodevelopmental outcome in cystic periventricular leucomalacia. *Neuropediatrics, 19,* 124–131.

Moore, G. A., & Calkins, S. D. (2004). Infants' vagal regulation in the still-face paradigm is related to dyadic coordination of mother-infant interaction. *Developmental Psychology, 40,* 1068–1080.

Moore, G. A., Cohn, J. F., & Campbell, S. B. (2001). Infant affective responses to mother's still face at 6 months differentially predict externalizing and internalizing behaviors at 18 months. *Developmental Psychology, 37,* 706–714.

Morelli, G. A. (1987). A comparative study of Efe (Pygmy) and Lese one-, two-, and three-year-olds of the Iture Forest of northeastern Zaïre: The influence of subsistence-related variables, and children's age and gender on social-emotional development. *Dissertation Abstracts International, 48/02B,* 582 (UMI No. 8710487)

Morelli, G. A., Rogoff, B., Oppenheim, D., & Goldsmith, D. (1992). Cultural variation in infants' sleeping arrangements: Questions of independence. *Developmental Psychology, 28,* 604–613.

Morgan, A. C., Brushweller-Stern, N., Harrison, A. M., Lyons-Ruth, K., Nahum, J. P., Sander, L., Stern, D. N., & Tronick, E. Z. (1998). Moving along to things left undone. Infant Mental Health Journal, *(19),* 324–332.

Mrazek, D. A., Casey, B., & Anderson, I. (1987). Insecure attachment in severely asthmatic preschool children: Is it a risk factor? *Journal of the American Academy of Child and Adolescent Psychiatry, 26,* 516–520.

Mullen, M., Snidman, N., & Kagan, J. (1993). Free-play behavior in inhibited and unihibited children. *Infant Behavior and Development, 16,* 383–389.

Murray, L. (1992). The impact of postnatal depression on infant development. *Journal of Child Psychology and Psychiatry, 33,* 543–561.

Murray, L., & Cooper, P. (Eds.). (1997). *Postpartum depression and child development.* New York: Guilford.

Murray, L., Fiori-Cowley, A., & Hooper, R. (1996). The impact of postnatal depression and associated adversity on early mother-infant interactions and later infant outcome. *Child Development, 67,* 2512–2526.

empton, C., Woolgar, M., & Hooper, R. (1993). Depressed mothers' infants and its relation to infant gender and cognitive development. *sychology and Psychiatry, 34,* 1083–1101.

., ,. ^., & Weissman, M. M. (1980). Use of a self-report symptom scale to detect depression in a community sample. *American Journal of Psychiatry, 137,* 1081–1084.

Nachmias, M., Gunnar, M., Mangelsdorf, S., Parritz, R. H., & Buss, K. (1996). Behavioral inhibition and stress reactivity: The moderating role of attachment security. *Child Development, 67,* 508–522.

Nahum, J. (1994). New theoretical vistas in psychoanalysis: Louis Sander's theory of early development. *Psychoanalytic Psychology, 11,* 1–19.

Nakagawa, M., Teti, D. M., & Lamb, M. E. (1992). An ecological study of child-mother attachments among Japanese sojourners in the United States. *Developmental Psychology, 28,* 584–592.

Napiorkowski, B., Lester, B. M., Preier, M. C., Brunner, S., Dietz, L., Nadra, A., et al. (1996). Effects of in utero substance exposure on infant neurobehavior. *Pediatrics, 98,* 71–75.

Needlman, R., Zuckerman, B., Anderson, G. M., Mirochnick, M., & Cohen, D. J. (1993). Cerebrospinal fluid monoamine precursors and metabolites in human neonates following in utero cocaine exposure: A preliminary study. *Pediatrics, 92,* 55–60.

Neuspiel, D. R., Hamel, S. C., Hochberg, E., Greene, J., & Campbell, D. (1991). Maternal cocaine use and infant behavior. *Neurotoxicology and Teratology, 13,* 229–233.

New, R. (1979). *Mothers and others: A review and preliminary analysis of infant-care-taker interaction.* Unpublished monograph, Harvard University.

Noam, G. F. K. (1996). *Development and vulnerability in close relationships.* Mahwah, NJ: Erlbaum.

Ogden, T. (1994). The analytic third: Working with intersubjective clinical facts. *International Journal of Psychoanalysis, 75*(1), 3–20.

O'Hara, M. W., Zekoski, E. M., Phillips, L. H., & Wright, E. J. (1990). Controlled prospective study of postpartum mood disorders: Comparison of childbearing and non-childbearing women. *Journal of Abnormal Psychology, 99,* 3–15.

Oro, A. S., & Dixon, S. D. (1987). Perinatal cocaine and methamphetamine exposure: Maternal and neonatal correlates. *Journal of Pediatrics, 111,* 571–578.

Osofsky, J. D. (1992). Affective development and early relationships: Clinical implications. In J. W. Barron, M. N. Eagle, & D. L. Wolitzky (Eds.), *Interface of psychoanalysis and psychology* (pp. 233–244). Washington, DC: American Psychological Association.

Osofsky, J., & Danzger, B. (1974). Relationships between neonatal characteristics and mother-infant characteristics. *Developmental Psychology, 10,* 124–130.

Ostrea, E. M., Brady, M. J., Gause, S., Raymundo, A. L., & Stevens, M. (1992). Drug screening of newborns by meconium analysis: A large scale, prospective epidemiologic study. *Pediatrics, 89,* 107–113.

Ostrea, E. M., Brady, M. J., & Parks, D. C. (1989). Drug screening of meconium in infants of drug dependent mothers: An alternative to urine testing. *Journal of Pediatrics, 115,* 474–477.

Paneth, N., Rudelli, R., & Monte, W. (1990). White matter necrosis in very low birth weight infants: Neuropathologic and ultrasonographic findings in infants surviving six days or longer. *Journal of Pediatrics, 116,* 975–984.

Papousek, H. (1967). Experimental studies of appetitional behavior in human newborns and infants. In H. W. Stevenson, E. H. Hess, & H. L. Rheingold (Eds.), *Early behavior* (pp. 24–47). New York: Wiley.

Papousek, H., & Papousek, M. (1983). Biological basis of social interactions: Implications of research for an understanding of behavioral deviance. *Journal of Child Psychology and Psychiatry, 24,* 117–129.

Papousek, H., & Papousek, M. (1986). Structure and dynamics of human communication at the beginning of life. *European Archives of Psychiatry and Neurological Science, 236*(1), 21–25.

Papousek, H., & Papousek, M. (1987). Intuitive parenting: A didactic counterpart to the infant's precocity in integrative capacities. In J. D. Osofsky (Ed.), *Handbook of infant development* (2nd ed., pp. 669–720). New York: Wiley.

Parmalee, A., Kopp, C., & Sigman, M. (1976). Selection of developmental assessment techniques for infants at risk. *Merrill-Palmer Quarterly, 22,* 177–199.

Parke, R. (1979). Perspectives on father-infant interaction. In J. Osofsky (Ed.), *Handbook on infant development.* New York: Wiley.

Parke, R., & Asher, S. (1983). Social and personality development. *Annual Review of Psychology, 34,* 431–463.

Parke, R. D., O'Leary, S. E., & West, S. (1972). Mother-father-newborn interaction: Effects of maternal medication, labor, and sex of infant. *Proceedings of the 18th Annual Convention of the American Psychological Association, 7*(1), 85–86. Washington, DC: American Psychological Association.

Pawlby, S. J. (1977). Imitative interaction. In H. R. Schaffer (Ed.), *Studies in mother-infant interaction* (pp. 203–224). New York: Academic Press.

Peery, J. C., & Stern, D. (1976). Gaze duration frequency distributions during mother-infant interaction. *Journal of Genetic Psychology, 129,* 45–55.

Peiper, A. (1928). *Die Hirntatigkeit des Sauglings.* Berlin: Springer.

Peiper, A. (1963). *Cerebral function of infancy and childhood.* New York: Consultants Bureau.

Pelaez-Nogueras, M., Field, T. M., Hossain, Z., & Pickens, J. (1996). Depressed mothers' touching increases infants' positive affect and attention in still-face interactions. *Child Development, 67,* 1780–1792.

Peters, D. A. (1988). Effects of maternal stress during different gestational periods on the serotonergic system in adult rat offspring. *Pharmacology, Biochemistry, and Behavior, 31,* 839–843.

Peters, D. A. (1990). Maternal stress increases fetal brain and neonatal cerebral cortex 5-hydroxytryptamine synthesis in rats: A possible mechanism by which stress influences brain development. *Pharmacology, Biochemistry, and Behavior, 35,* 943–947.

Petiti, D. B., & Coleman, C. (1990). Cocaine and the risk of low birth weight. *American Journal of Public Health, 80,* 25–28.

Piaget, J. (1954). *The construction of reality in the child* (8th ed.). New York: Basic Books.

Piaget, J. (1968). *Six psychological studies.* New York: Vintage Books.

Pickens, J., & Field, T. (1993). Facial expressivity in infants of depressed mothers. *Developmental Psychology, 29,* 986–988.

Piek, J. P. (1996). A quantitative analysis of spontaneous kicking in two-month-old infants. *Human Movement Science, 15,* 707–726.

Piek, J. P., & Gasson, N. (1999). Spontaneous kicking in fullterm and preterm infants: Are there leg asymmetries? *Human Movement Science, 18,* 377–395.

Porges, S. W. (1992). Vagal tone: A physiological marker of stress vulnerability. *Pediatrics, 90,* 498–504.

Porges, S. W. (1995). Cardiac vagal tone: A physiological index of stress. *Neuroscience and Biobehavioral Reviews, 19,* 225–233.

Porges, S. W. (2001). The polyvagal theory: Phylogenetic substrates of a social nervous system. *International Journal of Psychophysiology, 42*(2), 123–146.

Porges, S. W. (2003). The polyvagal theory: Phylogenetic contributions to social behavior. *Physiology and Behavior, 79,* 503–513.

Porges, S. W., Doussard-Roosevelt, J. A., Portales, A. L., & Greenspan, S. I. (1996). Infant regulation of the vagal "brake" predicts child behavior problems: A psychobiological model of social behavior. *Develomental Psychobiology, 29,* 697–712.

Porges, S. W., Doussard-Roosevelt, J. A., Portales, A. L., & Suess, P. E. (1994). Cardiac vagal tone: Stability and relation to difficultness in infants and 3-year-olds. *Develomental Psychobiology, 27*, 289–300.

Porges, S. W., Doussard-Roosevelt, J. A., Stifter, C. A., McClenny, B. D., & Riniolo, T. C. (1999). Sleep state and vagal regulation of heart period patterns in the human newborn: An extension of the polyvagal theory. *Psychophysiology, 36*(1), 14–21.

Prechtl, H. F. (1958). The directed head turning response and allied movements of the human baby. *Behaviour, 13*, 211–242.

Prechtl, H. F. R. (1972). Patterns of reflex behavior related to sleep in the human infant. In C. D. Clemente, D. P. Purpura, & F. E. Mayer (Eds.), *Sleep and the maturing nervous system* (pp. 287–301). New York: Academic Press.

Prechtl, H. F. R. (1974). The behavioral states of the newborn infant. *Brain Research, 76*, 185–212.

Prechtl, H. F. R. (1977). *The neurological examination of the newborn infant* (2nd ed.). Clinics in Developmental Medicine, No. 63. London: Lavenham Press.

Prechtl, H. F. (1981a). Assessment methods for the newborn infant: A critical evaluation. In P. Stratton (Ed.), *Psychobiology of the human newborn* (pp. 21–52). New York: Wiley.

Prechtl, H. F. R. (1981b). The study of neural development as a perspective of clinical problems. In K. J. Connolly & H. R. Prechtl (Eds.), *Maturation and development: Biological and psychological perspectives* (pp. 198–215). Philadelphia: J. B. Lippincott.

Prechtl, H. F., & Beintema, D. (1964). *The neurological examination of the newborn infant*. Clinics in Developmental Medicine, No. 29. London: Lavenham Press.

Prigogine, I., & Stengers, I. (1984). *Order out of chaos: Man's new dialogue with nature*. New York: Basic Books.

Provence, S., & Lipton, R. C. (1962). *Infants in institutions*. New York: International Universities Press.

Radke-Yarrow, M. (1987, April 23). *A developmental study of depressed and normal parents and their children*. Paper presented at meeting of Society for Research in Child Development, Baltimore, MD.

Radloff, L. S. (1977). The CES-D scale: A self-report depression scale for research in the general population. *Journal of Applied Psychological Measurement, 1*, 385–401.

Rakic, P. (1978). Neuronal migration and contact guidance in primate telencephalon. *Postgraduate Medical Journal, 54*(Suppl. 1), 25–42.

Ramsay, D., & Lewis, M. (2003). Reactivity and regulation in cortisol and behavioral responses to stress. *Child Development, 74*(2), 456–464.

Redfern, P. A. (1970). Neuromuscular transmission in newborn rats. *Journal of Physiology, 209*, 701–710.

Reznick, J. S., Kagan, J., Snidman, N., et al. (1986). Inhibited and uninhibited children: A follow-up study. *Child Development, 57*, 660–680.

Richards, J. E. (1987). Infant visual sustained attention and respiratory sinus arrhythmia. *Child Development, 58*, 488–496.

Richards, M. P. M., & Bernall, J. F. (1972). An observational study of mother-infant interaction. In N. B. Jones (Ed.), *Ethological studies of child behavior* (pp. 175–197). Cambridge, UK: Cambridge University Press.

Richardson, G. A., & Day, N. L. (1991). Maternal and neonatal effects of moderate cocaine use during pregnancy. *Neurotoxicology and Teratology, 13*, 455–460.

Richman, A. L., Miller, P. M., & LeVine, R. A. (1992). Cultural and educational variations in maternal responsiveness. *Developmental Psychology, 28*, 614–621.

Ricks, M. (1981). *Predicting one-year competence from earlier infant behavior: A methodological inquiry*. Master's thesis, University of Massachusetts, Amherst.

Rijt-Plooij, H.H.H.C. van de, & Plooij, F. X. (1993). Distinct periods of mother-infant conflict in normal development: Sources of progress and germs of pathology. *Journal of Child Psychology and Psychiatry, 34*, 229–245.

Robins, L. (1974). *Deviant children grown up.* New York: Krieger.

Robins, L., Cottler, L., & Keating, S. (1991). *NIMH diagnostic interview schedule, version III* (rev. ed.). Rockville, MD: National Institute of Mental Health.

Robinson, J. L., Little, C., & Biringen, Z. (1993). Emotional communication in mother-toddler relationships: Evidence for early gender differentiation. *Merrill-Palmer Quarterly, 39,* 496–517.

Robson, K. S. (1967). The role of eye-to-eye contact in maternal-infant attachment. *Journal of Child Psychology and Psychiatry, 8,* 13–25.

Roozendaal, B., Quirarte, G. L., & McGaugh, J. L. (1997). Stress-activated hormonal systems and the regulation of memory storage. In Yehuda, R. & McFarlance, A., *Psychobiology of posttraumatic stress disorder* (pp. 247–258). New York: New York Academy of Sciences.

Rose-Jacobs, R., & Fetters, L. (1989). Quantitative assessment of the development of reaching in healthy preterm infants at 7, 9 and 12 months. *Pediatric Physical Therapy, 1,* 183.

Rosenbaum, J. F., Biederman, J., Gersten, M., Hirshfeld, D. R., Meminger, S. R., Herman, J. B., et al. (1988). Behavioral inhibition in children of parents with panic disorder and agoraphobia: A controlled study. *Archives of General Psychiatry, 45,* 463–470.

Rosenbaum, J. F., Biederman, J., Hirshfeld, D. R., Bolduc, E. A., & Chaloff, J. (1991). Behavioral inhibition in children: A possible precursor to panic disorder or social phobia. *Journal of Clinical Psychiatry, 52*(11, Suppl.), 5–9.

Rosenblith, J. F. (1961). The modified Graham behavior test for neotates: Test-retest reliability, normative data and hypotheses for future work. *Biology of the Neonate, 3,* 174–192.

Rosenblum, K. L., McDonough, S., Muzik, M., Miller, A., & Sameroff, A. J. (2002). Maternal representations of the infant: Associations with infant response to the still-face. *Child Development, 73,* 999–1015.

Rosenblum, K. L., & Muzik, M. (2004). Mothers' representations of their infants and infant still face response: Individual differences from 7 to 15 months. *International Conference on Infant Studies.*

Rothbart, M., & Derryberry, D. (1981). Development of individual differences in infant temperament. In M. Lamb & A. Brown (Eds.), *Advances in developmental psychology* (pp. 37–87). Hillsdale, NJ: Erlbaum.

Rothbart, M., & Derryberry, D. (1984). Emotion, attention and temperament. In C. Izard, J. Kagan, & R. Zajonc (Eds.), *Emotion, cognition and behavior* (pp. 133–156). New York: Cambridge University Press.

Rutter, M. (1981). *Maternal deprivation reassessed* (2nd ed.). New York: Penguin.

Rutter, M. (2006). *Genes and behavior.* Malden: Blackwell.

Rutter, M., & Garmezy, N. (1983). Developmental psychopathology. In M. M. Haith, J. J. Campos, & P. H. Mussen (Series Eds.), *Handbook of child psychology* (Vol. 2, pp. 775–911). New York: Wiley.

Rutter, M., Yule, B., Quinton, D., Rowland, O., Yule, W., & Berger, M. (1974). Attainment and adjustment in two geographical areas: III. *British Journal of Psychiatry, 123,* 520–533.

Ryan, J. (1974). Early language development: Towards a communicational analysis. In P. M. Richards (Ed.), *The integration of a child into a social world.* Cambridge, UK: Cambridge University Press.

Ryan, L., Ehrlich, S., & Finnegan, L. (1987). Cocaine abuse in pregnancy: Effects on the fetus and newborn. *Neurotoxicology and Teratology, 9,* 295–299.

Ryan, T. A., Joiner, B. L., & Ryan, B. F. (1982). *Minitab reference manual* (Minitab Project). University Park: Pennsylvania State University, Department of Statistics.

Sackett, G. P. (1968). The persistence of abnormal behavior in monkeys following isolation rearing. In R. Porter (Ed.), *The role of learning in psychotherapy* (pp. 3–37). London: Churchill.

Saint-Anne Dargassies, S. (1977). *Neurological development in the full-term and premature neonate.* New York: Elsevier North Holland.

Sameroff, A. J. (1978). Organization and stability of newborn behavior: A commentary on the Brazelton Neonatal Behavioral Assessment Scale. *Monographs of the Society for Research in Child Development* 43(5–6, Serial No. 177).

Sameroff, A. J., & Chandler, J. J. (1975). Reproductive risk and the continuum of caretaking causality. In R. D. Horowitz (Ed.), *Review of Child Development Research, Vol. IV.* Chicago: University of Chicago Press.

Sameroff, A., Seifer, R., & Zax, M. (1982). Early development of children at risk for emotional disorder. *Monographs of the Society for Research in Child Development, 47*(7, Serial No. 199).

Sander, L. W. (1962). Issues in early mother-child interaction. *Journal of the American Academy of Child Psychiatry, 1,* 141–166.

Sander, L. W. (1975). Infant and caretaking environment: Investigation and conceptualization of adaptive behavior in a system of increasing complexity. In E. J. Anthony (Ed.), *Explorations in child psychiatry* (pp. 129–166). New York: Plenum.

Sander, L. W. (1976). Issues in early mother-child interaction. In L. Rexford, W. Sander, & T. Shapiro (Eds.), *Infant psychiatry: A new synthesis* (pp. 127–147). New Haven, CT: Yale University Press.

Sander, L. W. (1977). The regulation of exchange in the infant-caregiver systems and some aspects of the context-contest relationship. In M. Lewis & L. Rosenblum (Eds.), *Interaction, conversation and the development of language* (pp. 133–155). New York: Wiley.

Sander, L. (1980). New knowledge about the infant from current research: Implications for psychoanalysis. *Journal of the American Psychoanalytic Association, 28,* 181–198.

Sander, L. W. (1983a). Polarity, paradox, and the organizing process of development. In J. D. Call, E. Galenson, & R. L. Tyson (Eds.), *Frontiers of infant psychiatry* (pp. 333–345). New York: Basic Books.

Sander, L. W. (1983b). A twenty-five-year follow-up of the Pavenstedt Longitudinal Research Project: Its relation to early intervention. In J. D. Call, E. Galenson, & R. L. Tyson (Eds.). *Frontiers of infant psychiatry* (pp. 225–230). New York: Basic Books.

Sander, L. (1987). Awareness of inner experience. *Child Abuse and Neglect, 2,* 339–346.

Sander, L. (1988). The event-structure of regulation in the neonate-caregiver system as a biological background for early organisation of psychic structure. In A. Goldberg (Ed.), *Frontiers in self psychology* (pp. 64–77). Hillsdale, NJ: Analytic Press.

Sander, L. (1991). *Recognition process: Specificity and organisation in early human development.* Unpublished manuscript.

Sander, L. (1995). *Thinking about developmental process: Wholeness, specificity, and the organization of conscious experiencing.* New York: American Psychological Association.

Sander, L. (1997). Paradox and resolution. In J. Osofsky (Ed.), *Handbook of child and adolescent Psychiatry* (pp. 153–160). New York: John Wiley.

Sandler, J. (1987). *Projection, identification, projective identification.* New York: International Universities Press.

Sandler, J., & Fonagy, P. (Eds.). (1997). *Recovered memories of abuse: True or false.* London: Karnac Books and International Universities Press.

Scanlon, J. W., & Hollenback, A. R. (1983). Neonatal behavioral effects of anesthetic exposure during pregnancy. In E. A. Freidman, A. Milusky, & A. Gluck (Eds.), *Advances in perinatal medicine* (pp. 165–184). New York: Plenum.

Schaefer, E. S., & Bell, R. Q. (1958). Development of a parental attitude research instrument. *Child Development, 29,* 339–361.

Schaffer, A. J., & Avery, M. (1971). *Diseases of the newborn* (3rd ed.). Philadelphia: Saunders.

Schaffer, H. R. (1977a). Early interactive development. In H. R. Schaffer (Ed.). *Studies in mother-infant interaction* (pp. 3–18). New York: Academic Press

Schaffer, H. R. (Ed.). (1977b). *Studies in mother-infant interaction.* New York: Academic Press.

Schaffer, H. R. (1984). *The child's entry into a social world.* New York: Academic Press.

Schaffer, H. R., Collis, G. M., & Parson, G. (1977). Vocal interchange and visual regard in verbal and pre-verbal children. In H. R. Schaffer (Ed.), *Studies in mother-infant interaction* (pp. 291–325). New York: Academic Press.

Schebesta, P. (1933). *Among Congo pygmies.* London: Hutchinson.

Scheibel, M. E., Davies, T. L., & Scheibel, A. B. (1973). Maturation of reticular dendrites: Loss of spines and development of bundles. *Experiments in Neurology, 38,* 301–310.

Scherer, K. (1982). The assessment of vocal expression in infants and children. In C. E. Izard (Ed.), *Measuring emotions in infants and children* (pp. 127–163). Cambridge, UK: Cambridge University Press.

Schiff, W. (1965). Perception of impending collision: A study of visually directed avoidant behavior. *Psychology Monographs, 79*(11), 1-26.

Schneider, J. W., & Chasnoff, I. J. (1992). Motor assessment of cocaine/polydrug exposed infants at age 4 months. *Neurotoxicology and Teratology, 14,* 97–101.

Schore, A. N. (1994). *Affect regulation and the origin of self: The neurobiology of emotional development.* Hillsdale, NJ: Erlbaum.

Schore, A. N. (2001). Effects of a secure attachment relationship on right brain development, affect regulation, and infant mental health. *Infant Mental Health Journal, 22,* 7–66.

Schwaber, E. (1998). The non-verbal dimension in psychoanalysis: "State" and its clinical vicissitudes. *International Journal of Psycho-Analysis, 79,* 667–680.

Schwartz, G. G., & Rosenblum, L. A. (1983). Allometric influences on primate mothers and infants. In L. Rosenblum & H. Moltz (Eds.), *Symbiosis in parent-young interactions.* New York: Plenum.

Schweinfurth, G. (1874). *The heart of Africa* (2 vols., W. Reade, Trans.). New York: Harper.

Seashore, M. H., Leifer, A. D., Barnett, C. R., & Leiderman, P. H. (1973). The effects of denial of early mother-infant interactions on maternal self-confidence. *Journal of Personality and Social Psychology, 26,* 369–378.

Seifer, R. (1995). Perils and pitfalls of high-risk research. *Developmental Psychology, 31,* 420–424.

Seligman, M. E. P. (1975). *Helplessness: On depression, development and death.* San Francisco: W. H. Freeman.

Seligman, S. (1994). Applying psychoanalysis in an unconventional context: Adapting infant-parent psychotherapy to a changing population. *Psychoanalytic Study of the Child, 49,* 481–510.

Seligman, S. (1999). Integrating Kleinian theory and intersubjective infant observations: Observing projective identification. *Psychoanalytic Dialogues, 9,* 129–159.

Sepkoski, C. M. (1985). Maternal obstetric medication and newborn behavior. In J. W. Scanlon (Ed.), *Perinatal anesthesia* (pp. 131–173). London: Blackwell Scientific.

Shapiro, B., Fagen, J., Prigot, J., Carroll, M., & Shalan, J. (1998). Infants' emotional and regulatory behaviors in response to violations of expectancies. *Infant Behavior and Development, 21,* 299–313.

Shea, E. (1982). *The development and evaluation of a scale to measure maternal self-esteem.* Masters thesis, University of Massachusetts, Amherst.

Shea, E., & Tronick, E. (1982). *Maternal self-esteem as affected by infant health and family support.* Paper presented at the annual meeting of the American Psychological Association, Washington, DC.

Shedler, J., Mayman, M., & Manis, M. (1993). The illusion of mental health. *American Psychologist, 48,* 1117–1131.

Shereshefsky, P. M., & Yarrow, L. J. (1973). *Psychological aspects of a first pregnancy and early postnatal adaptation.* New York: Raven.

Sherrington, C. S. (1906). *The integrative action of the nervous system.* New Haven, NJ: Yale University Press.

Shore, A. N. (1994). *Affect regulation and the origin of the self: The neurobiology of emotional development.* Hillsdale, NJ: Erlbaum.

Silver, J. (1978). Cell death during development of the nervous system. In M. Jacobson (Ed.), *Handbook of sensory physiology* (Vol. 9, pp. 419–436). Berlin: Springer/Verlag.

Smythe, J. W., McCormick, C. M., & Meaney, M. J. (1996). Median eminence corticotrophin-releasing hormone content following prenatal stress and neonatal handling. *Brain Research Bulletin, 40*(3), 195–199.

Spangler, G., & Grossmann, K. E. (1993). Biobehavioral organization in securely and insecurely attached infants. *Child Development, 64,* 1439–1450.

Spietz, A. L., & Eyres, S. J. (1977). Instrumentation and findings: The environment. In K. E. Barnard & S. R. Rartner (Eds.), *Nursing child assessment project.* Washington, DC: Division of Health, Education, and Welfare.

Spinelli, D. N. (1987). Plasticity triggering experiences, nature, and the dual genesis of brain structure and function. In N. Gunzenhauser (Ed.), *Infant stimulation: For whom, what kind, when, and how much?* (pp. 21–29). Still man, NJ: Johnson and Johnson.

Spinelli, D. N., Jensen, F. E., & Viana di Prisco, G. (1980). Early experience effect on dendritic branching in normally reared kittens. *Experimental Neurology, 68,* 1–11.

Spitz, R. A. (1963). Ontogenesis: The proleptic function of emotion. In P. H. Knapp (Ed.), *The expression of the emotions in man* (pp. 36–64). New York: International Universities Press.

Spitz, R. (Ed.). (1965). *The first year of life: A psychoanalytic study of normal and deviant development of object relations.* New York: International Universities Press.

Spitz, R. A., & Cobliner, W. G. (1965). Emotional deficiency diseases of the infant. In R. A. Spitz (Ed.), *The first year of life: A psychoanalytic study of normal and deviant development of object relations* (pp. 267–284). New York: International Universities Press.

Spitz, R. A., & Wolf, R. M. (1946). The smiling response: A contribution to the ontogenesis of social relations. *Genetic Psychology Monographs, 34,* 57–125.

Spitzer, R. L., Williams, J. B.W., Gibbon, M., et al. (1988). *Structured clinical interview for DSM-III-R.* New York: Biometric Research, New York State Psychiatric Institute.

Sroufe, L. (1979a). The coherence of individual development: Early care, attachment, and subsequent developmental issues. *American Psychologist, 34,* 834–841.

Sroufe, L. (1979b). Socioemotional development. In J. D. Osofsky (Ed.), *Handbook of infant development* (pp. 462–516). New York: Wiley.

Sroufe, L. A. (1998). The role of infant-caregiver attachment in development. In J. Belsky & T. Nezworski (Eds.), *Clinical implications of attachment* (pp. 18–38). Mahwah, NJ: Erlbaum.

Sroufe, L., & Waters, E. (1977). Attachment as an organizational contact. *Child Development, 48,* 1184-1199.

Stack, D. M., & Muir, D. W. (1990). Tactile stimulation as a component of social interchange: New interpretations for the still-face effect. *British Journal of Developmental Psychology, 8,* 131–145.

Stansbury, K., & Gunnar, M. R. (1994). Adrenocortical activity and emotion regulation. In N. A. Fox (Ed.), *The development of emotion regulation: Biological and behav-*

ioral considerations (59 ed., pp. 108–134). Monographs of the Society for Research in Child Development.

Stechler, G. (1996, April). *Self disclosure and affect.* Paper presented at the American Psychological Association Division 39 meeting.

Stechler, G., & Halton, A. (1982). Prenatal influences on human development. In B. Wolman (Ed.), *Handbook of developmental psychology.* Englewood Cliffs, NJ: Prentice-Hall.

Stechler, G., & Kaplan, S. (1980). The development of the self: A psychoanalytic perspective. *Psychoanalytic Study of the Child, 35,* 85–105.

Stechler, G., & Latz, M. A. (1966). Some observations on attention and arousal in the human neonate. *This Journal of the American Academy of child Psychiatry, 5*(3), 517–525.

Stein, A., Woolley, H., Cooper, S. D., & Fairburn, C. G. (1994). An observational study of mothers with eating disorders and their infants. *Journal of Child Psychology and Psychiatry, 35,* 733–748.

Stengers, I., & Prigogine, I. (1997). *The end of certainty.* New York: Simon & Schuster.

Sterba, R. F. (1940). The dynamics of the dissolution of the transference resistance. *Psychoanalysis Quarterly, 9,* 363–379.

Stern, D. A. (1971). A micro-analysis of mother-infant interaction: Behavior regulating social contact between a mother and her 31/2 month old twins. *Journal of the American Academy of Child Psychiatry, 10,* 501-517.

Stern, D. N. (1974a). The goal and structure of mother-infant play. *Journal of the American Academy of Child Psychiatry, 13,* 402–421.

Stern, D. N. (1974b). Mother and infant at play: The dyadic interaction involving facial, vocal, and gaze behaviors. In M. Lewis & L. Rosenblum (Eds.), *The effect of the infant on its caregiver* (pp. 187–213). New York: Wiley.

Stern, D. N. (1976). A microanalysis of mother-infant interaction: Behavior regulating social contact between a mother and her 3-1/2-month-old twins. In L. Rexford, W. Sander, & T. Shapiro (Eds.), *Infant psychiatry: A new synthesis* (pp. 113–126). New Haven, CT: Yale University Press.

Stern, D. (1977). *The first relationship.* Cambridge, MA: Harvard University Press.

Stern, D. (1985). *The interpersonal world of the infant: A view from psychoanalysis and developmental psychology.* New York: Basic Books.

Stern, D. N. (1994). One way to build a clinically relevant baby. *Infant Mental Health Journal, 15,* 9–25.

Stern, D. N. (1995). *The motherhood constellation.* New York: Basic Books.

Stern, D., & Gibbon, J. (1978). Temporal expectancies of social behaviors in mother-infant play. In E. Thoman (Ed.), *Origins of the infant's social responsiveness* (pp. 409–429). New York: Erlbaum.

Stern, D. N., Hofer, L., Haft, W., & Dore, J. (1985). Affect attunement: A descriptive account of the inter-modal communication of affective states between mothers and infants. In T. Field & N. Fox (Eds.), *Social perception in infants.* Norwood, NJ: Ablex.

Stern, D., Sander, L., Nahum, J. P., Harrison, A. M., Lyons-Ruth, K., Morgan, A. C., et al. (1998). Non-interpretive mechanisms in psychoanalytic therapy. *International Journal of Psychoanalysis, 79,* 903–921.

Stifter, C. A., & Braungart, J. M. (1995). The regulation of negative reactivity in infancy: Function and development. *Developmental Psychology, 31,* 448–455.

Stifter, C. A., & Fox, N. A. (1990). Behavioral and psychophysiological indices of temperament in infancy. *Developmental Psychology, 26,* 582–588.

Stifter, C. A., Fox, N. A., & Porges, S. W. (1989). Facial expressivity and vagal tone in 5- and 10-month-old infants. *Infant Behavior and Development, 12,* 127–138.

Stifter, C. A., & Jain, A. (1996). Psychophysiological correlates of infant temperament: Stability of behavior and autonomic patterning from 5 to 18 months. *Developmental Psychobiology, 29,* 379–391.

Stolorow, R. D., & Atwood, G. (1992). *Contexts of being.* Hillsdale, NJ: Analytic Press.

Stolorow, R. D., Atwood, G., & Brandchaft, B. (Eds.). (1994). *The intersubjective perspective.* Northvale, NJ: Jason Aronson.

Strachey, J. (1934). The nature of the therapeutic action of psychoanalysis. In M. Bergmann & F. Hartman (Eds.), *The evolution of psychoanalytic technique* (pp. 331–360). New York: Basic Books.

Sullivan, H. S. (1953). *The interpersonal theory of psychology.* New York: Norton.

Svejda, M. J., Pannabecker, B. J., & Emde, R. N. (1982). Parent-to-infant attachment: A critique of the early bonding model. In R. N. Emde & R. J. Harmon (Eds.), *The development of attachment and affiliative systems* (pp. 83–94). New York: Plenum.

Teti, D. M., & Gelfand, D. M. (1991). Behavioral competence among mothers of infants in the first year: The mediational role of maternal self-efficacy. *Child Development, 62,* 918–929.

Teti, D. M., Gelfand, D. M., Messinger, D. S., & Isabella, R. (1995). Maternal depression and the quality of early attachment: An examination of infants, preschoolers, and their mothers. *Developmental Psychology, 31,* 364–376.

Teti, D. M., Gelfand, D. M., & Pompa, J. (1990). Depressed mothers' behavioral competence with their infants: Demographic and psychosocial correlates. *Developmental Psychopathology, 2,* 259–270.

Thelen, E. (1985). Developmental origins of motor coordination: Leg movement in human infants. *Developmental Psychobiology, 18,* 1–22.

Thelen, E. (1986). *Development of coordinated movement: Implications for early human development.* Boston: Martinus Nijhoff.

Thelen, E. (1995). Motor development: A new synthesis. *American Psychologist, 50*(2) 79–95.

Thelen, E., & Fisher, D. M. (1983). From spontaneous to instrumental behavior: Kinematic analysis of movement changes during very early learning. *Child Development, 54,* 129–140.

Thelen, E., Jensen, J. L., Kamm, K., Corbetta, D., Schneider, K., & Zemicke, R. F. (1991). Infant motor development: Implications for motor neuroscience. *Tutorials in Motor Neuroscience, 62,* 43–57.

Thelen, E., & Smith, L. B. (1994). *A dynamic systems approach to the development of cognition and action.* Cambridge, MA: MIT Press.

Thoma, H., & Kachele, H. (1987). *Psychoanalytic practice: Vol. 1. Principles.* Berlin: Springer-Verlag.

Thomas, E. A. C., & Malone, T. W. (1979). On the dynamics of two-person interactions. *Psychological Review, 86,* 331–360.

Thomas, E. A. C., & Martin, J. A. (1976). Analyses of parent-infant interaction. *Psychological Review, 83,* 141–156.

Toda, S., & Fogel, A. (1993). Infant response to the still-face situation at 3 and 6 months. *Developmental Psychology, 29,* 532–538.

Tomasello, M. (2001). *The cultural origins of human cognition.* Cambridge, MA: Harvard University Press.

Torgeson, S. (1983). Genetic factors in anxiety disorders. *Archives of General Psychiatry, 40,* 1085–1089.

Touwen, B. C. L. (1976). *Neurological development in infancy.* Clinics in Developmental Medicine, No. 58. Philadelphia: Lippincott.

Trevarthen, C. (1974). Conversations with a two-month-old. *New Scientist, 896,* 230–235.

Trevarthen, C. (1977). Descriptive analyses of infant communicative behavior. In H. R. Schaffer (Ed.), *Studies in mother-infant interaction* (pp. 227–270). London: Academic Press.

Trevarthen, C. (1979). Communication and cooperation in early infancy: A description of primary intersubjectivity. In M. M. Bullowa (Ed.), *Before speech: The beginning of interpersonal communication* (pp. 321–349). Cambridge, UK: Cambridge University Press.

Trevarthen, C. (1980). The foundations of intersubjectivity: Development of interpersonal and cooperative understanding in infants. In D. Olsen (Ed.), *The social foundations of language and thought: Essays in honor of J. S. Bruner* (pp. 316–342). New York: Norton.

Trevarthen, C. (1989a). Development of early social interactions and the affective regulations of brain growth. In C. von Euler & H. Forssberg (Eds.), *The neurobiology of early infant behavior.* New York: Macmillan.

Trevarthen, C. (1989b). Signs before speech. In T. A. Sebeok & J. Umiker-Sebeok (Eds.), *The semiotic web.* Berlin: Mouton de Gruyter.

Trevarthen, C. (1990). Growth and education of the hemispheres. In C. Trevarthen (Ed.), *Brain circuits and functions of the mind* (pp. 334–363). Cambridge, UK: Cambridge University Press.

Trevarthen, C. (1993a). Brain, science and the human spirit. In J. B. Ashbrook et al. (Eds.), *Brain, culture and the human spirit* (pp. 129–181). Lanham, MD: University Press of America.

Trevarthen, C. (1993b). The function of emotions in early infant communication and development. In J. Nadel & L. Camaioni (Eds.), *New perspectives in early communicative development* (pp. 48–81). London: Routledge.

Trevarthen, C., & Hadley, P. (1978). Secondary inter-objectivity: Confidence, confining and act of meaning in the first year. In A. Lock (Ed.), *Action, gesture and symbol: The emergence of language* (pp. 183–229). New York: Academic Press.

Tronick, E. Z. (1980). On the primacy of social skills. In D. B. Sawin, L. O. Walker, & J. H. Penticuff (Eds.), *The exceptional infant: Vol. 4. Psychosocial risks in infant-environmental transactions* (pp. 144–158). New York: Brunner/Mazel.

Tronick, E. (1981). Infant's communicative intent. In B. Stark (Ed.), *Language behavior in infancy and early childhood* (pp. 5–16). Holland: Elsevier.

Tronick, E. Z. (Ed.). (1982). *Social interchange in infancy: Affect, cognition, and communication.* Baltimore, MD: University Park Press.

Tronick, E. Z. (1985). Stress and coping in young infants. In T. Field, P. McCabe, & N. Schneiderman (Eds.), *Stress and coping, Vol. 2.* Hillsdale, NJ: Erlbaum.

Tronick, E. Z. (1987). The Neonatal Behavioral Assessment Scale as a biomarker of the effects of environmental agents on the newborn. *Environmental Health Perspectives, 74,* 185–189.

Tronick, E. Z. (1989). Emotions and emotional communication in infants. *American Psychologist, 44,* 112–119.

Tronick, E. Z. (2002). Dyadically expanded states of consciousness: And the process of normal and abnormal development.

Tronick, E. Z. (Ed.). (1998). Interactions that effect change in psychotherapy: A model used on infant research. *Infant Mental Health Journal, 19,* 1–290.

Tronick, E. Z. (2001). Emotional connections and dyadic consciousness in infant-mother and patient-therapist interactions. *Psychoanalytic Dialogues, 11*(2), 187–194.

Tronick, E. Z. (2002a). A model of infant mood states and Sandarian affective waves. *Psychoanalytic Dialogues, 12,* 73–99.

Tronick, E. Z. (2002c). The increasing differentiation and non-transferability of ways of being together: The primary attachment is specific, not prototypical. *Journal of Infant, Child and Adolescent Psychotherapy, 2*(4), 47–60.

Tronick, E. Z. (2002d). *Making and breaking human connections: Dyadic expansion of consciousness and moving away from entropy.* Paper presented at: Symposium on Affective Interaction: A Tool for Social and Cognitive Development. International Conference on Infant Studies, Toronto.

Tronick, E. Z. (2005). *Relational models need to grow up and understand the change in meaning systems from infancy to adulthood.* Manuscript in preparation.

Tronick, E. Z. (2003a). Infant moods and the chronicity of depressive symptoms: The co-creation of unique ways of being together for good or Ill. Paper 1: The normal process of development and the formation of moods. *Zeitschrift für Psychosomatische Medizin und Psychotherapie, 4,* 408–425.

Tronick, E. Z. (2003b). Of course all relationships are unique: How co-creative processes generate unique mother-infant and patient-therapist relationships and change other relationships. *Psychological Inquiry, 23*(3), 473–491.

Tronick, E. Z. (2004). Why is connection with others so critical? Dyadic meaning making, messiness, and complexity-governed selective processes which co-create and expand individuals' states of consciousness: The assembling of states of consciousness and experiential impelling certitude from the messiness of age-possible meanings of emotions, actions and symbols. In J. Nadel & D. Muir (Eds.), *Emotional development* (pp. 262–293). New York: Oxford University Press.

Tronick, E. (in press). The stress of normal development and interaction leads to the development of resilience and variation. In B. Lester, A. Masten, B. McEwen (eds.), *Resilience in children.* New York Academy of Sciences.

Tronick, E. Z., Als, H., & Adamson, L. (1979). The structure of early face-to-face communicative interactions. In M. Bullowa (Ed.), *Before speech: The beginning of interpersonal communication* (pp. 349–372). Cambridge: Cambridge University.

Tronick, E. Z., Als, H., Adamson, L., Wise, S., & Brazelton, T. B. (1978). The infant's response to entrapment between contradictory messages in face-to-face interaction. *Journal of the American Academy of Child and Adolescent Psychiatry, 17,* 1–13.

Tronick, E., Als, H., & Brazelton, T. B. (1977). Mutuality in mother-infant interaction. *Journal of Communication, 27,* 74–79.

Tronick, E., Als, H., & Brazelton, T. B. (1979). Early development of neonatal behavior. In F. Faulkener & J. M. Tanner (Eds.), *Human growth* (Vol. 3, pp. 305–328). New York: Plenum.

Tronick, E. Z., Als, H., & Brazelton, T. B. (1980a). The infant's communicative competencies and the achievement of intersubjectivity. In M. R. Key (Ed.), *The relationship of verbal and nonverbal communication* (pp. 261–274). The Hague: Mouton.

Tronick, E., Als, H., & Brazelton, T. B. (1980b). Monadic phases: A structural descriptive analysis of infant-mother face-to-face interaction. *Merrill-Palmer Quarterly of Behavior and Development, 26,* 3–24.

Tronick, E. Z., & Beeghly, M. (1999). Prenatal cocaine exposure, child development, and the compromising effects of cumulative risk. *Clinics in Perinatology, 26,* 151–171.

Tronick, E. Z., Beeghly, M., Fetters, L., & Weinberg, M. K. (1991). New methodologies for evaluating residual brain damage in infants exposed to drugs of abuse: Objective methods for describing movements, facial expressions, and communicative behaviors. In M. M. Kilbey & K. Asghar (Eds.), *Methodological issues in controlled studies on effects of prenatal exposure to drug abuse* (Monograph Series No. 114, pp. 262–290). Rockville, MD: National Institute on Drug Abuse.

Tronick, E. Z., Beeghly, M., Weinberg, M. K., & Olson, K. L. (1997). Postpartum exuberance: Not all women in a highly positive emotional state in the postpartum period are denying depression and distress. *Infant Mental Health Journal, 18,* 406–423.

Tronick, E. Z., & Brazelton, T. B. (1980). The infant's communicative competencies and the achievement of intersubjectivity. In M. R. Key (Ed.), *The relationship of verbal and nonverbal communication* (pp. 261–274). The Hague: Mouton.

Tronick, E. Z., Brazelton, T. B., & Als, H. (1978). The structure of face-to-face interaction and its developmental functions. *Sign Language Studies, 18,* 1–16.

Tronick, E. Z., Bruschweiler-Stern, N., Harrison, A. M., Lyons-Ruth, K., Morgan, A. C., Nahum, J. P., et al. (1998). Dyadically expanded states of consciousness and the process of therapeutic change. *Infant Mental Health Journal, 19,* 290–299.

Tronick, E. Z., & Cohn, J. F. (1987). *Revised monadic phases manual.* Unpublished manuscript.

Tronick, E. Z., & Cohn, J. F. (1989). Infant-mother face-to-face interaction: Age and gender differences in coordination and the occurrence of miscoordination. *Child Development, 60,* 85–92.

Tronick, E. Z., Cohn, J., & Shea, E. (1986). The transfer of affect between mother and infants. In T. B. Brazelton & M. W. Yogman (Eds.), *Affective development in infancy* (pp. 11–25). Norwood, NJ: Ablex.

Tronick, E. Z., & Field, T. (1986). *Maternal depression and infant disturbance: New directions for child development, Vol. 34.* London: Jossey-Bass.

Tronick, E. Z., & Gianino, A. (1980). An accounting of the transmission of maternal disturbance to the infant. *New Directions for Child Development,* 5–11.

Tronick, E. Z., & Gianino, A. (1986a). Interactive mismatch and repair: Challenges to the coping infant. *Zero to Three: Bulletin of the National Center for Clinical Infant Programs, 5,* 1–6.

Tronick, E. Z., & Gianino, A. (1986b). The transmission of maternal disturbance to the infant. In E. Z. Tronick & T. Field (Eds.), *Maternal depression and infant disturbance* (Vol. 34, pp. 31–47). San Francisco: Jossey-Bass.

Tronick, E., Krafchuk, E., Ricks, M., Cohn, J., & Winn, S. (1980). *Social interaction "normal and abnormal" maternal characteristics, and the organization of infant social behavior.* Paper presented at the Seminar on the Development of Infants and Parents, Boston.

Tronick, E., Krafchuk, E., Ricks, M., Cohn, J., & Winn, S. (1985). *Mother-infant face-to-face interaction at 3, 6, and 9 months: Content and matching.* Unpublished manuscript.

Tronick, E. Z., & Morelli, G. A. (1991). Foreword: The role of culture in brain organization, child development, and parenting. In J. K. Nugent, B. M. Lester, & T. B. Brazelton (Eds.). *The cultural context of infancy: Multicultural and interdisciplinary approaches to parent-infant relations* (2nd ed., pp. ix–xiii). Norwood, NJ: Ablex.

Tronick, E. Z., Morelli, G. A., & Ivey, P. K. (1992). The Efe forager infant and toddler's pattern of social relationships: Multiple and simultaneous. *Developmental Psychology, 28,* 568–577.

Tronick, E. Z., Morelli, G. A., & Winn, S. (1987). Multiple caretaking of Efe (Pygmy) infants. *American Anthropologist, 89,* 96–106.

Tronick, E. Z., Ricks, M., & Cohn, J. (1982). Maternal and infant affective exchanges: Patterns of adaptation. In T. Field & A. Fogel (Eds.), *Emotion and interaction: Normal and high risk infants* (pp. 83–100). Hillsdale, NJ: Erlbaum.

Tronick, E. Z., & Weinberg, M. (1980). Emotional regulation in infancy: Stability of regulatory behavior. Paper presented at *International Conference on Infant Studies.*

Tronick, E. Z., & Weinberg, M. K. (1990). *The Infant Regulatory Scoring System (IRSS).* Unpublished manuscript, Children's Hospital/Harvard Medical School, Boston.

Tronick, E. Z., & Weinberg, M. K. (1997). Depressed mothers and infants: Failure to form dyadic states of consciousness. In L. Murray & P. J. Cooper (Eds.), *Postpartum depression and child development* (pp. 54–81). New York: Guilford.

Tronick, E. Z., & Weinberg, M. K. (2000). Gender differences and their relation to maternal depression. In S. L. Johnson, A. M. Hayes, T. M. Field, N. Schneiderman, & P. M. McCabe (Eds.), *Stress, coping, and depression* (pp. 23–34). Mahwah, NJ: Erlbaum.

Tronick, E. Z., Weinberg, M. K., Beeghly, M., & Olson, K. L. (2003). *Short-term stability and change in infant, maternal, and mutual regulatory behavior during the face-to-face still-face paradigm.* Paper presented at the biennial meeting of the International Conference on Infant Studies, Chicago.

Tronick, E., Wise, S., Als, H., Adamson, L., Scanlon, J., & Brazelton, T. B. (1976). Regional obstetric anesthesia and newborn behavior: Effect over the first ten days of life. *Pediatrics, 58,* 94–100.

Truwit, C. L., Barkovich, A. J., Koch, T. K., & Ferriero, D. M. (1992). Cerebral palsy: MR findings in 40 patients. *American Journal of Nursing Research, 13,* 67–78.

Tsuang, M. T., & Faraone, S. Y. (1990). *The genetics of mood disorders.* Baltimore, MD: Johns Hopkins University Press.

Turnbull, C. M. (1962). *The forest people.* New York: Touchstone.

Twitchell, T. E. (1965). The anatomy of the grasping response. *Neuropsychologia, 3,* 247–259.

Uzgiris, I. C., Benson, J. B., & Vasek, M. E. (1983, April). *Matching behavior in mother-infant interaction.* Paper presented at the meeting of the Society for Research in Child Development, Detroit.

Vaal, J., van Soest, A. J., Hopkins, B., Sie, L. T. L., & van der Knaap, M. S. (2000). Development of spontaneous leg movements in infants with and without periventricular leukomalacia. *Experimental Brain Research, 135,* 94–105.

Valenstein, A. F. (1973). On attachment to painful feelings and the negative therapeutic reaction. *Psychoanalytic Study of the Child, 28,* 365–392.

van der Heide, J. C., Paolicelli, P. B., Boldrini, A., & Cioni, G. (1999). Kinematic and qualitative analysis of lower-extremity movements in preterm infants with brain lesions. *Physical Therapy, 79,* 546–557.

van Emmerik, R., & Wagenaar, R. C. (1996). Effects of walking velocity on relative phase dynamics in the trunk in human walking. *Journal of Biomechanics, 29,* 1175–1184.

Villar, J., Smeriglio, V. L., Martorell, R., Brown, C., & Klein, R. (1984). Heterogeneous growth and mental development of intrauterine growth-retarded infants during the first 3 years of life. *Pediatrics, 74,* 783–791.

Volpe, J. J. (1992a). Effect of cocaine use on the fetus. *New England Journal of Medicine, 327,* 399–407.

Volpe, J. J. (1992b). Value of MR in definition of the neuropathology of cerebral palsy in vivo. *American Journal of Neuroradiology, 13,* 79–83.

Von Bertalanffy, L. (1968). *General systems theory: Foundation, development, applications.* New York: Braziller.

von Hofsten, C. (1979). Development of visually directed reaching: The approach phase. *Journal of Human Movement Studies, 5,* 160–178.

Vygotsky, L. S. (1967). Play and its role in the mental development of the child. *Soviet Psychology, 5,* 6–18.

Vygotsky, L. (1978). *Mind in society.* Cambridge, MA: Harvard University Press.

Wagenaar, R. C., & Beek, W. J. (1992). Hemiplegic gait: A kinematic analysis using walking speed as a basis. *Journal of Biomechanics, 25,* 1007–1015.

Wagenaar, R. C., & Van Emmerik, R. E. A. (1994). Dynamics of pathological gait. *Human Movement Science, 13,* 441–471.

Wallach, H., & O'Connell, D. N. (1953). The kinetic depth effect. *Journal of Experimental Psychology, 45,* 205-217.

Wasz-Hockert, O., Lind, J., Vuorenkoski, V., Partanen, T., & Valanne, E. (1968). *The infant cry.* Clinics in Developmental Medicine, No. 29 (pp. 1–42). London: Lavenham Press.

Watzlawick, P., Beavin, J. H., & Jackson, D. (1967). *Pragmatics of human communication.* New York: Norton.

Weinberg, M. K. (1989). *The relation between facial expressions of emotion and behavior in 6-month-old infants.* Unpublished master's thesis, University of Massachusetts, Amherst.

Weinberg, M. K. (1992). *Sex differences in 6-month-old infants' affect and behavior: Impact on maternal caregiving.* Unpublished manuscript.

Weinberg, M. K. (1996, April 18). *Gender differences in depressed mothers' interactions with their infants.* Paper presented at International Conference on Infant Studies, Providence, RI.

Weinberg, M. K., Beeghly, M., Olson, K. L., et al. (2002, April). *Preschoolers' reactions to their still-faced mother.* Paper presented at International Conference on Infant Studies, Toronto, Canada.

Weinberg, M. K., Tronick, E. Z., Cohn, J. F., & Olson, K. L. (1998). Gender differences in emotional expressivity and self regulation during early infancy. *Developmental Psychology, 35,* 175–188.

Weinberg, M. K., & Olson, K. L. (1995). Maternal depression and infant gender differences. *American Academy of Child and Adolescent Psychiatry.*

Weinberg, M. K., Olson, K. L., Beeghly, M. & Tronick, E. Z., Making uup is hard to do, especially for mothers with high levels of depressive symptoms and their infant sons. *Journal of Child Psychology and Psychiatry, 47*(7), pp. 670–683.

Weinberg, M. K., Olson, K. L., Beeghly, M., & Tronick, E. Z. (2007). Effects of maternal depression and panic disorder on mother-infant interactive behavior in the face-to-face still-face paradigm. *Infant Mental Health Journal.*

Weinberg, M., & Tronick, E. Z. (1989). Facial expressions of emotion and social and object-oriented behavior are specifically related in 6-month-old infants [Abstract]. *Society for Research in Child Development.*

Weinberg, M. K., & Tronick, E. Z. (1992). Sex differences in emotional expression and affective regulation in 6-month-old infants [Abstract]. *Society for Pediatric Research, 31*(4), 15A.

Weinberg, M. K., & Tronick, E. (1994). Beyond the face: An empirical study of infant affective configurations of facial, vocal, gestural, and regulatory behaviors. *Child Development, 65,* 1495–1507.

Weinberg, M. K., & Tronick, E. (1996). Infant affective reactions to the resumption of maternal interaction after the still-face. *Child Development, 67,* 905–914.

Weinberg, M. K., & Tronick, E. (1997). Maternal depression and infant maladjustment: A failure of mutual regulation. In J. Noshpitz (Ed.), *The handbook of child and adolescent psychiatry* (pp. 177–191). New York: Wiley.

Weinberg, M. K., & Tronick, E. Z. (1998a). Emotional characteristics of infants associated with maternal depression and anxiety. *Pediatrics, 102*(5, Suppl.), 1298–1304.

Weinberg, M. K., & Tronick, E. Z. (1998b). The impact of maternal psychiatric illness on infant development. *Journal of Clinical Psychiatry, 59*(2), 53–61.

Weinberg, M. K., Tronick, E. Z., et al. (2003). Mother-infant mutual regulation at 3 months of age: Effects of interactive context, infant gender, and maternal depressive symptom status.

Weinberg, M. K., Tronick, E. Z., Beeghly, M., Olson, K. L., Kernan, H., & Riley, J. (2001). Subsyndromal depressive symptoms and major depression in postpartum women. *American Journal of Orthopsychiatry, 71,* 87–97.

Weinberg, M. K., Tronick, E. Z., Cohn, J. F., & Olson, K. L. (1999). Gender differences in emotional expressivity and self-regulation during early infancy. *Developmental Psychology, 35,* 175–188.

Weinstock, M., Fride, E., & Hertzberg, R. (1988). Prenatal stress effects on functional development of the offspring. *Progress in Brain Research, 73,* 319–331.

Weiss, B., & Spyker, J. M. (1974). Behavioral implications of prenatal and early postnatal exposure to chemical pollutants. *Pediatrics, 53,* 851–859.

Weissman, M. M., Leckman, J. F., Merikangas, K. R., et al. (1984). Depression and anxiety disorders in parents and children: Results from the Yale Family Study. *Archives of General Psychiatry, 41,* 845–852.

Weissman, M. M., & Paykel, E. S. (1974). *The depressed woman.* Chicago: University of Chicago.

White, B. P., Gunnar, M. R., Larson, M. C., Donzella, B., & Barr, R. G. (2000). Behavioral and physiological responsivity, sleep, and patterns of daily cortisol production in infants with and without colic. *Child Development, 71,* 862–877.

White, R. (1959). Motivation reconsidered: The concept of competence. *Psychological Review, 66,* 297–333.

Whiting, B. B. (1980). Culture and social behavior: A model for the development of social behavior. *Ethos, 8,* 95–116.

Whiting, B. B., & Whiting, J. W. M. (1975). *Children of six cultures.* Cambridge, MA: Harvard University Press.

Williams, E. A., & Gottman, J. (1982). *A user's guide to the Gottman-Williams time series analysis computer programs for social scientists.* New York: Oxford University Press.

Winn, S., Morelli, G. A., & Tronick, E. (1989). The infant and the group: A look at Efe care-taking practices. In J. K. Nugent, B. M. Lester, & T. B. Brazelton (Eds.), *The cultural context of infancy* (Vol. 1, pp. 86–109). Norwood, NJ: Ablex.

Winnicott, D. W. (1957). *The child and the family.* London: Tavistock.

Winnicott, D. W. (1976). In *Playing and reality.* New York: Basic Books.

Winnicott, D.W. (1971). *Playing and reality.* London: Tavistock.

Winnicott, D. W. (1975). *Through paediatrics to psycho-analysis.* New York: Basic Books.

Wolff, P. J. (1959). Observations on newborn infants. *Psychosomatic Medicine, 221,* 110–118.

Wolff, P. (1963). Observations on the early development of smiling. In B. M. Foss (Ed.), *Determinants of infant behavior* (pp. 113–138). London: Methuen.

Wolff, P. H. (1966). The causes, controls and organization or behavior in the neonate. *Psychological Issues, 5*(1), 1–105.

Wolff, P. H. (1968). Sucking patterns of infant mammals. *Brain, Behaviour and Evolution, 1,* 354–367.

Wolff, P. H. (1996). The irrelevance of infant observations for psychoanalysis. *Journal of the American Psychoanalytic Association, 44,* 396–392.

Yogman, M. W. (1977). *The goals and structure of face-to-face interaction between infants and fathers.* Paper presented at Society for Research in Child Development, New Orleans.

Zahn-Waxler, C., McKnew, D. H., Cummings, M., Davenport, Y. B., & Radke-Yarrow, M. (1984). Problem behaviors and poor interaction of young children with a manic-depressive parent. *American Journal of Psychiatry, 141*(2), 236–240.

Zetzel, E. R. (1956). Current concepts of transference. *International Journal of Psycho-Analysis, 37,* 369–376.

Zuckerman, B. (1991). Selected methodologic issues in investigations of prenatal effects of cocaine: Lessons from the past. *NIDA Research Monographs, 114,* 45–54.

Zuckerman, B. (1996). Drug effects: Search for outcomes. In C. L. Wetherington, V. L. Smeriglio, & L. P. Finnegan (Eds.), *Behavioral studies of drug-exposed offspring: Methodological issues in human and animal research* (pp. 277–287). Rockville, MD: National Institute on Drug Abuse.

Zuckerman, B., Amaro, H., Bauchner, H., & Cabral, H. (1989). Depressive symptoms during pregnancy: Relationship to poor health behaviors. *American Journal of Obstetrics and Gynecology, 160,* 1107–1111.

Zuckerman, B. S., Bauchner, H., Parker, S., & Cabral, H. (1990). Maternal depressive symptoms during pregnancy and newborn irritability. *Journal of Developmental and Behavioral Pediatrics, 11,* 190–194.

Zuckerman, B., Frank, D., Hingson, R., Amaro, H., Levenson, S. M., Kayne, H., et al. (1989). Effects of maternal marijuana and cocaine use on fetal growth. *New England Journal of Medicine, 320,* 762–768.

Index

mutual regulation model, 178–79, 319, 340–41, 352–54, 404–5
in older children, 175–76
see also depressed mothers
emotional functioning, infant's
affective synchrony in infant–adult interaction, 135, 148–49, 150, 252, 278, 281
appraisal system, 179
assessment, 231, 235
capacity to experience, 178–79, 230, 242, 244–45, 353–54
capacity to express, 169–70, 180, 182, 206, 230, 279, 341, 405
capacity to recognize facial expressions, 168–69
coherence among expressive modalities, 231–32, 235–45, 404–5
expressive flexibility, 244
facial expression as indicator of, 242–43
infant–mother emotional communication
characteristics of abnormal interactions, 171–72
constant low-intensity affective input, 458–59
content, 271–72
developmental significance, 164, 165, 172–75, 176
dyadic expansion of consciousness and, 406
examples of, 164–65
gender differences, 204, 279, 286, 308, 328–32, 334, 335, 336–37, 338, 339, 340, 343
infant goal-oriented behavior, 166–68
mutual regulation, 404–5
organization of infant emotions, 168–71
regulatory function, 272
therapeutic intervention to repair mismatched interactions, 176
see also mutual regulation
maternal depressed behavior and, 160–61, 288–89, 308, 328–38, 343, 344–45, 375–76, 392
moods. *see* moods
multiple caregiving among Efe people and, 119–20
normal mother–infant interactive stress, 158–60
object engagement, 240, 243, 279, 341
passive withdrawal state, 240, 241–42, 243, 279, 341
protest behavior, 240, 241–42, 243, 278–79, 300, 341
self-regulation in Mutual Recognition Model, 181–82, 191–92
sensitivity to mother's emotional state, 306

social engagement state, 236–39, 241, 243, 278, 279, 341
transfer of affect in mutual regulation model, 206, 212, 217
see also emotional functioning, generally
empathy, 260, 291, 347
energy
in expanding states of consciousness, 3
for meaning-making, 2
for open biological systems, 481
entraining stimuli, 117–18, 119, 218, 219, 226
evolutionary theory
attachment theory, 259
continuous and constant contact model of childrearing, 102, 103
Efe morphology, 114–15
hunting and gathering societies, 103–4
motivation for intersubjectivity, 289
experiential relational space, 472–73

face-to-face interaction
angry face, 355
assessment and categorization, 162, 195, 197, 198–99, 220–21, 235, 252–53, 297–98, 326–27, 344
bidirectional influence in, 218–20, 223–26, 280–81
coherence among emotional expression modalities in infant, 231–32, 235–45
coordination of infant–mother behaviors, 195–96, 199–205
developmental significance, 134–35, 262, 293
distribution of infant–mother affective expression, 341
distribution of infant–mother matches, 201
disturbances in maternal behavior, 253–57
face-to-face/still-face paradigm, 11–12, 162, 232, 295, 312, 322, 342–43, 383–84, 394, 402–3, 408
first year development, infant–mother, 196, 200–201, 203–4
gender differences, 279
Gusii mother–infant, 135, 137–38, 142–52, 174, 495–96
infant capacity for emotional expression, 169–70, 230
infant capacity to recognize facial expressions, 168–69, 272, 355
infant response to still face, 183–86, 210, 253–55, 268–71, 272–73, 283, 296–96, 312–13, 384–88
mutual regulation, 171, 355
neurophysiology, 384–88
normal infant behavior, 264–68, 279
regulation in Gusii society, 136–37
reparation of mismatches, 203–4, 312–13, 357

face-to-face interaction (*continued*)
  research methodology, 138–42, 195, 196,
    197–98, 207, 210, 220, 226–29,
    232–33, 263–64, 294, 297, 325–28
  reunion play following still face, 322, 328,
    330, 332–34, 335–36, 384
  stress of still face, 183, 271, 488–90
  synchrony, infant–mother, 196, 199–200,
    202, 204, 252–53, 277
  transitions between matched/mismatched
    states, 202, 203, 212
fantasy, 508
Fetters, L., 9
Field, T., 116, 256, 285, 313, 321
Fogel, A., 231–32, 478
Fonagy, P., 507
Foscha, D., 465
Freeman, W., 422, 471–72, 475, 478, 491
Freeman, Walter J., 2
Fuertes, M., 393

gender differences
  in affective expressiveness, 320
  depression symptoms in mothers of sons,
    365–66
  emotional expressiveness, 340
  emotional self-regulation, 286–87, 308, 340,
    345, 392
  infant–mother interaction, 174, 195, 204,
    279, 286, 308, 320
  maternal depression effects on infant
    responding, 286, 308, 321, 322,
    328–32, 334, 335, 336–37, 338, 339,
    340, 343, 344–45, 375–76
  object engagement, 320, 340
  outcomes of failed reparation of
    infant–mother interactions, 286–87
  sleep-wake behavior, 447
general systems theory, 422
Gianino, A., 157, 166–67, 173, 182, 183, 193,
    312
Gill, M., 433
glial cells, 22
goal-oriented behavior
  caretaker investment strategies, 99
  communication, 250
  critical processes for success, 275
  dyadic state regulation, 423
  in infants, 166–68, 206, 243
  mutual regulation model of mother–infant
    interaction, 178, 262, 423–24
  other-directed regulatory behaviors, 167
  psychobiological states of consciousness,
    478–79, 497–98
  reciprocal obligations, 260
  regulation of negative affect, 173
  resource acquisition strategies of children,
    98–100

self-directed regulatory behaviors, 167
social interaction goals, 206
therapeutic progress, 427
Gottman, J. M., 224
Green, A., 403
Greenberg, M. T., 213
Gunnar, M. R., 387
Guntrip, H., 421
Gusii people, 13
  mother–infant face-to-face interaction, 135,
    137–38, 142–52, 174, 280, 495–96
  research design for infant–mother
    interaction studies, 138–42
  social behaviors, 136–37, 151–52
  way of life, 136

Habermas, J., 260
habituation
  newborn behavioral capacities, 24
  prenatal cocaine exposure manifestations,
    65, 73
Haley, D. W., 387
Ham, J., 386
Hamilton, P., 172
Harlow, H. F., 122, 343
Harrison, Alexandra, 16
Haviland, J., 204
Hayes, A., 224
heroin, newborn exposure assessment, 35
Hinde, R. A., 122
Hofer, M. A., 276, 478
homeostatic regulation, 403–4, 406. *see also*
    temperature regulation
Hrdy, S. B., 116
hunting and gathering societies, 103–4, 109–10
hypothalamic-pituitary axis, 387

immunoglobulins, 108
immunophysiology, 491
  infant nursing and, 107–8, 113–14
impelling certitude, 478–79, 480
implicit relational knowing
  changes in, 421–22
  conceptual models, 421
  definition and scope, 413, 420
  development, 420–21
  experiential basis, 423
  forms of knowing in, 467–68
  integration of microinteractive knowings, 467
  metaprocedural knowing in, 467–68
  moments of meeting and, 421–22, 425
  in therapeutic relationship, 422
  therapeutic significance, 413–14, 437
infant–adult interaction
  adaptive context, 247, 256, 261
  adult self-esteem and, 212–16
  affective quality, 293
    infant sensitivity to, 296